Critical Approaches to Television

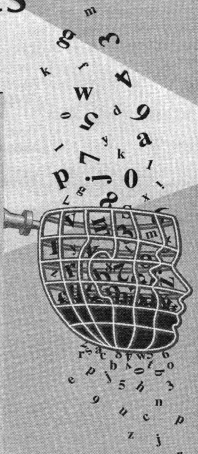

LEAH R. VANDE BERG
California State University, Sacramento

LAWRENCE A. WENNER
Loyola Marymount University

BRUCE E. GRONBECK
University of Iowa

Houghton Mifflin Company   *Boston   New York*

Sponsoring Editor: Mary Finch
Editorial Associate: Brigitte Maser
Production Design Coordinator: Bethany Schlegel
Senior Project Editor: Fred Burns
Manufacturing Manager: Florence Cadran

Cover Credit: Clockwise from upper left: © Debra Schuler-Murray; © Michael Skoglund; © Greg Friedler; © Michael Heiko.

Permissions acknowledgments may be found on page xxi.

Photo Credits:
Page 46: © Comedy Central/Photofest. Page 130: © Capital Cities/ABC, Inc./Photofest. Page 162: © CBS, Inc./Photofest. Page 212: Courtesy of *The Daily Iowan*; photo © AP/Wide World Photos. Page 206: © Photofest. Page 247: © CBS, Inc./Photofest. Page 371: © Capital Cities/ABC, Inc./Photofest. Page 415: © Fotos International/Archive/Getty Images. Page 464: © 1997 Warner TV/MPTV. Page 489: © Aaron Montgomery/JPI.

Printed in the U.S.A.

Library of Congress Control Number: 2001133362

ISBN-0-205-56466-6

2 3 4 5 6 7 8 9—MP—07 06 05 04

Critical Approaches to Television

Contents

PART TWO   Text-Centered Critical Approaches   65

PART THREE   Producer-Centered Approaches   229

PART FIVE Ethics and the Critical Approach 501

Alternative Contents

News/Talk

Preface

The twentieth century was called the ocular centric century. Mechanically produced visual displays such as poster art and photography played significant roles in fostering social-political awareness and change, and the electronically powered visual technologies—particularly film and television—revolutionized the community and the home. "Vision centeredness" marked that century, and continues into the current one, penetrating even farther into our daily social lives and psychological processes thanks to the computer and the digital revolution. The Global Village that so fascinated Marshall McLuhan exists in wired and wireless connections that allow you to hear from and see your neighbors on the other side of the world. DDS (direct satellite systems) and digitalization of the broadcasting spectrum multiply available audio and video channels by the hundreds. Television in particular has been adapted to your every need and whim: network news and entertainment channels, yes, but also religious experiences, cooking outlets, home shopping networks, music videos, sports of every kind from every sort of venue, courtroom drama, foreign programming, cartoons, weather, history, "adult" fantasy, more film channels than there are theatres in a multiplex movie complex, pay-per-view anything, and an array of sound-only channels. In the ocular centric age, television is parent, baby sitter, financial adviser, friend, moralist, sing-along accompanist, surveillance team, distraction, and, above all, a teacher of us all—or at least the ninety-nine percent of us in the United States with TV sets.

Whether you like it or not, significant portions of your life are probably centered on television. Even if you don't watch TV, most of the people you come in contact with use it for surveillance, authority, and entertainment. As television turned into a consumer product, especially in the United States some fifty years ago, it was popularly called a "window on the world." We have learned by now, however, that the window doesn't have clear glass: in part it's reflective, showing you part of yourself; in part, distortive, selecting and even recontextualizing what you're looking at; in part, fantasy, showing you an environment that never was or can be. Reflection, distortion, and fantasy are aspects of your viewing, whether you're looking at *Rugrats*, *The Wide World of Sports*, *All My Children*, *The Bernie Mac Show*, *Will & Grace*, or *Dateline*.

This book has been written and assembled to help you analyze television culture sensitively, systematically, and expertly. To confront television for what it is and what it can do to you, you must be able to distance yourself from the concept of "watching a little TV" by monitoring your own reactions to what has been constructed for you in sight, sound, and symbols. You'll understand television's ways and importance— *understanding* is the primary outcome of good criticism—only by studying the people who think up and construct programs, the coding systems used for a TV program, the descriptive and valuative content of what you see, characteristics of people who view and draw sustenance from TV, and the industrial behemoths that profit from your relationship with "the Box." This book seeks to make you a good television critic.

This book started out as *Television Criticism: Approaches and Applications*, written and edited by Leah Vande Berg and Lawrence Wenner in 1991. It was conceived of as a textbook and reader, a book with both methodologically oriented how-to-do-it instruction and samples of television criticism. Those who used it applauded the concepts behind the effort but wanted more material about general criticism, specific television criticism, various approaches to critical analysis, and writing.

So that's what we did when we wrote *Critical Approaches to Television*. The first edition in 1998 was built around advice users gave us, and in this second edition we have continued the effort to meet the needs of teachers and students wishing to take apart and reflect upon their televisual experiences. We've sought to make *Critical Approaches to Television* the most comprehensive textbook-reader on media criticism today.

- The title *Critical Approaches to Television* emphasizes the book's focus on the kinds of understandings and evaluations that television critics try to engender in their readers.

- We've reorganized the chapters into five parts: (1) theoretical and critical foundations, which introduces the subject, the history of television criticism, and the writing process; (2) text-centered critical approaches, which breaks out semiotic/structural, genre, rhetorical, and narrative criticism into separate chapters for fuller coverage; (3) producer-centered approaches, which permits interesting comparisons between and among auteur, production, and ideological criticism; (4) reception-centered approaches, where three types of viewer-sensitive methods (reader-centered, ethnographic, and cultural) carry us into the newest forms of critical study; and (5) a final chapter and television, ethics, and criticism—where television's effects on people's lives are probed. The book is now more comprehensive yet easier to teach.

- *Critical Approaches to Television* has two tables of contents: the primary Contents is built around approaches to criticism, while the Alternative Contents is organized around television genres (types of programs). The course and a student's reading, therefore, can be constructed around either of the two usual ways of drawing up courses in media criticism.

- Each of the chapters in Parts II, III, and IV is illustrated with sample essays. Because Chapter 15 deals with three kinds of cultural criticism—mythic, feminist, and psychoanalytic—it contains the most essays. The essays are introduced in the chapters themselves so that the critical concepts and advice associated with each approach to criticism can be tied directly to the essays.

- Essays have been updated where appropriate. Television is an ephemeral medium, with shows coming and going even in midseason. Most of the authors work with shows from the nineties and today, though we have included analyses of older programs such as *Dr Who, Doogie Howser M.D., Murphy Brown,* the 1984 Macintosh ad, and *Cheers* because they so clearly illustrate particular critical approaches and generally are available in syndication, CD format, or even Internet outlets. (And, if you're lucky, you'll find the Mac ad somewhere!)

■ Several approaches that were dealt with as parts of chapters now have been expanded into full chapters: semiotic/structural, genre, rhetorical, narrative, production context, ideological, and ethnographic criticism. Cultural criticism is so central that it's been turned into two chapters, one dealing with the general assumptions and operations of cultural criticism, and the other, with three of the many species that are associated culture-critique.

We have assembled, therefore, the most current ideas about television criticism generally and specifically in a textbook-reader accessible to undergraduates yet mindful of the larger, metacritical issues of particular interest to graduate students. We have offered examinations of both classic and contemporary TV shows to provide both an historical and a present-day context for critical understanding and writing. We are unalterably committed to theoretical-conceptual and critical-interpretive analyses that are central to college-level instruction and learning in the liberal arts, with an eye, always, to enough how-to-do-it advice to jump-start the beginning writer.

We have been helped in our endeavor by many. Special thanks are due to the anonymous reviewers of both the earlier versions of the book and its current version: Michael J. Porter (University of Missouri), Harry W. Haines (Trinity University), Barry Brummett (University of Wisconsin-Milwaukee), Robert Schrag (North Carolina State University), Christopher Francis White (Sam Houston State University), Raymond Gozzi, Jr. (Ithaca College), and Barbara Zelizer (Temple University). We thank, too, the authors of the sample essays, and Margaret Sewell, Houghton's former acquisitions editor who helped us develop the initial proposal for this book. We are deeply appreciative of professionalism and support provided by Houghton's editorial staff; we are especially grateful to our former Sponsoring Editor Adam Forrand, whose gentle encouragement and staunch support throughout every step of the revision process enabled us to turn *Critical Approaches* into a truly powerful textbook, and to Developmental Editor Brigitte Maser who gently but firmly shepherded us through the revisions process. Thanks to Development Editor Kristen Lefevre, and Senior Project Editor Fred Burns. Thanks also to Manufacturing Manager Florence Cadran. The expertise of Marketing Manager Barbara Lebuhn aided us in getting the book into your hands.

We offer our deepest thanks to the former teachers and students who used the book and cared enough to give us good advice on how to improve it. Only by meeting the needs of students and their mentors is any textbook worth the effort that goes into its making. The users we've come to know have inspired and directed our work. We appreciate their loving attention and exhortation. We hope that they like this edition ever better.

We hope that you become someone who'll never again "watch a little TV" without first engaging your critical faculties. Students often tell us that their television viewing has been ruined by this course because they find themselves analyzing and assessing the stuff they view. Life as a couch potato is not more. We smile knowingly when we hear that, telling them that it's all right. College education is supposed to disturb your ability to live life in a business-as-usual sort of way; it's supposed to alert and deploy your critical defenses. Adopting critical attitudes as you look at life, even life in front of a TV set, doesn't really ruin it. Rather, they allow you to enjoy life on two levels—the mundane and the critical, life-as-experienced and life-as-reflected upon.

So read this book and carry out the class discussions and writing assignments enthusiastically. If you do, you ought to be able to double your television-viewing pleasure.

Leah R. Vande Berg
Bruce E. Gronbeck
Lawrence Wenner

Acknowledgments

Matthew P. McAllister, "Recombinant Television Genres and *Doogie Howser, M.D.*," from the *Journal of Popular Film & Television*, vol. 20 (pp. 61-69). Copyright © 1992. Reprinted by permission of the Helen Dwight Reid Educational Foundation. Published by Heldref Publications, 1319 Eighteenth Street, NW, Washington, DC. 20036-1802. Copyright © 1992.

Richard Campbell and Jimme L. Reeves, "Television Authors: The Case of Hugh Wilson," from Robert J. Thompson and Gary Burns (Eds.), *Making Television: Authorship and the Production Process* (pp. 3–18). Copyright ©1990 by Praeger Publishers. Reprinted by permission of the Greenwood Publishing Group, Westport, CT.

Bonnie J. Dow, "Murphy Brown: Postfeminism Personified," from *Prime-Time Feminism: Television, Media Culture, and the Women's Movement Since 1970* (pp. 135–163). Copyright ©1996. Reprinted by permission of the University of Pennsylvania Press, Philadelphia, PA.

John Fiske, "Ideology: A Structuralist Reading of *Dr. Who*," from Willard D. Rowland, Jr. and Bruce W. Watkins (Eds.), *Interpreting Television: Current Research Perspectives* (pages 165–198). Copyright ©1984 by Sage Publications. Reprinted by permission of Sage Publications, Thousand Oaks, CA.

Heather L. Hundley, "The Naturalization of Beer in *Cheers*," from the *Journal of Broadcasting & Electronic Media*, vol. 39 (1995), pp. 350–359. Copyright ©1995. The Broadcast Education Association publishes the *Journal of Broadcasting and Electronic Media*.

Elana Levine, "Toward a Paradigm for Media Production Research: Behind-the-Scenes at *General Hospital*" from *Critical Studies in Media Communication*, vol. 18 (pp. 66–81). Copyright © 2001. Used by permission of the National Communication Association, Washington, DC.

Sonia Livingstone and Tamar Liebes, "Where Have All the Mothers Gone? Soap Opera's Replaying of the Oedipal Story," from *Critical Studies in Mass Communication*, vol.12 (pp. 155–175). Copyright ©1995. Used by permission of the National Communication Association.

Mark Orbe, "Constructions of reality on MTV's *The Real World*: An analysis of the restrictive coding of Black masculinity," from the *Southern Communication Journal*, vol. 64 (pp. 32–47). Copyright © 1998. Used by permission of the Southern States Communication Association.

A. Susan Owen, "Vampires, Postmodernity, and Postfeminisms: *Buffy, The Vampire Slayer*," from the *Journal of Popular Film & Television*, vol. 27 (pp. 24–31). Copyright © 1999. Reprinted with permission of the Helen Dwight Reid Educational Foundation. Published by Heldref Publications, 1319 Eighteenth Street, NW, Washington, DC 20036-1802.

Cathy Sandeen, "Success Defined by Television: The Value System Promoted by *PM Magazine*," from *Critical Studies in Mass Communication*, vol. 14 (pp. 77–105). Copyright ©1997. Used by permission of the National Communication Association.

Sarah R. Stein, "The 1984 Macintosh Ad: Cinematic Icons and Constitutive Rhetoric in the Launch of a New Machine," from the *Quarterly Journal of Speech*, vol. 88 (pp. 169–192). Copyright © 2002. Used by permission of the National Communication Association.

Lawrence A. Wenner, "The Dream Team: Communicative Dirt and the Marketing of Synergy," from the *Journal of Sport and Social Issues*, vol. 18 (pp.37–47). Copyright © 1994. Reprinted by permission of Sage Publications, Thousand Oaks, CA.

Robert Westerfelhaus and Teresa Combs, "Criminal Investigations and Spiritual Quests: *The X-File*s as an Example of Hegemonic Concordance in a Mass-Mediated Society," from the *Journal of Communication Inquiry,* vol. 22 (pages 205–220). Copyright ©1998 by Sage Publications. Reprinted by permission of Sage Publications, Thousand Oaks, CA.

Critical Approaches to Television

PART ONE

Theoretical and Critical Foundations

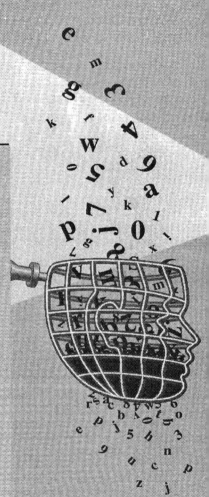

The Context
for Criticism:
Television and Society

CHAPTER 1

Chapter Outline

The Powers of Television

The Power to Entertain
The Power to Socialize and Educate
The Power to Create Community and Consensus
The Power to Inform

Characteristics of the Medium of Television

Television as Industry
Television as Appliance
Television as Flow
Television as Postmodern Fragments

The Need for Critical Analysis of Television

Preview of the Book's Organization

Television is ubiquitous. We watch it in Laundromats, bars, hospital waiting rooms, living rooms, and even minivans. Television's programs are available 24 hours a day, and we don't have to drive to a theater, stand in line, and buy a ticket to watch them. That's part of the reason that the TV set in the average American home is turned on for viewing 7 hours and 15 minutes a day. One result is that by the time most of you graduated from high school, you had spent far more time with this electronic storyteller—approximately 20,000 hours—than with your classroom instructors—11,000 hours (*Broadcasting & Cable Yearbook*, 1995; Kline, 1993)!

The goal of this book is to help you develop the critical viewing skills to explore the meanings and pleasures you have created through your interactions with television. We believe that for you, as it was for us, becoming a more informed and articulate critic of television will change your sense of self, your tastes, and your perception of television as a uniquely powerful social and cultural force.

The Powers of Television

Television's pervasive cradle-to-grave presence and its potential powers have been regarded by both critics and social scientists as sufficiently important reasons for subjecting the medium and its contents, uses, and effects to extensive scrutiny (see, e.g., Gerbner, Gross, Morgan, & Signorielli, 1994; Rubin & Step, 1997). Among television's powers are the power to entertain, to socialize and educate, to create community and consensus, and to inform.

The Power to Entertain

One of the most common reasons people watch television, according to researchers who study television's uses and effects, is for entertainment or diversion (Zillmann, 1982; Zillmann & Bryant, 1985). Television is a prolific provider of diversion, escape, and entertainment that requires no literacy, no mobility, and no direct purchase; indeed, children begin watching this tirelessly entertaining babysitter long before they can talk or read (see Gerbner et al., 1994; Silverstone, 1999, pp. 62–66).

For many of us, lounging on the couch watching episodes of *Friends, Frasier, The West Wing*, or MTV is a convenient, inexpensive way to relax after a stress-filled day of tests, work, and driving. However, television's power to entertain includes not only the capacity to divert and relax us but also the power to cheer us up. Zillmann and Bryant (1994) note that not only do adults turn to television entertainment programs when they need some cheering up, but that children as young as four years old use television to change their bad moods into good moods (see also Masters, Ford, & Arend, 1983).[1]

The Power to Socialize and Educate

When you think about television as a socializing agent or teacher, your first response may be to think about the studies on the efficacy of *Sesame Street* and *Mister Rogers' Neighborhood* in preparing children for school by helping them to learn the alphabet, simple rules of social courtesy, and intercultural cooperation (Silverman & Sprafkin, 1980). With a little more thought, you might also mention educational PBS documentaries like Ken Burns's *Baseball* or Bill Moyers's *A Walk Through the Twentieth Century, The Power of Healing,* and *The Language of Life;* the PBS science series *Nova* and *Nature;* and the programs on such cable outlets as the Discovery Channel. However, if we understand education in the larger sense to mean the acquisition of knowledge—including social, cultural, political, economic, scientific, philosophical, and religious information, generalizations, theories, and facts—then much of television is educational. As Gerbner et al. (1994) put it:

> Television is the source of the most broadly shared images and messages in history. It is the mainstream of the common symbolic environment into which our children are born and in which we all live out our lives. . . . Transcending historic barriers of literacy and mobility, television has become the primary common source of socialization and everyday information (mostly in the form of entertainment) of otherwise heterogeneous populations. (pp. 17–18)

From television's continuous and coherent use of visual, musical, aural-oral, and narrative codes, we learn to "read" television and other visual texts: we learn to identify (or decode) such visual indicators as flashbacks, dream sequences, chase scenes, and other simultaneously occurring events (created through editing techniques that Christian Metz, 1974, called alternating syntagms). We learn the power of the camera's "gaze" (Mulvey, 1975, 1989; Vande Berg, 1993); we learn to read musical soundtracks as signaling danger, suspense, humor, discovery, romance, or grief; and we learn from the laugh tracks what we are supposed to regard as funny and to anticipate when something humorous is about to happen (see Altman, 1986).

From the characters in television programs, performers in music videos, and sports celebrities' and actors' guest appearances and actions, we acquire social knowledge and cues about contemporary hairstyles and clothing styles (e.g., Madonna's underwear as outerwear), language use (e.g., Beavis and Butthead's "Hey, dude"), and behavioral mannerisms (e.g., baseball player Glenn Burke's "high five"). From soap operas, medical dramas, and made-for-television movies, we learn facts about heart disease, incest, and AIDS. From police and legal dramas, we learn about the criminal justice and judicial systems: what our *Miranda* rights are, what arrest procedures typically are like, and what prosecuting and defense lawyers do. Situation comedies and dramas teach us about contemporary social values and attitudes toward sex, family, and school, and they provide glimpses of various occupations.

Television's fictional and nonfictional entertainment also serve a socializing function by celebrating some characters and their deeds as admirable and heroic while ignoring and symbolically annihilating (i.e., failing to cover) other groups, thereby signifying their social status. Television can help demonize or canonize cultural heroes, create and destroy cultural myths, and shape people's perceptions and attitudes. For example, television coverage of President John F. Kennedy in the 1960s and in subsequent assassination anniversary specials and made-for-television movies such as *Kennedys Don't Cry, Four Days in November,* and *JFK: That Day in November* have helped create and maintain the American Camelot myth (Vande Berg, 1995). Television series about war (from *Hogan's Heroes, M*A*S*H, China Beach,* and *Tour of Duty,* to *Band of Brothers*), television series about doctors (from *Marcus Welby, M.D., St. Elsewhere, Chicago Hope,* and *Dr. Quinn: Medicine Woman,* to *ER* and *Scrubs*), and television series about cops (from *Car 54* to *Miami Vice, Hill Street Blues, Homicide: Life on the Streets,* and *NYPD Blue* to *Law and Order: Special Victims Unit*) help shape our understanding of history and contemporary culture (see, e.g., Real, 1996, pp. 208–236).

The Power to Create Community and Consensus

Television also helps create community and consensus. For instance, some 130 million American television viewers tuned in to watch Alex Haley's *Roots,* and at least as many tuned in to find out who shot *Dallas's* J.R. and to say "Goodbye, Farewell and Amen" to their friends on *M*A*S*H* (McNeil, 1991). Thanks to television, almost every adult American knows that Coke is "the real thing" and that "Air Jordan" is not the name of a commercial airline. And on September 11, 2001, we stayed glued to our television sets watching together the replays of the terrorist attacks and the heroic rescue efforts at the World Trade Center towers and the Pentagon.

Indeed, many of us regard our favorite television series' characters and newscasters as familiar friends whom we look forward to seeing each week. Scholars call this aspect of television its *parasocial function* because although watching our favorite character or cast of characters every week isn't really social interaction, for many people, weekly appointments with favorite shows and characters serve as partial functional replacement for social relationships (Horton & Wohl, 1956). In fact, many viewers apparently read the characters in television series quite realistically. For example, actor Tim Busfield, who played Elliot Weston on the prime-time serial *thirtysomething,* recalls a time when he was slapped in the face in a grocery store by a woman who told him that Elliot should not have left his wife (Zehme, 1989, p. 75). This incident happened, in part, because television uses social codes to create a sense of realism or verisimilitude (see Heide, 1995, and Chapter 3 in this book for further discussion of this).

Television also helps to create community by providing viewers with grist for social interactions. This *social utility function* of television can be seen, for example, in our work environments when we stop for a cup of coffee and engage in conversations with coworkers about what happened on last night's episode of *The West Wing, Six Feet Under,* or *Sex and the City*.

The Power to Inform

Closely related to television's power to educate and socialize is its power to inform. Television news and public affairs programming provide *surveillance* of our physical environment—functioning as an early-warning system about everything from tomorrow's rain predictions and tornado warnings to proposed actions by the U.S. Congress and state legislatures, to global warming and terrorist attacks. On television, we watched the first walk on the moon, the *Challenger* space shuttle explosion, and planes hitting the two World Trade towers.[2]

Apart from monumental events like these, however, many more events occur in a day than any one newscast (or any one newspaper, news magazine, or even an all-news cable channel, for that matter) can cover. Television news organizations must decide which of the myriad people, events, and issues to give airtime to. When a news organization decides to cover some events and issues and not others, it confers status on the events, issues, and people it covers and it marginalizes or symbolically annihilates those it does not cover. This *status conferral* function is one reason television critics constantly and critically examine television's gatekeeping choices.

Television not only confers status selectively on some issues and ideas; it also has the power to shape viewers' political and social agenda, though not by telling viewers what they should think or how they should vote; rather, by covering some issues rather than others, TV tells viewers what issues they should be thinking about (Fan, Brosius, & Kepplinger, 1994; McCombs & Shaw, 1972). Far fewer media studies scholars have explored television's agenda-setting function in the social and cultural areas of music, fashion, language use, behavioral mannerisms, myths, ideologies, and social norms than in the area of news.

Characteristics of the Medium of Television

Television has the power to entertain, inform, and socialize because it is simultaneously an industry, an electronic apparatus, a 24-hour nonstop flow of words and images, and a postmodern collection of images and sound fragments.

Television as Industry

That television is an industry means that it is a complex of organizations and individuals whose primary goal is economic profitability and only secondarily aesthetic excellence or public service. In 1999, the U.S. television industry encompassed one public and six commercial television networks, about 1,616 operating television stations, plus scores of program production companies, advertising agencies, talent agencies, and so on. Approximately 100.8 million U.S. homes (98 percent of all U.S. homes) had TV sets; 76 percent of these had more than one television set, and 68 percent were linked to cable television. For the television networks and cable outlets (which typically purchase programs from program creators to distribute to their owned and affiliated stations or systems) and advertisers, programming is merely the filler between the truly important television content: the advertisements. In 1999, $39.4 billion was spent on commercial TV advertising. The average 30-second prime-time television network commercial announcement cost $120,000, and 30-second spots on top-rated TV series cost $325,000 (Broadcasting & Cable Yearbook 2000, p. xxx). In 2001 advertisers paid $2.3 million per Super Bowl 30-second commercial to reach the estimated 135 million people viewing this sports event ("Super Bowl TV commercials, 2001, p. D5; see also Media Awareness Network, 2001, p. 2).

Because broadcast television requires no direct out-of-pocket purchase, we tend to think of it as free, but that is far from the case. Programs are financed by selling time to product producers for promoting their products within and between programs. The more viewers, or sometimes the more "quality" viewers with large disposable incomes, who watch a particular program, the more the advertisers are willing to pay the networks to try to reach those viewers with product promotions. So what is really being sold is us: the viewers. One important implication of commercialism for television criticism is that television stations, broadcast networks, and cable channels assess the goodness of a program in terms of the Nielsen aesthetic standard—how many viewers the program attract—and not in terms of a medium-based aesthetic standard of how effectively and creatively the program uses the unique characteristics of the television medium.

Television as Appliance

When we think of television, we also think of the appliance that sits in our living rooms (and bedrooms, dens, kitchens, and even our RVs). Our expectations of our television appliance are similar to expectations we have of such other household appliances as the refrigerator, microwave, dishwasher, and air-conditioner: we expect it to provide us a range of services of our choosing, on demand, at any and every hour of the day or night. While we may reasonably expect to find a book we like among the 10,000 offerings on the shelves at a bookstore any time we saunter in, without an equivalent number of channels, it is unreasonable to apply the same criteria to television. However, thinking of television as an appliance can lead to just such unreasonable expectations.

Furthermore, television's commonplace ordinariness as a household appliance is one reason that many viewers, critics, and educators have been slow to take television seriously as an art form and slower still to train students in elementary, secondary, and postsecondary classes to analyze television critically in the same way they are taught to analyze literature.

Television as Flow

Another key characteristic of television is flow: TV is a constantly changing yet seamless stream of images and sounds (Williams, 1974). Television programs are interwoven with advertisements, public service announcements, station identifications, program promotions, bumpers, teasers, and other materials designed to provide a constant flow of sight and sound. Since about 1976, thanks to videocassette recorders, we have had a means of arresting this flow and capturing the ephemeral, fleeting televisual experiences for closer study. However, the nonstop stream of entertainment, information, calls to civic duty, and consumer culture on 40 to 120 cable television channels makes television criticism extremely challenging and never dull (see Corner's 1999, pp. 60-69, discussion of debates over the concept of "flow").

Television as Postmodern Fragments

If part of what contemporary theorists mean by postmodernism is the fragmentation of temporal, linear narratives and their replacement by disjointed plots, disconnected elements, and aesthetics of excess, television is the quintessential postmodern art form (see Collins, 1992; Kellner, 1995). Despite television's perpetual flow of images and sounds, television comes to us in fragments. TV is, as Gronbeck (1984) has noted, "a series of islands, a patch here and patch there, chopped into 20-, 60-, and 90-minute narratives, each broken down into acts or episodes running anywhere from three to twenty minutes apiece, thanks to commercials" (p. 8). Many television programs are episodic, meaning that each series—like *Law & Order, Friends, The West Wing, JAG, CST,* and *Will and Grace*—comes to us in 13 to 22 weekly installments. Each weekly episode is a different, complete-in-itself narrative featuring the program's recurring characters. Furthermore, the structure of each weekly installment is also predictably fragmented into acts that include the introduction of the week's special situational problem, complication, confusion, and resolution (for comedies), or rising action, falling action, and denouement (for dramas). Each of the acts within a week's episode ends on a note of imminent suspense or romance designed to make sure we are still there watching after the commercial breaks.

Other television programs have a serial narrative structure, meaning that the story lines are not resolved at the end of each week's episode, but instead continue from week to week. Despite this continuous narrative flow, even serial television shows are fragmented: they end on peaks of action, suspense, or emotion. For example, daytime soaps such as *Days of Our Lives* and *The Young and the Restless,* prime-time soaps such as *Pasadena,* and prime-time serial dramas such as *NYPD Blue, ER,* and *The Sopranos* are broken up into weekly installments that usually end on a note of suspense designed to draw us back the following week to see what happens. To deal with such fragmentation in continuing story lines, television writers have developed a number of aesthetic strategies. For example, an announcer's introduction may verbally review highlights from the preceding week by saying something like, "Last week on *ER* . . ." as clips from last week's story lines flash across the screen. Another device writers use to deal with television's fragmentation and discontinuity is extradiegetic[3] voice-over narration by characters. For example, viewers, but not the characters around her, heard Ally McBeal's mental laments about the frustration and loneliness of being a hard-working young professional women as she walked home from the office, or hear *Scrubs's* J. D. Dorian's sarcastic but wisely unspoken thoughts about his intern supervisors during morning grand rounds at the hospital. Soap operas use a technique Allen (1987) terms *interepisodic redundancy* in which characters tell other characters what happened previously, thereby catching up both the character and the viewer on previous events that they did not witness.

The Need for Critical Analysis of Television

In fact, it is precisely because television is all of these things—industry, mundane appliance, nonstop flow of images and sounds, and postmodern fragments—that serious critical analysis of television is needed. Forty years ago, Moses Hadas (1962) noted:

> In literature, as we have observed, there is a tangible critical climate, guided and made articulate by professional critics, perhaps, but shaped by all who take books seriously and write and talk about them. The critical climate, in turn, determines what books are made available. A similar climate must be created for television; all who take education seriously in its larger sense—and not the professed critics alone—should talk and write about television as they do books. (p. 19)

Hadas's comments express several reasons that it is important for you to become a serious television critic. First, becoming a more articulate critic of television will help you interpret and understand your television-viewing experiences and those of your friends, neighbors, and children. Practicing television criticism will enable you to explain knowledgeably and articulately to others how and why some programs, series, and stories have engaged you, emotionally moved you, angered you, and amused you, while others have annoyed, depressed, and manipulated you (and them).

Second, learning and practicing television criticism will enable you to critically evaluate the subtle and overt ways in which encounters with television programs can shape aesthetic tastes; ethical, social, and cultural values; and political and ideological perspectives. Your understanding of the TV industry will change as you begin to study the various ways in which the industry packages, markets, and positions you as the commodity that is being sold, and so will your sense of yourself. Learning to use the various tools of criticism will help you discover how television's technical, social, conventional representational, and ideological codes work to position you to see and create some "preferred" meanings rather than "oppositional" meanings from the structured program elements.[4]

Third, by learning how to practice television criticism, you will be helping to create a critical climate within which television is viewed as seriously as books. As we have explained in this chapter, it is important to create such a critical climate because television, like books, is a powerful cultural and social force. Indeed, many educators believe that media literacy is a basic skill like reading and math, and they believe that all high school students should have to take media criticism or media literacy classes that teach how to "read television" in the same way that secondary students now take classes in which they learn to read writers like

William Shakespeare, William Faulkner, and Flannery O'Connor (see, e.g., Alvarado & Boyd-Barrett, 1992; Auferheide, 1993; Freire, 1985; McLaren, Hammer, Sholle, & Reilly, 1995; Potter, 2001). The goal of such television criticism classes is to enable people to become informed critics who can use critical tools to systematically examine the social, cultural, aesthetic, and political meanings of television programs and to share these insights with other television viewers, television program creators and industry decision makers, and other television studies students, scholars, and professionals.

Serious, careful television criticism provides informed, insightful explanations of particular television texts and groups of texts. It locates a text or a group of texts in one or more contexts, thereby encouraging and enabling viewers to understand their experiences with television in new and different ways. Serious television criticism invites viewers (or readers) of television to undertake new evaluations of their television experiences—sometimes appreciative, sometimes depreciative—in the light of systematic, substantive, stylistic criteria that it articulates for the reader.

As you can see, television critics are interpreters, teachers, and social and intellectual catalysts all rolled into one. In fact, because television criticism essays simultaneously provide a critical analysis and teach through example how to perform similar types of critical analyses on other television programs (or texts), all television criticism provides a pedagogical service.

Most of us who read and practice writing television criticism believe that if there were more informed, serious criticism and less unconsidered opining about television in newspapers, magazines, and books and classrooms, the television industry and the public would take television criticism and the television medium seriously—like the theater and literary communities have taken those mediums seriously for decades—to the great benefit of both. Indeed, given that according to Kubey and Csikszentmihalyi (1990, p. 1), on any given day some 3.5 billion hours will be spent watching television around the world, don't you think it's about time you started thinking critically about television?

Preview of the Book's Organization

This book will help you begin practicing television criticism. Chapters 2 and 3 provide a brief background and history of television criticism; they also discuss what television criticism is and what it isn't. Chapter 4 describes the general structure of critical essays about television and the criteria for evaluating criticism essays. You can use the general outline in this chapter as a model for writing your own critical essays and also as a template for examining how the sample critical essays in Chapters 5 through 15 are constructed.

Part Two (Chapters 5–8) introduces you to four types of criticism that focus on analyzing television texts, the precoded cluster of verbal, visual, musical and aural signs that viewers see and hear when they encounter TV programs. Each chapter begins with a methodological essay that explains the assumptions underlying each approach (or method), defines the central analytical terms and concepts, provides a brief overview of the procedures critics follow in using these constructs, and discusses some of the questions critics using each method ask and try to answer about television. Each chapter also includes one or two critical essays that illustrate how some writers have used this critical approach to analyze particular television programs or sets of programs. Chapter 5 overviews semiotic and structural criticism. Approaches to studying television genres are introduced in Chapter 6, and Chapter 7 discusses several of the many concepts and approaches that rhetorical critics can use to analyze television. Chapter 8 explores narrative analyses of television texts.

Part Three (Chapters 9–11) covers several critical approaches to studying the production context of television studies. Chapter 9 introduces auteur criticism, an approach used to study the "unique signatures" of influential producers—auteurs—of television texts. Approaches to critically studying the production and political and economic context of television texts, that is, the roles that the media industry, institutional, and organizational forces play in the production of television texts in American society, are the focus of Chapter 10, while Chapter 11 discusses approaches critics use to study the ways in which powerful political and economic ideas influence the form and content of television texts.

Part Four (Chapters 12–15) is concerned with reception contexts. Chapter 12 discusses reader-oriented perspectives that critics can use to identify and examine the ideal viewing positions (and ideal readers or spectators) "encoded" in television texts and to identify and describe the interpretive perspectives of actual television viewers. Audience ethnographic criticism, a critical approach in which the "texts" the critic analyzes are audiences' interpretations of television programs, makes up Chapter 13. Chapter 14 overviews general cultural frames—sociocultural and cultural studies—from which critics examine how television audiences approach and interpret television texts. Chapter 15 explores the use of mythic, psychoanalytic and feminist concepts to examine the unconscious reception of television texts' symbols and archetypes.

Finally, Part Five (Chapter 16) addresses some of the ethical issues and implications raised (and sometimes elided) in these and other critical analyses of television as a social and cultural force.

We sincerely hope you enjoy reading these chapters and trying your hand at practicing television criticism as much as we have enjoyed writing these chapters and our own television criticism essays.

Notes

1. The therapeutic powers of television entertainment do have some limitations, however. For example, researchers have found little support for television's cathartic power—that is, TV's ability to harmlessly discharge accumulated aggressive impulses merely by watching televised violence (see Gunter, 1994). In fact, the accumulated research on television suggests that viewing television entertainment can have a number of less-than-therapeutic effects. For instance, researchers have found a strong, positive correlation between watching a large number of violent television programs and approving the use of aggression to

solve conflicts, and they have found that this relationship persists even when such other contributing factors as education level, social class, aggressive attitudes, parental behavior, and sex role identity are controlled for. Among the research that has consistently found such troubling positive correlations are studies by Freedman (1984); Friedrich-Cofer and Huston (1986); Huesmann, Lagerspetz, and Eron (1984); Joy, Kimball, and Zabrack (1986); Liebert and Sprafkin (1988); and Williams (1986).

2. See, for example, Barbie Zelizer's (1992) and Bradley S. Greenberg and Edwin Parker's (1965) studies of the JFK assassination coverage, as well as the fall 1986 special issue of *Central States Speech Journal*, which is entirely devoted to coverage of the space shuttle *Challenger* disaster.

3. The word *diegesis* comes from the Greek word for narration. In film and television studies, diegesis refers to the world inside the story—the world in front of the camera to which the characters in the story have access. Formal, rhetorical features of the television text that occur outside the diegesis, like the musical soundtrack and the laugh track, are called extradiegetic or metadiegetic. Some features, like music, can be either diegetic (if the characters *and* the audience can hear it) or extradiegetic (if it is played by an off-screen orchestra or other sound source that only the audience, and not the characters in the story, can hear) (see Altman, 1986; Olson, 1987).

4. As we mention in Chapter 5, Stuart Hall (1980), a British professor and scholar who studies culture and media, has explained that there are three ways that audiences can "read" or decode television texts: through a *dominant* or *preferred reading*, we understand the text's signs in virtually the same way as the text's producers intended; through a *negotiated reading*, we understand the producers' encoded meanings but adjust some of them to better fit with our particular social experience, knowledge base, and position in society; and through an *oppositional reading*, we reverse the producers' understanding (e.g., treating a serious moment as laughable).

Further Reading

Silverstone, R. (1999). *Why study the media?* Thousand Oaks, CA: Sage. Silverstone's lucid book integrates mass media and critical theory into an accessible argument for the importance of studying the media and the importance of making courses in media literacy a basic part of contemporary education.

Webnotes

TV Guide Online. **www.tvguide.com**

Programs are listed by date, time, channel, and show type. Among the added features are polls, gossip, and soap opera updates.

Episode Lists for 1,600 TV shows. **http://www.epguides.com/**

Current series can be browsed by grid or alphabetically; new series are grouped by genre. Episode listings include season, show number, production number, original airdate, and title.

Learning Activities

1. Robert Rutherford Smith (1980) once reported that one of the major U.S. television networks purchased a full-page advertisement in the *New York Times* proclaiming that "nobody likes us but people." The ad proudly pointed out that although television critics had panned the network's season offerings, the ratings for many of its programs were very high. Such a contemptuous attitude toward critics' evaluations would be unthinkable in the other performing arts like music, theater, dance, painting, and even film. In the theater, directors and actors stay up opening night until the morning edition of newspapers comes out in order to read critics' evaluation of their work, knowing that what critics say can make or break their play's run and their future careers.

   Perhaps the network television executives who took out the *New York Times* ad were confused because they had not taken this course in television criticism; perhaps they just did not understand the role and function of television criticism. Your task is to help them by writing them a letter (begin it with "Dear Network TV Executives") in which you explain to them (a) some of the powers and characteristics of television that might lead people not to take TV seriously as a social, cultural, and educational force and (b) why it would be a valuable use of their time to read serious television criticism articles in journals and in books.

2. How would a letter that covers the same information but is written to (a) parents who are paying the college tuition for you to take a course in which you have to watch and write about television or (b) a childhood best friend who is majoring in aerospace engineering at a top technical college or university and thinks studying television is a waste of time differ from the letter written to the network TV executives?

3. Read the eight paragraphs under "The television text" in Heather Hundley's essay on *Cheers*, in Chapter 14, the first six paragraphs of Robert Westerfelhaus and Teresa Combs's essay on *The X-Files* in Chapter 15, and the first six paragraphs of Sonia Livingstone and Tamar Liebes's essay on the soap opera *The Young and the Restless* also in Chapter 15. Then, write a one-page single-spaced essay in which you (a) summarize the reasons they give for the importance of taking television seriously and for their specific studies of these television texts, and (b) compare their reasons with those discussed in this chapter.

4. In this chapter, we mention several different functions that television serves for individual viewers—including surveillance of the physical environment, parasocial relationships, social utility, and diversion and relaxation—which are all good reasons for taking television seriously and studying television texts, production contexts, and audiences. One tool that mass media scholars who do social scientific research use to explore the different reasons people watch television is a uses and gratifications effects survey. Following this paragraph are some standard items from such a survey. Make a photocopy of it, and verbally give it to three or four friends. Then take the results back for class discussion. Your instructor will explain which items on the survey tap each of the four television uses and will help you tabulate your findings. Once you have done this, you can discuss what this information suggests about reasons for studying the content of television texts.

(continued on next page)

Television Uses and Functions Survey

INSTRUCTIONS [which you say to the person you are interviewing]:

For a class project, I am talking to people to find out why people watch all kinds and types of television programs. Here are some reasons other people have given. As I read each reason, please tell me how much that reason applies to you. If the reason "Very Definitely" applies, give it a "5." If the reason "Does Not Apply at All," give it a "1." If it falls in between, give it a 2, 3, or 4, depending on how much it applies. Okay? Here are the reasons:

A. I watch TV because it helps me to relax.

    1   2   3   4   5

B. I watch TV to give me interesting things to talk about.

    1   2   3   4   5

C. I watch TV to help me make up my mind about social and political issues and topics.

    1   2   3   4   5

D. I watch TV to compare my own ideas to what the characters say.

    1   2   3   4   5

E. I watch TV because it allows me to unwind.

    1   2   3   4   5

F. I watch TV to find out about issues affecting people like myself.

    1   2   3   4   5

G. I watch TV because the characters are like people I know.

    1   2   3   4   5

H. I watch TV so I can pass on information to other people.

    1   2   3   4   5

I. I watch TV because it is often dramatic.

    1   2   3   4   5

J. I watch TV to find out what the latest fashions, music, and activities are.

    1   2   3   4   5

K. I watch TV when there's no one else to talk to or be with.

    1   2   3   4   5

(continued on next page)

L. I watch TV because it's something to do when friends come over.

   1   2   3   4   5

M. I watch TV so I can learn how to do things I haven't done before.

   1   2   3   4   5

N. I watch TV so I can forget about school, work or other things.

   1   2   3   4   5

References

Allen, R. C. (1987). *Speaking of soap operas.* Chapel Hill: University of North Carolina Press.

Altman, R. (1986). Television/sound. In T. Modleski (Ed.), *Studies in entertainment: Critical approaches to mass culture* (pp. 39–54). Bloomington: Indiana University Press.

Alvarado, M., & Boyd-Barrett, O. (Eds.). (1992). *Media education: An introduction.* London: BFI.

Auferheide, P. (1993). *Media literacy: A report of the National Leadership Conference on Media Literacy.* Washington, DC: Aspen Institute.

Broadcasting and Cable Yearbook. (1995). Year in review: Broadcasting and cable, 1994 (p. xxi). New Providence, NJ: Bowker.

Broadcasting and Cable Yearbook. (2000). Year in review: Broadcasting and cable, 1999 (p. xxx). New Providence, NJ: Bowker.

Collins, J. (1992). Postmodernism and television. In R. C. Allen (Ed.), *Channels of discourse, reassembled: Television and contemporary criticism* (2nd ed., pp. 327–353). Chapel Hill: University of North Carolina Press.

Corner, J. (1999). *Critical ideas in television studies.* New York: Oxford University Press.

Fan, D. P., Brosius, H., & Kepplinger, H. M. (1994). Predictions of the public agenda from television coverage. *Journal of Broadcasting and Electronic Media, 38,* 163–178.

Freedman, J. L. (1984). Effect of television violence on aggressiveness. *Psychological Bulletin, 96,* 227–246.

Freire, P. (1985). *The politics of education: Culture, power, and liberation.* South Hadley, MA: Bergin & Garvey.

Friedrich-Cofer, L., & Huston, A. C. (1986). Television violence and aggression: The debate continues. *Psychological Bulletin, 100,* 364–371.

Gerbner, G., Gross, L., Morgan, M., & Signorielli, N. (1994). Growing up with television: The cultivation perspective. In J. Bryant & D. Zillmann (Eds.), *Media effects: Advances in theory and research* (pp. 17–42). Hillsdale, NJ: Erlbaum.

Greenberg, B. S., & Parker, E. (Eds.). (1965). *The Kennedy assassination and the American public.* Palo Alto, CA: Stanford University Press.

Gronbeck, B. E. (1984). *Writing television criticism.* Chicago: Science Research Associates.

Gunter, B. (1994). The question of media violence. In J. Bryant & D. Zillmann (Eds.), *Media effects: Advances in theory and research* (pp. 163–212). Hillsdale, NJ: Erlbaum.

Hadas, M. (1962). Climates of criticism. In R. L. Shayon (Ed.), *The eighth art* (pp. 15–23). New York: Holt, Rinehart, Winston.

Hall, S. (1980). Encoding/decoding. In S. Hall, D. Hobson, A. Lowe, & P. Willis (Eds.), *Culture, media, language* (pp. 128–139). London: Hutchinson.

Heide, M. (1995). *Television culture and women's lives:* thirtysomething *and the contradictions of gender.* Philadelphia: University of Pennsylvania Press.

Horton, D., & Wohl, R. R. (1956). Mass communication and para-social interaction: Observations on intimacy at a distance. *Psychiatry, 19,* 215–229.

Huesmann, L. R., Lagerspetz, K., & Eron, L. D. (1984). Intervening variables in the television violence-viewing-aggression relation: Evidence from two countries. *Developmental Psychology, 20,* 707–716.

Joy, L. A., Kimball, M., & Zabrack, M. L. (1986). Television exposure and children's aggressive behavior. In T. M. Williams (Ed.), *The impact of television: A natural experiment involving three towns* (pp. 303–360). New York: Academic Press.

Kellner, D. (1995). *Media culture: Cultural studies, identity and politics between the modern and the postmodern.* London: Routledge.

Kline, S. (1993). *Out of the garden: Toys and children's culture in the age of TV marketing.* London: Verso.

Kubey, R., & Csikszentmihalyi, M. (1990). *Television and the quality of life: How viewing shapes everyday experience.* Hillsdale, NJ: Erlbaum.

Liebert, R. M., & Sprafkin, J. (1988). *The early window: Effects of television on children and youth* (3rd ed.). New York: Pergamon.

Masters, J. C., Ford, M. E., & Arend, R. A. (1983). Children's strategies for controlling affective responses to aversive social experience. *Motivation and Emotion, 7,* 103–116.

McCombs, M. E., & Shaw, D. L. (1972). The agenda-setting function of mass media. *Public Opinion Quarterly, 36,* 176–187.

McLaren, P., Hammer, R., Sholle, D., & Reilly, S. S. (Eds.). (1995). *Rethinking media literacy: A critical pedagogy of representation.* New York: Peter Lang.

McNeil, A. (1991). *Total television* (3rd ed.). New York: Penguin.

Media awareness network. *Media issues: Advertising and commercialism.* Available online: http://www.media-awareness.ca/eng/issues/stats/issad.htm#superad. Retrieved Oct. 30, 2001.

Metz, C. (1974). *Film language: A semiotics of the cinema* (M. Taylor, Trans.). New York: Oxford University Press.

Mulvey, L. (1975). Visual pleasure and narrative cinema. *Screen, 16*(3), 6–18.

Mulvey, L. (1989). Afterthoughts on "Visual pleasure and narrative cinema" inspired by King Vidor's *Duel in the Sun* (1946). In L. Mulvey, *Visual and other pleasures* (pp. 29–38). Bloomington: Indiana University Press.

Olson, S. R. (1987). Meta-television: Popular postmodernism. *Critical Studies in Mass Communication, 4,* 284-300.

Potter, W.J. (2001). *Media literacy,* 2nd ed. Thousand Oaks, CA: Sage

Real, M. R. (1996). *Exploring media culture: A guide.* Thousand Oaks, CA: Sage.

Silverman, L. T., & Sprafkin, J. N. (1980). The effects of *Sesame Street*'s prosocial spots on cooperative play between young children. *Journal of Broadcasting and Electronic Media, 24,* 135–147.

Silverstone, R. (1999). *Why study the media?* Thousand Oaks, CA: Sage.

Smith, R.R. (1980). *Beyond the wasteland: The criticism of broadcasting* (rev. ed.) Urbana, IL: ERIC Clearing house on reading and communication and the Speech Communication Association.

Super Bowl TV Commercials Slower to Sell. (2001, December 5). *Sacramento Bee,* p. D5.

Super Bowl ads hitting $1.3 million. (1997, Jan. 8). *Sacramento Bee,* pp. F-1, F-4.

Vande Berg, L. R. (1993). *China Beach,* Prime time war in the postfeminist age: An example of patriarchy in a different voice. *Western Journal of Communication, 57,* 349–366.

Vande Berg, L. R. (1995). Living room pilgrimages: Television's cyclical commemoration of the assassination anniversary of John F. Kennedy. *Communication Monographs, 62,* 47–64.

Williams, R. (1974). *Television: Technology and cultural form.* London: Fontana.

Williams, T. M. (Ed.). (1986). *The impact of television: A natural experiment in three communities.* New York: Academic Press.

Zehme, B. (1989, June 1). *thirtysomething:* The real-life angst and ecstasy behind TV's most serious series. *Rolling Stone,* pp. 70–72, 75–76.

Zelizer, B. (1992). *Covering the body: The Kennedy assassination, the media, and the shaping of collective memory.* Chicago: University of Chicago Press.

Zillmann, D. (1982). Television viewing and arousal. In D. Pearl, L. Bouthilet, & J. Lazar (Eds.), *Television and behavior: Ten years of scientific progress and implications for the eighties: Vol. 2. Technical reviews* (pp. 53–67). Washington, DC: U.S. Government Printing Office.

Zillmann, D., & Bryant, J. (1985). *Selective exposure to communication.* Hillsdale, NJ: Erlbaum.

Foundations
of Television
Criticism

CHAPTER 2

Chapter Outline

The Mass Society/Popular Culture Debate:
A Historical Overview

Television and the Mass Society/Popular Culture Debate
Television and Other Cultural Forms
The Emergence of Television Criticism

Popular Culture, Media, and Television Criticism

What Criticism Is
What Criticism Is Not
Standards for Evaluating Television Criticism Essays

Shall we allow the children to hear any stories that chance to be told by
anyone without distinction and to take into their souls teachings that are
wholly opposite to those we wish them to be possessed of when they are
grown up?
—PLATO, *The Republic,* Book II, 377B

Although Plato's language certainly is more stilted than that used today, some 2,400 years later, the issue he raised—whether popular art, because of its potential influence on children and adolescents, should present only heroic, ideal, socially conservative mainstream values, ideas, and actions or whether it should also be allowed to present gritty, realistic stories about humans and their societies—remains a hotly debated issue. In *The Republic,* his book about the ideal democratic state, Plato took the position that popular culture (plays in his day) should present only morally uplifting narratives. His contemporary Aristophanes also wrote about this issue; but Aristophanes addressed the topic in a play, not in a treatise.

In his play *The Frogs,* Aristophanes dramatically debated this question in terms of which of two "great" playwrights should be brought back from the dead: Aeschylus or Euripides. Aeschylus's plays reflected the view that art should present life as it ideally should be. Through themes, actions, and subjects, his plays provided audiences with morally uplifting instruction in proper social and personal ethics—not unlike such wholesome "family" television series as *Mysterious Ways, Seventh Heaven, Judging Amy,* and *Everybody Loves Raymond.* Euripides's plays, in contrast, reflected his view that art should present realistic reflections of human life in all its grittiness, crime, corruption, and immorality—not unlike the realistic depictions presented in such contemporary television series as *NYPD Blue, ER, The Practice, Law and Order* and *Oz.*

Although Aristophanes eventually decided to bring Aeschylus and not Euripides back from the dead, the debate over the appropriate function of popular art in society clearly did not end in 400 B.C. For example, the 1989 premiere of the prime-time animated cartoon *The Simpsons* generated an immediate, and huge, controversy. Well-known individuals who weighed in with negative critiques of the series included then-President George H. W. Bush and former U.S. Secretary of Education William Bennett, both of whom publicly castigated the series for its subversive and authoritarian nature (McAllister, 1997, p. 1494). Several years later, during the 1992 presidential campaign, Vice President Dan Quayle delivered a speech in San Francisco in which he blamed the spring 1992 Los Angeles riots on the collapse of traditional family values (especially among African Americans) and argued that the television series *Murphy Brown* had contributed to this erosion of social values.[1]

As these contemporary examples illustrate, the argument about the appropriate role and content of popular art and culture—whether popular cultural forms should present life realistically or idealistically—has continued to simmer in the 24 centuries since Plato and Aristophanes grappled with it. In media studies, this debate is known as the *mass society/popular culture debate.* In the next section, we provide a brief historical overview of the arguments for and against each position in this debate so that you have a better context for understanding controversies over such popular television texts as *The Simpsons, Murphy Brown,* and *Beavis and Butthead.*

The Mass Society/Popular Culture Debate: A Historical Overview

While concern about the potential impact of popular culture on ordinary citizens was rife over 24 centuries ago, as Plato's *Republic* and Aristophanes' *The Frogs* indicate, the issue became particularly controversial in Western European societies as medieval religious and monarchical empires began to crumble. As Gans (1974) succinctly explains:

> During the pre-industrial era, European societies were divided culturally into high and folk culture. The latter was sparse, homemade, and, because peasants lived in isolated villages, largely invisible. The former was supported by the city-dwelling elites—the court, the nobility, the priesthood, and merchants—who had the time, education, and resources for entertainment and art and were able to subsidize a small number of creative people to produce culture for them. Both artists and intellectuals were close to the sources of power and some shared the prestige and privileges of their employers and patrons. Because of the low social status and geographical isolation of folk culture, they also had a virtual monopoly on public and visible culture. (pp. 52–53)

With the death of feudalism, the demise of the all-powerful religious states, and the rise of industrialism came economical, political, and technological changes, and many artists lost their financial support when the power and economic resources of their aristocratic patrons declined. These artists, who had led highly privileged, liberally endowed lifestyles, were forced to look beyond the elite classes for audiences and patronage. "In this process the artists forgot the subordination and humiliation they had often suffered at the hands of their patrons . . . and had only contempt for the new publics on whom they depended for economic support, even though these offered artists greater rewards and more freedom than they had before" (Gans, 1974, p. 53).

Socioeconomic elites—formerly these artists' patrons—responded to their loss of power and privilege and the cultural works that artists began producing for popular rather than elite audiences by resurrecting the popular culture critique Plato had expressed centuries before. These social elites argued that "high" art would suffer and that the general public would be corrupted by exposure to popular art and would become unwilling to accept their appropriately subordinate station in life. They feared that popular culture might become a potent force in advancing a social revolution that would result in these elites' further loss of control—not only over what was considered art and good taste but over economic, educational, and political institutions as well.

Social critics who embraced the demise of powerful monarchies and the rise of democracy feared that popular culture would have the opposite effect: They worried that instead of fomenting a revolution, popular culture products would narcotize ordinary working people, causing them to become complacent, and certainly bring about the demise of authentic folk cultures (see Gans, 1974; Lowenthal, 1959).

When sensationalized dime novels, affordable by the newly literate working and middle classes, appeared in England and in the United States between 1860 and 1901, the debate again flared up, as it did with renewed vigor at the emergence of each new popular culture form in the early decades of the twentieth century. Both movies and jazz were reviled by many social elite and educated classes as potential threats to public morality and to "real" art (see, e.g., Gans, 1974). Conservative, liberal, and radical groups all have charged that various forms of popular culture—including film, popular musical genres like rap, and television—would have dire social and cultural consequences (see, e.g., Real, 1976).

Among the most outspoken participants in the mass society/popular culture debate that seethed in the United States from the 1930s through the 1950s were Dwight Macdonald, Edward Shils, and C. Wright Mills (see Carey & Kreiling, 1974; Himmelstein, 1981). Macdonald (1957) argued that popular culture was a blight on the aesthetic landscape that debased high art, and Mills (1956) called the media tools through which the power elite in a society manipulates the masses and destroys democratic community life.

Mills and other critics of popular art and culture who share this view believe that the mass media have helped to turn "the public" into a "mass"—a collection of geographically and psychologically isolated individuals whose anonymity, lack of interaction with each other, and lack of shared involvement in community organizations leaves them relatively free from informal, binding social obligations and makes them far more vulnerable to manipulation because there are fewer interpersonal social checks and balances (Lowenthal, 1959; see also Gerbner, Gross, Morgan & Signorielli, 1986 and Tönnies', 1957, description of this change from *gemeinschaft* to *gesellschaft* societies).

Other popular and scholarly writers have defended popular art and culture forms, including television and film. Edward Shils (1960), for example, argued that popular culture had not debased people's taste or exploited aesthetic reception any more than "brutal culture" (i.e., folk culture) and that much of what is labeled "high culture" is extremely mediocre in quality (p. 291).

Television and the Mass Society/Popular Culture Debate

Advocates of popular culture argue that television and other forms of mass-mediated popular have far more benefits than drawbacks. For example, Marshall McLuhan's (1964) book *Understanding Media* predicted that rather than destroying our sense of community, the mass media would retribalize the world by creating less insular, less xenophobic societies—in fact, a global village—through nearly instantaneous visual and verbal communication with fellow humans across the hemispheres. If you were watching CNN's worldwide television coverage of the dawning of the new millennium on January 1, 2000, you can confirm that thanks to satellite television coverage, McLuhan's prediction has come true: TV has indeed transformed our planet into a global village.

Another defender of television and popular culture, writer Walter Karp, has urged parents not to worry about violence in television cartoons. In fact, Karp (1987) argues that sanitizing the violence out of cartoons would be a serious disservice to children. According to Karp, television viewing of violent cartoons, like reading violent fairy tales, can be therapeutic for children because the characters' "ultimate triumph provides the heartswelling promise that the child, too, will find inner strength" in the belief that real as well as fictional "monsters can be slain, injustice remedied, and all obstacles overcome on the hard road to adulthood" (pp. 437, 438; see also Bettleheim, 1976; Gunther, 1994).

A second critique leveled against television as popular art regards television's texts as aesthetically questionable because television programs are not the work of a single artist expressing his or her unique creative vision within an established aesthetic tradition, but rather the collective work of a group of individuals. Further, this critique claims that popular art forms like television debase "real art" because they substitute commercialized, standardized, assembly-line products for individual aesthetic expressions, and they turn audiences into mere consumers.

Implicit in this critique is the assumption that there is a hierarchy of art forms that ranges from mass culture/art, at the lowest hierarchical level, to high or elite art at the apex, with popular art/culture and folk art/culture falling between these two extremes. In this aesthetic critique, *popular art* (like television) includes works that combine familiar conventional forms expressive of common cultural experiences with creative originality and individual stylization (see Gans, 1974; Real, 1976). Examples of popular art include William Shakespeare's plays—in his day, Shakespeare's plays were viewed as popular art, and Christopher Marlowe's plays were high art (see Craig, 1961); of course, today Shakespeare's dramas are considered "elite art"), the Beatles' music, and Steven Bochco's TV series *NYPD Blue* and *Murder One*.

Folk art works are individually performed or created but technically and thematically unsophisticated works produced as variations on common grass roots or local traditions shared by the artist and the audience. The music of Joan Baez and Peter, Paul, and Mary and hand-sewn quilts created by individuals not employed by a corporation are examples of folk art. In contrast, *elite art* consists of technically complex and thematically unique creative forms that are produced by an identifiable artist in accordance with (or in opposition to) an accepted canon of works and within a conscious aesthetic context (Real, 1976). Examples of elite art include the music of Mozart, the paintings of Edward Hopper, the novels of James Joyce, the movies of François Truffaut and Jean Renoir, and such television productions as the BBC's *I, Claudius*.

Mass art refers to commercially distributed, standardized artistic forms that lack the complex individualism typical of elite art, the shared traditions of folk art, or the unique mixture of these qualities that makes popular art the hybrid it is. Mass art is created solely as a money-making venture and views its audiences not even as consumers, but as a "market." An example of mass art includes collectible

Elvis Presley plates such as those advertised in *TV Guide*. As cultural studies scholar Raymond Williams (1974) has explained, in contrast to elite, folk, and popular culture, which are created *by* people who share common values, ideas, and perspective with their audiences, mass culture is created *"for* a people by an internal or external social group and embedded in them by a range of processes from repressive imposition to commercial saturation" (p. 15). Given these definitions, you should not find it surprising that all cultural forms except elite art are regarded as artistically deficient by critics of popular culture.

Defenders of popular culture, including television, respond that to reject artistic creations merely because they are created by a group rather than a lone individual is an elitist prejudice. Such a snobbish view, they note, is not compatible with the democratic notion of respect for the plurality of ideas, tastes, and traditions. They also point out that although Steven Bochco did not single-handedly create and complete *NYPD Blue*, neither did Michelangelo single-handedly paint the ceiling of the Sistine Chapel. Both had helpers (see Gans, 1974). Furthermore, advocates of popular culture remind its detractors that the same shared values and ties that bind both elite and folk artists to their audiences can also link popular culture creators to their audiences (see, for example, the ethnographic study of *thirtysomething* viewers in Heide, 1995).

Another critique leveled against popular culture like television and rock music is that it debases high art because it steals its artists and ideas. As a result of this talent and idea drain, high culture (the individualized expressions of novelists, painters, and others) loses potential creators of unique intellectually and aesthetically challenging work to formulaic, derivative generic popular art productions. For support, these critics point to the loss of "elite" art works never written when such well-known literary figures as John Cheever (*The Shady Hill Kidnapping*) and Paddy Chayefsky (*Marty*) were "lured" into writing for the well-paying television medium rather than writing another novel or a Broadway play.

Defenders of popular culture respond that "originality" is a comparatively new aesthetic standard. They point out that it was not until the Renaissance, a period of European history beginning in the fourteenth century and continuing until the early years of the seventeenth century, that originality of subject matter, form, and technique became the normative aesthetic standard. Prior to that period, imitation of classical models with only minor innovations was the dominant aesthetic standard. Further, these defenders point out that a number of elite art forms—for example, the sonnet and haiku—also are highly formulaic and conventionalized.

Supporters of television and popular culture also argue that detractors of popular art forms like television should remember that aesthetic standards (i.e., what is regarded as artistically excellent) change over time. They note, as we mentioned earlier, that in his era, Shakespeare's plays were popular entertainment, not high art. Shakespeare wrote for a broad popular audience, not merely the aristocratic classes (Craig, 1961). Some of Charles Dickens's novels (now studied as classics in literature classes), like television soap operas and prime-time serial dramas, were initially offered to audiences in serial form, and Jane Austen's "feminine" novels of manners, like soap operas, were once looked down on by literary doyens. In fact, they explain, the only reason we have access to such elite art works as John

Donne's "The Canonization" and Edmund Spenser's "Epithalamion" is that these poems have been reprinted in mass-produced and mass-distributed books.

Finally, defenders of popular art and culture argue that distinctions among elite art, folk art, popular art, and mass art are merely pretexts for social class distinctions, and this, they note, is problematic for a democracy. Sociologist Herbert Gans (1974) effectively summarizes the political ideology that underlies the historical mass society/popular culture debate and the reason it remains important for us to consider today:

> The so-called mass culture critique is important because it is concerned with far more than media fare and consumer goods. It is really about the nature of the good life, and thus about the purpose of life in general, particularly outside the work role. It is also about which culture and whose culture should dominate in society, and represent it as the societal or national culture in the competition between contemporary societies and in the historical record of cultures or civilizations. As such, the mass culture critique is an attack by one element in society against another: by the cultured against the uncultured, the educated against the uneducated, the sophisticated against the unsophisticated, the more affluent against the less affluent, and the cultural experts against the laity. In each case, the former criticize the latter for not living up to their own standard of the good life. (pp. 3–4)

Cultural forms (like paintings, television programs, films, novels) don't just appear; they grow out of the values and aesthetic standards of a society. As Gans (1974) explains, in homogeneous societies where there is little diversity, there is often only a single standard of beauty or style of art. However, in heterogeneous societies like the United States, there are a number of different aesthetic standards, or "taste cultures." People do not all agree on a single view of what is pleasurable, desirable, and beautiful. Unfortunately, people also are not all tolerant of differences or willing to accept that others' aesthetic tastes are as valid as their own. Typically, those who wish to impose their values, including their aesthetic values, on everyone else are those with the greatest economic, social, and political power. Thus, "although most taste cultures are not explicitly political, all cultural content expresses values that can become political or have political consequences" (Gans, 1974, p. 103).

Television and Other Cultural Forms

Defenses of popular culture do not ignore that there are production and aesthetic differences among forms of popular culture as a result of their different mediums of expression (for example, the printed page, film, television, and live theater). Television programs differs from books and film in that television texts are far more ephemeral than are films or books. Even with 82 percent of U.S. homes possessing at least one videocassette recorder (U.S. Census Bureau 1998), most first-run television episodes air only twice during a year. Television texts are also unlike newly released films that have multiple daily screenings, old films that you can rent at video stores, or books that you can buy at bookstores or check out of your university or local public library. Television series are made up of 13 to 22 episodes, and there is no single archive of all of them.[2]

Another difference between television and film is that television programs most typically are viewed in the home and in a fragmented, distracted way. About two-thirds of the time when we are watching television, we are also simultaneously engaged in other activities—work, housework, eating, talking, reading, caring for children, doing schoolwork or hobbies—and watching television in the presence of at least one other person, who may periodically enter and leave the room, talk with us, and engage in other activities (Kubey & Csikszentmihalyi, 1990; LoSciuto, 1972, p. 59).

In contrast to the typically inattentive and distracted way we watch the most recent episodes of television series, when we watch the newest theatrical films, we go to cinema theaters. There, we sit in a quiet, dark room with others who are doing what we are doing: concentrating our focused, uninterrupted attention on the images being projected from behind our heads onto the large screen in front of us. These characteristics of theatrical film viewing have led a number of film scholars to recognize the similarities between watching films and dreaming and to use psychoanalytic theories to explain our relationship with films. For example, Peter Wood (1976) has argued that we can gain important insights into the meanings and functions of television, as well as film, by studying TV using psychoanalytic perspectives. We take up Wood's notion that television is our collective dreamwork in more detail as part of our discussion of psychoanalytic critical approaches to television in Chapter 15.

The Emergence of Television Criticism

Initially, television texts received little attention by critics in the popular press, in part because television was viewed (by newspaper owners) as competing with newspapers for the public's attention (and advertising dollars). Indeed, although trade publications like *Broadcasting* and *Variety* have chronicled television's industrial, production, or regulatory news since the 1950s, most newspaper writers assigned to the television beat—unlike writers assigned to review books, art exhibitions, and theatrical productions—have not treated television texts with the same serious attention that other cultural texts have received (Himmelstein, 1981).

Among the early journalistic writers and critics who did give serious critical attention to television as an important social and aesthetic force and provided thoughtful critical commentary on television texts were Laurence Laurent, John J. O'Connor of the *New York Times,* and Michael Arlen of the *New Yorker* (see, e.g., Arlen, 1977). More recently, this list has included Pulitzer Prize–winning media critics Tom Shales of the *Washington Post* and Howard Rosenberg of the *Los Angeles Times,* as well as David Zurawick of the *Baltimore Sun,* Thomas Feran of the *Cleveland Plain Dealer,* and David Bianculli of the *New York Daily News.*

Until the mid-1970s, little serious critical analysis of television could be found in scholarly journals and books, much less in popular periodicals. David Thorburn (1985), for example, writes that in the 1950s, many academics hid the fact that they watched television from their colleagues for fear they would be ridiculed for spending time with this quotidian mass medium.

Television and the critical analysis of television began to acquire some measure of academic respectability when Marshall McLuhan, a brilliant, unconventional Canadian literary scholar who began to study popular culture and media, was given a prestigious university distinguished chair and a six-figure salary (which was even more money 25 years ago than it is today). Shortly after McLuhan broke the academic snobbery barrier, literature and American studies scholars from prestigious universities, such as John Cawelti (1971, 1976) at the University of Chicago, began to write seriously about popular film and television. In 1967, when the popular literature division of the national scholarly English literature association, the Modern Language Association, began publishing the *Journal of Popular Culture*, the critical study of popular culture (and television) became almost academically respectable (Gronbeck, 1986, p. 335). This watershed point was achieved a few years later when America's first academic television critic to focus his scholarly lens solely on television, Horace Newcomb, published his book-length genre study, *TV: The Most Popular Art* (1974). Newcomb's scholarly work, including the 1976 publication of his first anthology of critical essays on television, *TV: The Critical View*, provided a scholarly foundation for the newly emergent area of television criticism (see also Newcomb, 1979, 1982, 1987, 1994, 2000b).

This attention to television by serious scholars in the mid-1970s coincided with what Newcomb (1986) has termed "television's renaissance."[3] This period included Larry Gelbart and Gene Reynold's *M*A*S*H*, MTM's[4] *The Mary Tyler Moore Show*, Norman Lear's *All in the Family* and *Maude*, and Garry Marshall's *Happy Days*.[5] As Newcomb put it, "for richness and complexity, challenge and delight" these popular culture texts were definitely worth taking seriously and writing critically about (1986, p. 220). Michael Real introduced American scholarly television critics to cultural studies when he published *Mass-mediated Culture* (1976), and noted rhetorical critic Bruce Gronbeck turned his attention from parliamentary rhetoric to the criticism of television (1978, 1979, 1984). As a result, an increasing number of communication studies departments in U.S. universities began offering courses at the undergraduate and graduate levels in television criticism.

Journalism also began taking the review and criticism of television texts more seriously. In 1978, a group of young journalists who were university trained in television and film criticism and were concerned about the quality of television programming, created the Television Critics Association. Today, the association publishes a bimonthly *TCA Newsletter* that includes interviews with writers, producers, directors, and network and cable executives, as well as examples of members' critical columns. It holds semiannual meetings during the members' twice-yearly trips to Universal City, California, to view the next season's lineups offered by the networks, public television, and independent production companies, and at these meetings it has panel sessions with presentations (sometimes by academic scholars) on such topics as academic television criticism, research on violence and television, and children and television.

Popular Culture, Media, and Television Criticism

Meanwhile, a different type of serious analysis of popular culture was developing in Great Britain. Beginning in the 1960s in Great Britain, an approach to the analysis of popular culture that blended several strands of critical and social theory emerged in the writings of Raymond Williams, Stuart Hall, and John Thompson. British Cultural Studies, as this approach came to be called, crossed the Atlantic in the early 1970s and further stimulated the fledgling American television criticism studies.[6] Especially influential for the evolution of U.S. television criticism was a work by two of the second generation of British Cultural Studies scholars, John Fiske and John Hartley: *Reading Television* (1978).

Arguably, the publication of John Fiske's *Television Culture* in 1987 truly marked academic television criticism's passage from adolescence to adulthood (see Gronbeck, 1988). This textual study of television combined the study of codes (a rule-governed system of signs, or symbols, that convey meaning), discourses (systems of representation that convey shared meanings about topics), and audiences (socially situated readers of television texts who actively negotiate the meanings encoded into television texts). It began a new era of television criticism by elegantly incorporating multiple approaches (neo-Marxist/ideological, semiotic-structural, feminist, psychoanalytic, screen theory, auteur, institutional, and audience ethnographies) into studies of gender, class, and race in media. Fiske's recent critical studies of television (1990, 1994a, 1994b) have extended these concerns and reconnected television criticism and social criticism.

Now that you have a grounding in the history of television criticism, it's time to talk about what exactly (television) criticism is and what it is not.

What Criticism Is

The act of criticism involves organizing, systematically and thoroughly describing, analyzing, interpreting, and evaluating the patterned relationships among symbols in texts in order to share an informed perspective with others. Critical essays have three absolutely necessary components:

1. A thesis statement, which expresses the central, overarching interpretation, critical insight, or evaluation that the rest of the criticism essay expands on

2. Logical arguments that develop the thesis, which may be framed as either a question or an interpretive proposition

3. Concrete and specific supporting evidence, including examples of dialogue; plot and scene descriptions; other details from specific television program episodes; quotations from other published critical analyses or theoretical articles that define critical concepts and illustrate their application to other television texts; and testimony from expert and authoritative sources (e.g.,

about a series' popularity, census or viewership data, a network's reasons for canceling a series, actual viewers' responses to programs)

Without any one of these three elements, an essay is not criticism.

As Wander and Jenkins (1972) aptly put it, "Criticism, at its best, is informed talk about matters of importance" (p. 450). This definition of television criticism contains several implicit assumptions. The first is that television is a popular art form that is potentially just as socioculturally and aesthetically meaningful and important as literature, theater, painting, music, and arts and therefore just as deserving of serious critical analysis as are they. Second, this definition assumes that television criticism, like criticism generally, is epistemic. By this, we mean that writing critical analyses of television generates knowledge and understanding about what television texts are, the meanings television texts provoke, and the nature of the relationships among television, society, and ourselves.

Critical Methods   Critics use a variety of tools, called methods or approaches or perspectives, to talk about and analyze television. Critical methods (or approaches) are simply sets of technical vocabularies, analytical constructs, and normative assumptions that allow critics to organize their observations and communicate their insights and interpretations systematically and efficiently. As Gronbeck (1980) has pointed out, critical methods are really shared codes that critics and their readers have learned to understand and use. Parts Two, Three, and Four of this book introduce you to some of the different methods you can use to analyze and explain the meanings of television programs.

Writing Criticism for Various Audiences   As you learned in your basic speech and composition classes, all public presentations (and writing is a public presentation) need to be adapted for the audiences that will be receiving them. One explains the physics of top spin in tennis very differently to a seventh grader than to a nuclear scientist. Similarly, television critics write their essays somewhat differently depending on which of three general types of audiences they have in mind for a specific essay: (1) the academic audience of students, television and communication scholars, and other academics, (2) the television industry audience composed of writers, directors, producers, and program decision makers, or (3) the general public audience. The principal differences in critical essays written for these audiences are the depth of supporting argumentation, the nature and amount of supporting evidence cited, and the extent to which the method and theoretical assumptions that the critic used to arrive at the critical interpretation are explicitly laid out for the reader.

The essays in this book were written for the academic audience of students like you, television and communication scholars, and other academics. As a result, they will provide a more thorough definition of the theoretical and analytical concepts the critics used to examine television texts, and longer, more well-developed, and well-supported explanations of their critical conclusions than you would find in critical essays in popular magazines and newspapers.

What Criticism Is Not

It should be clear from the preceding discussion that television criticism is not everyday unsupported opinion, whether offered by ordinary TV viewers, paid journalists, Hollywood executives, or university students and professors. It also should be clear that criticism is not necessarily negative; criticism also can be appreciative systematic analysis.

Criticism also is not the same thing as history. Although a critical essay may trace the evolution of a genre of television programming or map the relationships among the medium of television, the programs airing during a particular era, the regulatory policies operative at that time, and societal events, criticism, unlike history, does not stop there. That is because television critics write such essays for different reasons than historians do. In contrast to the historian, who focuses on questions of what and why, the critic typically is more concerned with how and what it means. As Gronbeck (1980) explains, the critic "is more concerned with generating than finding meaningfulness" (p. 13). Criticism, then, is concerned with providing insightful interpretations that stimulate viewers to look at a television program or group of programs in a new and different way.

Criticism also is not social scientific hypothesis testing, although critics do sometimes count things (see Porter, 1987). Unlike the social scientist who primarily is interested in making predictions about how things work in order to control them, the critic's primary interest is understanding how things work—in post hoc, not predictive, explanations of meaning construction. The critic's goal is to better understand television texts as meaningful sociocultural symbolic forms and forces.

Finally, criticism is not theory. A well-written critical analysis often moves beyond interpreting a particular program or viewing experience to make a contribution to our theoretical understanding about the processes of meaning production and audience reception at work in television programs. However, the primary goals of criticism are understanding, explanation, and appreciation, not theory building. Thus, criticism is not constructed or delivered as a theoretical treatise, although critics rely on theoretical concepts, and their insights often advance critical television theory.

Standards for Evaluating Serious Television Criticism Essays

Now that we have a general understanding of what television criticism is (and what it is not), we can identify appropriate standards for evaluating the merits of television criticism essays. For example, because television criticism is not social scientific research, the social science standards of validity, reliability, and significance—whether a main effect at the specified level of statistical significance was found—are not appropriate standards for evaluating the merits of a serious television criticism essay. Similarly, because criticism is not personal opinion or diatribe, the personal bias standard (i.e., whether the central critical proposition and the writing seem right or wrong according to my individual biases as a reader) is not an appropriate standard.

The standard you should use in evaluating the merits of television criticism essays—both the example essays provided in this book and your own critical essays—should be the thoroughness and elegance with which the critical essay meets four criteria:

Four Criteria for Evaluating Television Criticism Essays

1. Does it possess internal consistency?
2. Does it provide sufficient, appropriate evidence for the claims implied by the thesis and advanced in the essay?
3. Does it offer a plausible rationale for its cultural, critical, theoretical, or practical significance?
4. Does it cause an astute reader to accept the critical interpretation or explanation argued for in the essay as a reasonable one?

Let's examine each of these four criteria that make up our evaluative standard.

Internal Consistency Internal consistency refers to the goodness of fit among the three elements we talked about earlier: the central critical proposition (the critical interpretation or thesis that the rest of the essay develops and supports), the arguments and the evidence used to support the arguments, and the general conclusions or implications the critic draws from the results of the analysis. The arguments and concluding implications the critic arrives at must follow logically from the essay's thesis or central interpretation.

Evidence The criterion of ample, appropriate evidence is one of the important differences between criticism and everyday opinion. A critic must provide sufficient evidentiary support so that a reasonable reader can judge the plausibility of the critic's interpretation. Of course, there is no magic yardstick for deciding if the amount of evidence is sufficient to make the critic's argument plausible. However, this criterion assumes that the evidence the writer has provided is sufficient if you think it would convince an open-minded but demanding critical reader that this interpretation of the television text is one that a reasonable, educated person could arrive at.

Significance This standard requires that the critic explain the cultural, critical, theoretical, or practical significance of the critic's analysis. Thus, this criterion requires that the critic explain to the reader both why the time the critic spent to research, analyze, and write this particular critical essay was worthwhile and why a reader would be well served by reading the results of the critic's analysis.

Reasonableness The final criterion is a statement about the nature and degree of persuasion that must be accomplished by the critical analysis. Notice that this standard does not specify that a critical essay offer "the truth" or "the right explanation." Rather, this standard requires that the critical essay must provide *one* (but not the only) insightful interpretation and explain the systematic, reasoned analysis that led the critic to arrive at this explanation.

Criticism is rigorous, systematic analysis, but it is also subjective, not objective.[7] The critic *is* the analytical instrument; critical theories and methods are just tools the critic uses to deconstruct television texts in order to understand some of their potential meanings better. The reader does not have to be persuaded that an essay provides *the* definitive explanation or interpretation of a television text (or group of texts). Indeed, in criticism, we assume that there are multiple reasonable interpretations, or readings, of each television program. The reader also doesn't have to be persuaded to arrive at moral, aesthetic, or political agreement with the critic's beliefs and perspective. However, an open-minded reader does need to be persuaded by the arguments, evidence, and conclusion by each critical essay that the critic's interpretation is plausible, sufficiently well supported, and concerned with a socially, critically, or aesthetically important issue, construct, or text. An essay that meets these standards is indeed good criticism.

Looking Ahead

In this chapter, we looked briefly at the foundations of television criticism, including the historical debate about popular culture and the development of academic television criticism. We also provided a working definition of what television criticism is and what it is not. We described the essential elements a critical essay must have and the standards for evaluating the quality of critical essays. In Chapter 3, we discuss some of the ways in which television criticism can be classified, some of the problems critics face in choosing a critical approach, and how to get started writing your first television criticism essay. Then in Chapter 4, we provide a model outline of what a television criticism essay generally should look like—what its parts are and how it is organized—recognizing that models are general blueprints, not rigid molds.

Notes

1. See Fiske (1994b) for a discussion of media coverage of the speech and the ensuing brouhaha.

2. Most theatrically released films are available on videotape (at your neighborhood video store) or in archives at major universities. However, there are no comparable repositories of old television programs. True, your local video store may have a few videotapes or DVDs with several episodes of *I Love Lucy, Dragnet,* or *Star Trek* on them, but remember that most TV series produce 20 to 22 episodes a year. Good luck finding a copy of the four episodes of Steven Bochco's *Cop Rock* (1990) series or the six episodes of his *Bay City Blues* (1983) series that aired on prime-time television. Not even the Museum of Broadcasting in New York City, the Museum of Television and Radio in Beverly Hills, or even the Library of Congress has all the episodes of all American television series. Each of these archives has only selected episodes of selected series.

3. See also Thompson (1996).

4. MTM is the acronym for the Mary Tyler Moore Company, an independent Hollywood production company established in 1970 by Mary Tyler Moore, her manager, Arthur Price, and her husband, Grant Tinker.

5. Soon other American scholars also began writing serious television criticism. Two influential edited collections, Adler's *Television as a Cultural Force* (1976) and Cater and Adler's *Television as a Social Force* (1975), reprinted television criticism papers that had been presented at conferences on television studies sponsored by the Aspen Institute for Humanistic Studies. Scholarly conferences such as the Television Drama Conferences at Michigan State University in the early 1980s, the 1984 University of Iowa Television Criticism Symposium (organized by Bruce Gronbeck), the Visual Communication Conferences (brainchild of Robert Tiemans of the University of Utah and Herb Zettl of San Francisco State University), and the feminist Console-ing Passions conferences all have contributed to the development and legitimization of television criticism as a significant area of study (see Gronbeck, 1988; Newcomb, 1986, 2000a; Vande Berg,1997).

6. As Gronbeck (1999) has explained, a separate, more anthropological American cultural studies tradition also exists.

7. Indeed, as Tuchman (1978) and others have noted, objectivity is really just a strategic ritual for performing certain tasks efficiently and with a minimal number of challenges.

Further Reading

Thompson, R. J. (1996). *Television's second golden age: From* Hill Street Blues *to* ER. New York: Continuum. In this smooth aesthetic history of television, Thompson argues that with the appearance in 1982 of *Hill Street Blues* and continuing through the mid-1990s, it is clear that the "golden age" of television was not the 1950s but rather the 1980s and 1990s. He then develops eleven characteristics of quality TV and uses these in his book-length aesthetic analysis of the decade of prime-time "quality dramas" that aired on U.S. television networks between 1982 and 1992.

Webnotes

U.S. Census: Statistical Abstract of the United States, 1999. **http://www.census. gov/statab/www/index.html**

In addition to this abstract, there is the complete 1,045-page report, **http:// www.census.gov/prod/www/statistical-abstract-us.html,** which is the most recent statistical report of economic and social conditions in the United States. One new feature in the 1999 report is a section titled "20th Century Statistics," which provides historical data from 1900 on such subjects as education, population, the U.S. labor force, and ownership of television sets.

National Opinion Research Center: The Emerging 21st Century Family. **http:// www.norc.uchicago.edu/online/emerge.pdf**

The National Opinion Research Center at the University of Chicago conducts general social and international social surveys. In January 2000, as part of its research, it released a report on the American family that revealed, among other interesting data, that in 1972, 45 percent of American households were composed of married couples with children, while in 1998 only 26 percent of U.S. households were made up of married couples with children. Such data raise interesting questions about the "ideal" and "realistic" depiction of families on prime-time TV, and provide ideas for critical analyses of television series.

Learning Activities

1. Using the *Reader's Guide to Periodical Literature* or an online database that includes daily newspapers and newspapers, look up four or five articles written by one of the Pulitzer Prize–winning television critics (Howard Rosenberg of the *Los Angeles Times* or Tom Shales of the *Washington Post*), or legendary journalistic critics about television (such as the *New Yorker* magazine's Michael Arlen, who wrote for the magazine in the 1970s and 1980s, or the *New York Times*'s John J. O'Connor), or contemporary journalistic critics regarded as opinion leaders by their news and academic peers (such as David Zurawik of the *Baltimore Sun*). Describe the topics of their articles. For which of the three audiences described in this chapter do you think the critic is writing? What evidence in their essay leads you to this conclusion? Use the four criteria for evaluating the quality of critical essays discussed in this chapter. Do their essays stand up well under this kind of critical scrutiny? In which of these areas are they weak? What about newspaper or magazine publication do you think might account for areas in which these journalistic articles do not meet the criteria for solid criticism essays?

2. Do a search for the word *television* using Lexis/Nexis or a comparable search engine in newspapers and news magazines for a one-week period. How many citations did you get? How many were in the entertainment section? In sports? In national and world news (usually section A)? In the metropolitan area? What does this tell you about the important role that television plays in all aspects of our lives?

References

Adler, R. (Ed.). (1976). *Television as a cultural force.* New York: Praeger.

Aristophanes. (1962). *The frogs* (R. Lattimore Trans.). Ann Arbor: University of Michigan Press. (Original work published circa 450–385 B.C.)

Arlen, M. J. (1977, Nov. 23). The prosecutor. *New Yorker,* 166–173.

Bettelheim, B. (1976). *The uses of enchantment: The meaning and importance of fairy tales.* New York: Random House.

Carey, J., & Kreiling, A. (1974). Popular culture and uses and gratifications: Notes toward an accommodation. In J. G. Blumler & E. Katz (Eds.), *The uses of mass communication: Current perspectives on gratifications research* (pp. 225–248). Thousand Oaks, CA: Sage.

Cater, D., & Adler, R. (Eds.). (1975). *Television as a social force: New approaches to criticism.* New York: Praeger.

Cawelti, J. G. (1971). *The six-gun mystique.* Bowling Green, OH: Bowling Green University Popular Press.

Cawelti, J. G. (1976). *Adventure, mystery, romance: Formula stories as art and popular culture.* Chicago: University of Chicago Press.

Craig, H. (Ed.). (1961). *The complete works of Shakespeare.* Glenview, IL: Scott, Foresman.

Feuer, J., Kerr, P., & Vahimagi, T. (1984). *MTM "quality" television.* London: British Film Institute.

Fiske, J. (1987). *Television culture.* London: Methuen.

Fiske, J. (1990). Ethnosemiotics: Some personal and theoretical reflections. *Cultural Studies, 4,* 85–99.

Fiske, J. (1994a). Audiencing: Cultural practice and cultural studies. In N. K. Denzin & Y. S. Lincoln (Eds.), *Handbook of qualitative research* (pp. 189–198). Thousand Oaks, CA: Sage.

Fiske, J. (1994b). *Media matters: Everyday culture and political change.* Minneapolis: University of Minnesota Press.

Fiske, J., & Hartley, J. (1978). *Reading television.* London: Methuen.

Gans, H. (1974). *Popular culture and high culture: An analysis and evaluation of taste.* New York: Basic Books.

Gerbner, G., Gross, L., Morgan, M., & Signorielli, N. (1986). Living with television: The dynamics of the cultivation process. In J. Bryant & D. Zillmann (Eds.), *Perspectives on media effects* (pp. 17–40). Hillsdale, NJ: Erlbaum.

Gronbeck, B. E. (1978). Celluloid rhetoric: On genres of documentary. In K. K. Campbell & K. M. Jamison (Eds.), *Form and genre: Shaping rhetorical action* (pp. 139–162). Falls Church, VA: Speech Communication Association.

Gronbeck, B. E. (1979). Television criticism and the classroom. *Journal of the Illinois Speech-Theatre Association, 33,* 1–12.

Gronbeck, B. E. (1980, Nov.). *Meaning and epistemic claims in criticism.* Paper presented at the annual meeting of the Speech Communication Association, New York.

Gronbeck, B. E. (1984). *Writing television criticism.* Chicago: Science Research Associates.

Gronbeck, B. E. (1988). The academic practice of television criticism. *Quarterly Journal of Speech, 74,* 334–347.

Gronbeck, B. E. (1999). The triumph of social science: *The Silent Language* as master text in American cultural studies. In T. Rosteck (Ed.). *At the intersection: Cultural studies and rhetorical studies* (pp. 266–291). New York: Guilford Press.

Gunter, B. (1994). The question of media violence. In J. Bryant & D. Zillmann (Eds.), *Media effects: Advances in theory and research* (pp. 163–212). Hillsdale, NJ: Erlbaum.

Heide, M. J. (1995). *Television culture and women's lives:* thirtysomething *and the contradictions of gender.* Philadelphia: University of Pennsylvania Press.

Himmelstein, H. (1981). *On the small screen: New approaches in television and video criticism.* New York: Praeger.

Horace. (1919–1974/65–8 B.C.). Ars poetica (N. DeWitt, Trans.). In A. Preminger, O. B. Hardinson, Jr., & K. Kerrane (Eds.), *Classical and medieval literary criticism* (pp. 158–170). New York: Frederick Ungar.

Karp, W. (1987). Where the do-gooders went wrong. In H. Newcomb (Ed.), *Television: The critical view* (4th ed., pp. 433–444). New York: Oxford University Press.

Kubey, R., & Csikszentmihalyi, M. (1990). *Television and the quality of life: How viewing shapes everyday experience.* Hillsdale, NJ: Erlbaum.

LoSciuto, L. A. (1972). A national inventory on television viewing behavior. In *U.S. Surgeon General Scientific Advisory Report on Television and Social Behavior* (pp. 33–86). Washington, DC: U.S. Government Printing Office.

Lowenthal, L. (1959). A historical preface to the popular culture debate. In N. Jacobs (Ed.), *Culture for the millions? Mass media in modern society* (pp. 28–42). Boston: Beacon Press.

Macdonald, D. (1957). A theory of mass culture. In B. Rosenberg & D. M. White (Eds.), *Mass culture: The popular arts in America* (pp. 59–73). Glencoe, IL: Free Press.

McAllister, M.P. (1997).*The Simpsons:* U.S. cartoon situation comedy. In H. Newcomb (Ed.), *Encyclopedia of television* (pp. 1493-1495). Chicago: Fitzroy Dearborn.

McLuhan, M. (1964). *Understanding media.* London: Routledge & Kegan Paul.

Mills, C. W. (1956). *The power elite.* New York: Oxford University Press.

Newcomb, H. (1974). *TV: The most popular art.* Garden City, NY: Doubleday.

Newcomb, H. (Ed.). (1976). *Television: The critical view.* New York: Oxford University Press.

Newcomb, H. (Ed.). (1979). *Television: The critical view* (2nd ed.). New York: Oxford University Press.

Newcomb, H. (Ed.). (1982). *Television: The critical view* (3rd ed.). New York: Oxford University Press.

Newcomb, H. (1986). American television criticism 1970–1985. *Critical Studies in Mass Communication, 3,* 217–228.

Newcomb, H. (Ed.). (1987). *Television: The critical view* (4th ed.). New York: Oxford University Press.

Newcomb, H. (Ed.). (1994). *Television: The critical view* (5th ed.). New York: Oxford University Press.

Newcomb, H. (2000a). Television and the present climate of criticism. In H. Newcomb (Ed.), *Television: The critical view* (6th ed., pp. 1–16). New York: Oxford University Press.

Newcomb, H. (Ed.). (2000b). *Television: The critical view* (6th ed.). New York: Oxford University Press.

Plato. (1962). *The republic, Book II.* In A. Gilbert (Ed. & Trans.), *Literary criticism: Plato to Dryden.* Detroit: Wayne State University Press. (Original work published circa 429–347 B.C.)

Porter, M. J. (1987). A comparative analysis of directing styles in *Hill Street Blues. Journal of Broadcasting and Electronic Media, 31,* 323–334.

Real, M. R. (1976). *Mass-mediated culture.* Englewood Cliffs, NJ: Prentice Hall.

Shils, E. (1960). Mass society and its culture. *Daedalus, 89,* 228–314.

Thompson, R. J. (1996). *Television's second golden age: From* Hill Street Blues *to* ER. New York: Continuum.

Thorburn, D. (1985, Apr.). *An aesthetic approach to television criticism.* Paper presented at the University of Iowa Symposium and Conference on Television Criticism, Iowa City.

Tönnies, F. (1957). *Gemeinschaft und gesellschaft* (Trans. by C. P. Loomis as Community and Society). East Lansing: Michigan State University Press. (Original work published in 1887)

Tuchman, G. (1978). *Making news: A study in the construction of reality.* New York: Free Press.

U.S. Census Bureau. (1998). *Statistical abstract of the United States.* Washington, DC: Government Printing Office.

U.S. Surgeon General's Scientific Advisory Report on Television and Social Behavior. (1972). Washington, DC: U.S. Government Printing Office.

Vande Berg, L. R. (1997, Nov. 21). *Television criticism: A wealth of critical approaches.* "Sharing the Wealth" presentation at the annual National Communication Association convention, Chicago.

Wander, P., & Jenkins, S. (1972). Rhetoric, society, and the critical response. *Quarterly Journal of Speech, 58,* 441–450.

Williams, R. (1974, Nov. 23). On high and popular culture. *New Republic,* p. 15.

Wood, P. (1976). Television as dream. In R. Adler (Ed.), *Television as a cultural force* (pp. 17–36). New York: Praeger.

Critical Approaches to Television Discourse:
An Overview

CHAPTER 3

Chapter Outline

Three Ways to Classify Types of Television Criticism

Horace Newcomb: Subject Matter

Raymond Williams: Pluralistic Criticism

Aspen Institute Program: Critical Approaches

Types of Television Criticism: Problems and Solutions

Essentialism

Pluralism

Partiality or Perspectivism

The Issue of Televisual "Realism"

Overcoming the Problems

Often people believe that the essence of criticism is judgment: "I like water-melon," "I hate polkas," "The Statue of Liberty is magnificent," "Steven Se-gal movies assault humanity." Such thinking reflects the everyday use of the term *criticism*. Colloquially, "to criticize" means to say something extraordi-narily good or bad about somebody or something. Actually, criticism—especially the kinds generated by intellectuals, scholars, and liberally educated students—is designed to engage other people in acts of analysis, interpretation, and assess-ment. So if you say the president delivered a disgusting speech on drilling for oil in the Alaskan tundra or that *Shrek* was a cleverly designed racist and sexist movie, you'll likely face challenges to explain and defend yourself. A critical argument is a statement—often a judgment, yes—plus reasons that justify thinking that the statement is acceptable and important.

If you're to be understood as making serious critical arguments, then you'll have to go beyond mere judgment and into the world of "good reasons."[1] You'll have to argue: "The president's speech on drilling in Alaska was disgusting *because* he demonstrated a complete disregard for the environment and sidestepped com-pletely the issue of American overconsumption of oil" or "*Shrek* is racist and sexist *because* its characters are visually and vocally coded in racial and gender stereo-types and hence help to perpetuate destructive images, especially of African Americans and females." The "because" clauses make criticism into something more than knee-jerk praise or condemnation. They also become ways that we can define different types of approaches to critical essay writing.

We say "essay writing" because the interpretive arguments that critics make are complete thoughts, usually with an introduction, a body, and a conclusion (Brock-riede, 1974). A good critical essay introduces its subject matter in a way that sug-gests its importance. The following statement tells the reader of your piece on *Shrek* that this animated film should be taken seriously: "Because films are bigger than life and because cartoons usually are thought of as entertainment rather than as sources of cultural education, the moral visions of life that they propagate need to be explicitly examined and evaluated." And good criticism has conclusions. Critics don't just stop writing; rather, they work to suggest implications of the ma-terial they've analyzed and interpreted. They address the question "So what?" So what if *Shrek* is racist and sexist? That "So what?" question should lead to serious discussion of children's media experiences—about cartoons as learning environ-ments with especially potent social lessons embedded in them and about the so-cial and political consequences of film fantasies. And what's true of judgments about presidential speeches and children's movies is true as well of television pro-grams.

If television criticism is to be a valuable intellectual enterprise, we must know what kinds of texts or discourses comprise the televisual experience and try to un-derstand the ways in which those texts or discourses can be approached critically. The purpose of this chapter is to examine some of the ways that critics have ap-proached television texts so that we can offer an informed and reasonable scheme for talking about types of television criticism in the rest of this book.

Three Ways to Classify
Types of Television Criticism

The work of television critics can be divided in multiple ways. Three approaches to the classification of types of criticism, however, have dominated the history of televisual studies. Horace Newcomb (genre), Raymond Williams (pluralism), and the editors of the Aspen Institute Program's Workshop on Television (critical perspectivism) each featured a different method for classifying the work of TV critics.

Horace Newcomb: Subject Matter

In his 1974 book, *TV, the Most Popular Art,* Horace Newcomb followed a time-honored practice of literary studies: he classified approaches to criticism by types of television program. Just as you're likely to see literary criticism divided by type of literature (poetry, drama, novels, essays), so Newcomb showed his readers how to do critical analyses of different kinds of TV programs. He reviewed the principal genres or kinds of shows: situation and domestic comedies, westerns, mysteries (police and detective shows), doctors and lawyers (professional shows), adventure shows, soap operas, news/sports/documentary, and what he called new shows (shows that defied generic classification because they mixed elements from several genres).

For each of these genres, Newcomb suggested formulaic ways of analyzing that sort of program by examining character types, plots, and the environment (setting). By studying character, plot, and setting, Newcomb argued, we are able to understand television formulas, that is, the habitual ways particular types of programs are put together. His interest in formulas came not from a desire to put down television as predictable and simplistic, but from a hope that reforming formulas can help us better understand our culture—the beliefs, attitudes, hopes, and fears of a citizenry—as it is presented to us daily by TV. Newcomb articulated his goal in this way:

> Each chapter deals with a separate formula or with a group of related formulas. While we explore the sense of cultural significance, it is also possible to define a set of artistic techniques, aesthetic devices that contribute to some unique capabilities on the part of television. The things that television does best are directly related to the most formulaic and popular works. They are developed in various ways by the various formulas we examine and build into a set of possibilities that allow television, like other media, to go beyond the popular and into works of great artistic complexity and cultural significance. (1974, pp. 23–24)

Newcomb's interest in the artistry of television led him to conclude the book with a chapter titled "Toward a Television Aesthetic," in which he discussed television as a medium characterized by intimacy, (dis)continuity, and history. Our sense of intimacy, he noted, was due in part to the smallness of the screen and in part to the ways in which good directors shoot a TV show, with many close-ups that rely on concreteness of detail and the emotional impact of direct involvement. Second, the lack of continuity on most television programs—the characters of most shows seemingly have no memory of what happened in previous weeks—means that television creates no artistic probability and little analytical force. Because episodic shows end with their problems neatly resolved on a weekly basis, there is little chance for sophisticated studies of human turmoil, except in some multipart specials such as *Roots, A Band of Brothers,* or *Masterpiece Theatre* episodes. The lack of continuity (memory, reflection) limits television's serious effect in our lives, according to Newcomb. And third, television is strongly historical. Not only does the recent past provide the plots for most programs, but the more distant past—the mythic past of the United States—provides the underlying formulas for many stories. Television seeks whatever depth it has through myth (see Chapter 12).

Newcomb, in other words, classifies television programs by program type or genre and then asks critics to investigate the formulas typical of each type so that we can understand the breadth of television's aesthetic.

Raymond Williams: Pluralistic Criticism

In his 1974 book, *Television: Technology and Cultural Form,* Cambridge University professor Raymond Williams explored relationships between television as a governmentally regulated communications technology and television as a social experience. The book was written while he was at Stanford University, so he was able to compare British and American experiences with the technological and cultural form.

To Williams, it is important for critics to examine not only characteristics of a technology and the social uses to which a technology is put, but also the economic links between technology and social uses. A new communications technology, after all, is not developed unless someone can make money selling it, and then the actual delivery of communication messages must be paid for as well. Technology and culture are linked in societies by economics, in the case of democracies, or politics, in the case of fascist regimes (1974, p. 24).

Williams was convinced that no critic can adequately analyze television without examining (1) the institutions of the technology (governmental, economic, artistic), (2) the forms of television (the types of programs inherited from other media or newly developed for TV), (3) the distribution and flow of programming (how consumer markets are divided up and regulated through sequences of programs on a station or network), and (4) the effects of the consumption of the technology by a society (the way that television is used in particular societies and measurable effects of those uses). These four ideas are represented in the central chapters of the book.

In other words, Williams saw technological development and expansion, economic and political institutions, and the social uses of television locked up in direct relationships with each other. Criticism therefore had to be pluralistic: a combination of technological history, examination of economic and political controls, a content analysis of program offerings on different channels, the close study of flow of programs on specific days of specific weeks, and the social scientific study of effects. For Williams, a critical analysis of a TV program such as *COPS* could not proceed without an understanding of the economics of inexpensive (VHS system) production, the programming that local channels need to supply between their news hour and the beginning of prime-time network fare, the formulaic aspects of cop shows, the electronic-digital distribution of shows from independent producers to stations, and the public's interest in law-and-order issues in the late twentieth-century.[2] In his view, criticism that ignored some aspects of the television production and delivery system was flawed. Pluralism—many things at onceness–should characterize TV criticism.

No one (except Williams himself) has ever really executed this pluralistic analytical task completely, yet his influence on British and American television critics is immense.[3] His insistence on tying together technologies, economics, politics, and social impact can be seen in studies of the political economy underlying programming, studies of relationships between television as technology and television as social force, and the new ethnographic studies of how real people make meaning from TV in real social situations. He and Newcomb together launched contemporary television criticism (Gronbeck, 1988).

Aspen Institute Program: Critical Approaches

The Aspen Institute for Humanistic Studies in Washington, D.C., set up its program in 1971 to foster analysis of public broadcasting, government and media, and the sociocultural aspects of television. Under the directorship of Douglass Cater, the Aspen Institute Program launched workshops for researchers and critical scholars to explore television's role in society. Its first two publications were *Television as a Social Force* (Cater & Adler, 1975) and *Television as a Cultural Force* (Adler, 1976). The 1975 volume was sensitive to the economic, political, regulatory, and social aspects of television—primarily institutional studies. The 1976 volume was important in the history of TV criticism.

Richard Adler, associate director of the institute, opened the 1976 volume with a definition of television as a medium, citing its four primary characteristics: (1) diversity (a great variety of types of programs shown weekly), (2) intimacy (we accept it uncritically as a familiar friend), (3) flow (television is composed of programs but viewed across time in larger or at least regularized ways, making it difficult for textual critics to know what to analyze), and (4) simplicity (a childish medium that makes it difficult for critics to access it fairly). Adler also noted its small screen, which hampers television's ability to show spectacle, and its low-fidelity sound system, giving its music a thin quality. TV is much better for sports, news, and public affairs than it is for opera or spectacular movies (Adler, 1976).

The chapters in the 1976 volume were highly diverse, reflecting different kinds of programs and, more important, different approaches to critical analysis. Peter Wood used a psychoanalytic approach to analyze television as dream. Paula Fass explored television comedy as a part of our cultural equipment. Kenneth Pierce examined *All in the Family*'s mixing of comedy and news genres. David Thorburn viewed television programming as melodrama, and Robert Alley explored the morality documented in medical shows. A method for examining how television shows might aid the moral development of children was featured in Kevin Ryan's chapter, and Sharon Lynn Sperry argued that the narrative form of news controls the way we experience the world. In other words, the Aspen Institute Program book suggested structurally that television programs could be studied through a variety of methods or approaches. The critical approaches view of television criticism was born that year.[4]

Contemporary Television Criticism

By now, most books on television criticism are variations and extensions of one of these three approaches: by subject matter, by multiple or pluralistic modes of attack, and by type of criticism. Types of criticism—critical approaches—receive the most emphasis in our time. For one thing, a types approach recognizes that criticism is a way of looking at the world, with each approach or type of criticism representing a different way of looking at a program or the medium. Cultural criticism places the program in its broadest social context, and psychoanalytic criticism in its most secret and private dimensions; genre criticism is centered on the ways literatures can be classified, and feminist criticism on the ways women are gazed on and portrayed in series. The different critical approaches show us different questions people ask about their world.

The critical approaches school of TV analysis is also popular because it puts primary emphasis on the television program—what we refer to as the text. Most critics do their best work when faced with a text: a musical score, a poem, a novel, a film, or a videotape of a TV program. Most critics have been trained to read closely, that is, to dissect particular aspects of texts. The critical approaches school of television criticism is generally textually oriented. We are not suggesting that it is easy to define what the text is (see Chapter 5), only that textual analysis dominates television criticism, as this book illustrates.

Williams's concerns with history, the industry, and viewers' experiences cannot be forgotten; nor should Newcomb's early emphasis on types of programs be ignored. We must remember that *television* is an ambiguous word, referring to a technology, an industry, a piece of furniture, a lifelong experience, and the specific programs viewers watch. Our explorations of television must reflect those ambiguities. The interests of Williams are reflected in the institutional studies in Chapter 11, and the Alternative Table of Contents is constructed around Newcomb's generic emphases.

Types of Television Criticism: Problems and Solutions

We have arranged this book by critical approaches, yet there is a series of obstacles involved in constructing any typology of critical approaches. The phrase *critical approaches* is ambiguous and abstract enough to need specification, and yet it must be broad enough to have some intellectual flexibility. To illustrate these requirements, consider four problems we confront when talking about critical approaches: essentialism, pluralism, partiality, and realisticness.

Essentialism

Too often, critics assume that each type of criticism is a pure form that must be maintained in pristine condition when being used. If you are doing a psychoanalytic analysis of *NYPD Blue,* you might think that you should talk only in Freudian or Jungian terms and not mention cop shows as a genre or the aesthetic quality of the program. Or you might want to approach *60 Minutes* with an interest in the auteur ("author") of the program, given the relentlessness of its anti-institutional crusades, ignoring techniques of production or comments on the genre of the show. Drive such purist thoughts out of your mind. In fact, many of the questions critics ask demand the use of analytical techniques from various types or schools of analysis.

Suppose you wanted to study the interesting narrative structure of *Highlander*—the way it used a mythic past and future to frame its stories in the present. To study the unfolding of its stories, you would probably want to talk about its mythic background, the semiotics of its primary symbols (the swords, eyes as windows to near-eternal souls, distinctions between indoor and out-of-door spaces), and even the adventure genre as a vehicle for exploring larger social issues of truth, goodness, and perseverance. If you asked the question, "Why was *Highlander* constructed the way it is?" you'd want to know something about the movies that preceded the program, the industrial practices involved in spinning off a TV program from a film, the author and his or her background, and the special attractiveness of such a mythic-adventure show to audiences of the late 1980s and early 1990s, perhaps through interviews of regular viewers. The question, "Why was *Highlander* constructed the way it is?" requires the use of more than one critical approach if you are to offer a good answer to it. The point is this: although critical methods can be defined in pure forms, your critical studies should be guided by the questions you ask, not the methods you want to use.

Pluralism

Your problems in using a particular critical approach are complicated by the fact that none of them appears in only one form. So you might define *ideology* as (1) false consciousness, (2) a set of ideas held by a society to be true, or (3) discourse in the service of power. Each definition would suggest a different kind of analysis of, say, *Law and Order.* Exploring false consciousness in that program would lead you to look for pro-police and pro-lawyer values disguised as facts in the program. You might try to inventory American ideals about crime and punishment by examining statements made by citizens (and criminals) in particular episodes. To study the ways that discourse is used to legitimate the criminal justice system, you might take apart the trials described in two or three episodes. Different definitions of ideology would seem to suggest different sorts of criticisms. Furthermore, if you then moved on to *Law and Order: Special Victims Unit,* you'd be faced with questions about the traces of feminist ideology in the program's plots dealing with victimization and empowerment.

One of the ways that critical studies stay fresh and alive, actually, is through the construction of new definitions—new theories of language that ask critics to study something they weren't studying before those theories came along, for example, or new understandings of male-female relationships that tell us our old ways of looking at *Father Knows Best* or *Ozzie and Harriet* in the 1950s disguised the real dynamics of family power. To look at a western such as the classic *Bonanza* as an instantiation of frontier myth will get you into the program, probably, as it was constructed from 1959 to 1973; but to redefine that myth not simply as a frontier story but as a patriarchal story changes the direction of your mythic analysis in significant ways. Each critical approach described in this book must be thought of as multidimensional—as multivocal concepts. Although the world would be neater if a particular word had only one meaning, only multidimensionalism guarantees that all critics will not end up saying the same things.

Partiality or Perspectivism

A third problem created by the critical approaches theory of televisual analysis is that of partiality: Each critical approach allows us to see only part of a program. That is, each approach is but one perspective on an object. Consider the old story of the blind men of India. They came upon an elephant and asked each other what it was. The one holding the tail said, "Oh, it is a long, thin animal with a beard on one end." "No, no," said the second, holding the trunk. "It is long and round, not thin, but rather tubelike with air moving through it." The third, touching a foot, said, "You're both crazy, for it's ponderous, flat, and armored with hard nails." Grabbing the ear, the fourth noted, "Heavens, no, it is flat, but soft and pliable, covered with an alluring fuzz." The fifth blind man, knowing that the rib cage he was feeling was for all the world like a giant drum, thought they were all witless. And so the dispute went on into the night, as each man was doubly blind: blind by nature and blinded by the perspective he had on the elephant, controlled as it was by the part he first seized.

And so it goes with television program analysis. A feminist approach to *ER* usually ends up ignoring the racial and class questions raised by that program. If you focus on the mythic dimensions of the Super Bowl, you might well ignore the economic force of the event. A narrative study of the evening news is interesting but may blind you to the kinds of people whose stories are never told by Dan Rather or Peter Jennings.

Examining only particular aspects or parts of something leads to the problem of perspectivism: each critical approach is a perspective—more or less a point from which to look at a program. And as the blind men of India found out, if you look at an elephant from only one point, you'll miss a lot. There's always a sense of incompleteness in a piece of criticism.

The Issue of Televisual "Realism"

Formally, *realism* can be defined as "the use of representational devices (signs, conventions, narrative strategies, and so on) to depict or portray a physical, social or moral universe which is held to exist objectively beyond its representations by such means, and which is thus the arbiter of the truth of the representation" (O'Sullivan, Hartley, Saunders, Montgomery, & Fiske, 1994, p. 257). Were you to apply that term to what you see on prime-time and public affairs television, you'd argue that television is our window on the world—a transparent glass behind which lies the world as it actually is. Because sitcoms arise out of everyday family and community problems depicted in commonsensical ways and because news crews are "on the scene," we often consider TV portrayals as life as it is.

John Fiske (1987) warns us that TV portrayals are not, however, real depictions. They are realistic. They are depictions, not reproductions, of reality. Your television set is not a window but an artistic surface on which creative artists, selective reporters, and talented production personnel remanufacture reality. Fiske wrote this about the O.J. Simpson trial:

> There was no clear and obvious distinction between electronic mediation [on television] and physical happenings, or between media figures and real people. This is not to say that there is no nonmediated reality—Nicole Simpson *was* murdered, Rodney King *was* beaten—but that the mediation of the murder and the beating modified or magnified what they really were. . . . O.J. Simpson's case was not just shown on television, it was a product of television, just as O.J. himself was. . . . We can no longer think of the media as providing secondary representations of reality; they affect and produce the reality that they mediate. We live in a world of media events and media realities. (1994, pp. xiv–xv)

It is television's realisticness—its real-seeming-ness—that causes people to worry about the accuracy or fidelity of its depictions of the world. The problem is that we cannot assume that something "real" always exists behind its images, for its images are every bit as much a source of information, opinion, and judgment for you as are your closest friends or family members. And therein lies a problem, as Parenti (1993, p. 3) notes: "Far more insidious and less open to conscious challenge are the notions that so fit into the dominant political culture's field of established images that they appear not as biased manipulations but as 'the nature of things.'" That's the problem of realisticness.

Overcoming the Problems

Essentialism, pluralism, partiality, and realisticness can hamper your work as a critic, messing with your thinking about your intellectual tasks if you're not careful. Here are some ways for you to overcome these problems.

The Centrality of "the Question" Critics always must remember that the question—the question that they want to answer in their work—is central to criticism. The questions you ask help you select methods or approaches, suggest what aspects of a program to explore, and become the conclusions that are the outcome of good work. If you find yourself worrying more about critical methods than about critical questions, you've got your priorities mixed up. Saying that you want to do a cultural study of *South Park* is likely to encourage you to focus on cultural approaches to criticism rather than on the show; instead, asking a culturally sensitive question—In what ways do the social parodies of *South Park* sensitize Americans to their cultural excesses?—will keep your eyes on the program even as you pursue a cultural study.

Approaches and Audiences A second point to think about is that the kind of study you do often defines its own audience, which is to say, a group of readers interested in the perspectives you take. If you're doing a feminist analysis, you're more likely to be read by other feminists than by farmhands. If a person despises the intricacies of semiotic analysis, he or she is unlikely to read a critical analysis of the sign systems used to suggest class in *Judging Amy*. A focus on types of criticism therefore is as much a focus on audience interests—others' questions—as it is on critical machinery. Hence, you should expect most criticism to be partial. That's even the point!

Another important point to remember about your work as a critic is that there will be people who find it worthless. In the example essays that follow in this book, there will be some you enjoy and others that you despise. (If you don't like any of them, you're probably in the wrong course.) If your favorite chatroom is dealing

"They killed Kenny . . . !" *South Park* (1997), Trey Parker and Matt Stone's popular animated series starring four third-graders—Stan, Kyle, Kenny, and Cartman, known for their foul language—has been the recipient of both complaints and awards, including a Cable Ace Award (1997).

with a topic you're not interested in, you sign off. The same is true about television criticism: you'll avoid the discussions of aspects of programs or approaches to them that you don't like. Criticism is partial, therefore, in two senses of the word: it's never a complete study of anything, and it produces kinds of knowledge of particular interest to only part of a population.

Constructedness of Reality   What Fowles (1996) says of advertising is true of television in general: "[Television] draws on popular culture's repository of symbolic material (images or text or music) in an attempt to fabricate new symbols with enlivened meanings. The older symbolic material had always been accepted by people as an ingredient in their culture. All [television] can do is recondition the public's symbols and pray that [it] will supply agreeable meanings to the new creation" (p. 9). Just because television presents you with images, texts, and music—with representations—rather than actual rocks or rockets, however, is no reason to disparage it or consider it harmless diversion. Televisual representations are significant aspects of personal and social life. Just ask the woman who wrote on a computer bulletin board after Simpson's arrest: "The media has another Black man to show the world as being a REPRESENTATION of ALL BLACK MEN. I HATE THAT!!!!" (Fiske, 1994). Her point as well is that those representations are neither harmless or diverting. Television does not broadcast reality but rather it constructs it—it fabricates new symbols, as Fowles says. It's up to TV critics to examine those fabrications very, very closely.

Centeredness   If you think long about the importance of the guiding question, the audiences who might be interested in how someone answers it, and the constructedness of life experiences through television programming, you can see that critical approaches are not prisons within which you do criticism but rather centers from which you launch projects. You might start a context-centered study of *Green Acres, The Beverly Hillbillies,* and *Petticoat Junction* by asking, "Why were these programs so popular in the 1960s?" Such a question would lead you to probe the 1960s, the decade of revolution and of the breakdown of many political, economic, and social institutions. You'd probably soon discover that mere description of that context was not enough; you'd want to explore the ideological battles of that decade, seeing the popularity of comedies in a rural setting as a conservative backlash, and you might even want to talk a little semiotics—about rural characters as signs for innocence in the face of too much knowledge, for simplicity in the face of an increasingly complex world, and for the guilelessness of the farm in the face of corrupted cities. (*Green Acres* especially often featured the corrupted city.) The key here is to remember what your center is: the question, which ought to suggest kinds of analyses to you, would provide parts of the answer to the question.

Centeredness, then, is the key to understanding what we are doing in this book. Not only can criticism be diffused so long as it is centered, but also our arrangement of critical approaches to television criticism is centered—in this case, centered on the classic communication model shown in Figure 3.1. That model suggests that the communication process—and television is assuredly a medium of one-to-many communication—can be examined in terms of the following:

Sender: the producers, directors, technicians, actors, and so on, who are the authors (auteurs) of television series and individual episodes

Messages: the texts of the programs, including verbal, visual (deep backgrounds, sets, costumes, icons, people), and acoustic (voice qualities, music) codes

Receivers: the audiences of television, viewers as understood by gender, race, class, and other social markers that can affect how they make meanings out of television programs.

Situation: the contexts of a show, including the period in which it was developed and exhibited, the kinds of worlds (work, family, foreign, historical) it depicts, and the ideological dynamics of the program and the period in which it was shown

Institutions: the primary and secondary institutions (network, production house, government regulatory agency, economic sponsor) controlling or in other ways affecting the way programs are produced, exhibited, and watched

Culture: the culture of a program, including social structures, rules for living, definitions of social roles and how they are played, and the use of television in different societies

FIGURE 3.1   **Critical Approaches to Television Arranged by Communication Model**

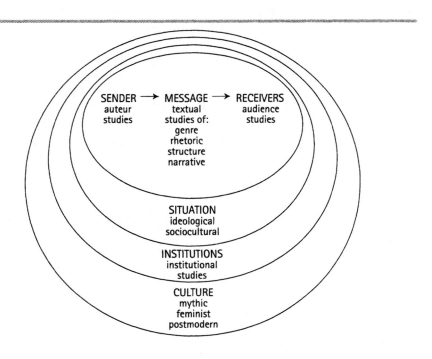

Each of these descriptions is expanded significantly in later chapters of the book. But perhaps this listing helps you understand the rationale for the way this book is laid out—how it is centered. These are the centers for criticism, though again, you should remember that just as you seldom talk about a message sender without saying something about the message, so too are you unlikely to do an auteur study of a television production company such as MTM Productions without mentioning some of its messages (programs) such as *The Mary Tyler Moore Show* and *Hill Street Blues*.

Looking Ahead

The rest of this book leads you through a types-centered approach to television criticism. An array of types—not all types, of course, and not all variations of each type—is offered. We discuss each type in terms of its origin, some of the variations available within it, its operating assumptions about the world of television, some of the analytical concepts it uses, and its problems or potential shortcomings. Then, we present example critical essays that show you how at least a few people have worked within the assumptions of a particular approach. You can skip around, not necessarily reading the chapters in order, because the approaches are more or less independent of each other. That's the way it is with perspectives. Any of the blind men of India could have spoken first.

As a result of reading this book and its essays, you should leave this course with a basic understanding of each of the principal kinds of television criticism, you should have seen each kind at work, and you should understand the range of meanings television produces in Americans about American society. You should understand in fundamental, concrete ways that criticism is not just judgment, that it's a matter of advancing interpretive propositions that are well supported and make a difference in how those who accept them understand the world.

Notes

1. Karl Wallace (1963) suggested that "good reasons" are those that audiences find convincing, grounded in a society's dominant values, and reasonably based on evidence.

2. Williams offered a similar analysis of newspapers in his earlier book, *Communications* (1962).

3. A book on television programming that comes close is Michael Curtin's *Redeeming the Wasteland: Television Documentary and Cold War Politics* (1995), a study of network documentaries, especially in the 1950s and 1960s. Curtin approaches his subject from the viewpoints of the U.S. government, the networks' news departments, production crews and styles, and program content. Although the book feels somewhat disorganized, it is a good example of responding to Williams's cry for pluralism.

4. That same year Horace Newcomb brought out his anthology, *Television: A Critical View* (1976). It too was organized by different kinds of shows and different

approaches to them—20 essays in all. The critical-approaches pattern was formally recognized as such by Arthur Asa Berger in 1982 and fully developed into textbook form by Robert C. Allen in 1987.

Further Reading

O'Sullivan, T., Hartley, J., Saunders, D., Montgomery, M., & Fiske, J. (1994). *Key concepts in communication and cultural studies* (2nd ed.). New York: Routledge. This is a highly useful scholarly dictionary with one- to three-page discussions of important terms in media studies and, more generally, communication theory. Concepts such as ideology, structuralism, semiotics, realism," and hegemony get clear, expert treatment. This is a great resource for starting to build your theoretical-critical vocabulary.

Webnotes

Communication Theorists. **www.popcultures.com/theorists/**

This site includes web pages on communication theorists from Adorno and Zizek. Raymond Williams is included among them.

Debates on the Future of Television, Benton Foundation. **www.benton.org/Policy/ TV/debate.html/**

Here is a series of articles, regularly changing, on future technical and social developments of television and is a useful place to stimulate ideas for a range of critical essays. Recent topics include the future of high-definition TV, the V-chip and children's programming, and free airtime for political candidates.

Learning Activities

1. Examine the opening paragraphs of three different critical essays reprinted in this book. Isolate statements in those introductions that articulate the critical approach being taken by the author to the analysis of television programs. (a) Are the statements clear? If not, how could they be improved? (b) Does the essay clearly suggest what you should learn about television, its place in your life, or your view of yourself or your world as a result of reading the essay? (c) Is there a clear connection between the approach and what you should come to know or understand as a result of reading the essay? If not, how could the connection be made stronger? (d) If there's time, get together with at least two other students who looked at one of the essays you did and compare notes. In what ways are your comments similar to or different from theirs? Why?

2. Get on the Internet and do a search of the names "Raymond Williams," "Horace Newcomb," and "Richard Adler." Write a brief statement on each person's background and what you learn about his career and his approach to the analysis of television.

References

Adler, R. (Ed.). (1976). *Television as a cultural force.* New York: Praeger.

Allen, R. C. (1987). *Channels of discourse: Television and contemporary criticism.* Chapel Hill: University of North Carolina Press.

Berger, A. A. (1982). *Media analysis techniques.* Thousand Oaks, CA: Sage.

Brockriede, W. (1974). Rhetorical criticism as argument. *Quarterly Journal of Speech, 60,* 165-174.

Cater, D., Adler, R. (Eds.). (1975). *Television as a social force: New approaches to criticism.* New York: Praeger. [Published with the Aspen Institute Program on Communications and Society.]

Curtin, M. (1995). *Redeeming the wasteland: Television documentary and cold war politics.* New Brunswick, NJ: Rutgers University Press.

Fiske, J. (1987). *Television culture.* New York: Methuen.

Fiske, J. (1994). *Media matters: Everyday culture and political change.* Minneapolis: University of Minnesota Press.

Fowles, J. (1996). *Advertising and popular culture.* Thousand Oaks, CA: Sage.

Gronbeck, B. E. (1988, August). The academic practice of television criticism. *Quarterly Journal of Speech, 74,* 334–347.

Newcomb, H. (1974). *TV: The most popular art.* Garden City, NY: Doubleday/Anchor.

Newcomb, H. (1976). *Television: The critical view.* New York: Oxford University Press.

O'Sullivan, T., Hartley, J., Saunders, D., Montgomery, M., & Fiske, J. (1994). *Key concepts in communication and cultural studies* (2nd ed.). New York: Routledge.

Parenti, M. (1993). *Inventing reality: The politics of news media* (2nd ed.). New York: St. Martin's Press.

Wallace, K. (1963). The substance of rhetoric: Good reasons. *Quarterly Journal of Speech, 49,* 239–249.

Williams, R. (1962). *Communications.* Harmondsowrth, England: Penguin.

Williams, R. (1974). *Television: Technology and cultural form.* New York: Schocken Books.

Writing Television Criticism

CHAPTER 4

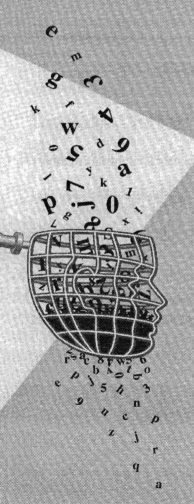

Newspapers and news magazines have sections about television and film for the same reason they have sports sections: to increase their profits. People buy newspapers and magazines to find out what is new in various areas, including what is new on television today. Newspapers and magazines are not philanthropic enterprises or benevolent institutions whose publications are produced solely to promote the general happiness and further the education of the general public. Newspapers and magazines are commercial businesses whose purpose is to make a financial profit. They publish articles and journalistic critical reviews of television because one reason many people buy their publications is to read about the latest shows, celebrities, and industry events. In contrast, although academic television criticism may generate a limited profit when it is published in a book or anthology (scholarly journals never pay authors for articles), its primary purpose is rarely financial gain. Rather, scholarly television criticism is written to stimulate further critical insights about television, teach both writers and the readers more about particular television texts, and enhance our understanding of television as a social and cultural form and force.

Stages of Critical Analysis

This may surprise you a bit, but criticism doesn't begin when you sit down at your computer to begin to write your critical essay. It actually begins somewhere in the uncharted chambers of your mind. In fact, criticism is a three-stage communication activity that begins with a personal critical reaction or a critical question. This stage eventually leads to the sharing of your critical insights, for example, by writing a critical essay (the second stage). And in the third stage, other readers (your teacher, your classmates, roommates, fellow television fans) give you feedback on your critical observations.

Stage One: Thinking About Television

Gronbeck (1984) calls the first stage of writing criticism *cerebration* (from the word *cerebral*, meaning "involving the brain or intellect"). In this stage, you select the text you are going to analyze,[1] the critical question you want to answer, and the tools that you think will best help you analyze that question. In general, there are two ways we can go about selecting the text and the critical questions: aha! reactions and systematic searches.

Aha! Reactions   The idea for a critical essay can come about through a sudden critical reaction as you are reflecting on a particular program or group of programs. Gronbeck (1984) compares this critical reaction to Archimedes' "Eureka!" formulation of the principle of specific gravity. For example, an aha! reaction was the first step when Heather Hundley wrote the critical essay on *Cheers* that is found in Chapter 14 of this book. Hundley was taking a television criticism class (from Professor Vande Berg) and facing her first paper assignment. Having been an avid fan of *Cheers,* a series set in a bar in Boston, for several years and having years of episodes on videotape, Hundley decided to start looking at episodes of the program and see if she could identify something to write her paper on. As she watched and took notes on videotaped episode after episode, she suddenly had an "aha! moment: She was struck by the realization that not only was the series set in a bar, but also that in episode after episode, the characters—especially main characters Norm, Cliff, and Frasier—drink beer after beer and develop only camaraderie, never hangovers. She noticed that neither Norm nor Cliff ever got drunk or ever experienced any ill effects from drinking beer, even though in most episodes, they drank beer from the moment they got off work until the bar closed. As she examined more episodes, Hundley realized that over its 11-year-run, *Cheers* had shown viewers weekly that excessive beer drinking is a natural, normal, unproblematic activity. This, she felt, was problematic. To help identify, understand, and explain the strategies *Cheers* had used to "naturalize" beer drinking, Hundley looked in her "methodological toolkit" and realized that structural analysis—specifically the concepts of discourse, naturalization, and paradigmatic oppositions—could help her understand just how *Cheers* had encouraged viewers to think of beer not as a potentially harmful alcoholic drug, but rather as a harmless beverage, as natural and perhaps as healthy as water. When you turn to Chapter 14, you can read about the three strategies she identified after watching and analyzing 24 half-hour episodes of the series.

Categorical Searches   A second way that critical essays can come about is through systematic searches for critical methods or concepts that can help explain and interpret a television text. For example, Lawrence Wenner went searching for a concept that would help him explain what he saw as a complex relationship among commercialism, nationalism, and sports in the 1992 "Dream Team" ads. After considering several approaches, Wenner decided that the insights he gained from viewing these ads could best be organized and explained by combining a critical method called reader-oriented criticism with media scholar John Hartley's use of the anthropological concept of "dirt." In Chapter 12, you can read the critical essay that resulted.

Once critics have (1) formulated a critical question (through an aha! reaction or a categorical search), (2) found an existing critical approach or formulated a new one using theoretical or analytical concepts (remember, critical approaches or methods, which, as we mentioned earlier, consist of analytical concepts and the procedures for using them),[2] and (3) used these analytical tools to deconstruct particular television texts and answer their question, these critics are ready to communicate that insightful answer to others—for example, by writing a critical analysis paper.

Stage Two: Communicating Critical Insights

Because criticism is the process whereby we communicate thoughtful, considered interpretations of the meanings of television texts with other people, we cannot keep the insights we gained from our critical analysis to ourselves. Criticism is not, as we discussed in Chapter 2, merely opinion. Serious criticism involves using critical approaches or methods (theoretical assumptions, analytical concepts, and procedures for using them) to explain your insights about television texts to others.

When this communication is done in writing, the creative insights are packaged in essays that more or less follow certain writing conventions. As we noted in Chapter 1, one of these conventions is that, at a minimum, all critical analyses must include three elements:

1. A clear thesis that states a critical interpretation (the answer to the research question the critic had posed and answered using the critical method)
2. Well-developed arguments that explain how the critic used analytical concepts to answer the research question and arrive at his or her interpretation
3. Specific supporting evidence so readers can see for themselves how the critic got from question to answer—in this case, critical interpretation

Only if all three of these elements are present can readers decide for themselves if the critic's interpretation seems reasonable, valid, and insightful.

If the critic is writing a critical analysis essay for presentation at an academic conference or for publication in a scholarly journal, the analysis needs some other elements as well, including a discussion of the critical method (or critical-theoretical concepts) that enabled the critic to arrive at this interpretation and a brief review (generally no more than one to two sentences each) of other relevant critical analyses that have looked at the same or similar television texts or have used this particular critical method or concept.

By now, you may have noticed that we use *critical question* and *critical interpretation* or *proposition* interchangeably. That is because the central critical proposition (the main idea or thesis) of a serious television criticism essay may be framed as either an interpretive statement or a question, although you, as the writer, already will have answered the question before you start writing.

Gronbeck (1984) has explained that serious criticism essays can be written in one of two styles: a *deductive* style, which begins with a critical proposition expressed in the form of a statement, or an *inductive* style, which begins with a critical proposition expressed in the form of a question. Hundley's essay, for example, illustrates a deductive approach: she begins with the critical proposition that *Cheers* legitimized (or "naturalized") beer drinking by presenting it as a normal, acceptable everyday activity. She then goes on to discuss three strategies through which the series accomplishes this. Cathy Sandeen's essay in Chapter 14 illustrates an inductive style; it begins with the questions, "Although *PM Magazine* was promoted for its unique production style, syndication arrangement, appeal to regionalism, and local community needs, was the program really unique in terms of its overall message?" and "What values did the program promote as being most important?" She develops answers to these questions after a categorical search for the underlying value system of the program. To do this, she examined 225 *PM Magazine* stories for the formal elements (e.g., patterns and emphases in topics covered, production variables including complexity of coverage, use of special effects, multiple locations and interviewees, and implicit and explicit statements of values).

In both deductively organized and inductively organized criticism essays, however, the introduction should convey the essay's central critical interpretation, phrased in either question or statement form, provide a rationale for why the critic believes this analysis is important enough for the reader to spend time carefully reading it; mention the analytical concept(s) the critic used; and preview the general organization of the rest of the essay (i.e., provide the reader with a brief road map of what is to follow).

The body of the essay, then, should describe the text being analyzed, set out the analytical concepts (i.e., critical method) used to analyze the text, and develop the ideas implied in the thesis by walking the reader through well-organized and amply supported arguments that show how the critic used these concepts to analyze the text and arrive at the interpretive, evaluative conclusion.

The essay conclusion should restate (in slightly different words) the central critical interpretation, and should discuss the implications of the critic's insights for better understanding this text, other television or cultural texts, and the relationship between television and society.

If we were to remove the specific content from most television criticism essays and leave only the skeletal frame visible, we would find that the underlying structure of most criticism essays can be reduced to an outline like this:

INTRODUCTION

I.   Begin with an interest-arousing opening paragraph.

II. Set out the rationale for writing (and reading) the essay.

III. Mention the critical approach or analytical concepts that you (the critic) used in analyzing the television text.

IV. Cogently preview the major sections of the essay (i.e., provide your readers with a brief road map so they can more easily follow the arguments you use to develop and explain your thesis).

BODY

I.   Succinctly overview the text you analyzed for this essay. Provide a *brief* (try to keep this to a page) summary of the series' premise and indicate the particular episode(s) you analyzed.

II. Provide a clear explanation of the critical approach and/or definition of the analytical concepts you used to analyze the text.

III. Develop the ideas embedded in the essay's thesis or central critical proposition or question by

     A. explaining to your readers what you discovered when you used these analytical concepts to examine the text(s), and

     B. supporting this explanation with, concrete, detailed description of specific plots, characters, scenes, lighting, music, camera angles, mise-en-scènes, and so on from specific program episodes (that's why it is a good idea to videotape the text you are going to analyze); quotations from or references to relevant theoretical or critical scholarly sources; quotations from other relevant sources (e.g., newspaper articles, reviews); attributed facts from authoritative sources (polls, U.S. Census Bureau, Nielsen ratings); definitions (of analytical concepts)

CONCLUSION

I. Summarize briefly any additional conclusions you arrived at as a result of the ideas, arguments, and evidence presented in the analysis.

II. Discuss the implications of your analytical conclusions and insights for one or more of the following: enhanced understanding of this program/text; future critical analysis of television texts using this method or construct; the relationship among the television-viewing public, the television industry, and/or society generally; and/or the advancement of our understanding of television criticism, critical theory, and television studies.

Of course, all formal papers also need to have a separate title page and a separate Reference Pages section where you provide the complete bibliographical information for the sources (alphabetically by the author's last name) of any of materials from which you took ideas, quotations, or facts that you used or referred to in the essay. The References section usually also should contain a videography (bibliographical information on the series episodes you discussed, listing the title of the episode, date aired, writer, producer, director, and production company); you generally can get this information from program web sites.

Stage Three: Responses and Feedback

Because serious television criticism is written primarily for those interested in viewing and studying television as a form of popular culture, television criticism essays appear primarily, though not exclusively, in academic journals published by scholarly associations or academic institutions (e.g., *Critical Studies in Media Communication, Journal of Popular Film and Television, Journal of Film and Video, Journal of Communication Inquiry, Wide Angle*), and in books and anthologies of television criticism. For many of these critical essays, their authors presented earlier versions of the essays at scholarly conferences and then used the feedback that they received from listeners to revise their work before sending them out to be published. Readers of scholarly journals and books on criticism do not usually write back to the authors of the essays and books, though that does happen occasionally. Most often, however, critical responses to published critical essays appear when the published articles are cited and commented on by other scholars when they are reviewing the published literature relevant to their own analyses.

For the critical essays you will be assigned to write for your classes, feedback will certainly come from your instructor and perhaps from the other students in the class. If you ask your roommate, significant other, or a friend in class to read your essay, you can also receive valuable critical responses to your interpretation. These readers can tell you if you have explained the critical method and analytical concept you used well enough so that they can understand it and could use it when they are viewing and thinking about other programs. Usually the audience members we tell our own students to write for are those intelligent, curious, well-informed members of the general public who read periodicals like the *New Yorker* but may not be familiar with this particular show nor have taken a TV criticism class. Essays aimed at this audience should be literate and fairly sophisticated but not filled with critical jargon. You will need to clearly explain and define the critical approaches and analytical concepts you used to arrive at your insightful interpretation because you cannot assume that your readers are thoroughly familiar with them. If these readers find your essay accessible, informative, and insightful, you will have made an important contribution to education in the larger sense. And this, as we discussed in Chapter 1, is one of the major goals of television criticism.

The purpose of writing critical essays is to stimulate a critical dialogue about television texts and about television generally—that is, the aim of television criticism is to stimulate others to take television, and critical thinking and writing about television, seriously. Indeed, the worst fate a critic can imagine is to be ignored. "Criticism's worth is measured by the degree to which it causes others to reflect on, interpret, and evaluate their own experiences with the [television] object in question" (Gronbeck, 1984, p. 11).

Some Differences Between Academic and Journalistic Writing about Television

Writing about television texts is done by academics (in scholarly journals and books) and by journalists writing for magazines and newspapers. Much of the writing about television in daily newspapers consists of short previews or industry news, although some Sunday newspapers (e.g., the New York *Times*, Los Angeles *Times*, Baltimore *Sun*, Washington *Post*) publish sociocultural TV criticism essays. Indeed, a few journalistic writers have received Pulitzer Prizes for their television criticism written for newspapers (e.g., Howard Rosenberg from the Los Angeles *Times* and Tom Shales from the Washington *Post*). However, typically serious academic criticism differs from journalistic previews and reviews of television in five ways: timeliness, vocabulary, length, proofs, and style.

Timeliness

For serious television criticism essays, timeliness is far less important a consideration than it is for journalistic writers who write articles for the television section of the daily paper.[3] The reason for this difference is that the primary aim of serious television criticism is not to provide timely viewing advice, but solely to share a detailed, insightful interpretation of a television text. As a result, television critics can analyze historical, esoteric, and unusual programs and episodes. Journalistic writers generally lack the luxury of being able to write about something other than current television texts because their foremost responsibility is to use their critical television analysis skills to sell the current issue of a newspaper or magazine.

Vocabulary

Just as chefs use specialized vocabulary terms such as *puree, zest,* and *roué* to describe processes, ingredients, and products, television critics' vocabularies include specialized terms such as *genre, discourse,* and *mise-en-scène.*[4] They use such specialized terms not to make their analyses inaccessible or show off their specialized knowledge, but rather to refer cogently to the assumptions and constructs that underlie their analysis.

When critics begin writing critical analyses, they generally rely on using established critical theories, methods, or constructs to analyze television texts—for example, rhetorical criticism methods such as fantasy-theme analysis (Bormann, 1972, 1982) and representative anecdote analysis (Burke, 1967; Brummett, 1984, 1985) genre theory (Altman, 1986; Jamieson & Campbell, 1982)), structural analysis (Fiske, 1984; Fiske & Hartley, 1978), or concepts like hegemony (Gramsci, 1971). However, critics also can create their own unique critical approaches by adapting or combining existing theoretical or critical concepts. This is what Rushing and Frentz (1978) did when they developed their social values model of narrative analysis and what Gumpert and Fish (1990) did when they developed the concept of mediated therapeutic communication.

When critics do create their own unique approach, they need to take particular care to provide clear contextual or stipulative definitions for terms and analytical concepts that may be unfamiliar to readers. And all critics must be careful to explain criticism terms whose everyday use differs from the way the same terms or concepts are used in critical studies. For example, in our everyday activities, we use the term *discourse* to mean "conversation"; however, in television criticism, *discourse* has a somewhat different meaning. As Fiske (1987) explains, in media criticism, a discourse is "a language or system of representation that has developed socially in order to make and circulate a coherent set of meanings about an important topic area" (p. 14).

Length

Critical analyses of television vary in length, but most are between 10 and 20 pages of double-spaced typescript. Although that may seem long, remember that you need to introduce your critical idea, provide a brief summary of what the series or episode is about, describe the critical approach or concepts that you used as tools to conduct the analysis, and then explain how you used the concepts to arrive at your critical interpretation, as well as provide several supporting examples and discuss the implications of your analysis. Once you have written all of this, you will be amazed at how quickly you have written 8 to 12 pages. Length is not a goal in itself in critical essays; the simple fact is that thorough discussion and adequate proof take a fair amount of space.

Proofs

In academic television criticism essays, the critic must support the interpretive proposition (thesis) or answer the critical question posed as the essay's thesis by elaborating on the ideas or arguments implied in the thesis or question and providing confirming, corroborating evidence for these arguments. This supporting evidence typically includes specific details and descriptions of exemplary scenes, dialogue, lighting or camera work, or citations from other television criticism essays, theories, and facts from reputable sources. Sometimes, in the case of institution-centered, auteur-centered, or audience-centered critiques, the proofs may include quotations from interviews conducted by the critics (see, for example, Campbell and Reeves's essay in Chapter 9).

Style

Academic television criticism follows formal stylistic writing conventions. That means it relies on well-developed arguments and specific supporting examples from texts, and it cites the sources for terms, concepts, ideas, and information garnered from other authoritative sources. It also means using correct grammar, punctuation, and usage. Critical essays, like other kinds of formal and journalistic writing, use headings and subheadings as signposts to help readers follow the development of ideas.

However, not all criticism essays look alike. Some critical essays are written in third-person voice and others in first person. Sometimes the choice to use one voice rather than the other is personal preference, and at other times (e.g., for ideological and feminist criticism) the choice is a reflection of the theoretical and ideological assumptions that undergird the critical approach.

Journalistic television criticism and academic television differ in their style: journalistic writers typically use a far livelier and more informal, casual style, in part because they need to attract as large a readership as possible. Consequently, in journalistic writing, being entertaining is as important as, if not more important than, analyzing and informing.

Looking Ahead

As we explained in Chapter 3, critics can use many different approaches to analyze and answer their questions about television. In Chapters 5 through 15, we explain a number of these methods and provide example essays to illustrate how some critics have used these critical approaches to examine television.

Notes

1. In all likelihood, the texts you will be analyzing in this class will be television episodes or series. However, if you were to do a production ethnography critical analysis, the text you would be analyzing would be the transcripts of your media organization interviews and your notes on your observations at the media pro-

duction site. If you were doing an ethnographic study of the meanings that specific audiences construct from watching a television text, the texts you would be analyzing would be the transcripts of tape-recorded interview or participant observation sessions in which you talked with audience members about what the meaning of television programs is.

2. See Foss's discussions (1989, pp. 18–19; 1996, pp. 483–486) of how critics create new critical methods that do not rely on constructs, theories, or approaches that other scholars have developed.

3. As you may have noticed, we have been careful about not using the term *criticism* to describe all journalistic writing about television because much of the writing about TV that appears in newspapers and magazines lacks one or more of the essential components of criticism. We can classify journalistic writing in the popular press in many ways: by the medium in which it appears (e.g., daily newspapers, weekly magazines, monthly magazines), by length, by subject, by the author's stated or inferred motive, or by its function or use for readers (Smith, 1980). The most common schema used to classify journalistic writing about television is by its probable use for readers. According to Gronbeck (1984), there are five general types or categories of journalistic writing about television: personality or star gossip, industry news updates, previews, reviews, and sociocultural and opinion essays. Of these five categories, only sociocultural essays fit the definition of criticism being used in this textbook.

4. Mise-en-scène, as film critic Andrew Sarris (1977) has cogently explained, "includes all of the means available to a director to express his [*sic*] attitude toward his subject. This takes in cutting, camera movement, pacing, the direction of players and their placement in the decor, the angle and distance of the camera, and even the content of the shot" (pp. 52–53).

Further Reading

Fiske, J. (1987). *Television culture*. London: Methuen. Using a cultural studies approach (a combination of semiotic, poststructural, and Marxist theoretical concepts), Fiske provides one of the most thorough, accessible introductions to critically analyzing the textual strategies through which television as a cultural agent attempts to control the meanings and pleasures of its viewers. He also examines the various ways that active audiences can negotiate or resist these strategies and use television texts to create their own pleasurable readings.

Webnotes

Communication Institute for Online Scholarship (CIOS). **http://www.cios.org**

CIOS is an organization supported primarily through individual and institutional memberships, through publication of the *Electronic Journal of Communication*, and through sales of software products to assist communication scholarship (e.g., ComIndex). CIOS, inaugurated in 1990, was designed to function as a parent organization for the set of online activities that had been initiated in 1986 as the Comserve service. CIOS indexes over 75 communication journals—some in full text, some in abstracts, and some just for the journal issues' Table of Contents.

Learning Activities

1. Have a copy of the Contents page of this textbook with you, and go to the *Readers Guide to Periodic Literature* or an online index (e.g., Nexis/Lexis or Academic Index) your library offers that indexes articles in major metropolitan newspapers and popular periodicals, including *Time, TV Guide, Rolling Stone,* and *Entertainment Weekly.* Look under "Television," then "Programs," then "Reviews," and locate a review about one of the series analyzed in the academic essays included in this book (e.g., *Buffy, the Vampire Slayer, Cheers, The Real World,* the *X-Files, Murphy Brown*). Write a one-page summary of the differences between the essay about television in this book and the review you found in which you compare and contrast the academic and the journalistic essay in terms of the vocabulary each uses, the amount of evidence offered, the timeliness, intended audience, and length.

2. Look at five to seven copies of a major newspaper (e.g., New York *Times,* New York *Daily News,* Los Angeles *Times,* Chicago *Sun-Times,* Chicago *Tribune,* Baltimore *Sun,* Washington *Post,* Cleveland *Plain Dealer,* New Orleans *Times-Picayune,* Boston *Globe,* Miami *Herald*), a weekly magazine (e.g., *New Yorker, Time, Newsweek*), or a monthly magazine (e.g., *Rolling Stone, Cosmopolitan, Jet*), and list how many of each type of essay about television (review, preview, industry news, star or industry gossip, or sociocultural or critical essay) appear in this publication. Now look at the Contents pages for one year (these journals are only published four times a year) of the following scholarly journals: *Journal of Popular Culture, Journal of Popular Film and Television, Wide Angle, Television and New Media, Journal of Communication Inquiry,* and *Journal of Film and Video.* What conclusions can you draw about the kinds of writing about television that appears in popular periodicals? Where should you go if you want to read serious, in-depth critical analyses of television programs?

References

Altman, R. (1986). A semantic/syntactic approach to film genre. In B. K. Grant (Ed.), *Film genre reader* (pp. 26–40). Austin: University of Texas Press.

Bormann, E. G. (1972). Fantasy and rhetorical vision: The rhetorical criticism of social reality. *Quarterly Journal of Speech, 58,* 396–407.

Bormann, E. G. (1982). A fantasy theme analysis of the television coverage of the hostage release and the Reagan inaugural. *Quarterly Journal of Speech, 68,* 133–145.

Brummett, B. (1984). Burke's representative anecdote as a method in media criticism. *Critical Studies in Mass Communication, 1,* 161–176.

Brummett, B. (1985). Electronic literature as equipment for living: Haunted house films. *Critical studies in mass communication, 2,* 247–261.

Burke, K. (1967). *Philosophy of literary form* (rev. ed.). Berkeley: University of California Press. (Original work published 1941)

Fiske, J. (1984). Popularity and ideology: A structuralist reading of *Dr. Who.* In W. K. Rowland & B. Watkins (Eds.), *Interpreting television: Current research perspectives* (pp. 165–197). Thousand Oaks, CA: Sage.

Fiske, J. (1987). *Television culture.* New York: Methuen.

Fiske, J., & Hartley, J. (1978). *Reading television.* New York: Methuen.

Foss, S. K. (1989). *Rhetorical criticism: Exploration and practice.* Prospect Heights, IL: Waveland.

Foss, S. K. (1996). *Rhetorical criticism: Exploration and practice* (2nd ed.). Prospect Heights, IL: Waveland.

Gramsci, A. (1971). *Selections from the prison notebooks* (Q. Hoare & G. Nowell-Smith, Eds. & Trans.). New York: International.

Gronbeck, B. E. (1984). *Writing television criticism.* Chicago: Science Research Associates.

Gumpert, G., & Fish, S. (Eds.). (1990). *Talking to strangers: Mediated therapeutic communication.* Norwood, NJ: Ablex.

Jamieson, K. H., & Campbell, K. K. (1982). Rhetorical hybrids: Fusions of generic elements. *Quarterly Journal of Speech, 48,* 146–157.

Rushing, J. H., & Frentz, T. S. (1978). The rhetoric of *Rocky:* A social-value model of criticism. *Western Journal of Speech Communication, 41,* 63–71.

Sarris, A. (1977, July–Aug.). The auteur theory revisited. *American Film,* 49–53.

Smith, R.R. (1980). *Beyond the wasteland: The criticism of broadcasting* (rev. ed.). Urbana, IL: ERIC Clearinghouse on reading and communication, and the Speech Communication Association.

PART TWO

Text-Centered Critical Approaches

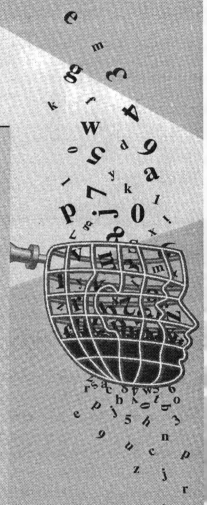

Semiotic/ Structural Criticism

CHAPTER 5

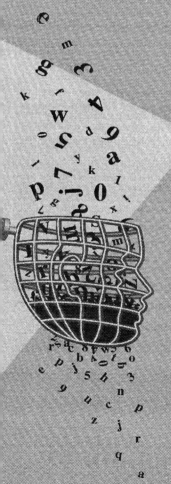

Chapter Outline

The Ambiguous Status of the Text
Stability-Instability
Production-Reception
Multiple Codes

Assumptions Grounding Semiotic Approaches to Television Criticism

Assumptions Grounding Structural Approaches to Television Criticism

Some Examples of Semiotic/Structural Criticism

Writing Analyses of Verbal, Visual, and Acoustic Signs and Structures

An Example Essay: John Fiske's "Popularity and Ideology: A Structuralist Reading of *Dr. Who*"

Writing about the televised coverage of the 1972 Olympics, Raymond Williams argued that the events were not so much sport as politics:

Nobody could have been watching and not seen the conventional politics. Of the nation state, above all: the flags, the delegations, the chefs de mission. Everybody says that the medals table between states is unofficial and virtually everyone compiles and broadcasts or prints it. The victory ceremonies are submilitary, with national anthems and the raising of flags. At the official opening, in and through the marching columns, there was often a pleasant lightness of touch: people waving and smiling: the dancing and the pigeons. All the time, in fact, behind these marvellous young men and women were the posses of appointed and self-appointed people who derive a right to control them. (O'Connor, 1989, pp. 22–23)

Such an analysis of a sporting event raises many questions—about sports and nationalism and about television's penchant for presenting the dramatic in ever more dramatic terms. It also raises a bedeviling question for the critic: What is the text of television programs? Obviously, Williams thought the text of the 1972 Olympics was political, especially that olympiad, perhaps, where seventeen people, including eleven members of the Israeli Olympic team, were shot to death by members of the Black September guerrilla group. Television was showing parades of athletes, competitions, and celebratory moments, but Williams saw only political actions whereby one country was seeking advantage and power, even in murderous ways, at the expense of others. To Williams, during the 1972 Olympics, "an arranged version of what the world is like was invaded by an element of what several parts of the world are actually like" (p. 24).

You might ask how he could provide evidence for that claim or, in the language of criticism, what texts drew his attention. Notice what they were: flags, the parades of athletes and others in their national delegations, the medals, human actions such as waving, and even pigeons (actually, probably doves). He supported his claim about the politics of the 1972 Olympics by (1) isolating objects and actions to which he attached particular meaning or significance and (2) setting them in relationships to each other in ways that helped him claim that the essence of Olympic activity in 1972 was political. The texts that he worked from did not include everything viewers could see on television that day. Rather, he identified particular elements as especially meaningful, relating them to each other structurally so as to provide support for his critical claim that "nobody could have been watching and not seen the conventional politics."

The heart of television criticism—perhaps all criticism—is the construction of a text out of some larger, thicker set of events and one's perception of them, which becomes the center of attention and the sources of evidence for critical claims. The idea of text will be our first concern in this chapter. Then we can move on to talk about elements or particular items of texts semiotically and the arrangements or groupings of those elements and items structurally. We will be suggesting that critics weave texts out of the objects (often called "works" after Barthes, 1975) and then engage those texts semiotically and structurally. Sometimes semiotic/structural analysis stands as a kind of criticism all by itself. At other times, it is but the basis for other kinds of analysis. We will finish this chapter discussing that duality.

The Ambiguous Status of the Text

What is the text? This is such a simple question, but the answer is difficult because it depends on how you look at the question. The idea of the text is actually an ambiguous concept in three ways.

Stability-Instability

A common understanding of the word *text* is a written composition with a beginning, a middle, and an end—a sort of Aristotelian understanding of a literary work; yet technically the word means almost the opposite. More specifically, we get our word *text* from the Latin verb *texere*, meaning "to weave." In a classical sense, therefore, a text is something—something verbal—being made: not already made, but being constructed, being textualized. The word *text* came into general use after 1953, when the French literary and social critic Roland Barthes contrasted a text with a work (*oeuvre*): to Barthes, a work is a complete, closed or finished object, while a text is an open, even infinite process of meaning making and remaking (Johnson, 1990, esp. p. 40).

Barthes's work-versus-process tension suggests that a text is both stable, as a work, and yet never stable, even instable, because it always is in process, always being remade by somebody for some purpose. As we saw, Williams selected from all of the TV images he viewed a few out of which he made a text capable of supporting his claims.

Furthermore, to Barthes, the tension that can exist between a particular signifier such as a word or a picture and a mental image such as an idea is simultaneously stable, because the word or picture exists objectively, and unstable, because the meanings attached to a signifier can vary from time to time or situation to situation, even from an awake state to a dream. Signifiers may be stable, but signifieds can be variable—that is, in process—because meanings change across time and setting. So *The Man from U.N.C.L.E.* was viewed as a television adventure story in the 1960s, but now would be understood better as a Cold War fantasy, similar to the recent program *Alias*. The signifiers are the same, but the signifieds, that is, the meanings we attach to those signifiers, have changed. So, the signs can be stable, but either through selectivity or through recontextualization—that is, examining only selected signs or looking at a whole work from a different time and place—signification becomes instable and hence potentially always ambiguous.

Production–Reception

A text is ambiguous because its meaning depends in part on who's doing the weaving, the constructing of meanings. "Texts are the sites of conflict," argues John Fiske, "between their forces of production and modes of reception" (1987b, p. 14). What the makers of a television program may have intended and what the viewers of that program actually see can be wildly divergent, and, further, different sets of viewers may "see" quite different shows. Many white viewers thought they were getting an inside view of black America in *The Cosby Show,* while many African-American viewers thought the show was a sellout to white America, erasing the difficulties so many black Americans experience in this society (Jhally & Lewis, 1992). Some people see in NFL football exciting games that showcase the best in stereotypically male values (teamwork, physical perfection, personal commitment to self-development), while others see in them some of the worst of presumably masculine values (celebration of the physical over the spiritual, ruthless competitiveness, revenge based on absolutist standards, rule-governed rather than creative interaction). Texts are ambiguous because people who read and see them tend to remake—to reweave—whatever they've read and witnessed in terms of their personal and social situations (see, e.g., Condit, 1989; Vidmar & Rokeach, 1974).

Multiple Codes

Particularly in the case of multimediated works such as television programs, the question, "What is the text?" becomes difficult to answer because so many codes are operative. From among the array of codes with which we are presented, out of what materials do we as viewers construct the meanings of TV programs? The written script? The performed action framed in a decorated set? The speeches of actors and the other aural codes such as sound effects and mood music? That is, are television's texts verbal, visual, or acoustic, or all three (see Figure 5.1)? As O'Sullivan, Hartley, Saunders, Montgomery, and Fiske (1994, pp. 317–318) argue, "A text, then, consists of a network of codes working on a number of levels. It is thus problematic and demands analysis." The notion of the text therefore is ambiguous because you must specify the codes with which you are working, the level (manifest or hidden, mundane or transcendent) on which you are attempting to read or interpret the text, and the degree to which you think the codes themselves interact.

In summary, the idea of textuality is an ambiguous concept because of problems of instability of meanings, variability in what people actually hear and see when they encounter a TV program, and multiplicity of codes comprising a televisual message. Yet in spite of—even because of—such problems, text-centered television criticism is popular and productive of vibrant critical television studies.

FIGURE 5.1   The Multiple Codes of Televisual Communication

Verbal Codes: Linguistic Units

Naming: how are people (girl, Ms., Joan, Dr. Maxwell) identified?
Attitudinal language: what words are used to express positive or negative judgments?
Valuative language: what values—sociological, psychological, legal, moral, religious, and aesthetic—are encoded in dialogue?
Metaphorical language: with what kinds of metaphors are people, events, places, and ideas talked about?
Ideological language: are examples of ideological language—democratic, heathen, scientifically proven—used in arguments and advice-giving talk?

Verbal Codes: Communication Acts

Grammatical orientation: who asks questions? who gives orders? who asserts something as a fact? do different characters use different kinds of grammar as signs of class, education, or status?
Verbal orientation (perspective taking): what perspectives or viewpoints are assumed in a character's speech? (As your father, I think . . . ," "You ladies always are . . . ," "Nine out of ten doctors recommend . . ."
Narrative orientation: what stories are told so as to emphasize what sorts of thoughts or actions?
Argumentative orientation: what kinds of arguments for or against some idea or action are offered?

Visual Codes: Orientation

Color: do particular colors in a shot carry special meanings?
Framing: are important people or objects centered or marginalized in key shots?
Light-dark: how does lighting control visual orientation?
Simplicity-complexity: are objects or people isolated in some shots (simplicity) or put into a multilayered picture (complexity)? (For example, many televised plays isolate characters giving soliloquies, whereas a show

such as *ER* often shows you activities in several areas at once to connote dynamism and excitement.)

Foreground-background relationships: what person or object is made the focus of a shot, and what people, objects, or scenes are made the context for the person or object in the foreground?

Conventionalized objects (icons): what icons—a flag, an identifiable kind of clothing, a way of standing or looking, a picture of a sunset—are used to convey particular meanings recognized across a society?

Visual Codes: Complex Meaning Systems

Emotionality: how are feelings coded into shots or sequences of shots?

Quotation: what characteristics of a particular shot or sequence evoke memories of similar shots or sequences from other visual artifacts?

Interaction with other codes: how do the verbal and acoustic codes affect the meaning of visualized people, places, things, or actions?

Acoustic Codes

Auditory signs: what sounds—a train whistle, a howling wolf, the sound of frying bacon—are used to convey particular meanings understood by members of a society?

Paralinguistic cues: what tones of voice—soothing, pleading, rasping, slurring, or whispering—are used to characterize physical or emotional states, relationships between people, and personality types?

Spatial organization: how is sound used to organize space (e.g., changing the sound of a train to signal its approach, arrival, and departure; two or three different auditory levels to indicate that some people are central, some farther away, and some still farther away, as in a busy shot in the emergency ward)?

Auditory echoes: what uses of sound trigger memories of one's previous experience with media (e.g., the theme song from a childhood cartoon) or important life or world experiences (e.g., "The Wedding March")?

Interaction with other codes: how is the meaning of sounds affected by what is said or what is shown?

Assumptions Grounding Semiotic Approaches to Television Criticism

Taking some of the ideas just encountered, we can formulate three primary assumptions underlying most text-centered TV criticism in our era.

1. *Texts are constructed out of sequences of signs arrayed in codes and capable of being experienced or interpreted in common ways by members of a society.* One of the key words in this assumption is *sign,* something accessible to your senses—for example, the spoken word *tree* (sound), the written word *tree* or a drawing of a tree (sight), the odor of burning wood (smell), a piece of wood carved into a duck (touch and sight). A sign is something with which meanings are associated. In the language of semiotics, a *sign* is a signifier or vehicle; that which is associated with it, what we usually call "meaning," is the *signified.* Taken together, a signifier plus a signified constitute a process of *signification.* A coherent series of signs—a string of words, for example, "Jack jumped over the candlestick"—makes up a sentence that is a communication act. Even a sequence of pictures can form a communication act, as when someone shows you a sunrise, then a picture of the sun overhead at noon, and finally a sunset, so as to suggest the passage of time through a day. A whole field of signs—the words in a language or recognizable clothing from particular countries—is called a *code.* Television, we already have noted, is experienced through verbal, visual, and acoustic codes.

2. *Signs are capable of multiple kinds and levels of interpretation.* The second key concept from the definition of *text* is "experienced or interpreted." For something to be a useful sign, the codes must be understood.[1] If I'm in Finland and don't know that the word *puu* is a sign Finns use when talking about a tree, that sign is not significant to me; it's not a sign I can experience in the way Finns do. When we defined texts in terms of "common ways," we were suggesting that unless people's understandings of signifiers and signifieds are similar, communication—the sharing of meaning—cannot occur.

This is not to suggest, however, that all signs have the same meaning for all people, even people of a particular society or region. Because meaning is grounded as much in personal experience as in common or shared experience, meanings are slippery and variable. Two people can and do construct different meanings from the same text, for several reasons:

> *Social situation.* The TV program *Law and Order* might be watched in one way by a rich person worried about crime in the neighborhood and in another way by a poor person who has been hassled by cops on his block. Males and females often look at sports programs in different ways. Your social situation and status can affect how you understand what you see on TV. Stuart Hall (1980) argued that you can decode or read television in three ways: a *dominant reading* understands the signs pretty much as the producer did, a *negotiated reading* adjusts some of the meanings, and an *oppositional reading* reverses them. A dominant reading of the 2000 Democratic political convention's introduction of candidate Al Gore with a slide show done by his wife, Tipper, produces

meanings consonant with the party hope that voters will find Gore warm, committed to public service, and loving; an oppositional reading might cause a viewer to laugh at Tipper's constant reliance on the word *love* and boo her attempts, which you view as feeble, to support liberal causes. Women might do a negotiated reading, as when they understand the political sentiments but see her as just one more woman being exploited by a male power figure.

Open and closed texts. Some texts invite you to make your own meanings; they are comparatively open. For example, weather programs often include outdoor shots over which a list of temperatures is scrolling. Those shots of the beach or wheat fields or mountains are open texts; you are invited to let your mind roam, to think of your own experiences or fantasies. The weather map, in contrast, is a comparatively closed text. The list of specific places with particular geographical relationships to each other and their temperatures is strongly oriented to the communication of specific information in unambiguous signs. The relative degree of openness of a text affects your ability to participate in or even take over the meaning-making process (see Eco, 1979; cf. Barthes on "readerly" and "writerly" texts, 1975).

Polyvalence. Celeste Condit (1989) suggests that people's value orientations affect how they experience televised scenes, for example, scenes concerning abortion. In her study, pro-life and pro-choice students interpreted an episode of *Cagney & Lacey* dealing with abortion in very different ways. They assessed the soundness of arguments made in the episode through their own values. Essentially, the pro-life and pro-choice students made different texts out of the episode. Signs thus can be interpreted in positive or negative ways by different people as they reflect on their own beliefs and values.

Recoding and poaching. The example of *The Man from U.N.C.L.E.* mentioned earlier illustrates another interpretive process. Especially across time, viewers can look at shows in wholly different ways. Michael Real (1989) calls this process *recoding,* that is, seeing a show in a totally alternative way, as many viewers of the channel Nickelodeon do when watching reruns from the 1950s and 1960s. They view the shows as illustrations of those decades rather than, say, as a sitcom or adventure show. Henry Jenkins (1992) suggests that viewers can go even further than that. With the help of a remote control and a VCR, they can build their own programs out of bits and pieces of material from multiple channels, or they can invent whole lives for characters, as the fans of *Star Trek,* the Trekkies, have done. Both of these activities are examples of what Jenkins calls *poaching.*[2] Meaning making thus can be almost wholly in control of the viewers, not the producers.

Overall, then, although texts are arrays of signs that have to a large extent been precoded, that is, come with shared meanings or signified associated with them, viewers have a series of interpretive strategies available.

3. *What texts mean varies with person, time, place, and context: with variations in sign or code users, the times or styles of an epoch, and the specific situations in which the texts are consumed.* This is a fact with which people—including critics—

must live. Human communication is never perfectly efficient; misunderstandings and alternative understandings are part of the human condition. Recognition of this fact could cause you to quit the business of criticism, but that's too radical a response. We suggest another. We propose handling the problem of the text in an arbitrary but serviceable way. We offer separate chapters on users (reception-centered criticism) and situations (producer-centered criticism) so that we can reserve text-centered criticism for kinds of analyses that focus on encoding processes, that is, on text making. Our focus is on textuality—how communication signs and acts are assembled, in our case by television producers, for the education and pleasure of viewers. This chapter features ways to analyze and interpret the arrays of signs that we call texts.

Assumptions Grounding Structural Approaches to Television Criticism

For reasons that should become clear shortly, semiotic analysis often is paired with structuralist analysis[3] by students of various sorts of works, including television shows. The study of how you think about and with such structures is called *structuralism*.[4] Three assumptions govern structuralist approaches to critical analysis:

1. *Structures are based on the ideas of wholeness and transformation*.[5] Human beings use structure to segment out a portion of what they are perceiving to create an idea of wholeness. Sitting at a track-and-field meet, starting with a sound (from a starter's pistol), you watch a group of people engaging in an activity you've learned to call sprinting for a little over ten seconds, identifying the order in which they finish, calling the whole thing a hundred-yard dash. You isolated those 10 to 12 seconds of activity from everything else those same people did before and after what you call "the race," defining a race as movement from the starter's pistol to the breaking of the tape at a mark on the ground called "the finish line." The use of structure to make a whole out of those people's activities that day is absolutely central to understanding what a hundred-yard dash is.

Such structures are never static, however. The same principles of wholeness that allowed you to isolate and recognize a hundred-yard dash likewise permit you to recognize other forms of races—for example, 5 kilometer and 10 kilometer races, half- and full marathons, even the Indy 500 or the Tour de France. Within the structures we acquire in our interaction with others are variable elements—in the case of races, variations in distances, racing techniques and strategies, even technologies for movement (e.g., with legs, machines)—that allow those structures to be transformed in various times and places. Yet the structure of activities that we call "a race" is recognizable in each. Similarly, the idea of transformation permits us to talk about types of TV programs (e.g., "reality television") and yet understand the variable manifestations of those forms in shows as diverse as *COPS*, *Survivor*, and *Larry King Live!*

2. *The structures with which human beings construct meaningful sequences of experience work at multiple levels of perception.* If only because "structures" are created by human beings in search of boundaries and order, they can operate at various levels of perception and human experience. They become part of the "already there" when you encounter a code; you've been taught to decode structural relationships as part of acculturation.[6] Perhaps the easiest way to comprehend this assumption is to consider levels of linguistic structures as a paradigm of five such levels:

Phonemic level. At this level are the smallest units of structural relationships that make a difference in human understanding. Relating a "p" sound to an "ig" sound creates an English sign different from the one resulting when an "f" is put into a structural relationship with "-ig." The same sort of thing happens visually when you put a chef's hat instead of a firefighter's hat on a picture of a man; that too makes a difference in what you perceive you're looking at.

Sentence level. The order of a series of signs in a single statement can be crucial to human understanding. "The boy tamed the lion" makes sense to you because of how the signs are ordered. Reverse them ("The lion tamed the boy") or scramble them ("Tamed the lion boy"), and either they mean something very different or become nonsensical. Again, visually, as you watch a TV program, you might see a sequence of action where a knocking sound is heard, a character looks at and then goes to a door, opening it just as the knocking sound is repeated. That is a visual-acoustic "sentence" or communication act—a stream of sound and action that creates a comprehensible (i.e., presumably motivated) set of human behaviors.

Paragraph level. In prose composition, a paragraph is a longer unit of signs that usually is marked by a topic sentence—a sentence asserting, describing, evaluating, or questioning some state of affairs—and then developing that topic through the illustrations, explanations, restatements, and authoritative testimony comprising the rest of the paragraph. The visual equivalent of a paragraph is a scene or episode. So if the knocking and door answering is the visual equivalent of a topic sentence, the rest of the scene is like a paragraph. The entrance of a new character into a scene can lead to plot, character, or ideational developments. The knocking on the outside door in *Macbeth* signals the entry of the outside world into the castle where Macbeth has murdered Duncan; the knocking on an office door in *Days of Our Lives* may introduce a lover, an investigator, or a close friend, any of whom can complicate the plot. Think of each scene or episode as a link in the chain of events we call the story or the narrative.

Artifactual level. And then there is the chain itself: the structuring of the scenes or episodes into a story. This is the level of structure that Aristotle in his *Poetics* identified as *mythos,* or what we call the *plot,* characterized, as he said, by a beginning, a middle, and an end. When Aristotle defined the beginning as that-before-which-nothing-else-need-come and the end as that-after-which-nothing-else-need-come, he was suggesting that human beings create terminus points or brackets around sequences of action that are understood to form a wholeness. When a fairy tale begins "Once upon a time" and ends "They all lived happily ever after," you know that you're to regard what occurs in between as a "story" with a plot. If the sequence doesn't clearly move from scene to scene, if you can't see connections, it's a bad (or at least complicated) story. Even films such as *Pulp Fiction* or *Memento,* which break normal narrative order, even relaying events backward, are built around recognizable stories that have wholeness.

Familial level. Finally, there are structural similarities between one story and others like it. Christopher Marlowe's sixteenth-century play *The Tragical History of Doctor Faustus* (about a scholar in search of supreme knowledge), Goethe's nineteenth-century play *Doctor Faust* (about an alchemist in search of the Eternal Feminine), Thomas Mann's *Doctor Faustus,* a twentieth-century novel (about a composer in search of perfect music in Nazi Germany), and even a 1978 episode of *Thundarr the Barbarian* (about evil wizards seeking to control the Helmet of Power) all draw their inspiration—and their narrative form—from a late medieval myth recorded in the German *Faustbuch.* The family resemblances among these works are clear, all structuring a series of character decisions within a story structure—what we'll call narrative structure in a later chapter—about human beings' search for powers exceeding normal human limits. Such relationships are based on what are called principles of intertextuality.[7]

The point here is that structuralist principles for creating wholeness and transformations by welding together in your mind varied perceptions become fundamental in multiple ways to how you organize and understand the world discursively.

3. *A principal vehicle for meaning making is perceptual relationship, though what is meant by that idea is ambivalent.* We have been using the word *relationship* throughout this chapter, though in varied ways. In the sentence "The boy tamed the lion," is the most important structural relationship in the mind of the author who wrote it, in the grammatical rules that permit an author and a reader to more or less understand each other, or in the perception of the reader who interprets it? In other words, is the meaning-making process that results from this structuring of linguistic units in the author's intention to communicate an idea or image, in the grammatical structures that make cognitively based communication possible at all, or in the reader who conjures up a picture as a result of encountering that sentence? The answer, of course, is yes: Authorial intention, grammatical rules for constructing relationships between signs, and readerly reactions are all ultimately matters of structuralist principles. That means that you'll have to be very careful to specify the mind-code relationship you're exploring in your criticism. In this chapter, however, we'll be focusing on sign-sign structures, given that we're exploring text-centered criticism.

For most beginning students of television criticism, semiotic studies of signs, the elements of a code, are the easier sorts of semiotic/structural analysis to perform. More subtle and more difficult are analyses of the structure of a sentence, a scene, an episode, or a program. As the Fiske example included in this chapter clearly illustrates, the structure of most sorts of texts can be fruitfully examined in two ways: by syntagmatic analysis and paradigmatic analysis.

Syntagms are coherent sequences of signs. A sentence, for example, is a syntagm. In the sentence "Jack jumped over the candlestick," the three primary signs are "Jack" (an agent), "jumped" (an action of the agent in some environment), and "candlestick" (an object defining that environment), and together they provide a set of signifieds that most users of English would understand. Most students of texts are interested in larger syntagms: whole stories, even whole TV programs (e.g., the changes in *M*A*S*H* or *ER* over time).[8] For example, whole types of programs can be defined by the sequencing of actions. A situation comedy was defined by Newcomb (1974), for example, as a sequence of four actions: setting a situation, complicating it, turning the world upside down in an episode of "uproar," and then resolving the situation (the denouement).

At the scenic level, what sorts of acts precede a police officer's shooting of a presumed criminal? The shooting will signify different motivations if it has been preceded by the criminal's (1) harming a member of the cop's family, (2) holding a hostage when cornered, (3) shooting at the police officer first, (4) running away from the scene of a capital crime, or (5) having repented and joined a monastery. Similarly, if a story about your state's financial crisis is followed by another on money the governor is spending on renovating his residence at state expense, the association of these two events almost demands that you question the governor's expenditures. Syntagmatically, one event can provide a context for our understandings of other events. Or if events tend to follow each other in predictable ways, as in the American western (Cawelti, 1970, pp. 34–45, argued that there are only seven narrative plots for all of them), then syntagmatic analysis is helping us to define basic forms for discourse.

Paradigmatic analysis is not so concerned with sequences of signs as with their substitutability or general resemblances to each other. A *paradigm*, in this sense, is a group of signs that, though different, are so related to each other that they either can (1) stand for general ideas or principles or (2) be exchanged for each other. O'Sullivan et al. (1994, p. 216) define *paradigm* as a "set of units from which one may be chosen to combine with units from other paradigms to form a syntagm (that is a combination of units into a signifying whole)." For example, "a Coke," "a soda," "a tumbler of water," "a glass of iced tea," "a lemonade," "a beer," or "a cold one" signify different chilled liquids, yet paradigmatically all are closely related. Each belongs to the family of liquids that is considered in Western thought to soothe and refresh. Similarly, the sentence "Your day of reckoning is here," the emergence of a Clint Eastwood or Arnold Schwartzenegger out of the shadows and into the vision of an evil-doer, and particular kinds of music used in Stallone or Segal films all participate in a paradigm we could call "signs of vengeance."

Some Examples of Semiotic/ Structural Criticism

Generally, most criticism focused on artifacts falls into one of four categories: semiotic/structural, generic, rhetorical, and narrative. Semiotic and structural analysis can occur in any of them. But in this chapter, we've focused narrowly on text-centered approaches clearly and directly using semiotic/structuralist vocabularies in pursuing their interpretive goals. We'll begin discussing semiotic/structural criticism with a study featuring semiotic analysis (Seiter, 1987), then move to two studies that combine semiotidc/structural analysis (Hodge & Tripp, 1986; Seiter, 1992) and end with our example essay, Fiske's analysis of *Dr. Who*, which is more clearly centered on structuralism (though do not push on this separation too hard).

Some critics are interested in the fine details of meaning making through structural relationships, in the careful (often called "close") analysis of particular aspects of encoding. Ellen Seiter (1987) did a shot-by-shot analysis of the opening credits (1985–1986 version) of *The Cosby Show*. She charted the visual, verbal, and acoustic signs as arranged in codes, talking about the kinds of shots, their sequence, their analogies to other shows in television history, and the overall impression left by the credits:

> *The Cosby Show* is itself a utopian representation of the family: money is no object; love and harmony is the rule; play abounds as a means of solving discipline problems; marriage is sexy; gender equality is the stated goal; parents and children enjoy stimulating, satisfying situations at work and in school; childcare and housework are either invisible or enjoyable. Like a musical, *The Cosby Show* presents the world not as it really is, but as it should be. (p. 38)

Such a study takes us squarely into the operations of coded signs and visual-acoustic structures on television. Seiter not only uses the shots, title cards, and musical style to ground her conclusions, but also looks at dress, stereotyped reactions to other characters, icons of wealth, and the dance steps of each character. Visual coding is broken down into subcodes so that she can assemble multiple kinds of semiotic evidence to back her claims.

Semiotic analysis is the basis for many kinds of criticism because of its focus on codes.[9] When paired with structuralist interest in syntagms and paradigms, that is, in sequences and oppositions among acts within the life world, semiotics helps us understand much of the dynamic, dialectical themes that engage television audiences.

In 1986, Robert Hodge and David Tripp did a semiotic/structural analysis of the children's cartoon *Fangface*. At the center of the program they found structured tensions between nature and culture, as well as, of course (this is a werewolf cartoon!), between animalness and humanness. Both halves of these oppositions were explored and shown in positive ways, and thus, they argued, "The result is not a single consistent message about the relations between the two. Sometimes nature is seen as threatening, sometimes as compatible with culture. *Fangface* is the focus of both ambiguity and ambivalence" (p. 28). Seiter (1992) shows that a similar analysis can be made of *Teenage Mutant Ninja Turtles*. This sort of analysis is typical of structuralism, which, as John Hartley notes, "shares with other twentieth-century enterprises—in physics and astronomy especially—attention to relations and systems as the framework for explanation" (1994, pp. 304–305). Oppositional structures, especially, create human interest and places for human decision making. Even a cartoon such as *Fangface* can have redeeming social value if it helps its viewers confront important problems where important choices have to be made. (See also Fiske's structural analyses: 1983, 1984, 1987b.)

Previously, we discussed family resemblances, arguing that once those resemblances are understood, individual signs can be used to evoke the whole family and draw meaning from them. We used a clearly familial example: the Faust myth. Resemblances, however, need not be so literal. The familial—paradigmatic—resemblances that John Fiske pursued in a study of particular characters in the British serial *Dr Who* are based on stereotypes. Stereotypical behavior in his study, which is the example essay at the end of this chapter, comes to represent oppositions between democracy and totalitarianism, freedom and slavery, peace and violence, plenty and scarcity, freedom and captivity, life and death, truth and lies, and good and evil. He suggests that some characters in that show—Dr. Who, Taris, Romana, and K9—line up with the ideologically positive values, whereas Adrasta, Palace, Karela, and Wolfweeds signify the binary opposites. Such arguments, and those from Hodge and Tripp (1986), depend on paradigmatic analysis.

Writing Analyses of Verbal, Visual, and Acoustic Signs and Structures

What sort of writing challenges face the semiotic/structural critic? The primary talents needed are those of the so-called close textual analyst, that is, talents in breaking down texts into discrete units that can be profitably interpreted or evaluated. Two talents are paramount: the ability to decode verbal, visual, and acoustic signs and the ability to work interpretively across multiple codes.

In a sense, all text-centered criticism begins with one sort or another of semiotic analysis: taking apart texts, isolating specific units of meaning that can be interpreted or evaluated. Unfortunately, there really aren't generally accepted, foolproof ways of decoding the verbal, visual, and acoustic signs that comprise a TV program. Figure 5.1 suggested some dimensions of those sign systems that might be explored.

The particular ways you'll decode texts will vary with your purpose. Suppose you're interested in male-female relationships in *Friends*. You'll probably want to focus on the valuative language employed by the males and the females (e.g., do they habitually emphasize different values?) and even their grammatical orientation (e.g., do males or females give more orders?). Argumentative orientation might be usefully examined to see if gender affects conflict and its resolution. If you're examining an advertisement for Crest toothpaste, however, ideological language would be important (e.g., what sorts of authorities are cited?), as is narrative orientation (e.g., what kinds of stories—based on fear or joy?—are told in Crest ads?).

Similarly, in thinking about visual and acoustic codes, your analysis of *Friends* may well be sensitive to how characters are arranged in the shots: Who's in the foreground and who's in the background? Who's centered and who's not? Who's lit and who's in the shadows? Are particular clothing styles associated with each character, and is that style important in his or her relationships to the other characters? Regarding acoustic codes, do males and females paralinguistically signal something about their power within the group? Or in looking at the Crest ads, how are the narrators dressed? How are fear at the possibility of tooth decay and joy when no decay is found conveyed acoustically?

Obviously, you can ask many more questions about verbal, visual, and acoustic coding in both *Friends* and toothpaste ads, depending on your purposes. However you proceed, always let your critical purposes guide your decoding practices.

Looking Ahead

As you prepare to read and then write your own semiotic/structuralist critiques, consider the limitations of and yet the promise offered by such approaches. In taking apart texts carefully and closely, you might be conceding too much power to languages or codes. Are not political acts, economic realities, and daily social practices more influential on our lives than episodes of *Friends* or *Frasier*? Maybe, but maybe not. You must at least think about that.

A second problem that can arise is that by emphasizing their texts (their messages), we might be tempted to forget about the text makers (the message makers). As will be noted in Chapter 9, producers should be studied more systematically, as should the authors of the political statements that are broadcast during political events. If semiotic/structural study keeps us from studying the people who craft those texts, then they are distracting us from serious social, political, and economic inquiry.

Finally, these studies can become so focused on such microscopic dimensions of codes as to obscure that which is presumably being studied. To analyze every single shot in a TV ad is possible, but you might be examining such particularized aspects of signs that you cannot say anything about meaning, which, after all, is your job.

But if textual critics might be tempted to avoid questions of real power, personalized motives, and the levels of consciousness at which meanings reside, they also face many rewards. When well done by sensible people, semiotic/structural television criticism reinforces the truism that meaning making is a process and that meanings are struggled with again and again. The best semiotic/structural critics allow us to see that the human world is inscribed in the languages by which we communicate with each other.

Textual studies also can become the bases for explicitly evaluative or judgment sorts of criticism. In tearing apart *CBS Evening News with Dan Rather, ESPN's Sports Center, Law and Order: Criminal Intent,* and the like, critics lay bare the ways in which our beliefs are manipulated in discourse, the two-valued thinking structured into news that so often forces us to see the world in terms of only good and evil, the springs of our socialization that form our social understanding of gender roles and racial attitudes, and the ways in which our perceptions of the world are filtered by the TV program that frames it for us.

Textuality is a powerful word that signals that systems of meaning are organized for citizens of a country in verbal, visual, acoustic, and behavioral texts that stand between those citizens and the direct experience of life. An important mission for all television critics, in fact, for all critics, is to penetrate and seize control of texts so as to comprehend and critique their hold on our personal and social existence. That certainly was Raymond Williams's goal when he sought to understand the textualizations he witnessed in TV coverage of the 1972 Olympics.

The Example Essay

Our example of a semiotic/structural criticism essay is John Fiske's analysis of *Dr. Who,* the world's longest continuously running television scrience-fiction series (Tulloch, 1987). Fiske's structural analysis of the British cult science-fiction series examines a four-part episode, "The Creature from the Pit." Using Seymour Chatman's (1978) narrative model, he first analyzes the syntagmatic structure of the episode narrative and identifies the narrative's existents (characters and settings) and events (actions). This, in turn, enables Fiske to identify the text's paradigmatic structures—the sets of binary characters and settings (and the values they signify), and to explain how these structured sets of oppositions articulate[10] five related discourses and generate mythically and ideologically preferred meanings that resolve certain textual and "real- life" value contradictions and affirm the social, political, and economic status quo.

Notes

1. In English (particularly in British pronunciation), there's a technical—a phonetic—difference between "coal" and "call," though not many people are likely to hear (to register, to understand) it. A difference in sounds that actually makes a difference in our comprehension or understanding—as between "tin" and "sin"—is a phonemic difference. A sign therefore can be attached to a concept (a signified) only through systems of meaningful difference. See Chapter 2 in Hawkes (1977).

2. Jenkins (1992) liberated the term from de Certeau (1984).

3. This is because in the original French versions of structuralism (especially the turn-of-the-century work of Ferdinand de Saussure), semiotics was a basic part of structuralism as an approach to language analysis. See O'Sullivan et al. (1994).

4. Much of this conceptual background, including this broad definition, is connected to the thought of Terence Hawkes in his classic work, *Structuralism and Semiotics* (1977), supplemented at points by Scholes (1982).

5. Hawkes (1977) suggests these two principles and a third idea as well, self-regulation, by which he means that nothing outside a system is necessary to account for how the system works. For example, you need only know the rules of grammar to be able to distinguish between "normal" ("Diana is great") and "inverted" ("Great is Diana"); grammar is self-regulating, based on a system of placement rules (subject-verb-predicate placements in indicative sentences, for example) and transformational rules (how to transform normal into inverted word order). Grammatically, language is self-regulating, though for people interested in what language does rather than how it's constituted, self-regulation is a limiting, even false, concept. What is the effect on listeners of hearing "Great is Diana" rather than "Diana is great"? Why did the ancient Greeks use the inverted word order in religious observations? Grammar cannot provide answers to such questions. Meaning making occurs in people and becomes conventionalized in actual situations, not in grammatical systems. That's why language and other sign systems are not self-regulating; communicative acts and the rules governing them are fluid, changing across time and space.

6. To quote Schleifer (1994, p. 698), "Structuralism . . . offers a framework of understanding in which what is structured is not simply 'content' but rather phenomena already structured on a different 'level' of apprehension, so that the isolated content implicit in literary 'formalism' . . . betrays the dynamic relational nature of meaning."

7. John Fiske (1987b) argues that there are three layers or kinds of intertextuality: the direct familial resemblances of the kind we've just described, those where somewhat similar characters with like (but not the same) motivations have a similar fate (think of the fall because of self-pride in *Oedipus Rex*), and those created by reading or talking with others about some work you've experienced. The variety of possible "intertexts" is explored in Scholes (1982) and explained nicely by Perron (1994).

8. The primary inspiration of syntagmatic study was Propp's *Morphology of the Folk Tale* (1968), actually a study from the 1920s. He studied hundreds of fairy tales, looking for the component parts of tales and the relationships among those parts as they gave meaning to tales as a whole. The basic unit of meaning he focused on was a cluster of signs that he called a function, which he defined as "an act of a character, defined from the point of view of its significance for the course of action" (p. 21). Among the functions that he identified are initial situation, absentation, interdiction, violation, reconnaissance, delivery, trickery, lack and/or villainy, mediation, counteraction, departure, donor, reaction, struggle, liquidation, pursuit, rescue, and transfiguration/punishment. These were generated by looking at what happened in folktales, though the list could be easily adapted to other kinds of texts. Propp's formal-analytical techniques can be used to define recurrent literary structures, to interpret whole narratives by how their conclusions are put together (see Picarillo, 1986; White, 1981), or even to disassemble a program.

9. Semiotic analysis is often combined with other kinds of criticism. For example, Schwichtenberg (1983) combined it with psychoanalysis and ideological analysis in her study of the prime-time soap *Dynasty*.

10. Articulation (in semiotic/structural, ideological, and cultural studies analysis) describes a hierarchical joining of two or more things, so they are "structured in dominance" (see O'Sullivan et al., 1994, pp. 17–18).

Further Readings

Fiske, J., & Hartley, J. (1978). *Reading television.* London: Methuen. This is the work on television criticism that theorized and popularized semiotic/structuralist critiques of television programming. The authors also worked some basic psychoanalytical principles into their studies.

Hall, S. (1997). The work of representation. In S. Hall (Ed.), *Representation: Cultural representations and signifying practices* (pp. 13–74). Semiotics, structuralism, and cultural studies are combined in a theory of representation, with representation understood as the processes by which signs both describe (depict) and symbolize (adding meaning to) the world. Hall provides a vocabulary for studying representation processes, exercises, and some short readings from the history of semiotics, (especially French) structuralism, and (especially British) cultural studies.

Webnotes

Semiotics. **http://carbon.cudenver.edu/~mryder/itc_data/semiotics.html**

This is perhaps the master international site giving you access to semiotics: basic resources, conferences, readings, backgrounds on the principal theorists and critics, and communication theories grounded in semiology. The study of semiotics itself is broken down into biosemiotics, computer semiotics, social semiotics, cultural semiotics, cognitive-semiotic studies, and visual semiotics.

Cambridge classics: Structuralism. **http://www.classics.cam.ac.uk/Faculty/structuralism.html**

An equivalent site devoted to structuralism is this "Cambridge Classics" site from Cambridge University. It provides brief synopses of so-called landmark publications, a bibliography of structuralism in classics literature, an introduction to the related theories of hermeneutics and poststructuralism (including a brief section directly relevant to television studies, on reception theory), and a look at developments in structuralism in the age of the Internet, followed by basic works on feminist and Marxist criticism, historical approaches, and cognitive studies done within structuralist assumptions.

1. Divide sheets of paper into three columns, labeling them "Visual," "Literate," and "Acoustic." In teams of three (or six, so that you have two people for each column), write down the visual, literate, and acoustic signs you're presented within a short—say, 15- to 45-second—television news story or advertisement you've videotaped. You'll have to play it several times to transcript the acoustic (especially verbal) texts and the range of visual images. Lay a description of what you heard and saw on the sheets of paper, so that pieces of spoken language are arranged directly next to the pictures and print language that accompanied them. Then as a team, prepare an in-class report with the subject, "The Newscast [or Advertisement] as a Communication Act." Try to figure out how the signs in one column are affected by the signs in the other columns—for example, how printed words affect your comprehension of pictures or how pictures provide particular understandings of the words used in spoken monologues or dialogues.

2. With the help of sources in the References list accompanying this chapter, as well as library and Internet searches, write a two- to three-page report on the theories of semiotics or structuralist thought (or both) built by one of the following people: Roman Jakobson, Thomas Sebeok, Ferdinand de Saussure, Roland Barthes, Carlos Colon, John Fiske, Göran Sonesson, Umberto Eco, Robert Scholes, Charles Sanders Peirce, Claude Levi-Strauss, or another approved by your instructor.

References

Barthes, R. (1975). *The pleasures of the text*. New York: Hill & Wang.

Cawelti, J. (1970). *The six-gun mystique*. Bowling Green, OH: Bowling Green State University Press.

Condit, C. M. (1989). The rhetorical limits of polysemy. *Critical Studies in Mass Communication, 6*, 103–122.

deCerteau, M. (1984). *The practice of everyday life*. Berkeley: University of California Press.

Eco, U. (1979). *The role of the reader: Explorations in the semiotics of texts*. Bloomington: Indiana University Press.

Fiske, J. (1983). The discourses of TV quiz shows or school + luck = success + sex. *Communication Studies, 34*, 139–150.

Fiske, J. (1984). Popularity and ideology: A structuralist reading of *Dr Who*. In W. Roland & B. Watkins (Eds.), *Interpreting television: Current research perspectives* (pp. 165–198). Thousand Oaks, CA: Sage.

Fiske, J. (1987a). *Cagney and Lacey*: Reading character structurally and politically. *Communication, 9*, 399–426.

Fiske, J. (1987b). *Television culture*. New York: Methuen.

Hall, S. (1980). Encoding/decoding. In S. Hall, D. Hobson, A. Lowe, & P. Willis (Eds.), *Culture, media, language* (pp. 128–139). London: Hutchinson.

Hartley, J. (1994). Structuralism. In T. O'Sullivan, J. Hartley, D. Saunders, M. Mont-gomery, & J. Fiske (Eds.), *Key concepts in communication and cultural studies* (2nd ed., pp. 302–305). New York: Routledge.

Hawkes, T. (1977). *Structuralism and semiotics.* Berkeley: University of California Press.

Hodge, R., & Tripp, D. (1986). *Children and television: A semiotic approach.* Stanford: Stanford University Press.

Jenkins, H. (1992). *Textual poachers: Television fans and participatory culture.* New York: Routledge.

Johnson, B. (1990). Writing. In F. Lentricchia & T. McLaughlin (Eds.), *Critical terms for literary study* (pp. 39–49). Chicago: University of Chicago Press.

Newcomb, H. (1974). *TV, the most popular art.* Garden City, NY: Anchor Books.

O'Connor, A. (Ed.). (1989). *Raymond Williams on television.* New York: Routledge.

O'Sullivan, T., Hartley, J., Saunders, D., Montgomery, M., & Fiske, J. (1994). *Key concepts in communication and cultural studies* (2nd ed.). New York: Routledge.

Perron, P. (1994). Semiotics. In M. Groden & M. Hreiswirth (Eds.), *The Johns Hopkins guide to literary theory and criticism* (pp. 658–665). Baltimore, MD: Johns Hopkins University Press.

Picarillo, M. S. (1986). On the authenticity of televisual experience: A critical exploration of para-social closure. *Critical Studies in Mass Communication, 3,* 337–355.

Propp, V. (1968). *Morphology of the folk tale* (2nd ed.). Austin: University of Texas Press.

Real, M. (1989). *Super media: A cultural studies approach.* Thousand Oaks, CA: Sage.

Schleifer, R. (1994). Structuralism. In M. Groden & M. Kreiswirth (Eds.), *The Johns Hopkins guide to literary theory and criticism* (pp. 696–701). Baltimore, MD: Johns Hopkins University Press.

Scholes, R. (1982). *Semiotics and interpretation.* New Haven, CT: Yale University Press.

Schwichtenberg, C. (1983). *Dynasty:* The dialectic of feminine power. *Communication Studies, 34,* 151–161.

Seiter, E. (1987). Semiotics and television. In R. C. Allen (Ed.), *Channels of discourse: Television and contemporary criticism* (pp. 17–41). Chapel Hill: University of North Carolina Press.

Seiter, E. (1992). Semiotics, structuralism, and television. In R. C. Allen (Ed.), *Channels of discourse, reassembled: Television and contemporary criticism* (2nd ed., pp. 31–66). Chapel Hill: University of North Carolina Press.

Tulloch, J. (1997). *Doctor Who.* In H. Newcomb (Ed.), *Encyclopedia of television* (pp. 512-514). Chicago: Fitzroy Dearborn.

Vidmar, N., & Rokeach, M. (1974). Archie Bunker's bigotry: A study in selective perception and exposure. *Journal of Communication, 24*(2), 36–47.

White, H. (1981). The narrativization of real events. In W. J. T. Mitchell (Ed.), *On narrative* (pp. 249–254). Chicago: University of Chicago Press.

Popularity and Ideology:
A Structuralist Reading of *Dr Who*

John Fiske

The first episode of *Dr Who* aired on November 23, 1963, which makes it the British Broadcasting Corporation's (BBC) longest running fictional program ever. It is exported to over 40 different countries all over the world and has spawned a network of fan clubs and organizations: in Chicago in 1978, 100,000 fans attended a convention.

Its popularity, as argued by Tullock and Alvarado (1983), lies in the flexibility of its structure—the time can range over millions of years, the Doctor himself can be (and has been) played by a number of different actors who vary his personality, appearance, and age, and he can have a number of different helpers and companions. But this flexibility is always contained within a set of conventions. The Doctor is essentially good—he is nonviolent, selfless, and his missions in time and space are always to defeat evil, to free the oppressed, and to establish a harmonious free society in the worlds that he visits.

He is a "Timelord" with human form and human characteristics, but a nonhuman origin. He is a rebel, constantly ignoring the control of his masters in Gallifrey. His reliance on space-age technology is minimized. The Tardis, his space/time ship, is like a police box (a blue telephone kiosk) on the outside, but is an enormous network of corridors and control stations on the inside. It is extraterrestrial, and its operations therefore slide easily over that crucial boundary between magic and science. K9, the canine computer, is domesticated, friendly hi-tech, not technology to be in awe of or to wonder at. Dr. Who wins his struggles not by superior technology (which in science fiction generally means superior force—technology is both totalitarian and imperialistic) but by reason, fearlessness, humor, and curiosity. Science, for him, is not a means of controlling the world or taming nature, but an expression of man's eternal curiosity—the desire to find out and to understand. His is a humane, mentalistic science, not a hi-tech, antihuman one. This paper uses a structuralist analysis of one particular story in order to raise some issues about its specific popularity and about popularity in general. Structuralism and semiotics avoid terms like escape or diversion to describe the television genre to which Dr. Who belongs because they imply that the symbolic world of television drama is disconnected from the social world of the audience. The notion of popularity, however, suggests connections between the two worlds, and it is these connections and their ideological effect that this paper seeks to explore.

The story whose analysis enables me to raise these theoretical issues is called "The Creature from the Pit." It is by David Fisher, and was first broadcast in Britain in 1979, and consists of four 30-minute episodes. Let me summarize the plot briefly.

The Doctor, Romana, and K9 are brought by the Tardis to Chloris, a planet overrun with vegetation and short of minerals. They have picked up a distress call from what the Doctor identifies as a huge egg. During their investigation they are captured by soldiers and a "Huntsman" who controls "the

Wolf-weeds" (large balls of vegetation that kill by rolling over their victim). They are taken to Chloris's ruler Lady Adrasta, but before they reach her they are attacked by bandits in the forest and Romana is kidnapped. Adrasta is surprised that the Doctor has identified the mysterious object, as the best brains in her kingdom have been unable to. Her chief engineer is condemned to death for his failure to solve the mystery. His execution consists of his being thrown into the pit where the Creature exists ready to devour any human being with whom he comes in contact. Meanwhile Romana, with the aid of K9, has escaped from the Bandits but is rapidly recaptured by Adrasta's men.

As a strategy to save her, the Doctor jumps into the pit. In the pit, which is a series of worked out mine galleries, the Doctor meets Organon, an astrologer who has been thrown in there by Adrasta. He has made himself comfortable in the galleries and has learned how to keep out of the Creature's way. He explains to the Doctor that Adrasta owns the only mine on Chloris and thus all its mineral wealth. By means of this monopoly of metal she maintains her power. The Doctor guesses that the Creature is not a native of Chloris.

Adrasta keeps Romana alive because of what she knows about the egg and because of K9's abilities. She, Adrasta that is, has discovered the capabilities of the Tardis, which she wants to use to fetch metal from other planets, thus preserving her monopoly. She now has no use for the Creature; previously she had used it as a means of terror for maintaining her power, but the strengthening of her mineral wealth will serve the same function. So she takes K9 to the pit to kill the Creature.

Down in the pit the Doctor has followed the Creature to try and learn more about it and discovers traces of minerals that have not come from Chloris. He befriends the Creature, who draws the shape of a shield that the Doctor has seen in Adrasta's palace.

The bandits meanwhile attack Adrasta's palace in order to steal her metal, including the shield that the Creature has drawn. The shield mysteriously hypnotizes them, and makes them carry it toward the Creature. The Doctor places the shield on the

Creature who then uses it to communicate through the Doctor's voice. We learn that the Creature is called Irato and that he is an Ambassador from Tythonis on a trading mission to exchange vegetation (the food of the Tythonians, of which they are short, for metal, of which they have plenty). The mysterious "egg" is, in fact, his spaceship. Adrasta saw that free trade would break the power that her monopoly had given her so she imprisoned him in the pit.

The Huntsman shows doubts about Adrasta's autocratic leadership and after an argument sides with the Doctor and turns the Wolf-weeds against Adrasta. Irato kills both Adrasta and her Wolf-weeds. He is naturally cross about his long imprisonment and plans to leave Chloris immediately in the egg. But the Doctor has "borrowed" his photon drive without which he cannot leave. He is then forced to disclose the information that in 24 hours a neutron star will hit Chloris. The Doctor uses the photon drive as a bargaining counter to persuade Irato to spin a web of aluminum around the star and then use the Tardis's gravitation field to yank it off course. Reluctantly Irato agrees, but Karela (Adrasta's henchwoman) has stolen the photon drive and tries to make an alliance with the bandits to preserve the metal monopoly with them.

K9 is called in to destroy the metal that the bandits have. This simple lesson in economics, that metal is not of intrinsic value but that value is a function of scarcity, shows the bandits the fragility of their theory. The Doctor returns the photon drive and departs with Irato for Tythonis. He returns with a draft contract for a trading agreement, which he hands to the Huntsman who has now taken over power and will, by implication, establish a progressive, democratic, *good* government.

In this paper I intend to explore two closely related concerns: (1) the relationship between the syntagmatic, onward thrust of the story through time and the paradigmatic, atemporal discourses through which it is realized, and (2) the notion of popularity, which I define as "an easy fit between the discourses of the text and the discourses through which its model readers articulate and understand their social experience."

FIGURE 5.2   Structural Model of a Simple Narrative

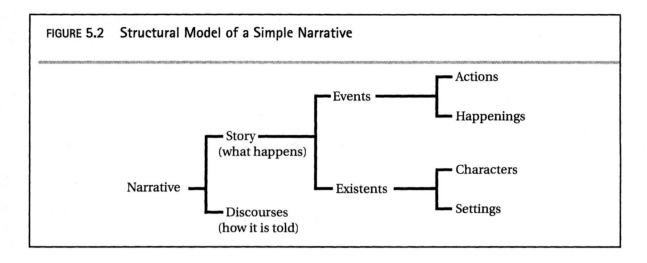

Let me use a simple structural model of a narrative as my starting point (Chatman, 1978). The reader should consult Figure 5.2. The top half of the model identifies first the comparatively unproblematic elements that can be schematized by a straightforward analysis of the manifest content. But the significance of these elements does not lie in their identification and nomination: but rather in the ways in which they are, or can be, interrelated.

And what is really at issue here is the relationship of discourses. For a number of discourses are used to realize the Doctor and his adversaries in the narrative. In this story, we find centrally the discourses of politics, morality, economics, and individualism used to establish the identity and difference of heroes and villains, while that of science and reason provides the common ground between them. The Doctor is realized by a neat interplay between the values of liberal democracy and those of "good" science, while his adversaries signify the values of totalitarianism and "bad" science. We will return to this point later; at the moment I wish only to establish the structuralist truism that significance lies in relationships, not in entities.

And these relationships are those among elements in the story (the top half of the model), among the discourses used to realize them, and between the elements and the discourses. Central to all these interrelationships is the notion of discourse, and this is one that I find most fruitful for it enables us to link text and society in a way that leads toward a theory of popularity.

A discourse, then, is both a topic and a coded set of signs through which that topic is organized, understood, and made expressible. Discourses, according to O'Sullivan et al. (1983), are "the product of social, historical and institutional formations, and meanings are produced by these institutionalised discourses. It follows that the potentially infinite senses any language system is capable of producing are always limited and fixed by the structure of social relations which prevails in a given time and place, and which is itself represented through various discourses." Discourse is the social process by which sense is made and reproduced. A discourse may be manifest in a text, but its origins and destinations are always social. It functions both in the production and reception of texts and in the production of meaning in social experience. Making sense of our social experience is at least a parallel activity to reading a text: indeed, I am tempted to go further and claim that the two are, in essence, identical. The notion of discourse is essential to both, for it is this that explains how we bring our social experience to bear upon our reading of texts and how we use our reading of texts to feed back into our social experience. In this, I differ only in emphasis from Morley (1980a):

> Thus the meaning of the text must be thought of in terms of which set of discourses it encounters in any particular set of circumstances, and how this encounter may restructure both the meaning of the text and the discourses which it meets.

The discourses available to the reader are obviously those available to the author for giving sense to the chain of events that constitute his story. And the interplay between textually located and socially located discourses is the process by which meaning is achieved in both text and society. And the interplay is two-way.

In the discourse of politics, for example, our social experience and our textual experience confirm each other in, for example, the positive connotations of democracy and the negative connotations of autocracy. But cultural consensus within a discourse can also be an agreement to differ: we agree that Marxism and monetarism, for example, can have positive or negative connotations within the same discourse depending on the speaker and context.

This points us to one of the crucial differences between discourses in society and the same discourses in a text, especially a popular text: those in a text operate with a higher degree of consensus and tend to exclude signs with alternative connotations. Popular texts are constructed from those areas of a discourse where consensus is high enough to be taken for granted—thus we find Dr. Who defined partly through democracy in the political discourse and his adversaries through totalitarianism, because these signs can be taken for granted.

Interestingly, and most importantly, this assumption of consensus is transferred to more controversial areas, such as free trade and individualism. But we will return to this later. At the moment I wish to make the point that it is in the nature of popular texts to operate within the high consensus areas of a discourse and then to extend this assumed and unquestioned consensus to more controversial areas.

Our social experience is, therefore, harder to read than a text, because it is fraught with the internal contradictions and sites of ideological struggle that are disguised, if not excluded from a popular text by its conditions of production and reception. Reading social experience is a struggle, and because of its open nature we find it difficult to be finally sure that our reading is adequate: Reading a text, however, is easier by far, and the greater closure within it is constantly working to reassure and convince us that this easy reading is adequate—totally adequate. A text, then, becomes popular when its readings, which are confidently believed to be adequate, fit neatly and naturally with readings of social experience that we use the same discourses to understand, but which are by definition, more complex, contradictory, and thus harder to read. Popular narratives prove in their own closed world the adequacy of discourses as explanatory, sense-making mechanisms: This adequacy is then transferred to the use of those discourses in the social world to the ultimate relief and reassurance of the reader. In this Dr. Who text, for example, we will see how the discourse of politics, economics, and morality enter into a mutually validating relationship within the narrative; this validity is then, through the sociotextual nature of discourse, itself transferred to the appropriate institutions that form their prime locations in society.

So discourses are not just social topics and a system of signs for realizing them: they are the means by which social experience is constructed and by which the social being is constructed. My history is the process by which I have acquired the range of discourses that enable me to exist as a social being.

Structuralism is concerned with the way that members of a culture make sense of their experience. It stresses that this sense derives not from any intrinsic meaning of an individual unit of experience, but from the relationship between the various units. Thus, later on in this article when I discuss the potential meanings of characters and settings in this story, I am able to do so only in terms of diagrams that relate characters and settings together according to certain criteria and value systems. The "meaning" of the character of Dr. Who emerges from two key sets of relationships—one with Romana and K9 (see Figure 5.3) and the other with Adrasta, Irato, and the bandits (see Figure 5.4). Similarly the meaning of the discourse of politics can be understood only in its relationship with the discourses of economics, morality, and individualism, and these in turn can be understood only in their relationships with the discourse of science/reason and the way it functions to transform nature into culture. Thus, for structuralism, meanings are not fixed or set either in a text or in an abstract system of languages: meanings are constantly generated and negotiated both by the structures that are dominant in any one text or in any one society at a particular period, and by the relationship between the discursive structures in a text and those in society as they come together in the crucial moment of reading. These various structures, and the relationships within and between them, are not arbitrary or random. All structures result from the operation of the human brain. This means that they all have something in common, and thus we should expect to find similarities between those found in, for instance, language, and those in, for instance, the kinship system, and those in, for instance, the cooking system (see Levi-Strauss 1955). The repeatability, or parallelism, of structures is the way that a culture produces a unifiable or coherable world view for its members. Structures that make sense of one facet of experience fit with those applied to another: This apparent harmony is essential to the smooth working of ideology. For without it, that is when contradictions and disunities are perceived; the arbitrariness of ideology, and therefore its partiality, is made apparent.

Developments in structuralism, which go under the name of post-structuralism, tend to emphasize the role of the reader in the construction of relationships both within structures and between structures. This sets structuralism on a different path from more traditional modes of textual analysis in that it prioritizes the reader over the author. The author's intention and even his "creativity"

are demoted from objects of crucial interest. The meanings of a text are not what the author intended or wished to put into it, but what the reader finds when using that text in a particular moment of space and time. Thus, the text can have different meanings for different readers at different cultural moments. This is not to say that the text is a wide-open potential of any meanings; far from it, for the structures of the text itself prefer some potential meanings over others and delimit the space within which meanings can legitimately be found.

Within this emphasis on the role of the reader can be found three main theoretical positions. The first, and this is one associated largely with Screen Theory, is that the reader is produced by the text. By cooperating with the text, the reader positions himself or herself in the appropriate discursive and social position to make the easy sense that the text itself prefers. This view has been challenged by work such as that of Morley (1980b), which asserts that the reader's social and cultural experience has at least as much bearing upon this negotiation of meaning as have the structures in the text. Both these positions differ from the third, which asserts that readings or interpretations exist in empirically definable individuals and are therefore assessible to empirical analysis.

Structuralism insists that meanings are located ultimately in subjectivities not in individuals. Subjectivity is the site of consciousness, which is produced by a number of cultural and textual agencies. O'Sullivan et al. (1983) write: "Subjectivity is a way of conceptualising text/reader relations without reproducing either as fixed unitary categories. At the level of analysis a lot of work has been done to show how cultural products (especially film and television) employ textual analysis and strategies like point-of-view, mode of address and narration to propose or fix a subject position from which they can be made sense of when read." This position of the reading subject need not coincide with the position of the biographically defined individual: classic Hollywood films position their readers as middle-class, white males. That is to say that they prefer to be read by the discourses that make sense of social and textual experience in a way that serves the interests of that particular social category. This means that blacks, or the working class, or women are positioned by the film in ways that contradict their social experience and are led to make sense of both the film and their experience via discourses that are not "theirs." In this sense, then, individuals are seen not as self-possessed and self-possessing entities, but as subjects in ideology constituted by the range of social discourses available to them (and these discourses, as we have seen, are both social and textual).

Barthes (1975) explains subjectivity as the "I" who reads the text: "This 'I' which approaches the text is already itself a plurality of other texts, of codes which are infinite or, more precisely, lost (whose origin is lost). . . . Subjectivity is a plenary image with which I may be thought to encumber the text, but whose deceptive plenitude is merely the wake of all the codes which constitute me, so that my subjectivity has ultimately the generality of stereotypes." He goes on to explain that "my task (as reader) is to move, to shift systems whose perspective ends neither at the text nor at the 'I': in operational terms, the meanings I find are established not by 'me' or by others, but by their *systematic* mark" (1975: 10–11). System, for Barthes, is a central term that refers to the structural properties of codes and discourses.

Subjectivity is thus available to analysis only via discourses, texts, and cultural practices, not by empirical investigation of individuals. Interpretation now becomes not a matter of matching an individual reader's response with an individual author's intention, but one of discovering within the text relationships of discourse, of characters, of settings, of narrative moments that parallel and reproduce structures found elsewhere in the culture and that will be available to the reader to bring, via the reader's discursive practices, to the making of the text.

This approach follows the priorities set by Todorov (1977) when he points out that there are two lines of force in a narrative: the vertical, which consist of the discourses of knowledge (e.g., the hidden cultural laws of class, politics, and sex roles), and the horizontal, which is the sequence of events. For Todorov, the vertical is the more significant.

Of the discourses of knowledge is this narrative, the first, and most obvious, is that of science; but science is not the value-free objective discourse it claims to be in society. As Tulloch (1982) has suggested, pure science is finally totalitarian—it allows no alternative, no oppositional view. In story after story in *Dr. Who*, "pure" or "cold" science is used to maintain or establish a totalitarian political order. Science is a means of power in an intergalactic version of feudal society. The Doctor typically defeats a totalitarian, scientific antagonist and replaces him or her with a liberal democratic humane scientist to take over and bring justice and freedom to the oppressed serf class.

While it is easy to oppose the values of liberal democracy to those of totalitarianism in the political discourse, it is less easy to oppose the values of totalitarian or "cold" science with the "warm" humane science whose values are embodied in the Doctor, and this is what the narrative works hard to achieve.

In this particular story, both types of existent, characters and settings, are used to structure our values, both within the discourse of science and in its relationships with other discourses such as politics or "humanism." In using this word we need to cut out many of its traditional associations with the "humanities," but to maintain its central concern with the "human," the nature of man (defined according to, as we shall see later, a postromantic, individualistic, capitalist set of criteria).

And at the heart of this humanism is the concept of the individual. Science, in our culture's common-sense understanding of it, at least, is anti-individualist: The objectivity of empiricism distrusts the individual in any role other than that of observer, analyst, or computer. Value-laden scales such as morality or politics are anathema to it.

The text then faces the inherent ideological problem of its genre—science fiction. It needs to reconcile the objective of inhuman values of

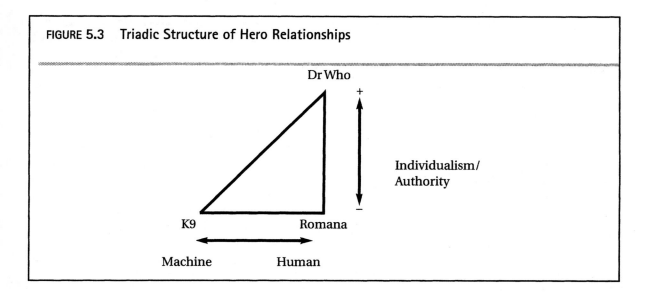

FIGURE 5.3   Triadic Structure of Hero Relationships

science with the individualistic and moral values of popular fiction. It does this by a careful structuring of heroes, villains, and discourses.

The triadic hero in this story consists of Dr. Who, Romana, and K9. Their basic relationships are structured on the dimensions of first, machines (controlled) to human (controller), and second, of degree of individuality, which goes with authority. The structure can be visualized as presented in Figure 5.3.

K9 is pure, technological science with two major exceptions—he is "domesticated," controlled by man, whom he constantly refers to as "Master" and "Mistress," and he is programmed to kill only in self defense. He has not only rigid scientific principles—he will not accept incompatible data, but also rigid, if fragile, moral principles. He can be significantly opposed to the Daleks in that he is science with the proper relationship to humanity, whereas they are antihuman. He is a domesticated Dalek, and this concept of the domestication of science is an important one. It is no coincidence that one of our commonest computer systems is called a PET. This is a similar pun to that contained in the name K9/canine, and both illustrate the ideological function of puns in bringing together opposing discourses and defusing the opposition

either by laughter or by demonstrating similarity of the signifier that overrides the more fundamental difference: in this case that between science as threatening to take over humans, and pets that are wild animals or nature domesticated, tamed and brought into households under human control. Science and nature become one in the K9/canine pun: the inherent threat in each is defused by the domestication common to both.

K9, then, is clearly a machine: Dr. Who and Romana are both Timelords in human form, but the Doctor is more "human" than Romana. Tulloch (1982) shows convincingly how the Doctor's ability to err is a way of structuring human or individualistic values into a "cold" scientist. He has other character traits that perform the same function: one is his schoolboyishness (Romana chides him for his untidiness and his collection of "useless" junk: he is also reading a child's book when the story opens), another is his hint of teenage rebelliousness (he will not plug in the transceiver so that he can receive orders from Gallifrey), similar to this is his trait of "randomness" (the Tardis is liable to materialize and land the Doctor almost anywhere: the acceptance of "chance" or "luck" seems another key value of the human when opposed to the coldly scientific) and another, of course, is his sense of humor. His eccentric dress performs much the same function. The romantic echoes of Bohemia in his hat and coat and the long scarf (apparently knitted by a myopic maiden aunt) both serve to individualize him. This individualism is set against the "objectivity" of cold science where the subjectivism of the individual observer/worker is distrusted and minimized: Dr. Who must, for ideological reasons, have a marked individualistic dimension.

The fact that his basic science is medicine—the most human and least objective of the sciences—is also significant, not least because it allows us to call him Doctor rather than Professor. Gerbner (1973) has shown how scientists in popular fiction tend to have negative connotations: they are usually evil and working against the common good of humanity. The Doctor, however, is essentially a healer, particularly of sick societies. Think how much colder the connotations would be if he were called "The Professor" instead of "The Doctor." Romana, however, lacks the Doctor's human frailties or imperfections and, therefore, lacks the flashes of inspiration and insight that in the Doctor's case accompany them. She works by pure logic, either when calculating their chances of survival (74,384,338 to 1) or when reasoning her way out of

the captivity of the bandits. She is, finally, less individualistic than he, for his eccentricity is a signifier of individualism.

A structure similar to that of the heroes relates the adversarial triad of Adrasta, Karela, and the Wolf-weeds, as depicted in Figure 5.4. The Wolf-weeds are tamed nature in the same way as K9 is tamed science. (Note that they are *Wolf*-weeds, i.e. *canine* and they are used for actions that are the evil equivalents of K9's good ones; for instance, they can and do kill whereas he merely stuns.) Twice the Wolf-weeds overpower K9 and render him helpless, paralleling Adrasta's capture and recapture of the Doctor and Romana, but more importantly reflecting the unbalanced situation on Chloris where nature is overpowering culture. Adrasta has power rather than the authority that the Doctor has. Her effectiveness relies on force, not on respect for her as an individual, and she therefore lacks the Doctor's touches of individualism, which are necessary to define his authority as a dominance achieved by individual worth exercised within a socially granted power role. Karela is an evil helper of the villain as Romana is the good helper of the hero.

But the two triads of heroes and villains do not operate alone; their values are extended and

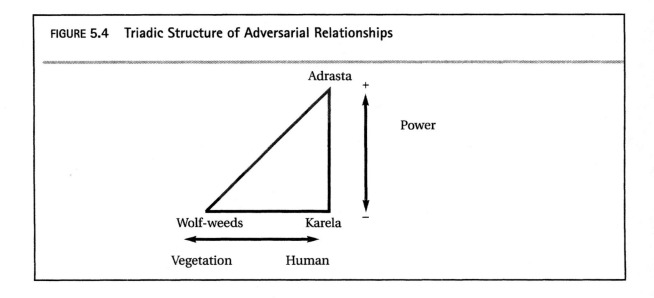

FIGURE 5.4   **Triadic Structure of Adversarial Relationships**

elaborated in their relations with minor characters and the settings of the story, that is, in its existents. The four main settings and the four main character groups are given identically structured relationships, as illustrated in Figure 5.5. The greater complexity of this model reflects the fact that negative and oppositional values have come into play as we take account of characters' roles other than the protagonists, that is, helpers and adversaries. The bottom left of Figure 5.5 is where humanism and science meet at the site of the heroes.

The Tardis exemplifies this meeting perfectly: on the inside it is pure science, on the outside idiosyncratically individualistic (see Tulloch, 1982); it is the mechanical equivalent of the Doctor, who also clothes his science in the garb of eccentric individualism. It is also a metaphor for control—spatial physics expands its interior presumably *ad infinitum*, whereas externally it is not only compact, but a police box—a metonym of social law and order.

The conflict in the narrative is between the left and right of this structure, that is between the humanistic and its opposite, not between science and nonscience. Indeed, the astrologer (nonscientist) Organon is the Doctor's only helper, and Irato becomes "friendly" by the end of the story. The pit itself was once mine workings, but now has become the underground equivalent of the forest. This structure elaborates our understanding of science, because it is seen as a site of conflict only in its relationship with the humanistic discourse, and this humanistic discourse merges into the political. Those on the right of the structure are totalitarian in that they are concerned to gain and exercise power over others for their own ends. All those on the left, including K9, are captured at one time or other by those on the right. The bandits are inefficient, deviant members of the same totalitarian ideology that Adrasta embodies. They are less evil and less of a threat than she is only because they are less "scientific" and therefore less logical. This means that they cannot organize themselves effi-

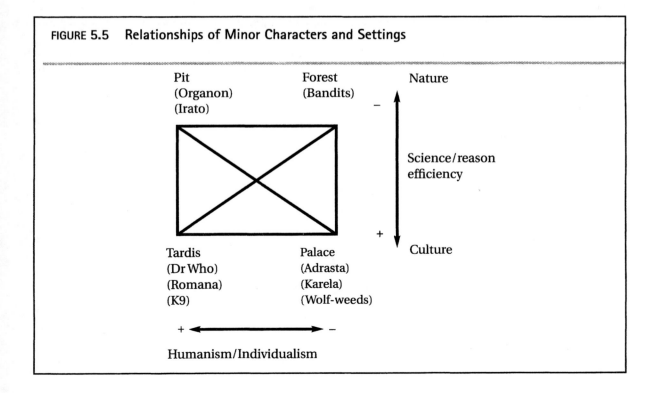

FIGURE 5.5   Relationships of Minor Characters and Settings

ciently into a leader and followers and they cannot understand how the economics of metal shortage is the key to political power.

Their social structure is a parody of the democratic. They have shapeless discussions that never reach a decision: they vote and then ignore the result, and they have a leader whose constant slips of the tongue show that he is in fact concerned solely with his own interests while pretending to have those of his followers at heart—"Bandit Leader: Metal, metal, metal, it'll make me—er, *us*—the most powerful people on Chloris." The bandits share with Adrasta a disregard for human life, both kill easily and callously, and after Adrasta's death they join with Karela to try and maintain the evil despotism based upon the monopoly of metal. They are properly on the right of the structure for they are binarily opposed to the "true" democracy embodied in the Doctor.

As the bandits are opposed to the Doctor and therefore aligned with Adrasta, so Organon is opposed to Adrasta and aligned with the Doctor. Adrasta threw him in the pit for his inefficiency, his nonscience, as she did with the hapless engineer at the start of the story. But he is properly on the left of the diagram because of his respect for the individual and his desire to help the hero. Irato has also been thrown into the pit but this is because he provided an opposition to Adrasta not on the science scale but on the political and economic scales.

On the left of the structure are the democrats, that is, those who value the rights and abilities of the individual, for the use of reason and persuasion rather than force to achieve social ends, and the belief in negotiation to arrive at a consensus. Irato is a diplomat from Chloris on a trade mission charged with the responsibility of achieving a trading agreement beneficial to both parties.

This brings us to another crucial discourse—the economics. Adrasta's power is maintained partly by her guards, but mainly by her manipulation of the economy so that she can maintain a monopoly of metal. In the past she owned the only metal mine: now this is worked out and she jealously guards the small remaining quantities of metal. The bandits' one aim is to steal as much as they

can, not because of its use-value—they do not care if it is in the form of swords, drinking cups, or ornaments—but because of its scarcity value. The shortage of metal has meant that the land cannot be cultivated, so the vegetation has run riot and the planet is almost completely overgrown.

Irato is a huge green shapeless monster who survives largely on chlorophyl from vegetation. He was sent from Chloris, which is a planet with a surplus of metal but a shortage of vegetation, in order to arrange trade with Chloris—a simple example of free trade that should, according to basic capitalist economics, have produced two balanced economies each supporting prosperous bourgeois democratic societies. But Adrasta saw that the end of her monopoly in metal would mean the end of her power, and that the increase in its availability would destroy her wealth by removing the scarcity value of her metal. She therefore captured Irato and threw him into the pit before any of her subjects could learn of his proposals. Adrasta's power, maintained by her "artificial" monopoly, is unbalanced because it is undemocratic, and is lacking the influence of the individual upon the ruling process. This social and political imbalance is "naturalized" by the rampant vegetation, which is nature out of balance with man. Both are the result of the artificial monopoly, both will then be cured, the implication goes, by natural free trade. The naturalizing of free trade into the obviously right system, indeed into the only possible system, is a central part of the ideological force of the narrative.

Toward the end of the story, Irato, the symbol of free trade, rolls over and kills Adrasta, the symbol of monopoly, and her Wolf-weeds. When he rolls off they are dead and monopoly is vanquished. The final action of the Doctor before dematerializing the Tardis is to produce a "mutually beneficial trading agreement" between Chloris and Tythonis. The actions in the narrative prove the structuring of the discourses.

The structure of Figure 5.5 illustrates that those on its left are free traders, whereas those on the right are monopolists. The discourse of economics exhibits a precise structural match with that of politics, and both fit with the underlying one of individualism. All three bear the same relationship to the discourse of science and, in fact, become the criteria for evaluating between "good" and "bad" science. The use of these value-laden objectives brings us on to the fourth crucial discourse, that of morality. The BBC is specific and precise about the morality of the show—the Doctor must be clearly good, and his adversaries clearly bad. The story admits of no blurred value judgments in the main characters, though minor ones may undergo a transformation through their meeting with the Doctor from apparently bad to really good (e.g., the Huntsman and Irato).

The significance of the Doctor lies partly in his structured relationship to gods and man. He is an anomalous creature in that he is neither God (or Timelord) nor man but occupies a mediating category between the two. He has a nonhuman origin and many nonhuman abilities, yet a human form and many human characteristics. In other words, he occupies the same space between humans and God as does Christ. Other Christ-likenesses include his consistent function of cleansing a society of evil and setting it on the paths of justice and goodness; the intergalactic timelessness of the Doctor is not unlike eternal heaven of Christ; his dislike of violence and his sexual abstinence are other shared characteristics, as is the fact that both are leaders. The fact that both are part of a trinity may be stretching the parallelism too far, but again, it may not.

Other motifs in the story support the theory that the discourse of morality is not just a humanistic one, but one with a strong religious base. Romana (echoes of Pax Romana?) is always dressed in white flowing robes with connotations of angels or vestal virgins and as such is structurally contrasted with the black of Adrasta who thus takes on Satanic connotations. We can also note here the traditional Christian motif on the bringer of evil into the world being a woman. The Huntsman's turning against his former mistress echoes the repentance of the sinner, and the defeat of Adrasta is the spiritual purging of the planet.

This structure of moral values, underwritten as it is by religious connotations, is the final naturaliz-

ing force in the ideological practice of the program, "the good" and "the bad" are clearly distinguished in the text, both by appearance, nature, or setting (that is as existents) and by behavior (that is by actions) as Figure 5.6 shows. Tabulated like this the fit between actions and existents is striking in its simplicity. In the narrative, however, the constant killing and capturing by the villains takes a variety of exciting forms that disguises the fundamental monotony or at least homogeneity. But this is typical of television where an attractive variety of signifiers commonly overlays a restricted range of signifieds and a simple repetitive self-reinforcing structure. Indeed, the attractiveness of the signifier is essential for the ideological effect because without it, the internal repetition of the structure would become manifest with the result that it would cease to be the hidden organizing device, and would then become apparent and therefore propaganda. In the discourse of morality the good is so clearly distinguished from the bad because its rightness is tested, found true, and finally rewarded by the narrative, and our affective sympathy with hero and villain is constructed to coincide with it, so that finally we are afforded practically no opportunity to question the basis or implications of this morality either in the text or in society. The ideological closure of the moral discourse is more final and complete than it can be of the political and economic discourses that would on their own admit of radically opposed or negotiated readings (see Hall, 1973).

The discourse of morality however allows little or no space for negotiation. It is difficult, if not impossible, to imagine a frame of reference that could be brought to bear upon Adrasta that could evaluate her as anything other than evil, and that therefore rejects her political, economic, and anti-individualistic values. The apparently innocent agreement of all discourses to fit the same structure and thus to support each other makes the text highly resistant to any other than its preferred reading. To clarify this we need to add the other discourses onto Figure 5.5. This elaborated structure is presented in Figure 5.6.

Here the discourse of morality functions to close off those other discourses whose values are

FIGURE 5.6   Parallel Relationships Between Actions and Existents in Text

The Heroes			The Villains		
	Existents		Existents		
Actions	Settings	Characters	Characters	Settings	Actions
Sharing information Befriending Caring Helping	Pit Decayed culture Reverting to nature			Forest Rampant nature Hostile to culture	Killing Taking captive Stealing Monopolizing
		Long hair and beards Inefficiency, lack of science, And deviation from the social norm			
Setting free Befriending Reasoning Revealing the truth Sharing	Tardis Futuristic culture			Palace Old-fashioned culture	Killing (including threats + orders to) Taking captive, lying Concealing the truth Monopolizing
		White Humanistic Individualistic	Black, Conformist De-individualized		
Stunning (i.e. not killing) Information storing Computing					Killing Capturing
		Tamed science	Tamed vegetation (nature)		

more open to question, particularly those politico-economic ones that are by definition specific to a Western industrialized democracy. And this is where the ideological effect of the onward drive of the narrative is so crucial. The constant unravelling of the mysterious or the flow of tension and release within suspense also functions to close off alternative readings. In nonnarrative television texts such as quiz shows (see Fiske, 1982) or current affairs shows (see Morley, 1980a), the relationships between discourses are more open, and therefore more variable readings are possible.

Here the onward syntagmatic flow of the narrative serves to restrict the potential range of the discourses, and thus the range of positions from which the reading subject can make sense of the text. I do not wish to take up the overdetermined position of some of the early screen theorists, which overemphasised the power of the text to construct the subject, but I do agree with them in their identification of the hegemony of the text in the enterprise of making sense. This text, in common with other popular narratives, constructs a restricted space within which the reading subject

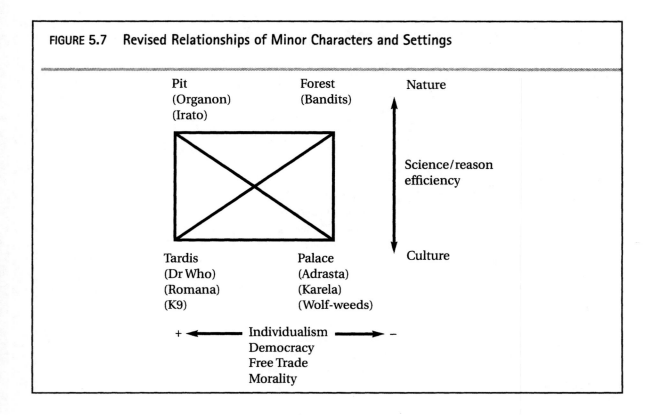

FIGURE 5.7   Revised Relationships of Minor Characters and Settings

must be positioned if she/he is to make the preferred sense, which is the easy natural sense of the text. The limits of this space can be determined by identifying in more detail the binarily opposed values by which the four main discourses are articulated. We can tabulate them thus:

Discourse of politics: Democracy : Totalitarism
Freedom : Slavery
Authority : Power
Progress : Stagnation
Peace : Violence
The Individual : The Ruler or State
Discourse of economics: Free Trade : State Monopoly
Use Value : Scarcity Value
Plenty : Scarcity
Balance : Imbalance
Discourse of individualism: Freedom : Captivity
Individuality/Eccentricity : Conformity
Life : Death
Discourse of morality: Truth : Lies
Good : Evil
Christ : Devil

The values on the left (those of the heroes) are clearly those of the Christian capitalist democracies, whereas those on the right are, by implication, those of communism (or at least the dominant Western view of it). So the deep structure, of which all the events, existents, and discourses of the narrative are transformations, is

Heroes : Villains : : Capitalism : Communism
(Heroes are to Villains as Capitalism is to Communism)

It is worth noting here that the story never refers explicitly to capitalism—indeed the word hardly ever occurs in any product of capitalist popular culture. This is because, as Hall (1977) points out, capitalism never calls itself such, but uses terms such as "democracy," which have a higher degree of social valorization. The same is true for communism, which is also not represented directly, but by the associated values of totalitarianism, state monopoly, and so on.

This text may be closed in its sense of delimiting the space within which a preferred reading can be arrived at. But within this space the reader has a certain amount of freedom. Schoolboys can use the discourses of science and morality to validate their school experience, and may subordinate those of politics and economics to the suspense of the plot. More skeptical adults can read the science discourse as a parody, but use the text's conflation of morality with capitalist democracy to validate their social experience. Different readers can place the discourses in a different hierarchical order, foregrounding them and relating them differently within the limits proposed by the text. But these limits are crucial: The text does not encourage us to correlate despotism with free market economics via the concept of the slavery of the one who may be exploited in the trading deal; neither does it allow us to perceive that the Doctor's liberal democracy requires dominant and subordinate classes just as clearly as does Adrasta's totalitarianism. These readings are radically opposed, ones that would be produced by readers who *dislike* the text, that is who put themselves outside the realm of its popularity.

The reading I am giving in this paper, one that derives from an academic discourse, is also radically opposed, in that it refuses to accept the ideological closure of the text; such radically opposed readers bring to bear on it discourses from their extratextual experience, or they find relationships among the textual discourses that the text itself does not invite. They look for the contradictions between the text and the world, or at least evidence of the arbitrariness of that relationship that the realism of the text seeks to hide. They see the text as a social construct that is the product of a particular social consciousness in a particular historical epoch whose laws and dominant values they may well not accept.

They would therefore read as significant the general absence of class identities. All characters speak with "classless" (i.e., middle-class) accents with the exception of the bandits. The bandits are criminals or deviants, and the opposed reader would note how the text displaces the working class into the criminal class: both are deviant from the middle class consensus. Dorfman and Mattelart (1975) have identified the same ideological practice in Donald Duck comics where criminals are consistently given working class characteristics—and they are the only characters who are. This displacement of class identities into criminal identities is a powerful tool in the naturalizing of the middle-class point of view from which to read the text.

Feminist oppositional readers would note a similar practice in the Adrasta-Romana opposition. Adrasta is female-dominant-evil; Romana is female-subordinate-good. The text emphasizes morality as the significant difference, and by so doing naturalizes the culturally more important value of subordination.

Interestingly, the individualizing character traits of the Doctor (e.g., inspiration, intuition, randomness) are ones normally associated with the feminine in our culture. Romana is therefore denied them, and her distinctive character traits are limited to femaleness—subordination, objective reasoning, and a proneness to victimization and captivity. Similarly, this feminist reading would note sardonically, if not angrily, that Adrasta's power is portrayed as unnatural not only because it depends on an artificial monopoly, but also because it is political power, which is traditionally confined to the male. The restoration of a male, the Huntsman, to dominance at the end is a hidden factor in the ideological closure, just as the trading agreement is a narratively foregrounded one.

But these "readings against the grain" require a conscious effort that can only be motivated from outside the text, or by the perceptions of contradictions between text and world. They deny the easy fit between the textual and social discourses of the reader, and refuse to allow the smooth harmony of the text to disguise the contradictory nature of material reality. They are produced by readers who insist on bringing extratextual discourses to bear in a way that opposes the inscribed preference of the text. They therefore define themselves in opposition to the "model readers." These are defined by Eco (1979) as ones who are "determined by the sort of interpretive operations they are supposed to perform." Model readers are subjects predicted by the text who willingly cooperate with that text in their own construction. They accept the textual hegemony by assisting in its ideological closure.

This notion of the relationship between the text and an active reader differs crucially from that posited by uses and gratifications theorists, who also assume an active reader. In uses and gratifications theories the media are seen as means of gratifying social or personal needs in the individual, and these needs frequently, if not normally, stem from lacks or absences in the lives of viewers: the media are seen as compensatory. Uses and gratifications theory finds its data in the stated gratifications of viewers: it ignores the content of the programs and prioritizes the viewer's ability to seek gratification for often unarticulated needs.

Structuralist/discourse theory, on the other hand, gives high priority to the text and seeks to discover in the text structures or discourses that can make sense of both it and the (potential) social situation of the reader. The subjectivities of readers are formed largely by their discursive experience, that is by the discourses available to them to make sense of their social experience, and of the multi-

tude of texts that they meet. Culture is the process of making sense, and discourses are central to this process. The individual reader's conscious or subconscious does not determine the meaning of the text, as uses and gratifications theory implies; rather, the reader's consciousness is determined by the discourses that produce him or her as a social subject, as a member of a culture (see Barthes, 1975). The model reader of the popular text relates to (or understands) authority, for instance, via particular forms of political and moral discourses. The belief that these same discourses in broadly similar articulations can make sense of Dr. Who's preference for the Huntsman over Adrasta, of the British actions in the Falklands, of the behavior of the father in the Western middle-class family, of the teacher in the school or of the policeman in his locality, makes the structured relationship of discourses in both text and society of greater importance than the individuality of any reader. Texts and social experience are both made and understood by discourses, and the reader's subjectivity, the site of this understanding, is equally a discursive product. A radical feminist, to take an instance already quoted, has/is a consciousness, a site of understanding, formed by the way that feminism interacts with the discourses of politics, of economics, of the family, of education, of work, and of all the formally and informally constituted institutions that form the framework of our culture, and that produce the discourses that produce the same. This consciousness, or structure of discourses, thus determines the sense she will make a of a television program such as this one, or of a moment of social experience such as a man opening a door for her, or of the language system with its characterization of the human as the male.

This emphasis on the discourse as the "maker of sense," rather than on the individuals (whether author or reader) involved in the process of communication is shared by many contemporary theorists.

Kristeva (1970) talks of a closed text as being one where the author disguises the productive work and tries to convince the reader that author and reader are the same. The insight is valuable here, though her emphasis differs slightly from mine.

Her implication is that the author, whether an individual or an institution, as in this case, is in some way being dishonest or underhanded in this enterprise. Barthes (1979) makes a similar point, though more positively, with regard to texts in general:

> The text requires an attempt to abolish (or at least to lessen) the distance between writing and reading, not by intensifying the reader's projection into the work, but by linking the two together in a single signifying process (*practique signifiante*).

My point is that the popularity of the text is directly attributable to the collapse of the difference between author and reader: the appropriate discourses by which the text is constructed and read are part of the commonsense experience of both. But popularity (then) is not just the willing consent of the model reader to the hegemony of the text, it involves a more active assessment of the effectiveness of the discourses in making sense of both the text and the world. And this fit between world and text is the prerequisite of what Genette (1968) calls verisimilitude or, more commonly, realism. Genette makes the point that the basis of a text's verisimilitude is to be found outside it, in the sociocentral assumed consensual values of society, that is in the intertextuality between the text and social behavior seen as a constructed text. The overall mode of this story is realism, despite the obvious fantasy of the characters and settings. This verisimilitude derives partly from the logic of cause and effect by which the actions are strung together, partly from the anonymous narrator evidenced in the objective camera work and motivated editing, but more importantly from the way that the discourses by which the text articulates its narrative structures are also those through which its model readers live their lives. The model reader and invisible author merge into one in the joint activity of making sense. The text is believable, it is verisimilar, because its discourses are part of the ideology of common sense. This cooperation denies any contradictions between world and text because it prioritizes the realism and, as McCabe (1974) points out, a defining feature of realism is its inability to deal with contradictions:

The unquestioned nature of the narrative discourse entails that the only problem that reality poses is to go and look and see what *things* there are. The relationship between the reading subject and the real is placed as one of pure specularity. The real is not articulated—it *is*. These features imply two essential features of the classic realist text:

(1) The classic realist text cannot deal with the real as contradictory.
(2) In a reciprocal movement the classic realist text ensures the position of the subject in a relation of dominant specularity.

Realism facilitates the easy interchange of discourses between text and world. If we assume that making sense of our social experience involves writing a narrative about it, that is making a text of it, then this text will, for the well-adjusted majority at least, be a realistic one. Realism is the most easily available mode of apprehending the world around us, particularly if we inhabit a science-based culture. For realism and science both assume an empirically verifiable universe with an objective existence that stands independent of the perception of it and which texts can refer to and signs can denote. Kristeva's author disguising the productive work is twin to the scientist observing natural phenomena objectively: both pretend their work is untainted by the stain of subjectivity or social consciousness, but instead attains a state of universal objectivity, of factuality.

The classic realist text of which this Dr. Who story is an example, is by definition a closed text, and it therefore becomes politically necessary to prise it open by the sort of semiotic or structuralist analysis. Let us return to these discourses, which are so crucial to the structure and the popularity of the text and which are shown in Figure 5.7. Those on the horizontal scale are culture-specific in the way that those on the vertical scale are not; they are instead assumed to be universal. Mankind is essentially rational, logical, scientific, and science and reason are the means by which man imposes himself on the world and in so doing turns Nature into Culture. Science and reason become central to the definition of human nature. But the culturally specific moral and political values of the horizontal dimension are the crucial ones in determining what sort of culture and what sort of identity this rational mankind actually creates for itself. The determining values of the narrative are those on the horizontal dimension; the vertical values provide the ground upon which the conflicts of the narrative and the oppositions of the other discourses are enacted.

An analysis of a scene from the story (see Table 5.1) will demonstrate how densely interwoven are the discourses of politics, economics, morality, and individualism, and how they are used to articulate the conflicts and the sequences of suspense and resolution in the narrative. The scene occurs toward the end of the story and is the crucial one in which Adrasta is finally overcome. It opens with K9 having been overpowered by the Wolf-weeds and Adrasta apparently in control.

The camera work exemplifies Kristeva's hidden productive work of the closed text. There are 36 shots in this four-minute, twenty-eight-second scene, and every one is changed by a cut—there are no dissolves, fades, or wipes. Every cut is motivated by the dialogue or action. The camera is objective, though placed slightly below eye level. Chatman (1978) suggests in his analysis of a frame from *Citizen Kane* that the low angle shot at crucial moments connotes the foregrounding of ideology, in that characters are seen from a less than realistic viewpoint. This may be true here, though the distance of the camera below eye level is less marked than in the *Citizen Kane* example, in fact none of my students have commented on it until the second or third viewing of the scene. The other piece of constructed camera work is that Adrasta is consistently shot in tighter closeup than the Doctor or his helpers. An unpublished study by one of my students has found evidence to suggest that villains are conventionally shot in tighter closeup than heroes in popular television fiction, and that this code is even extended to newspaper photographs. This sort of connoting, and therefore value-laden, camera work is subtle enough to escape conscious notice on first viewing but nonetheless signifies on the ideological level. The author in the realist text may be invisible but he is not absent. Discourses are visual as well as verbal, and ideology is the framework of meaning that holds the discourses together.

Here ideology is a pluralistic, as well as a slippery, concept. Though its final effect is to impose a false unity upon a contradictory world, it can perform this work in different ways. In Figure 5.7, for example, ideology functions differently in each of the two dimensions. In the vertical the ideology of our science-based world, with its concepts of history as progress, of man's right to impose himself upon and exploit nature, and of the supremacy of human reason, is placed beyond the possibility of conflict or doubt.

But on the horizontal dimension the values are clearly open to opposition. In the social world, as in the text, the dominant values of capitalist democracy are struggling to establish, defend, or extend themselves. The events of the story maintain the plot's constant forward drive from one expression of this struggle to another. This plot, in its outcome and closure, proves the supremacy of these values, as does our constructed sympathy for the characters and their settings on the left of the structure. The two dimensions come together in the effectiveness of science both in the value system and in the plot.

Though science and reason are common to both sides, the heroes are effective and finally victorious apparently because their science and reason are superior. At the start, the Doctor discovers the nature of the mystery object where Adrasta's engineers have failed, and at the end Irato and the Tardis together manage to save Chloris from destruction by a neutron star on a collision course. The Doctor's reason (together with the occasional flash of inspiration) is the means by which he controls the forward drive of the plot. As he uncovers each piece of the mystery, so one more battle against the opposition is won. The hero's science is not only more moral and humane than the villain's, but it is also more effective. It is this demonstrated effectiveness that brings together the twin ideologies of science and of capitalist democracy. They finally become the same ideology because the narrative demonstrates that they both work.

TABLE 5.1   Examples of Dialogue and Discourse from *Dr. Who*

Dialogue		Discourse
K9:	I am immobile, I was overpowered by the Wolf-weeds.	Hostil Nature overcoming tamed Science (Culture)
ADRASTA:	Order your dog to kill Tythonian.	Totalitarian disregard for life/the individual.
DOCTOR:	No.	
ADRASTA:	If you will not, your friend Organon dies.	Attempt to exploit the democrat's care for others.
DOCTOR:	Organon. Goodbye, old man, so sorry about this. Thanks for all the help.	The Doctor parodies totalitarian callousness, knowing Organon will be safe. Unexpected reaction = individualism.
ORGANON:	Doctor!	
DOCTOR:	If my deductions are correct, the well-being of two planets is at stake. Irato must not die.	The Doctor concerned for the health of societies.
ADRASTA:	Huntsman, set the Wolf-weeds on the Doctor.	Wild Nature (Wolf-weeds)/Death opposed to Science (the Doctor)/Life.
DOCTOR:	Now wait, that's all you've got on this planet, isn't it—weeds, weeds, forests, and weeds! You scratch about for food wherever you can, but you can't plough the land can you? You can't do anything until you've mastered the forest and the weeds, and you can't do that without metal.	Nature-Culture opposition articulated in discourse of Science (albeit primitive) that sets up the terms for an identical opposition in the discourse of Economics (see below).
ADRASTA:	Don't listen to him. It's just the ravings of a demented space tramp. Set the Wolf-weeds on him.	Attempt to discredit Doctor's reason/science. The falsity allies morality with science, repeated in the structure: Nature::Culture, Death::Life, Lies::Truth, Wolf-weeds::Doctor.
DOCTOR:	Do that and you hurl this planet back into the dark ages, and for what? To satisfy the petty power cravings of that pathetic woman.	Economic and political progress dependent on the transformation of Nature into Culture by Science.
ADRASTA:	Have a care, Doctor	Care = pun: care for *self versus for others.*
DOCTOR:	Have a care yourself. Care for your people for a change.	Democracy and individualism enter the fray!
ADRASTA:	Kill him!	Totalitarianism = anti-individualism (again).
HUNTSMAN:	Let him speak.	A convert to democracy and the rights of the individual.
ADRASTA:	Huntsman! I order you.	Totalitarian tone.
HUNTSMAN:	Let him speak.	First signs of conversion to democracy/free speech.

	Dialogue	Discourse
DOCTOR:	Now if my deductions are correct. . . .	Logic/reason allied to economics. . . .
ADRASTA:	They're not.	Another example of totalitarianism = falsity.
DOCTOR:	Irato came here 15 years ago to propose a trading agreement. Tythonis is a planet rich in metallic ores and minerals. Am I not right, K9?	Economic discourse articulated identically to the scientific (see above).
K9:	Checking data bank. Affirmative Master.	Scientific confirmation = truth of democrats contrasted with falsity of totalitarianism.
DOCTOR:	That was a good guess.	Individualism = inspiration.
ADRASTA:	Fool! You listen to the opinions of an electric dog.	Totalitarian misconception of science/truth.
DOCTOR:	Tythonians exist on ingesting chlorophyll, large quantities of it judging by their size. Now there is a superabundance of plant life on Chloris.	The universal objective logic of free-trade economics proved by its rationality and therefore scientificness.
ROMANA:	So, Irato came here to offer you metal in return for chlorophyll. Of course!	NB "offer"—free trade is generous "in return"—and fair.
DOCTOR:	Right. And who was the first person he met?	
ORGANON:	The person who held the monopoly of metal here.	Monopoly = totalitarian power. Free trade = democracy.
DOCTOR:	Right. And did she put the welfare of her struggling people above her own petty power? No. She's tipped the ambassador into a pit and threw Astrologers at him.	Politics, economics, and morality in one. Wit = individualism
HUNTSMAN:	Is this true, my lady?	Conversion to democracy marked by desire for truth.
ADRASTA:	Not a word of it. It's a pack of lies.	Totalitarianism = falsity (yet again).
DOCTOR:	Let's see if Irato agrees with me, shall we?	Irato : symbol of free trade.
ADRASTA:	That won't prove anything. You just take hold of that thing and say exactly what you like. You expect intelligent people to fall for your childish tricks?	Doomed appeal to reason.
DOCTOR:	Well, it's very simple really. Why don't you come over here, take hold of the communicator, and we hear the truth from you.	
ADRASTA:	What. No. Don't talk such rubbish. Huntsman, I order you to kill the Doctor.	The despot lies and kills.
HUNTSMAN:	My lady, I think we want to hear the truth of this. Go and speak with the creature.	The new democrat and his desire for truth.
ADRASTA:	No. I refuse. I utterly refuse.	
HUNTSMAN:	I think not, my lady. (He sets the Wolf-weeds on her).	The conversion is complete, even Nature turns against the despot in the end.
ADRASTA:	No! Back! Back!	

	Dialogue	Discourse
DOCTOR:	Just take hold of the communicator.	
IRATO:	Thank you, Doctor. Your deductions are of course correct. We are running dangerously short of chlorophyll on Tythonis, and have more metal than we need. Reports reached us of this planet Chloris, which has precisely the opposite problem, and we thought that a trading agreement would be mutually beneficial.	A mutually beneficial trading agreement—there are no losers, no one profits at another's expense—free market economics minus competition, minus exploiters and exploited, minus losers, minus anything that might disturb the ideological homogeneity.
ADRASTA:	It's lies, lies. It's all lies.	There she goes again!
IRATO:	No, it is you who were lying. Unfortunately I ran foul of this evil woman who tricked me into the pit. If you will forgive me, I have a score to settle.	Truth and free trade go together.
HUNTSMAN:	So, I think, have we. (The Wolf-weeds knock Adrasta down).	Nature destroys the one whose unbalancing and therefore unnatural monopoly gave it its unnatural power.
ADRASTA:	Aaaaaaah! (Irato rolls over Adrasta and the Wolf-weeds).	The symbol of free trade and freedom crushes the symbol of monopoly and slavery, and ingests the Wolf-weeds, the symbols of unbalanced Nature. Free trade becomes culture.
DOCTOR:	Dead!	
HUNTSMAN:	Yes. And with her die the dark ages for this planet.	Progress. Chloris moves into the "renaissance" and the birth of science, reason, individualism, free enterprise and trade, capitalism and the middle classes!

The only conflict is that between opposing ends of the horizontal scale, and its resolution is achieved by the superiority of the science of those on the left. The universality of science and reason naturalizes the culturally specific values of democratic capitalism and in so doing performs the mythic function of transforming history into nature (Barthes, 1972). For this story transforms the culturally specific (i.e., history) into the universal

(i.e., nature). Its final point of equilibrium is that point where science and democracy come together in an uncontradictory harmony at the bottom left-hand corner of the structure. If we take Todorov's (1977) definition of narrative as a sequence of events by which one state of equilibrium is disturbed and then transformed into another similar but different state, then we can see that the original equilibrium disturbed by the arrival of the Tardis was unnatural and therefore located on the right of the structure. The events of the story function to naturalize the restoration of the equilibrium to its "proper" place on the left. The mythic function of naturalizing history and the ideological practice of denying contradictions are one and the same, a similarity identified by Levi-Strauss (1955) when he proposed that "the purpose of myth is to provide a logical model capable of overcoming a contradiction." Here, the contradictions are those between science and politico-economic-moral values. The events of the story demonstrate that the Doctor and his helpers are successful because they are better scientists, but the structure of the discourses proposes that their success derives from their morality, politics, economics, and individualism. The story acts mythically in that the logic of its chain of events overcomes the contradictions inherent in a society whose ideology reconciles apparently unproblematically the totalitarianism of science with democracy and individualism. As Davies (1978–1979) points out, "narrative is a major agency in realism's attempt to deny contradictions." The popularity of the text derives from the reader's ability to transfer this uncontradictory reconciliation easily between text and society, a transference that becomes conventional because it is generic to the series of *Dr. Who* and even to the genre of science fiction.

This postulates an identity between an aesthetic/psychological need in the reader that is gratified by the deep structure of the text, and the ideological practice by which the text proffers dominant readings to its model reader. This need can be defined as the need to make unproblematic sense of an inherently self-contradictory area of the culture, and the practice can be identified as the conventional practice of realism. This similarity between reader's need and textual structure exists only in the reader's perception of the ease with which the text's power in overcoming contradictions and society's denial of structurally similar contradictions enter into a mutually validating relationship. The aesthetic structure of the text is satisfying only to the extent that it performs an ideological function in society.

This theory implies that popular art is not escapist, but mythic. It does not merely provide an imaginative refreshing alternative to the hard grind of an industrial existence, rather it enables and encourages the reader to make a particular kind of sense of that existence. The reader and the text are both active, and the text becomes popular only when the two activities are mutually supportive and when they can be replicated to make sense of that much broader, more open text that is our social experience.

There is a vast difference between the signifiers of these two texts (Dr. Who meeting shapeless green monsters on distant planets is not exactly an iconic reproduction of our daily commute into the city). The extent of this difference almost guarantees the effectiveness of the ideological work, which the similarity of the discourses performs. Because the same discourses can be related in similar ways to produce similarly satisfying structures of common sense out of such apparently diverse representations of reality, they must have a universal applicability. The divergence of the signifiers is yet another naturalizing force, which denies the historicity of the text's production and reception, and therefore of any difference between them. The only conflict is between opposing ends of the horizontal scale, and its resolution is achieved by the superiority of the science of those on the left.

Davies (1978–1979) makes a similar point:

> The creation of a narrative almost always entails the shaping of awkward materials into a smooth, closed structure. And this is the essence of myth. Like bourgeois ideology, most narrative cinema denies history, denies material reality as contradictory and denies the fact of its own production.

There is little doubt that this *Dr. Who* story is guilty of all the charges laid by Davies on narrative cinema. The big question is how effective the texts are in turning the reader into a passive consumer/spectator who willingly, though unknowingly, consents to the hegemony of the text. Davies (1978–1979) argues that they are highly effective, and many others working within the tradition of Screen Theory would agree with her. My disagreement rests on her negation of the role of reader in the negotiation of meaning. The text may well not invite reader activity, and may well prefer consumer/spectators to readers, but this does not account for its popularity, nor why some texts are more popular than others. For a text to be popular its discourses must fit those used by the reader in social experience, and thus it must be open to socially derived, as well as textually derived, inflections of meaning.

Here my position diverges also from McCabe's (1974), quoted above, in that I do not see the realist text as limiting the reader-subject to a position of mere speculary, but agree rather with Morley's (1980b) refusal to allow the textually constituted subject complete dominance over the socially constituted subject. The reader has a social life that is a structure of discourses just as the reader has a text that is also a structure of discourses, and reading is the activity in which the two are brought together. Work, as yet unpublished, by researchers at Murdoch University lends some support to this position. They investigated the finding of the 1981 Australian Broadcasting Tribunal that *Prisoner* and *Sale of the Century* were the two most popular shows amongst schoolchildren. They found that the appeal of *Prisoner* lay largely in the way that children could use it to validate and make sense of their school experience. The warders paralleled teachers, with a parallel hierarchy and parallel roles: some hard, some soft, some young and inexperience, some hard-bitten. The prisoners were like students, with their own code of ethics and behavior, their own pecking order, and their variety of forms of relationship with the staff. The prison was seen as the equivalent of school—an institution to which people were sent for a fixed term where there was as sense that real life existed only outside and where the inmates were made to think and behave in the way that society wanted them to. These discourses of social relationships, of power and authority, and of institutional behavior enabled the students to find in text and world a similar kind of sense by similar discursive means.

It is easy to hypothesize similarly about the appeal of *Sale of the Century*. It demonstrates how

knowledge or education can be turned into immediate reward: it collapses the temporal dimension of the sequence that children are constantly reminded of—a good education means a good job means good material rewards. Here the results flow instantly from the right answers. The discourses of education and economics bear a similar signifying relationship in the quiz text and the school world.

These relationships between discourse, text, and world constitute a system, for each element affects and is affected by the others. Texts and social experience enter a mutually supportive relationship, and each, and both, affect the discourses by which they are structured and understood. Barthes (1979) stresses this system of society, text, and discourse (or language): "A test is that social space that leaves no language safe and untouched." The fit between text and world not only tests each item, but also the discourses by which that fit is established.

Prisoner, Sale of the Century, and this *Dr. Who* story all illustrate how active readers can bring to bear upon the text discourses that they use to make sense of their social experience. The texts, with their neat closures and purified structures, prove the efficacy of the discourses as interpretative strategies, and reassure the reader that this effectiveness is transferable to the extratextual world. The relationship between world and text is not one of iconic reflection, nor a relationship of content or appearance. Rather it is a homologue of form, where what is shared is a structured relationship of discourses, so the realism, the verisimilitude, resides in what is represented, but in how. The final satisfaction of viewing is not escapist, nor a gratification of individually or socially generated needs, but a reassurance of the adequacy of the social discourses of the reader. And this is where a structural analysis is so important, because it reveals the ideology that is at work within the text and therefore the limits of the corresponding ideologies in society that can be validated by it within this relationship that we term "the popular."

Before I close, I must point out a possible weakness in my position: it could be seen to encourage a reactionary complacency. This is certainly not my intention. As much as anyone, I wish to encourage students and others to develop the distancing that defends them against the hegemony of the text. But I also wish to defend them against a possible misunderstanding of the work of some of the Screen Theorists whose high priorizations of the text can be seen to imply that the production of questioning, radical, contradictory tests will finally produce a radical audience. This inference that texts can change the sociopolitical structure of society is one that I find unacceptable because it ignores the fact that an art form that is radically opposed to dominant social discourses would not be popular, but would appeal largely to the converted, that is to those whose social discourses fit a priori, with those of the text. It would lose the mass appeal necessary for effective social change.

I would argue, conversely, that social change can start only in society. Socially responsible popular art can, in theory, articulate and thus encourage that change, but cannot originate it. Nor can it hasten it too quickly or it becomes in danger of losing its audience and thus its categorization as popular.

Popular art works generally, but not, I believe, necessarily, in favor of the *status quo*. What we now need is an understanding of popularity, of the intertext between work of art and social experience, and that is what I have attempted to move toward in this paper. The next enterprise is, for my money, the crucial one: it is to discover and analyze just how a work of popular art can be other than reactionary.

References

Barthes, R. (1972). *Mythologies*. London: Paladin.

Barthes, R. (1975). *S/Z*. London: Jonathan Cape.

Barthes, R. (1979). From work to text. In J. V. Harari (Ed.), *Textual strategies*. Ithaca: Cornell University Press. [Reprinted from R. Barthes (1977), *Image-Music-Text* (pp. 15–164). London: Fontana.]

Chatman, S. (1978). *Story and discourse: Narrative structure in fiction and film*. Ithaca: Cornell University Press.

Davies, G. (1978–79). Teaching about narrative. *Screen Education, 29*, 56–76.

Dorfman, A., & Mattelart, A. (1975). *How to read Donald Duck: Imperialist ideology in the Disney comic*. New York: International General.

Eco, U. (1979). *The role of the reader*. Bloomington: Indiana University Press.

Fiske, J. (1982). TV quiz shows and the purchase of cultural capital. *Australian Journal of Screen Theory, 13*, n.p.

Genette, G. (1968). Vraisemblance et motivation. *Communications, 11*, n.p.

Gerbner, G. (1972). Teacher image in mass culture. In G. Gerbner, L. Gross & W. Melody (Eds.), *Communications technology and social policy*. New York: Wiley-Interscience.

Hall, S. (1973). *Encoding and decoding in the television discourse*. Occasional Papers No. 7. Birmingham: Birmingham University Centre for Contemporary Cultural Studies. [Reprinted in S. Hall, D. Hobson, A. Lowe, & P. Willis (1980), (Eds.)., *Culture, media, language* (pp. 128–139), London: Hutchinson]

Halls, S. (1977). Culture, the media and the ideological effect. In J. Curran, M. Gurevitch, & J. Woollacott (Eds.), *Mass communication and society* (pp. 128–138). London: Edward Arnold.

Hall, S., Hobson, D. Lowe A., & Willis, P. (Eds.). (1980). *Culture, media, language*. London: Hutchinson.

Kristeva, J. (1970). *La texte du roman*. The Hague: Mouton.

Levi-Strauus, C. (1955). The structural study of myth. *Journal of American Folklore, 69*, n.p.

MacCabe, C. (1974). Realism and the cinema: Notes on Brechtian theses. *Screen, 15*, n.p. [Reprinted in T. Bennett, S. Boyd-Bowman, C. Mercer,

AUTHOR'S NOTE: An earlier version of this chapter, under the title "Dr Who, Ideology and the Reading of a Popular Narrative Text," appeared in *The Australian Journal of Screen Theory*, 1983, 14, pp. 60–100.

& J. Woollacott (Eds.), (1981), *Popular television and film* (pp. 310–313), London: British Film Institute/Open University.

Morley, D. (1980a). *The Nationwide audience*. London: British Film Institute.

Morley, D. (1980b). Texts, readers, subjects. In S. Hall, D. Hobson, A. Lowe, & P. Willis (Eds.), *Culture, media, language* (pp. 163–173). London: Hutchinson.

O'Sullivan, T., Hartley, J., Saunders, D., & Fiske, J. (1983). *Key concepts in communication*. London: Methuen.

Todorov. T. (1975). *The fantastic*. Ithaca: Cornell University Press.

Tulloch, J. (1982). Dr. Who: Similarity and difference. *Australian Journal of Screen Theory, 11–12,* n.p.

Tulloch, J., & Alvarado, M. (1983). Dr. Who: The unfolding text. London: Macmillan.

Genre
Criticism
Chapter 6

Chapter Outline

A Brief Walk Down the "History of Genre Criticism" Lane

The Evolution of Hollywood Genres
From Film and Radio to Television
Television Genre Criticism Comes of Age
Three Approaches to Genre Analysis

Writing Genre Criticism

The Genre Chicken or the Generic Egg: The Empiricist-Idealist
Genre Dilemma

Example Essay: Matthew P. McAllister's "Recombinant Television Genres and *Doogie Howser, M.D.*"

S*ituation comedy. Soap opera. Detective drama. Prime-time serial. Dramedy. Game show. Talk show. Adventure. Cartoon. Documentary. Western. Sports. News.*

What do all of these terms have in common? All are labels used to describe television program genres. A *genre* is a French word for type or category. To call a television program a situation comedy is to assert that it shares a set of characteristics with other TV programs in the paradigm we call situation comedies. Genres are complex fusions of formal, stylistic, and substantive features that over time become familiar, structural frameworks capable of arousing and satisfying the expectations of their audiences and producers (see Altman, 1985; Campbell & Jamieson, 1978; Foss, 1996; Gronbeck, 1978; Jamieson & Campbell, 1982; Schatz, 1981). While the collection of elements that comprise a genre may exist in other texts and even other groups of texts, it is the reoccurrence of this unique combination of these fused elements in all of its members that defines a genre.

A genre is both a static and a dynamic system. Schatz (1981) suggests that we should think of a genre as a game, like baseball or football: "A game is a system of immutable rules (there are three strikes in baseball) and components determining the nature of play. Yet no two games in a sport are alike, and a theoretically infinite number of variations can be played within the 'arena' that the rules provided" (pp. 16–17). Although all texts in a genre share certain common features (often called the genre's *conventions*), each individual program in a genre is somewhat unique (i.e., has some *innovations* in the genre's basic components).

Most popular story types or genres, Cawelti (1976) explains, are a combination of formulaic narrative or dramatic conventions specific to a particular culture and period that are used in a large number of individual works and larger plot patterns (e.g., recurring themes, discourses) that express cultural or archetypal moral tensions and fantasies. According to Cawelti, a popular culture genre

> is a means of generalizing the characteristics of large groups of individual works from certain combinations of cultural materials and archetypal story patterns . . . primarily as a means of making historical and cultural inferences about the collective fantasies shared by large groups of people and of identifying differences in these fantasies from one culture or period to another . . . or as a basis for aesthetic judgments of various sorts [about genres or individual members of genres]. (p. 7)

Genre criticism lies at the intersection of institutional, textual, and audience studies. On the one hand, genre analysis is intimately linked to the social institutions of Hollywood production companies and broadcast and cable networks. For these institutional program creators and distributors, genre formulas are a means of quickly and efficiently producing new texts with a track record of attracting large audiences. At the same time, genre criticism is deeply concerned with identifying and analyzing the textual features that provide the genre's rhetorical force—the potential sources of cultural, mythic identification and satisfaction genre texts provide for audiences (see Figure 6.1)

Popular culture texts, Cawelti (1976) argues, can satisfy two important psychological needs that audiences pursue through their imaginative leisure experiences with popular culture texts:

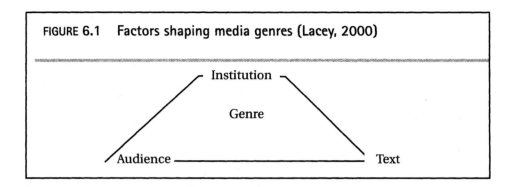

FIGURE 6.1   Factors shaping media genres (Lacey, 2000)

First of all, we seek moments of intense excitement to get away from the boredom and ennui that are particularly prevalent in the relatively secure, routine, and organized lives of the majority of the contemporary American and western European public. At the same time, we seek escape from our consciousness of the ultimate insecurities and ambiguities that affect even the most secure sort of life: death, the failure of love, our inability to accomplish all we had hoped for, the threat of atomic holocaust. . . . In the ordinary course of experience, these two impulses or needs are inevitably in conflict. The essence of the experience of escape [through watching and reading popular texts] is, I believe, that it temporarily synthesizes these two needs and resolves this tension. This may account for the curious paradox that characterizes most literary [and popular culture genre] formulas, the fact that they are at once highly ordered and conventional and yet permeated with the symbols of danger, uncertainty, violence and sex. (pp. 15–16)

The central problem for television program creators (e.g., Hollywood writers, producers, production studios) and distributors (i.e., the television and cable programming networks) is how to balance the tension between convention and innovation. Interesting, popular, quality genre texts, Cawelti (1976) explains, must clearly have both the essential features of the genre and something new: "To be a work of any quality or interest, the individual version of a [genre] formula must have some unique special characteristic of its own, yet these characteristics must ultimately work toward the fulfillment of the conventional form" (p. 10).

Although it may not seem that way because we grew up with television, television is a new medium compared to literature and film. While much television genre criticism has focused exclusively on the identification of obvious recurring formal and stylistic features, other genre criticism has looked beyond these surface characteristics to deeper, not-immediately-apparent visual, aural, narrative structures and their ritual and ideological functions. Early in the history of a medium, genre critics typically focus on semantic or formal and stylistic features. Only later, Bywater and Sobchack (1989) explain, do they begin to analyze the syntactic features and explore the relationships between popular genres and the society in which they are produced and consumed. To put television genre criticism in context, let's take a short walk down the "history of genre criticism lane" for some "backstory" on genre theory and criticism.

A Brief Walk Down the "History of Genre Criticism" Lane

We can thank Aristotle (384–322 B.C.) for the idea that there are various types (or genres) of texts that differ in terms of their subjects and techniques. In his *Poetics,* Aristotle separated literature (which for him was dramatic poetry) into various categories by their mode of presentation—drama (performed), epic (narrated), and lyric (sung)—and then analyzed these categories for the characteristics unique to each, for what each category does (its effects), and for the relative importance of each of these classes, or genres, of literature. During the Renaissance (roughly the fourteenth through sixteenth centuries), Aristotle's ideas about form became sedimented into rules about styles and forms—for example, "the three unities."[1] Literary authors in the neoclassical period (from around 1660 to the outbreak of the French Revolution in 1789) worried little about creating new literary forms and styles. Excellence in artistic achievement was defined in terms of adapting and perfecting extant literary forms rather than on developing new, original forms and styles of literary expression.[2] Writers of the romantic period (roughly 1798 through 1930) revolted against this mechanical, dictatorial, rule-governed approach to genre (see Buscombe, 1985) and emphasized creativity and originality. During this period, the novel developed, and the art-for-art's sake philosophy was widely embraced.

In the 1930s and 1940s, a literary movement referred to as the Chicago school of criticism developed. Reacting against the antihistorical perspective of the then-dominant "new criticism," the creative and scholarly work of Chicago school writers and critics sparked a renewed interest in Aristotle's notion of form (which focused on both structure *and* the dynamic shaping the structure), and the influence of writers on existing forms and conventions.[3] Their writings gave new life to literary genre theory and genre criticism, just in time to begin critically analyzing the array of new film genres that emerged during Hollywood's "golden age," the period between 1930 and 1960 when between 400 and 700 new movies were released each year (Schatz, 1981).

The Evolution of Hollywood Genres

Although film and television genres often are treated as if they are rigid, relatively unchanging formulas that magically appeared one day fully formed, genre films and television series develop out of the intersection of (1) the pragmatic needs of Hollywood production companies to maximize profits by simultaneously controlling production costs and developing a loyal body of consumers and (2) the tastes of audiences, who flock to some but not all of Hollywood's creations. Not every creative script that is successful enough to be made into a movie or a TV series ends up stimulating the development of a new genre. Think about Steven Bochco's failed attempt to fuse cop dramas and musicals in *Cop Rock* (1990). So, why don't all innovative new TV series and films develop into established genres? Because enduring media genres need to satisfy *both* the economic needs of the production-distribution system *and* the desires and tastes of the audiences. As Altman (1985) explains:

> Hollywood does not simply lend its voice to the public's desires, nor does it simply manipulate the audience. On the contrary, most genres go through a period of accommodation during which the public's desires are fitted to Hollywood's priorities (and vice versa). Because the public doesn't want to know that it is being manipulated, the successful ritual/ideological "fit" is almost always one that disguises Hollywood's potential for manipulation while playing up its capacity for entertainment. . . . The successful genre owes its success not alone to its reflection of an audience ideal, nor solely to its status as apology for the Hollywood enterprise, but to its ability to carry about both functions simultaneously. (p. 36)

When repeated texts develop into enduring genres, what has happened, Schatz (1981) explains, is that "the material economy, which motivated the studios to refine story formulas, translates into narrative economy for filmmakers and viewers." As the genre becomes established, it "incorporates a sort of narrative shorthand whereby significant dramatic conflicts can intensify and then be resolved through established patterns of action and familiar character types" (p. 24).

During the "classic" Hollywood film era, production studios capitalized on the success of popular films by making many more similar films. In fact, so many genre films were produced during this period that elite U.S. critics and independent foreign filmmakers and critics called Hollywood a "factory" system. This label evoked an invidious comparison between the Hollywood studio production system and the European tradition of independent films. Calling Hollywood production studios "factories" characterized Hollywood as an assembly-line industrial system of mass production and distribution, like the auto and steel factory system, that produced commodities, not the cinematic "art" of European independent filmmakers.

From Film and Radio to Television

Television genres that combined aspects of Hollywood film genres and network radio series began to emerge during the 1950s. Although television broadcasting had been exhibited at the 1939 World's Fair, broadcasting of regularly scheduled programs on television really did not begin until 1946 (Brooks & Marsh, 1999). In the period following World War II, the United States resumed postwar domestic manufacture of nonmilitary durable goods (including television sets), and by the 1950s television had begun to catch on as a form of popular home entertainment. The broadcast television programming that emerged in the United States in the 1950s reflected both the lessons that television networks had learned from the film industry's star-as-genre system and those they had learned from the success of weekly genre series on their parent radio networks NBC, CBS, ABC, and Dumont in drawing large, regular audiences.

Originally, television production was centered in New York City, at least in part because Hollywood film production studios, like most urban newspapers, regarded television as a dangerous interloper and competitor for people's leisure time. During the late 1940s and early 1950s, Hollywood studios shrugged off opportunities to produce what they considered "low-brow" television programs, and newspapers refused to carry television program schedules. Television programming clearly faced some challenges that film production did not. As Rose (1985) has explained,

> Television's voracious need for material, especially in its early years when the motion picture industry refused to cooperate, forced the networks to re-create and transform reliable formats in any way they could. . . . The genres that prospered on radio and made the move to TV were those which lent themselves to frequent interruptions, strong personality identification, mass audience involvement, and a conventional moral view unlikely to ruffle the sponsors. (pp. 3–6)

Indeed, since television was available in the family environment of the home many hours a day (although not 24 hours a day until decades later), one major challenge broadcast networks faced was how to keep this voracious program-eating creature fed. A related challenge was what to feed this creature, which, unlike the cinema, had a very small screen, displayed images lacking depth and shading, and derived economic support not from audiences' direct purchases but from product advertisers that initially underwrote entire programs and often hired the creative personnel who produced them. The answer that broadcast television developed initially emerged in response to budget issues and technical limitations of the television medium; however, it soon became an established medium-based aesthetic standard: "Since there was little money at first to shoot programs from scenic locations or to utilize elaborate sets . . . focusing on close-up shots of performers' faces and gestures, on the 'drama of personality'" and reactions to immediate conflicts rather than on large-scale action and sweeping panorama "became a practical way to compensate for what wasn't there behind them [the actors] (or could barely be seen if it was)" (Rose, 1985, pp. 3–4).

Economic considerations—the medium's insatiable appetite for programs, the need for advertising support to pay for the production of once-weekly programs viewers watched for "free," and advertisers' desire to have their products identified consistently with particular popular programs—contributed to television's medium-based aesthetic standard. So too did technical considerations unique to the television medium in the late 1940s and early 1950s: a small screen, black-and-white images lacking depth and shading, and the family environment viewing situation. Television programs that best used these unique economic and technical characteristics of television were those characterized by *intimacy* (in content and camerawork), *history* (television's unique mythic adaptations of history with "patterns of action and characters who seem familiar to our cultural consciousness . . . special versions of families, of certain types of doctors and lawyers" that cut across formulas and genres), and compensating for the (dis)*continuity* with continuing series in which familiar characters faced new problems each week (Newcomb, 1974, pp. 243–264). Clearly, television genres have developed as "dynamic fusions of substantive, stylistic, and situational elements and as constellations that are strategic responses to the demands of the situation and the purposes of the rhetor" (Campbell & Jamieson, 1978, p. 145).

Viewers' approval of the networks' genre series solution to their economic and programming exigencies was reflected in huge prime evening-time audiences that developed for television and the diminishing film audiences. Although television production had begun with New York City as its center, by the second half of the 1950s, Hollywood warmed to the new medium (or at least to the public's embrace of the medium) and began to produce programs for television. Still, although Los Angeles became the principal production center for network television entertainment series (Brooks & Marsh, 1999, p. xiii), television did not adopt Hollywood's film genres wholesale; instead, television transformed successful film and radio genres, making them uniquely televisual. For example, the action-packed western of the big Hollywood film screen became the psychological western of the small television screen. Some academic critics took note of these changes and began seriously analyzing television genres (see, e.g., Eaton, 1981; Kaminsky & Mahan, 1986).

Television Genre Criticism Comes of Age

Television genre criticism is rooted in both film genre theory and criticism and rhetorical genre theory and criticism. Film genre criticism began to blossom in the late 1950s and early 1960s: Simultaneously in the 1970s literary critics like Hernadi (1972) began reconceptualizing genre theory, and film auteur critics (discussed in Chapter 9) began to study certain individual film directors as a kind of genre in himself or herself. Several landmark essays provided the impetus for critical studies of Hollywood genre films. Among these were Robert Warshow's essays on gangster films and western films (1970), John Cawelti's studies of the western (1971) and crime and detective (1976) genres, and Will Wright's structural-rhetorical analysis of the western film genre (1975). Then, with the 1972 establishment of the *Journal of Popular Film* (now the *Journal of Popular Film and Television*) to provide a scholarly outlet for genre criticism, film genre theory and criticism moved from the academic shadows to center stage. Rhetorical genre analysis received a concomitant impetus with the publication of Edwin Black's *Rhetorical Criticism: A Study in Method* (1965) and the 1978 Speech Communication Association-sponsored conference 'Significant Form' in Rhetorical Criticism"(see also Fisher, 1980).

Additional stimuli contributing to the development of television genre studies included the Aspen Institute Program's *Television as a Cultural Force* (Adler & Cater, 1976) and *Television as a Social Force* (Cater & Adler, 1975), which were discussed in Chapters 1 and 3, and Arthur Asa Berger's analyses of popular television programs as representatives of various genres in *The TV-Guided American* (1976).[4] Two other influential academic critics who wrote seriously about television genres, despite the prevalent academic and journalistic disdain toward genre television at the time, were Bruce Gronbeck and Horace Newcomb.

Like Cawelti's (1971, 1976) and Wright's (1975) film genre studies, Bruce Gronbeck's 1978 essay, "Celluloid Rhetoric: On Genres of Documentary," argued that television and film genre studies needed to move beyond listing the various building blocks (or semantic features) of genres in order to understand the rhetorical force of genres. As Gronbeck explained, "Genres are nothing more than pigeon-holes capable of sorting artifacts if they do not include explorations of the cultural rules which give such configurations social force" (p. 156). What genre criticism should focus on, he argued, was trying to understand the relationship between audience expectations and the enduring popularity of generic texts by studying the ways in which "form, content, and culture" intersect in genres (p. 156).

Horace Newcomb's *TV: The Most Popular Art* (1974) was the first book-length analysis of television genres. In it Newcomb examined eleven television genres: situation and domestic comedy, western, mystery, doctor and lawyer dramas, adventure, soap opera, and reality entertainment (news, sports, documentary). His genre analysis was notable not only because it was the first relatively comprehensive examination of popular television genres, but more importantly, because it incorporated historical-aesthetic, ritual, and ideological approaches to genre.

Three Approaches to Genre Analysis

Surprisingly little scholarly television genre criticism has been published in the ensuing quarter-century, and very little of it has heeded Gronbeck's (1978) admonition to study the ways in which "form, content, and culture" intersect in genres (p.156). Instead, television genre critics generally have tended to adopt one of three perspectives on genre —an aesthetic approach, a structural approach, or an ideological approach—rather than combining these approaches to explore the ways in which the ways form, content, and culture merge in enduring popular genres.[5]

Aesthetic Approaches

Many television genre criticism essays have adopted an aesthetic approach to the study of television genres. Such aesthetic genre critiques typically have focused on identifying recurring formal and stylistic features (and innovations) of genre texts but have not analyzed their recurring syntax (the deeper cultural themes and oppositions articulated through these surface features). Two examples of such aesthetic genre critiques are Turner and Sprague's (1991) analysis of *Miami Vice*'s innovations in the cop genre and Vande Berg's (1989) study of *Moonlighting* as an example of the emerging genre, dramedy, a genre hybrid fusing elements of drama with elements of comedy. Turner and Sprague's essay looks at the relationship between the culture and the text's form and content in its discussion of the influence of MTV and baroque artistry on the innovations in look and sound that *Miami Vice* made in the typical cop genre. Vande Berg's essay uses Altman's (1985) theory about how new genres develop to explain how the fusion of formal and stylistic features in the detective series *Moonlighting* signals the emergence of a new genre—dramedy. However, the focus in both essays remains the recurring semantic formal and stylistic (surface) features of these genres and never extends to an analysis of the genres' substantive structures (the recurring patterns of cultural oppositions, themes, and discourses that define the genre's syntax). Thus, these analyses stop short of providing insights into the rhetorical force of these innovative genre texts.

Ritual Approaches

Ritual approaches to television genres generally have used semiotic/structural methods to describe and then analyze the recurring syntagmatic narrative structures and the sets of paired oppositions, themes, and discourses (paradigmatic structures) that constitute the genre's recurring conventions, and then related these textual structures to the cultural tensions and themes articulated in genre texts. Such critiques regard enduring popular television genres "as an exchange between industry and audience ... through which a culture speaks to itself" (Feuer, 1992, p. 143). Thus, changes in the basic genre features and the popularity of a genre are seen as emerging through unspoken negotiations among the media production industry, audiences, and the larger social and cultural context which both share.

One of the best examples of a ritual genre critique to date is Robert C. Allen's (1985) *Speaking of Soap Operas*. His study of the soap opera examines the genre as "narrative form, cultural product, advertising vehicle, and source of aesthetic pleasure for tens of millions of persons," and "map[s] out some of its historical, economic, aesthetic, and cultural features" (p. 4). Allen analyzes the paradigmatic complexity of the genre in terms of the three types of relationships—kinship, romantic, and social—that soap opera characters share. He also explains the link joining the television industry's economic needs, the soap opera genre's narrative economy, and the psychological and social pleasures provided to its devoted audiences by the genre's central treatment of "aspects of American life that have been marginalized in mainstream fictive narratives: parentage, family, the emotional consequences of romance, conflicting female role expectations, and so forth" (p. 94).

Ideological Approaches

These approaches see television program genres as instruments of power and control whose texts "naturalize" the dominant ideology of the capitalist system. From this perspective, genres are a tool used by the media production industry (including Hollywood production studios, the broadcast networks, and cable systems that bankroll the development and production of television series and distribute them to their affiliated stations and advertisers to take "advantage of spectator energy and psychic investment in order to lure the audience" into viewing the world from positions that ultimately benefit Hollywood and the network and cable owners (but not necessarily viewers) (see Altman, 1985; Feuer, 1992; Gitlin, 2000).

In describing several of the hegemonic processes (format, formula, genre, setting and character type, slant, and solution) through which prime-time ideology is articulated, Gitlin (2000) develops the argument that prime-time generic series are "performances that rehearse social fixity." He compares the superficial changes in prime-time schedules' replacement of one generic series with another to elections: both "seem to affirm the sovereignty of the audience while keeping deep alternatives off the agenda. Elite authority and consumer choice are affirmed at once—this is one of the central operations of hegemonic liberal capitalist ideology" (p. 578).

Judith Hess Wright (1985) concurs. She explains that genre texts do not stimulate people to look differently and critically at their social and economic situation because genre texts

> produce satisfaction rather than action, pity and fear rather than revolt. They serve the interests of the ruling class by assisting in the maintenance of the status quo, and they throw a sop to oppressed groups who, because they are unorganized and therefore afraid to act, eagerly accept the genre[s']. . . absurd solutions to economic and social conflicts. When we return to the complexities of the society in which we live, the same conflicts assert themselves, so we return to genre [texts] . . . for easy comfort and solace—hence their popularity (p. 41).

John Fiske's structural analysis of quiz shows (1983) is a powerful and timeless example of an ideological genre critique. Fiske focuses on four main discourses that structure quiz shows—capitalist economics, education, gambling, and sex—and explains how these discourses function to reproduce the social order by giving subordinate classes a superficial taste of the rewards of the capitalism and thereby buying their loyalty to an economic system that permanently disadvantages them.

Not all ideological critiques regard genre texts as regressive. An alternative ideological approach regards genre texts as potentially progressive—capable of revealing and critiquing, rather than naturalizing, the dominant ideology. As Klinger (1985) explains, a progressive genre text "literally makes a spectacle of ideology, and in so doing, elucidates, even materially objectifies, the presence and activity of ideology" (p. 74).[6] David Marc's (1984) analysis of *The Beverly Hillbillies* and Executive Producer Paul Henning's other situation comedies is examples of such an ideological critique.

Marc argues that Henning's situation comedies are microscopic commentaries on American society that foreground the continuing tensions between the idealized gemeinschaft (traditional, folk culture) of rural communities—including the values of hard work, self-reliance, and ethical integrity, and the technologically sophisticated gesellschaft (modern, urban culture) of the morally bankrupt wasteland of Beverly Hills, with its superficiality and selfishness. As Marc explains,

> Identification occurs not so much with one character or another as it does with one cultural point of view or the other. The antagonists are cultures. A pitched battle is fought in each episode between the homespun, right-minded values of the Clampetts, which represent a traditional, folkish, "real American" culture, and a cutthroat money-ruled technocracy, represented by the city people. . . . Henning . . . has created a nihilistic caricature of modern life. . . . the Clampetts' rejection of modern conveniences is still a wild slap at modern decadence. (1984, pp. 56–57)

Feuer (1992) notes that such ideological critiques are not limited to prime-time television. To illustrate, she points to the self-reflexive variety show *Saturday Night Live*, which, she observes, critiques not only the hegemony of social and political institutions but also the hegemony of television genres (e.g., with its tongue-in-cheek "Headline News") and the broadcast industry.

According to film theorist Christian Metz, the fact that *Saturday Night Live* critiques its own genre features is to be expected, given what he saw as the typical evolution of popular genres. Metz (1975, pp. 148–161) argued that genres generally progress through four stages: the "classic" stage, the parody stage, the contestation stage, and the critique or deconstruction stage. In the latter stages, Schatz (1981) has explained, the genre's established conventions emerge from "invisibility" and become the focus of the genre's narratives. At this point, "no longer does the genre simply celebrate the values of popular entertainment, it actually 'critiques' and 'deconstructs' them in the process" (p. 40).

Writing Genre Criticism

Armed with all of this information about television genre history and theory, let's say you decide to undertake a genre analysis of the political drama genre now popular on prime time (*The West Wing, Mister Sterling*), or the resurgence of the spy drama genre (*24, Alias, The Agency*), or PBS's *American Family* (a soap? a telenovela? another upscale drama?) Now what? You need to begin by considering the question of which comes first, the genre chicken or the generic egg.

The Genre Chicken or the Generic Egg: The Empiricist–Idealist Genre Dilemma

One theoretical and also very practical problem that genre critics face is where to start. The genre critic is caught in a circle. To do a genre criticism requires first that you identify the potential members of the genre. To do this, you need a set of criteria that make up the potential genre; however, you can develop this set of criteria only by analyzing common characteristics of a group of texts that seem to share most of the same features. For example, unless you already had an idea of what a soap opera was, how could you identify *Providence, Dallas, Dynasty, Titans* or *Pasadena* as a prime-time soap opera? Unless you had an idea of what soap operas, prime-time serial, and telenovelas were, how could you decide to which (if any) of these genres the *American Family* or *Betty LeFea* series belongs? Another name for this chicken-and-egg question is the *empiricist-idealist dilemma* (see Lacey, 2000; Tudor, 1985). Genre critics can respond to this circular problem in one of two ways: they can analyze the generic text or group of texts deductively or inductively.

Deductive Genre Analyses   Deductive genre analyses begin with the critic's assumption that a genre (like soap operas or telenovelas, dramedies, or spy dramas) already exists. Next, the critic needs to research theoretical or critical essays that have been written about this genre, and from these compile a list of formal, stylistic, and substantive features that apparently must be present and linked in a particular way in a text in order for it to belong clearly to the genre. Now the critic is ready to compare and contrast the characteristics of the particular text or television series she is studying with the list of genre features identified earlier. If the series has all or almost all of these features, the critic can conclude that the text belongs to this genre.

At this point, however, the critic's work is not over; in fact, she certainly is not yet ready to begin writing. Now, the critic needs to analyze the relationship between the genre (its formal, stylistic, and substantive features, including the recurring, oppositions, themes, and discourses that comprise its syntax) and the society in which it is produced and consumed. By analyzing the way "form, content and culture" intersect in this genre (Gronbeck, 1978, p.156), the critic can begin to develop an inferential explanation of some of the meanings this genre (and texts belonging to the genre) may have for viewers (including some ideas of the social, psychological, ritual, and ideological functions the genre may be serving), the media industry, and the society in which it is produced and consumed. As Lacey (2000) explains,

> Because genres are characterized by "the same but different," they are constantly evolving. Society, too, constantly changes, and the "repertoire of elements" allows us to tentatively make links between what makes a particular form of the genre popular at any one time and the social situation that produced and consumed the variant. (pp. 142–143)

Now, having completed the analysis, the critic is ready to develop an outline and then proceed to writing the critical essay that will explain the analysis and interpretation to others.

Inductive Genre Analyses   Inductive genre criticism does not begin with an a priori list of the semantic (formal, stylistic) and syntactic (underlying oppositions, themes, discourses) features that define a genre as deductive genre analyses do. Rather, inductive genre criticism begins with a critic's response to a group of texts[7]: "Eureka! I think there might be a genre here!" After this initial discovery, the critic then proceeds to develop a description of this potential genre's recurring features by identifying and analyzing the shared similarities among these texts.

In an inductive genre analysis, the critic carefully and systematically examines texts and identifies and describes the common semantic features (i.e., formal and stylistic building block elements) and syntactic features (i.e., the recurring substantive thematic relationships and discourses generated by oppositions and tensions expressed through the text's semantic features) shared by these texts. After defining the genre's characteristic elements (especially the genre's syntax—including the recurring oppositions and conflicts enacted through its narrative elements), the critic must analyze the relationship among these common features and discuss the meaning and importance of this generic discovery. In doing this, the critic links the genre's characteristics (especially hierarchical structures of oppositions, themes, and discourses) to the social world beyond the text in order to offer some insights into the potential social, psychological, ritual, and ideological meanings and functions of this genre for viewers. Once the critic has completed this part of the analysis, he is ready to begin writing the critical essay that explains the analysis and interpretation to others.

Critics often use an inductive approach when they believe they see a new genre emerging. The emergence of a new genre, Altman (1985) explains, is an important aesthetic and ideological moment. He theorizes that new genres come about in one of two ways: "Either a relatively stable set of semantic givens is developed through syntactic experimentation into a coherent and durable syntax, or an already existing syntax adopts a new set of semantic elements" (p. 34). On the other hand, critics often use a deductive approach when they are making aesthetic judgments about the quality of members of an existing genre.

Deciding Which Approach to Use

Whether you approach your genre analysis inductively or deductively depends on what you are trying to learn about a television genre. Ask yourself, "What question do I want to answer and then explain to others in a critical essay?" Another way to think about this decision is to reflect on why you want to analyze this text. In general, critics undertake genre analyses for several reasons. Some seek to make an aesthetic judgment about a text: others to explain a problematic text (i.e., to figure out to what genre it belongs). Some critics do genre analyses in order to compare or contrast two genres (in terms of their features and possible individual and social functions), where other critics undertake genre critiques to evaluate the quality of particular members of a genre, or trace the history of a genre in order to understand the relationship between the genre and the society in which it is produced. Such critics may be interested in analyzing the genre "primarily as a means of making historical and cultural inferences about the collective fantasies shared by large groups of people and of identifying differences in these fantasies from one culture or period to another" (Cawelti, 1971, p. 7). Critics undertaking genre analyses may also be interested in analyzing the genre as an ideological tool in order to identify how it reproduces the dominant ideologies and to assess its rhetorical force in positioning audience members to accept as "natural, right, and desirable" the dominant beliefs of the social, economic, and political system in which these genre texts are produced and consumed. And, of course, many genre analyses are undertaken for a combination of these reasons, and thus may combine aspects of aesthetic, ritual and ideological approaches.

Elements of Television Genres

Regardless of the reason motivating the critic, each genre is a group of texts "unified by a constellation of forms that recurs in each of its members" (Campbell & Jamieson, 1978, p. 20). As a result, genre critics begin by looking for the distinctive set of elements whose co-occurrence in a text signals that the text belongs to a particular genre. Here are some of the semantic (formal, stylistic) and syntactic features (the oppositions, themes, and discourses that constitute the genre's internal dynamic) that television genre analyses identify and analyze.

Semantic (Formal/Stylistic)Features

- Character types
- Location (in geography, time, space)
- Scene settings (indoors, outdoors, both)
- Characteristic types of shots, camera angles, camera work (e.g., unobtrusive versus handheld)
- Style of action (naturalistic versus stylized)
- Style of editing[8] (e.g., continuity editing)
- Use of time (compressed or prolonged)
- Single plot or multiple intersecting plotlines
- Iconography[9]
- Metatextual practices (e.g., self-reflexivity, intertextuality)
- Types of diegetic sound and extradiegetic sound (musical soundtrack, laugh track)
- Length of episodes
- Frequency of episodes (daily, weekly)
- Types of lighting (flat, bright versus chiaroscuro/noir)

Syntatic (Substantive) Features

- Narrative structure (open versus closed; episodic, serial, or anthology; Newcomb's four-part sitcom narrative structure, Thorburn's three-part melodrama, or Propp's syntagmatic narrative structure)
- Dialectic (i.e., structure of paired oppositions)
- Recurring themes
- Discourses[10]

Berger (1992), for example, uses a combination of Vladmir Propp's typology of syntagmatic narrative functions (1968) and Lévi-Strauss's paradigmatic analysis of the binary oppositions (1967) to develop a schema describing the paired oppositions in actions, characters, and goals in popular culture genres. We discuss narrative and form in more detail in this book in Chapter 8.

Example Essay: Matthew McAllister's "Recombinant Television Genres and *Doogie Howser, M.D.*"

Our example of a television genre criticism essay is Matthew McAllister's analysis of *Doogie Howser, M.D.* (ABC, 1989–1993), which is this chapter's example essay McAllister argues that the series was so successful (it was in the top 25 series) because it fused two established genres: the teen comedy genre and the medical drama genre. His analysis of the combination of stock types of characters and settings and narratives enacting the underlying cultural oppositions typifying both genres leads him to conclude that the popularity of the series can be explained by its fulfillment of industry commercial and economic functions (it succeeded in drawing large numbers of teen and women viewers) and audience ritual functions (it reassured audiences about the altruism of doctors in the face of recent transitions in American medicine and about the ultimate goodness of teenagers in the face of horrific examples of teen violence during the last decade).

Notes

1. Literary critics added to Aristotle's "unity of action" (the idea that a plot will be an artistic whole if it is a single, complete structure in which all actions contribute toward the intended conclusion and no incidents are unnecessary) the "unity of time" (the idea that verisimilitude, or the creation of a sense of reality in a theatrical production, required that the action be limited to approximately the amount of time it took to present the play—at the most, twenty-four hours), and the "unity of place" (the idea that the action in a play should be limited to a single location, like a single city). These rules were followed quite strictly in Italy and France during this time but less faithfully by many "high art" dramatists in Great Britain; indeed, more popular cultural innovators like Shakespeare violated these proscriptions repeatedly in thoroughly popular productions (see Abrams, 1971).

2. According to semiotician Umberto Eco (1985), postmodern aesthetics is largely an attempt to deal with issues of repetition, redundancy, and iteration—"the new aesthetics of seriality." Eco provides a typology of four kinds of artistic repetition or seriality in art—the retake, the remake, the series, and the saga–which he applies to various classic literary works to argue that nothing would prevent postmodern serial art creations using these types of repetition from being regarded "well done" in terms of "modern" conceptions of aesthetic value (i.e., every well-done work must "achieve a dialectic between order and novelty"—between innovation and convention—which must be apprehendable by the consumers of the art). He also discusses Italian postmodernist Omar Calabrese's argument that a new neobaroque or postpostmodern aesthetic sensibility concerned with similarities in works is emerging (see Berger, 1992, pp. 48-51).

3. The term *new criticism* became popular after John Crowe Ransom published his book *The New Criticism* in 1941. Subsequently, the term was used to describe a point of view and literary practice that developed from Ransom's book and also some ideas from I. A. Richards's *Principles of Literary Criticism* (1924) book and T. S. Eliot's critical essays. With Cleanth Brooks and Robert Penn Warren's literature textbook, *Understanding Poetry* (1938). This view of criticism became the dominant one in scholarly literary study. Essentially the new critics argued (1) that one should treat a literary work (a poem, a play, a novel) as a literary work in and of itself, and not focus on the presumed intent of the author, the biography of the author, the social context, or the presumed emotional, psychological, or moral effects on the reader, and (2) that one should study literary works through explication of the critic's detailed close reading of the ambiguous (capable of evoking "multiple meanings") elements of the literary work. Genres were largely ignored; new critics focused on words, images, symbols, and themes (rather than character

and plot) in order to identify the "structure of meanings" in a text (see Abrams, 1971).

4. More recently, in his *Popular Culture Genres: Theories and Texts* (1992), Berger argues that there are essentially four types of television programs: actualities (news, documentary), contests (sports and game programs), persuasions (ads), and dramas (soaps, sitcoms, action adventure, hospital/cops/lawyer dramas). Genres within each of these program types can be categorized (and their important elements explained) in terms of the polar opposition between their emotive aspects (generating feelings and excitement) and their objective aspects (concerned with events that actually happen rather than fictions involving make-believe events). Such categorization, Berger suggests, can help explain the appeals of various genres—the aesthetic, psychological, and social functions popular culture genres serve.

5. This and similar typologies of film genre approaches appear in many discussions of film genres. For example, Schatz, (1981) discusses expressive/aesthetic, social/mythic/ritual, and ideological approaches to genres; Bywater and Sobchack (1986) discuss aesthetic, structural, psychoanalytical, and sociocultural approaches; and Altman (1985) discusses structural, ritual, and ideological approaches. Feuer (1992) uses this framework to argue that television genre criticism can be separated into three types of approaches: aesthetic, ritual, or ideological.

6. According to Klinger (1985), some of the characteristics of "progressive" texts include a pessimistic (i.e., bleak, cynical, apocalyptic, or highly ironic) worldview and themes (or syntax) that demolish belief in the nature and role of social institutions (e.g., debunking the ultimate benevolence of the law, debunking the view of the family as an institution of social and sexual "salvation" for individual members of a couple, and especially women), narrative forms that expose ideological contradictions by minimalization (paring them down to their bare essentials) or excess (exaggerating the techniques of classic genre texts), endings that refuse closure and are ultimately unredemptive (see also Wood, 1985), visual styles that are self-consciously foregrounded, and the use of excessively sexually stereotyped characters to focus on "both the threat and enigma of female sexuality in all its complexity" (pp. 81–84).

7. However, Edwin Black (1965) and others (see Vande Berg, 1989) would argue that you can indeed have a genre with only one member.

8. In television and film, continuity editing is a technique used to make a text appear to be realistic. This is accomplished by editing that makes the action on the screen appear to be logical and continuous. For example, when two people are engaged in dialogue, the editing matches the eye levels in shot and reverse-shot sequences. Another editing "rule" used to create the sense of realism is the 180-degree rule: the camera keeps to one side of an imaginary line dividing the scene so that the audience has a constant reference point from which to view the action. If this rule is broken, the audience loses its frame of reference, and the sense of continuity is broken.

9. *Iconography* is a term art critic Erwin Panofsky (1955) coined to refer solely to the visual signs in a genre. Subsequent film critics expanded the meaning of the term to refer to visual and aural iconography; that is, to both the objects and sounds—both diegetic (sounds the characters in the narrative as well as the audience hear) and extradiegetic (sounds that only the audience hears, like the laugh track in comedies and the orchestral mood music in dramas) associated with a genre (see Lacey, 2000, pp. 138–139).

Further Reading

Allen, R. C. (1985). *Speaking of soap operas.* Chapel Hill: University of North Carolina Press. This book examines the American soap opera as textual system, commercial product, advertising tool, and source of viewing pleasure. The chapter on reader-oriented poetics explores how the genre's paradigmatic and syntagmatic structure and the variety of soap opera codes (stylistic, generic, textual, intertextual, and ideological) construct an ideal female reader and illustrate how reader response criticism can be combined with semiotic/structural analysis to provide a complex genre analysis—not only of soaps but of other television genres as well.

Webnotes

Retroactive TV Party! **www.tvparty.com**

This site provides essays, photos, and videos of programs from television's past, including memorable, forgettable, campy, and long-forgotten programs.

Daniel Chandler's Introduction to Genre Theory. **www.aber.ac.uk/Media/Documents/intgenr1.htm/**

This site provides an overview of genre theory. Included are links to appendices, papers, and other sites that discuss conventions of genre TV and film (e.g, narratives, characterization, themes, setting, iconography, filmic techniques, modes of address, subject matter) and taxonomies of genres.

Learning Activities

1. Check the TV guide listings for Nickelodeon, TBS, TV Land, USA, TNT, Lifetime, and other channels that carry old television series (those now in syndication), and compare similarities and note any changes in the semantic (formal and stylistic) and syntax (substantive, thematic) characteristics of two or three examples of series from the same genre but different time periods. For example, you might choose police dramas from 20 to 30 years ago (*Dragnet*, 1952–1970; *Hawaii Five-O*, 1968–1980; *Columbo*, 1971–1977; and *Starsky and Hutch*,1975–1979), fifteen years ago (*Hill Street Blues*, 1981–1987), and current series (*Homicide: Life on the Streets*, 1993–1999; *Law and Order*, 1990–present; *NYPD Blue*, 1993–present).

References

Abrams, M. H. (1971). *A glossary of literary terms* (3rd ed.). New York: Holt.

Adler, R., & Cater, D. (Eds.). (1976). *Television as a cultural force.* New York: Praeger.

Allen, R. C. (1985). *Speaking of soap operas.* Chapel Hill: University of North Carolina Press.

Altman, R. (1985). A semantic/syntactic approach to film genre. In B. K. Grant (Ed.), *Film genre reader* (pp. 26–40). Austin: University of Texas Press.

Berger, A. A. (1976). *The TV-guided American.* New York: Walker.

Berger, A. A. (1992). *Popular culture genres: Theories and texts.* Thousand Oaks, CA: Sage.

Black, E. (1965). *Rhetorical criticism: A study in method.* New York: Macmillan.

Bormann, E. G. (1976). Rhetorical criticism and significant form: A humanistic approach. In K. K. Campbell & K. H. Jamieson (Eds.), *Form and genre: Shaping rhetorical action* (pp. 165–187). Falls Church, VA: Speech Communication Association.

Brooks, T., & Marsh, E. (1999). *The complete directory to prime time network and cable TV shows, 1946–present* (12th ed.). New York : Ballantine.

Brooks, C., & Warren, R. P. (1938). *Understanding Poetry.* New York: Hult.

Burke, K.(1954). *Counter-statement.* Los Altos, CA: Hermes.

Buscombe, E. (1985). The idea of genre in American cinema. In B. K. Grant (Ed.), *Film genre reader* (pp. 11–25). Austin: University of Texas Press.

Bywater, T., & Sobchack, T. (1986). *Introduction to film criticism: Major critical approaches to narrative film.* New York: Longman.

Campbell, K. K., & Jamieson, K. H. (Eds.), (1978). *Form and genre: Shaping rhetorical action.* Falls Church, VA: Speech Communication Association.

Cater, D., & Adler, R. (Eds.). (1975). *Television as a social force.* New York: Praeger.

Cawelti, J.C. (1971). *The six-gun mystique.* Bowling Green, OH: Bowling Green University Popular Press.

Cawelti, J. (1976). *Adventure, mystery, and romance.* Chicago: University of Chicago Press.

Eaton, M. (1981). Television situation comedy. In T. Bennett, S. Boyd-Bowman, C. Mercer, & J. Woollacott (Eds.), *Popular television and film* (pp. 26–52). London: British Film Institute/Open University Press.

Feuer, J. (1992). Genre study of television. In R. C. Allen (Ed.), *Channels of discourse, reassembled: Television and contemporary criticism* (2nd ed., pp. 138–160). Chapel Hill: University of North Carolina Press.

Fisher, W. R. (1980). Genre: Concepts and applications in rhetorical criticism. *Western Journal of Speech Communication, 44,* 288–299.

Fiske, J. (1983). The discourses of TV quiz shows, or school + luck = success + sex. *Central States Communication Journal, 34,* 139–150.

Fiske, J. (1987). *Television culture.* New York: Maethuen.

Foss, S. K. (1996). Generic criticism. In S.K. Foss (Ed.), *Rhetorical criticism: Exploration and practice* (2nd ed., pp. 225–237). Prospect Heights, IL: Waveland.

Gitlin, T. (2000). Prime time ideology: The hegemonic process in television entertainment. In H. Newcomb (Ed.), *Television: The critical view* (6th ed., pp. 574–594). New York: Oxford University Press.

Grant, B. K. (Ed.). *Film genre reader* . Austin: University of Texas Press.

Gronbeck, B. E. (1978). Celluloid rhetoric: On genres of documentary. In K. K. Campbell & K. H. Jamieson (Eds.), *Form and genre: Shaping rhetorical action* (pp. 139–161). Falls Church, VA: Speech Communication Association.

Hernzdi, P. (1972). *Beyond genre: New directions in literary classification.* Ithaca: Cornell University Press.

Jamieson, K. H., & Campbell, K. K. (1982). Rhetorical hybrids: Fusions of generic elements. *Quarterly Journal of Speech, 68,* 146–157.

Kaminsky, S. M., & Mahan, J. H. (1986). *American television genres.* Chicago: Nelson-Hall.

Klinger, B. (1985). "Cinema/ideology/criticism" revisited: The progressive genre. In B. K. Grant (Ed.), *Film genre reader* (pp. 74–90). Austin: University of Texas Press.

Lacey, N. (2000). *Narrative and genre: Key concepts in media studies.* New York: St. Martin's Press.

Lévi-Strauss, C. (1967). *Structural anthropology.* New York: Anchor.

Marc, D. (1984). The situation comedy of Paul Henning: Modernity and the American folk myth in *The Beverly Hillbillies.* In D. Marc, *Demographic vistas: Television in American cultur*e (pp. 39–64). Philadelphia: University of Pennsylvania Press.

Metz, C. (1975). *Language and cinema.* New York: Praeger.

Newcomb, H. (1974). *TV: The most popular art.* Garden City, NY: Anchor.

Panofsky, E. (1955). *Meaning in the visual arts.* New York: Anchor Press.

Porter, M. J. (1998). The structure of television narratives. In L. Vande Berg, L. A. Wenner, & B. E. Grunbeck (Eds.), *Critical approaches to television* (pp. 140-157). Boston: Houghton Mifflin.

Porter, M. J., Larson, D. L., Harthcock, A., & Nellis, K. B. (2002). (De) filming narrative events: Examining television narrative structure. *Journal of Popular Film & Television, 3.0,* 23-30.

Propp. V. (1968). *Morphology of the folktale* (2nd ed.). Austin, TX: University of Texas Press. (Original work published 1928)

Ransom, J. C. (1941). *The new criticism.* Norfolk, CT: New Directions.

Richards, I. A. (1924). *Principles of literary criticism.* London, Routledge & Kegan Paul.

Rose, B. G. (1985). Introduction. In B. G. Rose (Ed.), *TV genres: A handbook and reference guide* (pp. 3–10). Westport, CT: Greenwood.

Schatz, T. (1981). *Hollywood genres: Formulas, filmmaking, and the studio system.* New York: Random House.

Scholes, R. (1974). *Structuralism in literature: An introduction.* New Haven: Yale University Press.

Thorburn, D. (2000). Television melodrama. In H. Newcomb (Ed.), *Television: The critical view* (6th ed., pp. 595-608). New York: Oxford University Press.

Turner, K. J., & Sprague, R. (1991). Musical and visual invention in *Miami Vice*: Old genre, new form. In L. Vande Berg & L. A. Wenner (Eds.), *Television criticism: Approaches and applications* (pp. 278–288). White Plains, NY: Longman.

Tudor, A. (1985). Genre. In B. K. Grant (Ed.), *Film genre reader* (pp. 3–10). Austin: University of Texas Press.

Vande Berg, L. R. E. (1989). Dramedy: *Moonlighting* as an emergent generic hybrid. *Communication Studies, 40,* 13–28.

Warshow, R. (1970). *The immediate experience.* New York: Atheneum.

Wood, R. (1985). Ideology, genre, auteur. In B. K. Grant (Ed.), *Film genre reader* (pp. 59-73). Austin: University of Texas Press.

Wright, J. H. (1985). Genre films and the status quo. In B. K. Grant (Ed.), *Film genre reader* (pp. 41–49). Austin: University of Texas Press.

Wright, W. (1975). *Six guns and society: A structural study of the western.* Berkeley: University of California Press.

Recombinant Television Genres and *Doogie Howser, M.D.*

By Matthew P. McAllister

Genre is a broad explanatory concept for cultural analysis, applicable to Shakespeare and Superman. One particular point of attraction of genre for many critics is its explanatory power for industrialized mediated production. Feuer (1987) argues that genre was applied very early to film by Adornoesque critics of "mass culture," who used it to highlight and condemn the assembly-line imperative of motion picture studies (p. 117). The set-up of the studio machines encouraged formulaic production: because the studios looked to past successes for future projects, and because each had specific personnel on contract who specialized in certain categories of production, studios began to specialize in certain genres of film.

Given the industrial and economic nature of television production, it would seem that the concept of genre would be a most fitting one for that medium as well. Because of television's economic thrust, its content should be even more likely than other cultural forms to be explained by genres. Certainly the industrial context and audience expectations of television encourage some sort of generic production, as the development of standardized formula allows the creative personnel of

Doogie Howser (1989–1993) was a half-hour situation comedy that followed the series' title character, a child prodigy who graduated from medical school and began his hospital internship while struggling with typical teen dilemmas. Although *Doogie* was a departure for executive producer Steven Bochco, who is best known for his innovations in the cop drama genre, this series illustrates Bochco's creative ability to blend genres, as McAllister argues in this essay.

television to constantly crank out programs and overall helps to guarantee a fairly predictable audience for different categories of shows.

But things are not that simple. Compared with the concept of genre in film, the same concept in television is problematic. In the motion picture industry, we can define one complete, uninterrupted entity—and these entities can easily be categorized as the cop film, the horror film, the gangster film, etc. In TV, on the other hand, the industrial imperative is to make the viewer forget the distinction between program and commercial, or program and program, and so the concept of genre becomes harder to apply. Moreover, the television show must generate numerous, specific plot episodes—the program premise. Given these factors, TV formats/shows/ads/genres tend to bleed into each other. With this lack of clear distinction, one wonders if the television program can even be said to have one, overarching defining element as the motion picture does (Feuer, 1987, p. 279).

Along these lines, when we try to classify recent television shows according to genres that have been established by film, radio, or early television, we may find that perfect "fits" are hard to locate. To use Gitlin's (1985) biological metaphor, there are very few "pure" gene pools found in television programming. TV shows often are "recombinants," or splices of two or more previously existing, and successful, types. Mixtures of comedies and dramas ("dramedies"), like *Sisters* or *Brooklyn Bridge*, may be found on the schedule during a given season. In fact, as Vande Berg (1991) notes (p. 91), the era of the dramedy may have been signified by *Moonlighting's* nomination as *both* best drama and best comedy during the 1985–86 season. Mixtures of comedies and game shows ("gamedies") may be the new descripters for shows like *Studs* and *Grudge Match*. Certain key personnel of the television industry (Fred Silverman, Steven Bochco) may specialize in developing recombinant television programs. Many of the most publicized programs of recent television have been recombinants, including the above-mentioned *Moonlighting* as well as *Hill Street Blues* (*Barney Miller* meets *Fort Apache, The Bronx*, Gitlin, 1985, p. 279), *Twin Peaks* (what *Newsweek* called a "soap opera/murder mystery"), *Cop Rock* (a "musical detective drama"), and *Eerie, Indian* ("*The Wonder Years* meets *Twin Peaks*," according to *TV Guide*). The point I wish to make is that often such a combination will especially "click," both industrially (it will be easy to produce and a ratings success) and ideologically (people will like it, and the elements of the two genres will fit together in such a way to reinforce or popularize their messages). *Doogie Howser, M.D.*, I believe, is such a program: an archetype of a recombinant TV genre, in which elements of two—the teen genre and the doctor genre—are spliced for a perfect iconic and ideological fit.

Doogie Howser, M.D. as a Recombinant Success Story

Because of his stellar track record, television writer-producer Steven Bochco was given a ten million dollar, ten television series contract with ABC. Bochco, of course, had previous recombinant hits with *Hill Street Blues*, *St. Elsewhere*, and *LA Law*. The first series produced as a result of this contract was *Doogie Howser, M.D.*, which premiered in September 1989 on Thursday nights. The show focuses on the (at first) sixteen-year-old child prodigy Doogie, a character reportedly inspired by Bocho's father, who was a child prodigy violinist (Marin, 1989). With Doogie having graduated from Princeton at age 10, medical school (at the top of his class) at 14, and beginning a hospital internship at 16, the show deals with the unlikely dilemmas faced by a teenager going through both puberty and pediatrics.

Although the program initially received mixed reviews (thumbs up by Zurawik of the *Baltimore Sun*; thumbs down by Millman of the *San Francisco Examiner*), it became the biggest, in fact the only, new hit of the 1990 fall season. Drawing on the demographics from its lead-in program (initially *Growing Pains*, and later *The Wonder Years*), the

show does well with teens and young women audiences, two markets very desirable for advertisers (Haithman, 1989). After the 1990–91 season, the program ranked 24 overall, just behind *LA Law*, with a 14.7 average rating (Brooks and Marsh, 1992, p. 1107). Although ratings slipped in the 1991–92 season, the fall premiere episode, where Doogie lost his virginity, scored a 16.8 rating (Miller, 1991, p. 36), and throughout the season the program usually won its time slot. Critically, the program receives occasional accolades. *TV Guide* listed *Doogie* as one of the "Best Teen Shows" for young people in a March 1992 issue. The program will be released into syndication in fall 1993 (Guider, 1992, p. 36), may be the most economically desirable mark of success, and first-run production will probably cease, at the latest, following the 1994 season, which the title character turns 21 (Beck, 1992, p. 3).

What makes this program so successful? In large part, it is its nearly brilliant combination of two established genres, one designed to pull in the teens and the other designed to pull in adults, especially women. These are the teen comedy genre and the medical doctor genre, each with its own specific characters, icons, and themes.

The Teen and the Doctor Television Genres

The two genres co-opted by *Doogie Howser, M.D.* are established cultural genres, both found in a variety of popular culture forms. Both also are traditionally very malleable and easily combined with other genres (as illustrated by the 1950s teen flick *I Was a Teenage Werewolf*, combining teens and horror; and NBC's *Quincy, M.E.*, combining medicine and detectives). However, before they could be merged *together* as successfully as they were in the ABC program, they had to undergo certain fairly recent changes in their formula.

The "teen comedy" is probably less established of the two. Although there certainly were precedents for very early popular culture aimed at teenagers (as Mickey Rooney would say, "Let's put on a show!"), Doherty (1988) notes that the teen genre as a definable product really came into its own in the mid-1950s as the motion picture industry tried to capture the street roving teenaged market through the creation of the teenpic. With the exception of *The Aldrich Family*, an adaptation from radio airing from 1949 to 1953, successful TV programs—in this case sitcoms—centering on teens began to slowly filter into prime time in the late 1950s and early 1960s, as illustrated by CBS's *The Many Loves of Dobie Gillis* from 1959 to 1963; ABC's *The Patty Duke Show* from 1963 to 1966; and ABC's *Gidget* (starring Sally Field) from 1965 to 1966. All three programs were influenced by the "teen trend" in movies, with the latter two explicitly so (*The Patty Duke Show* capitalizing on its star's Oscar and motion picture success; *Gidget* being a continuation of the movie series).

These shows and their movie influences introduced several enduring elements into the teen comedy formula. The programs featured middle-class, clean, loving kids trying to advance their social lives in high school. The shows with male leads often portrayed them as misfits—not quite successful in their search for high school elite acceptance. Maynard G. Krebs helped to solidify the character type of the goofy best friend who often caused problems and added comic relief. Themes of dealing with the opposite gender, popularity and fitting in, and high school social mobility tended to dominate the programs. The parents and teachers of the programs, although old-fashioned, generally were warm hearted and ultimately understanding. Often, the parents, especially the fathers, would impart wise advice that would save the day for the teens. Both Dobie Gillis and Gidget directly addressed the audience, a technique that continues today in teen movies and television shows and encourages a feeling that the shows were speaking immediately to the teens of America.

The genre underwent a significant mutation in the early to mid-1980s with the introduction of the mainstream, big-budgeted "teen *sex* comedy" in movies. *Risky Business* (1983), *Real Genius* (1985), *Fast Times at Ridgemont High* (1982), and the movies of John Hughes such as *The Breakfast Club* (1985), *Pretty in Pink* (1986), and *Ferris Bueller's Day Off* (1986) helped to refine the genre, especially when successfully translated into a form more savory for television (like *Parker Lewis Can't Lose, The Wonder Years, Blossom*, and the short-lived TV version of *Ferris Bueller*). Certain elements remained, of course, such as dealing with the opposite sex (in practically all of the above instances), popularity (stressed especially in *The Breakfast Club*), the goofy friend (like Miles in *Risky Business* or Cameron in *Ferris Bueller*), and using direct address. In *Ferris Bueller* and its TV clone *Parker Lewis*, the characters turn and talk directly to the camera; direct address is also implied in the retrospective narration of *The Wonder Years*.

Overall, though, the eighties teen films added an "edge" to the genre that was missing before, especially in television. Three key elements—additions that the TV versions picked up—especially highlight this edge: the emphasis on sex, the appropriation of the "us versus them" mentality from teen dramas, and the smart, hip teen hero.

Characters in modern teen sex comedies are not that concerned with dating, with going steady, or even with necking. They want to have sex. Joel in *Risky Business* calls a prostitute. Mitch, the 15-year-old brain in *Real Genius*, sleeps with his girlfriend. Even the TV versions of the genre have picked up this explicit sexual orientation: Becky Conner of *Roseanne* and Brenda Walsh of *Beverly Hills 90210* both faced sexual situations in the 1991–92 television seasons.

In the recent teen comedies, and to a lesser degree in the television versions, teen characters are pitted against the adult world. Becky Conner is much more likely to rebel than Patty Lane. This characteristic has been adapted from the teen drama, such as *Rebel Without a Cause* and *The Wild One*. In the new version, authority figures, especially school administrators (like the nurse in *Risky Business*, Mr. Rooney in *Ferris Bueller*, Principal Musso in *Parker Lewis*, and Professor Hathaway in *Real Genius*) are more bureaucratic, buffoon-like, and unreasonable than in previous versions. In the movie versions, parents tend to be also portrayed as silly and unsympathetic: however, in the TV versions, the parents are warm and understanding, if not completely with it (and dads still are the voice of reason). Also reinforcing this "us versus them" image is the continued use of direct address (talking to the teen audience directly, as if adults are not in the room), the use of fantasy sequences (as in the beginning of *Risky Business*), and the use of intertextuality, including unexplained references to teen culture (the insider joke technique).

Finally, the hero of the teen comedy has been changed. Although the social outcast can still be found in teen movies (*Porky's, Sixteen Candles, Revenge of the Nerds*), now the teen hero is as likely to be the smartest, the most technologically advanced, and the coolest character around. Ferris, in his Hawaiian shirts, is able to outsmart, and outgadget, Mr. Rooney; Chris Knight of *Real Genius* turns Professor Hathaway's house into a giant jiffy pop; Parker Lewis knows that, no matter how much trouble he's in, it's "not a problem"; Blossom is arguably the hippest and most mature character in her household. It is interesting to note, in fact, that three teen TV show *failures* of the 1980s, *Spencer, Square Pegs* and *The Marshall Chronicles*, featured misfits as the main characters, and that the mid-1970s' show *Happy Days* did not become a huge hit until the focus of the show shifted from the square Richie to the hip Fonzie.[1] Overall, these three alterations have made it easier to fit this genre with the stereotypical doctor television program.

As Turow (1989) points out, the medical genre also began to solidify in film before moving to television. Movie series of the thirties and forties like *Dr. Kildare* and *Dr. Christian*, contributed the initial supplies of the genre, which were later refined in television as that medium became almost the sole outlet of the fictional medical story. In the early 1960s, the popular competitor programs *Ben Casey* on ABC and *Dr. Kildare* on NBC picked up the film contributions and added a few key features. Further solidifying the doctor genre was the wave of medical programs in the late 1960s, including ABC's *Marcus Welby*, CBS's *Medical Center*, and NBC's *The Bold Ones*.

These cultural products shared certain characteristics that helped to define the medical formula. Overall the formula was extremely celebratory of certain mainstream elements of society. The stories were physician centered rather than focused on the patient or other medical personnel: the tele-hospital was clearly the "doctor's workshop" (Turow, 1989). The main physician was an extremely dedicated professional, often overcoming medical, psychological, and bureaucratic obstacles to save the lives of the patient. Typically medical strategies and ethos were discussed between "the young doctor" (Ben Casey, Dr. Kildare, Dr. Kiley) and "the old doctor," the mentor (Dr. Zorba, Dr. Gillespie, and Marcus Welby, respectively). Usually the young doctor was innovative, but immature, and the old doctor the calmer, wiser voice. The latest advances in medical technology (of which the main character was always knowledgeable) often were needed to cure the patient. The doctor movies and television programs, then, glorified the medical profession as a whole, as the rugged individualist doctor nearly always saved the day and the patient through the successful application of medical techniques and the medical model of treatment (seeing the human body as a machine to be quickly fixed). The politics and limited resources of medicine were either never shown or superficially portrayed (Alley, 1985; Turow, 1989). The hero-doctors, of course, were white, male, and middle class; usually the entire cast tended to be white, middle class (Alley, 1985). Occasionally, the pro-medicine message of the programs would be driven home in the epilogue, where the doctor characters would discuss, over coffee, the patient's (usually positive) prognosis.

Other stock characters began to be developed as the genre matured. Nurses, more often than not, were young and very attractive (this caricature was solidified even more with Nurse "Ripples" in *Trapper John, M.D.* and Hawkeye's various conquests along with "Hot Lips" in *M*A*S*H*). Patients tended to be completely passive and ignorant about their condition (Alley, 1985) or, for varied sub-plot complications, even very detrimental to their own cure because of behavorial or psychological problems—i.e., "Why didn't you tell me your mother died on the operating table?" This was labeled by one writer of *Medical Center* as the storyline of "the patient as his own worst enemy" (Turow, 1989,

p. 146) and helped to fortify the doctor-character's symbolic power as the ultimate voice of authority in the health arena.

Medical shows of the 1970s and 1980s, including *M*A*S*H*, *Trapper John, M.D.*, *St. Elsewhere*, and *Quincy, M.E.* solidified many of the above characteristics (*Trapper John* featured the young/old doctor dynamic, for example) but also slightly refined the genre and made *Doogie Howser, M.D.*'s successful teen-doctor combination more likely. The character of the hospital administrator, although occasionally found in the early doctor programs, grew more salient in the newer versions. Characters like Arnold Slocum of *Trapper John, M.D.*, Dr. John Gideon of *St. Elsewhere*, Dr. Robert Astin of *Quincy, M.E.*, and Mike D'Angelo of *AfterMASH* were bureaucratic, image-conscious medical administrators out of touch with the human and healing needs of the physicians. Often these administrators, along with the patients, would be the most significant barriers to the physicians' completion of their duties.

Also added to the medical genre in the 1970s and '80s was humor. Many doctor shows took on a "dramedy" tenor. Although doctor sitcoms existed before this era (*Hennesey* and *Temperatures Rising*, for example), humor, in its proper place, became more prevalent in the medical dramas. *M*A*S*H* may be the show most responsible for this: beginning more as a pure sitcom but ending up mixing medical drama and commentaries about war. Doctors could be fun loving, as long as the fun did not interfere with their medical dedication (it rarely did). Hawkeye, Trapper John, Gonzo, and Wayne Fiscus of *St. Elsewhere* had their share of cut-up moments and wisecracks.

Finally, the physician's personal lives were perhaps stressed more than in the past. In *M*A*S*H*, Hawkeye wrote intimate letters to his dad back home; in *St. Elsewhere*, we learned about the love life of almost all of the physicians; indeed, sometimes these were the main plots of the programs (Turow, 1989, p. 236). Given these new additions to the medical genre, as well as the changes mentioned in the teen comedy genre, the stage was set for television mutation.

Doogie as Teen Comedy/Doctor Drama

Doogie Howser, M.D. contained separate elements of both genres. From the teen realm, for example, one finds the wacky best friend, Vinnie (who often has the funniest and/or most vulgar lines, such as his suggestion that Doogie should choose as his medical specialty "Plastic surgery, specializing in breast enhancement"). Doogie's room is filled with teenage icons, like pin-ups and silly bric-a-brac. Intertextuality is found in many episodes, including the strategic use of well-known popular music (Robert Palmer's "Addicted to Love" plays on the radio as Vinnie tries to put the moves on his girlfriend Janine). Scenes with a music video style appear in the program: the fun that Vinnie and Doogie have while (temporarily) living on their own or on Spring Break are conveyed with quick cuts and a montage of images accompanied by a rock score.

Likewise, elements from the medical genre are evident in *Doogie*. The resident sexy nurse at Eastman Medical Center is Curley. Specific techniques might be borrowed from medical forms: the cinema verité of *M*A*S*H* or *St. Elsewhere* is used when Doogie has to stabilize a victim of a motorcycle accident. The day-to-day workings of the hospital are not shown, unless they happen to center on the physicians. Medical treatment is a completely limitless economic resource. Patients often create their own barriers to recovery (in one episode, for example, Curley's father refuses to accept a pacemaker because his wife suffered a prolonged, painful death).

But the show does not just add the elements of the two genres together. Rather, the creators of the program also *combined* certain elements, highlighting the concordance of the genres with each other.

First of all, several characters often serve two functions at once: one function from the teen genre and another function from the doctor genre. Central to the show, of course, is Doogie Howser, the boy genius doctor. In the world of the TV doctor, he is the sensitive, dedicated, and medically brilliant physician-hero. Doogie is the nineties Dr. Kildare. Despite his age, Doogie has an incredible bedside manner. In one episode, he makes a young chemotherapy patient accept his inevitable hair loss by reminding the patient of Michael Jordan. Doogie is also willing to make personal sacrifices (such as giving up sexy dates; living with his parents) to fulfill his oath. And he is a medical genius: he develops an "experimental" technique that saves the life of the young patient described above.

But on the other hand, he is a teenaged hero, making him a cross between Hawkeye Pierce and Ferris Bueller (although more sedate than either). He is smart, technically gifted (like Ferris, he has a home computer), hip, wears funky clothes (as the opening credits highlight with a long shot of his outfit compared with other doctors), and thinks a lot about sex. Doogie does many of the things that a modern teen hero would do: worry about his virginity, head to Florida for "Spring Break," go on road trips. Occasionally, he will explicitly combine his two roles, such as when he holds a phoney First Aid demonstration to get his friend Vinnie some lip action. Recent changes in the two genres (the smart, hip hero in the teen genre and the addition of humor and the physician's personal life in the doctor genre) have made the combination of characteristics less strange, and more economically viable, than it would have been in the past. Doogie is perhaps the ultimate Nintendo teen: he's an expert at techno-medicine.

Likewise, the wise-father role of the TV teen sitcom and the older doctor role of the doctor genre is combined in the character of Dr. Douglas Howser, Doogie's father. Both his parents are shown as being out of the teenage loop (and humor is pulled from this—such as when his parents visit Doogie and Vinnie when the two kids get an apartment on their own, and the parents are appalled by how teenagers live) but are nevertheless wise and caring. Equally important, though, is the older doctor role that Dr. Howser plays. Dr. Howser runs a Marcus Welby–type family practice. In several episodes, Doogie and his dad have conversations about medical dedication and doctor-patient relationships that are right out of Robert Young's style guide. When Doogie is deciding whether to specialize in trauma surgery, for example, he goes to his father for advice about that track ("Maybe the question is, how are you going to deal with patients like that on a daily basis?" His father asks). When he and his dad volunteer for medical work in Central America, it is his dad who gives Doogie perspective on dealing with medical pressures.

Another character who performs double generic duty is Dr. Benjamin Canfield, the chief of services. Although not *quite* as cartoonish as his dual counterparts, Dr. Canfield is the equivalent of both the bureaucratic hospital administrator and the bureaucratic school administrator. He is constantly obsessed about the public relations image of the hospital. For example, he forces Doogie to do a series of hip public service TV spots that compromise Doogie's ability to perform medicine and allows a television crew (the self-reflexive "*LA Med*, starring Rick O'Neill as Dr. Miles Chambers") to disrupt the hospital. Other episodes reveal his function as an obstacle to youthful fun—he is startled when the hip orderly, Ray, gives him a high five; he bores Doogie with stories about the struggles over the hospital cafeteria budget.

The way each episode ends also shows how one element can combine two functions. Right before the closing credits, Doogie sits down with his home computer and types in his computer diary his conclusions about the events in the episode. In the first episode, for example, Doogie writes, "Kissed my first girl. Lost my first patient. Life will never be the same again." Doogie's computer diary combines both the medical show epilogue (in this case, the discussion occurs over a computer keyboard instead of a coffee cup) and the direct address technique of the teen shows. Often the computer messages drive home the themes and the lessons of the episode, and are usually quite legitimating of medicine and/or the family.

In fact, the most significant combination of genre elements comes in the presentation of *Doogie*'s themes and morals. Often, an episode will feature two plots. For example, one of the plots may be pulled from the teen genre and the other from the medical one. In the end, the two plots converge, with one providing the solution to the other. Generally, the plot with the most potential for celebrating mainstream values, feel-good resolutions, and dominant institutions (the family or medicine) is the governing resolution.

For example, the much publicized fall premier episode of the 1991–1992 season, where Doogie has sex for the first time, illustrates this recombinant formula.[2] The teen plot features Doogie preparing, right after his eighteen birthday, to lose his virginity during a well-orchestrated evening with his girlfriend, Wanda, who is leaving for school the next day (the episode starts off with a fantasy sequence that is a parody of the clay scene in *Ghost*). Doogie is anxious about the event because he feels that people snicker at him for not being skillful in "the art of love." But getting in the way of his teen plan is the medical plot. Doogie collaborates with a doctor whose patient, Mrs. Sherman, has developed a brain condition, a "traumatic subdural hematoma." On a variation of the "patient as her own worst enemy" plot, Mrs. Sherman suffers psychological stress and is under the delusion that Doogie is her long-dead husband. The two plots come together when Doogie is forced to stand-up Wanda so that he can comfort Mrs. Sherman the night before her operation. Although Wanda is furious about this, Doogie goes to her house the next day while she is packing to leave. They make up, and then make love. When asked later if having sex made him feel like a man, Doogie concludes, "No, having sex made me feel more like a confused kid than before. What made me feel like a man was sitting up 'til two in the morning with the patient in the hospital." Doogie learns yet again to value medical responsibility over teen lust.

Doogie's Recombinant Ideology

In the beginning of this essay I stressed the relevance of genre for the television industry. But obviously genre is connected to cultural as well as economic issues. Ultimately, from a cultural perspective, *Doogie Howser, M.D.* is a show about reassurance. The combination of the doctor show with the teen show reassures the audience both about the nature of medicine and the nature of teens.

On the surface, the show is a reaffirmation of American medicine. Alley (1985, p. 79) argues that one of the main reasons doctor shows tend to "deify" medicine is that television does not want to present information that is too disturbing to audiences: TV producers perceive that audiences *want* to believe that individual physicians are heroes. *Doogie* serves this function by glorifying medicine even more than medical shows of recent memory. Unlike *Marcus Welby* or *Trapper John*, Doogie is only a one-half-hour program. Also, its recombinant nature further limits the time devoted to medicine because part of the half hour is usually taken up with the teen plot. Thus, the writers are not given much time to explain and resolve the medical plot. Because reaffirming American medicine is easier, quicker, and more of a television tradition than criticizing (especially fundamentally criticizing) medicine, *Doogie*'s medical plots are usually very reassuring about the nature and state of health care. Doogie, or Doogie's dad, cures the patient in the twenty-two minutes of air time, either through the application of innovative medical technology or through the compassion and understanding of a healer. There simply is not enough time to explain the complexities of limited resources or medical politics, even if the writers wanted to.

One irony of this is that the eighties and, presumably, the nineties are times when American mainstream medicine is in a state of transition, as is evident by increasing government involvement ("Diagnostic Related Groups" are defining medical billing procedures for Medicaid; the increased push for National Health Insurance), rising costs of medical care, and greater corporatization of health (in the form of for-profit health maintenance organizations, for example). Doogie helps to alleviate anxieties that these changes are bringing. Medicine, personified by Doogie, is still dependable.

At a deeper level, though, Doogie also reassures viewers about the nature of American teenagers. As argued above, the teen comedy took a sharp turn with the popularity of the teen sex comedy in the eighties. Although Dohert (1988) argues that teen movies, including the modern teen sex comedy, ultimately legitimizes dominant values, for many parents the possibility of dealing with a real-life Ferris Bueller is a scary proposition. The "us-versus-them" nature of this genre can be perceived as threatening or alienating to older viewers, especially. Likewise, the social context of these generic changes raises questions about the nature of teenagers for many adults. In 1989, reports of teenaged "wilding," of sexual assaults by teenagers upon the mentally disabled, of gang activity, of "skinheads," led magazines such as *Time* to speculate about "Our Violent Kids" (Toufexis, 1989). Many in the country wondered if teenagers are changing for the worse, and if media are encouraging this change.

Why did producers create a show that is so reassuring to its audience? Television producers, of course, want to plug into the popular. They want to create successful programs by stealing successful ideas from elsewhere. The teen sex comedy appeals to youth, a very desirable market for television, and one that ABC is increasingly targeting (Miller, 1991, p. 26). But to adapt the new teen sex comedy for television, given the increasing coarseness of this form and the social tensions about wild teens, is risky. It is risky in that the genre will not have a wide enough appeal for longevity, and it is risky in that it might anger adult viewers. And as Gitlin argues, the TV industry tends to avoid the risky: "Safety first is the network rule" (Gitlin, 1985, p. 63). Network television has to placate mass audiences, advertisers, and affiliates. The recombinant strategy, however, helped to fulfill the safety requirement of television and the reassurance requirement of many of the viewers; the *combination* of the teen sex comedy *with* a more adult-oriented genre helped to smooth out the former's rough edges. *Doogie Hoswer, M.D.* premiered in September 1989, before any of the other teen adaptations of the new teen type: *Beverly Hills 90210, Ferris Bueller,* and *Parker Lewis Can't Lose* premiered a year later. Doogie, then, led the way for television.

Combining the teen genre with the doctor genre means that you *really* don't have a Ferris Bueller in your living room: you have a hip, funny (but noble) doctor visiting you. The doctor genre takes the edge off the teen genre. It assures adults, including

parents, that kids are okay. Here's a teen, smart and hip, who is a dedicated physician. Here's a kid that you would want your daughter to date.[3] Teens still like him, but first and foremost he's a doctor. Even if he does occasionally screw up, his wise doctor-father, in the nuclear family context, can set him straight.

Brian Rose (1985, p. 8) argues that when television genres mutate, it is often the result of industry imperatives (such as attracting a new market) rather than the result of cultural tensions. Taking this one step farther, the TV industry often tries to co-opt cultural tensions for its imperatives. In the case of *Doogie Howser, M.D.,* two genres were combined to help one genre fit in with the mainstream of television. This example thus illustrates how TV can merge two or more genres in a way that transforms them and makes their message acceptable to the industrialized needs of television. A recombinant can help make separate genres acceptable for mass audiences and safe for the television industry.

Notes

1. It is also interesting to note, as Goostree does, that the late 1960s' show *The Monkees* had many of these characteristics. In *The Monkees,* the teen characters were smarter and hipper than the adults, and there was a strong use of direct address and intertextuality. Perhaps this TV show was simply 15 to 20 years too early for the formula to be widely copied.

2. Although not receiving as much attention as the Dan Quayle–*Murphy Brown* controversy, the virginity episode of *Doogie Howser* was likewise criticized by a politician, in this case Ross Perot. In September 1991, Perot said that he felt that the episode would encourage teenagers to have premarital sex. Perot's opinion of the episode really didn't receive much press until after Dan Quayle's statement hit the stands.

3. Likewise, as Brooks and Marsh (301) point out, when we compare the main characters of the teen TV shows *Ferris Bueller* and *Parker Lewis Can't Lose,* we note that Ferris was much meaner than

Parker, which may help explain why the latter survived longer than the former. Rose (4) argues that because we consume TV in our home, we in essence are inviting TV characters to pay us a visit. Intense characters, unlikable characters, or those too smart-assed are not likely to be invited back very often.

References

Alley, R. S. (1985). Medical melodrama. In B. G. Rose (Ed.), *TV genres: A handbook and reference guide* (pp. 73–89). Westport, CT: Greenwood.

Beck, M. (1992, March 7–13). Doogie's diagnosis. *TV Guide*, p. 3.

Brooks, T., & Marsh E. (1992). *The complete dictionary to prime time network TV shows 1946–present.* New York: Ballantine.

Doherty, T. (1988). *Teenagers and teenpics: The juvenilization of American movies in the 1950s.* Boston: Unwin Hyman.

Feuer, J. (1987). Genre study and television. In R. C. Allen (Ed.), *Channels of discourse* (pp. 113–133). Chapel Hill: University of North Carolina Press.

Gitlin, T. (1985). *Inside prime time.* New York: Pantheon.

Goostree, L. (1988). The Monkees and the deconstruction of television realism. *Journal of Popular Film and Television, 16*(2), 50–58.

Guider, E. (1992, 13 January). What's up, doc? Syndicated Doogie. *Variety*, p. 36.

Haithman, D. (1989, 23 November). Doogie: Crossing the generations. *Los Angeles Times*, n.p.

Marin, R. (1989, September 19). Terminal cases of TV malpractice. *Washington (D.C.) Times*, n.p.

Miller, S. (1991, 30 September). Mid-week weak at season's start. *Variety*, p. 30).

Miller, S. (1991, 4 November). Finding fountain of youth not as easy as ABC. *Variety*, p. 26.

Rose, B. G. (1985). Introduction. In B. Rose (Ed.), *TV genres: A handbook and reference guide* (pp. 3–10). Westport, CT: Greenwood.

Toufexis, A. (1989, June 12). Our violent kids, *Time*, pp. 52–58.

Turow, J. (1989). *Playing doctor: Television, storytelling, and medical power.* New York: Oxford University Press.

Vande Berg, L. R. E. (1991). Dramedy: Moonlight as an emergent generic hybrid. In L. R. Vande Berg & L. A. Wenner (Eds.), *Television criticism: Approaches and applications* (pp. 87–111). New York: Longman.

Rhetorical Criticism

CHAPTER 7

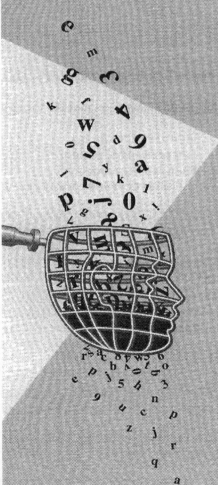

W hile introducing her book *Prime-Time Feminism: Television, Media Culture, and the Women's Movement Since 1970* (1996), Bonnie Dow felt it important to indicate why a rhetorician ought to be examining televisual discourse. In part, she wrote:

> To attempt to understand past and present reactions to feminist movements without attending to television's frequent attempts to offer visions of the "new women" produced by women's liberation is to overlook the medium's considerable power in making sense of social change. Moreover, it is also to dismiss the pleasure that those representations have brought to many viewers, particularly those who, like me, searched for progressive portrayals of women among prime-time schedules filled with passive housewives, sultry sex objects, and helpless female victims. (p. xix)

If the study of rhetoric is centered on important questions intellectuals ask about the power of public discourse—the effects, ethics, and techniques of discursive power—then of course televisual discourse is of great concern to rhetoricians. Or, to reverse that thought, rhetorical approaches to television criticism lead us to think about the affective powers of televisual works. Television programs, as Dow and other rhetoricians show us, have the power to influence our conceptions of ourselves and others, our social-political relationships, and the world around us. We've known since the 1940s (Herzog, 1944), for example, that soap operas have taught people how they are expected to act in life, and indeed, what life itself is like. Halloran (1978) analyzed the televised texts of the House Judiciary Committee's debates over articles of impeachment against President Richard Nixon in order to understand how it is that such public proceedings on television create in our heads visions of what it means to be an American citizen. Three years later, Robert Schrag, Richard Hudson, and Lawrance Bernaboe (1981) examined the "new humane collectivity," that is, the caring circles of friends and associates that appeared as surrogate families in television sitcoms of the 1980s. Jane Connelly Loeb's (1990) analysis of the prime time serial drama *thirtysomething* concluded that it endorsed and propagated ideological conservatism.

As rhetorical critics have moved from the study of political speechmaking or pamphleteering into the world of electronically reproduced images, they not only have taught us how to explore the persuasive appeals of those images, but they also have been affected themselves by that encounter: their understanding of persuasive processes has been broadened as they have struggled to explore the text-based influences of television on people's beliefs, attitudes, values, behaviors, and conceptions of the world. Hence, in this chapter, we will examine some of the assumptions underlying rhetorical criticism; offer a brief introduction to a rhetorical vocabulary; review different types of rhetorical studies of prime-time programming, news, politics, and advertising; and then consider how rhetoricians tend to write up their analyses before concluding.

Some Assumptions Underlying Rhetorical Criticism

We cannot provide a complete introduction to rhetorical criticism (for that, you might try Sillars & Gronbeck, 2001), but we can explore some assumptions underlying it and offer enough vocabulary to get you started:

1. *Rhetorical criticism is always, to one degree or another, focused on persuasive processes.* The idea of rhetoric was invented in the fourth or fifth century B.C.E. to provide a way to talk conceptually and evaluatively about persuasive speeches (Schiappa, 1990). Thus, rhetoric should not be equated with persuasion. *Persuasion*—to be persuaded—is a state of mind. *Rhetoric* is the study of how persuasion occurs: how listeners, readers, and viewers have their minds changed, why techniques work (or not), in what sorts of social, economic, and political climates people are susceptible to particular kinds of appeals, what aspects of verbal and many nonverbal coding systems affect people's minds and behaviors, and the ethics of all of these things.

2. *Consequently, rhetorical criticism is always, to one degree or another, concerned with discursive power.* The quintessential mission of rhetorical study is to come to grips with what signs do to those who consume them and how that doing gets done. The search for "what" is the exploration of the vehicles of rhetorical effect, while the search for "how" is the identification of what aspects of signs and their structures have the potential to change audiences' ideas, actions, or perceptions of the world.

For example, Randall Bytwerk (2000) has been working, among other projects, on the Nazi Nuremberg rally of 1927. To get at the "what" of that event, he has documented multiple tools used to affect Germans' beliefs about and attitudes toward Nazis: speeches, songs, parades, regional costumes and banners, torch-lit grounds, and uniforms. Multiple communication channels were employed to weld the some 223,000 people attending the two-day rally into a coherent group of Nazi supporters. But how did all of these channels work? The "how" requires an examination of (1) the reconstruction of German history and the identification of Nazi ideology in the speeches; (2) the coming together into a single display of regional costumes and banners (making a oneness out of the many, *e pluribus unam*); (3) the traditional songs that recalled the past associated with the new anthem (*Deutschland über alles*) that pointed toward the future; (4) the sheer enormity of 30,000 men in uniform marching past spectators for one and a half hours; and (5) the torch-lit ring that cut off the outside world at night so that the only perceivable reality was the Nazi space inside the circle. Putting together the "what" and "how" of rhetorical discourse provides, ultimately, a "why": an interactive explanation of "why did the discourses have the power that they did?"

3. *Rhetorical criticism therefore focuses on multiple dimensions or aspects of discursive acts, either individually or collectively.* Rhetorical critics must choose how to conceive of communication acts within any particular study. And they have plenty of choices when looking at literary (written-verbal), acoustic (spoken-verbal

and other sounds), and visual communication media. Sillars and Gronbeck (2001, p. 29) offer an initial list of nine dimensions of works explored by rhetorical critics:

Themes—statements that indicate a point of view [or perspective]

Attributions—characterizations of persons, places, or things

Subject matter—characterization of what subject is being discussed or of its contrast with the same or similar sources at another time and place

Probable cause—statements that were likely caused by another phenomenon, statements that are likely to cause another phenomenon

Stylistic features—distinctive syntax, word [image or sound effect] choice, figures of speech, one style compared to another

Values, attitudes, beliefs—speaker [writer-producer-videographer] or cultural pattern

Argumentative features—argument forms, evidence

Intentions, psychological states—statements that reflect a communicator's inner state or intention

Political relations—statements that reveal political or power relations[1]

As this list suggests, rhetorical critics look for the engines of discursive power in various dimensions of written, spoken, and visual codes. It is, of course, impossible to examine every conceivable source of power in any particular message as it operates in a specific context. Rhetorical critics generally, as we saw Raymond Williams doing in the previous chapter, select specific signs from among the whole array available to focus on. The point is that your attention when approaching works as complex as television programs should be tied to particular dimensions or aspects of those works when seeking to understand the power of televisual discourses.

A Traditional Rhetorical Vocabulary

Rhetorical critics focus much of their work on public discourse in the service of power. The texts they make out of works, including television programs, public service announcements, ads, and other telecast materials, are woven so as to be amenable to the analysis of their persuasive techniques, whether one is examining form or content, verbal or nonverbal communication systems. The fundamental vocabulary for executing such studies is ancient, marked often by the Greek and Latin terms from which it sprang. The terms were selected and defined from the viewpoint of the message maker—the speechmaker in the classical period, the writer/producer, filmmaker, broadcaster or videographer in later times. Some of that basic vocabulary is recorded in Table 7.1. Except for the section of effects, which reflects today's conceptions of rhetorical power, all of these concepts have endured for two millennia.

TABLE 7.1 A Basic Rhetorical Vocabulary

I. The arts of making rhetorical messages (the *officia*)	*Inventio:* finding or assembling the material (content) of a message *Dispositio:* arranging the materials into parts or segments of the whole *Elocutio:* making sign and structural choices to create a feeling or style *Memoria:* making the message easy to remember *Pronunciatio, actio:* delivering the message to others using channels
II. Genres of speeches (expand when discussing other kinds of messages)	Legal: speeches about past actions delivered in courts Legislative: speeches about the future delivered in assemblies Epideictic (ceremonial): speeches about present accomplishments or failures
III. Kinds of proof (leading audiences to *pistis*, or a state of conviction)	*Logos:* rational proofs drawn from audiences' beliefs (from *doxa*) *Pathos:* proofs drawn from feeling states created in audiences *Ethos:* an audience's perception of the speaker's sense, goodwill, and morals
IV. Rhetorical effects	Reinforcement or change of beliefs, attitudes, and values Reinforcement or change of personal or public behaviors Reinforcement or change of self-identity or sense of personal agency Reinforcement or change of group identity or sense of group agency Reinforcement or change of orientation toward the world (*Weltanschauung*)

This list is only a start, for the vocabulary was honed carefully, including words for dozens of lines of argument (called enthymemes and examples); some 200-plus different stylistic manipulations of language (schemes were manipulations of syntax, and tropes, of signifieds attached to signs); the emotional significance of different kinds of gestures and physical stances; and so on. The vocabulary thus provides tools for manufacturing, and analyzing, presumably powerful content, forms, and modes of presentation. In our time, the terms have been supplemented by the kinds of supporting materials (e.g., testimony, statistics, explanations) or the language needed to describe not only verbal language but also visual languages (e.g., foreground-background, color, density, symmetry), yet the basic purpose is the same: to provide you with tools to analyze the engines of discursive or rhetorical power in messages. We will use some of that vocabulary in the rest of this chapter, and you'll certainly find it in the critical studies of television executed by rhetoricians.

Some Types of Rhetorical Analyses of Television

Rhetorical critics have used multiple methods based on the concepts listed above to analyze television.[2] Rather than discuss types of rhetorical analyses methodologically, we will organize this section of the chapter by kind of television programming, because each kind of televisual experience reviewed here—prime-time programming, news, political coverage, and advertising—presents unique challenges to the TV critic. Each presumably creates its own sorts of rhetorical effects.

Prime-Time Programming

One of the earliest studies of prime-time programs done rhetorically was Gronbeck's (1984) study of the 1970s program *Family*. The program centered on the lives of a five-person family with two teenagers and an adopted younger child, all struggling to lead their own lives even while holding the nuclear family together. Envisioned by film director Mike Nichols, the program was an aesthetic and, for a while, commercial success. Its heart was Sada Thompson's rendition of mother; the program demonstrated that all wisdom for living the good life flowed from a solid family, with a matriarch as the font of most of that wisdom. In Gronbeck's analysis, this stress on motherly intuition and on family as sources of both wisdom and life's best pleasures made the program ideologically resistant to what was happening on the rest of television in the mid-1970s, where most adult women (as in the hit *One Day at a Time*) were struggling with job and family and most solutions to people's programs came from doctors, lawyers, and even a coroner (*Quincy, M.E.*). Rhetorically, the program reinforced traditional matriarchal ideology even as the women's movement was moving into high gear.

This study of *Family* is based on the close analysis of dialogue in several scenes of a single episode; it focuses on how problems are introduced and the ways in which solutions to those programs are articulated, almost always by the mother. The visual and acoustic (especially musical) codes are discussed only to the degree that they echo or reinforce the moods created verbally. Rhetoricians often are more comfortable analyzing verbal rather than visual or acoustic languages. That shows through here.

A different approach to prime-time programming is seen in Gray's study of *The Cosby Show* in his 1994 book, *Watching Race: Television and the Struggle for "Blackness."* Gray is a critical sociologist rather than a practicing rhetorical critic, yet his approach to *discursivity*—to how visions and ideas are articulated in verbal and visual codes—has a strong rhetorical feel to it. He positions the show against the history of TV's portrayal of African Americans, from *Amos 'n' Andy* in the 1950s to the "authentic" experiences of poor blacks in the 1970s shows, *Good Times, Sanford and Son,* and *What's Happening!!* and then in the shows with upwardly mobile African Americans, including *The Jeffersons, Benson, Webster, Diff'rent Strokes,* and *Gimme a Break* in the early 1980s.

Gray depicts *The Cosby Show* as having "reconfigured the aesthetic and industrial spaces within which modern television representations of blacks are constructed" (p. 79). In a fascinating analysis of race and class, Gray argues that with the Huxtables' upper-middle-class status, Americans' conception of race gets reworked: "Discursively, the show appropriated the genre of situation comedy and used it to offer a more complex representation of African American life than had been seen previously" (p. 81), even presenting "a black universe as the norm, feeling no need to announce the imposition of African American perspectives" (p. 82). To be sure, race was marked in *The Cosby Show,* but racism, writes Gray, was made to seem foolish. These interpretative characterizations are traced back to Bill Cosby's viewpoints: he regularly stated the mission of this show in press interviews. Bill Cosby thus was a rhetor, a persuader, at work inside television's prime-time space.

As these examples illustrate, whether one is doing a scene-by-scene textual analysis or a study of the rhetorical purposes of a show and its creators, rhetorical studies of prime-time shows help us understand the force of programs in affecting the beliefs, attitudes, values, orientations, and even the self- and group identities of their viewers. That is the force of the latest rhetorical work on prime-time programs (e.g., Bellon, 1999; Hanczor, 1997; Thompson, 1997, esp. chap. 7).

News

Newscasts and other news department programs such as *60 Minutes* have been subjected to a variety of rhetorical studies. Consider the following examples: Condit and Selzer (1985) compared press coverage of a murder trial with a trial transcript to see the effects of press storytelling techniques. Corcoran (1986) found that the news coverage of Russia's shooting down of flight KAL 007 heightened the disaster and rationalized U.S. responses. Barkin and Gurevitch (1987) explored the melodramas of the unemployed carried by television, while Campbell (1987) did the same for stories on *60 Minutes,* working especially on the personae of the journalists offering tales of struggle. Farrell (1989) dissected the social dramas offered in TV coverage of the 1984 Olympics, and a whole issue of *Critical Studies of Media Communication* (March 1990) was devoted to similar analyses of the portrayal of science and technology on television.

Useful to students of news and public affairs telecasting are essays and book chapters that provide tools for thinking about rhetorical processes and the news. Sharon Lynn Sperry's (1976) classic "Television News as Narrative" can be supplemented with Chapter 8 on narrative in this book or with Black's (1992) essay and then employed to study ways in which news stories—narratives—construct particular understandings of newsworthy people, their actions, and the places within which significant human actions occur. Such stories take on the status of public social drama when analyzed through the lenses of Kenneth Burke (see Sillars & Gronbeck's discussion of Burkean approaches to cultural narrative, 2001, esp. pp. 229–233; see also Brummett, 1984, 1985). Mumby and Spitzack's (1983) critical essay on the metaphors that dominate political news stories—politics as game, as war, and as drama—takes you into some of the principal linguistic resources of news reporting. The utility of their understanding of metaphors shows through in a critical study of reporting of the last two weeks of the 2000 presidential campaign (Alsina, Davies, & Gronbeck, 2001).

The most ambitious studies are book length rhetorical analyses, often of specialized news programming, which is easier to record than entire news broadcasts across the networks. Campbell's (1987) article was expanded into a book, *60 Minutes and the News: A Mythology of Middle America* (1991), in which he took the themes from the article (which he reviewed in his chapter on news as narrative and reporters as characters in news stories) and developed them much more fully in additional chapters on *60 Minutes*'s view of social-political mysteries, on the program's work as therapy or as tool of arbitration, and on its reinforcement of the myth of individualism in America. He then utilized these chapters to deftly explore the effects of the program on individual, social, political, and economic dimensions of life.

A more complicated book doing much the same sort of analysis of television documentaries, especially of the 1950s and 1960s, is Michael Curtin's *Redeeming the Wasteland: Television Documentary and Cold War Politics* (1995). Curtin weaves together the story of Cold War relations with the Soviet Union, the rise of network documentary units well trained in telling dramatic stories, a consuming public interested in television's information-gathering and advice-giving capabilities, a government willing to use private corporations' help in fighting communism, and the global reach of the whole enterprise. Along the way, he provides two-to-three page analyses of TV documentaries that support his critical arguments.

One last study that should be mentioned is Postman's (1985) book on televised political news. Postman finds television totally distortive of public information because of its chattiness and attempts at amusement, its short stories, and its greater reliance on pictures than words. He is one of many rhetoricians concerned that visual media such as TV will drive people away from print media such as newspapers.

Political Coverage

While many more rhetorical studies of televised politics have been offered to the media community, few of them have focused on what television does to and for political processes. To most rhetoricians, television seems to be simply a conduit with pictures—a good way to connect politicians and audiences but not much else. One work that helped enormously to move the field forward was Kathleen Hall Jamieson's (1988) *Eloquence in an Electronic Age*. Her primary argument was simple but important: the up-close-and-personal aspects of how television is shot and edited creates a kind of intimacy in a politician's relationship with an audience, and so simple, sincere stories, offered in what she called a feminine style, work well in televised politics. Jamieson argued that the master of such techniques was then President Ronald Reagan.[2] Her subsequent study, *Dirty Politics* (1992), went further in two ways: first, she carefully took apart political ads and second, she used those analyses to both test truth claims and ground larger arguments about democracy in trouble in an era of distorting verbal and visual political discourse.

Robert Tiemens (1978) and Tiemens, Susan Hellweg, Phillip Kipper, and Steven L. Phillips (1985) have gone further yet in examining the visuality of TV politics. Tiemens' series of studies of how presidential debates and other political events are shot, examined the composition of shots, camera angles, and amount of time politicians are shown to audiences. In the 1985 study which integrated visual and verbal analysis, he argued that such matters yield evidence of how visual presentations affect politicians' credibility and substantive effectiveness. Whereas Tiemens essentially believes that televised politics has given the citizenry more and better access to politicians, Hart (1999) finds that it gives audiences a false sense of emotional identification with politicians and political processes generally, seducing rather than instructing the people in political life.

Advertising

Advertising is nothing more than economically or politically driven persuasion, and hence it is preeminently rhetorical. Although political (especially negative) advertisements have been analyzed to the point that they represent a cottage industry in rhetorical studies (for reviews of studies, see Cartee-Johnson & Copeland, 1991; Gronbeck, 1994), few rhetorical studies have looked at product advertisements. One exception is Sarah Stein's analysis of the "1984" Macintosh ad, which is included at the end of this chapter as an example essay. One interesting piece is Meister's (1997) examination of Jeep Cherokee ads of the late 1990s as places where nature and environmental concerns generally are reconciled with the imagery of the Cherokee's technology, allowing it to provide not environmental destruction but protection and comfort. More sophisticated is Lester's (1997) reading of a direct mail package of print and video materials on the Nissan Pathfinder. She reads the material semiotically at the first level (where a rhinoceros stands in for the SUV), rhetorically (from the advertiser's motivational viewpoint) at a second level, and then culturally (ideologically) at a third level, where the SUV is to be understood as a tool of dominance for "us" over wildness and "the other."

Still more ambitious is Jean Kilbourne's (1999) *Can't Buy My Love*, a book-length treatment of her popular slide show and video presentations of the impact of product advertising on younger and older women. The book argues, chapter by chapter, that women and girls are being sold not just products but self-images, ways of seeing the environments within which they live, methods for building relationships, addictive mind-sets, and even attitudes toward violence and rebellion. She relies on examples of both visual and verbal texts, primarily print and TV ads, for her evidence.

Of further help for those wanting guidance into the rhetorical world of advertising is an essay by Foss (1994) on visual imagery and a book-length treatment of visual advertising by Messaris (1997).

Overall, as one might expect given that the focus of rhetorical studies is the power of public discourse, rhetorical critics have done most of their work on the flow of public information (in news and public affairs programming) and politics. Much more remains to be done in our time, with the worlds of electronic and digital communication technologies. This is especially true when it comes to television: studies are forcing the development of a whole new subfield of rhetorical studies, called *visual rhetoric*. The excitement that Bonnie Dow described in the introduction to her book on prime-time feminism was born of the act of taking the ancient art of verbal, public persuasion and adapting it to a whole new medium of public information, advice, identity, and policy. Analyzing examples of visual persuasion in ways discussed in this chapter will help the field of rhetoric, too often thought about merely as oral or written composition, redefine its missions in the electronic age.

Writing Rhetorical Criticism

Rhetorical studies provide a unique route into the analysis of televisual discourses even as the study of such discourses redefines that ancient art.

The Example Essays

We provide two example essays in this chapter. The first is Bonnie Dow's "*Murphy Brown:* Postfeminism Personified," a chapter in her 1996 book, *Prime-Time Feminism.*[3] This study demonstrates the usefulness of placing a rhetorical analysis of a TV program in its historical context. Dow spent earlier book chapters showing the entrance of women's issues and female culture into television in such shows as *The Mary Tyler Moore Show, One Day at a Time,* and *Designing Women.* In this, the fourth chapter, she explores the historical shift from feminist to postfeminist thought, presumably the result of altered social, economic, and political conditions for American women. Murphy's pregnancy provides the clearest issue for examining the struggle between feminist and postfeminist themes. Dow thus writes this chapter with an eye to historical context, ideological battles within society over the women's movement, and dialogical and characterological markers of the rhetorical warfare occurring in that show.

The second essay is Sarah Stein's 2002 analysis of the classic "1984" MacIntosh ad, which aired only once, during the halftime of the 1984 Super Bowl, and launched Apple as the home desktop computer. In this rhetorical analysis, Stein uses Maurice Charland's conception of constitutive rhetoric to examine the historical and cultural context within which the ad was aired and the ways in which the sexes' mythic and culturally coded narrative allusions combined to defuse the threat of mechanistic technology and reaffirm a cultural belief in the ultimate goodness of the technological progress.

Notes

1. Sillars and Gronbeck (2001) adapted this list from Krippendorff (1980).

2. These methods have included fantasy theme analysis (e.g., Bormann, 1982; Foss & Littlejohn, 1986; Nimmo & Combs, 1982; Schrag, 1981), Burkean Pentadic analysis (e.g., Blankenship, Fine & Davis, 1983; Ling, 1970), Burkean representative anecdote analysis (Brummett, 1984, 1985), mythic analysis (e.g., Blair, 1982; Gronbeck, 1991), narrative analysis (e.g., Dobkin, 1992; Schrag, 1991; Schwichtenberg, 1987), ideological analysis (e.g., Dow, 1992; Japp, 1991; Loeb, 1990; Vande Berg, 1993; Wander, 1976), institutional analysis (Tucker & Shah, 1998), feminist analysis (e.g., Dow, 1995; Rabinowitz, 1989; Projansky & Vande Berg, 2000), audience ethnographic analysis (e.g., Rockler, 1999), genre analysis (e.g., Timberg, 1987), psychoanalytic criticism (e.g., Torres, 1989), social values analysis (e.g., McGuckin, 1968; Ryan, 1976; Williams, 1991), and aesthetic criticism (Feur, 1984). For textbooks in rhetorical criticism that reflect these and other approaches, see Sillars and Gronbeck (2001) and Foss (1998).

3. We suggest taking the time to contrast this example with Dow's original article on *Murphy Brown* (1992) to see her fuller development of a historical overview of developing feminist themes on 1970s and 1980s television.

Further Readings

Hartley, J. (1992). *The politics of pictures: The creation of the public in the age of popular media.* New York: Routledge. This study show how citizens are represented on television screens and the printed pages of news organs, with examples drawn from books, manuals for photography, television, print ads, newspaper pictures, and other media.

Sillars, M. O., & Gronbeck, B. E. (2001). *Communication criticism: Rhetoric, social codes, cultural studies.* Prospect Heights, IL: Waveland Press. This book on rhetorical criticism and its methods is written broadly enough to be adapted to the analysis of both television and film discourses.

Webnotes

Ad Watch Toolkit. **http://www.pbs.org/pov/ad/ads/toolkit_list.html**

This site provides 10 categories for the analysis of political ads: candidate myths, background, props, emotions, appeals, music, editing, clothing, depicted actions, and code words. The categories are useful for rhetorical analysis of televisual materials.

http://www.lcc.gatech.edu/gallery/rhetoric

One of the best web sites devoted to rhetorical studies, this site includes an overview essay on rhetoric, brief background essays on figures in the history of rhetoric, issues in contemporary rhetorical theory, and terms, as well as links to other web sites on rhetoric.

Learning Activities

1. Examine an episode of *Friends*. In groups of four, subdivided into pairs, list the basic values underlying the conversation and action of the male and the female characters. (Chapter 9 of Sillars & Gronbeck, 2001, is devoted to value analysis. Or go to **http://www.geocities.com/Heartland/Acres/9890/SelfTest.html**, which is a self-test used to investigate male and female value compatibility; it should help you compare and contrast the lifestyles or value orientations of the *Friends* characters.) After you've completed the value analysis and gender comparisons, discuss the sorts of role models for teens and twentysomethings being presented on this program.

References

Alsina, C., Davies, P. J., & Gronbeck, B. E. (2001). Preference poll stories in the last two weeks of campaign 2000. *American Behavioral Scientist, 44,* 2288–2305.

Barkin, S. M., & Gurevitch, M. (1987). Out of work and on the air: Television news of unemployment. *Critical Studies of Media Communication, 4,* 1–20.

Bellon, J. (1999). The strange discourse of *The X-Files:* What it is, what it does, and what is at stake. *Critical Studies in Media Communication, 16,* 136–154.

Black, E. (1992). Dramatic form in rhetorical transactions. In E. Black, *Rhetorical questions: Studies of public discourse* (pp. 147–170). Chicago: University of Chicago Press.

Blair, K. (1982). The garden and the machine: The *why* of *Star Trek.* In H. Newcomb (Ed.), *Television: The critical view* (3rd ed., pp. 181–197). New York: Oxford University Press.

Blankenship, J., Fine, M. G., & Davis, L. K. (1983). The 1980 Republican primary debates: The transformation of actor to scene. *Quarterly Journal of Speech, 69,* 25–36.

Bormann, E. (1982). A fantasy theme analysis of the television coverage of the hostage release and Reagan inaugural. *Quarterly Journal of Speech, 68,* 133–145.

Brummett, B. (1984). Burke's representative anecdote as a method in media criticism. *Critical Studies in Mass Communication, 1,* 161–176.

Brummett, B. (1985). Electronic literature as equipment for living. Haunted house films. *Critical Studies in Mass Communication, 2,* 247–261.

Bytwerk, R. (2000). Nazi propaganda archive [of Calvin College]. Available online: http://www.calvin.edu/academic/cas/gpa/rpt27c.htm/.

Campbell, R. (1987). Securing the middle ground: Reporter formulas in *60 Minutes. Critical Studies in Media Communication, 4,* 325–350.

Campbell, R. (1991). *60 Minutes and the news: A mythology of middle America.* Urbana: University of Illinois Press.

Cartee-Johnson, K. S., & Copeland, G. A. (1991). *Negative political advertising: Coming of age.* Hillsdale, NJ: Erlbaum.

Condit, M. C., & Selzer, J. A. (1985). The rhetoric of objectivity in the newspaper coverage of a murder trial. *Critical Studies in Media Communication, 2,* 197–216.

Corcoran, F. (1986). KAL 007 and the evil empire: Mediated disaster and forms of rationalization. *Critical Studies in Media Communication, 3,* 297–316.

Critical Studies in Media Communication (1990, March), Volume 7.

Curtin, M. (1995). *Redeeming the wasteland: Television documentary and cold war politics.* New Brunswick, NJ: Rutgers University Press.

Dow, B. J. (1992). Femininity and feminism in *Murphy Brown. Southern Communication Journal, 57,* 143–155.

Dow, B. J. (1996). *Prime-time feminism: Television, media culture, and the women's movement since 1970.* Philadelphia: University of Pennsylvania Press.

Dyson, M. (1989, Sept.). Bill Cosby and the politics of race. *Z Magazine,* 26–30.

Feuer, J. (1987). The MTM style. In H. Newcomb (Ed.), *Television: The critical view* (4th ed., pp. 52-84). New York: Oxford University Press.

Farrell, T. B. (1989). Media rhetoric as social drama: The winter Olympics of 1984. *Critical Studies in Media Communication, 6,* 158–182.

Foss, S. K. (1994). A rhetorical schema for the evaluation of visual imagery. *Communication Studies, 45,* 213–224.

Foss, K. A., & Littlejohn, S. W. (1986). *The Day After:* Rhetorical vision in an ironic frame. *Critical Studies in Mass Communication, 3,* 317–336.

Foss, S. K. (1998). *Rhetorical criticism: Exploration & practice* (2nd ed.). Prospect Heights, IL: Waveland Press.

Gray, H. (1994). *Watching race: Television and the struggle for "blackness."* Minneapolis: University of Minnesota Press.

Gronbeck, B. E. (1984). Audience engagement with *Family.* In M. J. Medhurst & T. W. Benson (Eds.), *Rhetorical dimensions in media: A critical casebook* (pp. 4–32). Dubuque, IA: Kendall/Hunt.

Gronbeck, B. E. (1990). Electric rhetoric: The changing forms of American political discourse. In *Vichiana* (pp. 141–161), Naples: Loffredo Editore.

Gronbeck, B.E., (1991). Mythic portraiture in the 1988 Iowa presidential caucus bio-ads, In L. Vande Berg & L.A. Wenner (eds.), *Television criticism: Approaches and applications* (pp. 254–273). White Plains, NY: Longman.

Gronbeck, B. E. (1994). Negative political ads and American self images. In A. H. Miller & B. E. Gronbeck (Eds.), *Presidential campaigns and American self images* (pp. 60–81). Boulder, CO: Westview Press.

Halloran, M. (1978). Doing public business in public. In K. K. Campbell & K. H. Jamieson (Eds.), *Form and genre: Shaping rhetorical action* (pp. 118–138). Washington, DC: National Communication Association.

Hanczor, R. S. (1997). Articulation theory and public controversy: Taking sides over *NYPD Blue. Critical Studies in Media Communication, 14,* 1–30.

Hart, R. P. (1999). *Seducing America: How television charms the modern voter* (rev. ed.). New York: St. Martin's Press.

Herzog, H. (1944). What do we really know about daytime serial listeners? In P. F. Lazarsfeld & F. N. Stanton (Eds.), *Radio research, 1942–1943*. New York: Duell, Sloan and Pearce.

Jamieson, K. H. (1988). *Eloquence in an electronic age*. New York: Oxford University Press.

Jamieson, K. H. (1992). *Dirty politics: Deception, distraction, and democracy*. New York: Oxford University Press.

Japp, P. (1991). Gender and work in the 1980s: Television's working women as displaced persons. *Women's Studies in Communication, 14*, 49–74.

Kilbourne, J. (1999). Can't buy my love: *How advertising changes the way we think and feel*. New York: Touchstone.

Krippendorff, K. (1980). *Content analysis: An introduction to its methodology*. Thousand Oaks, CA: Sage.

Lester, E. P. (1997). Finding the path to signification: Undressing a Nissan Pathfinder direct mail package. In K. T. Frith (Ed.), *Undressing the ad: Reading culture in advertising* (pp. 19–34). New York: Peter Lang.

Ling, D. (1970). A pentadic analysis of Senator Edward Kennedy's "Address to the people of Massachusetts, July 25, 1969." *Central States Speech Journal, 21*, 81–86.

Loeb, J. C. (1990). Rhetorical and ideological conservatism in *thirtysomething*. *Critical Studies in Media Communication, 7*, 249–260.

McGucken, H.E., Jr. (1968). A value analysis of Richard Nixon's 1952 campaign fund speech. *Southern Speech Journal, 33*, 259–269.

Meister, M. (1997). "Sustainable development" in visual imagery: Rhetorical function in the Jeep Cherokee. *Communication Quarterly, 45*, 223–234.

Messaris, P. (1997). *Visual persuasion: The role of images in advertising*. Thousand Oaks, CA: Sage.

Mumby, D. K., & Spitzack, C. (1983). Ideology and television news: A metaphoric analysis of political stories. *Communication Studies, 34*, 162–171.

Nimmo, D. & Combs, J.E. (1982). Fantasies and melodramas in network news: The case of Three Mile Island. *Western Journal of Communication, 46*, 35–55.

Postman, N. (1985). *Amusing ourselves to death: Public discourse in the age of show business*. New York: Penguin.

Projansky, S., & Vande Berg, L. R. (2000). Sabrina, the teenage . . . ? Girls, witches, mortals, and the limitations of prime-time feminism. In E. R. Helford (Ed.), *Fantasy girls: Gender in the new universe of science fiction and fantasy television* (pp. 13–40). Lanham, MD: Rowman & Littlefield.

Rabinowitz, L. (1989). Sitcoms and single moms: Representations of feminism on American TV. *Cinema Journal, 29*(1), 3–19.

Rockler, N.R. (1999). From magic bullets to shooting blanks: Reality, criticism, and *Beverly Hills 90210. Western Journal of Communication, 63,* 72–94.

Ryan, K. (1976). Television as a moral educator. In R. Adler & D. Cater (Eds.), *Television as a cultural force* (pp. 111–128). New York, Praeger.

Schiappa, E. (1990). Did Plato coin *rhetorike? American Journal of Philology, 111,* 457–470.

Schrag, R. (1991). Sugar and spice and everything nice versus snake and snails and puppy dogs' tails: Selling social stereotypes on Saturday morning television. In L. Vande Berg & L.A. Wenner (eds.), *Television criticism: Approaches and applications* (pp. 220–234). White Plains, NY: Longman.

Schrag, R. L., Hudson, R. A., & Bernabo, L. M. (1981). Television's new humane collectivity. *Communication Studies, 34,* 151–161.

Schwichtenberg, C. (1987). *The Love Boat:* The packaging and selling of love, heterosexual romance, and family. In H. Newcomb (Ed.), *Television: The critical view* (4th ed., pp. 126–140). New York: Oxford University Press.

Sillars, M. O., & Gronbeck, B. E. (2001). *Communication criticism: Rhetoric, social codes, cultural studies.* Prospect Heights, IL: Waveland Press.

Sperry, S. L. (1976). Television news as narrative. In R. Adler (Ed.), *Television as a cultural force* (pp. 129–146). New York: Praeger.

Thompson, G. (1997). *Rhetoric through media.* Boston: Allyn & Bacon.

Tiemens, R. K. (1978). Television's portrayal of the 1976 presidential debates: An analysis of visual content. *Communication Monographs, 45,* 362–370.

Tiemens, R. K., Hellweg, S. A., Kipper, P., & Phillips, S. L. (1985). An integrative verbal and visual analysis of the Carter-Reagan debate. *Communication Quarterly, 33,* 34–42.

Timberg, B. (1987). The rhetoric of the camera in television soap operas. In H. Newcomb (Ed.), *Television: The critical review* (4th ed., 1164–178). New York: Oxford University Press.

Torres, S. (1989). Melodrama, masculinity, and the family: *thirtysomething* as therapy. *Camera Obscura, 19,* 87–106.

Tucker, L.R., & Shah, H. (1998). Race and the transformation for culture: The making of the television miniseries *Roots.* In L. Vande Berg, L. A. Wenner, & B. E. Gronbeck (Eds.), *Critical approaches to television* (pp. 405–416). Boston: Houghton Mifflin.

Vande Berg, L. R. E. (1993. *China Beach,* Prime time war in the postfeminist age: An Example of patriarchy in a different voice. *Western Journal of Communication, 57,* 359–366.

Wander, P. (1976). *The Waltons:* How sweet it was. *Journal of Communication, 26,* 148–164.

Williams, S. (1991). Bugs bunny meets He-Man: A historical comparison of values in animated cartoons. In L. Vande Berg & L. A. Wenner (Eds.), *Television criticism: Approaches and applications* (pp. 210–219). White Plains, NY: Longman.

Murphy Brown: Postfeminism Personified

Bonnie J. Dow

For four years (1988–92), *Designing Women* shared "women's night" on CBS with *Murphy Brown*. Because I viewed them in tandem, I have often made sense of the two sitcoms in terms of their similarities and their contrasts with each other. For example, both were products of the growing minority of powerful female producer/writers in the 1980s; *Designing Women* was produced by Linda Bloodworth-Thomason and her husband, Harry Thomason. *Murphy Brown* was the product of the team of Diane English and her husband, Joel Shukovsky. The sheer novelty of the existence of female producers resulted in the lion's share of publicity being directed at the female members of these teams; moreover, because of their integral involvement with the actual writing of the shows, English and Bloodworth-Thomason always were featured as more directly involved with the creative aspects of the sitcoms. In short, *Murphy Brown* and *Designing Women* were frequently talked about as examples of programming written by women, about women, and for women.

Newsweek's 1989 cover story on the new "womanpower" in television, entitled "Networking Women," attributes the wave of new woman-centered programming to two factors: the heightened pursuit of the female audience for prime-time (in the wake of male viewers' defection to cable) and the presence of female talent behind the scenes (Waters & Huck, 1989, pp. 48–49). Relying on what Marjorie Ferguson (1990) has called the "feminist fallacy," the notion that media representations of women will improve as women rise in media industries, the article argues that the more powerful women on screen are "being cast in the formidable image of their behind-camera female creators" and that "only the sexual integration of TV's creative community could have blessed us with a 'Murphy Brown'" (Waters & Huck, 1989, pp. 49, 52).

"Networking Women" is a rather typical story in the "let's celebrate women's progress" media genre; it exaggerates the import of a few success stories, thereby implying that women's problems have all but disappeared. Its claim that female producers "in the post-Reagan, post-feminist '90s" are using their programming to tell women that "it's okay to work," "it's okay to be alone," "it's okay to mess up," and "it's okay to mouth off" is supported, primarily, by examples from *Roseanne* and *Murphy Brown*, hardly typical television women (Waters & Huck, 1989, pp. 50–51). Again, however, it is a media convention to highlight dramatic, deviant examples.

The tremendous attention paid to *Murphy Brown* on its debut in the fall of 1988 is attributable to a number of factors. It starred a highly visible film actress, Candice Bergen, in her first foray into series television. It was a relative ratings success at a time when the pressure on new shows to prove themselves quickly was fierce. Finally, and most interesting to me, it was a reworking of a television staple associated with 1970s feminism—the single, working-woman sitcom. The numerous comparisons between *Murphy Brown* and *Mary Tyler Moore* made this point hard to miss; as Waters and Huck put it, "the critics . . . haven't lavished so much attention on an unmarried woman since Mary Richards walked into that other TV newsroom in Minneapolis" (1989, p. 49).[1] In the same article, Linda Bloodworth-Thomason also spoke of *Mary Tyler Moore* as the baseline for representations of working women: "When Mary Richards threw that hat in the air for the last time, it stayed up. The contemporary TV woman is making it on her own" (Waters & Huck, 1989, p. 50).

The similarities between Mary Richards and Murphy Brown, which both focus on a single woman who works in a television newsroom, are overpowered by the differences, as popular critics have hastened to note. While *Mary Tyler Moore* was firmly within what Norman Lear called the "emerging woman" genre, there is no doubt that Murphy Brown has made it. She is no struggling producer-cum-secretary in local news but, rather, a powerful network co-anchor of a prime-time news magazine. Murphy Brown presumably proves that "TV women have come a long, *long* way since Mrs. Cleaver whipped up her last breakfast for the Beav" (Waters & Huck, 1989, p. 48).

This point is made again and again in media treatment of *Murphy Brown.* Not only was a CBS special focusing on the twentieth anniversary of *Mary Tyler Moore* broadcast on a Monday evening (February 18, 1991) with *Murphy Brown* as its lead-in show, but the special was advertised as "An Evening with Murphy and Mary." *Primetime Live*, the ABC news magazine show, introduced a July 25, 1991, feature on *Murphy Brown* by placing the show on a continuum of "liberated woman" sitcoms that included *That Girl* and *Mary Tyler Moore.*

In virtually all comparisons between the two sitcoms the purpose is to demonstrate how far women have come since *Mary Tyler Moore.*[2] If Mary Richards was the feminist television icon of the 1970s, then Murphy Brown is the postfeminist icon for the 1990s. The show's producers have claimed that they "intend Murphy to be for the 90's what Mary Richards was for the 70's" (Horowitz, 1989, p. 1H), and a headline in *USA Today* described the sitcom as "Mary Tyler Moore Updated for the Eighties" (quoted in Alley & Brown, 1990, p. 204). Critic Jane Feuer has perhaps put it most explicitly by claiming that *Murphy Brown* is a "program based almost entirely on intertextuality," and that "the two shows [*Mary Tyler Moore* and *Murphy Brown*] really represent a continuation of the same cultural theme—the earlier show riding the crest of the feminist movement, the later one detailing its ebb in the 'postfeminist' era" (1992, p. 156).

To return to my original comparison, unlike *Designing Women, Murphy Brown* was treated, from the outset, as a sitcom with feminist implications. While *Designing Women* was positioned in media accounts as a sitcom with a *gendered* consciousness (e.g., women talk to women about things women really talk about), *Murphy Brown* was treated as a show with a *feminist* (or, as I will argue,

a *postfeminist*) consciousness. Several possible explanations for this reaction exist. One has to do with the power of television conventions. Previous television trained viewers and critics to see single, white, working-woman sitcoms as the paradigmatic form for feminist representation. *Designing Women's* characters are white, single, working women, but the sitcom lacks other essential characteristics, such as the liberal feminist emphasis on women in a man's world (journalism is a masculine occupation, whereas interior design is feminine). Possibly, for critics, *Designing Women's* feminism is undercut by its context, revealing the implicit sexism in media perceptions of women's progress; that is, media assume that feminism is being represented when women do what men traditionally do, making male values the standard for measuring women's advancement.

A second explanation is that *Designing Women* questions the reigning postfeminist ethos promulgated by mainstream media. *Designing Women's* frequent reiteration of the ongoing need for feminism, as well as its consciousness-raising about that need, hardly fits a view of the world that increasingly saw changes wrought by women's liberation as part of the problem in women's lives rather than as the solution.

If *Designing Women* resists postfeminism, *Murphy Brown* exemplifies it, both in its validation of women's progress embodied in the power of the lead character and in its exploration of the costs of that progress. Although media treatment of *Murphy Brown* emphasizes the sitcom's progressive portrait of a professional woman, it also contains subtler themes about the lessons of liberation. The *Newsweek* article discussed above, for example, claims that "beneath their self-assured veneers," television's new, powerful women "carry stretch marks on their psyches. They've been roughed up by life and are coming to terms with their limits" (Waters & Huck, 1989, pp. 50–51). Candice Bergen adds to this theme in a 1989 *Playboy* interview in which she notes that "Murphy is at the top of her profession but . . . she is, in a very realistic way, paying the price for it" ("Candice Bergen," 1989, p. 62).

A *People* article calls Murphy Brown a "feminist figurehead" and a "merciless careerist" while contrasting the character's persona with the happy home life of the actor who portrays her (Jerome, 1991, pp. 162, 160). This issue of *People* features Candice Bergen on the cover, with a caption that reads: "*Murphy Brown* is a hoot, but her [Bergen's] heart's at home with Chloe, 6, and her French husband, Louis Malle, the man who saved her 'from the loneliness I was so used to living with.'" In fact, the many articles about Bergen consistently note the contrast between the star's happy, satisfied life as a wife and mother and the "desolate personal life" of Murphy Brown (Rosenblatt, 1992, p. 258). At another point in the *Playboy* interview, Bergen says "I don't know if I could have played this part if I weren't married and didn't have a child. It would have been too painful for me" ("Candice Bergen," 1989, p. 69).

Esquire magazine's annual "Women We Love" issue for 1992, which featured Bergen on the cover as their "Woman of the Year" adds further strength to this positioning of Murphy Brown as an example of postfeminist fallout: "A product of the Eighties backlash against women Having It All, Murphy embodies a belated recognition that it is not possible all-at-once to do the deal, cook the dinner, give a man good lovin', and still flounce about with a chirpy Mary Tyler Moore bob and smile" ("Candice Bergen," 1992, p. 79).[3] Diane English, the sitcom's producer, perhaps put it most succinctly in her comment in a *New York Times Magazine* profile that *Murphy Brown* is "a sort of cautionary tale about getting what you wished for" (De Vries, 1993, p. 20).

I have reviewed popular press treatments of *Murphy Brown* at length here because they indicate the ambivalence of attitudes toward women's progress both in the sitcom and in reactions to it. Elsewhere, I have interpreted *Murphy Brown* solely as a "cautionary tale," connecting it to the backlash against women's liberation (see Dow, 1992a, 1995). Today, I am less sure of the totalizing power of that interpretation. As a viewer, I have always been reserved in my positive reaction to the sitcom because I felt that feminism had not come far enough

for me to take comfort in a show that made a buffoon out of a powerful female character. However, continued watching of *Murphy Brown,* and the gathering of reactions from many self-identified feminist viewers who unabashedly enjoy it have confounded the simplicity of this view. *Murphy Brown* is tremendously sophisticated comedy, and it is perhaps the model of what critics mean when we say there is no such thing as a closed text.

That *Murphy Brown* has import for women's roles is something everyone seems to agree on, an interpretation that was strengthened by then–Vice President Dan Quayle's attack on Murphy's single motherhood. However, the substance or ideological content of that import is difficult to pin down. As the press coverage indicates, there is a doubleness to the perceived meaning of the sitcom; it is discussed, at once, as an affirmation of women's progress and as a reminder of the problems such progress has created. This is, of course, precisely the doubleness represented by postfeminist attitudes, as I discussed in Chapter Three of *Prime-Time Feminism* (1996). My reading of *Murphy Brown* in this chapter, then, is an exploration of this postfeminist ambivalence as it is constructed in the character of Murphy Brown and the narrative themes that fuel the sitcom. *Murphy Brown* illustrates particularly well, I think, the way in which popular texts gain appeal from exploiting and reworking cultural contradictions at particular historical moments.

Postfeminist Womanhood

The regulars on *Murphy Brown* consist primarily of Murphy's colleagues at "FYI," the weekly prime-time news magazine show of which she is a coanchor. The other primary anchor on "FYI" is Jim Dial, an older, experienced television newsman known for his rigid, uptight nature and his stiff, laconic style. Miles Silverberg, the executive producer of "FYI" and Murphy's boss, is less experienced and younger than Murphy, a situation that Murphy finds consistently irritating in early seasons of the sitcom. Two other regulars are Frank Fontana and

Corky Sherwood, reporters for the program. Frank is an experienced investigative reporter and Murphy's closest friend in the group.

In contrast, Corky has little journalistic experience. She is an ex–Miss America who was hired at "FYI" for her beauty queen status. Corky is young, pretty, and perky, a softer character than Murphy, and she provides a traditionally feminine foil for Murphy's feminist character. Murphy's relation to Corky is competitive rather than cooperative. Corky's role on "FYI" is to produce "soft" news features (e.g., "Twelve Angry Women in Hairdresser Horror Stories," "Dinner with the Van Patten Family") that appeal to female viewers. Although the two women become friends over time, Murphy does not see Corky as her professional equal, and a strong theme in their relationship is Murphy's disdain for Corky's journalistic ability. Two other regulars on *Murphy Brown* are not connected to "FYI." They are Murphy's ever-present housepainter, Eldin Bernecky, who appears in most of the scenes set in Murphy's home,[4] and Phil the owner of a bar frequented by the "FYI" staff.

This review of characters shows kinship between *Murphy Brown* and *Mary Tyler Moore.* Like Mary Richards, Murphy is "a woman in a man's world." However, unlike Mary Richards, Murphy does not achieve success by playing a domestic role in the workplace; rather, she has adapted successfully to the masculine culture of television journalism and made her way to the top of her profession through rugged individualism. The fact that Murphy's professional competence is never an issue on *Murphy Brown* shows progress since *Mary Tyler Moore.* Murphy is a media "star," a knowledgeable, driven, investigative reporter who has won numerous awards. Unlike *Mary Tyler Moore,* in which the narrative problematic was "can she make it on her own?" *Murphy Brown* has moved beyond such a question. She has indeed made it on her own, becoming in the process what Phyllis Japp calls " a male persona in a female body" (1991, p. 71). Indeed, Murphy could be considered the fictional embodiment of the liberal feminist hegemony Hewlett and Friedan assumed when they argued that women's liberation required that

women "clone the male competitive model" (Hewlett, 1986, p. 186).

Murphy Brown signifies Murphy's masculinized persona in numerous ways. Her name is not traditionally feminine; generally, "Murphy" would be more likely to refer to a man than a woman. Moreover, although Candice Bergen is a strikingly beautiful woman, her style, as Murphy Brown, is not traditionally feminine. Indeed, much of the humor that arises from Murphy's character is connected to the incongruity of Bergen's glamorous and patrician persona in combination with the deemphasized femininity, abrasive personality, and physical aggressiveness of Murphy Brown.

Murphy's clothing is severely tailored, and she tends to wear high collars and boxy suits with straight lines. Even her less formal clothes have a masculine aura; when Murphy is relaxed, she often wears a baseball cap, tennis shoes, and baggy, man-tailored slacks. The contrast of Murphy's look and manner with that of the ultrafeminine Corky give Murphy's "difference" additional weight. Reinforcing the idea that she and Corky are two extremes on a spectrum, Murphy's tendency toward black, brown, and strong colors are a clear contrast to Corky's frequent pastels, soft scarves, and bows. While Murphy often wears flats, Corky always wears high heels. Murphy's subdued makeup and hair also are striking in comparison to Corky's teased, bleached hair and bright lips. Corky's appearance is part of her general performance of femininity, while Murphy's style reflects the goal of gaining credibility in a male world.

Murphy's physical presence also is noteworthy in defining her character. Her stride is aggressive, her gestures are strong, her manner of speaking is forceful, and she commands primary attention in any scene in which she is involved. Murphy's physical and facial expressions are excessive; she often does double-takes, and her expressions of distaste, amazement, or triumph are exaggerated. She is the primary focus in most camera shots in which she is involved, and her strength and autonomy are underscored by the way in which camera angles often show her physically isolated from other characters in a scene.

Murphy's physical aura is reinforced by her aggressive communication style. She is supremely confident about her own opinions, and she expresses them easily, often with little regard for others' feelings. For example, in "The Strike"[5] (1989), Murphy is disgusted by the way the men around her are handling a management-union dispute. She accuses them of being blinded by male pride, and comments, "just pull down your pants, I'll get a ruler, and we'll settle this once and for all." This line, in fact, illustrates the double edge to Murphy's character. It can be taken, simultaneously, as a salient feminist comment on a masculine obsession with power at the expense of reasonable problem-solving *and* as further evidence of Murphy's insensitivity and her taste for harsh sarcasm.

The latter interpretation is bolstered by Murphy's habit of playing hostile practical jokes, another typically male-associated trait that defines her character. When angry at her producer, for example, she has pizzas delivered to him every half-hour all night long, later hiring a polka band to play outside his window. Upset with Corky, she sends religious missionaries to Corky's house. Even Murphy's closest friend, Frank, does not escape. When Frank finally wins a prestigious journalism award that he has coveted for years, the victory goes to his head and he becomes obsessed with his own importance. To deflate Frank's ego, Murphy hires actors to tell him that the award has been rescinded because it was based on a mathematical error.

A clear message of *Murphy Brown* is that the personality traits alluded to above, such as aggression, competitiveness, and lack of interpersonal sensitivity, are key to Murphy's professional success in a patriarchal world. For example, in "The Unshrinkable Murphy Brown" (1989) Murphy is so relentless while interviewing a subject that he has a heart attack and dies on the air. Guilt-stricken, Murphy vows to be a nicer person, and in subsequent scenes she is uncharacteristically polite and considerate to her colleagues. They are shocked and dismayed at the change in her behavior, concerned that it is affecting the quality of her work. This episode is instructive, because it implies that Murphy's display of traditionally "nice," feminine qualities is not only shocking, but incompatible with her success as a journalist. In order to be successful she must be tough and competitive, and must reject behaviors that contradict such a persona. While other reporters on "FYI" are also capable and successful, notably Jim Dial and Frank Fontana, they do not behave as ruthlessly as Murphy. To compete in a male culture, Murphy becomes an extreme version of it, a caricature of the consequences of liberal feminism. Alison Jaggar notes that a typical liberal feminist argument is that "women are capable of participating in male culture and of living up to male values" (1983, p. 250). In *Murphy Brown*, consistent with postfeminism, this success has its costs. A theme in early seasons is Murphy's recovery from alcoholism, a disease that she attributes to her driven lifestyle. She has little success with romantic relationships and does not bond easily with other women.

All of these factors are, of course, fodder for comedy, contributing to the intriguing ambivalence of the sitcom's message. At the same time that Murphy is a "new" (read: liberated, autonomous, and powerful) woman on television, much of the humor attached to her character is derived from the incongruity of these characteristics in a woman. The prevailing tone in *Murphy Brown* is irony: Murphy is funny because she consistently acts as we do not expect a woman to act. Rather than rejecting naturalized prefeminist conceptions of "good womanhood," the sitcom depends on them to make sense. The troubling aspect of this dynamic is that laughter is linked most often to the absurdity of Murphy rather than to the absurdity of conventional expectations for womanhood, indicating that the postfeminist presumption of women's equality is premature. As Andrea Press notes in her brief discussion of *Murphy Brown*, given that Murphy's "harsh personality becomes the focus of so much of the show's humor, . . . were a man in her role, one suspects that the humor would have to be focused entirely differently" (1991, p. 41).

The earlier seasons of *Murphy Brown* are the most direct about exploiting aspects of Murphy's stereotypical liberal feminist character. A recurring theme, for example, is that Murphy's competitiveness and ambition are excessive. In "Devil with the Blue Dress" (1988), Miles assigns Corky to assist Murphy on a difficult story, claiming that Corky needs "seasoning as a reporter." After expressing her displeasure to Miles in competitive terms ("I won't work with her on my story. I was an only child—I never learned to share"), Murphy finally agrees. Hoping to discourage Corky, Murphy sends her on various humiliating old-goose chases (such as searching through a suspect's garbage cans), but Corky eventually discovers a piece of information that proves to be the key to the story.

Murphy dismisses the value of the information in front of Corky so that she can pursue the angle herself. Corky later discovers this maneuver but responds graciously, saying, "When I realized what you'd done with that crucial piece of information I gave you . . . there it was, the perfect example of what makes you the best. . . . I have learned so much from you and I respect you so much. Thank you for allowing me to work by your side." Murphy assuages the guilt engendered by this reaction by telling Corky that she may introduce the story during the FYI broadcast before turning it over to Murphy.

However, Corky reads the entire story and takes full credit for it. After the show, Murphy is furious, but she must admit respect for Corky, saying, "You saw your brass ring and you went for it. It took a lot of chutzpa. I have to respect a person for that." This episode illustrates a pattern in *Murphy Brown* in which Murphy's aggressive, competitive personality creates a problem that leads to her humorous comeuppance. In this episode, Murphy rejected cooperation and nurturing (qualities of traditional femininity) in favor of competition and ruthlessness (qualities of the patriarchal public sphere). While the latter qualities presumably have led to Murphy's past success, she is reproved for them in this situation, creating a classic double-bind for her. Through plotlines such as this, *Murphy Brown* exploits the perceived conflict between femininity and professional success.

That the competition is between two women is additionally interesting in this case. Murphy consistently compares herself to other newswomen, but not other newsmen, in a fiercely competitive way. In various episodes, she measures her success against that of Lesley Stahl, Connie Chung, and Linda Ellerbee, exemplifying the sitcom's reliance on humor generated by intertextual references and reinforcing the idea that there are limited spaces for women at the top. To help Corky to join such a club threatens Murphy's status rather than presents her with an opportunity for female solidarity. *Murphy Brown*'s almost total lack of realistic female community sets it apart from other examples of "postfeminist postfamily" television such as *Kate and Allie, The Golden Girls*, or *Designing Women*. These shows, to varying degrees, contain the message that female friendship and support are important and valuable to women; that message is arguably a primary reason for their popularity with women audiences and offers some resistance to postfeminism's rugged individualism. Murphy Brown, on the other hand, embraces individualism so thoroughly that she is seemingly incapable of deep emotional ties.

Murphy has none of the nurturing qualities so common in television's female characters. She is rarely physically affectionate, usually stiffening when others are demonstrative toward her. When Jim Dial comes to her for advice on a personal problem, her first response is, "Don't you have a family priest or someone?" In a later season, when Corky is married and is considering an affair, she asks Murphy for advice and receives essentially the same response: "I don't know, Corky. I'm not good at this stuff. Isn't there some all night radio station you can call?"

Murphy's interpersonal difficulties extend into her private life, where she enacts the stereotype of a driven career woman with no time or talent for relationships. Outside of the newsroom, her closest relationship is with Eldin, her housepainter. When she is not invited to the inaugural ball, she ends up spending the evening with Eldin. When she is suspended from work, it appears that Eldin is the only person to keep her company. There is no real or implied romantic connection with Eldin, but Murphy seems to have no other friends outside her job. In a 1988 episode, Murphy first thinks of becoming a single mother. However, it proves difficult to find someone to father her child. Forty years old, Murphy fears her time for motherhood is running out, and she bemoans the fact that her "most enduring relationship is with the skycap at Dulles airport."

Unmarried, childless, and without a satisfying romantic relationship, Murphy's character embodies what media constructions of postfeminism posit as the negative consequences of female independence. For example, *Time*'s 1989 cover story asking "Is there a future for feminism?" maintains that many career women resent feminists for not foreseeing the sacrifices women would have to make, noting that "the bitterest complaints come from the growing ranks of women who have reached 40 and find themselves childless, having put their careers first" (Wallis, 1989, p. 82). *Murphy Brown*'s emphasis on Murphy's barren personal life enacts this postfeminist scenario. Although Jim Dial, who is closest to being Murphy's peer, has a successful marriage (and a wife who is a fulltime homemaker), such a choice is precluded for Murphy.

Several episodes of *Murphy Brown* comment on the effect of Murphy's life choices on her personal relations, offering the message that her professional ambition precludes lasting personal relationships. For example, in a 1988 episode, Murphy's ex-husband, a political activist to whom she was married for five days twenty years earlier, appears on "FYI." They reignite their attraction and decide to marry again. However, Murphy cannot find time for a wedding and they give up on the idea. Her excuses range from "I gotta fly to Moscow to interview Gorbachev" to "I can't plan that far in advance—I've got to be ready to hop a plane at a moment's notice." Murphy's devotion to her work seems extreme in this circumstance, with the result that she sacrifices her own personal happiness.

In the 1990–91 season, Murphy began a relationship with Jerry Gold, an abrasive talk show host. In their first try at a relationship, Murphy eventually called it off, saying, "I'm good at a lot of things, but this isn't one of them. I start saying things I don't normally say, I start doing things I

don't normally do. . . . Oh, God, I'm wearing an apron. See what I mean?" This remark comes after a failed dinner party that Murphy concocted to introduce Jerry to her colleagues. It is telling that Murphy equates her failure at the relationship with her unsuitability for a domestic role, reinforcing the dichotomy between the private and public spheres.

In the next season, Murphy and Jerry try again to be a couple, but it ends when Jerry takes a job in California and Murphy is too busy to pursue a long-distance romance. Again, however, this episode creates an inverse relationship between Murphy's personal happiness and her professional success. Murphy and Jerry are brought together when a new "FYI" segment requires that they debate political issues each week. Their sharply contrasting political views make this a lively and popular segment. However, after they rekindle their romance, Murphy is no longer aggressive and sharp-witted in the debate segment; instead, she exhibits traditionally feminine qualities. She is supportive, polite, and willing to compromise with Jerry's extremist views. Her colleagues are horrified, concluding that her romance with Jerry has affected her professional performance.

This episode reiterates that personal happiness and professional success are incompatible for Murphy, implicitly arguing that, for women, the qualities the public world requires are radically different from those necessary for success in the private world of relationships. Murphy simply cannot win. *Murphy Brown* implies that she must act one way to be professionally successful and another to be personally fulfilled. For many female viewers, Murphy's difficulties could strike a responsive chord. However, the episodes of *Murphy Brown* that deal with this issue present these conflicts as the result of Murphy's *choices* rather than as a result of contradictory cultural expectations. The ultimate rugged individualist, Murphy is no one's victim. Rather, she sabotages herself. This dynamic is what makes *Murphy Brown* so vividly postfeminist. Unlike *Designing Women*, *Murphy Brown* gives no "presence" to patriarchy. Instead, women's problems (or Murphy's problems) flow from their own choices.

A final, classic example of *Murphy Brown*'s depiction of Murphy's self-sabotage again highlights the personal/professional dichotomy that defines her character. In "The Morning Show" (1989), the major plotline concerns Murphy's week-long stint as the substitute co-anchor of "Today America," a program much like "Good Morning America." Murphy ridicules the "soft news" orientation of the program, and she is unhappy to discover that Corky is to be her co-host. Corky is excited by the assignment and spends significant time preparing. Murphy, in contrast, does not see the job as challenging and does no preparation.

The contrasts between Murphy and Corky as co-anchors are the context within which Corky's traditional femininity is validated, while Murphy's aggressive competitiveness only creates difficulties. In the first morning show, they interview the male author of a popular children's book. While Corky praises the inventiveness and popularity of the book, Murphy asserts that the setting of the book, "the Land of the Woogies," emulates a male-dominated society, and that the story represents the larger culture's "struggle for sexual equality in the workplace." The author protests that his characters are not gendered, but Murphy is relentless, claiming that the "Fifis," another group in the book, are female and represent "an oppressed minority of sorts." At this point, Corky steps in, soothes the author and ends the interview.

The contrast between Murphy's feminism and Corky's femininity are clear in this scene. Murphy personifies the intensity and humorlessness of the stereotypical feminist ideologue, refusing to enact the supportive, gracious role required in such a situation. While her argument that the children's book is sexist indeed may be correct (and some viewers may see it as a salient point to make), within the context of the episode, the laugh track encourages the audience to view her claim as absurd and her behavior as inappropriate for the situation. Corky, in contrast, is at home in the "soft news" format which reflects traditionally female interests.

While Corky is praised for her performance, Murphy is described by colleagues as "acerbic, hu-morless, inflexible, and unprepared." The next day, Murphy panics when she hears that she must participate in a segment with a bake-off champion, and she moans, "The last time I tried to bake brownies, I had to call an industrial cleaning service." During the segment, Corky startles Murphy by separating an egg with one hand. Corky's baking expertise is manifest, and Murphy is challenged. She becomes obsessed with learning to separate eggs and annoys the bake-off champion. Murphy ruins the segment as she and the bake-off champion do verbal (and nearly physical) battle and have to be pried apart by Corky. Murphy's dearth of culinary skills, and her inability to acquiesce graciously to Corky's superiority in this arena further demonstrate her lack of stereotypical feminine qualities.

By the end of this episode, Murphy is humbled, and she must admit that Corky did the better job. Murphy is humiliated because she is not traditionally feminine enough, in terms of social facilitation or cooking skills, to fulfill the assigned role. Despite the fact that her particular traits have led to success in "hard news," when she fails at "soft news," she is punished. Again, Murphy is the victim of conflicting expectations. Corky, whose more traditionally female skills are appropriate for the situation, shines on the morning show, although she has failed in the past at "hard news" assignments.

This episode adds strength to a theme that dominates early seasons of *Murphy Brown*: a woman cannot both be professionally successful and retain traditional qualities of femininity. Murphy is rich and famous but not a "real" woman in personality or personal relationships. Corky, in contrast, is more traditionally feminine in appearance and behavior but is professionally competent only in the feminine province of lower-status "soft" news situations. In *Murphy Brown*, neither major female character can be totally complete, and the "weaknesses" of each are highlighted through contrast with the other. The sitcom allows only polar conceptions of womanhood, refusing to permit integration of traditionally bifurcated masculine and feminine qualities attached to the public and private spheres.

The sharp contrast between Murphy and Corky

The contrast between perky, petite, feminine Corky and ascerbic, serious feminist fictional television news producer Murphy Brown illustrates the politics of media representations, and as Bonnie Dow explains, the rhetorical strategy of using Murphy as a comic scapegoat for postfeminism's ills.

that feeds the dichotomy in *Murphy Brown* between professional and personal competence lessens in later seasons of the sitcom, largely as a result of the development of Corky's character through her marriage, divorce, and increasing professional ambition. Corky's ultimately unsuccessful marriage to a man from her hometown in Louisiana (resulting in the comical married name of "Corky Sherwood-Forrest") extends *Murphy Brown*'s message about the incompatibility of personal and professional success to encompass Corky's life as well. The disintegration of Corky and Will Forrest's marriage, although it receives little attention in the sitcom's narrative, is linked to the pressures of their dual careers and the fact that they rarely see each other.

Although Corky still handles only soft news features, she becomes more competent, successful, and ambitious in later seasons of *Murphy Brown*. Interestingly, one of the hallmarks of Corky's development as a journalist is her adaptation of Murphy's style of "going the distance" to get what she wants, even if it involves manipulation and/or misrepresentation. However, despite Corky's development, the disturbing element of competition that fuels Murphy and Corky's relationship is never lost. Corky frequently uses her new skills at Murphy's expense, which feeds the competition between

them *and* functions to discipline Murphy for her excesses. A 1991 episode, in which Corky is given a network special of her own, is illustrative.

Corky decides to frame the special as a tea-party, in which she will interview people such as Mrs. Fields (of Mrs. Fields' cookies fame) and Mary Ann Mobley and Gary Collins (best known as hosts of the Miss America pageant). Corky also wishes for Murphy to be a guest, a request Murphy disdains ("What self-respecting journalist would let himself[6] be interviewed at a tea-party?"), until Miles manages to talk her into it by appealing to her ego. On the day the special is to be broadcast live, a newspaper columnist ridicules the special so thoroughly that Corky is completely demoralized, convinced that she can never be as good as the other members of "FYI," that she will never be able to "ask the tough questions." Uncharacteristically, Murphy offers Corky encouragement and convinces her to go ahead with the special. Corky promises that she will "try to live up to your [Murphy's] standards."

During the special, instead of asking Murphy questions about her professional experiences, Corky turns the conversation to Murphy's troubled personal life with question such as "Earlier in your career, you were, in your own words, a 'major booze hound.' I was just wondering, could America trust your accuracy and judgment in reporting information?" Corky's relentless probing eventually leads to various highly personal revelations from Murphy, such as "Maybe I deliberately sabotage my personal relationships because I fear losing some professional edge." After the special, Murphy is completely humiliated, convinced that her reputation has been destroyed. When she confronts Corky, threatening to "kill" her, Corky's reply is that she was modeling herself after Murphy: "I did what I thought you would have done in the same situation . . . I'm right, aren't I, Murphy?"

Murphy is hoisted on her own petard in this episode. She has disdained Corky's abilities for years while asserting her own superiority as a journalist, only to be the unwitting victim when Corky finally is able "to ask the tough questions" (it is doubly interesting, of course, that Murphy's dysfunctional personal life is the focus). Murphy suffers this kind of deflation regularly in *Murphy Brown,* frequently at Corky's hands. In true sitcom style, Murphy never really learns her lesson (to do so would eliminate the "sit"), and she keeps returning for yet more comeuppances.

I find it particularly meaningful that Corky is so often the catalyst for Murphy's symbolic punishments, feeding the postfeminist media theme of divisions among women and the implicit message that the possibility of female solidarity was a feminist fantasy. In much postfeminist pop culture, women have replaced patriarchy as women's worst enemy. Journalists lavish attention on the conflicts between mothers who work outside the home and those who do not, between women of different races, and between feminists and nonfeminists—conflicts that are strengthened by their vivid representation in television programs like *thirtysomething;* films such as *Fatal Attraction* (1987), *Jungle Fever* (1991), *The Hand That Rocks the Cradle* (1992), and *Disclosure* (1994); and public controversies like the Thomas/Hill hearings, in which much was made of Clarence Thomas's preference for women with light complexions and of the divergence in white and black women's responses to Hill's charges.[7]

Generally, the episodes I have discussed thus far illustrate what I believe to be a powerful rhetorical strategy in *Murphy Brown:* Murphy's function as a comic scapegoat representing postfeminist ills. By sacrificing Murphy through humiliation, embarrassment, or ridicule, *Murphy Brown* turns the tables on the basic project of liberal feminism, which is to critique how the public sphere excludes women. Instead, Murphy is a vision of liberal feminist success, and the scapegoating of her character is a recurring reminder of the problems that success creates. Murphy is too abrasive, confident, outspoken, and powerful (for a woman) to be left unchecked. In *Murphy Brown's* postfeminist vision, patriarchy is no longer the problem; feminism (and the problems it creates for women) is.

Kenneth Burke argues that the general attitude of classical comedy is "charitable," designed to promote cooperation and resolution of differences (1959, p. 166). This is also the basic philosophy of

television situation comedy narrative, which centers on problem-solving. The way in which problems are resolved says much about the values promoted by a series. For example, the controlling value of patriarchal authority is evident in 1950s sitcoms like *Leave It to Beaver* or *Father Knows Best,* in which the correct resolution of a problem inevitably follow the wisdom of the father (Leibman, 1995).

In *Murphy Brown,* Murphy's extreme personality and behavior most often create (or significantly contribute to) the problem that must be solved, and the solution involves some kind of symbolic discipline for Murphy as the comic scapegoat. The comic scapegoating in *Murphy Brown* is simply another example of a classic comedic strategy, in which a character serves as a representation for ideology or behavior that is ridiculed or debunked in the process of disciplining the character.[8] The treatment of Archie Bunker in *All in the Family* is the paradigmatic example of this strategy in television situation comedy. Archie was the repository for the conservative bigotry that Norman Lear wished to attack. Poking fun at Archie was a way to debunk the ideology he represented. However, audience interpretation of this strategy is unpredictable. Although critics might assume that audiences were always complicitous with Lear's intention to ridicule Archie, research shows that many viewers loved Archie *because of* his contentious conservatism (Adler, 1979).

Reaction to Murphy is similarly ambivalent, I think. Although *Murphy Brown* troubles me because Murphy's consistent function as a sort of feminist buffoon whose ritual humiliation functions to contain the threat that a powerful woman poses, I can see why she is so appealing for many viewers with feminist sympathies. Television programming offers so few representations of powerful, funny, smart, belligerent women (the massive amounts of attention that *Murphy Brown* and *Roseanne* receive often blinds us to how unusual and outnumbered they are) that we take what pleasure we can get from the ones we have.

Patricia Mellencamp (1986) has made a similar argument about the appeal of *I Love Lucy's* (1951–61) portrayal of Lucy Ricardo's desperate, and always futile, attempts to escape domesticity for show business. That is, although Lucy is always chastened by episode's end and returned to her traditional role, for many women this outcome does not wholly diminish the appeal of Lucy's struggle. Just so with Murphy Brown. Although my position is that the series does not encourage a view of Murphy as a victim of conflicting expectations that continue to be enforced by a patriarchal culture, it is quite possible that feminist viewers construct that interpretation for themselves, filling in a context that the sitcom's narrative does not provide. Such an interpretation would make Murphy a sympathetic character rather than a comic scapegoat. As is always the case, the possibility of such a reading of Murphy Brown depends on the experiences a viewer brings to a text as well as on the work s/he is willing to do in decoding it.

The Politics of Single Motherhood

Major shifts in narrative premise often spell disaster for situation comedies. A large part of the appeal of sitcom is its regularity, circularity, and predictability in terms of character function and plotline. Major shifts in characters or in situation can diminish that appeal. Some very popular and long-running sitcoms successfully manage shifts in character (witness, for instance, the many changes in *M*A*S*H*, and to a lesser extent, in *Cheers*), but major shifts in situation are harder to manage. For example . . . the appeal of Rhoda Morgenstern in *Mary Tyler Moore* was largely linked to her situation as an underdog single woman. In *Rhoda*, when she became a satisfied wife, the situational dynamics changed so much that her previous appeal for the audience was lost.

At the conclusion of the 1991 season, *Murphy Brown*'s producers presented the possibility of a drastic alteration in the narrative premise of the sitcom when Murphy discovered that she was pregnant. As I will discuss in a moment, Murphy's decision to become a single mother ultimately had little effect on the dynamics of the sitcom. However, the series of events surrounding Murphy's pregnancy and birth, both inside and outside the

text of *Murphy Brown*, deserves discussion for its illustration of the intersections of postfeminism, politics, and media intertextuality.

Press reaction to Murphy's pregnancy was mixed. Rather than viewing it as shocking, some writers (e.g., Charen, 1991; James, 1991) interpreted it as part of a trend on series television, which was experiencing a spate of baby-related storylines in shows such as *Designing Women* (in which Mary Jo considered having another child through artificial insemination) and *Cheers* (Sam Malone desired a child and enlisted the aid of his platonic friend Rebecca). The stigma of unwed motherhood as a plot device presumably had been diminished by successful storylines in recent years on *Moonlighting* (1985–89) (although the pregnant character rushed into a short-lived marriage and eventually miscarried) and *The Days and Nights of Molly Dodd* (1987–91) (in which the pregnancy led to the mother and father becoming engaged, until the father unexpectedly died).

Murphy's pregnancy did spark some moral outrage, from editorial columnists who accused television producers of irresponsibly weakening "the rule against illegitimacy [that] helps to prevent women and children from being abandoned by men" (Charen, 1991, p. 15A), to viewers who protested that the show was sending the wrong message about the joys of single motherhood ("Murphy Is Not Reality," 1992, p. 10A; "Mixed Messages," 1992, p. 10A). Even Candice Bergen herself, in *TV Guide*, made a point of asserting that "I myself, as a parent, believe that the ideal is that you have a two-parent family. I'm the last person to think fathers are obsolete" (Rhodes, 1992, p. 8).

However, given the possibilities, the handling of Murphy's pregnancy within the narrative of the sitcom was remarkably conservative. In the concluding episode to the 1990–91 season of *Murphy Brown*, both of Murphy's former loves reenter her life at the same time. Jerry Gold returns from California to resume a relationship with Murphy at the same time that Murphy's ex-husband, Jake Lowenstein, reappears. Murphy juggles the two men briefly, unable to decide between them. In the episode's final scene, Murphy is shocked by the result of a home pregnancy test, creating the cliffhanger question: Who is the father?

Murphy Brown takes care, in later episodes, to downplay implications of sexual irresponsibility. When Frank chastises Murphy for having unprotected sex with two men, Murphy reminds him that it was a fluke, that she has sex about as often as Democrats are in the White House. Moreover, the father turns out to be Jake, who makes the choice not to be involved in the pregnancy or the child's life, citing his commitment to political activism around the world. Finally, although Murphy considers abortion, she ultimately rejects it. By this point, it has been established that Murphy is not promiscuous, that the child has an aura of legitimacy derived from the fact that Murphy was once married to the father, that the father is deserting her through his own choice,[9] and that Murphy will not abort the pregnancy simply to avoid the inconvenience of single motherhood. Beyond the fact that Murphy engaged in unprotected extramarital sex in the first place, the portrayal of her journey to single motherhood is relatively timid.

Indeed, Murphy's surrender to women's supposed biological imperative, is, in my view, the ultimate postfeminist moment in *Murphy Brown,* giving credence to the claims about biological clocks, about the emptiness of childless career women, and women's "natural" destiny to mother. Various characters in *Murphy Brown,* including Murphy herself, reiterate that Murphy is unsuited for motherhood. After she had decided to keep the baby, Phil comments that her decision was "pretty gutsy for a woman with no maternal instinct whatsoever," to which Murphy replies, "Not everyone is born with maternal instincts, Phil. I can get some. I'm sure there's a class." At another point, Corky comments that she is sure Murphy will "make a wonderful mother. Once she gets a little practice and maybe some estrogen supplements."

Given her personality and lifestyle, Murphy's decision to bear the child hardly seems rational. It makes sense only as a reflection of the sexist adage that all women have a deep and irrepressible desire (duty?) to reproduce that is merely waiting to be triggered. Indeed, this essentialist interpretation of Murphy's motivation is given support in the "birth" episode from the end of the 1992 season—an episode viewed by some 38 million people. In the final scene, Murphy cradles her new infant in her arms, singing to him words from one of her favorite songs, "Natural Woman," by Aretha Franklin. The lines that Murphy sings, including "I didn't know what was wrong with me, 'til you helped me name it," and "You make me feel like a natural woman," take on a powerful meaning in this context. Having given birth, Murphy is miraculously transformed, albeit briefly, from an "unnatural" (professional) to a "natural" (maternal) woman.[10]

Apparently, then–Vice-President Dan Quayle did not view this episode before making his remarks about the poverty of family values represented by *Murphy Brown.* If he had, he might have noticed how closely it dovetailed with his wife's (and presumably his own) view, expressed at the Republican National Convention a few months later, that, contrary to feminist claims, "women do not wish to be liberated from their essential natures."

Given my position that *Murphy Brown*'s treatment of Murphy's pregnancy and birth is hardly radical, the most interesting aspects of the Quayle/ *Murphy Brown* media phenomenon to me is the way in which a popular sitcom, and the underlying values of the entertainment industry, became the dominant focus in reaction to a speech that was predominantly an attack on poor women. Focusing on the theme of family values, as though its implications were gender, race, and class neutral, both mainstream media and the text of *Murphy Brown* itself (through its intertextual appropriation and interpretation of Quayle's statement) created a debate that left untouched what bell hooks (1994) usefully calls "white supremacist capitalist patriarchy."

Quayle's famous comment about *Murphy Brown* occurred in a May 19, 1992, speech to the Commonwealth Club of California, an elite political group dominated by white men.[11] Attempting to make sense of the recent Los Angeles riots, Quayle argued that "the lawless social anarchy which we saw is directly related to the breakdown of family structure, personal responsibility, and social order in too many areas of our society." He went on to note that, while baby boomers such as himself participated in the "war against traditional values" waged in the 1960s and 1970s, now that the boomers are "middle-aged and middle-class . . . the responsibility of having families has helped many recover traditional values."

Quayle maintains that the poor, unfortunately, have never managed to regain those traditional values. The result is that "the intergenerational poverty that troubles us so much today is predominantly a poverty of values. . . . The anarchy and lack of structure in our inner cities are testament to how quickly civilization falls apart when the family foundation cracks." The Vice-President then asserts the necessity of male role models for inner-city children, touts marriage as "the best antipoverty program of all," and calls for a return to the moral stigmatization of illegitimacy.

At this point he mentions *Murphy Brown,* claiming that "it doesn't help matters when prime-time TV has Murphy Brown—a character who supposedly epitomizes today's intelligent, highly paid, professional woman—mocking the importance of fathers by bearing a child alone and calling it just another 'lifestyle choice.'" Moments later, Quayle extends his censure to the "cultural leaders in Hollywood, network TV, the national newspapers" who "routinely jeer" at moral values.

Quayle's remarks made the front pages of national newspapers—notably the *New York Times* and *USA Today*—and became the lead story on ABC's *World News Tonight,* the most popular national television newscast in America. In its May 20 edition, *USA Today* ran a photograph of Murphy Brown holding her baby next to the headline: "Quayle: Murphy No Role Model." The following day, the *New York Times* ran the same photograph of Murphy Brown on its front page, juxtaposed with photos of Quayle and White House spokesperson Marlin Fitzwater and the headline "Appeal of 'Murphy Brown' Now Clear at White House." The *New York Times* article made clear the extent to which Quayle's brief comment about Murphy Brown was influencing reaction to his

speech, noting that in his tour of Los Angeles, "Mr. Quayle was greeted at every stop and in six local television interviews with questions about the 'Murphy Brown' program" (Wines, 1992, p. A12). Press coverage of President Bush's trade talks with Canadian Prime Minister Brian Mulroney also was dominated by questions about the *Murphy Brown* issue (pp. A1, A12).

Generally, reports on Quayle's remarks were dominated by analysis of the White House campaign strategy to emphasize family values, by the comical contradictions in Quayle's and Fitzwater's follow-up remarks, and by reactions from *Murphy Brown* producers. Fitzwater, for instance, noted that Murphy's decision to bear the child "'[exhibits] pro-life values which we think are good'" (Wines, 1992, p. A1), an opinion that Quayle later countered, claiming that *Murphy Brown* "'does not represent pro-life policies'" ("Quayle vs. Brown," 1992, p. A1). Quayle's disagreement with Fitzwater was no doubt prompted by the widely reported response of Diane English to the Vice-President's attack: "'If the Vice-President thinks it's disgraceful for an unmarried woman to bear a child, and if he believes that a woman cannot adequately raise a child without a father, then he'd better make sure abortion remains safe and legal'" (Rosenthal, 1992, p. A11).

English's comment was one of the few that made it into coverage of the incident that indicated even a slight sense of the substance and the politics of Quayle's speech. However, even English overlooked Quayle's classism. Quayle did not suggest that *women in general* could not raise children adequately without fathers; rather, he suggested that *poor women,* in particular, were "bearing babies irresponsibly." Murphy Brown's contribution to the crisis was that she was failing to provide a worthy role model for poor women, apparently a key issue in the "trickle-down theory of values" which holds that prime-time television is a major influence on inner-city mothers (Pollitt, 1994, p. 32). A point that was never raised in the debate over Hollywood's poverty of values was that, in fact, the overwhelming majority of families on television have always been headed by two parents, a factor that has apparently made little difference in checking the "anarchy and lack of structure in our inner cities."

Quayle's claims in his speech that poverty is traceable to a lack of moral fiber, that single, poor women are inadequate mothers, that poor mothering is responsible for inner-city problems, and that marriage will save the inner city from decline are the most interesting and disturbing claims in his speech to the Commonwealth Club. That these claims were largely overlooked is fairly easy to explain. First, the mass media love to inflate their own importance and found it far more interesting to highlight their own minor role in Quayle's speech than to examine the implications of the Vice-President's remarks for welfare and urban policy. Second, it is a media convention to focus on an individual—even a fictional one—rather than to grapple with the structural problems (e.g., lack of economic opportunity, racism, sexism) that contribute to inner-city poverty.

Media emphasis on the "Murphy Brown angle" transformed a vicious attack on poor, presumably black (given the emphasis on the inner cities and the L.A. riots) women into a debate about Hollywood liberalism, middle-class morality, and the constitution of the nuclear family.[12] *Murphy Brown* itself, in its famous and much hyped response to Quayle in the premiere episode of the 1992 fall season, frames the debate in this fashion. Continuing the series tradition of intertextual references (which had been seen most recently in a baby shower for Murphy attended by Katie Couric, Joan Lunden, and other real-life newswomen), this episode's pivotal moment is a scene in which Murphy and Frank see Quayle's remarks on the evening news. Murphy, who has been struggling to learn to care for her new infant, is frustrated, exhausted, and unkempt in her pajamas, having recently moaned that "this mother stuff is the hardest thing I've ever done. And I'm one of the fortunate ones. I have a secure job, a fairly stable life, I'm educated—last night I bit the head off a stuffed bunny."[13]

Indeed, this episode establishes that almost everyone around Murphy (all men, interestingly enough) is better at motherhood than she is. Murphy is incompetent at interviewing nannies in the beginning of this episode, and Eldin eventually takes over that task. When Murphy shows up at the office, it is Miles who tells her that she is not ready to come back. Later, Frank must show her how to hold her baby so that he will stop crying, prompting the following exchange:

MURPHY: Oh, great, Frank, you've got better maternal instincts than I do.
FRANK: Murphy, would you stop writing this stuff down? You can't go at it like a reporter. You've gotta just feel your way through it.

This episode is the first indication that motherhood will not alter Murphy's personality and that postbaby episodes will retain the earlier comedic dynamic of deriving humor from Murphy's lack of feminine qualities and of placing her in situations where her failure is humorous.

After hearing Quayle's brief remarks about her "lifestyle choice," Murphy explodes:

Glamorize single motherhood? What planet is he on? Look at me, Frank, am I glamorous? . . . And what was that crack about just another lifestyle choice? I agonized over that decision. I didn't know if I could raise a kid myself. I worried about what it would do to him, I worried about what it would do to me. I didn't just wake up one morning and say "Oh, gee, I can't get in for a facial, I might as well have a baby!"

Murphy's debunking of Quayle's characterization of her motives is humorous, but it takes Quayle's comments largely at face value and ignores their context, as did media accounts. As the controversy escalates (in additional intertextual moves, *Murphy Brown* visually features several of the actual headlines following Quayle's remarks), Murphy decides that she must make a response to the Vice-President on "FYI." Although media accounts positioned this episode as an oppositional response to the Vice-President, the substance of Murphy's argument on "FYI" is consistent with the framing of the debate as a referendum on the proper definition of a family:

These are difficult times for our country, and in searching for the causes of our social ills, we could choose to blame the media, or the Congress, or an administration that's been in power for twelve years, or we could blame it on me. . . . I doubt that my status as a single mother has contributed all that much to the breakdown of Western civilization. . . . The Vice-President says he felt it was important to open a dialogue about family values, and on that point we agree. Unfortunately, it seems that for him, the only acceptable definition of family is a mother, a father, and children, and in a country where millions of children grow up in non-traditional families, that definition seems painfully unfair. Perhaps it's time for the Vice-President to expand his definition and recognize that, whether by choice or circumstance, families come in all shapes and sizes, and ultimately what really defines a family is commitment, caring, and love.

Following this speech, Murphy proceeds to introduce a group of adults and children (from various racial backgrounds, but predominantly white) representing a variety of definitions of family.

By the time that this episode aired in September of 1992, both the White House and the producers of *Murphy Brown* were enjoying the fruits of the publicity the incident had created. Candice Bergen, only partly tongue-in-cheek, thanked Quayle in her acceptance speech after she won the Emmy for best actress in a comedy series. Quayle obtained yet more attention when he arranged to watch the episode with a group of single mothers. The producers of *Murphy Brown* benefited from the ratings boost and the rise in advertising prices that the incident gave the sitcom (Elliott, 1992: "Murphy to Dan: Read My Ratings" 1992), and the Bush administration gained publicity for its "family values" campaign agenda. The only losers were the poor women of the inner cities, who became invisible in a debate that began with an assertion of their moral failings.[14]

Despite *Murphy Brown*'s relentless topicality and media characterization of it as a forum for liberal values (Zoglin, 1992), the sitcom is actually much less likely than *Designing Women* to engage with feminist politics, particularly when they are complicated by race. Like *Designing Women*, *Murphy Brown* built an episode around the Thomas/Hill hearings. In this episode, Murphy is called before the Senate Ethics Committee to testify about

how she obtained a leaked Senate report that she used in a story. The episode takes a number of shots at the senators who question Murphy (who are thinly veiled caricatures of the members of the Senate Judiciary Committee that grilled Anita Hill), and Murphy delivers an entertaining diatribe denouncing them for their "grandstanding and shameless self-promotion." For all this, however, the issues of gender, race, and sexual harassment that were central to the Thomas/Hill hearings (and that figured in the *Designing Women* episode) are completely ignored. Similarly, a 1994 *Murphy Brown* episode, modeled on O.J. Simpson's then alleged murder of his wife and his flight down an L.A. freeway, is recast as a plotline about "FYI"'s difficulties covering a story about a famous white astronaut who has allegedly murdered his brother. Again, race and sex, central to the O.J. case, were eliminated from the narrative.

Postfeminist Politics in *Murphy Brown*

Despite all of the controversy, Murphy's child, Avery, makes little difference in the patterns of Murphy's character or in the narrative of *Murphy Brown*. Avery is not featured in every episode, and Murphy's personality remains largely unchanged. Generally, the child functions as a comic device to plotlines for Murphy's antics. Various episodes center on child-derived plotlines, such as Murphy's attempt to create a perfect, traditional Christmas for Avery (which turns into an exploration of her dysfunctional extended family), the problems that result when Murphy takes Avery to the White House Easter egg hunt, or the difficulties she creates when she attempts to join a mothers' play group.

In fact, at least one article, originally published in the *Los Angeles Times*, featured complaints from a number of women and child-care experts (including baby guru T. Berry Brazelton) that Murphy was unrealistically well-adjusted to working motherhood and that she was not "guilty, anguished, or exhausted" enough. The consensus among those interviewed in this article was that *Murphy Brown*, having defended Murphy's right to be a single mother, has "failed to prove Dan Quayle wrong" by neglecting to portray Murphy as a classically "good" mother and refusing to focus on "what [her] child's life was like" (Smith, 1993, p. E6). Harry Stein, critic for *TV Guide,* made a similar argument in an article in which he claimed that *Murphy Brown* featured "parenthood as designed by people with zero love for children. . . . Say what you will about the much-mocked Ozzie and Harriet, in their world the kids came first. In Murphy's, as in ours, they far too often come last." Indeed, Stein comments in this same column that he had looked forward to the possibility that Murphy, whom he views as overly self-involved, would change: "Would she—like most real moms, working and otherwise—have a visceral understanding of the depth of her child's needs, and, in meeting them, take on a new depth of her own?" (Stein, 1992, p. 31).

Putting aside the obvious arguments that could be made about the possibilities for realism in television, I find a number of fascinating postfeminist contradictions at work in critiques of Murphy's motherhood. The postfeminist working mothers who dominated television in the 1980s never inspired such a reaction, even though they were hardly realistic in that their highly paid professional jobs never seemed to interfere with their constant availability for family matters. However, these women were characters in sitcoms about *family,* not work. *Murphy Brown,* in turn, has always been a sitcom about *work,* not family.

However, the possibility that, after initial adjustment, Murphy's professional life might continue largely unaffected by her maternity is interpreted by critics of *Murphy Brown* as irresponsibility on the part of the show's producers (as if Dan Quayle was really concerned about the maternal fitness of white, wealthy, career women in the first place). For some reason, Murphy's motherhood should dominate her life. Such a move would have brought *Murphy Brown* even closer to the "unstated but ever-present normative implication of postfeminist television . . . that women should combine work with family, and that normal women prioritize the latter" (Press, 1991, p. 146).

To its credit, in one of its rare refusals of postfeminist ideology, *Murphy Brown* refuses to provide this satisfaction. After a brief flirtation with essentialist womanhood in the "natural woman" scene, the sitcom seems to take the position that Murphy's dedication to her job, and her personality as a strong-willed, belligerent woman, will not be drastically altered by motherhood. In a sense, *Murphy Brown* is simply being consistent with its original premise—that Murphy approaches life much like a man would. Her brand of parenting is more stereotypically masculine than feminine in that her life as a professional and her life as a mother seem rather compartmentalized (the masculine model) rather than overlapping (the feminine model). However, her ability to do this is as much a product of class (i.e., her ability to afford a fulltime mothering substitute) as a product of personality. Like postfeminist family television, *Murphy Brown* generally avoids dealing with integration of an employed woman's personal and professional lives. In family-based sitcoms, such as *The Cosby Show,* viewers see only the mother's home life. *Murphy Brown,* in contrast, focuses on the mother's work life. There is little attention, in either case, to the difficulties of juggling the two spheres and their different demands.[15]

In the 1994–95 season, *Murphy Brown* toyed with the idea of Murphy marrying an "FYI" correspondent, Peter Hunt, who became a recurring character in the 1993–94 season and with whom she had been having an on and off romance. Their relationship was a focus in only a few episodes, as Peter was often out of town on assignment. However, in a spring 1995 episode when the two are caught in a hurricane, Peter asks Murphy to marry him and she accepts. In the final episode of the 1995 season, however, with the wedding only days away, both have doubts. They finally conclude that they are too impulsive and that neither really wants marriage. This is a rather unsatisfying episode; the romance was never well developed and there is little investment in its outcome. Certainly, Murphy's marriage would have complicated the show's narrative going into its eighth season.

The most interesting aspect of this episode is its

last scene. After Peter and Murphy agree marriage would be a mistake and Peter leaves Murphy's home, Avery comes downstairs, complaining that he cannot sleep. Murphy picks him up and dances around the room with him to a song from which the refrain is "You're all I need to get by." The clear message here is that Murphy has all the family that she needs, and that her son, rather than marriage, will supply her emotional satisfaction. As it did in the birth episode, *Murphy Brown* descends here into a profound romanticization of motherhood, and one that rings rather false, given Avery's near invisibility in the series narrative. The ending claim of this episode, that Murphy can reject marriage and find fulfillment in motherhood instead, does little but reinforce the general message of the series that a successful career cannot be the basis for a satisfying life for a woman.

This interpretation of Murphy's motherhood has a number of ideological edges, as does Murphy's character generally. *Murphy Brown* gives in to the postfeminist notion that a woman's life is incomplete without reproduction, but does not, in turn, use Murphy's motherhood to further essentialist ideas about the effect of maternity on women's thinking and/or behavior. Nor does it argue that careerism and motherhood are incompatible (for those of us who would have preferred that Murphy remain child-free, this is meaningful and keeps us watching). Likewise, Murphy's difficulties with the tasks of motherhood and her lack of "maternal instincts" can be interpreted as subtle debunking of essentialized constructions of motherhood *or* as further demonstration of how Murphy's stereotypical feminist lifestyle has "defeminized" her and made her (humorously) unsuitable to be a mother—furthering her general function as a comic scapegoat.

More than any other popular television show, *Murphy Brown* represents and comments on various strands of postfeminist thought in the late 1980s and early 1990s: the personal costs of professional success, the conflicts between work and motherhood, and the emphasis on the "choices" women make. Despite the clear coding of its main character as a liberal feminist success story—

prompting even Katha Pollitt to call it "the most feminist sitcom in TV history" (1994, p. 32)—*Murphy Brown* still leaves room for ambivalence.[16]

For profeminist viewers, Murphy is a rare and satisfying portrait of a powerful woman. From this perspective, even Murphy's frequent comeuppances, from which she always bounces back to endure yet more of them, can be viewed as evidence of the continuing discomfort of Americans with powerful women and of the need for continued feminist struggle (certainly, media obsession with Hillary Clinton's persona provides intertextual support for this idea). However, for an audience uncomfortable with the confrontation that feminism presents for many cherished assumptions, Murphy's function as a comedic character, whose extreme personality traits are often the source of humor, provides the relief necessary to keep her character appealing. The fact that Murphy "suffers" for her success makes it easier to accept her rejection of traditional womanhood. Ultimately, *Murphy Brown*'s potential to satisfy viewers from both camps (if only partially) tells us something about why it is so popular.

However, a sitcom's potential to enable diverse evaluations by viewers does not necessarily mean that any of those evaluations are powerfully oppositional; it is possible that "popular texts offer viewers a multiplicitous but *structured* meaning system in which instances of multivocality are complementary parts of the system's overall hegemonic design" (Cloud, 1992, p. 313). Even with its potential doubleness, *Murphy Brown* stops far short of offering any substantive challenge to postfeminism in the same way that *Designing Women* does. For example, *Murphy Brown* reiterates the profoundly disturbing silences of mass-mediated postfeminist discourse on issues such as male responsibility, female solidarity, sexual politics, *and* the significant differences in women's experiences and problems created by race, class, and sexual identity. *Designing Women*, in contrast, gave some attention to all of these factors, though to differing degrees.

This emphasis on individualistic solutions and women's "choices" is classic postfeminism, and it is sustained in the text of *Murphy Brown* and in reactions to it. *Murphy Brown* appears to eschew any acknowledgment of women's collective problems or of the need for collective action to solve them.[17] To me, the fact that so much of the humor generated by Murphy's character derives from her failure to meet conventional expectations for womanhood indicates that we are far from living in postpatriarchy. However, as *Murphy Brown* tells it, Murphy sabotages herself and pays the price for it. Even those critics of *Murphy Brown* who claim that Murphy integrates motherhood and work too easily are not motivated by a desire to dramatize the need for structural change to benefit working mothers. Rather, they are concerned that Murphy is failing to fulfill adequately her responsibility as a postfeminist role model. The onus is not on a workplace, or government, or cultural mindset that has failed to adapt to the realities of women's lives; it is on the woman, the character (or those who write her).

Indeed, it is difficult to view someone as privileged and powerful as Murphy as a victim because she is the kind of woman who has benefited the most from the liberal feminist advances of the past two decades: she is white, wealthy, and well educated. For me, this is the ultimate problem of uncritically accepting Murphy Brown as a representation of what feminism hath wrought: In doing so, all we are gaining is the possibility for a kind of rugged individualism on the part of exceptional women whose lives are cushioned by privileges of education, race, and class. In doing so, we are encouraged to overlook the profound inequalities that burden women who are *not* like Murphy Brown (a category that, in fact, includes most women). The Quayle/*Murphy Brown* incident reveals, at once, just how easily Murphy Brown has been accorded status as the icon of liberated womanhood *and* how different her circumstances are from the poor, black women who have benefited little from liberal feminism and who were Quayle's primary target.

Murphy Brown is a popular sitcom because it taps into the postfeminist anxieties of both those who think feminism went too far and those who think it did not go far enough. In the end, however,

I view *Murphy Brown* as a sitcom which, beyond the "lifestyle feminism" popularized more than twenty years ago by *Mary Tyler Moore*, has no genuine feminist politics of its own, no sense that women's problems can be understood "not as symptoms of individual failure but as symptoms of oppression by a system of male dominance" (Jaggar, 1983, pp. 85–86). That *Murphy Brown* can be so widely interpreted as a vision of feminist success is a testament to how firmly postfeminist attitudes and expectations have taken hold of popular consciousness.

Notes

1. Although many articles on *Murphy Brown* stressed the comparison with *Mary Tyler Moore*, particularly noteworthy is a review of *Murphy Brown* in *The Christian Century* which builds its entire analysis of the sitcom around the comparison, concluding that Murphy is a substantial improvement over Mary (Rebeck, 1989).

2. For other examples of press coverage that make this claim, see Alley and Brown, 1990; Elm, 1989; Horowitz, 1989; O'Connor, 1989; O'Reilly, 1989; Wisehart, 1989.

3. *Esquire*'s connection of *Murphy Brown* with the backlash mentality is interesting—and ambiguous. That is, while the comment seems to cast the backlash as unfair, it also seems to agree with the substantive claim of the backlash—that women simply cannot have it all. Moreover, like backlashers, *Esquire* does not explore how the continuance of patriarchy limits women's capacity to "have it all." Equally interesting is the fact that in *Backlash*, *Murphy Brown* is one of the few television programs that Susan Faludi does not critique as antifeminist (1991, p. 158).

4. In the 1994–95 season, Eldin left *Murphy Brown* (the actor that played him, Robert Pastorelli, began his own sitcom). By this point, Eldin's primary purpose was serving as the nanny for Avery, Murphy's child, and he was replaced in this position by his mother.

5. The names that identify the episodes used in this analysis are from Alley and Brown, 1990.

6. Remarkably, Murphy does indeed refer to herself with a masculine pronoun in this comment.

7. For excellent discussion of these issues in relation to the Thomas/Hill hearings, see Crenshaw, 1992; Lubiano, 1992; Painter, 1992.

8. Hugh Duncan, drawing on Burke, explains the function of a comic scapegoat as a representation of values that pose a threat to the dominant social order (1962, p. 395). Functioning as a caricature of the values in contention, the scapegoat is comically sacrificed, through ridicule, embarrassment, or humiliation, and the social order is protected from the threat it represents (Duncan, 1962, pp. 401, 378).

Such a comic strategy ultimately is aimed at acceptance of the scapegoated character; however, that acceptance must come on the terms set by the dominant cultural group. As Duncan notes: "There is hostility in our laughter, but it is not the hostility of derisive laughter which ends in alienation and hate. . . . Such joking is really a form of instruction, a kind of social control, directed at those we intend to accept once they learn to behave properly" (1962, p. 389). As Duncan explains it, this is the conservative function of comedy; it requires sacrifice of the scapegoat so that authority can be maintained (1962, p. 380).

9. After Jake leaves, Murphy and Jerry Gold make a brief attempt to live together, but they cannot get along. Murphy decides that their relationship makes her feel too dependent and "needy." Murphy's most consistent companion throughout her pregnancy is Eldin, her housepainter, who is motivated, he claims, by the realization that whereas Murphy would be a rotten mother, he would be an excellent one. Indeed, Murphy eventually hires Eldin to be the child's nanny. While Eldin's skill at child-rearing could be viewed as a feminist statement (i.e., men can be caretakers as well as women), it can also be viewed as underscoring Murphy's maternal incompetence (i.e., an itinerant housepainter can be as good a mother as she can).

10. The troubling implication of this scene was not lost on some viewers. In response to a *USA Today* editorial about *Murphy Brown*'s glorification of single motherhood, at least two viewers wrote letters expressing their dissatisfaction with the sitcom's message. One wrote, "Television writers, take a hint: Not every woman has to be fulfilled through the joys of motherhood" ("Aghast at Writers," 1992, p. A10), while another had a more expansive analysis: "Why can't she 'feel like a natural woman' without a child? Why does the entertainment industry insist on showing childless women as less than whole? . . . Is having a child supposed to 'tame' Murphy and make her softer and more feminine? The entertainment industry's message seems to be that liberation has made women unhappy and unfulfilled. What's wrong with exalting an intelligent female character who is happy with her life and her choices?" ("A 'Natural Woman'?" 1992, p. A10)

11. All quotations from the Quayle speech that I use here are from "Excerpts from the Vice-President's Speech on Cities and Poverty," the *New York Times*, May 20, 1992, p. A11.

12. For example, the *Chicago Tribune*, alongside an analysis of the response to the *Murphy Brown* flap from politicians and members of the television community, ran a story entitled "Single Mom: Quayle Stance Is Ludicrous," which featured a single, white, female business executive describing the joys of motherhood. The woman concludes that "she knows 'other single women who have children and who are strong and financially able— and they deserve to have a child if they want to'" (Kleiman, 1992, p. 1:2). By featuring a white, economically privileged woman, even this seemingly oppositional story fails to challenge the politics of race and class raised in Quayle's speech and, in fact, implicitly participates in the distinction between deserving and undeserving mothers that Quayle creates.

13. This remark, in which Murphy refers to herself as "fortunate," is the closest this episode comes to acknowledging the differences between Murphy and the women Quayle was attacking.

14. Katha Pollitt, one of the few journalists to point out the race, class, and gender politics that infused Quayle's speech, offered an incisive analysis of the Quayle/*Murphy Brown* incident that has greatly influenced my thinking about the issues involved. (See Pollitt, 1994, pp. 31–41).

15. A few episodes following the birth did pay some attention to the difficulties created by a new baby. In the 1992 season premiere, a running joke concerns Murphy's inability to find time to take a shower. In another episode, the opening sequence of shots shows Murphy being forced to change her shirt three times because the baby keeps spitting up on it. Another plotline is driven by the problems caused when Murphy brings the baby to the office. After the 1992–93 season these issues largely go away, and there are many episodes when the baby is never seen or mentioned.

16. I use the term "ambivalence" for two reasons. First, I do not see much potential for denotative flux in *Murphy Brown;* hence my avoidance of the term "polysemous." The issue, for me, is not whether viewers are encouraged to see Murphy as carrying meaning about the progress of American women (I think it is clear that they are) but, rather, how they might *evaluate* Murphy's representation of that progress. Second, following Dana Cloud's (1992, p. 314) arguments about depiction of racial difference in *Spenser: For Hire,* I see potential evaluations of *Murphy Brown* "as contained within a *binary* meaning system"; hence the term "ambivalence" rather than "polyvalence."

17. It's useful to note here that Robert S. Alley and Irby B. Brown, in their book-length study of the making of *Murphy Brown,* claim that "the fictional characters on *Murphy Brown* relate to one another as if feminism had succeeded. . . . In the world of FYI . . . Murphy and her colleagues have transcended sexism. They probably do reside in a post-feminist world, a world we would argue rests firmly on the causes championed by the feminist movement" (1990, p. 100).

References

Adler, R. (1979). *All in the family: A critical appraisal.* New York: Praeger.

"Aghast at writers." (1992, May 20). *USA Today,* p. 10A.

Alley, R. S., & Brown, I. B. (1990). *Murphy Brown: Anatomy of a sitcom.* New York: Delta.

Burke, K. (1959). *Attitudes toward history.* Boston: Beacon Press.

"Candice Bergen." (1992, August). *Esquire,* 79.

Charen, M. (1991, August 26). Sitcoms treat unwed motherhood as laughing matter. *The Cincinnati Post,* p. 15A.

Cloud, D. (1992). The limits of interpretation: Ambivalence and the stereotype in *Spenser: For Hire. Critical Studies in Mass Communication, 9,* 311–324.

Crenshaw, K. (1992). Whose story is it anyway? Feminist and antiracist appropriations of Anita Hill. In T. Morrison (Ed.), *Race-ing injustice, engendering power: Essays on Anita Hill, Clarence Thomas, and the Construction of Social Reality* (pp. 402–440). New York: Pantheon.

De Vries, H. (1993, January 3). Laughing off the recession all the way to the bank. *New York Times Magazine,* 19–21, 24, 26.

Dow, B. (1992). Femininity and feminism in *Murphy Brown. Southern Communication Journal, 57,* 143–155.

Dow, B. (1995). Prime-time feminism: Entertainment television and women's progress. In C. Lont (Ed.), *Women and media: Content, careers, criticism* (pp. 199–216). Belmont, CA: Wadsworth.

Duncan, H. D. (1962). *Communications and social order.* New York: Oxford University Press.

Elliott, S. (1992, September 17). Contretemps lifts ad rate for *Murphy. New York Times,* p. C8.

"Excerpts from the Vice-President's speech on cities and poverty." (1992, May 20). *The New York Times,* p. A-11.

Feuer, J. (1992). Genre study and television. In R. Allen (ed.), *Channels of discourse, reassembled: Television and contemporary criticism* (2nd ed., pp. 138–160). Chapel Hill: University of North Carolina Press.

Hewlett, S. A. (1986). *A lesser life: The myth of women's liberation in America.* New York: Warner.

hooks, b. (1994). *Outlaw culture: Resisting representations.* New York: Routledge.

Horowitz, J. (1989, April 19). On TV: Ms. Macho and Mr. Wimp. *New York Times,* pp. 1H, 36H.

Jaggar, A. M. (1983). *Feminist politics and human nature.* Totowa, NJ: Rowman & Allanheld.

James, C. (1991, October 16). A baby boom on TV as biological clock ticks cruelly away. *New York Times,* pp. B1, B7.

Japp, P. (1991). Gender and work in the 1980s: Television's working women as displaced persons. *Women's Studies in Communication, 14,* 49–74.

Jerome, J. (1991, December 2). Murphy's laws. *People,* 157–166.

Kleinman, C. (1992, May 21). Single mom: Quayle stance is "ludicrous." *Chicago Tribune,* p. 2.

Liebman, L. (1994, February). The savior of Saturday night. *New Woman,* 28.

Lubiano, W. (1992). Black ladies, welfare queens, and state minstrels: Ideological war by narrative means. In T. Morrison (Ed.), *Race-ing injustice, engendering power: Essays on Anita Hill, Clarence Thomas, and the construction of social reality* (pp. 323–363). New York: Pantheon.

Mellencamp, P. (1986). Situation comedy, feminism and Freud: Discourses of Gracie and Lucy. In T. Modleski (Ed.), *Studies in entertainment: Critical approaches to mass culture* (pp. 80–95). Bloomington: Indiana University Press.

"Mixed Messages." (1991, May 20). *USA Today,* p. 10A.

"Murphy is not reality." (1991, May 20). *USA Today,* p. 10A.

"Murphy to Dan: Read my ratings." (1992, October 5). *Time,* 25.

"A natural woman." (1992, May 20). *USA Today,* p. 10A.

Painter, N. I. (1992). Hill, Thomas, and the use of racial stereotype. In T. Morrison (Ed.), *Race-ing injustice, engendering power: Essays on Anita Hill, Clarence Thomas, and the construction of social reality* (pp. 200–214). New York: Pantheon.

Pollitt, K. (1994). *Reasonable creatures: Essays on women and feminism.* New York: Knopf.

Press, A. (1991). *Women watching television: Class, gender, and generation in the American television experience.* Philadelphia: University of Pennsylvania Press.

"Quayle vs. Brown." (1992, May 21). *The Cincinnati Post,* pp. 1A, 8A.

Rhodes, J. (1992, September 19). When baby makes two. *TV Guide,* 6–10.

Rosenblatt, R. (1992, December). Candy can. *Vanity Fair,* 223–227.

Rosenthal, A. (1992, May 20). Quayle says riots arose from burst of social anarchy. *New York Times,* pp. A1, A11.

Smith, L. (1993, January 24). Critics say selfish "Murphy Brown" is failing as career mother who wants it all. *St. Paul Pioneer Press,* p. 6E.

Stein, H. (1992, November 14). Our times. *TV Guide,* 31.

Wallis, C. (1989, December 4). Onward, women! *Time,* 80–89.

Waters, H. F., & Huck, J. (1989, March 13). Networking women. *Newsweek,* 48–55.

Wines, M. (1992, May 21). The appeal of *Murphy Brown* now clear at White House. *New York Times,* pp. A1, A12.

Zoglin, R. (1992, September 21). Sitcom politics. *Time,* 44–47.

The 1984 MacIntosh Ad: Cinematic Icons and Constitutive Rhetoric in the Launch of a New Machine

Sarah R. Stein

Half time at the 1984 Super Bowl featured a sixty-second commercial, one that has since taken on legendary status as "the biggest single splash in the history of advertising" (Malone, 1999, p. 274).[1] Its purpose was to announce the release of the Macintosh, Apple Corporation's new personal computer. Titled "1984," the ad evokes the dystopic George Orwell novel of the same name, with its Big Brother figure ceaselessly intoning the slogans of Newspeak. "1984" was directed by Ridley Scott, the highly regarded director of *Alien* (1979) and *Bladerunner* (1982). The ad is elegant, filmic, and, despite its abbreviated form, a powerful cinematic narrative containing allusions to legendary films and cultural myths and icons. *Advertising Age* declared "1984" the Commercial of the Decade for the 1980s (Johnson, 1994) and then in 1995 named it the "greatest commercial" of the last fifty years ("The Best," 1995, p.3). It was the first U.S. commercial to win a Grand Prix award at Cannes (Malone, 1999, p.276). In 1999 *TV Guide* named it the best commercial ever made (Enrico, 1999, p.2). "1984" cost $400,000 to produce and $500,000 for the advertising slot in which it ran.[2] As an advertisement broadcasting nationally, it ran only once (Levy, 1994).

In retrospect, it was a defining moment, not only of the heralded computer revolution but also of what has become our media landscape: "It turned the Super Bowl from a football game into advertising's Super Event of the year. And it ushered in the era of advertising as news: The three major TV networks replayed parts or all of the spot as a story on nightly news programs" (Johnson, 1994, p.1).[3]

The ad broadcast was followed with a highly orchestrated promotional scheme: television and print ads displaying the Macintosh computer and touting the simplicity of its use ("1984" never showed the product), press releases, T-shirts—an integrated marketing strategy that the president of the American Association of Advertising Agencies called the "beginning of a new era" (Johnson, 1994, p.1). With the launch of the Macintosh, the personal computer began its evolutionary course to its current status as an indispensable object in millions of everyday lives. Although Atari and IBM had already been manufacturing personal computers, it took Apple's Macintosh to change the nature—and the perception—of individual computing. At the same time, the Macintosh ad opened the floodgates of computer hype. Images of computer-based technologies poured forth, images that were themselves increasingly generated by the very technologies they were promoting.

This study provides a critical look at the ways that mass media help to shape a culture's incorporation of new technologies, and in doing so, contribute to our ongoing understanding of the hegemonic processes engaged in technological dissemination. Its focus is the cultural constructions circulated by television commercials, specifically the Macintosh "1984" ad, early in the introduction of computers into everyday lives. If, as Hartley (1992) claims, "the popular media of the modern period are the public domain, the place where and the means by which the public is created and has its being," (p.1), then mass media texts, such as new technology ads, form part of that public domain and thereby influence public perception of the desirability and efficacy of technological mediation of everyday social and economic interactions. Advertising thus can be seen as a significant locus of cultural production to be understood, as Schudson (1986) argues, not simply as a system of corporate persuasion but as a "distinctive and central symbolic structure" in society (p. 210).

In the cultural transformation wrought by the widespread dissemination of the personal computer over the last two decades, the "1984" ad represents a key rhetorical moment. Its tropes of freedom and revolution made possible by a computational device still dominate popular discourses, both commercial and philosophical. In Aristotelian terms, it was a kairotic moment, the right cultural product appearing at the right time, a critical juncture in the emergence of an information economy and computer-mediated social world. IBM had overtaken the Apple II in the early 1980s corporate market with a personal computer that foregrounded computational complexity. The Macintosh ad was to launch accessible computing for the non-expert public.

Although the "1984" ad has been the subject of ongoing popular media attention, it has not been subjected to extensive critical examination.[4] Its standing as a rhetorical text of enduring power and status warrants a closer look at its internal dynamics as well as its cultural impact, and criticism provides the means by which this may be accomplished. In examining this text for its complex interweaving of ideologies and cinematic icons that elevated the cold rationality of a machine into the realm of fantasy and the mythic, this essay contributes to an understanding of the integral role ads play in contributing to and drawing on ideological and cultural discourse.

The analysis is based on a synthesis of three theoretical frameworks: Maurice Charland's (1994) treatise on the rhetorical constitution of a particular public that is ideologically based and grounded; Robert Goldman (1992) and others' work on the significance of advertisements in social and political relations; and Walter Benjamin's concepts of the role of cinematic representation and of mass-mediated re-enchantment (1968; see also Buck-Morss, 1994). By combining the literature on meaning making in advertising discourses with Charland's view of constitutive rhetoric, this analysis contributes to a theoretical understanding of the strong constitutive, ideological function of advertising texts.

The first section of the essay surveys the theoretical frameworks that are the basis for the analysis of the Macintosh ad. Charland's theory of constitutive rhetoric is connected with analyses of ads as key cultural symbol systems to reveal the workings of ideological discourses in an emergent period of our computer-mediated society. The first section concludes with a brief history of the Macintosh marketing strategy, and the rhetorical context in which the "1984" Macintosh ad first appeared.

Theoretical Frameworks

In the emergence of a new technology, and particularly one as foreign as a computer was to most people outside scientific or corporate domains, speculative discourses often shape expectations more than substantive assertions. Popular media representations such as ads then play a central role in the hegemonic production and reproduction of perspectives on new technologies in our culture. In investigating such representations both the ideological codes that construct them and the audiences they address are important.

Charland's (1994) conception of constitutive rhetoric was developed to illuminate the workings of political discourse, yet it provides a framework to understand how audiences are rhetorically constructed by advertising texts. Charland builds on Kenneth Burke's proposal in *A Rhetoric of Motives* to use "identification" rather than "persuasion" as the key term of the rhetorical process in which "audiences are constituted as subjects through a process of identification with a textual position. This identification occurs through a series of ideological effects arising from the narrative structure of constitutive rhetoric" (Charland, 1994, p.228). Audiences are not considered to exist outside rhetoric as the subjects of its address, but rather to "live inside" the rhetoric that constructs them:

A theory of constitutive rhetoric leads us to call into question the concept, usually implicit to rhetoric's humanist tradition, of an audience composed of unified and transcendent subjects. If we are left with a subject, that subject is partial and decentered. History, and indeed discourse itself, form the ground for subjectivity. (p.228)

The theoretical move toward understanding audiences as embodying and, thus, participating in the discourses that attempt to persuade them allows for a rhetorical view of ideological discourse:

> Because ideology forms the ground for any rhetorical situation, a theory of ideological rhetoric must be mindful not only of arguments and ideographs, but of the very nature of the subjects that rhetoric both addresses and leads to come to be. Indeed, because the constitutive nature of rhetoric establishes the boundary of a subject's motives and experience, a truly ideological rhetoric must rework or transform subjects. (p.229)

In 1984, generating consumer awareness of the computer outside of scientific or corporate realms and as something beyond a game console meant not only introducing a radically different personal computer to the marketplace. It entailed transforming the social identity of the consumer into that of a personal computer user, at the time an identification held by few outside of a narrow work context. This transformation requires a rhetorical re-positioning, as Charland (1994) suggests:

> What is significant in constitutive rhetoric is that it positions the reader toward political, social and economic action in the material world and it is in this positioning that its ideological character becomes significant. For the purpose of analysis, this positioning of subjects as historical actors can be understood as a two-step process: First, audience members must be successfully interpellated; not all constitutive rhetorics succeed. Second, the tautological logic of constitutive rhetoric must necessitate action in the material world; constitutive rhetoric must require that its embodied subjects act freely in the social world to affirm their subject position. (p.221)

Charland developed his theory of constitutive rhetoric through his analysis of the sovereignty claims made by Quebec in its bid for independence from Canada. The discourse he examined focused primarily on a "White Paper" that sought to convince a specific population to vote for secession, a population that had to recognize themselves as the rhetorically framed "Québécois." In a similar fashion, the Macintosh ad sought to engage viewers in assuming the mantle of an information freedom fighter who could withstand the brainwashing techniques of a despot, an identity that would then mobilize them into the computer-mediated world.

Charland's (1994) theory posits three ideological effects: (1) the process of constituting a collective subject through narratives that foster an identification superseding divisive individual or class interests; (2) the positing of a transhistorical subject; and, (3) the illusion of freedom and agency of the narrative's protagonist. The third ideological effect is of particular utility in revealing the constitutive rhetoric of the Macintosh ad. It provides a means of understanding how the ad's narrative connects to social action, in this instance reconstituting audiences as personal computer users:

> Constitutive rhetorics are ideological not merely because they provide individuals with narratives to inhabit as subjects and motives to experience, but because they insert "narrativized" subjects-as-agents into the world.... In particular,... the constitution in action of a motivated subject, that orients those addressed toward particular future acts. (Charland, 1994, p.223)

Advertising discourse constitutes viewers as deficient in some quality, attribute, or value such as happiness or liberty, a deficiency constructed as happily remedied through the consumption of material objects. In the terms of Charland's third ideological effect, ad narratives construct us as subjects motivated by lack, sent into the world as acquisitive agents. The ideological and rhetorical work involved in this transformation of viewers into subjects can take place at two different levels, the cognitive and the emotional, including aesthetic practices that extend the reach of ideological rhetoric beyond political public address. As will be demonstrated later in the analysis, the "1984"

Macintosh ad is inclusive of both levels theorized by Charland: a narrative that provides strong possibilities for identification as well as a visually compelling aesthetic employing innovative computer-generated special effects.

The concept of constitutive rhetoric enriches our understanding of the ideological aspects of advertisements, particularly those that promote new technologies. Although Charland provides an overarching look at how audiences are constructed within ideological discourses, critics of advertising texts provide a sense of how the ideological codes that produce the narrative work. As cultural critics such as Goldman (1992) point out, advertising images are ideologically powerful because they draw sociocultural meanings from viewers' lives as well as from the mass media themselves, meanings reframed as inherent to the products. Goldman views ads as "maps to the cultural reproduction of commodity hegemony":

> In a society that is fundamentally structured by commodity relations—by the relations of private property and wage labor—ads offer a unique window for observing how commodity interests conceptualize social relations....This search for the underlying social grammar of meaning in ads is an essential step toward grasping the deeper ideological significance of ads in our cultural and political lives. (p. 2)

To further the search for meaning, Goldman incorporates Williamson's (1978) analytic framework to parse the system of value exchanges in ads, illuminating their influence on viewers. In ads the meaning of one thing is made equivalent to another, the visual signifier is substituted for the product's signified: "signifieds are quickly transformed into signifiers: what reflects us will soon create us too, the symbols of our feelings will become the bounds of our feelings" (Williamson, 1978, p. 47). The meaning produced by viewers, through their work of exchanging values of signifiers, exists in a transformational space in which we as subjects are constituted as well. Viewers are part of the meaning-making process; at the same time, the meanings made help to shape viewer subjectivities.

Expectations and assumptions about new technologies are particularly susceptible to symbolic negotiations and narrative symbolizations (see Rosenthal, 1991). Repetitive media images such as ads have the power to establish frames of reference and mark the boundaries of public discussion as an integrative common language. Such frames of reference inform Marchand's (1986) cultural critique of print ads in mass circulation publications of the 1920s and 1930s. Marchand identifies the verbal and visual patterns used to frame the valorization of "modernity" by consumer capitalism during the time of the first great wave of immigration in the twentieth century:

> If the metaphors, syntactical patterns, and verbal and visual "vocabularies" of our common language establish our parameters of thought and cut the furrows along which our ideas tend to flow, then advertising has played a significant role in establishing our frames of reference and perception. (p. xx)

Brief though it is, the "1984" Macintosh ad is such a richly layered narrative that contributes to frames of reference that mark the transition into the Information Age: a world saturated in vibrant color and fantasy, a world made free by the freeing of information, a world of tomorrow brought into the present by a radically new technology. Yet the "1984" ad is also highly reminiscent of Ridley Scott's *Bladerunner*, evoking its "cyberpunk film noir" sensibility and the fears in society that make such cultural products so compelling: alienation of the human spirit, abandonment of the body, increasing estrangement from the natural world, displacement in the work force—all are fears that continue to feed the tension between humans and machines. In the face of such hopes and anxieties, the promoters and advertisers of computer-based technologies employ rhetorical strategies and visual tropes that foreground the power and wonder of technological innovation.

Promotional rhetoric has long been a corollary to the introduction of new technology. Mass-mediated discourses have fostered the shifts in public consciousness necessitated by the introduction of every mass communication technology since the telegraph (see Marvin, 1988; Spigel, 1992). New technology ads have fostered the adoption of the personal computer by non-technical users in ways both parallel to and divergent from earlier communication technologies. The electric light, the telegraph, telephone, radio, and television are all communication technologies that materialized in forms foreign to early adopters; their introduction required the production of cultural conventions targeted at non-expert consumers. Yet none of these prior media forms have required the level of technical expertise computers demand of mainstream users. Neither tuning into a television program nor the often intimidating job of programming a VCR are comparable to the level of skills required in the use of a personal computer, an unstable medium prone to frequent breakdowns with rapidly changing software applications that must be learned and updated. How computers are made to speak to overcome their very foreignness requires the type of non-expert, everyday discourses in which ads excel.

Walter Benjamin expressed a similar perception of the function of mass culture in *Passagen-Werk,* (1972) his study of the nineteenth-century Parisian arcades, or the first mega–shopping mall. He saw in mass culture a move toward the "re-enchantment" of the social world through commodities and images that brought about a "reactivation of mythic powers" (quoted in Buck-Morss, 1994). His notion of re-enchantment played off Max Weber's (1904) social theory that pointed to the valorization of abstract and formal reasoning in the eighteenth and nineteenth centuries as the source of the disenchantment and rationalization of economic and political structures as well as cultural forms. Benjamin perceived a level below this systematic rationalization, an unconscious dreamworld fueled by the projection of ancient mythic symbols onto present commodity images, the re-enchantment from which the collective needed to be awakened. Goldman's (1992) conceptual framework of meaning making in ads rests on the socio-cultural knowledge viewers bring to their interpretation, and Benjamin (1972) provides us with one source of the shared values that constitute that

knowledge. As is later elaborated, Benjamin's notion of re-enchantment through commodity images correlates with one of the cultural icons invoked in the Macintosh ad.

Cinematic representations were the early twentieth century's cultural realization of the visual. Benjamin saw the language of film as a bridge during a period of transition, helping people to navigate within the changing conditions of their world. In a time of physical dispersal of human populations, the new medium of film afforded people the means to connect with each other, to see one another clearly through the distance-obliterating closeups afforded by the camera lens. Further, Benjamin remarked on the state of distraction in which audiences perceived architecture and film at the turn of the century, a state very like the one mass media advertisers rely on for optimum persuasion today.

Mirroring what Benjamin (1972) perceived to be the role of cinematic technology in a fundamental shift in viewing the world, ads for new technologies project computer-generated special effects and images of digital technologies that provide a guide to changing modes of cultural behavior and perception. The "1984" Macintosh ad, a commercial that is itself one of the most cinematic in form and content of any produced, promotes a product that promises re-enchantment, bringing color and art to the gray, rationalized world of computation.

The "1984" Macintosh ad in particular lends itself to an analysis utilizing the frameworks discussed above because of its appearance in the emergent personal computer evolution and its use of a cinematic and cultural vocabulary. Charland's (1994) view of audiences, not as transhistorical subjects addressed by a persuasive appeal, but rather first *constituted* as "narrativized subjects-as-agents" propelled into the world supports an exploration of the Macintosh ad in its ideological and rhetorical constitution of its subjects-as-acquisitive-agents. Synthesizing such an investigation with Goldman's (1992) work on the interpretation of ads helps reveal the ideological codes embedded in the formal as well as the narrative elements of the "1984" ad. Drawing on Benjamin's (1972) work on the important orienting function of cinematic representations at a time of profound social change and his notion of the re-enchantment of commodities in the form of dream images that keep a society enthralled provides a more nuanced understanding of the role of the numerous cultural icons evoked by the ad. The synthesis of these theoretical frameworks will aid in understanding how the "1984" ad continues to resonate for contemporary critics and viewers.

The sections that follow look at the making of the Macintosh in terms of its promotional team's designs, and the historical context in which the ad first appeared. The history of the Macintosh reveals how the advertising industry addresses the notion of the constitution of an audience. In particular, the formulation of the Macintosh promotional strategies reveals a remarkably intentional rendering of constitutive rhetoric's third ideological effect: the constitution of narrativized subjects-as-agents in the material world.

The Rhetorical History of the Macintosh

The marketing of the Macintosh computer was a process intertwined with the marketing of its creator and his vision. Apple Computer Corporation was founded in 1976 by Steve Jobs and Steve Wozniak. Part of the California hobbyist scene, Jobs and Wozniak had been working together since 1971 building "blue boxes," electronic devices that allowed for illegal access to the long-distance phone system (Campbell-Kelly & Aspray, 1996). Wozniak was the engineering wizard of the two, and in 1975, when the first hobbyist computer kit launched the personal computer revolution, Wozniak joined the Homebrew Computer Club in Berkeley, bringing Jobs with him to meetings (Rose, 1989). Its premise was to "seize control of technology, to transform the computer from an Orwellian instrument of oppression to a liberating force . . . not [through] massive mainframes but from computers so small they could sit on a table" (p.31). The early hobbyists were computer game-players, a background that led to a desire for ease

in human-computer interactions. The Homebrew Computer members, with Jobs particularly attuned to their vision, regarded the creation of an easy-to-use personal computer as a counterattack on the establishment, a liberatory movement:

> The personal computer of Homebrew's dreams would combine the coolest design features with the purest individuality, built by enterprises that undermined the predatory world of Big Business, and priced to liberate the common man. It would be not just a personal computer but a revolutionary act (Malone, 1999, p. 54).

The Sixties' counter-cultural goals for revolution through technology have been characterized by Roszak as "a wishful alliance of the reversionary and technophiliac visions" (Roszak, 1985). It brought together the desire for a return to economic simplicity and self-reliance and mixed it with a view of high tech as a politically egalitarian force. Apple's origins grew out of such a sensibility and reflected the early manufacture of personal computers as a sort of cottage industry.

The prototype for the Apple II was built in a garage and began selling in 1977; its enormous success was among computer programmers, designers, and game players, securing a part of the market ignored by the leading computer manufacturer. IBM, the leader in business computers, stayed out of the personal computer arena until 1981. In that year, IBM hired the advertising agency Chiat-Day (ironically, the same agency that would later create the "1984" Macintosh ad that would demonize IBM) and mounted a highly successful campaign featuring a Charlie Chaplin lookalike to give IBM a "human face" (Caputi, 1988). By 1983 IBM's personal computer surpassed the Apple in sales to become the industry standard, largely because of the availability of business-related software programs that ran on IBM compatible clones such as Compaq (Campbell-Kelly & Aspray, 1996, p. 257).

Jobs's vision for Apple was to create a "user-friendly" computer with an intuitive interface for the domestic market and to reclaim the dominant position in personal computing. By 1979, Apple began developing the Apple III, the Macintosh (with Jobs in charge), and the Lisa, Apple's bid to penetrate the corporate consumer world controlled by IBM and its clones (Malone, 1999, p.236). Lisa's complicated functionality and expensive price tag made it a failure at its launch in 1983, and Apple desperately needed a new breakout product to replace its now aging Apple II technology. The Macintosh, with its mouse and graphical user interface, observed by Jobs in 1979 in a more primitive form at Xerox PARC, was that breakthrough product as far as Jobs and his engineering team were concerned. They would utilize the Lisa graphical interface and produce a personal computer that was affordable and easy to operate for the general public. Jobs named his working group "pirates" and fired them with the revolutionary rhetoric and zeal that had energized him since the sixties. Macintosh was going to change the world. What it needed was a marketing strategy.

Stanford University is the recipient of archived documents from the Apple Computer Corporation and has made them available through a website called "Making the Macintosh" (Stanford University, "Making the Macintosh," 2001). In citing the significance of the materials, Stanford's posted narrative speaks of the Macintosh story as a "kind of Ur-text for Silicon Valley," thereby contributing to the ongoing propagation of the mythic elements of the personal computer industry. This "Ur-text" marked the beginning of popular culture's now familiar casting of programmers, engineers, and technically savvy entrepreneurs as heroic, brilliant rebels against the "system." The Macintosh ad continued in that vein, setting the stage for popular culture's and the advertising world's increasingly fantastic depiction of the world of computers.

Apple's goal for the Macintosh was to establish it as the industry standard for personal computers along with their own Apple II and the IBM-PC. "The Evolution of a Computer," a video produced in 1983 for Apple, featured Apple CEO John Sculley: "We wanted a product that was really going to change people's lives. Where the personal computer could be as important in people's lives as the telephone has been over the last century" (Stanford University, "Making the Macintosh," 2001).

The tone of the documented marketing strategy echoes the computer games that had first popularized the personal computer in the form of the Atari. Referring to the competition, the report states that "IBM will be using its successful corporate positioning approach known as FUD to thwart Apple success in the worldwide business marketplace. FUD stands for Fear, Uncertainty, and Doubt."

The marketing plan targeted "knowledge workers," defined as "professionally trained individuals who are paid to process information and ideas. . . . In general, their psychographic profile correlates very closely with SRI's Values and Lifestyles Study (VALS) group known as 'achievers.' Excluded from our definition of the knowledge worker are CEO's and secretaries/clerks. . . . Macintosh is an advanced *personal productivity tool* for knowledge workers"[3] (Stanford University, "Making the Macintosh", 2001; emphasis added).

What is clear in this statement is the intended penetration of a Tayloristic workplace mentality into the personal space of the home. The marketing plan, then, is rooted in the movement toward a greater colonization of leisure time and the enlistment of the white-collar workforce in extending its own labor. Ironically, that control and productivity of personal space and time is fundamental to the futuristic world of Orwell's *1984*, a bleak reality the Macintosh was designed to subvert.

The public relations firm of Regis McKenna was hired to market Apple products. McKenna's philosophy of high-tech marketing indicates his strategy, "Markets are Made, Not Won":

> [T]raditional marketing was fine for mature markets (like, say, soft drinks), but for new technologies, a more comprehensive approach is necessary.... This *requires defining who users are.... It also requires constructing the rules by which a product would be evaluated—inventing the concepts, terms of evaluation, and discourse that would define a product.*
>
> Markets for high-tech products don't exist, in other words: they have to be created. Thus, high-tech marketing involves not just convincing buyers that a product is right for them; *it involves convincing them to think of themselves as members of a group who would—almost by definition—be interested in that*

product. As sociologists of technology would put it, the technology and its market are co-productions.

Successful marketing would thus define the product, define the way to think about a product, define who its market is, and help customers figure out if they are potential buyers. This sounds subjective, but subjectivity is intrinsic to public perceptions of high-technology products (Stanford University, "Making the Macintosh", 2001; emphases added).

Clearly, personal computers were not yet able to "speak" for themselves, having gained no hold in the social identity or cultural imagination at the time. In a striking echo of constitutive rhetoric's theoretical claims, this ad campaign recognizes the need to define who users are—that is, constitute audiences who as narrativized subjects-as-agents fulfill their subject identities through being propelled into the world to buy computers. The marketing strategists recognize that audiences do not exist outside rhetoric, but, as Charland (1994) states, "the very moment of recognition of an address constitutes an entry into a subject position to which inheres a set of motives that render a rhetorical discourse intelligible" (p.228). What is observable, then, is that elements of a theory meant to *critique* ideological rhetoric are apparently being used to *script* the same rhetoric. It is not only critics of advertising that utilize these principles, but also those within the advertising industry.[5]

Regis McKenna's theory of marketing also applies the logic of the commodity form identified by Goldman (1992) as central to interpreting the impact of advertisements:

A logic is a framework within which social practices are defined and enacted. The logic designates the cognitive and procedural rules which mediate exchanges between people. These rules are evident in the formally rationalized contractual and juridical codes of capitalist society but, more significantly, they comprise tacit and underlying principles which define what is "real" about individuals and the social relations they form (p.19).

Regis McKenna perceived the powerful combination of imagination and identification in selling computers and framed Apple's ads in the image of hip rebels, contemptuous of the conventional corporate world, and whose mission to make the world freer and better through personal computing positioned Apple as a "style, an attitude, a *movement*"(Malone, 1999, p.231). McKenna recognized the necessity of supplementing advertising with "Macmessages" fed to "influencers," such as journalists and industry analysts whose "appearance of objectivity and disinterestedness" was an essential ingredient in orchestrating the coverage of a new technology product (Stanford University, "Making the Macintosh", 2001).

Much of this radiated around and from the public relations personification of Steve Jobs, portrayed as not "just a high-tech intellectual . . . but that elusive combination of visionary and evangelist" (Malone, 1999, p.368). One story that is continually repeated is that of Jobs' visit to Xerox PARC in 1979, where he saw for the first time the graphic user interface and mouse that would later be the design framework for the Lisa and the Macintosh. Jobs' genius and charisma were frequently extolled, and Guy Kawasaki, Apple's chief software evangelist, characterized the "meaning" of the creation of the Macintosh as, "a small team of bright, fearless, and ambitious punks led by a charismatic high priest trying to do the right thing can defeat mediocrity and the status quo"(Kawasaki, 1990, p.25).

In the voluminous press generated about Macintosh from press, evangelists, critics, and biographers, talk of dreams, magic, mission and passion abounds. Macintosh is a philosophy—the *Macintosh Way*—and an expression of fervent belief on the part of Jobs, the Mac developers, and the myriad software developers who provided the programs for the Macintosh to use:

In a world of empty and cynical claims for "revolutionary" toilet bowl cleaners and diet aids, Apple and its agency believed in a higher power. "1984" was "truth in advertising," says Joanna Hoffman, one of 18 original members of the Macintosh engineering and marketing team and now VP-marketing at General Magic, a software company.

Macintosh, Mr. Hayden [the Chiat/Day copywriter of "1984"] says, was "leading a revolution . . . taking the power away from big business and big government and putting it in the hands of people.

"You've got to understand that was the rallying cry in the hallways of Apple. Computing had been held by a close-knit elite, and we were going to bust up the cabal and give the power to the people."

"This spot resonated because it was dealing with fundamental issues at the change of an age," Mr. Hayden says. "'1984'—or any great commercial, any great thing—*operates on a super-rational level, and so it carries with it a lot of freight that has nothing whatsoever to do with what's being said, and nothing whatsoever to do with the product in question*" (Johnson, 1994, p.2; emphasis added).

The statements above are clear examples of what Goldman (1992) and other theorists refer to as "commodity-as-sign," maintaining that modern advertising teaches viewers to consume the sign, not the product. The reference to the "super-rational level" in the discourse above echoes as well Benjamin's (1972) concept of "dream images," messages of re-enchantment that lurk below and in resistance to the hyper-rationalized empirical worldview. Most important, the promotional strategists' statements delineate the central ideological code of the narrative: revolution and freedom.

The impact of the "1984" ad is clearly evident in several media initiatives: News coverage of "1984" began the practice of reporting on advertising as news, and of most significance turned the Super Bowl into an advertising event for new campaigns, a veritable hymn to capitalism.[6] News now regularly reports nearly as much on the commercials the day after the Super Bowl as on the game, and the computer industry and Internet-related companies have been major advertisers at that event. The price of the commercial airtime is currently about $2 million for a thirty second spot, about four times the cost of the same time slot when the Macintosh ad was aired (Linnett & Friedman, 2001).

Although the "1984" Macintosh ad ran only once in a commercial spot, forty-six percent of U.S. households were tuned in (Johnson, 1994, p.2), and it has been broadcast repeatedly on news and award programs. Ironically, however, "1984" al-

most was not broadcast. The Board of Directors saw it just days before the air date and loathed it. The ad contained nightmarish depictions of dehumanization through technology, and worse, it never displayed the product. Jobs and the marketing team were ordered to sell the time and pull the spot (Malone, 1999, p.273). In addition, the ad received the lowest-ever score for a business machine commercial in focus group testing that was commissioned by the Macintosh marketing team to change the Apple Board's minds (Goldberg, 1994, p.21). One of the two minutes that had been purchased was sold; when the other minute couldn't be sold off, the decision was made, just days before the Super Bowl, to run the ad.

The Apple Board's response is interesting as their inability to grasp the ad's rhetorical and aesthetic power placed them outside of what Charland referred to as the narrative's "identificatory" function necessary to the successful constitution of subjects (223). As Rose stated, "what they failed to realize—what they couldn't realize, being businessman and capitalists rather than dreamers—was that Macintosh wasn't a computer, it was a crusade"(Rose, 1989, p.133). In time, the tone-deafness on the part of those businessmen to the Macintosh ad would prove prophetic: while the ad itself resonated powerfully and created an immediate spike in Macintosh sales, the corporate world never adopted it to the degree Apple's "revolution" had prescribed. The ad's rhetoric constituted its subjects as rebels against the "system." In the widespread dissemination of the personal computer in the years following the Macintosh's release, Apple's marginal status in the industry has never afforded its subjects another role (Yaukey, 2001, p. C-1).[7]

As this rhetorical history makes clear, the theoretical themes developed by Charland, Goldman, and others are present in the advertising discourse. The principles spelled out by the theorists also functioned in producing the Macintosh ad: constituting the audience and subject positions for new technologies in the framework of commodity logic were paramount marketing strategies in the emergence of the personal computer.

The Rhetorical Context
of the "1984" Ad

The Macintosh ad "1984" appeared in a year in which several themes coalesced that continue to inform our present computer-based information society. In 1984, Ronald Reagan was elected in a landslide victory to a second term of the presidency. Reagan not only embraced the ultimate high technology in the form of the Strategic Defense System (dubbed "Star Wars") but also continued to push his anti–big government agenda (at least rhetorically), a chord that would resonate in the Macintosh narrative itself.

On the cultural front, William Gibson's *Neuromancer* was published in 1984, coining the term "cyberspace" for the realm of networked electronic communications, and thus making a seminal contribution to the burgeoning cyberculture of the 1980s and 1990s. Further, *The Terminator* was released in 1984, bringing stardom to Arnold Schwarzenegger and supplying the world with a prototype for the cyborg as consummate evil, an anti-human life-form created by the coming to consciousness of the globe's networked computers. Finally, Sherry Turkle's study of young computer programmers at MIT, *The Second Self*, was published in 1984, and introduced the notion that humans invest spirituality in their dealings with computers and even accord independent intelligence to the computers themselves.

One further movement in the media environment of 1984 is worthy of note: a shift in advertising strategy that marked the Association of American Advertising Agencies' attempt to re-engage jaded viewers. Goldman (1992) reports on their ad campaign in that year, "Advertising. Another Word for Freedom of Choice," that headlined the questions, "Is advertising a reflection of society? Or is society a reflection of advertising?" (p.3). The use of the phrase "freedom of choice" resonated with the short-lived marketing strategy targeting independent women as consumers (see Goldman, Heath & Smith, 1991).[8] The Advertising Association's ad also set the stage for the opaque and ambiguous (and often entertaining) advertising narratives that pervaded the commodity culture by the 1990s. The 1984 campaign's advertising narratives denied the symbolic equivalence exchange between the viewer and the commodity ideal (Williamson, 1978) by incorporating criticism of advertising into the ads, utilizing overt elements within commercial narratives to "recognize" viewer sophistication, and reflexively foregrounding the conventions that inform the routine reading of ads. The Association's market research found this new breed of ads to be highly effective in grabbing and keeping audience attention, requiring the viewer to decipher obscure symbolic narratives and even what product is being sold.

The years preceding the introduction of the Macintosh were those in which attitudes toward personal computers exhibited more technophobia than celebration. Reed's investigations of instructional and popular media in the 1970s and 1980s found cultural management of technophobia to be a primary concern in the mainstreaming of the personal computer (Reed, 2000). Women were especially cast as fearful of the effects of the personal computer as it encroached on the domestic sphere, and mainstream magazines made a considerable effort to cajole the U.S. housewife into accepting this new technology as a constructive pastime for her husband and children. Feminist critics such as Doane (1990) and Wajcman (1991) have noted the fundamental opposition between discourses of the technological and of the feminine, with the technological "always promising to control, supervise, regulate" the latter (Doane, 1990, p.163). The "1984" Macintosh ad, however, cast a female as its victorious protagonist. It is with these tensions, contradictions, and anticipations in the larger rhetorical context that I turn to the text of the ad itself.

Description of the Text

"1984" begins with an extreme long shot of a line of men, dressed uniformly in gray prisoner-style clothing, marching in a circular tunnel, much like that in an underground train system. The audio, which extends for most of the piece, consists of a rumbling background with the sound of marching feet and a sustained electronic tone. Mixed over this, at first almost inaudibly and then in full force, is the voice heard throughout; its first intelligible words are: "Today we celebrate the first glorious anniversary of the information purification directives."

The image cuts to a mere flash (a quarter of a second) of a woman running, carrying a long-handled hammer. The woman is in color. She is dressed as a track and field athlete, with short blond hair, a white sleeveless T-shirt with a schematic drawn on the front, and vibrant red shorts. Her entrance is heralded by two electronic notes, a high D, followed by another, one octave below, whose decay seems to ring out continuously underneath the following shots, until the high D is sounded again. This audio motif acts as a clarion call that announces each one of the shots of the woman running.

The next shot is a close-up of the workers' faces as they march by. Only white males are visible, all with shaven heads and blank, fixed stares, a few wearing gas masks (Levy, 1991, p.171). The pallor and sickliness of the workers are accentuated. The air is thick with smog, a bluish-gray haze overlaying everything, reminiscent of Scott's vision of the bleak, rainy misery of the future Los Angeles in *Blade Runner.* The image cuts to a brief shot of men in face-obscuring helmets, running with rifles in their hands. The long shot of the marchers in the tunnel reappears, the camera positioned to cut their heads out of the frame. Their bodies move along mechanically, arms hanging inertly. Television monitors are attached to the walls every few feet along the way. The camera cuts to a close-up of their feet, marching in lockstep.

The runner appears, again briefly. The voice has intoned over the last three shots: "We have created, for the first time in all history, a garden of ideology where each worker may bloom, secure from the pests of contradictory truths," the word "truths" hitting over the image of the runner. The image cuts to reveal for the first time the source of the relentless voice. In an extreme long shot, a huge hall is seen filled with workers already seated as others march in. The hall is monumental, the line of marchers/workers appears endless. The back wall of the hall is an enormous screen, filled by the talking head of an elderly man in glasses. The screen resembles that of a computer monitor, and computer code can be glimpsed along its borders. The man's face is framed so that the top of his head and the bottom of his chin are cut off. He appears hollow-cheeked and steely-eyed, the cinematic stereotype of the cold-blooded tyrant. As he speaks, his words appear in white font on the screen below his mouth, each word preceded by a round dot of light, the proverbial bouncing ball.

We see the runner for the first time in full-body, flanked by enormous marble columns. Noticeable now are the red shoes on her feet, and the power of her stride. Behind her the cadre of guards appears. The camera cuts to a panning shot of the workers, staring passively at the screen as if mesmerized. The words "Our unification of thought is more powerful a weapon . . ." are heard from the screen. Once again the camera pans over workers sitting inertly, one or two now visible as quite young. The voice builds in intensity: ". . . than any fleet or army on earth. We are one people . . ." Cut to the runner in slow-motion in an extreme long shot that reveals the vast and imposing hall. ". . . with one will." Cut to a medium shot of the faceless guards: "One resolve." Then the camera reveals the full computer screen, the tyrant's face filling most of the frame: "One cause. Our enemies shall talk themselves to death . . ." The image cuts over the last words to the runner stopping and beginning to spin with the great hammer. For the first time we can just make out the drawing on her shirt—the Macintosh logo of the bitten apple and monitor-keyboard. The guards are approaching in the background. The image cuts to a medium shot of the guards running fast.

The runner spins again. The voice continues, with the image cutting in mid-sentence to a full-frame closeup of the face on the screen, venomously proclaiming as the bouncing ball follows the words: "And we will bury them with their own confusion."

The runner makes her final windup and lets go

of the hammer with a loud cry, as the guards are almost upon her. We see the hammer in slow motion flying through the air, then a wide shot of the screen with the hammer approaching. The on-screen presence finishes in diabolical triumph "We Shall Prevail," just as the hammer shatters the screen in a blinding flash and the sound of a detonation. A synthetic chorus of wordless cries is heard, behind which is a sound like rushing wind. The camera pans over the workers, flooded with white light, their mouths opened in awe, hands gripping the benches beneath them, uniforms blown back against them. A title, its text in black font, rolls up the white screen, as we hear the familiar television advertising voice of authority of the cultured, white male:

On January 24th,
Apple Computer will introduce
Macintosh.
And you will see why 1984
won't be like "1984."

The screen fades to black, then reveals the last image we see: the multi-color graphic of an apple, with a bite taken out of it.

The ad's production values are those of high-budget feature quality. The great visual lushness of the images presents a futuristic scene at once frightening and enticing, reminiscent of the feel of the lighting of Scott's *Blade Runner*. The cinematic technology, with its telephoto lenses and mattes, is supplemented by the then cutting-edge computer-generated special effect of the slow motion flying hammer and the blinding white light that fills the hall at the end of the spot.

The formal structures of the commercial add to its power. The accelerating pace of the cuts juxtaposing the lone woman, the faceless band of guards in pursuit, and the giant, bodiless face on the screen, produce a kinesthetic experience of danger and urgency triumphantly resolved with the contact of the hammer with the computer screen and its satisfying explosion.

The aural code is complex. The meaningless sloganeering of the tyrant puppet on the screen continues unceasingly, destructive of thinking, of reflection. The marching feet, the great hall ambiance, the electronic rumble, all work to create an aura of dread, of industrialized enterprises and great human oppression. The multilayered sound seems designed to mesmerize. The body is prevented from contacting itself when sound intrudes that way, creating a kind of disorientation on so cataclysmic a level that it is impossible to reconnect the mind and the body. The body becomes an automaton, running on pilot, programmed by the aural bombardment (see Turkle, 1984, p.362). Then the clarion call, announcing the running woman: an alarm, an audio hailing, something that has escaped from the iron-fisted control of the aural environment.

Analysis

One of the most striking aspects of the Macintosh ad on first viewing is that it casts the introduction of the ultimate rational device—a computational machine—into a mythic narrative of Manichean struggle. This version of a David triumphing over a Goliath projects the promise of a future freed from tyranny and the constraints on an unbridled creative renaissance. Yet its intertextual resonance with *Blade Runner*'s tale of robotic replicants created and controlled by a ruthless master—a powerful dystopic narrative of unchecked technological progress—is also present. The tensions and ambivalence so often present in dreams of technological salvation and enchantment are strongly evident here: the dehumanized and brainwashed legions of workers, their bodies as broken as their minds are shackled, alienated from their surroundings and each other, mesmerized by the lure and the cadence of high technology.

The ad makes manifest two other cultural preoccupations that have resurfaced throughout popular culture in relation to new technology. The roboticized, automaton-like workers materialize the fears expressed from Thomas Carlyle on that not only will machines become more human, but that humans also will become more like machines. In a less overt way, these figures evoke the haunting specter of joblessness, of the displacement of humans by machines, an anxiety complicating the reception of technological advances since the Industrial Revolution.

The other cultural anxiety hinted at in the text is that of the obsolescence of the physical body. If the computer is an invention and extension of the human mind, the bodiless head floating on the screen is a symbolic reenactment of the human body becoming obsolete, a fear that is materialized in even more threatening terms in *The Terminator* which was released the same year.[9]

Much of the ongoing fascination with the "1984" Macintosh ad—and a significant facet in its hold on viewers' and critics' imaginations—can be attributed to its reconfiguring of popular cultural icons. The most obvious articulation is with the novel that gives the ad its name, *1984*. George Orwell's novel, written in 1948, is a critique of power, directed specifically at Stalin and his gulag and evident in the mass of prisoner/workers assembled on the screen in the "1984" ad. The incantations of the voice emanating from the screen evoke the Newspeak of the novel, a form of ideological brainwashing that ruthlessly curtailed the words permitted expression in the totalitarian society of 1984. That society was policed night and day by "Big Brother," a panoptic presence on countless television screens.

The ad's use of this theme suggests some intriguing political inflections. The IBM culture was famous for its rigid rankings and insistence on a uniform, blue-suited corporate look and attitude. Steve Wozniak and Steve Jobs, Apple's founders, had already been brought into the public eye by media stories highlighting their hippie, garage-grunge style and anti-corporate, anti-hierarchical stance. The baby-faced, long-haired Jobs, with his slingshot aimed at the IBM giant, was the personalized basis for the David and Goliath myth evoked by the ad.

The identification of Big Brother and Stalin with IBM/Big Blue is clearly intentional, although IBM, it might be argued, is quintessentially representative of capitalism. The reversal of that identification, the equation of IBM with the communist dictatorship of Stalin, allows a reiteration of the conflation of capitalistic competition (suppressed

by IBM in this narrative) with democracy and freedom, represented by the Macintosh. That this is at odds with the professed Sixties "power to the people," anti-capitalist sensibilities of Jobs and the other developers of the Macintosh is an issue addressed later in this essay.

As discussed above, Charland developed his theory of constitutive rhetoric to understand the workings of political discourse in Quebec's movement toward independence. One aspect of the rhetoric used to constitute the Quebec people was to frame the existing government as not real, as illegitimate in its claim to represent the Québécois. In a parallel fashion, in the Macintosh ad, the equation of IBM with Orwell's Big Brother and its authoritarian control over language and thought negates it as a source of information (which longs to be free), rendering it inauthentic as a leader of the computer revolution. The cognitive processes—ways to think, to communicate—are imprisoned, the robotic bodies become metaphors for the shackled and brainwashed mind. Apple is equated with the real leader of the information revolution as it frees the computer users from subjugation to IBM and its operating system, DOS.[10]

Orwell's dystopic tale is the most directly quoted framework for the ad's narrative structure, but there are other important cultural symbols invoked along with it. The opening shot of the marching workers is taken from Fritz Lang's 1927 *Metropolis*, a film that depicted the destructiveness of capitalism and the misery of the working class in a plea for compassion and equity. The futuristic world of *Metropolis* is dependent on the advanced technology that has created a soaring, awe-inspiring colossus of glass, steel, and flying bridges above ground, yet it is a world that buries the darker side of its technological progress underground. In the endless tunnels undergirding the great city are nightmarish scenes of mechanized industrialism where the relentless push toward greater profit and productivity for the corporate "Master" drives the human laborers to the edge of destruction.

Metropolis begins with a series of shots of the bent and exploited workers in a circular tunnel, directly quoted in the Macintosh ad, leading to their underground city and the machines they die maintaining. The hall in the Macintosh ad in which the head on the screen addresses the mass of men mirrors architecturally the oppressive Master's building in *Metropolis.* Orwell's narrative projected stasis and immutability in the totalitarian state of 1984; Lang's story, however, allowed for resistance and the redistribution of control, a theme central to the Macintosh ad's industrial agenda as well as to its narrative.

Drawing such a classic film into play associates the introduction of the Macintosh with a political sensibility, transforming consumerism into a revolutionary act against authoritarian tyranny and dehumanizing technological progress. Computer choice—and acquisition—wrest control from the tyrannical Master and deliver it into the hands of the individual user. Commodity hegemony, in Goldman's term, is reproduced as democratic principles of free thought and expression are defended and secured through the *real* technological salvation. The media representation of an individual tyrant is a staple of hegemonic ideology, the projection of an isolated and specific instance of abuse that deflects attention from the systemic forces of capitalism and technological development.

In interpreting the ideological codes in "1984," the collective masses here are inimical to freedom. In *Metropolis,* a narrative motivated by more socialistic sensibilities, the massed workers led by a courageous female rebel are the force necessary to the overthrow of the tyranny. In "1984," the U.S. ideological faith in the individual supersedes the potential of the massed workers and is triumphant *despite* the collective. Thus, we have a rhetorically constituted subject who is a political activist by virtue of a choice of a consumer object and who is free to do so because of the *independence* from the masses afforded by capitalism's free market.

Casting a woman in the "1984" ad as the liberator of information technology and thus the savior of the free world was counter to identifications that had surfaced before in popular culture's depictions of technology and femininity. Huyssen (1986) found the attitudes toward technology in *Metropo-*

lis to present two diametrically opposed views: the expressionist fear of technology as oppressive and destructive, and the *Neue Sachlichkeit's* [11] fascination with and belief in technological solutions. Huyssen notes that the balance between male and female sexual identity in eighteenth-century androids gave way to a marked preference in the literature of the nineteenth and twentieth century for a machine-woman. He proposes that in *Metropolis,* male projections result in a homology between woman and technology. This homology encapsulates the myth of the dualistic nature of women, the binary of virgin-mother versus prostitute-vamp projected onto technology, which in turn is perceived as either neutral and obedient or out-of-control and threatening.

In *Metropolis,* the threat of a raging femininity succeeds in displacing the threat of technology. When the robot made in the likeness of the chaste female leader of the workers is burnt at the stake, Huyssen observes, "Sexuality is back under control just as technology has been purged of its destructive, evil, i.e., 'sexual,' element through the burning of the witch machine" (1986, p.81). The expressionist fear of technology and the displacement of male fears of female sexuality projected onto the machine-woman are thus exorcised, leaving intact capitalism's ideological stake in the technological realization of social progress.

In an analogous situation, messages about technophobia tied to women in the popular media discourses examined by Reed also implicate women as obstacles to the social progress realizable through technological innovation. The difference in the instance of emergent computer technologies was that women's *anxieties* rather than their uncontrolled (and uncontrollable) *sexual* appetites threatened the unimpeded march of civilization.

The Running Woman of the Macintosh ad reverses these depictions, displaying a courage, strength, and determination usually reserved for her male counterparts, and fostering an identification necessary to the constitution of subjects. It is a role that resonates with another classic U.S. narrative, one whose inflection is evident in the "1984" ad as well. This is the role of Dorothy in the *Wizard of Oz*, and it contributes in significant ways to the enduring popularity of the ad.

Allusions to the *Wizard of Oz* appear in several of its visual codes. The Running Woman is in color, her blonde hair and red shorts in sharp contrast to the hazy, bluish black and white of the other scenes, paralleling Dorothy's entry into Oz and color, from the black and white of the Kansas scenes. The computer screen talking head is reminiscent of the disembodied head of the Wizard consulted by Dorothy and her friends. The hammer shattering the screen in the Macintosh ad echoes Toto's revelation of Frank Morgan behind the curtain, exposing the virtuality of the Wizard and unmasking the artifice. When the Running Woman is finally shown in full shot she can be seen to be wearing red shoes, and the fully saturated colors of the Apple logo lighting up the screen after it is shattered tells us we are not in Kansas anymore.

Based on this associative link to the Emerald City, Benjamin's concepts of dream images and re-enchantment are illuminating. William Leach (1989) calls the author of the *Wizard of Oz*, L. Frank Baum, one of the "earliest architects of the dream life of the consumer age" (p.107). Baum was the first significant advocate of the aesthetic display of consumer goods and believed fervently in "the virtues of consumption and leisure and in lifting taboos on the expression of desire." The late nineteenth century saw the move from an agrarian to an industrial society, transforming the nation from the "Land of Comfort" to the "Land of Desire." The visual vocabulary of desire was expressed in new forms of representation, reconstructing both the look and the meaning of commodities and commodity environments.

The aesthetic energies mobilized on behalf of consumption were fed by technological developments in the production of colored glass and electrical light. Baum's fascination with these fueled his success in creating a new language of commodity interpretation, influencing merchants and department stores to create visual environments for goods that evoked magical associations. Baum's animation of products, according to Leach, helped to accustom Americans to living in artificial environments, even to finding them superior to the natural, a preference significant in light of our contemporary virtual communities and mediated communication networks.

In Leach's words, "Display was fantasy, childhood, theater, technological play, and selling all rolled into one for Baum, as it would be for later display artists infatuated with the same urban commercial forms." The show window was of primary importance to Baum, leading him to exhort department stores and fellow merchants to ever-larger windows in which theatrical effects and a new enchantment could be offered for the consumer's imagination (1989, p.110).

When Baum began writing his fictions in 1900, after 25 years as a merchant, his literary works followed the aestheticization of machinery begun in the mid-nineteenth century and culminating around 1915 with the pleasure palaces and their new "aesthetic of artificiality." In a statement that bears a strong resemblance to descriptions of computer morphing and multimedia for which Macintosh provided the lead, Leach (1989) likened Baum's stories to "the literary apotheosis of commodity flow. In the Land of Oz, things are always animated, always metamorphosing; landscapes shift again and again in color and hue, boundaries are magically crossed, and pathways go in many directions at once. Gender lacks fixity" (p.108).

Anne Friedberg (1993) comments on the analogy between Baum's conception of the display window and the cinema screen, because both feature an inaccessible yet visible tableau. Friedberg characterizes the "mobilized virtual gaze" of both window shopping and cinema spectatorship and refers to the late nineteenth-century shop window as "the proscenium for visual intoxication, the site of seduction for consumer desire" (p.65). Window shopping and cinematic spectatorship rely on a gaze that is acquisitive yet distanced, "an integral feature of both cinematic and televisual apparatuses: a *mobilized 'virtual' gaze*. The *virtual gaze* is not a direct perception but a *received* perception mediated through representation" (p.2).

Baum   transformed   consumer   items   into

commodities by transforming the department store window into a theatrical stage, captivating the attention of passersby, ultimately luring them through the doorways to revel in (and purchase) intoxicating objects. The allusions in the Macintosh ad to the *Wizard of Oz* point to an equivalent seduction by dream images, the lure of a different window. Almost a century later, the computer screen offers the same enchantment, luring consumers in as surely as Baum's shop windows, as the Internet is gradually transformed into a virtual shopping mall. The acquisitive drive for goods and information is an additional element to the frenetic consumption particular to our culture—beyond goods, in an information economy, accumulating and consuming information is rapidly becoming both a recreational pastime and a prerequisite for staying employed.

Benjamin's (1972) concept of dream images in the service of capital and the commodification of everyday dimensions of life is strongly echoed in Baum's enthusiastic embrace of the seduction of image and display. In 1984, the emergence of a new form of computer that was to revolutionize the consumer market called on new ways of representing re-enchantment. Macintosh brought color and light to the world of computing, reawakening aesthetic pleasure and appreciation. The magic glimpsed through the early department store windows is evoked in this new promise of an enchanted computer screen, a promise realized later in the multimedia capabilities of the mid-nineties. These new commodities signal a shift in their use value, from the Big Blue world of business and commerce to leisure and designer lifestyle.

Baum proved a significant force at a time of transition in which discursive conventions were being formed for new ways of relating to commodities, in a period when leisure and consumption became the focus of individual fulfillment. Friedberg (1993) sees a progression in the cultural shifts "resulting from the organization of the look in the service of consumption and the gradual incorporation of the commodified experience into everyday life" (p.3):

From the middle of the 19th Century, as if in a historical relay of looks, the shop window succeeded the mirror as a site of identity construction, and then—gradually—the shop window was displaced and incorporated by the cinema screen. Cinematic spectation [was] a further instrumentalization of this consumer gaze. . . . (Friedberg, 1993, p.66).

We can posit a further progression from the cinema to televisual apparatuses and then on to the computer screen, where a new level of identity construction and instrumentalization of the consumer gaze is observable. Extending the progression even further is the projection of an exteriorized identity in the form of adopted personae, virtual avatars in digital environments (see Turkle, 1995).

By incorporating elements interpretable through the *Wizard of Oz,* the Macintosh ad works on a number of levels. It defuses the negative association with computers in the "1984" dystopia represented. By introducing themes of fantasy and wonder, the association is forged between a repressive corporate sensibility and 1984, rather than between computer technology and the invasion of human freedom and spirit graphically depicted, an associative link that could easily contaminate the perception of the Macintosh computer as well as the IBM PC. Quoting the *Wizard of Oz* facilitates a move into the realm of fantasy fiction and magic and invokes the playful, inventive possibilities of the new computers.

The tension nevertheless exists in the 1984 Macintosh ad between these elements of magical play and cinematic delight and the technophobia that has repeatedly been found in cultural responses to technological development. In the ad, bodies and machines are in antagonistic relation to each other. The bodies of the mass of prisoner-workers have been stripped of cognition and volition, rendered automatons by bureaucratic machinery as well as technological development. The narrative in this sense is modernist, expressing the fears and distrust of industrialization. The bodies are inscribed with the marks of a disciplinary society, in which in Foucault's (1993) terms a body becomes a useful force only if it is both a productive body and a subjected body.

Power is present as a destructive force and rendered visible in the technology, the inimical all-seeing presence of Big Blue/Big Brother. The split between body and mind is paramount: the disembodied talking head on the huge computer screen controls the collective body, the roboticized masses at the will of the master. But power, as Foucault points out, is always local and unstable (1990, p.93), and in the "1984" ad, it is depicted as vulnerable to Apple's surrogate, the Running Woman.

The woman in the "1984" Macintosh ad is a significant figure in contrast to depictions in later technology commercials. She represents a powerful body able to execute a plan with great risk, formulated with a mind capable of maintaining its autonomy, a figure that provided a heroic narrative figure for the identification at the base of Charland's (1994) theory. She equally represents a political figure, one aware of the repressive powers of advanced capitalism and willing to use revolutionary tactics in response. The rigorous training of her body, then, is in protest and defiance of the docile, subjected bodies of the roboticized masses of DOS users. Recall that Apple retained at that time an image of the maverick, of an anti-corporate, individualistic U.S. entrepreneurship, and the runner reflects that cultural myth. Hers is the uncontainable, disruptive body, the body aligned with and an appropriate vehicle for a courageous and independent mind.

Casting a woman as the heroic rebel who shatters Big Blue/Big Brother marks several discursive strategies at once. In 1984, the feminist movement, although already facing some of the backlash against women in the public sphere that continues to this day, would still have allowed for a wide familiarity with a woman as signifier of the iconoclastic rule-breaker. In fact, in the summer of 1984 the first and only woman was selected as a running mate for a major presidential candidate.[12] The Running Woman of the "1984" Macintosh ad presents a formidable figure, but one that will not be repeated in the later ads. The clarion call and the

subversion of the established order that the runner represents are about to nose-dive into the backlash of the '80s. The patriarchal oligopoly that Big Blue represents is mobilizing in this period to move to subvert the feminist movement and the interventions made against sexual, racial, and economic inequality. The Running Woman may narratively have survived her assault on Big Brother in 1984, but she will not survive the mass media's symbolic annihilation of her kind in the technology ads of the 1990s.

In the "1984" ad, the Running Woman hurls a sledgehammer, a salute to David's slingshot as well as an ironic co-optation of the communist symbol as an anti-totalitarian weapon. The hammer, made of stone or metal, also resonates with Roszak's assertion of a reversionary-technophiliac synthesis attempted by the sixties' counterculture. He remarks on the vision that energized the early techno-utopians, of a "technophiliac route forward that would lead to a reversionary future":

> For many in the counter culture, the result of high industrial technology would be something like a tribal democracy where the citizenry might still be dressed in buckskin and go berry-picking in the woods: the artificial environment made more artificial would somehow become more . . . natural...The motto of the philosophy might almost have been "Forward to the Neolithic!" (Rozak, 1985)

An even more distant past, reaching into one the West's myths of origin, is evoked, however, with the principal signification visible: the bitten apple's reference to Eve and the Tree of the Knowledge of Good and Evil. Invoking the Edenic myth, with its associations of pain and death as well as the pleasure and knowledge the woman's act precipitates, points us to Leo Marx's (1964) reading of the "machine in the garden." Marx tracks the metaphor of contradiction pervasive in U.S. literature and thought: the idealization of the pastoral in the face of the grim realities of nineteenth-century industrialization and the increasing domination by the machine in the visible world. That this metaphor of contradiction is again present in the "1984" ad affirms the tenacity of the pastoral ideal in our cultural imagination. The Macintosh computer in the ad is the sign of "the fruit of an Edenic tree, with its links to notions of a clean technology, free from polluting and robbing the planet's resources, while making the Tree of Knowledge within everyone's grasp" (Marx, 1964, p.7).

As so often occurs in the most complex popular discourses, however, other cultural chords are sounded. The tensions that exist in the larger culture in response to women asserting their own power must evoke an ambivalence to the portrayal of a rebellious and, therefore, dangerous woman. Many feminist theologians have noted the metaphoric equating of "woman" with "nature" or the earth, and the corresponding edict in Genesis to subdue "her" (see Johnson, 1993; McFague, 1987). As Jane Caputi (1988) points out, the Apple logo replaces the material symbol of knowledge with an inorganic icon representing artificial intelligence, knowledge, and understanding stripped of their elemental material dimensions (p.514). The Running Woman thus represents the artificial paradise or, as Caputi observes, the artificial *as* paradise (p.514).

The numerous links to cultural themes and the complexity of embedded sociocultural codes coalesce to make the "1984" Macintosh a constitutive rhetoric of a select group of narrativized subjects. At the same time, the "1984" ad has such staying power and force because its ideological and cultural codes resonate with viewers' social knowledge. Charland theorizes that all of these facets constitute us in ways that make us less aware *because* of the complexity itself; the more multifaceted and the more subtle those elements are, the more possibilities for identification. These different strands come together to constitute subjects in a more ideologically gripping, yet opaque, way.

Conclusion

This analysis of the Macintosh "1984" ad comes full circle from a political sensibility evoked through the ad's homage to Orwell's *1984* and Fritz Lang's *Metropolis* into social action ultimately realized as

consumer choice of commodified dream objects. The ideological codes represented in the ad of the lone hero defeating the monstrous agent of repression are much cherished myths of Western culture. Freedom through revolution is the central theme of the ad, the power to revolt against tyranny and to act freely as an individual. The narrative constitutes its audience as revolutionaries, cast into the marketplace to realize their subjectivity as warriors in the crusade for the freedom of information. As Charland (1994) frames it, these subject positions are driven to act in the illusion of agency to fulfill their narrativized roles of breaking free from authoritarian suppression of choice. The objects of this fulfilling act are computational devices reconfigured as dream machines, Baum's department store windows recast as portals to digitized global markets. The co-optation of individual rebellion via mass culture manifested by the Macintosh ad resonated strongly with then President Reagan's rhetorical glorification of the individual opposed to big government while his actions empowered and valorized big business and the military. The "1984" ad promised rebellion but actually delivered further obedience, further submission to the hegemony of the market.

The Running Woman is successful at shattering the image of Big Brother in the "1984" ad, but that is as far as her revolutionary power extends, not unlike the Macintosh itself that never took over the corporate market, the only market that would really count. Furthermore, the panoptic presence depicted in the "1984" ad has become a much *greater* reality as computer-mediated communication networks such as the Internet have elevated monitoring and surveillance technologies to disturbing new heights.

Evocations of radical social, economic, and political change become subverted by commodity hegemony. As pointed out by Roszak (2000), the misguided notion that information is sufficient for radical social change continues to drive the rhetoric of the telecommunications industry. The synthesis of the technophiliac with reversionary sensibilities, that early perception of the home-brewed personal computer as a means of democratization and political activism combined with a return to a pastoral lifestyle, was resolved, in Roszak's words, with the "technophiliac values of the counter culture [winning] out." Notions of technologically facilitated freedom and revolution fueling the creation of the Macintosh have been appropriated to such ends as Microsoft's freedom of "travel" via the web ("Where Do You Want To Go Today?"), or the instrumentalization of African Americans and civil rights songs to promote the "freedom" afforded by Toshiba's cellular phones.

Ultimately, the message of the Macintosh ad is an old one echoing cultural faith in the machine and in technology-engendered progress. Technology per se does not yield the Big Brother figure and its control over brainwashed and roboticized masses. It is the *wrong* technology that creates such a state. The right technology—in this case the Macintosh—will provide salvation. The solution to the problems of technology is always a better technology.

This analysis has suggested that in understanding the rhetorical constitution of the audience through ideological codes used to construct the narrative we can begin to fathom how commodity technodiscourses work in our lives. The computer revolution in the advanced Western societies insinuates electronic mediation into communications to an unprecedented degree and increasingly dictates how our social and economic relationships will be played out. In the absence of public education and deliberation over the merits and pitfalls of far-reaching technological development, advertising discourses play a crucial role, contributing to expectations of computer technologies and a sense of identity in relation to them.

Notes

1. The "1984" Macintosh ad was broadcast only once, in 1984, to launch a personal computer that could be easily used by non-expert consumers, but the ad has remained in the public eye via numerous television and advertising award ceremonies. Applying a theory of constitutive rhetoric with analysis of the ideological codes and cinematic narratives that construct the ad, this essay explores the integral role ads play in the cultural discourse of new technologies. Ultimately, the ad's rhetoric of freedom and revolution is used to constitute consumers, not rebels, leaving intact capitalism's ideological investment in the technological realization of social progress.

2. There are conflicting reports on the cost of the production and of the airtime: Malone (1999) states that the ad cost $500,000 to produce, while Rose (1989) states that the cost was $900,000 for the sixty-second time slot.

3. While Levy (1994) reports that the ad ran once in December 1984 in a local Midwest market to qualify for that year's advertising awards, it should also be noted that the "1984" ad has run numerous times from its Super Bowl air date to the present in the context of advertising award shows and television features on the Super Bowl.

4. For a semiotic analysis that includes a study done on student interpretations of the ad, see Berger (2000). for a political reading of the "1984" narrative and an online video of the ad, see Friedman (1997).

5. I am not claiming that Regis Mckenna read Charland (1999) or Goldman (1992), but rather that the same principles inform the advertising discourse as arise in the theoretical writing. The former uses these principles to perpetuate, while the latter uses them to critique.

6. Thanks for Jo Tavener for this phrase.

7. As Yaukey (2001) noted, while the Macintosh controls only five percent of the computer market, it has retained the "rebel" image portrayed in the "1984" ad.

8. Goldman et al. (1992) provide an excellent discussion of advertising's transformation of feminist ideals into lifestyle signifiers.

9. The threat of unemployment and the marginalization of the human body come together in Hollywood actors' response to the release of *Final Fantasy*, a film released by SONY that uses a case made up entirely of computer-generated humanlike actors (Lyman, 2001).

10. In the mid-nineties, IBM launched an ad camp[aign under the rubric "Solutions for a Small Planet." Nakamura (2001) notes that the racial and ethnic boundaries central to the conceptual frame of the ad—having characters from non-technological societies talk "computer-speak": IBM's hegemonic power through its information networks causes everyone to speak the same language (p. 21).

11. This is the term given to the mix of art and technology that surfaced during the Weimar Republic.

12. Geraldine Ferraro was chosen by Walter Mondale; the pair was defeated overwhelmingly by Reagan's second election bid in November 1984.

References

Benjamin, W. (1968). The work of art in the age of mechanical reproduction. In H. Arendt (Ed.), *Illuminations* (pp. 217–251). New York: Schocken Books.

Benjamin, W. (1972). *Gesammelte schriften (passagen-werk)/Walter Benjamin: Unter mitwirkung von Theodor W. Adorno und Gershom Scholem hrsg.* Von Rolf Tiedemann und Hermann Schweppenhauser (Eds.). Frankfurt am Main: Surkamp.

Berger, A. A. (2000). *Ads, fads, and consumer culture.* Lanham, MD: Rowan & Littlefield.

Buck-Morss. (1994). Dream world of mass culture: Walter Benjamin's theory of modernity and the dialectics of seeing. In D. M. Levin (Ed.), *Modernity and the hegemony of vision* (pp. 309–338). Berkeley: University of California Press.

"The best of TV's 50 years of pitching. (1995, March 15). The *Houston Chronicle*, p. 3.

Campbell-Kelly, M., & Aspray, W. (1996). *Computer: A history of the information machine.* New York: Basic Books.

Caputi, J. (1988). Seeing elephants: The myths of phallotechnology. *Feminist Studies, 14,* 487–524.

Charland, M. (1994). Constitutive rhetoric: The case of the Peuple Québéçois. In W. L. Nothstine, C. Blair, & G. A. Copeland (Eds.), *Critical questions: Invention, creativity, and the criticism of discourse and media* (pp. 211–232). New York: St. Martin's Press.

Doane, M. A. (1990). Technophilia: Technology, representation, and the feminine. In M. Jacobus, E. Fox Kellner, & S. Shuttleworth (Eds.), *Body/politics: Women and the discourse of science* (pp. 163–176). New York: Routledge.

Enrico, D. (1999, July 3). The fifty greatest commercials of all time. *TV Guide, 147* (2), 4–34.

Foucault, M. (1979). *Discipline and punish: The birth of the prison.* New York: Vintage Books.

Foucault, M. (1990). *The history of sexuality: Vol. 1. An Introduction.* New York: Vintage Books.

Friedberg, A. (1993). *Window shopping: Cinema and the postmodern.* Berkeley: University of California Press.

Friedman, T. (1997, October). *Apple's 1984: The introduction of the Macintosh in the cultural history of personal computers.* Paper presented at the Society of the history of Technology Convention, Pasadena, CA. Available: *http://www.duke.Edu/~tlove/mac.htm.*

Goldberg, F. (1994, January 31). Recalling "1984" spot. *Advertising Age,* p. 21.

Goldman, R. (1992). *Reading ads socially.* London: Routledge.

Goldman, R., Heath, D., & Smith, S. (1991). Commodity feminism. *Critical Studies in Mass Communication, 8,* 333–351.

Hartley, J. (1992). *The politics of pictures: The creation of the public in the age of popular media.* London: Routledge.

Huyssen, A. (1986). The vamp and the machine. In A. Huyssen, *After the great divide: Modernism, mass culture, postmodernism* (pp. 65–81). Bloomington: Indiana University Press.

Johnson, B. (1994, January 10). Ten years after "1984": The commercial and the product, that changed advertising. *Advertising Age Online*, pp. 1–7. Available *http://www.adage.com.*

Johnson, E. A. (1993). *She who is: The mystery of god in feminist theological discourse.* New York: Crossroads.

Kawasaki, G. (1990). *The Macintosh way.* Glenview, IL: Scott Foresman.

Leach, W. (1989). Strategists of display and the production of desire. In S. J. Bronner (Ed.), *Consuming visions: Accumulation and display of goods in America, 1880–1920* (pp. 99–132). New York: Norton.

Levy, S. (1994). *Insanely great: The life and times of Macintosh, the computer that changed everything.* New York: Viking.

Linnett, R., & Friedman, W. (2001, January). No gain: Super Bowl ad pricing is flat. *Advertising Age*, p. 1. Available on line at http://www.adage.com. Retrieved 1 August 2001.

Lyman, R. (2001, July 8). Movie stars fear inroads by upstart digital actors. *The New York Times.* Available online at *http://www.partners.* Nytimes.com/2001/07/08/technology/08FANT.html. Retrieved 10 July 2001.

Malone, M. S. (1999). *Infinite loop: How the world's most insanely great computer company went insane.* New York: Doubleday.

Marchand, R. (1986). *Advertising the American dream: Making way for modernity.* Berkeley: University of California Press.

Marvin, C. (1988). *When old technologies were new.* New York: Oxford University Press.

Marx, L. (1964). *The machine in the garden: Technology and the pastoral ideal in America.* London: Oxford University Press.

McFague, S. (1987). *Models of God: Theology for an ecological nuclear age.* Philadelphia: Fortress.

Nakamura, L. (2000). Where do you want to go today? In B. E. Kolko, L. Nakamura, & G. B. Rodman (Eds.), *Race in cyberspace* (pp. 15–26). New York: Routledge.

Reed, L. (2000). Domesticating the personal computer: Technology and cultural management of a widespread technophobia, 1964—. *Critical Studies in Media Communication, 17,* 159–185.

Rose, F. (1989). *West of Eden: The end of innocence at Apple Computer.* New York: Viking.

Rosenthal, P. (1991). "Jacked-In: Fordism, cyberpunk, Marxism. *Socialist Review, 21,* 7–103.

Rozak, T. (1985, April). Machines of loving grace. In From Satori to Silicon Valley, Alvin Fine Memorial Lecture. Lecture delivered at San Francisco State University, San Francisco, CA. Available online at http://www.library.stanford.edu/mac/primary/docs/satori/machines.html, pp. 1–5. Retrieved 7 February 2001.

Schudson, M. (1986). *Advertising: The uneasy persuasion.* New York: Basic Books.

Spigel, L. (1992). *Make room for TV.* Chicago: University of Chicago Press.

Standford University. *Making the Macintosh.* Available online at *http://www.library.stanford.edu/mac.* Retrieved 4 March 2001.

Stanford University. *Making the Macintosh: Macintosh production introduction plan.* Available online at *http://library.stanford.edu/mac/primary/docs/pip83.html*

Turkle, S. (1984). *The second self.* New York: Simon & Schuster.

Wajcman, J. (1991). Technology as masculine culture. In J. Wajcman, *Feminism confronts technology* (pp. 131–167). University Park, PA: Pennsylvania State University Press.

Weber, M. (1985). *Protestant ethic and the spirit of capitalism.* London: Counterpoint. [originally published in 1904]

Williamson, J. (1978). *Decoding advertisements.* London: Boyars, 1978.

Yaukey, J. (2001, 24 July). Mac mystique: What is it about these stylish computers that has created an almost cult-like following? *Asheville Citizen-Times*, pp. C1, C5.

Narrative
Criticism
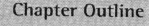

CHAPTER 8

Chapter Outline

Some Assumptions Governing Narrative Criticism

Vocabularies for Narrative Analysis
  Traditional Aristotelian Vocabulary
  Structuralist Vocabulary
  A Visualist Vocabulary

Writing Narrative Criticism

An Example Essay: Bruce E. Gronbeck's, "The Visual and Narrative Rhetoric of Redemption: American Culture Responds to 9/11"

The events of September 11, 2001, were shocking and disorienting to Americans. A look at **www.Poynter.org/Terrorism/gallery** will take you to 237 front pages of newspapers from around the world—special editions for September 11 and regular editions for the day after, Wednesday, September 12.[1] Around the world, front pages showed the scenes of awe-inspiring destruction of the World Trade Center and portions of the Pentagon; New Yorkers running from the clouds of debris or walking, covered with a gray residue; citizens in other parts of the country and the rest of the world watching television sets, wearing looks of sadness, disorientation, and horror; firefighters and police officers helping the wounded, digging for the dead; and, sometimes, a picture of Osama bin Laden as the presumed perpetrator or of President George W. Bush as the official U.S. spokesperson, labeling the act as evil and promising revenge.

Fully absorbed television viewers soon found themselves awash in stories about what came to be called simply 9/11. As those stories coalesced, three tended to dominate: a story of institutional failures, a story about an emerging New World Order, and a third story about American renewal after tragedy.

> *The story of institutional failure.* One way to account for the terrorist attacks was to blame the CIA for not knowing what was happening, airport security officials for their laxness and inability to train security personnel, and the crisis response plans (not) in place in most major American cities. What was presented as needed in these stories was some overhaul of these kinds of governmental and business operations, not any fundamental change in American life.

> *The story of the new world order.* Here was a tale of the post–Soviet Union international community, which could come together as a brother- and sisterhood now that the Cold War between democracy and communism was over, to create shared economic, social, and even political and military systems. "Rogue nations" such as Iraq and "terrorist operations" such as al Qaeda could be disciplined by a united world, not just the military force of the United States.

> *The story of American renewal.* The preferred tale was the story of the United States looking backward, not forward, in times of trouble, as it did during the Great Depression or following the attack on Pearl Harbor. What we needed to do to save ourselves in the future was to look back to traditional values, patriotic commitments to collective action, and even a return to the industrial economy—"manly" jobs—to work ourselves back into shape as an economy and a body politic.[2]

Many variations on these stories appeared following 9/11, but the central point here is that in a time of disorientation and fear, the United States turned to stories. Further, not only did such stories dominate news and public affairs telecasting, but they also appeared in prime-time programming. *The West Wing* opened its season with a plot focused on a possible terrorist in the White House. By late fall, *NYPD Blue* regularly made references to the attacks, showed "United We Stand" banners in background shots, and even devoted an early 2002 episode to the story of a Middle Eastern family whose small business was vandalized. *Law and Order* aired a story about New York minority populations afraid of how they'd be treated by law enforcement agencies that questioned their politics and commitment. Even *The Education of Max Bickford,* in January 2002, depicted its campus as one that now required identification cards and was suspicious of students of Middle Eastern descent.

An important avenue toward understanding a society's culture—how it sees itself valuatively and characterologically, where it sees itself coming from and tending toward, by what mechanisms it passes on guidance and wisdom to later generations—is to study stories that circulate widely through that society. As Richard Campbell (1998, p. xvi) says: "The mass media play a role in all of our autobiographies. We watch television and go to movies to find stories that remind us of our own experience or transport us to remote times and places. . . . We go to the mass media for stories about our neighbors and our world."

To take that claim seriously is to argue that mass-mediated stories play central roles in how we understand ourselves, other people with whom we have contact (neighbors), and people and even places with whom and with which we're likely never to have any contact whatsoever—the rest of the world and beyond. Telling stories in televised news and fictive programs is serious business. This chapter will consider some assumptions that students of stories (narratives) make, examine some ways of analyzing television's stories, and then set up a sample narrative analysis to help you see how narratives work.

Some Assumptions Governing Narrative Criticism

The first assumption is that *human beings construct their understandings of themselves and their lives, their immediate environments, and even worlds outside their direct experience using stories.* Fisher (1987) essentializes people as *homo narrans* because he takes storytelling to be that which defines us as sentient animals. To Fisher, our abilities to organize and make coherent our lives and even lives beyond the ones we now live mark us as unique on this planet. Ask, "So how did your day go?" and you'll get a story from a best friend or intimate. The questions "Where did I come from?" and "Where am I going?" generate grand tales of origin ("In the beginning God created heaven and the earth") and destiny ("And whosoever believeth in Him shall not perish but have eternal life"). When challenged, people justify decisions they've made narratively ("Well, when I saw what had happened, I grabbed . . . and . . ."). We read our children stories—Aesop's fables, Mother Goose and Dr. Seuss rhyming narratives, basic books with positive morals—in order to socialize them, that is, to teach them to behave in the company of others.

Second, *human beings use stories to construct coherence in the world and guides for living within it.* You've been taught so well to see life in terms of stories that you're probably not even conscious of doing it. Yet you do. So when you're asked, as we just noted, "How did your day go?" you don't just answer the question with

"Rotten!" or "Gloriously!" Instead, you almost inevitably tell a story: "First, I . . . And then, wouldn't you know it, I came across . . . Finally I found time for lunch, but . . ." And on and on. What we identified as narrative structure in Chapter 5 is a symbolic tool for creating something understandable. Just as an individual's life so often is experienced as an unfolding story with little beginnings, middles, and endings, so also are larger aspects of your environment. We organize time in the passage from morning until nightfall, weeks from Sunday to Saturday, months from the first to the last day, years in decades, centuries, and millennia that seem to pass before us in story-like ways. We create coherent stories about "the Roaring Twenties," "the Thirties Depression," "the Sixties," or the "Post–Cold War Nineties" so that we can understand the past in comprehensible pieces.

Finally, *stories gain their coherence horizontally and vertically.* One aspect of narrative structure is the "And then . . . and then . . . and then" part—that is, the unfolding of experience. Stories must be structured, at least most of the time, horizontally in what seems to be a rational, almost cause-and-effect way. There certainly can be what Wolfgang Iser (1976) termed gaps and indeterminacies in a narrative, but audiences for stories usually can fill those in, cementing them over in their heads. So when a TV program breaks for some ads, you run to the refrigerator and come back in time to pick up the story, and do so even though it might have shifted locations and even characters. The links between actions in a story, as you move through them, are understood *syntagmatically,* even if a story is told backward, for example, using flashbacks.

As well, of course, a story's structure may be recognizable to you because you've experienced others like it; such links between one story and another are understood *paradigmatically* (see Chapter 6). The link may even be material. For example, the chair from *Who Wants to Be a Millionaire?* in 2002 was remade and became a game show of its own, *The Chair,* which in turn was remanufactured again for a heated and lit box in *The Chamber.* All three programs were not only game shows; they also were works cut from the same paradigm: shows where contestants, while confined, had to fight through growing psychological pressures to win. "The chair" was literally there, but paradigmatically it stood for the theme of all three programs.

Vocabularies for Narrative Analysis

In referencing the ideas of syntagmatic and paradigmatic structure, we're already invading the world of technical vocabulary. Herein lies a problem: narrative theory is such a robust and engaging arena of study that multiple vocabularies for analysis have been developed. (See Martin, 1986, for one of the standard summaries.) We'll introduce three of them here—traditional Aristotelian, structuralist, and visualist vocabularies—because each is used by a segment of the community of television critics.

Traditional Aristotelian Vocabulary

When Aristotle sought to analyze the elements that combined to form a tragedy, he worked with two sets of analytical tools: (1) modes of presentation and (2) formative elements. That is, he sought both to distinguish tragedy (drama) from other kinds of poetic discourse and to break down the elements of performance that combined to make a play. He distinguished among three kinds of poetic discourse, with each kind defined primarily by its mode (or radical) of presentation: epic poetry (recited or narrated), lyric poetry (sung), and dramatic poetry (performed). Drama thus had no storyteller to Aristotle, no controlling hand, as the script or story was taken into people's bodies and acted out on a stage or set. Given such a definition of drama, Aristotle identified two sets of three formative terms that, to him, comprised drama:

Traditional Narrative Vocabulary

The Contents of Dramatic Stories

1. *Plot:* sequence of actions
2. *Character:* those performing the actions
3. *Thought* (theme, more generally): subject matter of a play

The Vehicles of Dramatic Stories

4. *Diction:* spoken language
5. *Melody:* vocalizations of language (both song and recitation)
6. *Spectacle:* bodily performance within some environment[3]

These elements are more or less listed in order of their importance to Aristotle: plot is the most significant aspect of drama, for it is in the acting out of human stories that they reflect or comment on the life world; character is the second most important element because actions are executed by human agents; while to Aristotle, spectacle is the least important element, for the "tragic effect is quite possible without a public performance" (Aristotle, 1954, p. 232, 1450b). (This belief is challenged by visual theorists.)

The Aristotelian or traditional understanding of the dramatic genre led to many additional ways of classifying kinds of stories. Northrop Frye (1957), for example, viewed plot types as coming in four varieties, each associated with a season: (1) *romances* are spring, with problems or complications worked out when characters follow society's advice about actions and relationships or find creative ways even to remake the world; (2) *comedies* are summer, the season of foolishness, guile, and the bringing down of braggadocio bureaucrats and avaricious old men, a time even to critique social norms of acceptable behavior; (3) *tragedies* inhabit the coolness of autumn, in situations where individuals through pride or other dangerous motivations bring about their own fall from station or fall from grace; and (4) *ironic literature* is winter, where the world is subjected to Kafkaesque tyrannies and hidden dictators, where the human spirit all but dies—in hopes of being reborn in spring. From such a traditional understanding of genres come our vocabularies for subgenres: melodramas as overly sentimentalized romances, sitcoms as particular, limited kinds of comedies, and many science fiction shows as ironic commentaries from alternative universes on our own life world.

Pieces of television narrative criticism working from a traditional vocabulary often reduce their focus to matters of plot, character, and setting (environment), where plots are discussed generically (sitcoms, cop shows, talk shows, sports-casts), characters as socially or professionally defined, and settings as definitional of group culture (the home as social culture, the workplace as institutional culture, the out-of-doors as a natural environment). Newcomb's original book, *TV, The Most Popular Art* (1974), was built around plot, character, and setting analyses of sitcoms, family comedies, crime shows, westerns, and other forms. Schrag, Hudson, and Bernabo (1981) employed a similar kind of analysis to demonstrate that family-like social arrangements, which they called "the new humane collectivity," were becoming central to workplace-centered programs such as *The Mary Tyler Moore Show* or *The White Shadow*. Even a newer work such as Bonnie Dow's analysis of *The Mary Tyler Moore Show* (1996), while embedded in a feminist vocabulary, depends on definitions of the show's theme—"the independent woman trying to 'make it on her own'"—as well as its plot structures (problems and their patriarchal solutions), the "patterns of interaction of characters," and a work setting emphasizing "a family paradigm" (pp. 40, 44).

A traditional narrative vocabulary thus can be elaborated with rhetorical or ideological or psychoanalytical perspectives and provide insightful access to television narratives.

Structuralist Vocabulary

We introduced this vocabulary generally in Chapter 6, and now we elaborate on aspects of semiotic/structuralist thought that focus particularly on stories. What is most useful about the semiotic/structuralist vocabulary so far as narrative analysis is concerned is its approach to plot, particularly the form of plots.

The usual starting point is to note, with Chatman (1978), the difference between *story* (in French, *histoire*) as a chain of events and existents (happenings-actions/characters-settings) and *discourse* (*discours*, the actual relating of those events and existents in some discursively constructed way. (Notice that the word *discourse* has taken a very different meaning from the one it had in Chapter 6.) Events are just happenings; they must be shaped in what structuralists sometimes call acts of *emplotment* (see White, 1973). To emplot is to form into coherent narratives with beginnings, middles, endings; to identify key events or turns in our understanding of those existents; to give presence or power, sometimes to the narrator; and to spin out the political, social, or personal implications of that narrative for reader-viewers' lives. Acts of discoursing are therefore the ways human beings make events understandable and interpretively powerful or significant. The analytical vocabulary used by semiotic-structuralists to analyze narratives has been constructed to help you deal with the elements of the stories and their shaping by storytellers:

Semiotic-Structural Narrative Vocabulary

Narrator: actual or implied agent providing the discourse that shapes the story

Actual time: the literal and across-time order of the events comprising a story

Discourse time: the shaping of events into the plot of a particular duration

Forms (emplotments): the usual relationships between events in traditional narrations, such as romance, satire, comedy, and tragedy (White, 1973)

Narrative structure: internal relationships between actions in a story—for example Todorov's (1975) five-part equilibrium model: a statement of equilibrium, disruption of equilibrium, recognition of the disruption, attempts to repair, reinstatement of the equilibrium

Functions of actions: the particular force of each action in moving the structure along—for example, Propp's (1968) 31 kinds of actions that have consequences for a plot

Structural relations between actions: the ways that actions are put into consonant or dialectical relationship with each other

Nonliteral significations: the ways in which first-order signs come to have second-order (mythic) or even unconscious (psychoanalytical) force

Now, not all of these terms or even all of these considerations appear in every semiotic/structural analysis of narratives. Particular studies usually focus on only particular questions. For example, John Fiske (1984) studied Great Britain's longest-running television program, *Dr. Who,* a science-fiction show about a time traveler who gets around in a space-age phone booth, by focusing on structural relationships between the actions and mental attributes of heroic and villainous characters (see Chapter 5). Semiotically, he attributed particular signifieds to characters' talk and actions, and then structurally, he put the characters into consonant (positive) and oppositional (negative) relationships with each. He drew on Chatman's (1978) understanding of relationships between events (actions, happenings) and existents (characters, settings) in order to examine the meanings of *Dr. Who*'s consonant and oppositional relationships.

Dr. Who's character is reinforced and resonates with a computer dog, K9, and a logical thinker, Romana; their modes of rationality blend with his more intuitive and humane mode of thinking and acting virtuously to make them a positive triangle of characters. This triangle of heroic relationships is contrasted with the negativity of another triangle: the evil triangle of Wolfweeds, Karela, and the powerful Adrasta. Fiske then extends his analysis to minor characters, which permits him to contrast the dialectical relationship between the two "civilized" triangles (Who/ K9/Romana and Wolfweeds/Karela/Adrasta) and the "naturalized" dialectical relationships in the episodes being examined between the deadly pit creature (Organon) and forest bandits. In other words, Fiske creates a square (see Figure 8.1), with humanistic/selfish signifieds forming the horizontal dialectical contrast and cultural versus natural signifieds forming the vertical contrast. The sequence of actions that comprise the plot therefore features constantly evolving confrontations along the horizontal, vertical, and even diagonal dimensions of the square.

Fiske thus explains *Dr. Who*'s popularity in terms of both complex structural relationships between characters, who stand in mythically for eternal human oppositions (other-directedness versus self-directedness, civilized rationality and control versus natural yielding to feelings and freedom), and the plots that are driven by near-constant conflict between dialectically opposed forces.

Nick Lacey (2000, pp. 53–60), in contrast, uses Todorov's conception of narrative structure and Propp's list of functions of actions to analyze the film *Se7en* in order to account for its popularity; a popularity that, he argues, came not through a traditional reinforcement of values and myth but through the film's breaking of convention. *Se7en* was a 1995 film about a serial killer who was dispatching people whose lives epitomized the Seven Deadly Sins. Lacey suggests that this neo-noir detective film was disturbing to audiences because it disrupted our understandings of conventional forms and our expectations of consequences for actions committed by heroes and villains. The "hero" rookie cop, Mills, who solved the crime also became a "villain"—a murderer—because he was forced, after his wife became a victim, to live out one of the Seven Deadly Sins (wrath) that was the patterning device for the serial killer. The outright villain, serial killer John Doe, was executed by Mills, but given that death was what Doe craved, the bloodletting was not retribution but rather a kind of twisted reward. In the end, Mills solved the crime but had to be punished.

Thus, the Proppian actions of these characters had consequences that violated viewers' expectations: we expect the struggle between good and evil to be clear

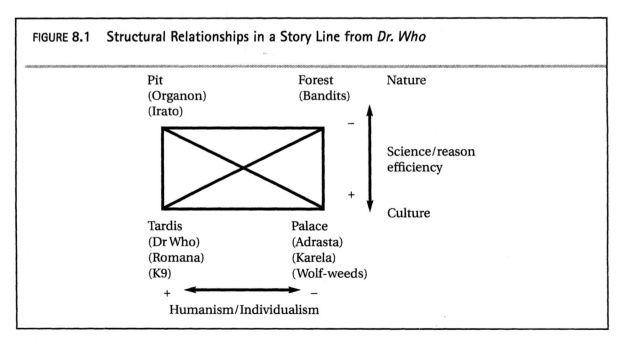

FIGURE 8.1   Structural Relationships in a Story Line from *Dr. Who*

Source: This is a diagram from the 1979 episode of Dr. Who entitled "The Creature from the Pit," written by David Fisher and broadcast across four episodes.

and plots to move from equilibrium to disequilibrium and restoration. That did not happen in *Se7en*. The very violation of traditional structures and action sequences gave the film its power. Why? Because, according to Lacey (2000), such violation forced audiences to examine their own assumptions about societal values, law and order, and relationships between virtue and the living hell of contemporary urban environments.

These are just two examples of semiotic/structuralist analyses of narratives, but they illustrate that such analyses are very useful in coming to grips with both story lines and characters' thoughts and behaviors within stories. As acceptable or unacceptable motives and values are attached to characters' talk and actions semiotically and as talk and action are emplotted syntagmatically into story lines, a fictive universe within which audiences can explore their own values, perceptions of the world, and sense of its operations is built. Within that universe, the underlying psychoanalytic structures of life, as well as the overarching mythic struggles to find higher meaning in the life world, are worked on paradigmatically through the signs and structuralist principles made manifest in narrative emplotments. And exploring such narrative meaning is one reason critics use semiotic/structural analysis to examine stories.

A Visualist Vocabulary

As Aristotle reminded us, dramatic works have no narrator, no controlling voice. That, of course, is not always true of television programs. The 1950s programs *Death Valley Days* and *Alfred Hitchcock Presents* had narrators—Ronald Reagan and Alfred Hitchcock, respectively—who presumably were in charge of the telling and showing stories. Author Earl Hammer, Jr., introduced and offered general and autobiographical interpretive commentary through the use of a voice-over narrator—the older John Boy character—on episodes of *The Waltons,* and the 1980s program *Wonder Years* employed a similar authorial voice. A disembodied voice set the scene for *Star Trek* episodes, and even contemporary programs such as *Law and Order* and *Scrubs* narratively articulate the basic premise of those programs before launching episodes.

Still, in the main, the Aristotelian dramatic imperative—the so-called fourth-wall convention—is observed: no one talks directly to us through the vast majority of television's stories. But yet, we suggest, those stories in fact are being told. How? By the camera. The camera leads us in and out of characters' lives, provides background or environmental shots against which close-up action is shown, and manufactures the raw material that another kind of narrator, the video editor, puts together to make "a show." To say that the camera and its accomplice, the editor, are narrators is to take us into the subject matter of the next chapter on auteur criticism. Insofar as a program's "authors" are telling stories, they are at least implied narrators. We will save more details about that idea for Chapter 9. For now, we need not go that far. Let us concentrate on the camera as narrator, for it is in the shooting and editing of whatever has been shot that a story materializes before our very eyes. To talk about that story, one needs a visualist vocabulary:

A Visual Vocabulary

Color: coding people, objects, and environments using color

Framing: centering or marginalizing people or objects within the picture frame

Light-dark: controlling visual orientation through the use of light

Shot depth: use of close-up, medium (head-and-shoulders), or long shots

Simplicity-complexity: the number of layers or items of sight captured in a shot

Foreground-background relationships: persons or objects made the focus, with others made the interpretive context in the background

Icons: flags, uniforms, or other conventionalized objects used to convey particular signifieds recognized by the audience

Visual quotations: stereotyped shots (e.g., the "V for victory" hand gesture, the football player who assumes the pose from the Heisman Trophy statue) that are recognized by the audience

Interactions of/with others: ways in which visualized people, places, things, or actions are affected by signs in verbal and acoustic codes

Mise-en-scène: all of the available means that directors, producers, and editors have in creating a scene, including camera placement and movement, pacing, positioning of actors, and set decoration, that, when assembled in the camera shot, convey the feelings, attitudes, style, or personality of directors, producers, and editors

How, you might ask, can one use a visual vocabulary to discuss storytelling? Think, for example, of Spike Lee's classic film, *Do the Right Thing* (1989). Not only did its plot center on visualization—Whose pictures would be exhibited on Sal's Famous Pizzeria's Wall of Fame?—but the movie itself depended on shot selection and sequencing to drive its themes. Sal's wall recognized ethnic adaptation and achievement, but it contained only pictures of famous Italian Americans, like Liza Minnelli, Frank Sinatra, Joe DiMaggio, and Mario Cuomo, to the exclusion of famous African Americans, with whom Sal's predominantly African-American customers could relate. The Wall of Fame in all of its whiteness dominated the African Americans who made up Sal's clientele. As one of the neighborhood characters, Buggin' Out, looked at the wall rising above him, the film made the argument for African-American exclusion from a kind of public space in the following way:

Framing: Buggin' Out was pictured in the lower part of the shot, the wall towering over him (see the photographic still of this scene on the next page).

Light-dark contrast: Buggin' Out was in the shadows, but the wall was in the light.

Foreground-background juxtapositioning: Buggin' Out was in the foreground, but the wall of white heroes was the context within which he felt himself being assessed.

Icons: In contrast to the icons of success on the wall, Buggin' Out was a poor black man left in his neighborhood, standing for the omission of African Americans from the society's dream.

The wall of white heroes overlooking Buggin Out and other African American patrons serves as a constant reminder of African Americans' exclusion from public space and the society's dream.

This center of Lee's narrative was depicted visually. To be sure, arguments and counterarguments for diversifying the wall were articulated verbally, but the force of *Do the Right Thing* came down to how the film was shot: Sal's act of menacing Buggin' Out with an icon of white violence toward blacks, a baseball bat, and later smashing Radio Raheem's boom box—his rap music, and thus his cultural identity—with that weapon, or Smiley's integration of the Wall of Fame during the race riot by pinning a picture of Martin Luther King, Jr., and Malcolm X amid the pictures of Italian Americans. The dialogue of the film was important, but the key turns in the plot and the actual significance of characters' actions depended on the film's visual grammar—on how the movie was shot and edited. (For further commentary, see Mitchell, 1994, pp. 371–396, who compares the visualizations of Lee's film with photos of Chinese students erecting their "Goddess of Democracy" statue during the Tiananmen Square riots that same year.)

A larger question about visualization is raised by this example: the *politics of representation.* One of the important questions the politics of representation addresses—presence versus absence of representation—was central to Lee's movie: If African Americans are absent from the Wall of Fame, what does that say about their political status, that is, the status of their citizenship? Equally important in the narratives we construct with African Americans actually in them is this: How are they shown? If blacks are depicted only as they were in TV's first African

American shows in the 1950s—*Amos 'n' Andy* (low-class hustlers), *Beulah* (black domestics), and *The Jack Benny Show* (black servant)—then the audience's vision of the African American community is flattened socioeconomically and, of course, racially. Even the 1970s shows—*Good Times, Sanford and Son,* and *What's Happening!!*—drew their characters from stereotypically poor urban communities. Only with the coming of *The Cosby Show,* argue Gray (1995, esp. p. 79) and Real (1989), did we get a general shift away from the socioeconomic, racial, and gender stereotypes that had served to inhibit or contain blackness on American television.[4]

Narratives, therefore, are tellings, but how they're *shown* can provide the rhetorical or ideological force of the stories. As Hartley (1992) argues:

> No picture is pure image; all of them, still and moving, graphic and photographic, are "talking pictures," either literally, or in association with contextual speech, writing or discourse. Pictures are social, visual, spatial and sometimes communicative. . . . Pictures are objective traces of socio-semiotic struggles (conflict), allegiances (consensus), and ideologies (sense-making practices), right across the spectrum from big-deal public politics to intimate personal culture. (pp. 28, 29)

The visualist aspect of television's storytelling therefore becomes a tremendous source of its power to control audiences' understandings of the world, their associations with others, and even themselves.

Writing Narrative Criticism

The secret to writing engaging narrative criticism is to be a good storyteller yourself. What narrative critics are actually doing is retelling a story, but from some larger (say, mythic or ideological) or some submerged (psychoanalytical) perspective. We—your authors and W. J. T. Mitchell—worked hard to help you understand *Do the Right Thing* as an attack on civil rights myths of the United States by retelling the film's story. Martin Luther King, Jr.'s dream is not yet a reality in Lee's movie, but then the threat of force that flowed from the lips of some of Malcolm X's followers is not an answer, either. We thought that Lee's movie demanded that more social progress be made, though it didn't exactly point the way as to where we must go. That conclusion is supported by (1) an analysis fuller than we've offered of the characters and plot of the movie, (2) careful citation of specific events or shots from the film that provide evidence for claims, and (3) an interpretive move to macro (mythic-ideological) or micro (psychoanalytic) themes supported by the analysis and evidence. The narrative critic builds a story parallel to the one being examined—an interpretive story overlaid on the manifest or actual story. If the interpretive story seems to fit well, the reader accepts it as an account of what's really going on in a work.

A second feature of critical writing is especially important to narrative criticism: solid description. The narrative critic has to draw readers into the guts of the story being analyzed. That takes a person adept at relaying details to appeal imaginatively to readers. When Michael Curtin (1995) wrote a book analyzing American Cold War documentaries, he regularly had to describe scenes, such as this brief one from the 1961 NBC documentary *Panama: Danger Zone*:

> At the beginning of the next segment, the calypso band segues out of the commercial singing the praises of Fidel, and the camera then cuts to Castro speaking at a microphone before an adoring crowd of Cubans. This scene is crosscut with shots of various groups of Panamanians listening intently to their radios. Furthermore, the images are connected by the sound of Castro's speech, which runs uninterrupted throughout the scene. The overall effect is to suggest contemporaneous actions by Castro and his Panamanian audience. We do not know if they are in fact listening to the very speech that is featured in this specific footage, but the editing suggests a bridging of spatial barriers, a growing influence of Castro on the western shores of the Caribbean. (p. 207)

Notice how carefully Curtin interweaves his argument about the association of Cuba and Panama, visual and verbal-acoustic evidence from the documentary, and hints about his larger interpretive claim (Cold War documentaries overlaid political ideologies on descriptive footage through editing). This is good critical writing. Curtin is offering his political story about Cold War documentaries by inscribing on the documentary film stories he is studying with evidence good enough to convince his readers.

Narrative critics often are poetically gifted writers who use those talents to enchant as well as enlighten their readers.

An Example Essay

Bruce Gronbeck's analysis of what he saw as the three predominating stories about 9/11 playing on television and in print journalism through the rest of 2001 and into the middle of 2002 is this chapter's example essay. The stories are the three we identified at the beginning of this chapter. His analysis expands on the idea of what Mitchell (1994) called *imagetexts*—texts where the verbal/literate and the visual are woven together, even fused, producing what he calls the rhetoric of seeings and tellings. Stories were told, but then could be rehearsed or evoked at later times through images associated with them; taken together, the tellings and the showing worked in unison to position American citizens, that is, to orient their responses to 9/11. Each of the three stories, Gronbeck argues, suggested a different response and a different place for 9/11 in the cultural history of the United States generally.

Notes

1. Should the Poynter Institute pull down its gallery of 9/11 front pages, they'll remain at **http://www.uiowa.edu/~policult.**

2. See Gronbeck's essay on 9/11 at the end of this chapter. For verbal-visual web sites related to 9/11, see Communication Studies (2002).

3. The language of "diction," "melody," and "spectacle" reflects Bywater's translation of Aristotle's *Poetics* (1954). The other important English word he uses is *fable* for "plot," with both words being translations of the Greek word *mythos*, with his choice coming from the Latin word for story, *fabula*. *Plot*, we think, is a more neutral translation.

4. Gray's argument is not quite so simple. The breakthrough shows started much earlier with *The Nat "King" Cole Show, I Spy,* and in the late 1970s and early 1980s, *Benson,* and in between, TV specials such as *Roots* and *The Autobiography of Miss Jane Pittman.* It was only with *The Cosby Show,* however, that he believes there was an actual aesthetic, cultural, and even industrial shift in how American television generally depicted African Americans.

Further Readings

Frye, N. (1957). *Anatomy of criticism: Four essays.* Princeton, NJ: Princeton University Press. Here is the foundation of much of twentieth-century narrative theory—a difficult but rewarding text, especially the essay on the theory of genres.

Lacey, N. (2000). *Narrative and genre: Key concepts in media studies.* New York: St. Martin's Press. This work includes collage of narrative theories, genre theories, and sample narrative and generic studies of (especially) film and television.

Webnotes

Narrative Television Network. **www.narrativetv.com.**

> This site for the visually challenged contains links to movies and television programs that include a narrative describing the visual treatment of the stories.

Narrative Inquiry. **www.clarku.edu/~narrinq**

> *Narrative Inquiry* is an electronic journal that is an extension of an older print work, the *Journal of Narrative and Life History.* It provides an online source of articles on narrative theory and criticism.

Television Narrative and Discourse. **www.brown/edu/Departments/MCM/ courses/MC11/outline/TV_narrative_outline.htm**

> This is a short course lecture outline on "Television Narrative and Discourse," which extends some points made in this chapter and adds others.

1. Videotape a half-hour sitcom. Then write three paragraphs explaining how you would describe and interpret it using a traditionalist, a structuralist, and a visualist vocabulary. Which would you likely use to write a full analysis? Explain your choice.

2. Videotape and then examine a major story from national or local news. Carefully chart the story in three parallel columns: shots, verbal language (oral and written on the screen), and sounds. With the aid of your chart, write a short interpretive essay on how the story was told: the role of visual, verbal, and acoustic media in giving the story direction, coherence, and rhetorical force.

References

Aristotle (1954). *Rhetoric; Poetics* (W. R. Roberts & I. Bywater, Trans.). New York: Random House.

Campbell, R. (1998). *Media and culture: An introduction to mass communication.* New York: St. Martin's Press.

Chatman, S. (1978). *Story and discourse: Narrative structure in fiction and film.* Ithaca: Cornell University Press.

Communication Studies [University of Iowa website] (2002). 11 September Attacks. http://www.uiowa.edu/~commstud/resources.

Curtin, M. (1995). *Redeeming the wasteland: Television documentary and cold war politics.* New Brunswick, NJ: Rutgers University Press.

Dow, B. J. (1996). 1970s lifestyle feminism, the single woman, and *The Mary Tyler Moore Show.* In B. J. Dow, *Prime-time feminism: Television, media culture, and the women's movement since 1970* (pp. 24-58). Philadelphia: University of Pennsylvania Press.

Fisher, W. R. (1987). *Human communication as narration: Toward a philosophy of reason, value, and action.* Columbia: University of South Carolina Press.

Fiske, J. (1984). Popularity and ideology: A Structuralist reading of *Dr. Who.* In W. B. Roland & B. Watkins (Eds.), *Interpreting television: Current research perspectives* (pp. 165-198). Newbury Park: Sage.

Frye, N. (1957). *Anatomy of criticism: Four essays.* Princeton: Princeton University Press.

Gray, H. (1995). *Watching race: Television and the struggle for "blackness."* Minneapolis: University of Minnesota Press.

Hartley, J. (1992). *The politics of pictures: The creation of the public in the age of popular media.* New York: Routledge.

Iser, W. (1976). *The act of reading: A theory of aesthetic response.* Baltimore, MD: Johns Hopkins University Press.

Lacey, N. (2000). *Narrative and genre: Key concepts in media studies.* New York: St. Martin's Press.

Martin, W. (1986). *Recent theories of narrative.* Ithaca, NY: Cornell University Press.

Mitchell, W. J. T. (1994). *Picture theory: Essays on verbal and visual representation.* Chicago: University of Chicago Press.

Newcomb, H. (1974). *TV, the most popular art.* New York: Anchor.

Propp, V. (1968). *Morphology of the Russian folktale.* Austin: University of Texas Press.

Real, M. R. (1989). *Super media: A cultural studies approach.* Thousand Oaks, CA: Sage.

Schrag, R. L., Hudson, R. A., & Bernabo, L. M. (1981). Television's new humane collectivity. *Western Journal of Communication Studies, 45,* 1–12.

Todorov, T. (1975). *The fantastic.* Ithaca, NY: Cornell University Press.

White, H. (1973). Metahistory: *The historical imagination in nineteenth century Europe.* Baltimore: Johns Hopkins University Press.

Bruce E. Gronbeck's The Visual and Narrative Rhetoric of Redemption: American Culture Responds to 9/11

Bruce E. Gronbeck

Now, the world is my town
and we are at war
geopolitics will not be denied
But first I must understand
what their faces looked like, what they saw
in that disavowal
of one's humanity
I want to believe the look on his face
explains it all
—"Facing the Enemy," MARIANNA TAYLOR
(2001)

The poet's consciousness of probing the countenance of otherness even while realizing that the world is her town and that geopolitics will not be denied is but one of myriad incongruities by which we gain perspective on the September attacks. We identify the day nimbly, simply, as 9/11, a gruesome play on 9-1-1. Yet, to evoke "9/11" among people still too close to the event is to call up in the mind's eye an album of snapshots: stop-action slices from video of the planes; the firefighters' tableau created when they raised a flag on site; the array of nineteen head shots of the evil-doers; a pentagonic building missing a side; some New Yorkers fleeing before a gray cloud of debris, and others who had not escaped the cloud just standing, looking for all the world like statues.

My own memories are incongruous in that I was to fly to Finland that Wednesday, and so was interspersing viewing and videotaping with ironing and packing. When I finally did go on September 19, the most striking image I took was the day-after front page of the University of Iowa's newspaper, the *Daily Iowan.* That single image synecdochally captured the principal problem that the United States faced following the World Trade Center and Pentagon attacks: How are we to define, to understand, and to remanufacture ourselves following the traumas of September 11, 2001? Three features of the *Daily Iowan* front page comprised entrées to that query:

1. The headline, "Day of Infamy." This phrase is an historical marker that recoups a past trauma in the words of President Franklin Delano Roosevelt on December 8, 1941—another day-after. "Day of Infamy" resurrects the collective horror of Pearl Harbor and for some—at least those who had viewed the eponymous movie playing the previous summer—calls up the collective strength demonstrated by a country that sent its men to war, its women along with Rosie the Riveter to factories, and its children into a lifeworld of rationing and fears of "Krauts" and "Japs," yet ultimately created a culture that Tom Brokaw three years' previous had labeled *The Greatest Generation* (1998). In times of crisis, countries often reconstruct themselves out of the stability, strength, and resolve that flowed from earlier shocks. The United States was no exception.

2. The photo of people fleeing skyscrapers engulfed by an immense cloud of dust and debris. To some viewers, this shot, which appeared in so many newspapers around the world (Poynter Institute, 2001), doubtless evoked a visual memory from the film *Independence Day* (Devlin & Emmerich, 1996) with its uncannily analogous shots. Here was a vivid reminder from a fictive past focused on U.S. and even worldwide disaster, yet one that was survived through presidential leadership and the pluck of a people who answered the call of citizenship and who made the ultimate sacrifice in an act of redemption. In that film, a drunken veteran/crop sprayer, Russell Casse (Randy Quaid), flew a suicide mission into the alien craft to save the planet. In the popular imagination, it took no effort to equate the aliens of that movie with the non-American, the un-American aliens who flew the planes into the twin towers and the military nerve center of the country, and to wonder where Russell Casse was now.

3. A box with a quotation from 11-year-old Colleen Russo of Iowa City: "I never thought

something like that would happen. I thought all the wars were over, and people wouldn't do that stuff anymore." Colleen captured the loss of innocence that Americans experienced. Her fundamental understanding of life was fractured, she faced an uncertain future. The rules of the games of life were disrupted for who knew how long.

4. Captured in the front page images of September 12, then, were not only depictions of

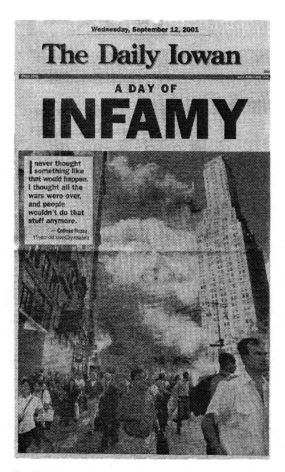

This *Daily Iowan* front page intertextually references FDR's December 8, 1941 words, the *Independence Day* film shot of people fleeing skyscrapers engulfed by clouds of smoke and debris, and the feeling of lost innocence Americans experienced after 9/11.

terrorist events but also a verbal-visual symbolization of a cultural crisis of extraordinary dimensions. Here we had what W. J. T. Mitchell (1994) has termed an *imagetext*, but one that went beyond an interpenetrating weaving of words and pictures to criss-cross time and literal as well as cognitive space. In the front page imagetext we were given signifieds dwelling in both yesterday and today, in both the social and the fictive realms of representation. The evocative power of that front page lay in iconic visions of today, yesterday, and an uncertain tomorrow, and in its hints of a narrative that could structure relationships between that past, present, and future.

September 11, indeed, likely will become a pivotal intersection of cultural time and space in the history of the United States, a time when we redefine our cultural trajectory and reposition ourselves rhetorically in an evolving lifeworld. At the least, it has plunged us into a struggle to understand who we are and what powerful sociopolitical forces pushing us collectively to and fro we face. The various conceptions of who Americans are as a people—whether backward-looking for a revival of some imagined strength-of-character from the past or forward-looking to retooled *ethoi*—are captured in verbal-visual symbolizations tracing through the public sphere.[1]

The Rhetoric of Seeings and Tellings

In this essay I explore some of the resources available to Americans (and others) in the public sphere for talking about and visualizing themselves, individually and collectively, in the wake of 9/11. The conversations, the tellings, are important because they permit social beings as a collectivity to fit 9/11 into the broad outlines of cultural history—into preferred narratives of where we came from, where we are, and where we are going—along the way, positioning ourselves as characters in those stories. The diegetic constructions assembled via

non-diegetic connections between events and people participating in them give narratives their rhetorical power (Lacey, 2000, esp. 13–23).

To call accounts of events "narratives" is to emphasize that the accounts are (1) selective (not everything is told), (2) verbal (a human telling), (3) formed (starting and ending in ways that make the events—usually—coherent and connected), and (4) told (explicitly or implicitly narrated or controlled). As well, (5) they usually are purposive—told to someone for a reason. That reason may be simply that storytelling helps pass time, or, more complexly, that stories can be employed propagandistically to control the ways in which listeners understand themselves (identity) and the ways of the world (culture). As selected events are turned into language and formed into sequences-of-events by someone often for some purpose, the resulting narratives can become very, very powerful. And so social narratives, that is, narratives about the lifeworld, especially, should be thought of as rhetorical. The "rhetoric of narrative" focuses on the power of storytelling in affecting people's beliefs, attitudes, values, behaviors, and identities.

In this essay, however, I will be dealing not only with storytelling but also story-showing—the pictures in newspapers and magazines, posters, ads, recollective publications, websites, television newscasts and primetime programs, and films. Now, Lacey (2000, p. 116) sees "a fundamental tension in narratives between the *telling* explicitly or *showing* the events of the narrative." He understands tellings to be the non-diegetic products of (narrative) voices and showings to be diegetic, event-centered presentations that, especially in the era of mechanically reproduced images, empower a realist aesthetic mimicking observation. However, it becomes clear as he explores the "observational documentary" (p. 116) of showings that he conceives showings to be as rhetorically manipulated as tellings. So do I. In the words of Hartley (1992, p. 28), "No picture is pure image; all of them, still and moving, graphic and photographic, are 'talking pictures', either literally, or in association with contextual speech, writing or discourse.

Pictures are social, visual, spatial, and sometimes communicative." Consider this:

1. Showings are sequenced, producing not only a sense of storytelling but of a story where particular events are shown (and hence more important), other events are not (and hence are less important, even irrelevant). So, the Kevin Costner film *13 Days* made no attempt to tell the whole story of the Cuban Missile Crisis, but instead focused its cause-effect narrative chain on inner-circle debate and decision making within the Kennedy White House. It achieved a kind of documentary-like distance from the events because the narrator was a minor observer, not a major player.

2. Showings are framed. The edges of the picture both direct viewers to look inside the box and prevent them from looking at anything outside the box.

3. Showings are coded semically (Barthes, 1974, as expanded upon by Cook, 1985). That is, inside the frame characters take on symbolic meanings through dress, speech, and action, often in stereotyped ways. Environments are marked—houses as Victorian or prairie representations of class, mountains or oceans as majestic, etc. Icons are semic: the hammer and sickle of the Russian worker-farmer coalition, the switch blade of the ghetto street fighter.

4. Showings position their audiences; they put them in their places, in subject positions (Mulvey, 1975; for an introduction, see Sturken & Cartwright, 2001, esp. 73–76). Here is the Foucauldian idea that viewers are invited, called, by the "contents" of images to look at them in particular ways. More mechanically, of course, the construction of a showing forces one to see its existents within the frame from a particular place: above or below, head-on or to the side, panoramically or up-close-and-personal. Subject positions are matters of both vision and psychocultural conditioning.

More could be said about showings, but perhaps the point is made: both the narrative structurings of stories-as-told and controls over selecting, framing, detailing, and orienting images meld as imagetexts, that is, as textual encounters wherein the verbal and the visual are experienced as a unit, to direct the perception and other cognitive processes of their listener-reader-viewers. In this conception, relationships between tellings (narratives) and showings (graphics, pictures) are integral to rhetorical force; "the inescapable heterogeneity of representation" (Mitchell, 1994, p. 418) is experienced as a totality. Perceptions are formed, beliefs and attitudes are reinforced or changed, and values and other aspects of cultural orientation are evoked at the intersection of verbal and visual textualizations.

Narratives, to be sure, are more clearly marked as temporal, and visual images, as spatial. Narratives are particularly powerful at suturing past, present, and future into coherent, conceptual wholes; pictures, yes, let us see the stories, and in the age of mechanically and electronically reproduced still and moving images, seeing is believing, comprehending, remembering, the evidence for claims. Even further, however, visual symbolizations permit us to emphasize, individually and collectively, the spatial environments within which we (should) act, and in showing us acting in those environments, they reinforce our conceptions of who we are as persons and as people. The showings can function as idealized and yet empirically grounded performances. Yet, while tellings and showings can—and should—be analyzed separately, they are experientially interlocked by those who consume them.

One last point about showings: They need not reveal all to evoke all. That is, episodes or even single images can trigger memories of stories learned in earlier times. Just as the punchline of a joke can call it to mind or a partial phrase can set a song ringing in your head, so even a single image can act as what Aristotle in *De memoria et reminiscentia* (McKeon, 1941) called a reminiscence or recollection. He understood a recollection to be a memory of some event recalled in its duration and in its surrounding human contexts. Memory rehearses the details of events; reminiscences include the important personal and collective associations accompanying events. So, a painting of George Washington crossing the Delaware River or of Joan of Arc having a vision can call up the major outlines of their life events, even the social-political or social-religious significations associated with those life events. A single image, to put this another way, can trigger cognitive framing (Gronbeck, 1993)—narrativized framing as we will pursue that idea. This is very much like what Toby Miller (1998) means by "technologies of truth": just as smoke is an index of a fire, so a picture can be indexical of the whole narrative, bringing it to mind and reinvigorating its rhetorical demands.

The sort of rhetoric being examined in this essay, therefore, is understood to be persuasive in three fundamental ways: Verbal, visual, and even acoustic discourses are understood as circulating through publicly accessible channels—the public sphere—with the power to reinforce particular subject positions of citizenship, to affect both cognitive and behavioral aspects of individuals' lives, and to remake or remanufacture cultural understandings of a collectivity's past, present, and future.

The public sphere, in this case, is more than the non-institutionalized places where the governed can hide from and work independently of the governors (Habermas, 1989). Rather, it is composed of what Todd Gitlin called "sphericules" (qted. in Bennett, 2001, 77), or publicly accessible sites where localized groups of people find common information and ideas, engage shared concerns, and even compatible grounds for concerted action. As similar messages appear in newspapers from around the country (and world), over broadcast television programs, and in websites attracting a significant number of people, the sphericules are threaded together. Indeed, *thread* is a useful metaphor, for it permits us to see how similar stories and similar depictions in varied places make it possible for those who are unconnected in other ways to share discourses. In sharing similar, verbally, visually, and acoustically coded discursive formations, a disparate or fragmented people can participate,

virtually yet publicly, in shared identities, cognitive and behavioral actions, and cultural narrativizations of their histories.

No one member of a people, of course, can experience all of the messages circulating at any one moment; no one has all of the threads in hand. But, items in the archive of popular discourses circulating through a society are similar to and resonant enough with each other to guarantee that some of the discursive formations are dominant and, at least roughly, experienced by most members of the collectivity in similar ways. These stories are told repeatedly, usually in part, and indexed often through images that evoke them. Such stories are "popular logics" (Miller, 1998, p. 5) that "are *telling* technologies; they tell stories about who and how 'we' are, in ways that make a difference to what they define and explain. . . . The technologies produce truths about and for the very people who provide their receptive targets *and* their diegetic subjects" (p. 59).

Within the public sphere, then, explanations in storied forms become constructed through bits and pieces of news reports and commentary, at first illustrated but subsequently recollected evocatively through the visualizations that come to become melded inseparably with them. These explanations, in their turn, both publicly textualize social understandings and accounts, and provide visions of identity for those who are actors in the stories and also readers of them. And so, supplied with such images and narratives, a society periodically can reconstruct itself, including in times when it faces traumatic circumstances in the here-and-now of daily life. It is one such rhetoric of seeings and tellings that this essay explores.

The Trauma That Was/Would Be September 11

Before we examine the tellings that were offered to the country in the post 9/11 sphericules, we must return briefly to that day. On 10 March 2002, CBS broadcast a two-hour documentary, *9/11*, from footage shot by French documentarists Jules and Gedeon Gaudet. This video allowed audiences to re-live that Tuesday morning and the breathtaking, numbing events that generated confusion, fear, and anger (cf. Tvnews3, 2002). Live-TV coverage available at the time guaranteed total audience involvement, and print coverage in special editions of newspapers on 9/11 and in those from the day-after saturated Americans with five groups of images:

1. The acts themselves: violent, spectacular, awesome in their enormity of conception and their effects on buildings and the people in and around them;

2. The stunned New Yorkers near "Ground Zero," with that very metaphor evoking the older disaster narratives of nuclear war;

3. Glazed, crying citizens: some in New York, but also shots of worried viewers watching television around the country and the world;

4. A resolute President Bush: labeling the events as evil, calling for a response, but yet offering no specific information on what could be done; and,

5. The soon-deified firefighters and law enforcement personnel: providing the only glimmers of hope, particularly in the internationally circulated image of firefighters' reenactment of the raising of the U.S. flag on Iwo Jima.[2]

As one might remember, most of the pictures in newspapers were of helpless victims, not self-confident citizens in control of their lives or environment. The day-of and the day-after were depicted as occasions of mass disorientation, productive of a statement-of-mind that the warfare gamesters had predicted would happen only with the use of WMD—weapons of mass destruction ("Talk," discussion of 9/12/2001). Airplanes full of fuel and fanatics had compellingly demolished the rules of international contestation. Terrorism worked its worst during those days.[3] As a society, the United States collectively buried itself in narratives from those WHO barely survived and about those who didn't, expressions of unbridled anger and sleepless sorrow, and shared bewilderment. So, what could the U.S. tell itself to restore confidence, to move on?

Three Narratives of Cultural Definition and Redefinition

Many stories about the state and direction of American society have threaded their way through American sphericules. Some never developed into broad, elaborate, thick narratives. Such was true for Rev. Jerry Falwell's account that "the pagans, the abortionists, and the feminists, and the gays and the lesbians who are actively trying to make that an alternative lifestyle, the ACLU, People of the American Way, all of them who have tried to secularize America, I point the finger in their face and say, 'You helped this happen'" (*The 700 Club*, 9/13/01, qted. in *Adbusters*, 2002, Jan./Feb.). Similarly, the call to de-urbanize the country, "turning to nature in a time of crisis" (*Audubon*, 2002 Jan.), did not chain through the popular imagination.[4] Falwell's assertion could not explain the complex action of nineteen suicide terrorists, while few Americans were willing to give up the technological society for an agrarian one. Three narratives, however, did have sufficient breadth and near-constant revisualization to deserve our attention. Those three narratives were sturdy enough, as well, to provide distinctive cultural definitions or redefinitions.

Story #1: The Story of Institutional Failures

One story that was running at full throttle the day of the attacks on the World Trade Center and the Pentagon was a narrative about institutional shortcomings, even failures. Often shown in split-screen so we could see both the investigative and the material specialists working for us, expert after expert on security and military affairs, especially, was dragged onto radio and television interview programs to explain how the attacks could have occurred.

Three centers of institutional failure—governmental antiterrorism activities, airport security procedures, and U.S. crisis response planning—were explored with special closeness: First, the CIA, the FBI, and other parts of the international espionage community: Why were there failures in intelligence? Why could not Al-Qaeda be penetrated? How is its network organized and maintained internationally? How could the terrorists live so invisibly in the U.S. and even acquire flight training sophisticated enough to let them handle 747s? So, for example, on CNN the evening of September 11, correspondent Wolf Blitzer assembled electronically Sen. Christopher Dodd (D–CT), Warren Christopher, former Secretary of State under Clinton, and Jim Steinberg, Clinton's Deputy National Security Advisor, to answer the question, "Was someone asleep at the switch?" The query prompted Dodd to note that Senate Democrats and many Republicans approved of missile defense shields but saw "a higher degree of danger to be faced from the very kind of thing we saw today" (9/11/01). (Cf., e.g., "Attacks exposes intelligence failure," *DI*, 9/13/01, p. 6A.)[5]

Second, airport and in-flight security: Why were not security checkers better trained? How can pilots be overcome so easily? Why does it take our air defense planes so long to scramble? The Federal Aviation Administration tried to quiet questioners by announcing new security measures on September 13, yet kept almost all except diverted flights grounded until the next week (ibid., p. 7A; *ICP-C*, 9/14/01, 6A). Discussions of arming pilots, reinforcing cockpit doors, federalizing airport personnel, instituting still more stringent check-in procedures, and training more sky marshals kept these questions on the public mind long after 9/11.

And third, crisis response procedures in the United States: While major cities had thought in terms of disaster relief plans in the case of massive attacks, such as nuclear assault, why had not more people been working on terrorism, especially since the Oklahoma City bombing of 1995? Most of NPR's September 12, 2001, broadcast of "Talk of the Nation" (2001) featured disaster relief experts warning the country that much more had to be done to help cities and states through similar incidents in the future. New York City's program came

under particular scrutiny when Mike Bloomberg became mayor that fall; the tourists would not return if the city didn't provide better security and control.

In the story about institutional failures, America and Americans were fundamentally good people on the right track through life, but were victimized as much by governmental systems' corner-cutting and incompetence as by the terrorists. This narrative was a contemporary Roman comedy—a story of foolish governors, braggadocio generals, bumbling investigators and spies, naïve and untrained security personnel. All of these institutional clowns were ridiculed on news interviews and talk shows by retired generals, private security directors, and disaster planners who insisted that no one ever listened to their expertise until it was too late.

The story of institutional incompetence had sticking power. The debate over airport and in-flight security, especially, regularly resurfaced. In January 2002, new airport security requirements involving hand searches, luggage matching, X-rays, and bomb-sniffing dogs went into effect with front-page stories and televised pictures of dogs and the technologies (e.g., CNN, 1/18/02). And on the 11 March 2002 six-month anniversary of 9/11, reviews of how much safer (or not) we were made newspapers, radiocasts, and telecasts across the country (e.g., *ICP-C*, 3/11/02, 7A). Debate over handguns or taser (stun) guns for pilots, public identification cards, and security checks of nationals from selected countries continues to fill newspaper inches and talk shows. Even a Department of Homeland Security, carved out of twenty-two government agencies including the Immigration and Naturalization Service, Coast Guard, and the Federal Emergency Management Agency, was put on the public's plate by President Bush in June 2002.

Overall, this was a populist narrative that, like classic comedy, assembled storylines of citizen innocence, institutional failures, and the ever-popular hope that things will be better tomorrow with just a little tinkering or changes in personnel. Individual plot lines coalesced into an overarching narrative structure pointing to a common Moral of the Story: look what happens when officials with responsibilities for public well-being fail to do their institutional jobs in competent and coordinated fashions. The capture of the shoe-bomber Richard Reid and the incompetent pilot-in-training Zacarias Moussaoui seemed to demonstrate institutional progress; and by 21 January 2002 *Newsweek* (p. 33) stories emphasized that 9/11 was not the product of CIA failure, though that judgment was questioned in the 10 June 2002 issue of the same magazine (p. 7). The appointment of Homeland Security Director Tom Ridge, the detention policies of Attorney General John Ashcroft, and the ballyhooed passage of the Patriot Act in October 2001 were bureaucratic dams that diverted the flood of criticism into the things-will-be-better-tomorrow segment of the narrative. By early 2002, the "homeland defense" strategies of today were being associated with similar actions reaching back to John Adams' proposal for the Alien Act of 1798 (Perret, 2002). The story of institutional incompetence was being retrofitted into the much larger historical tale of American self-protectionism.

The protectionist theme carried over into the economic world, with exhortations to get America back to work. The weaknesses of our economic institutions—and, in particular, the situation of the service economy and dot-coms—were emphasized by the free-falling stock market after 9/11. Product and service advertising soon came onboard to emphasize the strength of American economic institutions and their ability to sustain recovery. So, a Fidelity Investments ad (2002) had Peter Lynch talking about the underlying supports in the economic system—Social Security, unemployment dollars, a budgetary surplus, and a strong housing market—that made the country strong. As Lynch explained it: "We've had nine recessions since World War II. We've had nine recoveries since World War II. We've had a perfect score. Betting against America's been a bad bet in the past. It's going to be a bad bet in the future." General Motors joined in the parade of pious predictions. A Chevy ad (2001) opened with a shot of the Statue of Liberty at sunrise, followed by three racially diverse workers in hard-hats walking toward the camera as the narrator assured us, "For ninety years, Chevrolet has helped keep America moving, and we're not about to stop now." After mentioning interest-free financing, he patted his sponsor on the back: "it's one way we can help keep America rolling forward. We'll be there."

The industrial economy, the durable goods markets particularly, thus showed their patriotic stripes. President Bush, as well, periodically left the District to visit factories around the country; so, when he first journeyed to Iowa on 14 January 2002, he addressed John Deere workers. The post-industrial economy of services did not receive his attention; it was a time of trouble, so solid manufacturing—cars, agricultural implements, and appliances, not the flighty financial empires or web-based ventures—was emphasized in the President's travels. As the story percolated through the public prints and airwaves, another set of institutions was contributing to a happy ending of the first story; consumers were asked to spend their way toward normalcy. That consumer spending in fact held up through the winter holidays and well into 2002, with the stock market exhibiting signs of recovery, kept the first story on newspaper front pages and electronic news leads. Continued reform of governmental organizations along with a can-do spirit of American manufacturing and public confidence in industry possibly could give the comedic post-9/11 story a sweet resolution.

Story #2: The Manufacture of the New World Order

The narrative that I heard and saw most clearly while in Finland, when I was receiving my news from the BBC World and CNNI newscasts, was the story of the United States taking still another run at what George Bush Sr. had called a "New World Order." The tale spun here was a post-USSR international scenario wherein the world was uniting in fellowship, organized to the mutual benefit of sovereign nations and, conversely, against anyone or any collective that would seek to violate the rules of friendship and social-political cooperation. Positively, the central narrative depicted cooperative international coalitions that would act to benefit all economically and even socially by distributing the military, economic, and personnel requirements for mutual defense and order. Negatively, because the First-, Second-, and Third-World stratifications would disappear as nations evolved into an interdependent order, new categories of enemies were articulated: "rogue nations" such as Iraq–which, with Iran and North Korea, Bush called an "axis of evil" in his 2002 State of the Union Address—could be segregated (boycotted) until they agreed to live by the laws of humanity, and "terrorists," who could be sought out, chastened, and punished for their disruption of transnational tranquility.

This story had a new dialectical core formed around new depictions of good and evil. The conflict was articulated in monumental proportions, beginning in President Bush's speech to the Joint Session of Congress, with British Prime Minister Tony Blair present, when he said: "Every nation in every region now has a decision to make: either you are with us [the international coalition] or you are with terrorists" (9/20/01). The old dialectic with the Red scare had been replaced by one with invisible guerrillas and their burqa-clad women. The new talk resonated through at least Western media, as country after country either volunteered materiel and technical support for the U.S. military operations or promised humanitarian aid to Pakistan and Afghanistan. Most allowed U.S. flyovers across their domestic airspace, and pledged to pursue terrorists working inside their borders (BBC broadcasts, 9/20–10/1/01); videos of planes high overhead accompanied these stories, presumably showing what was being promised.

As this story developed in the first few weeks following 9/11, the United States was granted sympathy from the rest of the world; strings of Internet pictures of flowers and other icons of sorrow were laid especially at U.S. embassy gates worldwide (September11, 2002 news).[6] That sympathy was turned into action on 7 October 2001 with the launching of Operation Enduring Freedom— nighttime air and missile strikes deep within Afghanistan against Taliban and/or Al-Qaeda command posts and strongholds. Prime Minister Blair led the way for non-American countries involved, discussing a three-pronged strategic response (military, humanitarian, and diplomatic), while Secretary of State Donald Rumsfeld offered America's justification for its assault on a beleaguered Afghanistan:

> I want to reiterate a point that President Bush has made often and that he made again today in his remarks. The United States has organized armed coalitions on several occasions since the Cold War for the purpose of denying hostile regimes the opportunity to oppress their own people and other people. In Kuwait, in northern Iraq, in Somalia, Bosnia, and Kosovo, the United States took action on behalf of Muslim populations against outside invaders and oppressive regimes. The same is true today. We stand with those Afghans who are being oppressed by a regime that abuses the very people it purports to lead, and that harbors terrorists who have attacked and killed thousands of innocents around the world, of all religions, of all races, and of all nationalities. While our raids today focus on the Taliban and the foreign terrorists in Afghanistan, our aim remains much broader. Our objective is to defeat those who use terrorism and those who house or support them. The world stands united in this effort. (CBS News special, 10/7/01.)

By November 2001, a second act of this story began developing, as pictures of meetings in Germany to set up a new government for Afghanistan filled newspapers with depictions of the New World Order at work. By December, plans to push multinational initiatives for economic reform in the Middle East, reduction of tensions between India and Pakistan, and a deceleration of growing Arab-Israeli confrontations added an air of optimism to this narrative. Initially, during the week following 9/11, Clear Channel radio programmers identified John Lennon's song "Imagine" (rpted. *Adbusters*, 2002, p. 3) as one of 150 potentially "insensitive" tunes. Soon, however, it was playing regularly, capturing the New World Order vision in its lyrics.

As these lyrics suggest, the New World Order narrative was a classic utopian romance, replete with the darkness before the dawn of a new day in a whole new World of Tomorrow. In this telling, our fear, grief, and ignorance will disappear only if we embrace a utopian worldwide brother- and sister-hood. This narrative was referenced regularly, especially through fall 2001. President Bush offered photo and conversation opportunities to visiting and telephoning world leaders, including Prince Saudi al-Faisal of Saudi Arabia and Tony Blair (9/20/01), Thai Prime Minister Thaksin and Canadian Prime Minister Jean Chrétien (9/24/01), Prime Minister Junichiro Kozumi of Japan (9/25/01), Dutch Prime Minister Kok and Kazakhstan President Nazarbayev (9/26/01), Prime Minister Howard of Australia and President Arroyo of the Philippines (9/29/01), Czech President Havel and Malaysian Prime Minister Mahathir (10/1/01), the Emir of Bahrain, the President of Poland, the President of Mexico, and the Emir of Qatar (10/4/01). As well, the American Muslim and Sikh community leaders were invited into the White House in late September for conversations about restoring domestic peace. (See *George W. Bush*, 2001.)[7]

The story of the New World Order, of course, already was being lived out economically in the age of transnational corporations and aggressive international investment initiatives cross-stitching the world together. The question now was, could it be turned, politically and socially, into the next chapter of American history? Given the power in the U.S. of the myth of American exceptionalism (Zullow, 1994), it would have a most difficult time getting written. Throughout the twentieth century, the U.S. has steadfastly refused to surrender any of its sovereignty to transnational organizations. It refused to join the League of Nations altogether, and by statute limits the U.N.'s and International Court's jurisdiction in matters it believes to be of pressing national interest. We envision ourselves as exceptional, genetically constructed out of every other people in the world, and destined for greatness in and through our own works. We would not fit easily into the New World Order, which explains why, even though the story periodically emerges, it has little staying power. Among the three dominant post-9/11 narratives, this one receives the fewest retellings. It lives the smallest corner in the public sphere.

Story #3: Looking Back Toward the Future

> I want to thank America for the outpouring of support. I want to thank Americans for their strong will. We're still the greatest nation on the face of the earth, and no terrorist will ever be able to decide our fate. —President Bush's radio address to the nation, 9/15/01 (*George W. Bush*, 2001, p. 37).

The most widespread and oft-referenced narrative following 9/11 was the story of recovering and reinstituting past values and collective orientations as guides to America's future. Talk soon started emphasizing the people's lack of commitment to fundamental American values in the recent past and their institutional agents' lack of memory of what had made America great in earlier generations. What was needed, in this story, were new exemplars of Brokaw's "Greatest Generation," though heroes in these days, given the multicultural world of the New Century, would have to have the wisdom and tolerance for diversity needed to reassemble a great nation. This set of developing themes was illustrated nicely in the 13 January 2002 episode of the first-season Sunday night TV show, *The Education of Max Bickford*. Professor Bickford's (Richard Dreyfus's) small all-female college was being made safe by security patrols and identification cards, yet Middle Eastern students and their visitors were being hassled. The episode's resolution involved a reassertion of traditional American values—fairness, justice, tolerance, and love—even while maintaining the vigilance espoused by the security patrols.

"Looking back toward the future" thematically depends upon the recovery of a past so as to hammer it into a template for the future. This is, for Americans, a fascinating and powerful story, emphasizing self-blame (laxness) but also individualized redemption (self-reliance). It is a narrative driven by the kind of thinking that President Bill Clinton emphasized in his first inaugural: "There is nothing wrong with America that cannot be cured by what is right with America" (Clinton, 2002). Salvation lies within the enduring value orientations already available and malleable enough to be retrofitted for the new, post-9/11 complexities. This narrative was iconized in the now-famous shot of firefighters raising an American flag in the rubble of the World Trade Center, expanded in any number of TV ads and magazine pictures showing American strength in those whom President Ronald Reagan had called the everyday heroes in his 1981 inaugural address, and made concrete less in national action than in local lifeworlds.

The localization of redemptive acts was most obviously visible in New York City itself. Mayor Rudy Giuliani said "I love New York" at every opportunity, and soon other New Yorkers given presence on the electronic media followed suit. The public service announcements that were being broadcast by late fall included collections of New Yorkers—Broadway entertainers, hotel employees, CEOs of major corporations—who turned the amorous declaration into a chant.

News broadcasts showcased local heroes and heroics, as cheering, flag-waving citizens and visitors lined the streets when fire fighters and law enforcement officers went back and forth to Ground Zero to continue the digging.

Locales around the country reflected similar public commitments. Memorial services were reported nationwide. Other heroic acts of rescue by fire fighters or police officers made headlines wherever they occurred. A *Reader's Digest* (2002, Feb.) article lionized a group of teenaged girls who were trained and maintained an effective rescue squad in a small Alaskan town. Small-town fire brigades marched off to New York City to help in the removal of rubble. By Thanksgiving 2001, the "Give Thanks America" digital hookup, sponsored by Compaq and its partners Digital Island and Sorenson Media, allowed citizens to e-mail personalized video greetings and thanks to military personnel, police, and fire fighters; a mobile "movie studio" swung to smaller cities so as to provide the same service to less urbanized people (PRNewswire, 2002).

And, everywhere, everywhere, the American flag, often embroidered with the first-week slogan "United We Stand," was impossible to avoid, given its presence in or on newspaper pullouts, flag pins and other designer jewelry, clothing (especially entertainers' costumes and sports uniforms), the sets and outdoor establishing shots for primetime television programs, displays of the WTC tattered flag at the World Series and the Olympics, cereal boxes, Pop-Tarts packages, red-white-and-blue M&Ms, bumper stickers and auto antennas, eighteen wheelers, store windows, bed spreads, and collectibles kits in hobby stores. Thanks to the sanctimony of the flags associated with the site of destruction, any display could evoke both the horror and the subsequent pledge to never forget.[8] The mundane lives of everyday Americans were lived against a background of reminders, evocative of the events of 9/11 and of the multivocal commitments of citizens everywhere to stand united.

As Toby Miller (1998, p. 11) has noted, "popular culture is an opportunity to uncover collective and individual weakness and strength, for the purposes of either cultural mapping and resistance or policy enumeration and advice." A book could be written illustrating that truism from 2001–2002. Product advertisements, as we noted earlier, were arrayed with patriotic symbols, demonstrations of the American can-do spirit, and articulations of the resilience of a people who were rediscovering the mindsets and (especially consumer) acts that made them great. The President had requested that our inward looking include economic activity: "I ask your continued participation and confidence in the American economy" (Joint Address to Congress, 9/20/01, *George W. Bush*, 2001, p. 38). Ralph Lauren, among other manufacturers, answered the call, and appeared in Polo ads, wearing a knit flag design on his sweater in both print and TV ads.

Not only American commerce but also the film industry responded to 9/11, in particular following another of Bush's lines in his 9/20/01 Joint Address: "I ask you to uphold the values of America" (2000, p. 31). It piously waited until the turn of the calendar, then released a torrent of war-and-revenge films after the first of the year: *Behind Enemy Lines*, *Black Hawk Down*, *We Were Soldiers*,[9] and *Hart's*

War and the DVD re-release of the summer 2001 *Pearl Harbor* treated heroic, all-American military actions in Kosovo, Somalia, Vietnam, and World War II; *Collateral Damage* showed a one-man wrecking crew (Arnold Schwartzenegger) responding to a terrorist bombing, while the *Count of Monte Cristo* remake enacted a classic avenge-and-revenge story.

The United States may have forgotten its valuative and behavioral commitments to the previous generations' legacy temporarily, but they were lost no longer, was the theme of this story. In the wake of 9/11, the country was reawakened by symbolic markers of this story in its daily environments and in the flow of representations in popular culture of localized service to others, patriotism, investment in one's own future, and even a willingness to make the ultimate sacrifice, if necessary, that might be required if America were to survive the outsider-enemies.

Certainly the fullest articulations of narrative structures encasing these themes were primetime television programs, especially those set in governmental halls and East Coast cities. The *West Wing* delayed its season-opener to broadcast a video-taped play featuring a doubled narrative that toggled between the grilling of a White House worker feared to be a terrorist and the civics lessons being taught to touring high school students about tolerance, personal rights, and the difficulties true democracies have in responding to terrorism. Later episodes that season gave vent to the frustration of White House advisers who were expected to remain cool and open-minded in the face of constant danger. On *NYPD Blue* a love affair between its African American leads was interrupted because of all of the tension in their work following 9/11, and the retaliatory bombing of a Middle Eastern business as one of its January 2002 plots. As well, its set always showed American flags on the streets of New York. *Law & Order* exhibited similar characteristics: One of its stories featured a suspect who could be traced in part because a New York art exhibit had a controlled guest list and ID wristbands in the wake of 9/11 fears. *The Practice* offered an episode in which a Middle Easterner

was held by the FBI without bail or explanation, which provoked a judge's speech about citizen rights even in times of fear. On such programs the tension between democratic openness and national multiculturalism over and against the willingness to give up civil liberties and the desire to escape from aggressive otherness was illustrated time and again.

In all such events in American popular culture, the country was arising from the ashes of the towers and the Pentagon striving to become great again. There was no need for non-Americans in this narrative. The backward-looking was also an inward-looking—an act of spiritual regeneration and then righteous action. The backward-looking, too, was amnesiastic: it erased the horror of 9/11 by looking over and beyond it, binding a more distant past, better times, to the hoped-for future. This narrative form was a favorite of Puritan preachers when addressing community tragedies such as killer storms, deaths of infants, and the like. Called the jeremiad after the warnings of the Old Testament prophet Jeremiah, this rhetorical genre (1) emphasizes that a people is responsible for its own fate, suffering when lax and prospering when vigilant and committed, and (2) suggests that good always can be fetched out of evil when acts of righteousness and redemption follow the evil.[10]

Among the heroes of Story #3 were Americans working by themselves, not with others, in efforts reminiscent of all of the war movies circulating through the winter and spring of 2002. The people were proud and commanding, in direct contrast to the day-after shots that filled the front pages of newspapers in September. They were celebrated in the patriotic gore that flowed through Super Bowl XXXVI, and of course, the 19th Winter Olympics in Salt Lake City. Like the metaphor that was featured in NBC's Olympic opening six-minute feature (2/9/02), heroic Americans in fact were "a light in the darkness." The American World Order articulated here, as opening night at those Olympics made clear, had but one leader—a tall-walking Texan who was working with the blessing of a public job-approval rate hovering between eighty and ninety percent (PollingReport.com, 2003).

Seeing and Telling Cultural History

So where are we in the narrative study of the reconstruction of American collective identity? What can be said about 9/11's impact on Americans' understanding of themselves as a people, as a government, and as a force in the world? And what is the place of shared showings and tellings as the instruments of cultural redefinition?

First, as has been suggested, the varied stories told in and around 9/11 bring back into focus debates about the United States' place in the world—a debate that has raged at least since George Washington warned the young country in his farewell address to avoid entangling alliances: To what degree are our obligations to help others to be inwardly or outwardly directed? Do we continue to serve the world—its tired, its poor, its huddled masses yearning to breathe free—or do we focus upon ourselves, getting our own house in order before obligating ourselves to others in ways that are not simply self-serving? Attached to such questions are classic issues that have rung out in congressional debates across the nineteenth and twentieth centuries: isolationism, the virtues and vices of serving as the world's police force, tariff debates (these days particularly, the North American Free Trade Association and our relations with Mexico/Mexican laborers), membership obligations to international associations. These issues, of course, are not directly referenced in 9/11 conversations, but they do get inscribed back into public consciousness. Debates over the President's military budget, legislative debates over who is eligible for state social services, and economic stimulus/airline bailout bills all bring back into focus foundational questions of the United States' place on the planet.

Additionally, 9/11 stories do not simply raise questions about our economic, political, and military obligations to others, though those questions are important. These narratives also implicate such socio-ideological questions concerning our conceptions of others as:

1. How open are we/should we be to others?
2. How do we define otherness as a country?
3. How seriously do we take questions of equal opportunity, affirmative action, and, in terms of a decade-long debate, multiculturalism?

These are socio-ideological questions that must be wrestled with openly before Americans can advance serious proposals to solve policy conundrums: While we all work within a multinational, globalized economic system, how far are we willing to go in that direction—the direction of the New World Order—politically? How liberal are we willing to become domestically, in legislation that legalizes various domestic partners arrangements, that deChristianizes public space, that opens publicly supported health services to varied medical practices and patient needs, that provides social services for non-citizens as well as citizens, and that extends the reach of the Freedom of Information Act? The Patriot Act of October 2001 is one indexical sign of current answers to these questions, as were spring 2002 discussions of identity cards for both American citizens and particular groups of non-citizens. So are actions of state legislatures that make English the official state language, that seek to erase references to multicultural education from the state codes, or that declare the United States the greatest country that has ever existed on earth. The first of these became law in Iowa in February 2002, and the other two declarations were debated in congressional committee. All three actions perform nothing less than the state-sanctioned devaluation of otherness. Answers to such socio-ideological questions will be affected by the story of 9/11 that we tell ourselves next year and the years after that. Of course the country curled into a fetal ball when the planes hit; but how long will it remain so tightly, defensively, self-absorbed?

I suggest that debates about cultural definition and redefinition that flow through the public sphericules and are depicted graphically in the pictures and videos that fill newspapers, television news holes, and Internet sites, and that saturate our visual environment via items of food, clothing, bodily and building decorations, and mass-mediated fictive stories have astonishingly far-reaching, definitional consequences.

These consequences may well be the most important collective results of the terrorist actions that Tuesday morning in September. The narrative forms that these definitional debates take enable a people to superimpose familiar structures on the storied episodes of their lives. These different types of narratives—the comic frame (incompetence), the romantic or utopian frame (New World Order), and the resurrection or post-tragic frame (looking back toward the future)—articulate alternative visions of the future; no one of them controls the social-political world initially because they must be manufactured in an unfocused here-and-now. What we have to work with in the here-and-now are generic conventions and a cultural past that we have inherited; traditional narrative forms are our surest guides to comprehensible futures because they are metalanguages (Lacey, 2000, p. 248) that suggest how we can read that-which-is-as-yet-unknown, that-which-is-as-yet-unseen.

The precise configuration of narrative frames working within any particular historical setting is largely a matter of availability (see Frye, 1957, on the historicization of literatures). The comic frame in the history of Western literature has been a means by which the less-powerful are able to critique the actions of the more-powerful; it is a tool of complaint and a way to demand conformity to social expectations (see Frye, 1957). It assumes that the social-political world will function well enough until someone allows it to break down. When that happens, blame must be placed—in the comic frame, often through public ridicule or humiliation—so that offending minions can be eliminated and the social universe can be restored to harmony. The comic frame works from a comparatively conservative societal outlook, one that assumes that the system is generally sound and hence only in need of changes in personnel and perhaps some tinkering. On the dark side, it is the story told by mobs calling for firings or worse; in its brightest versions, the comic narrative encourages optimism because so little has to be done, especially by the people, to make the world right once more.

More interesting, perhaps, is the utopian frame. On the one hand, utopian literature has always sought reform of or escape from the here-and-now through the positing of an alternative, assuredly a better, world, as in Sir Thomas More's (1615) *Utopia*. Such a world is liberal in that word's original sense—freeing. On the other hand, because that world is almost inevitably unattainable, it serves, perhaps paradoxically, to make readers more accepting of where they are now (Marius, 1995). Utopias also are easily turned into imprisoning societies, as in Aldous Huxley's (1931) *Brave New World* or George Orwell's (1948) *Nineteen Eighty-Four*. And, one might add, dystopias always inevitably involve the surrender of individual or group rights to a collectivist central agency. The romantic vision of the New World Order, therefore, faced not only the usual arguments about American exceptionalism we noted earlier, but, additionally, the problem all utopian visions face: beautiful dreams of brotherhood evolve all too easily into nightmares of enslavement-to-others. The rhetoric of the New World Order, while initially reassuring to people looking for friends in times of trauma, loses its power when we recover from the shock of attack and become ready to make our own future.

And so we come to the resurrection narrative frame, where apparent tragedy metamorphosizes into heroic triumph. Given U.S. history, the telling and showing of a reborn people became the most virulent post-9/11 story. The September attacks were most easily understood in terms of World War II, Vietnam, Somalia (or Grenada), the Gulf War, and Bosnia-Kosovo—the most clearly envisioned war-related stories circulating in the 2001 collective psyche of the country. World War II, with the sneak attack of Pearl Harbor the most usual starting point in its narrativizations, provided the most vivid of the historical parallels—and hence the most powerful of the wartime pasts available as a source of the Moral of the Story. The values dominating American advertising, sporting events, and electronic media productions through the fall of 2001 and the spring of 2002 came from that framework. For that matter, even Story #1 could be absorbed into the resurrection narrative; FBI Director Robert Mueller in May 2002 acknowledged past problems but promised a revitalized Agency as he created an Office of Intelligence and sought computerized hookups between his agents and those of other intelligence and antiterrorism organizations (*Newsweek*, 2002, May 27, p. 39).

Though the third story was the most forceful in the post-9/11 public sphere, all three continuously circulated, and were regularly evoked in electronic, print, and material media. The debates over the best and most enduring of 9/11 legacies were depicted in pictorial and material forms because within the symbols we array in photographic, televisual, and Internet images as well as bodily decorations and visual displays are stop-action visualizations of the meanings of life—the human values, the fears, and the hopes that help the stories our own lives take on broader significance. Stories are evocative of deep memories and hence primal emotions, individual and collective identities, and can be brought to surface every time we see a flag or fire truck, pass an Afghan restaurant, or hear a fleeting reference to the American spirit in a Chevy ad. No one, really—not counting essays such as this one—tries to tell the stories of cultural definition or redefinition whole, all at once. Rather, those stories are gathered out of bits and pieces of news, listservs and e-mail attachments, store fronts, movies, radio talk shows, advertisements, and the cold cereal aisles of grocery stores. They are assembled, fully or not, clearly or not, in the consequential or inconsequential lives of individuals, each of whom is working with different-though-similar, redundant pieces of information and impression. Individual sphericules are not much different from the "public sphere" generally. A picture here, a piece of jewelry there—these bring the stories back to mind because they are markers of imagetexts as Mitchell understood them (1994).

In our contemplative moments, we ask ourselves, what will happen to us next? And the answers we give to that question depends, finally, on how we've managed to remanufacture American history in the wake of 9/11. And in that way the rhetoric of seeings and tellings will have done its work—made us, for better or worse, whole again.

The stories of 9/11, I think, will go down in United States cultural history as extraordinarily significant. That date will take its place among other culturally potent temporal identifiers: the 1620 landing of the Pilgrims, the Declaration of Independence on the 4th of July, the 11th hour of the 11th day of the 11th month that become Armistice Day for two generations. Extraordinary events that affect our understanding of our own history—of its twists and turns, of who we are in time and space—are marked and remembered, and that will happen to 11 September 2001. U.S. citizens will find a ways—most likely with the help of the resurrection tellings and showings—to absorb that Tuesday in September into the grand narrative of what Boorstin (1958, 1965, 1973) so simply and self-reflexively called "The Americans." In the words of Joe Kubert and Peter Carlsson in the last panel of their cartoon tribute in *9/11* (2002, vol. 2, p.215):

> I've lived long enough to see the worst turn into something better. The efforts of people with conscience will result in a better and stronger nation, and a world that must eventually live in peace. There is no alternative, after all.

Notes

1. I've been gathering largely visual web-based materials at Gronbeck (2002), http://www.uiowa.edu/~commstud/resources. Links to print resources soon will be mounted on http://www.uiowa.edu/~policult.

2. The Poynter Institute (2002) website contains 240 front pages of newspapers from around the world, for 9/11/01 and 9/12/02, arranged alphabetically. It is from examining these sources that the five categories of images have been drawn.

3. One interesting set of records of 9/11 was assembled by "the world's finest comic book writers and artists." 9-11, volumes 1 and 2, are collectors' editions of 9/11 cartoons. Volume 1 appeared January 2002, was published by Dark Horse Comics,

and featured sketches inspired by the day itself. Volume 2 came soon after, was put out by DC Comics, and had more range. Its comics were broken into six sections: Nightmares, Heroes, Recollections, Unity, Dreams, and Reflections. Volume 2 included panels that reflected much of what we'll discuss as Story #3.

4. The *Audubon* January 2002 special section was entitled "This Land is Your Land: Turning to Nature in a Time of Crisis," and ran 17 pages, filled with lush pictures and with naturalist essays by William Cronon ("Introduction"), Scott Russell Sanders ("Loving the Land"), Barbara Kingsolver ("Saying Grace"), Carl Safina ("Wild Comfort"), Sallie Tisdale ("Seeing Clearly"), Annick Smith ("Sacred Ground"), Janisse Ray ("Weaving the World"), John Daniel ("The Flow of Life"), and Diane Ackerman ("Finding the Time Pool"). The escapist vision was articulated repeatedly, with redemption from 9/11's hell coming through decollectivizing action. It was beautiful; it did not spread.

Another story that floated through the press and, especially, Internet sites was the tale of the architectural loss when the WTC went down. The loss of those buildings, both literally and symbolically, led to moral, technological, economic, and political consequences. For varied lines of thought, see essays in *Preservation* (2002): Vincent Scully, "Risen to the Scale of the Vast Sky"; Witold Rybczynski, "Fairy Tales and After"; Adele Chatfield-Taylor, "The Violent Vanishing of Buildings"; Richard Moe, "Anchors in an Uncertain World"; Brian Doyle, "Down"; Hugh Hardy, "Celebrating Contrast"; Stanley Abercrombie, "The Shape of Things to Come"; and David McCullough, "Who We Are" (62–69).

5. By May–June 2002, these questions took on special force. Before 9/11, the Department of Justice had rejected FBI requests for more counterterrorism analysts, the alleged twentieth hijacker Zacarias Moussaoui had been arrested (with a note indicating that he might be flying something into the World Trade Center), Bill Kurtz from the FBI's international terrorism section had warned that bin Laden associates might be using U.S. flight schools for training, the central offices of the FBI had ignored Minnesota agents' (especially Coleen Rowley's) warnings from the field, CIA operatives knew of the January 2000 Kuala Lampur (Malaysia) summit of Al-Qaeda leaders (including U.S.-based members who were allowed back into the country), and both the CIA and the FBI kept information from each other that, had it be put together, would have made the Moussaoui memo credible. Story #1 has legs (Newsweek, 5/27/02, 6/10/02).

6. As of this writing, the most complete website for 9/11 photos in a variety of categories is this one. For live broadcasts from 9/11, go to http://tvnews3.televisionarchive.org/tvarchive/html.

7. The publisher of this and other commemorative magazines devoted to 9/11 was the Florida company that was mailed anthrax in October. It's also the publisher of the best-selling tabloid newspapers, *National Enquirer* and *Star*.

8. For a popular essay on relationships between flag idolatry and cultural consciousness, see Lutz (2002). Cf. http://www.usflag.org/.

9. "We Were Soldiers" was a cover headline of the 3/18/02 *Newsweek*, which pitched its coverage of Afghanistan's Operation Anaconda as a replay of that Vietnam film.

10. On the jeremiad, see Miller (1953); on its regular American use in and around the theme of fetching good out of evil, see Bormann (1985).

References

The 700 Club [television program, Christian Broadcasting Network] (2001).

9-11 [books]. (2002). Vol. 1: Artists respond. Milwaukie, OR: Dark Horse Comics. Vol. 2: The world's finest comic book writers & artists tell stories to remember. New York: DC Comics.

Adbusters: Journal of the Mental Environment [magazine] (2002, Jan./Feb.).

"Attacks expose intelligence failure." (2001, September 13). *Daily Iowan*, p. 6A.

Audubon [magazine] (2002, Jan.).

Barthes, R. (1974). *S/2* (R. Miller, Trans.). New York: Hill & Wang.

BBC [television channels] (2001–2).

Bennett, W. L. (2001). *News: The politics of illusion.* (4th ed.). New York: Longman.

Boorstin, D. J. (1958, 1965, 1973). *The Americans* [three-volume cultural history]. New York: Random House.

Bormann, E. G. (1985). *The force of fantasy: Restoring the American dream.* Carbondale: Southern Illinois University Press.

Brokaw, T. (1998). *The greatest generation.* New York: Random House,.

CBS News [television channel] (2001–2).

Chevrolet [televised advertisement] (2001).

Clinton, W. J. [electronic text] (2002). President Clinton's first inaugural address (1993). http//www.law.ou.edu/hist/clinton.html.

Cook, P. (Ed.) (1985). *The cinema book.* London: British Film Institute.

CNN [television channel] (2001–2).

DI [*Daily Iowan,* Iowa City, IA] (2001).

Devlin, D. (Producer) & Emmerich, R. (Director). (1996). *Independence day* (motion picture).

Fidelity investments [televised advertisement] (2002).

Frye, N. (1957). *Anatomy of criticism: Four essays.* Princeton, NJ: Princeton University Press.

George W. Bush: The making of a wartime president [photo magazine]. (2001.) Boca Raton, FL: American Media, Inc.

Gronbeck, B.E. (1993). The spoken and the seen: Phonocentric and ocularcentric dimensions of rhetorical discourse. In J. F. Reynolds (Ed.), *Rhetorical memory and delivery: Classical concepts for contemporary composition and communication* (pp. 139–155). Hillsdale, NJ: Lawrence Erlbaum Associates.

Gronbeck, B. E. [websites] (2002). http://www.uiowa.edu/~commstud/faculty/Gronbeck and http://www.uiowa.edu/~politcult/.

Habermas, J. (1989). *Structural transformation of the public sphere: An inquiry into a category of bourgeois society.* Cambridge, MA: MIT Press.

Hartley, J. (1992). *The politics of pictures: The creation of the public in the age of popular media.* New York: Routledge.

ICP-C [*Iowa City Press-Citizen]* (2001–2).

Independence day (film). (1996).

Lacey, N. (2000). *Narrative and genre: Key concepts in media studies.* New York: St. Martin's Press.

Lutz, S. (2002, February/March). Seasons of the flag. *American Heritage,* 56–61.

Marius, R. [electronic text] (1995). *Utopia as a mirror for a life and times.* Keynote address, Early Modern Literary Studies conference, Baltimore, MD.   http://www.shu.ac.uk/emls/iemls/conf/texts/marius.html.

McKeon, R. (Ed.) (1941) *The basic works of Aristotle* [De memoria et reminiscentia]. New York: Random House.

Miller, P. (1953). *The New England mind: From colony to province.* Cambridge: Harvard University Press.

Miller, T. (1998). *Technologies of truth: Cultural citizenship and the popular media.* Minneapolis: University of Minnesota Press.

Mitchell, W. J. T. (1994). *Picture theory: Essays on verbal and visual representation.* Chicago: University of Chicago Press.

Mulvey, L. (1975). Visual pleasure and narrative cinema. *Screen, 16,* 6–18.

Perret, G. (2002). Of doves and swords: A brief history of homeland defense. *America's New War,* 70–74.

Poynter Institute [website] (2001). Covering the attack: Front page galleries. http://www.poynter.org/Terrorism/gallery.

PRNewswire [website, s.v. "local fire fighters," 11/20/01 release]. (2002). http://www.FindArticles.com.

Roeger, K. [electronic text] (2001). Archetypal works of dytopian literature. http://www.gwu.edu/~english/kaleidoscope/Essaypages/Essay14.htm.

September11news [website] (2002). http://www.september11news.com/InternationalImages.htm.

Sturken, M., & Cartwright, L. (2001). *Practices of looking: An introduction to visual culture.* New York: Oxford University Press.

Talk of the nation [radio program] (2001).

Taylor, M. (2001). Facing the enemy [poem]. *Infinite respect, enduring dignity: Voices & visions on the September attacks* [conference program]. Iowa City: Project on Rhetoric of Inquiry, University of Iowa.

Tvnews3 [website] (2002). http://tvnews3.televisionarchive.org/tvarchive/html.

Zullow, H.M. (1994). American exceptionalism and the quadrennial peak in optimism. In A. H. Miller & B. E. Gronbeck (Eds.), *Presidential campaigns and American self images* (pp. 214–230). Boulder, CO: Westview.

PART THREE

Producer-Centered Approaches

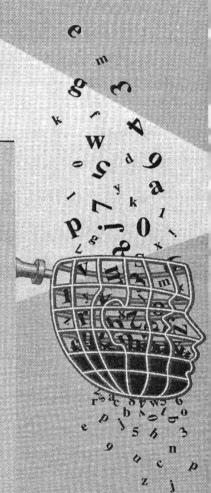

Auteur
Criticism
CHAPTER 9

Chapter Outline

The Evolution of Auteur Theory and Criticism

Auteur Television Criticism

Writing Auteur-Centered Criticism

Example Essay: Richard Campbell and
Jimmie L. Reeves's "Television Authors:
The Case of Hugh Wilson"

> One of the essential attributes of auteur analysis is its structural approach: Its method
> is to uncover the "deep structure" the .., [authorial signature] in order to interpret
> and evaluate the "surface structure" (his or her movies/[television series]). The socio-
> economic imperatives of Hollywood [production]. . . . however, indicate that there
> are a number of deep structures—industrial, political, technical, stylistic, narrative,
> and so on—which inform the production process (Schatz, 1981, p. 9).

A uteur-centered approaches came to television criticism from film studies,
specifically with the film criticism and theory written in the 1950s by a
group of French New Wave film director/critics for the French cinema journal *Cahiers du Cinéma.*

Auteur is a French term for the artist whose vision and personality is "written"
into a text—the "author." Auteur-centered criticism is based on the view of art as
"the expression of the emotions, experience and 'worldview' of an individual
artist" (Caughie, 1981, pp. 9–10). This rather romantic view sees artists as creatively obsessed individuals who manage, despite the collective nature of film production and the commercial-industrial context within which (American) films are
produced and distributed, to put their own unique signature or stamp on their
films. André Bazin (1957) once described auteur criticism as a critical approach
that involves "choosing in the artistic creation the personal factor as a criterion of
reference, and then postulating its permanence and even its progress from one
work to the next" (p. 14). Another way of saying this is that the critic really regards
the whole body of work by a particular artist (e.g., director or executive producer)
as a sort of genre in itself. As Schatz explained, "In fact, the auteur approach, in asserting a director's [or producer's] consistency of form and expression, effectively
translates an auteur into a virtual genre unto himself [*sic*], into a system of conventions which identify his work" (1981, p. 9).

The Evolution of Auteur Theory and Criticism

Auteur criticism came to television from film studies. As we discussed in Chapter
6 on genre criticism, most feature-length films produced in Hollywood have been
collaborative efforts involving screenwriters, a director, the studio producing and
financing the film, and expectations developed from previously produced and distributed films (genre). During the silent film era, some directors supervised every
aspect of their films' productions. Charlie Chaplin, for example, wrote the screen-
plays and musical scores, financed their production, cast the performers, acted in
the production, performed the music, and directed the production. Other famous
early film directors such as D. W. Griffith and Sergei Eisenstein also were known to
have been responsible for all aspects of their films. However, with the coming of
sound and the evolution of cinematic technology, filmmaking became increasingly complex and expensive. In Hollywood, this meant that the director's control
diminished and the studio's control increased. Hollywood studios' decisions were

concerned primarily with attracting, keeping, and increasing the size of the audiences of movies—hence, the reliance on tried-and-true successes and the development of genre films, as we discussed in Chapter 6. Hollywood movie audiences went to films for the stories and the stars in familiar, pleasurable types of stories, and they paid little attention to who had directed the films. The Hollywood director of that era generally was viewed as part of the invisible production crew; the director was told to produce a given type of film with the script, the cast, and almost everything else already decided. The director's job was to assemble these raw materials into a coherent film (see Caughie, 1981; Sarris, 1968; Schatz, 1981).

In Europe, however, "art films" remained the popular norm. There, highly individualistic films continued to be produced and directed by identifiable independent directors who oversaw every aspect of their films and were regarded as being totally responsible for them, until World War II pretty much shut down film production in Europe. The films of these European directors were viewed as the individual visions of their creators, like the individual works of novelists; hence, much early criticism relied heavily on biographical information about film creators (see Sarris, 1968, p. 30). In contrast, the films of American Hollywood directors of this era were viewed by many Europeans as mass-produced, industrial products and not the reflection of identifiable creators' visions.

Prior to World War II, European film directors, film patrons, and literati—writers, artists, poets, and film buffs—had gathered regularly in fairly luxuriously appointed film salons. At these ciné clubs, they sat around tables, sipped espresso and wine while they screened films, and then spent hours discussing them until World War II put a damper on this activity. As Peter Wollen (1972) points out, during the war, which extended from the late 1930s through the mid-1940s, American films were banned from France. Furthermore, in Europe, little filmmaking besides propaganda films went on during the war.

When the war finally ended and the European film industry was beginning to recover, Hollywood films were among the few new films available for screening in French film clubs. European film audiences were not particularly excited about watching what they regarded as primitive, factory-produced, commercial fare. Indeed, as Wollen explains, "directors who built their reputations in Europe were dismissed after they crossed the Atlantic, reduced to anonymity. American Hitchcock was contrasted unfavorably with English Hitchcock" (1972, p. 532).

Given these views of Hollywood film, it is easy to understand why French filmmakers and other French film aficionados sitting around their salon tables after World War II were astonished to discover among those Hollywood movies they previously had looked down on that some Hollywood directors had managed, in spite of the Hollywood studio system's genre and star constraints, to place their unique stylistic and thematic signatures on their films. This realization led to a renewed interest in American and European film directors' works, and fueled development of auteur theory in the articles published by French filmmaker-critics in *Cahiers du Cinéma*, under editor André Bazin. In the 1950s and 1960s *Cahiers du Cinéma* published critiques by Truffaut and others who argued that Hollywood directors like Orson Welles, John Ford, and Fritz Lang, no less than European "art" cinema directors, had transformed their film material into personal artistic statements (Wollen, 1972).

Many film histories date auteurism as a unique critical perspective from the publication of a 1954 article in *Cahiers du Cinéma* written by French film director and critic François Truffaut (Caughie, 1981, pp. 15, 35–38). Truffaut's article attacked the then-dominant critical view that the writer was the central creative force behind a film and the director merely a translator who realized the writer's creative vision (i.e., translated words into film images). Instead, Truffaut insisted that the real creative force in film was the director. However, he argued, not all directors were equal, and critics needed to distinguish between directors who merely did a competent job of transferring the writer's work to the screen and directors who turned scripts into their own unique, artistic visual expression through the *mise-en-scène* (a term that describes the aspects of the film image that occur in front of and in relation to the camera, in contrast to editing that occurs after the image is captured on the film). Thus, these early auteur critics, many of whom were film directors as well, began to reexamine the films of expatriate European directors now working in Hollywood (such as Alfred Hitchcock) and American directors whom previous European filmmakers and critics had snubbed as too commercial.

Les politiques des auteurs, as Truffaut called this critical perspective, did not emerge initially as a fully developed theory and critical method. Rather, like most other critical methods, it evolved slowly through the film criticism and film theory articles published in *Cahiers du Cinéma,* the British journal *Movie,* and the writings of Andrew Sarris and others in the American journals *Film Culture* and *Film Quarterly.* Today, auteur criticism is a method of analyzing film texts that combines elements from structuralist, aesthetic, and historical and cultural methods. Auteur critics analyze films in order to discover whether, behind the superficial contrasts of subject matter, there exist stylistic and thematic patterns in the whole body of a director's films that constitute his or her artistic signature. As Wollen (1972) explains, it is "the pattern formed by these motifs [that] gives an author's work its particular structure, both defining it internally and distinguishing one body of work from another" (p. 532). What makes one director an auteur in contrast to just a competent journeyman or journeywoman director is the ability to establish and communicate his or her artistic vision within the constraints of the film production system, the genre, and the culture in which the director is working.

Early auteur critics began studying the influence of film directors in reaction to the dominant types of criticism—content-oriented simple plot and theme analysis and historical and biographical criticism—of the script's writers, not directors. Like the criticism they were reacting against, these early auteur critics initially also relied fairly heavily on biographical interviews with directors in their analysis of an auteur's works (Sarris, 1968). Later auteur critics, however, used a structural perspective to analyze the auteur "signature" in a body of works; many even put the auteur's name in quotation marks to indicate the distinction they drew between the flesh-and-blood director and the auteur, which they regarded as a critical construct, a signature that they saw written into the works (see Nowell-Smith, 1967; Wollen, 1969, 1981).

Today, auteur criticism is an emerging type of television criticism that provides an insightful alternative to biographical criticism on the one hand and genre criticism on the other. Auteur criticism includes some discussion of the genre (and industry) and looks at how the auteur has managed to stamp his or her own unique signature onto these generic texts. However, unlike genre criticism, it does not regard genre conventions as the most powerful shaping influence on the form and content of an auteur's work. Instead, auteur analysis regards the auteur as a sort of genre in himself or herself, and looks at the ways in which the auteur creatively managed to place her or his uniquely consistent artistic signature on all her or his works, despite the constraints of the Hollywood production and network and cable television industry. As Wollen (1972) explains, auteur analyses must examine both the redundancies (similarities) *and* the system of differences and oppositions in an auteur's works. In fact, Wollen argues, the real test of an excellent auteur analysis is not its ability to explain what he calls "the orthodox canon of a director's works, where resemblances are clustered," but rather the identification of repeated thematic motifs, oppositions, and stylistic features in even those works "which at first sight may seem eccentricities" (1981, p. 139).

The two-pronged focus of contemporary auteur criticism is on the stylistic and thematic features common to the entire body of the individual's work, including all the television, film, and video works that the auteur wrote (alone or as a staff writer), produced, or directed. Specifically, auteur criticism involves a close visual and textual examination of these two aspects of the auteur's work—stylistic features, or the mise-en-scène, and the pattern of thematic motifs[1] that occur across the entire body of an author's work—that are the "defining characteristics of an author's work [although they] are not necessarily those which are the most readily apparent" (Wollen, 1972, p. 532).

Film theorist John Caughie (1981) has argued that one of the strengths of auteur criticism is that at addresses aesthetic matters: because it focuses on mise-en-scène, auteur analysis provides the critic with a way of "accounting for the text as pleasurable, pointing to its fascination as well as its meaning" (p. 13). Thus, auteur criticism can help critics explain what it is in Aaron Spelling's, Stephen Bochco's, David E. Kelley's, or Aaron Sorkin's work that audiences may find so enjoyable that they flock to watch premieres of each new series by these television producers. If we substituted the title of any prime-time television series in the following comment by French director-auteur critic Fereydoun Hoveyda, we'd find she could just as easily have been talking about Aaron Spelling's *Beverly Hills 90210*, David E. Kelley's *Ally McBeal*, or Stephen J. Cannell's *The A-Team* or *The Rockford Files*: "If one insists on thinking that *Party Girl* is rubbish, then I proclaim: Long live this rubbish which so pleases my eyes, fascinates my heart, and gives me a glimpse of the kingdom of heaven" (pp. 13–23).

Auteur Television Criticism

Auteur film criticism did not develop until film had been around as an art and entertainment form for more than 50 years, so it should not surprise you to discover that auteur television criticism is just starting to appear. Indeed, it wasn't until August 1948 that seven-day-a-week, four-network broadcasting[2] began in New York (McNeil, 1991), so national American television has only recently celebrated its fiftieth birthday.

Auteur television criticism shares many similarities with the film auteur criticism from which it has emerged. Like film auteur analyses, auteur television criticism assumes that television can be an art form and that some television creators deserve to be regarded as authors/auteurs. Like film auteur studies, auteur television criticism values the inscription of the auteur's personal signature into television texts precisely because of the barriers (genre, industry, cultural) to individual creative expression posed by the collective nature of the Hollywood production and distribution industry. Finally, like film auteur criticism, auteur television criticism assumes that by using an auteur approach that combines concepts from structural, aesthetic, genre, and historical analysis, an auteur television study can uncover—behind the superficial contrasts of subject, actor, and genre—the recurring stylistic and thematic motifs that signify the creative presence of the auteur in and on these texts.

Despite these similarities, there are also some important differences between film and television auteur criticism. One difference is the person regarded as the most influential creative force—that is, the person who typically is regarded the auteur. Film has focused almost exclusively on the director as the auteur, though there are some studies of film companies and executives that essentially argue for their auteur status. The reason for this difference between the typical film auteur (the director) and the typical television auteur (the executive producer) is that in film, the director is the individual with the greatest legal, financial, and creative responsibility for the final artistic product. The film director is the person in charge of hiring and firing members of the production crew, establishing the creative vision, viewing the "dailies," keeping the production on budget, and keeping the cast and crew cooperative. In television, the executive producer has the primary responsibility for the above-the-line and below-the-line production decisions and budgets, and also for the overall continuity and quality of the final program (see Cantor, 1971).

The importance of the role of the executive producer is the reason that Horace Newcomb and Robert S. Alley (1983) call television "the producer's medium." This also explains why almost all auteur television criticism has focused on the (executive) producer as the auteur. For example, in one of the earliest essays on television auteurs, David Marc (1981) mentions four television candidates whom he thinks deserve to be regarded as auteurs: producers Paul Henning (e.g., *The Beverly Hillbillies, Petticoat Junction, Green Acres*), Norman Lear (e.g., *All in the Family, Sanford and Son, Maude, Good Times, The Jeffersons*), Garry Marshall (e.g., *The Odd*

Couple, Happy Days, Laverne and Shirley, Mork and Mindy), and Aaron Spelling (e.g., *The Mod Squad, The Rookies, Starsky and Hutch, Charlie's Angels, Hart to Hart, Hotel, Dynasty, Beverly Hills 90210, Melrose Place, Pasadena, Titans, Family, Seventh Heaven,* and *Charmed*).[3] Don Davis (1984) argues that Norman Lear and Garry Marshall deserve to be regarded as television auteurs, while Robert Thompson (1989, 1990) explains why Stephen J. Cannell is an auteur.

Despite the strong arguments for regarding the executive producer as the person who deserves the utmost authorial credit for television series, there are several other possible candidates for the title of television auteur, including writer-producers, directors, production companies, and even television executives. David Marc and Bob Thompson's (1992) *Prime Time, Prime Movers* provides essays and videographies (i.e., lists of all the writing, directing, producing, and acting credits for books, films, plays, and television) for writers Paddy Chayefsky, Reginald Rose, Rod Serling, and for writer-producer hyphenates[4] Irna Phillips, Agnes Nixon, and Ken Burns, as well as 24 producers they think should be regarded as auteurs.

Jane Feuer, Paul Kerr, and Tise Vahimagi (1984) provide a convincing argument for regarding MTM, the Mary Tyler Moore Company, as a corporate auteur whose reputation as a quality production company stems from its corporate philosophy of putting quality considerations above financial considerations in producing its programs, and its consequent ability to consistently draw "quality" (higher-educated, higher-income) audiences. Indeed, as Feuer (1984) points out, "The fact that MTM has a public image is significant in itself. Most TV production companies remain invisible to the public" (p. 32). MTM's authorial signature, they argue, can be seen in shared features of series it produced, regardless of producers, writers, or directors: its transformation of the situation comedy into the "warm-edy." In contrast to typical television comedies in which the humor was centered on the unique, problematic "situation" the characters had to deal with that week, MTM comedies, Feuer explains "operated almost entirely at the level of character," emphasizing comic reversals of expectations rather than physical sight gags. MTM's comedies and dramas featured techniques typically associated with "high art," such as intertextuality and self-reflexivity. MTM's dramas used multiple plot lines, ensemble casts of coworkers, and literate dialogue; emphasized the personal dimensions of public issues; and featured ambiguous narrative closure reflecting its series' grappling with moral ambiguities in contemporary urban life.

Still other as yet unexplored potential auteurs include network television executives such as Fred Silverman, Grant Tinker, Brandon Tartikof, and Roone Arledge, all of whom clearly placed their unique stamps on their television networks' programming, and television directors such as Jay Sandrich, Gregory Hoblit, Gene Reynolds, Jackie Cooper, Bruce Paltrow, Georg Stanford Brown, Randa Haines, and David Anspaugh.

Discovering "authors" in any form of industrialized collectively produced popular cultural art form like the television industry is not an easy task, for it requires hundreds of people to produce those finished half-hours of *Malcolm in the Middle* and *Frasier.* In fact, the difficulty of identifying the precise contribution and signature of particular individuals is exactly what Robert Thompson's auteur analysis of

St. Elsewhere (1998) illustrated. However, despite the multiple authorial signatures that can be identified in television, film, and many other popular culture texts, someone eventually assumes the final decision-making responsibility for a television text. As Marc and Thompson (1992) note:

> The elements of personal style that emerge from such choices remain beyond the purview of what can be accomplished by interoffice memos, programmable machines of generic inertia. Despite all odds, the necessity—as well as the mystique—of the individual artist has survived the late industrial age. By some measures it is resurgent. The growing desire of marketers to slap "designer labels" on every kind of mass-produced product from evening gowns to ice cream cones provides evidence of an increasing public awareness that the mass-culture apparatus is not some kind of self-sustaining engine but, rather, a distribution system for the products of a new class of designers and artists. Though there can be no doubt that the relationship of artist to audience has been altered by the nature of mass-distributed culture, it has not been destroyed. Surely if we can attribute the cut of our blue jeans to authorial influences, we can do at least as much for the substance of our national drama—television. (p. 4)

Auteur criticism needs to be careful to avoid the intentionalist fallacy (second-guessing the author and asserting what an author and a text "really mean" to say). You can do this by focusing on tracing the stylistic and thematic characteristics that chain throughout a body of creative works rather than trying to infer from these features the meanings you "think" the author intended to convey through the text. Indeed, the difficulty of identifying the contribution of any potential auteur to a collection of works on which she or he worked is why many film auteur critics regard the auteur as a critical construct rather than a flesh-and-blood person and put her or his name in quotation marks when they attribute creative responsibility to the person having the greatest formal authority (the director in film, the executive producer in television). Furthermore, as we discuss in Part IV, increasingly many media studies scholars argue that the ultimate authors of a text are really the audience members, who take the raw material of a television program and create meanings through their interactions with it.

Writing Auteur-Centered Criticism

Auteur criticism can be a difficult kind of analysis for students to do as a class paper, primarily because of the difficulty in locating samples of the auteur's work to analyze. However, with the help of cable television's syndicated programming, we have some "archives" of television series coming into our homes. Thanks to these syndicated reruns and some of the sources listed at the end of this chapter, a number of students have done thorough and insightful auteur studies during the course of a term.[5]

The first step in writing an auteur analysis is to select the auteur whose work you want to study. Look at the credits of television series you regularly watch and enjoy: notice for each episode who is listed as the executive producer, episode producer, director, and writer. Other sources of possible auteurs are collections of short auteur biographies, for example, David Marc and Robert Thompson's (1992) *Prime Time, Prime Movers* and Horace Newcomb and Robert Alley's (1983) *The Producer's Medium: Conversations with Creators of American TV.* The References at the end of this chapter list a number of general television program credit sources that you can consult (Brooks & Marsh, 1999; Eisner & Krinsky, 1984; Gianakos, 1978, 1980, 1981, 1983; Marill, 1984; Marc & Thompson, 1992; Newcomb, 1997; Newcomb & Alley, 1983; Parish, 1973, 1978, 1982; Perry, 1983, 1991; Ravage, 1978; Shapiro, 1989; Slide, Hanson & Hanson, 1988; Wicking & Vahimagi, 1979; Terrance, 1986, 1991; Thompson, 1996; Thompson & Burns, 1990; Wolley, Malsbary & Strange, 1985). Of course, since these books are already in print, they won't cover the most recent television seasons. To update them, you will need to check sources like Gale Research's *Contemporary Theatre, Film and Television,* as well as indexes like *Reader's Guide to Periodical Literature* (which indexes *TV Guide*) and *Guide to Business Periodicals* (which indexes articles in trade magazines such as *Broadcasting, Electronic Media, Entertainment Weekly, Variety*) under the auteur's name. These sources will point you to articles about the auteur (e.g., Aaron Spelling, Linda Bloodworth-Thomason, Aaron Sorkin, Barry Levinson, Dick Wolf, Edward Zwick, Diane English) and recent television and movie productions with which he or she was involved that have appeared in such popular periodicals as *TV Guide* (the annual fall preview issues are especially useful), *Variety, Entertainment Weekly,* and *Broadcasting.*

The next step is the most difficult one: You need to locate example episodes of all or almost all of the television series and films by the auteur. Possible sources of sample episodes, in addition to those programs you manage to record from cable television, include your instructor, the media library at your university, and video rental stores. Some sources useful for this stage of your research also are listed in the References at the end of this chapter (Balkansky, 1980; Black, 1990; Black & Moersh, 1990; Culbert, 1984; Godfrey, 1983; Mehr, 1977; Rouse & Loughney, 1989; Rowan, 1980; Schreibman, 1983; and Thompson, 1985). Additionally, the Library of Congress in Washington, D.C., has more than 15,000 programs; the Academy of Television Arts and Sciences (ATAS)/UCLA Television Archives has more than 20,000 titles; and the Museum of Broadcasting in New York City and the Museums of Television and Radio in New York City and Beverly Hills have representative copies of more than 17,000 radio and television broadcasts. Of course, since most of these archives do not make copies of series' episodes for you, you would need to travel to them to view the sample episodes (which is one factor that undoubtedly has limited the amount of auteur television criticism that has been done). However, in the case of the Library of Congress National Archives, you can request that a limited number of episodes be sent to a presidential library or one of its 13 regional archives (like the one in San Francisco), where you can go to view the tapes (see Adams & Schreibman, 1978).

Assuming that you have located examples of all of the auteur's television series (and films), the next step is to examine them for two sets of characteristics: (1) recurring stylistic features and (2) recurring thematic motifs evident in the texts' syntagmatic and paradigmatic structures. Of course, you need to take careful, detailed notes while you are doing so. In the case of Aaron Spelling, this process would involve analyzing sample episodes from the six television series on which he served as a staff writer, sample episodes from the 60-plus television series he personally has produced, and a representative sample (perhaps about one-quarter of the total) of his 150-plus television and feature films on which he has been the executive producer or which his production company produced.

In the case of a prolific television creator such as Aaron Spelling, you can see that the amount of screening time is another constraint critics face in doing auteur-centered analyses.

Recurring stylistic features across the various series and films your auteur was responsible for certainly would include such aspects of the mise-en-scène as the use of lighting (e.g., flat or chiaroscuro) and sound (including the use of dialogue, diegetic sound—that is, sound within the scene that the characters hear), the types of actors or specific actors used in multiple series (e.g., Steven Bochco has used James Sikking, Dennis Franz, and Barbara Bosson in several series), the camera work (including pans, zooms, dollies, soft focus, typical settings/sets/ locations, and the length of takes). Mise-en-scène, as Andrew Sarris (1977) cogently explains, "includes all of the means available to a director [or producer] to express his attitude toward his subject. This takes in cutting, camera movement, pacing, the direction of players and their placement in the decor, the angle and distance of the camera, and even the content of the shot" (pp. 52–53). Other recurring stylistic features (not part of the mise-en-scène) certainly would include the use of extradiegetic sound, including the musical soundtrack or the laugh track, types of edits used between scenes, and whether the program is shot on film or video.

In the case of Aaron Spelling, for example, an auteur critique of his stylistic authorial signature would include a discussion of the following elements found in his works ranging from his action-adventure/romantic dramas of the 1970s to prime-time serial dramas of the 1980s and 1990s, and his forays into daytime soaps:

- His recurring use of lavish, glamorous sets that emphasize wealth, class, and conspicuous consumption
- Heavily orchestrated musical themes
- Ritual introductory sequences that serve to introduce the regular cast members, the series' typically urban(e) settings, and the various plotlines to be explored in that week's episode (a convention later borrowed by many other producers)
- Heavy use of high-key lighting and a stylized symmetrical use of close-ups, two shots, three shots, and long shots
- The gratuitous display of nearly naked, almost entirely Anglo bodies (more often women's rather than men's).

Analysis of an auteurial signature also requires that the critic analyze and trace recurring themes and conceptual and ideological oppositions that appear throughout the auteur's work regardless of genre. For Aaron Spelling, this would lead the auteur critic to discuss some of the following themes (or thematic motifs) that reoccur in Spelling's series and films:

- Social relevance. In the 1960s, this included the youth rebellion, the rehabilitation of these errant youths or criminals, and their subsequent incorporation into law enforcement or the justice system (e.g., *The Mod Squad*). In the 1990s, relevance included problems of yuppie teens and ambitious middle-class young adults (e.g., *Beverly Hills 90210*).

- Valorization of wealth and capitalism, specifically, the affirmation of the altruistic capitalism myth that one can be both economically and morally successful. This is seen most obviously in *Charlie's Angels, Hart to Hart, Matt Houston, Hotel*, and *Fantasy Island*.

- The myth of the caring company, which dominated *Hotel* and *Love Boat*.

- The maxim that money can't buy love, seen in *Dynasty, The Colbys, Beverly Hills 90210, Family, Seventh Heaven*, and *Titans*.

- The myth that the grass always looks greener but rarely is, clearly featured in *Fantasy Island, Beverly Hills 90210, Melrose Place*, and *Titans*.

- The myth that good eventually triumphs over evil, found in all Spelling series, including *Mod Squad, The Rookies, Charlie's Angels, Dynasty, Hotel, Hart to Hart*, and *Seventh Heaven (see Vande Berg, 1997)*.

Once you have analyzed the stylistic and thematic features that reoccur across the various series and genres in which the auteur has worked, you are ready to summarize the distinctive signature of this auteur and share your analysis with others in a critical essay, which should follow (more or less) the general outline for criticism essays provided in Chapter 4. Obviously, there are variations from one auteur critique to another, but this essay should provide a solid foundation for your efforts at writing an auteur-centered critical analysis.

The Example Essay

Now that you've learned something about the origins of auteur critical theory and about how critics go about doing auteur-centered television criticism, you can critically evaluate the example of auteur-centered criticism that follows. Richard Campbell and Jimmie Reeves's auteur analysis of the work of Hugh Wilson focuses on Wilson's series *Frank's Place* as illustrative of Wilson's artistic signature. They acknowledge several other significant creative influences on *Frank's Place*, notably Tim Reid; however, they argue that analysis of three aspects of the series—its regional and professional cultural orientation, its cinematic look, and its ethnically and racially collaborative writing and crew—affirms Wilson's authorial voice.

As you will see when you read their essay, their analysis includes face-to-face conversations with Wilson about his work, along with the historical research (on Wilson's videography and filmography) and close textual analysis of the stylistic and thematic features that signify television series he produced as his. Although direct communiqués certainly add interesting insights to auteur critiques, such access to television producers and directors is not typical. One certainly can write thorough, insightful auteur analyses by combining close textual analyses of multiple examples of the auteurs' texts (the television series, plays, and movies she or he has written for, produced, or directed) with the historical/biographical information located through library research. In fact, in many cases, through library research, you can locate published media interviews with television auteurs and include these auteur comments in your essay.

Beyond Hugh Wilson, the authorial "signatures" of a plethora of other potential television auteurs have yet to be studied, including Steven Bochco, Aaron Spelling, Diane English, Norman Lear, Gary David Goldberg, Quinn Martin, Glen Larson, James L. Brooks, Garry Marshall, Marcy Carsey and Tom Werner, and David E. Kelley, David Lynch, Aaron Sorkin, Dick Wolf, and Barry Levinson, to name only a few.

Notes

1. A motif is a recurring element—ranging from a type of incident or setting to a stock type of character to a significant phrase. A theme is a thesis or idea which is conveyed through the syntagmatic and paradigmatic structures of a work. As Abrams (1971) notes, sometimes, the two terms are combined or used interchangeably, as in thematic motif or *leitmotif* (or guiding theme).

2. These were NBC, ABC, CBS, and Dumont (which lasted from 1946 to 1955).

3. Marc (1981) argues that Henning's immensely popular but critically disdained comedies contrasted solidly democratic, old-fashioned rural American virtues (e.g., those of the Clampetts, especially Jed) with the moral bankruptcy and incorrigible greed of sophisticated, urban consumer society in ways that entertained and articulated cultural tensions that resonated with audiences. Indeed, Marc (1984) argues, Henning's comedies (and *The Beverly Hillbillies* was almost always in the Nielsen Top 20 during its nine-year run) illustrate Kenneth Burke's observation that "drama gets its material from the historical conversation of a given culture" (p. 40). (David Marc is quoting this Kenneth Burke statement that appeared as an epigram in Sherman Paul's (1976) *Repossessing and renewing: Essays in the green American tradition*. Baton Rouge: Louisiana University Press.)

4. Hyphenate is the term for someone in television production who receives screen credits for more than one area of production responsibilities. The most common hyphenate is that of writer-producer. Richard Levinson and William Link were a writer-producer hyphenate team whose memoir, *Stay Tuned: An Inside Look at the Making of Prime Time Television* (1981), traced their productive collaboration from their days as junior high friends through their production of *Columbo*; their docudrama *The Execution of Private Slovik* (NBC, 1974; Martin Sheen played Private Slovik), which received a Peabody award and nine Emmy nominations; *Murder She Wrote*; and many other series and made-for-television movies.

5. For example, our television criticism students have done auteur analyses of producers David Lynch, Steven Bochco, Gary David Goldberg, Glen and Les Charles, and Edward Zwick and Marshall Herskovitz and also of actor-producer Bill Cosby.

Further Reading

Marc, D., & Thompson, R. J. (1992). *Prime time, prime movers: From* I Love Lucy *to* L.A. Law—*America's greatest TV shows and the people who created them.* Boston: Little, Brown. Their book contains short auteurish essays of 24 television producers, plus short paragraphs about "honorable mentions" whose work was primarily in comedy, drama, or "other genres." Although this book is more history and biography than close textual analysis, it is indispensable to the serious television critic.

Webnotes

Hollywood biographies. **http://www.hollywood.com**

This site lists current television series and movies and the 10 Nielsen-rated series for the week. It can be browsed for series information, celebrity information and bios, upcoming productions, and other information.

Sitcoms Online. **http://www.sitcomsonline.com**

Hundreds of links to situation comedies, including episode guides and theme songs.

TV Creative Directory. **www.tvtome.**

Features over 70,000 people associated with television—writers, directors, producers, actors—and provides a partial list of their media credits.

Learning Activities

1. Film theorist and critic Peter Wollen (1981) has said that the real test of an excellent auteur analysis is not its ability to explain what he calls "the orthodox canon of a director's works, where resemblances are clustered," but rather the identification of repeated thematic motifs, oppositions, and stylistic features in even those works "which at first sight may seem eccentricities" (p. 139). Choose two apparently very different works by a television auteur—for example, Aaron Spelling's *Seventh Heaven* and *Beverly Hills, 90210*, David E. Kelley's *Ally McBeal* and *The Practice*, Steven Bochco's *Doogie Howser, M.D.*, and *NYPD Blue*, or Marcy Carsey and Tom Werner's *The Cosby Show* and *Roseanne*. Then write a one-page paper analyzing and describing the auteurial signature evident in the resemblances (shared themes, oppositions, and stylistic features) shared by these apparently opposite sorts of texts by the same auteur.

References

Abrams, M. H. (1971). *A glossary of literary terms* (3rd ed.). New York: Holt, Rinehart & Winston.

Adams, W., & Schreibman, F. (Eds.). (1978). *Television network news: Issues in content research.* Washington, DC: George Washington University School of Public and International Affairs.

Adler, R. P. (Ed.). (1979). *All in the family: A critical appraisal.* New York: Praeger.

Balkansky, A. (1980). Through the electronic looking glass: Television programs in the Library of Congress. *Quarterly Journal of the Library of Congress, 37,* 458–475.

Bazin, A. (1957). De la politique des auteurs. *Cahiers du Cinéma, 70,* 2–11. [English Ed. & Trans in 1966 by P. Graham, *The new wave.* London: Secker & Warburg.]

Bedell, S. (1981). *Up the tube: Prime time TV in the Silverman years.* New York: Viking.

Black, S. (1990). *Thesaurus of subject headings for television: A vocabulary for indexing script collections.* Phoenix: Oryx Press.

Black, S., & Moersh, E. S. (Eds.). (1990). *Index to the Annenberg television script archives (Vol. 1: 1976–1977).* Phoenix: Oryx Press.

Brooks, T., & Marsh, E. (1999). *The complete directory to prime-time network TV shows, 1946–present.* (7th ed.). New York: Ballantine.

Campbell, R., & Reeves, J. (1990). Television authors: The case of Hugh Wilson. In R. J. Thompson & G. Burns (Eds.), *Making television: Authorship and the production process* (pp. 3–18). New York: Praeger.

Cantor, M. (1971). *The Hollywood TV producer.* New York: Basic Books.

Caughie, J. (Ed.). (1981). *Theories of authorship.* London: Routledge & Kegan Paul.

Culbert, D. (1984). Television archives. *Critical Studies in Mass Communication, 1,* 88–92.

Davis, D. (1984). Auteur film criticism as a vehicle for television criticism. *Feedback, 26,* 14–18.

Eisner, J., & Krinsky, D., (1984). *Television comedy series—An episode guide to 153 TV sitcoms in syndication.* Jefferson, NC: McFarland.

Feuer, J. (1984). The MTM style. In J. Feuer, P. Kerr, & T. Vahimagi (Eds.), *MTM "quality" television* (pp. 32–60). London: British Film Institute.

Feuer, J., Kerr, P., & Vahimagi, T. (Eds.). (1984). *MTM "quality" television.* London: British Film Institute.

Gianakos, L. J. (1978). *Television drama series programming: A comprehensive chronicle (Vol. 2: 1959–1975).* Metuchen, NJ: Scarecrow.

Gianakos, L. J. (1980). *Television drama series programming: A comprehensive chronicle (Vol. 1: 1947–1959).* Metuchen, NJ: Scarecrow.

Gianakos, L. J. (1981). *Television drama series programming: A comprehensive chronicle (Vol. 3: 1975–1980).* Metuchen, NJ: Scarecrow.

Gianakos, L. J. (1983). *Television drama series programming: A comprehensive chronicle (Vol. 4: 1980–1982).* Metuchen, NJ: Scarecrow.

Godfrey, D. G. (Comp.). (1983). *A directory of broadcast archives.* Washington, DC: Broadcast Education Association.

Hoveyda, F. (1976). La réponse de Nicholas Ray. In B. Nichols (Ed.), *Movies and methods.* Berkeley: University of California Press.

Levinson, R., & Link, W., (1986). *Off camera: Conversations with the makers of prime-time television.* New York: Plume/New American Library.

Marc, D. (1981, Nov.). TV auteurism. *American Film,* 52–55, 65, 81.

Marc, D. (1984). The situation comedy of Paul Henning: Modernity and the American folk myth in *The Beverly Hillbillies.* In D. Marc, *Demographic Vistas* (pp. 39–64). Philadelphia: University of Philadelphia Press.

Marc, D., & Thompson, R. J. (1992). *Prime time, prime movers.* Boston: Little, Brown.

Marill, A. H. (1984). *Movies made for television—the telefeature and the miniseries 1964–1984.* New York: Zoetrope.

McNeil, A. (1991). *Total television—A comprehensive guide to programming from 1948 to the present.* New York: Penguin.

Mehr, L. (Ed.). (1977). *Motion pictures, television and radio: A union catalogue of manuscript and special collections in the western United States.* Boston: Hall.

Newcomb, H. (Ed.). (1997). *Encyclopedia of television.* Chicago: Fitzroy Dearborn.

Newcomb, H., & Alley, R. S. (1983). *The producer's medium: Conversations with creators of American TV.* New York: Oxford University Press.

Nowell-Smith, G. (1967). *Visconti.* London: Secker & Warburg (Cinema One).

Parish, J. R. (1973). *Actor's television credits, 1950–1972.* Metuchen, NJ: Scarecrow.

Parish, J. R. (1978). *Actor's television credits, Supplement I, 1973–1976.* Metuchen, NJ: Scarecrow.

Parish, J. R. (1982). *Actor's television credits, Supplement II, 1977–1981.* Metuchen, NJ: Scarecrow.

Paul, S. (1976). *Repossessing and renewing: Essays in the green American tradition.* Baton Rouge: Louisiana University Press.

Perry, J. (1983). *Universal television—The studio and its programs, 1950–1980.* Metuchen, NJ: Scarecrow.

Perry, J. (1991). *Screen gems: A history of Columbia Pictures Television.* Metuchen, NJ: Scarecrow.

Ravage, J. W. (1978). *Television: The director's viewpoint.* Boulder, CO: Westview.

Rouse, S., & Loughney, K. (Comps.). (1989). *Three decades of television: A catalog of television programs acquired by the Library of Congress, 1949–1979.* Washington, DC: Library of Congress, Motion Picture, Broadcasting, and Recorded Sound Division.

Rowan, B. G. (1980). *Scholars' guide to Washington, D.C. film and video collections.* Washington, DC: Smithsonian Institution Press.

Sarris, A. (1968). *The American cinema.* New York: Dutton.

Sarris, A. (1977, July–Aug.). The auteur theory revisited. *American Film,* 49–53.

Schatz, T. (1981). *Hollywood genres: Formulas, filmmaking and the studio system.* New York: Random House.

Schatz, T. (1984). Film archives. *Critical Studies in Mass Communication, 1*, 83–88.

Schreibman, F. (1983). *Broadcast television: A research guide.* Los Angeles: American Film Institute.

Shapiro, M. E. (1989). *Television network prime-time programming, 1948–1988.* Jefferson, NC: McFarland.

Shapiro, M. E. (1990). *Television network daytime and late-night programming, 1959–1989.* Jefferson, NC: McFarland.

Slide, A., Hanson, P. K., & Hanson, S. L. (Comps.). (1988). *Sourcebook for the performing arts: A directory of collections, resources, scholars, and critics in theatre, film, and television.* Westport, CT: Greenwood Press.

Stacey, J. (1994). *Star gazing: Hollywood cinema and female spectatorship.* New York: Routledge.

Terrace, V. (1986). *Encyclopedia of television: Series, pilots, and specials* (3 vols.). New York: Zoetrope.

Terrace, V. (1991). *Fifty years of television: A guide to series and pilots, 1937–1988.* New York: Cornwall.

Thompson, R. J. (1985). Capturing the ephemeral texts: Reference literature on American television programs. *Feedback, 27,* 37–41.

Thompson, R. J. (1989). Stephen J. Cannell: An auteur analysis of adventure/ action. In L. Vande Berg & L. Wenner (Eds.), *Television criticism: Approaches and applications* (pp. 112–128). White Plains, NY: Longman.

Thompson, R. J. (1990). *Adventures on prime time: The television programs of Stephen J. Cannell.* New York: Praeger.

Thompson, R. J. (1996). *Television's second golden age: From* Hill Street Blues *to* ER. New York: Continuum.

Thompson, R. J. (1998). Too many cooks don't always spoil the broth: An authorship study of *St. Elsewhere.* In L. Vande Berg, L. A. Wenner, & B. E. Gronbeck (Eds.), *Critical approaches to television* (pp. 78–92). Boston: Houghton Mifflin.

Thompson, R., & Burns, G. (Eds.). (1990). *Making television: Authorship and the production process.* New York: Praeger.

Truffaut, F. (1954). Une certaine tendance du cinéma français. *Cahiers du Cinéma,* 31, 15–28. [English translation]. Reprinted in B. Nichols (Ed.), *Movies and methods.* Berkeley: University of California Press, 1976.

Vande Berg, L.R. (1997). Aaron Spelling. In H. Newcomb (Ed.), *Encyclopedia of television* (pp. 1545–1547). Chicago: Fitzroy Dearborn.

Wicking, C., & Vahimagi, T. (1979). *The American vein—Directors and directions in television.* New York: E. P. Dutton.

Wollen, P. (1969). The auteur theory. In P. Wollen, *Signs and meaning in the cinema* (3rd ed., pp. 530–541). London: Secker & Warburg.

Wollen, P. (1972). The auteur theory. In P. Wollen, *Signs and meaning in the cinema* (4th ed., pp. 530–541). London: Secker & Warburg.

Wollen, P. (1981). The auteur theory (extract). In J. Caughie (Ed.), *Theories of authorship* (pp. 138–151). London: Routledge.

Woolley, L., Malsbary, R. W., & Strange, R. G. (1985). *Warner Brothers Television: Every show of the fifties and sixties—episode by episode.* Jefferson, NC: McFarland.

Television Authors: The Case of Hugh Wilson[1]

Richard Campbell and Jimmie L. Reeves

Wilson, the creator and executive coproducer of *Frank's Place*, accepted our invitation to attend the seminar in New Orleans. Because of our previous experience with prime-time TV producers (who shall remain nameless), we expected Wilson to be a fast-talking mercenary—brusque and aloof—with an ego the size of Alaska. When he turned out to be a chivalrous southerner who wears his humor and humanity on the sleeve where some people wear their religion, we were, quite frankly, caught off guard. A down-home raconteur in the tradition of Mark Twain and Will Rogers, Wilson seemed to treat the seminar as an opportunity to get a lot of things off his chest. By the end of the day we were left with the feeling that Wilson genuinely relished this encounter with a live audience who appreciated the artistry of *Frank's Place*. As he put it, "making a television show is like sending out a message in a bottle. You never know if anybody ever gets your message."

Frank's Place featured the tragicomical experiences of Frank Parrish (played by Tim Reid), a professor of Italian Renaissance history. Parrish is forced to give up his affluent life in Boston when his estranged father dies and Parrish inherits a New Orleans restaurant. The program was one of the most highly acclaimed series of the 1987–88 television season. For example, Michael Pollan, writing for *Channels* magazine, declared *Frank's Place* "revolutionary," "a sitcom of uncommon freshness and a 'black' show of uncommon dignity." And, in an interview with *Newsweek*, Alvin Poussaint (the Harvard psychiatrist who consults for *The Cosby Show*) went so far as to describe *Frank's Place* as a "breakthrough," "the first black show since *Roots* to take black culture seriously." This enthusiasm was shared by many other critics. *Electronic Media*'s semi-annual poll of newspaper reviewers rated *Frank's Place* among the top three shows of the year; only *L. A. Law* and *The Wonder Years* ranked higher.

Unfortunately, after winning three Emmys, *Frank's Place* was cancelled because of low ratings just as the show was set to produce 13 new episodes as a mid-season replacement during the 1988–89 season. Although *Frank's Place* premiered well in fall 1987 (14.9 rating/25 share), its final airing on October 1, 1988, garnered dismal numbers that ranked it among the week's lowest rated network shows (5.6 rating/10 share). As any viewer who tried to follow the show knows, the chief reason for its failure was inept scheduling and promotion on the part of Kim LeMasters, head of CBS's entertainment division. In twelve months, LeMasters moved the show into six different time slots on four different nights. Both Wilson and Reid claim that, eventually, even their own mothers could no longer find the show on the schedule.

Since the forum took place only about a month after CBS finally cancelled the series, Wilson was still hurting from the experience. However, Wilson was not at all reticent about discussing the tragedy of errors that resulted in the demise of the program.

Frank's Place was one of the most highly acclaimed series of the 1987–1988 television season, both for its genre innovations and for its serious, positive portrayal of working and middle class African Americans living in New Orleans. Pictured here are several of the ensemble cast: (standing) main characters Bubba Weisberger, Anna-May, Dr. Frank Parrish, Cool Charles, and (seated) Miss Marie, and Tiger Shepin.

As to why *Frank's Place* failed, I don't think I've got what would be considered a clean test here. When it was run on Saturday night in reruns, we were only on in 82 percent of the markets. Even in Atlanta they weren't running it—they were running a game show. I was really surprised. We were the lowest rated show on television one week. And we were cancelled the next week. My reaction by the time we got cancelled was: "Please. Do it. This is embarrassing. And I'm mad." I like Kim LeMasters a lot, personally. And so does Tim [Reid]. And that's one of the reasons we haven't just raised holy hell over this thing.

Wilson predicts that the failure of *Frank's Place* will have long-term consequences on the future of both television comedy and "black" shows.

Most of the letters I got were from people in the business saying, "My God. How did you do this? How did you pull this off? How did you get the network to go along with this?"? If *Frank's Place* had succeeded, it

would have had enormous impact. As it turned out, the cancellation was a real blow. The day it got cancelled, every schlockmeister in town used *Frank's Place* as a prime example of what not to do: "You see what happens when you do that?" When a bad show fails, nobody says, "Let's learn our lesson." When a good show goes down, everybody goes, "Ya see?"

. . . In editing [Wilson's] transcript, we have tried to emphasize the following four areas of special interest to media scholars concerned with questions of authorship: the making of a television producer; achieving creative control; the Wilson imprint; and orchestrating a collaboration.[2]

The Making of a Television Producer

Wilson, who is white, earned a journalism degree from the University of Florida in the 1960s. And his journey to *Frank's Place* began at the Armstrong Cork Company in Lancaster, Pennsylvania, where he went to work writing linoleum brochures. Strangely enough, at this job in the heart of Amish country, Wilson met Jay Tarses (who most recently produced *The Days and Nights of Molly Dodd* and *The "Slap" Maxwell Story*) and Tom Patchell (who now produces *Alf*). During their time at Armstrong Cork, Wilson assisted Tarses and Patchett in the staging of an amateur stand-up comedy routine. "Just as a hobby," Wilson remembers, "we'd go out on the weekends and I would sort of work the lights. They did a Nichols and May type thing—but it was not very good. I had to signal the pay-off. You know, if I didn't turn out the lights at the end, the audience didn't know when Tom and Jay delivered the big joke."

Wilson characterizes this early connection with Tarses and Patchett as "a great stroke of luck." Later, both of the future television producers would play decisive roles in aiding and promoting Wilson's early career in Hollywood.

After the Armstrong Cork episode, Wilson went back down south. Settling in Atlanta, he joined an ad agency and became a specialist in radio advertising. Inspired by Stan Freberg's work, Wilson wrote funny radio commercials that won several national awards. Significantly, he stayed in contact with Tarses and Patchett during this period, and earned their gratitude by using them as voice-over talent on some of the radio spots. He lived in Atlanta for ten years, becoming the copy chief and then creative head of the ad agency.

But then Wilson made an audacious career move. In his words:

> I became very bored with the advertising business—and I grew not to like it. By this time, Tom and Jay had gone out to Hollywood and their stand-up career was finished, as it rightfully deserved to be. They had gotten jobs on Carol Burnett's writing staff, which was a great place to be. So, I went out to L.A. to shoot a television commercial and I stayed with Jay.

Tarses helped Wilson set up a meeting with Grant Tinker, who was then the head of MTM Productions. At that meeting, Tinker told Wilson that the only job opening was as student-trainee, a position normally filled by fresh-faced kids from USC or UCLA.

Wilson took the student-trainee position and was a quick study: "Because all the other trainees were 21 and I was 32, they never asked me to get sandwiches or coffee. I would just sit there in the stands and watch them make the *Mary Tyler Moore Show*. And I realized that the writer-producer was really the key guy. At that time on *Mary Tyler Moore* there were two: Allan Burns and Jim Brooks." Allan Burns went on to be the writer-producer of *Rhoda* and *Lou Grant*, while James Brooks has moved into filmmaking, receiving writer-producer-director Oscars for *Terms of Endearment*. Of the two, Brooks left the deepest impression on Wilson. In Wilson's words: "I would have to say watching Jim Brooks work was a real education."

After this crash course in producing comedy television, Wilson wrote scripts for several MTM Productions, specializing in the original *Bob Newhart Show*. Then, when Patchett and Tarses created *The Tony Randall Show* in 1976, they hired Wilson as a staff writer. Although the Randall sitcom was cancelled after only two years, Wilson still managed to improve his lot:

> One day, Grant Tinker came around and said, "Ah, the leaves are falling. It must be pilot time. Think of

something." We all did. I used to frequent a bar in Atlanta where what passed for our glitterati gathered—media people from local radio and television stations. I always enjoyed the radio guys. I had a friend who was a morning man. So, I started thinking about developing what would turn out to be *WKRP in Cincinnati*.

Achieving Creative Control

WKRP ran for four seasons. Although it did not score great ratings during its initial run, it has earned the MTM company over $100 million in syndication. For Wilson, producing *WKRP* was a frustrating and exhausting experience. Perhaps his greatest frustrations involved network scheduling. *WKRP* was developed when Robert A. Daly was head of CBS Entertainment. Daly scheduled *WKRP* right after *M*A*S*H*, which, according to Wilson, was "the most wonderful place to be." Unfortunately, Daly moved on to Warner Brothers in 1980 and Harvey Shepherd became the CBS executive in charge of programming. Wilson believes Shepherd is responsible for killing *WKRP*:

> Harvey Shepherd didn't like me, and didn't like the show. He had nothing personal at stake with the show. And he moved us all over. That show was a hit and he just wore it out. He just killed it off trying to promote his other stuff. I'd always maintained to Harvey and to Bud Grant [former president of CBS Entertainment] that *WKRP* was not an eight o'clock show—and that they had to get me out of there because I was beating my brains out against *Happy Days* and *Little House on the Prairie*. I knew *WKRP* was a nine o'clock show. But they thought with the rock-and-roll music it had kid appeal.

Wilson confesses that the creative, intellectual and physical demands of television's assembly-line storytelling had also taken their toll:

> I told everybody involved in *WKRP*, all the actors, that I would never do another television series again because of the unrelenting nature of this thing. I'm a writer. It's easy to act in a series, once you get a handle on the character. But the writing is like Sisyphus rolling the rock up, and every Friday night, it rolls back down again. And you start all over. It's just eating

up material. In essence, you're asked to write twelve hours of comedy in a matter of twenty-five weeks, and then turn around and do it again.

Despite these bad memories, Wilson is very proud of his work on *WKRP*.

However, he gives the impression of being ashamed of the next stage in his career. In his words, "I wanted very much to get involved in movies, having the mistaken conception that you could do better work in movies. Of course, this was completely ludicrous. By the time the *Animal House* thing had taken over movie comedy, and the sixteen-year-old male was king in terms of the audience they were going for. I helped to perpetuate this ugly trend."

Leaving television, he began working as a "script doctor" hired to punch up film comedies for money and no screen credit. When he was given the script of the original *Police Academy* to rewrite, Wilson says he initially refused the assignment:

> They couldn't find anyone in town to direct it. It was such a mess. But, by then, I was determined that I wanted to direct movies. So, I said I would rewrite it for free, if they would let me direct it. After I did my rewrite, I told my wife, "These people are going to be so impressed." They saw it, and they said, "O.K. Time out. Five on the play." And they sat me down and I watched, in one afternoon, *Porky's*, *Fast Times at Ridgemont High*, *Stripes*, and *Animal House*—four movies I'd never seen before. And then we started again. They used some of my script and some of the old script. We shot it in Toronto, for what Hollywood would call cab fare, thinking it was a drive-in movie—which it was—for teenage boys. I cut this thing and I told my wife, "I'm finished. I'm dying. We're moving back to Georgia." And we took it out and tested it. They brought in a young audience, 15 to 23, emphasis on males. And they went crazy. Just crazy.

Police Academy grossed $132 million. But although Wilson would direct other features, he remained frustrated by the limitations of film comedy. As he puts it: "I became very disappointed in myself for getting involved in the machine, in the packages, and whatnot. And I began to realize that I could have more creative freedom and do more interesting work on television than I could in

the movies—because I was the *Police Academy* guy. It was a coat I couldn't take off."

In returning to network television production as the "*Police Academy* guy," Wilson achieved the creative control and relative autonomy necessary for television authorship. The first project of his second career in television was the *Easy Street* pilot for Loni Anderson (who played Jennifer Marlow on *WKRP*). Tim Reid (who played *WKRP*'s Venus Flytrap) then talked Wilson into doing a pilot with him. As Wilson recalls it:

> William Morris, who represented both of us, saw *Package*, which is what their life is all about. Packages. And they went to CBS. And CBS had an idea. We went in and sat down with two gentlemen, Kim LeMasters and Gregg Maday [former CBS vice-president for comedy program development]. They said, "We've always heard you'd like to do something about the South." I've always been pretty vocal about Hollywood's inability to deal with the South in any sort of believable fashion. So they said, "How about New Orleans? And how about Tim inherits a restaurant down there?" So, CBS had the bones of the idea. I liked that because I always felt—and I've been proven wrong here—that if they thought of it as their baby, they'd nurture it and look after it and take care of it.

It's worth noting in passing that there are several interesting parallels between the Wilson-CBS arrangement that resulted in *Frank's Place*, and the Welles-RKO arrangement that resulted in *Citizen Kane*. Most importantly, both *Frank's Place* and *Citizen Kane* fit into a pattern of invention and innovation connected to inferior market positions. A desperate company is more likely to seek out new ideas and new talent, more likely to sponsor experimentation, more likely to take risks—and less likely to interfere in the creative process. In the case of *Citizen Kane*, the financially troubled RKO lured Orson Welles away from his spectacular radio and stage career with an unprecedented six-film contract that promised the "boy genius" complete creative control over his projects. In the case of *Frank's Place*, CBS was not holding its own with the other networks and so desperately wanted the Wilson/Reid package that Wilson was able to negotiate a "complete hands-off deal."

In fact, Wilson readily acknowledges that ABC and NBC would not have given him such creative freedom:

> CBS, they were desperate. They were struggling. They weren't [number] three—yet. Consequently, they were the best people to work for from a creative standpoint. NBC behaves just like ABC did when they were number one. They are sure they have it all figured out, and that it's not just dumb luck. But if Bill Cosby hadn't walked in there, they would be in as much trouble as they were before. Since they are absolutely sure they have it all figured out, they want to get into your stuff. They think they can fix shows by changing scripts, by changing attitudes, by adding characters.

The Wilson Imprint

Of course, it's a mistake to think of television authorship solely in terms of the expression of an individual's artistic vision. *Frank's Place* is clearly not Wilson's private property. Instead, Wilson worked in dialogue with the network, who provided the basic premise, with Tim Reid, who shared executive production duties and was active in the early stages of series development, and with other creative personnel who would play decisive roles in shaping the look and feel of the program.

Even so, Wilson's was still the strongest voice in the creative collaboration—and he definitely left his imprint on the series. We suggest that this imprint is apparent in three areas of the show: the cultural orientation; the cinematic look; and the writing philosophy.

The Cultural Orientation

Here, Wilson's imprint is apparent along two symbolic planes: region and profession. These planes intersect in the very setting for *Frank's Place*: the Chez Louisianne, a Creole restaurant located in a black neighborhood in New Orleans.

Offended by TV's *Dukes of Hazzard* treatment of things southern, Wilson was determined to create a more authentic vision of his native region. According to Wilson, CBS had originally intended the restaurant to be located on Bourbon Street: "They

were hoping to cash in on the Cajun-cooking craze that was sweeping the nation, and they were thinking a French Quarter, straw hat, showboat-type ambience."

However, Wilson and Reid had other ideas. "We decided that it would be more interesting to put it in a black community," Wilson remembers. "So, when we came down here, we just skipped Bourbon Street and went into the black community. And we did some good research down here. In fact, we worked just like oral historians. We'd just go around with tape recorders."

In our telephone interview with Tim Reid, he referred to this crucial research stage as "venturing into history"—something that Reid feels is sorely lacking in most network programming. Indeed, the quest for authenticity during this research stage is at the heart of what Michael Pollan celebrates as the show's "painstakingly evoked locale" and what Horace Newcomb describes as the show's profound "sense of place."

Interestingly, Wilson says this crucial research stage was heavily informed by both his experience as a civil rights worker and his experience as a TV writer.

> I had done a little bit of civil rights when I was at the University of Florida. When we would go into these little towns in northern Florida, there would be the minister and the funeral home director and, usually, a restauranteur. But it was always the minister and the funeral home director that seemed like the key guys. We were thinking he [Reid's character, Frank Parrish] would inherit a funeral home and restaurant and some apartments. Because I'm a writer, I always look for lots of venues, you know. Otherwise, I'm going to be stuck after eight shows. On *WKRP*, we did four shows and we said, "Well, that's all we know about radio. What now!?" So, I wanted funerals and restaurants and tenants and all that.

Perhaps the most important person Wilson and Reid encountered during their time in New Orleans was Austin Leslie, who runs a Creole restaurant named the Chez Helene. In fact, the Chez Helene would be the inspiration for the Chez Louisianne and Leslie would be the model for Big Author, the head cook on the series. As further evidence of Wilson's commitment to authenticity, Leslie would even come to Los Angeles to talk to the writers about running a restaurant.

Which brings us to the second dimension of the cultural orientation of *Frank's Place*—profession. One of the hallmarks of Wilson's oeuvre is his exploration of the world of work. Even *Police Academy* is about occupation and profession. And Wilson's passion for the world of work is evident in his valuation of other comedy series.

He is particularly outspoken about his admiration for *M*A*S*H* and *Barney Miller*. In Wilson's words:

> *M*A*S*H* made bad writers good. I'm not talking about Gene Reynolds and Larry Gelbart. I mean outside writers. They'd write for *M*A*S*H* and be wonderful—and then they'd get stuck on something like *The Montefuscos*, which is really hard to write. *M*A*S*H* was easy to write because it was the ideal setup. [I would think of *M*A*S*H*] when we were sitting around at three o'clock in the morning in a writers' meeting at *WKRP* trying to figure out how to blow the show off. [I'd think,] "How do we end this sucker? How do we end it? How do we end it?" And I would have given anything in the world if radio stations had in-coming wounded. Because, at *M*A*S*H*, they always had this wonderful device of saying, "Hey, we've all kidded; we've all laughed; jokes are over; incoming wounded; music up; people running out the door." It had devices—and I don't mean that in a pejorative sense. It had wonderful devices. I like to write about people at work, obviously, and these were people at work, but it was their home as well.

Given Wilson's preoccupation with the world of work, it's not at all surprising that he also admires *Barney Miller*. In fact, as a writer, he sees certain similarities between what he calls the "setup" for *Barney Miller* and the "setup" for *Frank's Place*:

> In *Frank's Place*, the stories were coming pretty easy to us. I always thought that the reason for this was that it [the restaurant] was a public place. A story could walk in the door. I wrote something called "The Bum Out Front" which was one of these episodes. It was about Frank, but it was also about this [homeless] guy who wouldn't go away. You know, he was singing for spare change, and hanging around. But that's a *Barney Miller* setup. A story can come in the door. *Barney*

> *Miller*'s wonderful. You have three stories and they walk in every week. One of the reasons I have never wanted to do a family show is that I don't know what the hell to do with this [setup]: [You've got] mom and dad; and you've got a dining room set and a kitchen. [In L.A.] you walk through one sound stage after another full of dining rooms and kitchens. I think that it is really hard to write for that setup.

The Cinematic Look

According to Wilson, the quest for authenticity—or as he puts it, "getting it right"—also motivated the cinematic look of the show. After "venturing into history" in the research stage, Wilson reports that he then

> went to CBS and said, "You know, I'm one of the few guys working on television that has also directed features. I could make this thing look like a feature. And I think that might be key, because I can't do this three-camera/live-audience and capture what I want of New Orleans. I think I'm going to need steam, and smoke, and music, and food." And I got everybody real excited about that. And they forgot that these things cost money.

In initially creating the look of the series, Wilson enlisted the talents of William A. Fraker, a veteran cinematographer. Fraker, whose screen credits include *Rosemary's Baby, Bullitt,* and *Close Encounters of the Third Kind,* has been nominated for six Academy Awards. Wilson remembers approaching Fraker about shooting the pilot for *Frank's Place:* "We had done this movie together—a very bad movie, I must say—and become great friends. I so admired him. So, he agreed to lower his price, or whatever. He was waiting around to shoot *Baby Boom,* the movie, and they were being delayed. So, he shot the pilot."

Although Fraker returned to filmmaking after shooting the pilot, Wilson says Fraker's look was perpetuated by his replacement, Marvin Rush:

> We couldn't keep Fraker on because he really doesn't do television. We got a young guy who Tim and I knew from *WKRP*. He was the B Camera. The B Camera is the one in the middle [in three-camera sitcoms] that carries the master shot. And it's the hardest to shoot.

As a matter of fact, he had done a couple of things that Tim had produced—low budget, nonunion projects. He was moving into film. And he knew a lot about lights. So, he came in and looked at Fraker's work and he copied it. His name was Marvin Rush. And he was the glue as far as the look because he lit all of the shows. He was the continuing force down there.

In fact, according to Wilson, Fraker's look (as copied by Rush) imposed limits on what the show's directors could do on *Frank's Place:*

> The various directors would come in. Each person would have a slightly different approach. But it was incumbent upon all of them—as it is in all television—to continue the look. If you're going to do *L.A. Law,* you're going to sit down and look at a bunch of *L.A. Laws.* You can't impose something that is inappropriate on what they are doing. So, the directors, they had Marvin there. And he was going to light it the way he was going to light it. Sometimes camera movements would be different. Directors, traditionally, are not involved in lighting too much. They just want it to be real good. But they will decide where to put the camera. Each one is a little different. Some direct the camera. It's called that, you know. And the actors will get hardly any input. Others, particularly if they have a stage background, will concentrate on the Stanislavski stuff with the actors—and they will say to the cameraman, "Where should I put the camera?" So, it varies. But on *Frank's Place,* they all had to copy the [Fraker] look. And most of them were delighted to do it. So, that's how there is continuity there.

The look that Wilson and Fraker devised for the series had other important consequences. As Welles discovered after *Citizen Kane* failed at the box office, hands-off deals are ephemeral creatures that often perish in the heat of competition. But, interestingly, the cinematic look of *Frank's Place* enabled Wilson to sustain creative control throughout the season.

> The hands-off agreement stuck because of the way we shot it. If you do a three-camera sitcom, you rehearse it much like a stage play. And the networks send people down to look at run-throughs. You turn around, and they've all got their scripts out saying, "I feel like on page so-and-so. . . ." And some of them

have amazing nerve. But we started shooting film style at seven o'clock in the morning. Bing! The lights were on. We rehearse it, shoot it, and shoot it out of order. There was no run-through to see. Consequently, we were left totally free. CBS people would look at the dailies—but they didn't know how to look at dailies because they weren't movie people. They'd just kind of look at them and say "OK?" Or they would call and say, "Gee, that scene . . ." and I'd say, "Well, when we cut it all together, it'll be good."

According to Wilson, in addition to sustaining his creative control over the series, the cinematic look also caused him to abandon the laugh track. Where Wilson thinks the laugh track is appropriate in standard TV comedies using three-camera/live-audience production techniques, he discovered that the laugh track was extremely awkward using a one-camera/filmic approach. As he puts it:

> As far as the laugh track goes, Jay Tarses—this is the *Molly Dodd* man—he carries the cross about the laugh track. He's out to get it. But I have no problem with laugh tracks. I like a live audience. I think that's good. I think in [situation] comedy, the track is very appropriate. Laughter is a form of agreement. I know that if you screen a movie comedy in front of three people and a couple of critics, you might as well blow your brains out. But if you watch a comedy with a crowd, it changes everything. So, I don't have any problem with the laugh track. But, because of the look, we just couldn't get the laugh track to work on *Frank's Place.* For some reason, because of the sound track, the [laugh track] audience had to be in the room. But they couldn't be in the room, because gradually, we were shooting all the way around. You got a strong feeling of "Where the hell are these [laughing] people?"

Unfortunately, a new programming category was invented by newspaper reviewers as a device for describing the appearance of several new shows that did not conform to the laugh track or three-camera conventions of situation comedy. *Frank's Place, The "Slap" Maxwell Story, The Days and Nights of Molly Dodd,* and *Hooperman*—all got tagged with the label of "dramedy." And Wilson believes that because this label became associated with low ratings, "guilt by association" with these shows helped doom *Frank's Place*. Like the *Police Academy* coat, the dramedy albatross was something that Wilson couldn't shed.

The Writing Philosophy

The cultural orientation and cinematic look of *Frank's Place* were reflected in the philosophy that governed the writing of the series. Wilson hired four writers, including African-American playwright Samm-Art Williams, to join him in the creative process. And, according to Wilson:

> We, or I should say I, decided right off that we would go for it—that we would not do the sitcom number on this thing because the look was already beginning to dictate the writing. And I had it in mind that we should try to—I mean, I would never say this to a network—but we should try to take the great American dead art form, the short story, and think of ourselves as short story writers. Although, of course, obeying the rules of drama—climax, resolution, building action, and whatnot.

With the short story as a model, Wilson also asked his writers to "regionalize" their thinking: "[I felt] we should bone up on southern authors to see what we could steal. Or to at least let some of that rub off on us."

A corollary of Wilson's short story philosophy was the avoidance of any storyline that faintly resembled the machinations of the conventional situation comedy. Because most sitcoms are primarily vehicles for showcasing comedic star performances, the individual episodes often become highly predictable and painfully contrived variations on a well-established theme. This theme, in fact, is the very "situation" that gives the formula its name and it is embedded in the ongoing relationships between the regular characters. Wilson and his ink-stained comrades essentially tried to write the "situation" out of television comedy. In Wilson's words:

> People, myself included, would yell, "No, that's *Laverne and Shirley*. That's just right out." Laverne and Shirley, for some reason, became the shorthand for any kind of setup, setup, punch, setup, punch. Also actors saying things that were out of character—or interrupting the dramatic flow of something to get a joke out of it. Also, I decided that these stories didn't necessarily have to be funny. Our main thrust was story, story, story! What I was after was good stories. Let's do good stories.

Orchestrating a Collaboration

> Where better to observe the circumscribed role of the author in contemporary cultural production than in commercial television? Because of the technological complexity of the medium and as a result of the application, to television production, of the principles of modern industrial organization (mass production, detailed division of labor, etc.), it is very difficult to locate the "author" of a television program—if we mean by that term the single individual who provides the unifying vision behind the program. (Allen, 1987, p. 4)

Because of what Allen terms "the circumscribed role of the author in contemporary cultural production," television authorship always takes place in the context of collaborative storytelling. In this context, television authorship does not in any way conform to the romanticized literary model of an individual artist writing in isolation. Instead, television authorship is more like coaching a championship football team or conducting a superb symphony orchestra. Like the coach and the conductor, the television author must coordinate and facilitate the concerted efforts of a large and complex team.

We have already addressed certain aspects of Wilson's orchestration of the *Frank's Place* collaboration: how Wilson's regional background and artistic commitment transformed CBS's basic premise; how Wilson's institutionalization of the "Fraker look" guided not only Marvin Rush's work, but also informed the performances of the various directors who worked on the show; how Wilson's writing philosophy encouraged his writing staff to subvert the conventionality of the typical situation comedy. As the coach and orchestrator of *Frank's Place*,

Wilson was involved in everything from hiring cast and crew to supervising post-production editing.

In fact, Wilson tells an interesting story about locating the amateur actor who played the role of Shorty, a cook on the show. We include this story because it lends insight into both Wilson's commitment to authenticity and the importance attached to casting in the television industry. He first met Don Yesso during the research stage of the project:

I was flying to New Orleans and I had stopped smoking. But the plane started bouncing all over the place and there was lightning outside the window, so I said, "I'm getting out of here." I went back to the smoking section and Donny was there. I bummed a cigarette and started talking to him. And he had the accent I wanted. There's that strange New Orleans accent that first sounds like it's coming from Brooklyn and then it's from Jackson, Mississippi, or Biloxi. I had it in the back of my mind that I would have to find a New Orleans actor. I was scared to death of accents because American actors don't do good Southern accents. British actors do, for some reason I don't understand. But I wanted to use that accent. So I started talking to him and I was mainly picking his brains about New Orleans. I was just a sponge. And it occurred to me in the conversation that this guy had a certain aliveness about him that I liked very much. I ordered a couple of drinks and said to him, "You ever act?" And I think he thought right there, "This guy's gay and trying to hit on me." So there was a long pause there.

Wilson couldn't prove on the plane that he was a genuine television producer who was only interested in Yesso as an actor because he doesn't carry business cards. According to Wilson, in the television business, "by the time you get the business cards printed, you get cancelled." However, once the plane landed in New Orleans, Yesso began to believe Wilson's professed occupation and motives: "We got to the airport and they had, per Hollywood style, arranged for a limousine to pick us up. So then Donny decided that maybe I was legit."

Even with Wilson's "hands-off deal," however, the network still retained final approval of casting decisions. But, ironically, because Wilson and Reid were lagging so far behind in putting the show to-

gether, they were able to push through unconventional talent like Yesso. As Wilson explains:

The way you do casting with the networks is that you cast the show with your casting director and then they're all sent to the networks for approval. And there are God-awful, terrible, terrible things that they do when these actors have to go in to read for the network people. It's usually in somebody's office. Or sometimes they have this big room where they do it. At NBC they had this idiotic setup where they forced so much light on the actor that you can't see who's watching. So, it's like a line up. They're just put in the most uncomfortable situations. And then they read— and you hope so much that they like who you picked.

So we cast the show very, very quickly. And I used the great excuse of "I'm so busy getting the sets ready and everything that I can't come." So Tim [Reid] went to read with the cast, and even he hadn't met a lot of them [the actors]. They got over there and the network was really surprised when Donny came in. Donny was so nervous that he went completely nuts. He had never read for me. I had just hired him. And he overacted terribly. It scared everybody, including myself. But they let me have him because I said, "Well, I can't make your delivery date unless you give me these actors."

As this story illustrates, Wilson's relationship with Reid was central to the vitality of the collaboration. And as with most of Wilson's working relationships, his association with Reid was cemented by friendship.

Reid and I are very close personal friends. He and his wife [Daphne Maxwell Reid, who plays mortician Hanna Griffin on *Frank's Place*] are godparents of my middle daughter. After *WKRP* we stayed in close touch and we like one another very much. But I would have never, ever, in my wildest dreams have given an actor any kind of responsibility—including president of the United States, I might add. Even so, I did that with Reid. Reid and I sat down. We said, "We've got to have a united front here. This is a biracial effort." And also . . . this is a show about black people and there's this one white guy running it with a Southern accent!? [I felt] this was inappropriate and Reid agreed. So we decided that we would be the coexecutive producers and that would be how we'd represent ourselves to the public. But in addition to that, what we would do within the show was kind of break things in two. I would, in essence, run the office, and he would run the stage. That's how we did it. I had control of the editing and writing and he ran the stage. I never had any problems with directors because most of those things were straightened out by Reid down there. So, I didn't have to run back and forth.

As a matter of strict policy, Wilson and Reid set about hiring a racially mixed crew. According to Wilson:

We made a commitment [to hire black crew members]. And I was more aggressive about this, in a way, than Tim was, although it was more appropriate that I be aggressive about it. When you came down on the stage, the camera operator was black and the first assistant director was black and second assistant director was black and the guys watching the trailer were black and it went on and on. It was an absolutely concerted effort on our part to do that. Everywhere we had equal talent, we would hire blacks. And one of the reasons we did this was because it was only fair. Because white males run the show out there, they [black crew members] really have trouble. Nobody, when you're doing *Dynasty*, nobody says, "Uh, just get a black gaffer."

Tim Reid is also proud of this hiring policy, estimating that, of the just over 100 members of the cast and crew, 45 to 50 percent were black—and of that percentage, half were black women. Most significantly, as Reid is quick to point out, two of the show's directors were black women. That kind of hiring, according to Reid, "is almost unheard of today in network television."

Wilson contends that the mixed crew was a key ingredient in the *Frank's Place* collaboration. Because there was no live audience, Wilson says crew members became a surrogate audience and their reactions to the script and set provided a crucial "read" on whether "we were getting it right": "If you had a whole bunch of white people making that show, you couldn't read anything from the crew. They wouldn't know any more than *I* do." Reid agrees, adding, "If the crew didn't get into it, we knew we were in trouble."

Of course, the mixed crew also provided un-usual challenges to Wilson and Reid. These challenges are perhaps best illustrated by an anecdote related by Wilson that concerned the name of a cat that appears in the series:

The disagreements—of a racial nature—that came up while we were making the show were few, but funny. [For example] we had this cat that we used for a while, which I often refer to as "that goddam cat." Anyhow, we named him, or I named him, Jesse Jackson. That was the cat's name—Jesse Jackson. Well, Frances Williams, who played Miss Marie, said, "I object to that. I think that is demeaning to Jesse Jackson." So, I talked to Reid. Reid said, "Aww, that's nuts. But I don't want to make Frances angry." So, what do we call the cat? The only thing I can come up with is Hank Aaron. But that's not alliteration. Jesse Jackson is an alliteration. It's funny. It's topical. I think Frances is really wrong. So, everybody talked to Frances. And then we were all going around talking—white people were pairing up with black people. You would see a white writer with a black makeup lady saying, "Uh, I want to talk to you about this cat." The vote, finally, was 50–50. Then Tim got into one of the most embarrassing experiences in his life. He goes to Chicago to make a speech and he's heard that Jesse's gonna be there. He's met Jesse before, so he says to me, "You know what? I'm just going to ask him about the cat." He goes there, and Jesse doesn't show up, but some friends of Jesse's are there. Reid says, "Is Jesse coming?" And they say, "No." And he said, "Oh darn. I wanted to ask him something." And they said, "Well he's not going to be here." And that was the end of it. Now, Jesse Jackson is running for president of the United States. Reid, sitting at home minding his own business, gets a phone call. "Tim, this is Jesse Jackson." Tim says, "Yeah, bullshit. Yeah. Who is this?" He says, "I'm not kidding you. This is Jesse Jackson. I was told to call you. You had a question?" [Reid thought,] Oh, no. He had just watched him [Jackson] on the *MacNeil-Lehrer Report*, you know, talking about foreign policy, and he's got Jesse Jackson on the phone. And he's got to say, "Well, Jesse, see, we got this cat on a television show. . . ." Oh, he was just dying. And Jesse gave him, I think, a politically smart answer. He says, "It doesn't offend me, but it may offend others."

The cat's name was, ultimately, changed to Hank Aaron. But, according to Wilson, Reid was so flustered by the incident that he called a meeting with the entire cast and crew that "saved us a lot of pushing and shoving and a lot of nonsense":

> After the first and second show with the cat, Tim had a meeting with everyone. He said, "We're not going to get into this. This is nonsense. There'll be no politics. There'll be no power plays. We're going to do this about a bunch of people in New Orleans who happen to be black. It'll be about their experience and I don't want any [pause] I'm just cutting it off right here."

Of course, everything is political. And seminar participant Herman Gray, an African-American sociologist at Northeastern University, has characterized this Wilson/Reid collaboration as disturbingly similar to the old plantation system where a white man "ran the office" and his black overseer controlled the field hands. But, in fairness to Wilson and Reid, the politics and division of labor at the producer level made sense, given Wilson's background as a writer and Reid's as an actor. It's also worth emphasizing that Wilson deserves credit for his extraordinary sensitivity regarding racial issues. In the struggle for racial equality in the television industry, Wilson is clearly part of the solution, not part of the problem.

Wilson's personal and professional identities are anchored in his status as a writer. Over and over again during the seminar, Wilson said, "I'm a writer." For Wilson, everything else—producing, directing, editing, managing resources, cutting deals—is secondary. Not surprisingly, Wilson took the highest profile in the collaboration in the area of scripting the series:

> The way this [the writing process] worked was, we would discuss the stories in a group. And we would talk these stories down. And we would talk and talk. And sometimes we would talk about a story for days and then decide to abandon it. Now, I don't want to mislead you. We did some unique things [on *Frank's Place*]. But, basically, it was a typical setup in terms of the writing. The reason there's so much discussion is—this is the best analogy I've ever heard for the type of writing I do—is that we're all safe crackers. And we're just sitting there going, "Twenty left. Nope. Twenty-two left. Ah!" It's like we're all detectives working on a nonexistent show. You sit in these meetings and somebody says, "Well, I don't know. Bob loses his

briefcase? Who knows?" Somebody else: "Well, you know . . . what's in the briefcase?" And it goes from there. And it either goes somewhere and begins to track, and people begin to get excited, and they stand up and all that—or, you just sit there. And, oh, it's so terrible. Nobody will speak for twenty minutes.

According to Wilson, the episode called "The Bridge" (which won him the Best Writing Emmy in 1988) started as a food poisoning premise and then "got talked into" a poignant tale of a terminally ill man who commits suicide by driving off a bridge so that his family can sue the Chez Louisianne for serving him his final drink.

Although the writing process was intensely collaborative, Wilson still had the final word. According to Wilson, after "talking the story down," the staff writer who had the assignment would then write an outline:

> We would all read the outline and then talk that to death. Then, the writer would write a draft, and sometimes a second draft. Then, he would give it to me, and I would write a third draft. This is egotistical of me to say, but that's why the shows sort of have a singularity of point of view. With the exception of one show, they all came through my final filter.
>
> Now, this is typical. I mean, there were many writers on *Barney Miller*—but in the end, it all came through Danny Arnold. There were many writers on *Soap*, but in the end it all came through Susan Harris. There were many writers on *Taxi*, but in the end it all came through Jim Brooks.

Wilson's "final filter" metaphor, though not entirely original, is still perhaps the best way of conceptualizing the circumscribed role of the television author.

The Wilson filter was particularly evident during one moment in a *Frank's Place* episode which explored the fall and rise of a New York business tycoon named Mitchell Torrance. Near the end of the episode, Torrance shares a "great piece of information" with Shorty, the cook: "Whether we're talking cooks, piano players, or hit men in the Mafia, none of the really A-plus people are doing it for the money. They're doing it 'cause . . . they're in love." Raconteur, creator, producer, director, the *Police Academy* guy, coach, orchestrator, writer, final filter, TV author—Hugh Wilson is clearly a man who is in love with his work. Although he admittedly gets by with a lot of help from his many friends—Jay Tarses, Tom Patchett, the morning radio man in Atlanta, Tim Reid, Bill Fraker, Austin Leslie, even Kim LeMasters—his passion for writing, for telling "good stories," for "getting it right," is ultimately what transformed this network of friendships into the artistry of *Frank's Place*.[3]

Notes

1. This chapter uses a close textual analysis of Hugh Wilson's Emmy-award winning television series *Frank's Place* and comments Hugh Wilson shared with us during his participation in a six hour seminar on his work at the Speech Communication Association in November 1989 to illustrate why Wilson is indeed a television auteur. In November 1988, we acted as coleaders of a day-long seminar on *Frank's Place* at the national convention of the Speech Communication Association. Fittingly enough, the host city for the convention was New Orleans (which is the setting for *Frank's Place*). We conceived of the seminar as a critical forum challenging scholars operating from diverse interpretive traditions to make sense of this highly acclaimed series. Television researchers from Louisiana State, Northeastern, Northwestern, Rutgers, Texas Christian, the University of Michigan, the University of Texas, the University of Wisconsin, and other institutions prepared papers for the forum that were based on close textual analyses of five representative episodes of the series.

2. The authors are especially indebted to Christopher Campbell, Herman Gray, Horace Newcomb, and Mimi White for their support and encouragement during the early stages of this project. The authors also express appreciation to David Barker, Lawrence M. Bernabo, Chad Dell, Jackie Byars, Christy Greene, Joe Moorehouse, Dana L. Pierce, Mark Poindexter, Alan D. Stewart, and Bernard M. Timberg for lending their support to the project by participating in the SCA seminar. Finally, the authors thank Carolyn Moses for volunteering to assist in transcribing the interview tapes.

References

Allen, R. C. (Ed.). (1987). *Channels of discourse: Television and contemporary criticism*. Chapel Hill, NC: University of North Carolina Press.

Newcomb, H. (1990). The sense of place in *Frank's Place*. In R. J. Thompson & G. Burns (Eds.), *Making television: Authorship and the production process* (pp. 29–37). New York: Praeger.

Pollan, M. (1988, May). New Orleans banquet. *Channels*, pp. 92–93.

Production
Context
Criticism

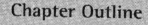

CHAPTER 10

W e tend to think of television in terms of what we see and hear. However, when we look at just the television screen, we get only part of the picture. Important things happen behind the scenes to influence programming. Decisions made by writers and producers, executive responses to competition or regulation, and changes in ownership or regulation are just some of the examples of production context issues that can shape content. *Production context criticism* seeks answers to how and why television programs, programming, and organizations have come to be as they are.

This approach assesses the dynamics of individuals, organizations, and institutions that influence what we see on television. Here, the creativity and actions of individuals working in television are influenced and constrained by organizations and an industry set in a cultural and historical context. In the United States, television is part of a complex culture industry where production is guided by the logic of democratic capitalism. Thus, successful competition in production necessitates being both strategic and responsive to the political context.

Perspectives and Assumptions

Production context criticism is done at three levels of analysis:

Macro-level criticism—focuses on big-picture questions such as how as concentration of ownership affects diversity in programming or how the battles of cable news titans CNN, MSNBC, and Fox have affected news coverage

Micro-level criticism—zooms in to look at pressures faced by television workers in doing their jobs

Mid-range criticism—provides case studies or critical, analytical histories of organizational dynamics within one company or niche of the industry

Two theoretical perspectives color production context criticism. The *political-economic perspective* relies on theories of capitalism and focuses on political and economic implications. The *organizational or industrial relations perspective* uses theories of industrial society to focus on sociological and organizational relations (Giddens, 1979; Murdock, 1982; Schudson, 1991). While both can focus on issues of power and control at macro and micro levels, studies from political economy typically involve broadly critical looks at allocative control, while industrial and organizational studies often focus more specifically on aspects of operational control.

Allocative control is the power to define an organization's scope, goals, and use of resources. In the corporate setting, allocative control directs policy and strategy formulation such as decisions on expansion and financial policies (Murdock, 1982). *Operational control* entails lower-level decisions about "the effective use of resources already allocated and the implementation of policies already decided upon at the allocative level" (Murdock, 1982, p. 122).

Production context criticism is concerned with organizational actions or organizational structures. *Actional analysis*, which looks at how people in media organizations act to gain compliance, often begins by identifying effective controllers and strategies used to enlist support for their ideas, interests, and policies. *Structuration analysis* (which is not the same as semiotic/structural analysis we discussed in Chapter 5) focuses on issues of determination; it often begins by examining how constraints in the economic, political, and organizational environments place limitations on effective media decision makers and controllers (Murdock, 1982). Key features of each of these perspectives are discussed below in terms of how critics use them to examine issues of control in television production.

Political Economy Critical Perspective

This approach grows from a Marxist conception of the socioeconomic order. It focuses on how the underlying structures (or base) of elite economic power promulgate television as a system (or superstructure) supporting the interests of economic and political elites through programming and advertising. Critics using this theoretical foundation for their analysis of media organizations and products see culture industries like television as having a special relationship between economic and cultural power (Murdock, 1982), though some opponents see the claim as an unbelievable "conspiracy" (Schudson, 1991). More refined explanations argue that the media advance the economic interests of economic and political elites primarily by domesticating rather than stifling social problems that raise questions about the legitimacy of prevailing arrangements (Gitlin, 1979). Television produces consensus, in this perspective, by showing the elasticity of consumer society and presenting as "natural" solutions that involve inconsequential give and take that do not challenge core elite interests. Elites thereby maintain social and ideological control through hegemonic consensus rather than confrontation. However, because this perspective views prevailing economic and political arrangements as problematic for all but the ruling classes, the focus of political-economic critiques is on the operational forms such ideological control takes and its potential political and economic consequences.

One type of political-economic analysis (here labeled *actional analysis*) sees television products as derived from industry economic structure. These critiques examine the implications of centralization of ownership on allocation and control of resources and corporate strategies by studying how the actions of individual companies serve to advance their corporate interests at the expense of the public's interests. More generally, such studies explore how television operates to improve the position of the dominant classes.

Another type of political-economic criticism (*structuration analysis*) focuses on the larger societal-level issues concerning the power of corporations. Such critiques focus on both the effects that competition has on television production and products (e.g., programs, news coverage), and on the limits to instrumentality by corporations posed by the larger logic of capitalism. Such critiques may focus, for example, on the limits that market conditions place on news gathering or new program development.

Industrial Relations Critical Perspective

This critical perspective is grounded in organizational sociology and the study of the industrialization of cultural production (Peterson, 1976). The focus of television industry criticism is on the social organization of television work, the relative power (or lack of power) of personnel, and the constraints that consumer behavior imposes on television productions. Key issues include the operational effects of professional values, bureaucratization of production, maintenance of creativity and decisional autonomy in media organizations, and the audiences' influences on media organizations and products.

One body of studies grounded in this perspective examines the actions of media managers, and another looks at the organizational culture of media organizations (Murdock, 1982; Schudson, 1991; Turow, 1991). Critical studies of professional managers and popular creators explore how and to what extent these media professionals exert control over media production and products. Some critical analyses study managers (e.g., executive producers, managing editors) as power brokers and examine the tensions between managerial control and the autonomy of star creative personnel. Other analyses explore the ways in which professional and organizational norms and practices limit and constrain the autonomy of managers and creators. Both types of analyses, however, see media production professionals as resourceful and creative individuals who are constrained by time, budget, and organizational routines (Molotch & Lester, 1974; Tuchman, 1978).

Structuralist critiques share this perspective and focus on the ways in which organizational workers, the range of television programs, the popularity of certain formats, the creation of new forms, and scheduling appear to be "limited by the power and veto of consumers" (Murdock, 1982, p. 129). Concomitantly, these critical perspectives also deconstruct this assumption of a responsive marketplace and examine the ways in which the television industry uses a consumerist stance to justify its actions as giving the public what it wants, often to defend problematic programming.

Frameworks for Production Context Criticism

In doing production context criticism, you begin by determining whether your concern is a macro-level or a micro-level issue or problem: Do you want to take on big issues of marketplace dynamics, or are you concerned with specific strategies in an organizational setting? Is your focus on the production process for a certain television genre or on the compromises creative personnel make to be successful? Answering questions like these is an essential first step.

Once this has been done, you will need to turn to a critical framework or foundation for some analytical tools to help you in your critical efforts. In the next section, we discuss two of them. Dimmick and Coit's (1982, 1983) analytical scheme provides a framework for examining the hierarchically ordered levels of decision making that influence television production, and Turow's (1991) typology focuses on power roles played by people involved in producing television.

Hierarchies of Decision-Making Power and Control

Dimmick and Coit's (1982, 1983) nine-level hierarchy provides a typology of levels of decision making and interdependence among the "systems that shape television," from the level of international organizations down to the individual production personnel level. Their model uses the gatekeeper (White, 1950) concept: at each level, an individual or group of individuals functions as a gatekeeper, controlling what ideas and information get through and what ideas and information are barred. Studies using their hierarchy examine the influence and exercise of power at and between hierarchical levels, looking at the ways that decisions made at one level affect decisions at others. In their model, most influence is seen as moving down the hierarchy, but some filters up from lower levels. Influence comes from both formal and informal hierarchies. *Formal hierarchies* reflect superior-subordinate patterns seen in organizational charts; influence stems from rank. *Informal hierarchies* reflect influence patterns from ongoing interaction and are sociometrically constructed. Formal and informal hierarchies exert different forms of influence.

Normative social influence stems from formal hierarchies where power is exercised by A and accepted by B because A controls resources that B needs (King, 1975). In this classic power model, for example, (1) legislative action might (2) fuel Federal Communications Commission (FCC) rule making, which in turn (3) affects corporate communication strategies (4) including decisions about network programming that (5) affect local station profits (see Luhmann, 1979). Normative social influence also occurs where no clear hierarchy exists between organizations or individuals. An example is the reporter-source relationship: the reporter needs the source to have a story to write about, and the source needs the reporter to convey his or her ideas to the public. Each needs the other: dependency, rather than a hierarchical position, guides the exercise of normative influence. In contrast, *informational social influence* stems from informal social or *liaison networks* that develop in order to get a job done within or between organizations (Rogers & Kincaid, 1981).

In practice, Dimmick and Coit's (1983) model often leads the critic to analyze media production at three levels: (1) the larger environment level of societal influences on the organization's function, (2) the organizational level, and (3) the small group and individual decision-maker levels (Lorsch & Morse, 1974). You could, for example, do a comparative case study of two media organizations. One way to start would be to pick two organizations that you would expect to be "most similar" or "most different" at a particular level of analysis (Przeworski & Teune, 1970). Studies that look at similar organizations seek to isolate key differences and find within- or between-level explanations for these, while studies of outwardly different organizations seek to identify similarities and find explanations for these.

Thinking about the following hierarchical levels of production context will help you get started in framing your critical examination of hierarchical influences on media production processes and content.

Supranational– and Pan–National–Level Influences In analyzing television, decisions made beyond the nation-state are often overlooked. International agencies and global agreements set compatible technical standards or mediate legal issues such as copyright that can shape the activities and products of media organizations. Some studies may focus on analyzing the pan-national influences by dominant producers or other media decision makers to set limits on "media imperialism" (Turnstall, 1977) or the "free flow" of information (Luther, 1988) using new technologies. For example, many countries, including Canada, have policies limiting the amount of foreign programming that can be aired. In terms of Canada, the government specifies a limit to the amount (20 percent) of the non-Canadian programming (including U.S. radio and television series) that any broadcast station can air. This clearly constrains the audience and market for prime-time and syndicated programs produced in the United States.

Societal–Level Influences Television is influenced at the societal level by law-making and political pressures. In the United States, the FCC has licensing and rule-making power over broadcast stations and cable networks, and the Federal Trade Commission (FTC) oversees television advertising. These governmental regulatory bodies make decisions about such matters as how many minutes of ads can be shown during an hour of television and whether the same corporation can own a newspaper and a television station in the same city.

Societal-level influences also come from threats by the executive or legislative branches (e.g., Congress has held multiple hearings at which Hollywood and network producers and executives were called to testify about violence and sex in television). Economic influences such as tax rates, investment rules, and consumer spending also affect television production.

Industry–Level and Interorganizational Influences The industry-level context within which television programs are produced includes relationships among networks, local stations, advertisers, and program suppliers. At the industry level, production context criticism focuses on competition and cooperation between organizations and the strategies these organizations use to garner resources necessary for television production, distribution, and exhibition. Hence, the changing face of competition in an oligopolistic market and the advance of horizontal and vertical integration are key topics in these critical studies, as are corporate partnering and the creation of advantageous synergies.

Supraorganizational Influences Corporate strategy is a supraorganizational level of influence that critics also study. When AOL, Viacom, or Disney, for example, takes over an entity, at least five *P*s change: *policies, procedures, programming, pricing,* and *personnel.* Pressures for economies of scale and synergies with the owner's stable of products affect the production context. Conglomerates often bring reduced risk taking and homogeneity of programming, while their infusions of financial resources can allow development in new marketplace niches (Turow, 1992). For example, when Disney acquired ABC, suddenly a rash of characters in ABC programs were taking vacations to Disney World, Epcot, and Disneyland.

Community or Market Influences   Specific community groups and organized pressure groups also can influence media production. Counterprogramming strategies, business policy changes in response to other media competitors, and shifts in news coverage due to pressure by community groups are all examples of influences at this level (see Montgomery, 1981)

Intraorganizational Influences   Here, the critic studies the influence of the organization's goals, formal structure, policies, work routines, and informal networks on decision-making processes and outcomes. For example, critics shadow and study key television executives as gatekeepers or power brokers who make decisions amid competing resources and political coalitions in order to identify and clarify the informal as well as formal criteria used in making programming decisions (Breed, 1955; Cyert & March, 1963). Decisions are influenced by two features of organizational life, policies and routines, each having a formal and informal side.

Organizational policies grow from debates over limited resources such as airtime, budget, or personnel. Television programming is influenced by turf battles that work out priorities in organizational goals, such as targets for ratings or advertising billings. Informal creative strategies, such as leading the newscast with blood and guts during sweeps weeks, may be a conscious or unconscious derivative (see Gitlin, 1983). Work routines influence decisions and creativity in other ways. Formal policies may dictate a required approval or cross-checking with two independent sources before running a news story (see Tuchman's 1978 analysis of news objectivity as a strategic ritual). Informal routines tend to be pragmatic practices, such as "back-timing" (i.e., the kind of reverse counting down of the week's schedule, such as you have with the Space Shuttle launch and New Year's Eve in Times Square) staff responsibilities in a situation comedy so it is ready for shooting with a studio audience at week's end. The press of policies, schedules, and routines necessarily affects creativity.

Formal or Informal Group Influences   Critics who analyze group behavioral influences on television program production must have a thorough understanding of the context, history, patterns of interaction, power relationships, and formal and informal forces within which the organizational group functions. To do this, the critic often uses interviews and firsthand observation of multiple organizational members in order to understand multiple perspectives. A critic may study the different criteria used by executives who hammer out a program schedule (Brown, 1971) or by the local newscast section editors who decide on how much time is allotted to national, local, sports, or weather stories in a given day.

Dyadic Communication Influences   Some important production decisions result from the interactions of pairs of individuals, for example, reporters and their editors or reporters and their sources. What stories will be covered from what angles are news production decisions that are negotiated by reporters with editors; reporters make bargains with sources, and segment producers reach agreements about topics with talk show guests (Tuchman, 1974). Personal relationships between executives often cement big production deals (Gitlin, 1983, esp. pp. 115–156).

Intraindividual or Cognitive-Level Influences   Individual personal decisions can affect whether a show is produced, a news story runs, or a cut needs reworking. How models of decision making change according to situation or over time and how the strategies of two decision makers in comparable roles differ are among the types of questions research into this level of the production process seek to answer.

Power Roles

A second analytical schema that critics can use to analyze the television production context critically is Joe Turow's (1992) typology of 13 power roles, or positions, from which influence is exerted in television program production. Media organizations, he explains, must negotiate with other organizations to achieve goals, and each negotiation is an opportunity to gain power. The goal of each power role holder is to use resources strategically to gain control over resources needed from others. These resources may be money, talent, information, supplies, or services. Television has many examples of resources that one organization has that another needs. Program producers have creative resources, but they lack the resources to distribute and exhibit their programs; for this, they need others. Advertisers bring economic resources; they invest money to get access to the benefits of the creative, distribution, and exhibition resources of both producers and networks.

Turow sees power roles as purposeful roles that organizations (for the most part) play in employing resources to gain others' compliance with their goals and plans. Keep in mind that organizations are not the same as power roles. Organizations can play more than one role; for example, NBC is a network serving in the producer role when it creates news programs, sports programs, and late-night talk programs. It is also a distributor and exhibitor when it distributes programs produced by independent production companies to its more than 200 network-affiliated independent stations around the country, trading airtime for ads in return for programs to air. Some roles, such as the creator (e.g., executive producer Aaron Spelling) and public power roles (Disney CEO Michael Eisner), tend to be played by individuals. Turow's model helps television critics focus their analysis on the influence of these and other power roles in television production.

The Producer Power Role   In television, the producer power role facilitates the creation of programming or advertising for release to an audience. This role is almost always played by complex organizations with vast resources and leverage to determine content, oversee production, and arrange for distribution and exhibition. The producer power role is not the same as that played by creators of television content, such as program producers, directors, or writers who lack power over such matters as placing or retaining a show on a network's schedule. However, as we discuss later, such creative personnel can have considerable leverage.

Television networks with monies to contract for programming in line with corporate goals and programming strategy play the classic producer power role. Creative personnel led by program producers pitch shows to networks, but they cannot begin to produce these shows until they are given a green light by these gatekeepers. Consequently, the producer power role controls creative personnel and, through them, the ideas aired on television. This role is also played by local stations, program syndicators, cable networks, cable multiple system owners, and local cable franchises. TV critics studying producer power roles might focus on relationships between network power producers and network stockholders or advertisers in order to understand financial pressures in the production context or tensions over creativity with writers or actors. TV critics examining issues of public responsibility versus private profit might focus on power relations among producers, public advocacy groups, and regulatory efforts.

The Authority Power Role   Governmental agencies legislate, regulate, and enforce actions among power role players. Authorities, including the FCC and FTC, provide leverage at three levels:

   The structural level. Regulations set the character and boundaries of media organizations. Congress's decisions to establish broadcasting as a commercial rather than government enterprise and FCC decisions to set limits on broadcast station ownership are structural-level authority and power.

   The technical level. Authorities' regulation of television's transmission standards affects how programming is produced and distributed.

   The content level. Regulations are vitally important because rulings on freedom of speech, copyright, and obscenity directly affect content. TV critics' examination of the workings of the authority power role in particular situations grows out of such societal concerns over television as ownership, children's programming, and diversity.

The Investor Power Role   Diverse organizations such as investment banks, mutual fund managers, insurance companies, and foundations attempt to influence television production by leveraging their positions as investors and underwriters of programs, production companies, and multinational conglomerates. Some of these organizations make such investments because they are looking for financial return, whereas others, such as foundations, may have different goals. The ability to attract investors influences the viability of television production organizations and programming.

The Client Power Role   As producers' customers, advertising industry clients provide an influx of money that is critical in determining program development and continuance. Television programs are designed to appeal to targeted demographics that advertisers want to reach. Thus, children's shows draw advertising support from cereal manufacturers, while sports shows attract the interest of auto manufacturers. Organizations in the client power role include businesses seeking to advertise, ad agencies, media buying firms, and production companies. The client power role is considerable; when influential advertisers talk about the right setting for products, program producers and distributors listen. Advertisers also may enter barter arrangements to underwrite producing programs. TV critics' studies of the client power role include analyses of the economics of advertising as well as ethnographic studies of sponsor-station interactions (see, e.g., Englehardt, 1986).

The Creator Power Role   In television, individual producers, directors, writers, actors, news reporters, set designers, editors, and others play creator power roles. Such creators gain clout when they are recognized for distinct or superior talent that contributes to a track record of success (Gitlin, 1983, pp. 115–142; Pekurny, 1982; Turow, 1992). Such star quality inflates labor costs, but producers view this investment as a cost of doing business. While critics need to distinguish creator power roles from the producer power roles, these can blur as creators gain clout. As writers such as Stephen Bochco or Dick Wolf build successful track records, they can become the key creative figure in television production: the writer-producer whose production company forms long-term deals with networks or syndicators that play formal producer power roles (Newcomb & Alley, 1983). Much power in the relationship between creators and production organizations comes from the need to keep star writer-producers and talent happy so they will stay in the controlling producer's stable. Production context criticism that focuses on the writer-producer role chronicles creativity in the face of corporate constraints and shares much with auteur criticism.

The Union Power Role   Because creators and production personnel have traditionally had little clout, job security, or control over working conditions, a guild system developed to provide leverage. Television production companies negotiate agreements with union groups representing directors, writers, actors, designers, and other technical and creative personnel. Although this group has been little examined by critics, the rules and tensions of labor influence the television product.

The Distributor and Exhibitor Power Roles   In television, distributor and exhibitor power roles are often merged or so interlinked that they are thought of as one. Technically, distributing programming means making it available to an exhibitor; distribution through networks, syndicators, or other organizations does not necessarily ensure exhibition or desirable scheduling of a program. For example, a network may distribute a program without specifying an airtime. Networks base successful distribution and exhibition on stations they own and operate while eliciting effective control of exhibition through contracts with affiliated stations. Given that networks also control production (through contracts and in-house efforts), this vertical integration of control over production, distribution, and exhibition has created powerful oligopolies. Syndicators can offer attractive alternatives to production organizations looking for distribution and exhibition. However, syndicators rely on a fragile group of stations, with clout coming from packaging rights to hot properties (such as *Friends*) with less desirable product. Television product is also affected by the distribution and exhibition clout of movie studios, cable networks, and multiple-system cable owners. Hollywood studios auction product to competing movie channels, cable networks vie for syndicated programming, and cable system owners can close distribution channels to production arms of competitors. Because much television marketplace action concerns the shifting arrangements producers face in getting programming through the gate of distributors and exhibitors, the savvy critic of production context must understand this power role dynamic.

The Auxiliary Power Role   Many organizations provide ancillary supplies and services to producers. Sets need to be designed and locations found for shooting scenes. Wardrobe and makeup have to be just so. Camera, sound, and lighting equipment need to be coordinated. Offices, equipment, transportation, security, maintenance, accounting, and insurance are required. These frequently overlooked roles in criticism can make or break a production.

The Linking–Pin Power Role   Linking-pin organizations move media material to television, such as promoting a new book or movie on television. Linking-pin power is often played by public relations or promotional agencies serving other media clients. Much linking stems from necessary cooperation between media producers. For example, a talk show producer might need a movie clip to attract a star guest, or a local station might need sports footage from ESPN for a story. Linking-pin organizations leverage a variety of resources needed in the production of television. These resources can be free when publicity is bartered or purchased.

The Facilitator Power Role   Organizations such as talent agencies, law firms, market research firms, and others play the facilitator power role. By bringing together talent in their stable, a powerful talent agency such as William Morris can offer an almost complete package of creative talent, leveraging organizations in the producer power role by simplifying the production task, saving time and money, and providing a safety net of talent with proven track records (Whiteside, 1981). Other organizations facilitate decisions by providing specialized information or services such as program testing, ratings research, financial support, and public relations.

The Public and Public Advocacy Power Roles   Whereas audiences exercise collective power through ratings, public advocacy organizations can make effective demands on producer, distributor, exhibitor, and client organizations that lead to change. Diverse organizations from Action for Children's Television to Mothers Against Drunk Driving can pressure for legislation to control content, organize boycotts of products, or use public relations and advertising to present their view. Advocacy efforts are evaluated on a cost-benefit basis by organizations that affect the producer power role. Often temporary fixes prevail, while longstanding disputes over sex and violence in programming ebb and flow with public advocacy efforts.

Permutations in Controlling Dependence and Risk   Organizations often play more than one power role in seeking to reduce resource dependence and control risk. For example, television networks not only play producer, distributor, and exhibitor roles but also often bring some auxiliary, linking-pin, and facilitator services in-house. Interorganizational coalitions develop to reduce risk, and these shift over time and circumstance. As these relationships change, centers of power shift in the television industry. Critical studies that assess historical processes in changing power role relationships can make important contributions to understanding the production context.

Writing Production Context Criticism

Identify your central question, and then determine your perspective. Do you want to explain why most network newscasts and most local newscasts (no matter where you are) look virtually the same and cover many of the same types of stories? Or are you interested in a big-picture critique—for example, explaining why there are no children's programs on early prime-time network or cable television (except for Nickelodeon) when millions of children under age 12 are in the TV audience each night? Are you interested in approaching these questions from a political-economic perspective or a consumerist perspective? In longer critiques, you can blend critical approaches. Combining a feminist perspective (see Chapter 15) with a culturalist view of organizational relations may help explain the absence of stories about women and the dearth of women newsmakers—both the experts who are interviewed and the journalists doing the interviewing (for social scientific rather than criticism studies of women journalists and media coverage of women, see Mills, 1997; Iyengar, Valentino, Ansolabehere, & Simon, 1997; Norris, 1997; and Weaver, 1997). Writing a critical audience ethnography may help explain the pleasures (and concomitant popularity) of viewing certain programs (see, e.g., Rockler, 1999).

In making your decision, you need to consider practical issues such as whether you can gain access to organizations for the observations and interviews you will need to do for your critical analysis or where to find a representative groups of audience members with whom to view programs and talk about the meanings they see these programs provoking. Such obstacles to access are one reason that few critics have published this type of critical analysis.

Choosing your writing approach requires matching research questions to the level of analysis. In writing production criticism, you may decide to adopt a historical perspective, an ethnographic perspective, or a particular example or case study perspective. All rely on gathering information about and critically analyzing the program production context.

Big-Picture Media Industry Critiques

As we noted in Chapter 1, criticism is not history. However, critics do sometimes adopt historical perspectives in writing critical analyses of aspects of television. Some genre critiques, some ideological critiques, and some production context critiques adopt a longitudinal, big-picture perspective. Critical analyses of production contexts necessarily have a historical component because they are attempting to explain, interpret, and evaluate production processes and practices that have developed over time within a particular historical-cultural context.

In writing production context criticism, you can use a political-economy perspective or an industrial relations–organizational socialization perspective. If you combine this approach with interviews and observations, you will be taking a grounded theory approach with one of these other theoretical perspectives to understand and analyze what you have observed. Big-picture media industry critiques involve reading others' accounts and research on this topic, doing interviews, perhaps reviewing institutional and industry data, and even using available statistical information. The media industry critic is an adventurer with many tools who in one analysis must make sense of an era, situation, personal judgments, and structural constraints.

Topics that critics doing big-picture media industry criticism explore should be significant, clearly defined, demarcated in time and space, and have continuity. Topics range from broad developments in national systems (Barnouw, 1975, 1978) to specific analyses of networks or shows (Metz, 1975, 1977). Research must be bibliographically sound, evaluating implicit and explicit meanings of primary and secondary sources. Facts need to be purposively collected, accurate, verifiable, and clearly documented. Interpretation should stem from facts at hand, with generalizations made in context rather than overstepping logical bounds. Writing media industry critiques presents challenges. Foremost is crafting the analysis. Good big-picture critiques are as engaging to read as literature: they are alive, present compelling evidence, rely on intuitive reasoning, and are well organized.

One example of such a critique is Michael Real's analysis (1996) of the production hegemony enacted in annual Hollywood award ceremonies. Real's analysis of the Oscar awards, primarily, but also the Academy awards, combines a political-economic perspective with an analysis of the media gatekeepers who produce the Oscar texts to explore cultural hegemony.

Case Study Approaches

The defining feature of the case study is its particularity in studying real life in context (Merriam, 1988). The production context case study is like a textual analysis of a particular situation comedy; it is accomplished the through analysis of a particular example.

There is no guide on how to do or how to write a media production case study. Your point of departure, as with any other criticism essay, should be a significant and clearly defined question and topic. Case study critiques are a useful way to approach critical analyses of the operational side of television. Case study criticism can describe and analyze the making of a particular program (Mayerle, 1991; Stipp, Hill-Scott, & Dorr, 1987), television newsroom practices (Browne, 1983), links between network profits and investment in new technology (Dimmick & Wallschlaeger, 1986), or organizations, groups, individuals, policies, or events. The material for case study critiques of media production processes comes from many sources, including published information about organizations, individuals, and the industry; interviews; and direct observation. In terms of writing, case studies typically rely on "thick" description and analysis that is grounded in specific observations, interviews, and documents gathered.[1] Because case study critiques can yield massive amounts of information, effectively summarizing and coherently analyzing the material in order to produce some general interpretive conclusions can be challenging. Organizationally, case study critiques may present the critic's interpretations as quest or problem and solution, as a chronological narrative, or in terms of particular themes that emerged from the analysis.

Case study criticism may be shaped by pragmatic issues, such as the analysis of power roles in particular media organizations and limited by the access and cooperation the critic receives from organizations or individuals.[2] An example is Michael Real's (1996) analysis of various accounts of the notorious American television quiz show scandal of the 1950s. His analysis takes the scandal as a sort of case study example in order to explore two larger critical questions: "What are the standards of truth when media represent history?" and "What are the lessons history offers for our media practices and ethics?" (p. 208).

Ethnographic Critiques

Many times production process criticism uses ethnographic methods to analyze media organizations and media production processes critically. Studying television work from this vantage point means going into the field to get an inside view of television organizations (see van Mannen, 1988). By observing the process in progress and discussing perceptions of participants, ethnographic criticism provides rich interpretive analyses of individuals and smaller groups within media organizations, as well as media production processes (see, e.g., Gittlin, 1983; Mayerle, 1991; McManus, 1994). Gaining access to media production organizations and gaining the trust of workers in the television production context in an ethnographic studies approach involves building relationships and blending into their daily dynamic. Media workers may initially be reticent to disclose information and feelings to critics because trade secrets or uncomfortable workplace dynamics may be at issue. Also, media workers may feel that candor over information would give a competitor an advantage or that disclosing true feelings about the work situation, bosses, or coworkers might create ill will and even put their jobs at risk. Thus, in studying production context, you must take care in being introduced into the organization, making your objectives clear, and providing ongoing reassurance about how sources will be attributed and how the information gathered will be used. It is not uncommon for researchers to come to agreements about how the identity of the organization and individuals will be handled in research reports, and often the critic creates a fictional name for the media organization and the media workers. Organizations may ask you to sign confidentiality agreements and to see, and even approve, your research reports prior to release.

In the ethnographic tradition, gathering data means approaching the observational environment as though it were anthropologically strange. Observation should be unobtrusive and nonjudgmental. In ethnographic criticism, the critic must strive to understand the media production situation or organization from the perspectives of the actors in the media organizational setting. Critical media ethnographers must focus on listening and trying to understand rules as perceived by participants rather than imposing their own logic on situations. The critic's goal is to gain a well-rounded, well-grounded understanding of the forces at play. Often critics combine observation, depth interviewing, focus group interviews, and institutional data to gain these understandings. Typically, as with most other criticism, the best critical analysis comes from an analytic induction process: continuously revise your initial assumptions by grounding them in experiences as understood by television workers (Glaser & Strauss, 1967) until you have a thorough understanding of the production context or process as it is perceived by those involved in it.

Developing themes and confronting tensions in creative ways make narrative critiques of the production context come alive. Though the list that follows is not exhaustive, the tensions it identifies are almost universal and used in both micro- and macro-level studies (see Ettema, Whitney, & Wackman, 1987):

Power and equity. In critical analysis of the overarching tension between power and equity in production, the critic needs to go beyond asking only about who has power and how it works. Questions about power beg others about those who do not have it and whether existing arrangements are fair. Critical inquiry examines this relationship in studies of power roles and decision making and searches for answers to questions of equity, fairness, and change.

Public responsibility and private profit. This tension pits two philosophically distinct beliefs about market regulation. While some believe regulation needs to protect viewers from the harms of television and abuses by its operators, others believe government should stay out of the speech, ideas, and business of television and let the free market resolve issues of public responsibility. Manifest in roles and decisions, this tension plays out from broad policymaking on down to the individual level, where ethical judgments and professional standards come into play (see McManus, 1994).

News and entertainment. Television is a two-headed monster: the market presses for its news to be entertaining, yet at the same time, its entertainment fare is necessarily informational. Its advertising also straddles the matter, informing viewers of the merits of products but in a way that entertains and leaves a warm afterglow. From issues such as choosing news reporters for their looks as much as reporting experience, to docudramas balancing drama with fact, the news-versus-entertainment tension is a fundamental one in television production context.

Globalism and localism. The advantages of producing television for global markets can conflict with meeting local needs (see, e.g., Rodriguez, 1996). Programs that easily cross borders and are long-lasting are attractive to investors, while local interests may be served by one-use community programming. Cultural imperialism is felt by less developed nations when global product dominates local agendas. Closer to home, a television station's broad reach dictates focus on region rather than community. Regulatory philosophies intersect these issues, with tensions evident in production decisions.

Conglomerization and fragmentation. Television's push toward globalization is linked with increasing conglomerization. As mergers and acquisitions consolidate the industry, networks, stations, production companies, and cable systems are owned by an increasingly smaller group of multinational conglomerates. They press to create vertical integration of production, distribution, and exhibition of television product and synergies among holdings. Much remaining competition fights to position a suite of products (like news, sports, or movies) that can synergize and collectively control shares of a fragmented marketplace.

Diversity and track records. Specialization in a fragmented market may not link to diversity. Television has more failures than successes. To control risk, decision makers rely on track records of success. There is a press for something new, but not too new; new shows often clone successful shows but with new twists. There is reliance on veterans who deliver on time and on budget. This limits creativity and diversity, as a homogeneous group anchored in past television success dominates power. Newcomers may be greeted with apprehension because there is less risk for managers to fail with talent with an established track record.

Routinization and creativity. Workplace routines and dependence on formula also work to constrain creativity. Shows must be produced on budget in a timely manner. A television "assembly line" produces programming according to professional standards reliant on proven formulas. Formulas set episode and segment length, number of characters, plot structure, variants in theme, and breaks in the action. Thus, in news shows, stories with action footage or easily accessible sources are more likely to be aired (Tuchman, 1978). Creativity is often inversely related to market position, with weak positions fostering creativity through risk taking.

The Example Essay

In the example essay at the end of the chapter, Elana Levine gets inside ABC's soap opera *General Hospital* to explore many of the issues discussed in this chapter. Her critical essay is a historically informed case study critique that uses ethnographic methods to study production processes. This approach merges structural and actional components of a political-economic model and the concept of hegemony with a culturalist perspective from industrial relations. Most important, her critical analysis describes and interprets the structural mechanisms and social consequences of constraint in the production setting.

Note

1. "Thick description" is the term Clifford Geetz (1973), one of the founders of cultural anthropoloigy, used to describe the practice and the end result of analysis based on participant observation of members of a culture engaged in their everyday life activities. As Geetz put it, "What we call our data are really our own constructions of other people's constructions of what they and their compatriots are up to" (p. 9). Ethnographers, Geetz explains, attempt to analyze and make sense of "the structure of significations," which inform people's lives and which emerge slowly through the researcher's involvement with the people s/he is studying.

2. Time, access, and page limits for your class assignment may limit you to a single case study. While great depth comes from a critique of a single case, the generalizations you can draw about program production processes from one example are limited. Doing multiple case study critiques allows you to look for shared patterns and make comparisons along the lines of a "most similar" or "most different" approach suggested by Dimmick and Coit's decisional hierarchy model (1983).

Further Readings

Compaine, B. J., & Gomery, D. (2000). *Who owns the media? Competition and concentration in the mass media industry* (3rd ed.). Mahwah, NJ: Erlbaum. The chapter in this book on the television and cable industry sets the standard for understanding the dynamics of the business behind the production context.

Longworth, Jr., J. L. (2000). *TV creators: Conversations with America's top producers of television drama*. Syracuse, NY: Syracuse University Press. Insightful conversations with the top creators of recent television drama provide the writer-producer's view of constraints on creativity in the production process.

Webnotes

National Association of Television Program Executives. **www.natpe.org**

> This is the web site for the leading professional group playing the power role in television. It features industry information and a very good Industry Hub link to resources on the television business.

Columbia Journalism Review. **www.cjr.org**

> This site's up-to-date Who Owns What link inventories the holdings of all of the corporate owners that are big players in the television business. It also features good insights into constraints in television news.

Learning
Activities

1. In the next week, watch three early evening news broadcasts on one television station in your local market. Pick three feature reports that you found most problematic. Outline the reasons for your evaluation in each instance, and determine which report troubles you the most. Then assume you are going to have the opportunity to interview the producer of that report to understand the handling of that story. Prepare a series of questions that will allow you to get at issues in the decision-making hierarchy that came into play and the influence of different people in power roles that shaped the story.

2. In Hollywood, it often seems that everyone is a producer. Research carefully what a television producer really does. Start by looking at what the Producers Guild of America has to say about the standards that should be met in assigning producer credits in television and film. Review its site at **www.producersguild.org** to find out more about the guild's credit fraud campaign. What is at the heart of this controversy? Write a job description that would summarize the skills and responsibilities needed to be a television producer.

References

Barnouw, E. (1975). *Tube of plenty: The development of American television.* New York: Oxford University Press.

Barnouw, E. (1977). *The sponsor: Notes on a modern potentate.* New York: Oxford University Press.

Breed, W. (1955). Social control in the newsroom: A functional analysis. *Social Forces, 32,* 326–335.

Brown, L. (1971). *Television: The business behind the box.* New York: Harcourt Brace Jovanovich.

Browne, D. (1983). The international newsroom. *Journal of Broadcasting, 27,* 205–231.

Cyert, R. M., & March, J. G. (1963). *A behavioral theory of the firm.* Englewood Cliffs, NJ: Prentice Hall.

Dimmick, J., & Coit, P. (1982). Levels of analysis in mass media decision making: A taxonomy, research strategy, and illustrative data analysis. *Communication Research, 9,* 3–32.

Dimmick, J., & Coit, P. (1983). Levels of analysis in mass media decision making: A taxonomy, research strategy, and illustrative data analysis. In E. Wartella & D. C. Whitney (Eds.), *Mass communication review yearbook* (Vol. 4, pp. 361–390). Thousand Oaks, CA: Sage.

Dimmick, J., & Wallschlaeger, M. (1986). Measuring corporate diversification: A case study of new media ventures by television network parent companies. *Journal of Broadcasting and Electronic Media, 30,* 1–14.

Englehardt, T. (1986). The shortcake strategy. In T. Gitlin (Ed.), *Watching television* (pp. 68–110). New York: Pantheon.

Ettema, J., Whitney, D. C., & Wackman, D. B. (1987). Professional mass communicators. In C. R. Berger & S. H. Chaffee (Eds.), *Handbook of communication science* (pp. 747–780). Thousand Oaks, CA: Sage.

Geetz, C. (1973). *The interpretation of culture.* New York: Basic Books.

Giddens, A. (1979). *Central problems in social theory: Action, structure, and contradiction in social analysis.* New York: Macmillan.

Gitlin, T. (1979). *The whole world is watching.* Berkeley: University of California Press.

Gitlin, T. (1983). *Hill Street Blues*: "Make it look messy." In T. Gitlin, *Inside prime time* (pp. 273–324). New York: Pantheon.

Glaser, B. G., & Strauss, A. L. (1967). *The discovery of grounded theory: Strategies for qualitative research.* Chicago: Aldine.

Iyengar, S., Valentino, N. A., Ansolabehere, S., & Simon, A. F. (1997). Running as a woman: Gender stereotyping in women's campaigns. In P. Norris (Ed.), *Women, media and politics* (pp. 77–98). New York: Oxford University Press.

King, S. W. (1975). *Communication and social influence.* Reading, MA: Addison-Wesley.

Lorsch, J., & Morse, J. (1974). *Organizations and their members: A contingency approach.* New York: Harper & Row.

Luhmann, N. (1979). *Trust and power.* New York: Wiley.

Luther, S. F. (1988). *The United States and direct broadcast satellite.* New York: Oxford University Press.

Mayerle, J. (1991). *Roseanne*—How did you get inside my house? A case study of a hit blue-collar situation comedy. *Journal of Popular Culture, 24,* 71-78.

McManus, J.M.C. (1994). *Market-driven journalism.* Thousand Oaks, CA: Sage.

Merriam, S. B. (1988). *Case study research in education.* San Francisco: Jossey-Bass.

Metz, R. (1975). *CBS: Reflections in a bloodshot eye.* Chicago: Playboy Press.

Metz, R. (1977). *The Today show: An inside look.* Chicago: Playboy Press.

Mills, K. (1997). What difference do women journalists make? In P. Norris (Ed.), *Women, media and politics* (pp. 41–56). New York: Oxford University Press.

Molotch, P., & Lester, M. (1974). News as purposive behavior: On the strategic use of routine events, accidents, and scandals. *American Sociological Review, 39,* 101–112.

Montgomery, K. (1981). Gay activists and the networks. *Journal of Communication, 31,* 49–57.

Murdock, G. (1982). Large corporations and the control of the communications industries. In M. Gurevitch, T. Bennett, J. Curran, & J. Woolacott (Eds.), *Culture, society, and the media* (pp. 118–150). New York: Methuen.

Newcomb, H., & Alley, R. S. (1983). *The producer's medium.* New York: Oxford University Press.

Norris, P. (1997). Women leaders worldwide: A splash of color in the photo op. In P. Norris (Ed.), *Women, media and politics* (pp. 149–165). New York: Oxford University Press.

Pekurny, R. (1982). Coping with television production. In D. C. Whitney & J. Ettema (Eds.), *Individuals in mass media organizations: Creativity and constraint* (pp. 131–143). Thousand Oaks, CA: Sage.

Peterson, R. A. (1976). The production of culture: A prolegomenon. *American Behavioral Scientist, 19,* 7–22.

Przeworski, A., & Teune, H. (1970). *The logic of comparative social inquiry.* New York: Wiley.

Real, M.R. (1996). Production/hegemony: "And the winner is . . . Hollywood!" In M.R. Real, *Exploring media culture: A guide* (pp. 148–170). Thousand Oaks, CA: Sage.

Rockler, N. R. (1999). From magic bullets to shooting blanks: Reality, criticism, and *Beverly Hills, 90210. Western Journal of Communication,63,* 72–94 .

Rogers, E. M., & Kincaid, D. L. (1981). *Communication networks: Toward a new paradigm for research.* New York: Free Press.

Schudson, M. (1991). The sociology of news production revisited. In J. Curran & M. Gurevitch (Eds.), *Mass media and society* (pp. 141–159). London: Edward Arnold.

Stipp, H., Hill-Scott, K., & Dorr, A. (1987). Using social science to improve children's television. *Journal of Broadcasting and Electronic Media, 31,* 461–473.

Tuchman, G. (1974). Assembling a network talk show. In G. Tuchman (Ed.), *The TV establishment: Programming for power and profit.* Upper Saddle River, NJ: Prentice Hall.

Tuchman, G. (1978). *Making news: A study in the construction of reality.* New York: Free Press.

Turnstall, J. (1977). *The media are American.* New York: Columbia University Press.

Turow, J. (1991). A mass communication perspective on entertainment industries. In J. Curran & M. Gurevitch (Eds.), *Mass media and society* (pp. 160–177). London: Edward Arnold.

Turow, J. (1992). *Media systems in society: Understanding industries, strategies, and power.* New York: Longman.

Van Mannen, J. (1988). *Tales of the field: On writing ethnography.* Chicago: University of Chicago Press.

Weaver, D. (1997). Women as journalists. In P. Norris (Ed.), *Women, media and politics* (pp. 21–40). New York: Oxford University Press.

White, G. M. (1950). The gatekeeper: A case study in the selection of news. *Journalism Quarterly, 27,* 383–390.

Whiteside, T. (1981). *The blockbuster complex.* Middletown, CT: Wesleyan University Press.

Toward a Paradigm for Media Production Research: Behind the Scenes at *General Hospital*

Elana Levine

This essay points to the dearth of media production studies conducted under the cultural studies rubric and calls for cultural studies of media production that fulfill the models of cultural circulation theorized by Stuart Hall and Richard Johnson. It argues that such a perspective must include analyses of both economic and discursive power. It presents five factors shaping the production process of a U.S. broadcast television network soap opera as provisional categories for scholarly exploration, as well as offering an in-depth look at the soap opera production process and its cultural implications.

Cultural studies of media have made significant contributions to our understanding of the social and political implications of mediated representation and the contextually-dependent meanings made of media by their audience members. The study of media production, however, has received much less attention from cultural studies scholars. This gap in research is *not* intrinsic to the field's models of cultural circulation. In fact, models such as those provided by Stuart Hall (1980) and Richard Johnson (1986/87) explicitly call for attention to cultural production and for the integration of production analyses and studies of texts, audiences, and contextual influences. In this essay, I argue that cultural studies scholarship can be usefully expanded and nuanced both by taking on more production-centered research and by drawing upon the media production scholarship of those working under other theoretical and methodological perspectives (Cantor, 1971; Cantor & Cantor, 1992; Gans, 1979; Tuchman, 1979). The development of theoretically and methodologically rigorous and sophisticated approaches to production studies can offer cultural studies researchers, as well as communications scholars working within other paradigms, new insights and heretofore unrecognized connections between media production, media texts, media audiences, and the social contexts within which they circulate. To demonstrate the benefits of such a broadened strategy, I here analyze the production process of *General Hospital,* a U.S. broadcast television network daytime soap opera, and suggest ways in which production factors relate to questions about texts, audiences, and social contexts.

The cultural studies bias toward analyses of texts and audiences over production has existed to varying degrees throughout the field's studies of media. Inspired by Stuart Hall's (1980) encoding/decoding model, various cultural studies projects of the early and mid-1980s did include industrial analyses along with their presentations of audience readings. But because the most revelatory aspect of Hall's model was its recognition of contextually-influenced variability in audience decoding, much of the scholarship in its wake focused disproportionately on audiences over industries. Studies of soap operas, including those by Hobson (1982), Ang (1982), and Brown (1994), have exemplified this trend, examining such issues as the gendered address of the soap opera text, the rewards and costs of soap viewing, and the negotiations audiences make with the raced, classed, and gendered norms of both the soap world and the social world within which soap viewing occurs.

This text- and audience-centered bias has understandable origins in cultural studies history. Founded, at least in part, as a reaction against economically determinist interpretations of commercial culture, cultural studies has logically emphasized the resistive power of audience readings over the constraining forces of production. At the same time, an ongoing debate between political economy and cultural studies has kept production-centered scholarship largely in the hands of political economists, where it serves as a reliable marker of difference from their less classically marxist cousins.[1] With production-oriented scholarship practiced for so long by those more interested in the circulation of money than the circulation of meaning, it has been difficult for cultural studies scholars to connect production practices to questions of discourse and power (aside from economic power) that the field most frequently addresses. While cultural scholars readily admit that capital plays a chief role in commercial media production, they tend to stop their thinking there, failing to look for the roles of discourse, knowledge, and daily practice in cultural production.

In attempting to broaden the cultural studies approach to media along such lines, this essay offers a case study of soap opera production and thereby puts Richard Johnson's (1986/87) circuit of culture model into practice. Johnson's model poses a mutually influential relationship between production, texts, audiences, and contexts. To get at this relationship, he urges a two-pronged analysis of production. The examination of material means and the capitalist organization of labor are one prong, but Johnson suggests that production scholarship should also engage in exploring a range of *cultural* elements, such as rules of language and discourse and classed, raced, and gendered struggles over these rules as they occur within the production sphere (p. 55). Having advocated this two-pronged analysis of the production process itself, Johnson also suggests two means of relating production to the other spheres of cultural circulation. First, he argues for the examination of production moments as distinct and particular, as specific acts, not just general conditions. Secondly, and at first glance contradictorily, he argues for a *lack* of distinction between production, texts, and audiences. He urges, for example, careful analysis of the "productive" elements in cultural *consumption*, thereby retaining the cultural studies insis-

tence upon active audiencehood (pp. 57–58). Instead of negating his call for the distinctiveness of production, this second suggestion avoids economic determinism while remaining materially grounded in audience experience and production practice.

How the various aspects of the production process contribute to texts and shape possibilities for audience readings are the foci of the rest of this essay. I here categorize, describe, and analyze five major factors that shape a particular kind of cultural production, U.S. broadcast network television production. Even more narrowly, I examine the production of one particular television soap opera. The five categories I outline—production constraints, the production environment, production routines and practices, the production of characters and stories, and the role of the audience in production—have grown out of interviews and observations I conducted on-site at the *General Hospital* studio. I spent two weeks of August 1997 on the set, in the control booth, and around the offices of the show. I chose this particular program largely because I had spent the last sixteen years as a devoted viewer and thus had an immense backlog of information about its storylines, style, and personnel. I gained access by writing a letter to the executive producer, explaining my academic project and my interest in *General Hospital*. The coordinating producer called me months later and invited me to visit. The ease with which these arrangements were made illustrates the potential accessibility of commercial production to interested scholars. The ease with which a long-time fan was able to become a critical researcher and a critical researcher was able to turn back into a long-time (albeit somewhat more jaded) fan has helped me to analyze the similarities and differences between audience experience and the production world in ways unavailable to the more traditionally "objective" researcher. While the resulting analysis should offer useful insights to those interested in television soap opera, my aim here is also to provide a model for further research of television production practices, and possibly even for other forms of commercial culture.

Production Constraints

This first area of cultural production focuses on the production history and constraints of *General Hospital* in order to better understand the way the production process is shaped by its own background. While production as a whole is seen as a limiting or constraining factor in theories of media culture, I here illustrate some of the large-scale constraints that shape not only the resultant text, but the rest of the production process, as well. While mainly economic in origin, these large-scale constraints also have cultural impact. They influence the environment within which employees work and the routines and practices they follow, as subsequent categories will demonstrate. This section focuses on the large-scale constraints of ownership structure, the program's own production history, and the status of soaps in the contemporary television industry. While constraints can be imposed by the histories and specificities of the medium, the genre, the show, and the people who create it, as well, the three constraints I touch on here were particularly salient during my research trip and seem particularly formative to *General Hospital*.

While most U.S. broadcast network television programming is produced by independent production companies that license their products to networks for a fee, *General Hospital* is wholly owned and produced by ABC/Disney itself. While all of ABC's soap operas are network-owned, they are the only one of the three major networks with that arrangement. As Joe Montrone (personal communication, August 20, 1997), ABC executive in charge of daytime production for the west coast explained, "Technically, everybody on the show is an employee of ours, whether they're contracted, daily hire, or full staff with benefits. They all get an ABC paycheck." Because of this, there is intense network involvement at every level, with ABC's west coast executive in charge of daytime programming attending weekly story meetings between the executive producer and head writers, ABC Daytime publicity handling media relations, and ABC network offices in New York holding the budgetary purse strings. As a result, when network

policies forbid guns to be held directly to character's heads or restrict the explicitness of sex scenes, the show's staff sometimes feels creatively constrained. Yet the backing of ABC and its parent company, Disney, has benefitted the show by providing a degree of financial security less likely for a soap owned by an independent production company. According to one *GH* staff member who had previously worked at a soap not owned by its network, *General Hospital* has larger budgets for sets, wardrobe, and other such necessities than does this other soap because the production company owning the other show is unwilling (or unable) to spend as much, given its smaller size.

The show's own history also affects its production, setting it apart from even the other ABC-owned soaps. The enormous success of *General Hospital* in the early 1980s not only changed the soap opera industry, but earned *GH* a certain status with its network from which it still benefits today. According to coordinating producer Marty Vagts (personal communication, August 12, 1997):

> What we heard in those days was that ABC Daytime . . . was dropping 67% of the network profits. Right to the bottom line. We were clearing 67%. . . . And the pack was led by *General Hospital*. It was a giant cash cow. . . . And *General Hospital* had the ability to go to the well, the network well, and say that we needed a prop budget of X number of dollars or we needed a scenery [budget] of X number of dollars and we would get it. The other shows did not have that ability.

The material benefits the show received during the 1980s continue to pay off in substantial backstocks of wardrobe, sets, and props; in the contractually secured earnings of star performers; and in the current studio space itself, which was constructed specifically for the show in the late 1980s and is substantially larger than the studios for ABC's New York–based soaps. Such historically earned perks set *GH* apart from other soaps, allowing it an opulence that is increasingly rare in the financially strained soap industry of the 1990s and 2000s.

Soaps are no longer the "cash cows" they once

were for the broadcast networks. The soap opera audience, at least as it is measured by Nielsen, has shrunk drastically since the 1980s, a change attributable to the increasingly fractured television marketplace and the growing numbers of women in the workforce. Both of these trends have eroded the industry's formerly solid base of housewife viewers and have kept the genre from attracting newer, young audiences, who, 20 years ago, might have begun watching with their mothers or grandmothers (Parney & Mason, 2000, p. 13). Since the early 1990s, soaps have lost more than 20 million daily viewers, or about 25% of their total audience (Johnson, 1999, p. 1E; McFadden, 1999, p. D1). As a result, today's highest-rated soap hovers around a 7.2 rating while the lowest-rated ones survive on ratings in the 2.0 range. In August 1997, at the time of this study, *General Hospital* floated in the middle of this range, rating a 4.6, at least 6 to 8 million viewers less than in the early and mid-1980s. As a consequence, ABC and the other networks are making less and less money on these productions, resulting in decreased budgets for the shows. One specific result has been the virtual elimination of remote location shooting, a practice *GH* once engaged in up to seven times a year. Another has been a reduction in the show's clothing budget. According to costume designer Bob Miller (personal communication, August 20, 1997), "Our budget next year will probably be the same budget that we had in 1986. And clothing has probably tripled [in cost]."

As with any kind of constraints, the show's staff works to maintain a certain level of quality within these budgetary limits. For example, the wardrobe department sells used clothing to a specialized television and film resale shop, returning $70,000 to their budget from one year of these proceeds. Miller and co-designer Steve Howard make 3 or 4 wholesale shopping trips to New York design houses each year, purchasing high-fashion clothing a season in advance at much-reduced prices. Part of the reason they are able to do this is Miller's 10-year employment history with the show, a background that has provided him with a strong sense of the clothing many characters will need. But the

wardrobe department's ability to reduce costs in this way is also assisted by the fact that, "Our gals are in a size range from 0–2 to 6 mainly" (B. Miller, personal communication, August 20, 1997). The clothing they purchase will fit, or else can be slightly altered to fit, a number of different actresses. Even the body types of performers shape the production process, their similar, extremely small, sizes allowing advance, wholesale wardrobe shopping that saves money and establishes a high-fashion, designer look.

This variety of physical and fiscal production constraints illustrates just a few of the distinctive shaping factors that media scholars might consider in analyses of television production. Though production is frequently understood as limiting or constraining texts and readings, these examples point to the constraints within such constraints. The limits of commercial culture are more complicated than simple profit motivation or the exploitation of workers. They can affect studio size and body size, the scope of the on-screen world and the scope of femininity. An understanding of such factors not only informs the interpretation of texts, but helps us to comprehend the priorities of capitalism, the imperatives of the television medium, and the reasons behind the products the medium offers. De-naturalizing the television world in these ways is the first step to not only knowing that world, but understanding the particular ways its power is shaped and its money and meanings are circulated.

Production Environment

Large-scale industrial factors, and the specific production details through which they have an impact, necessarily constrain the rest of the production process, even the environment in which ABC's employees work. Exploring this environment can uncover relevant economic determinants, such as the role of labor unions in the production process. But it can also provide insight to the cultural issues at stake within production situations. Hierarchies of gender and institutional positioning, for example, operate in *General Hospital* production and affect production routines and practices, as well as the television narrative constructed through the work process. Two aspects of the production environment that best bring to light these economically and culturally shaped processes are the overall workplace milieu and the organizational hierarchy.

Though the *General Hospital* work environment functions like any other television production in many ways, it is significantly different, as is any soap, because of the continuous, unending nature of the work. With preemptions no more than one or two times a year and production running only two to three weeks in advance of airing, the staff must produce an entire episode each day of the week. Thus, every task must be executed as efficiently as possible. The *General Hospital* studio must constantly negotiate high-level efficiency, technological intricacy, and creative selectivity. The tenuous blend of a tight production schedule and the emotionally-charged material endemic to soap operas escalates the tensions already present in any dramatic production.

These contradictory working conditions play out in the weekly production meetings, held one week in advance of the actual production. Here, issues up for discussion range from the kind of undergarments needed for a scene where a character disrobes to the maneuverability of the cameras in a new set. The meetings are a carefully balanced combination of practical or technical details and creative speculation on character motivation and story progression. While the director, who coordinates discussion of his or her particular episode, tends to work on the side of the practical and technical, questions of character motivation inevitably intervene, such as how vitally important it is for the abandoned-at-the-altar Brenda, now in a precarious emotional state, to rid herself of all remnants of her wedding, even her dress. This character motivation then requires practical back-up, as in the decision to slightly re-design Brenda's wedding gown to cover the undergarments she will wear as she sheds the dress in her hurt and angry post-wedding scene.

These tensions and their practical repercus-sions continue in daily production. While the director must be concerned with technical details of camera placement, lighting, and sound, he or she is also responsible for imparting performance notes to the actors. While these duties are no different than those of any television director, the pace at which the soap opera director must work, shooting 25–30 "items," or scene segments, per day, makes concerted attention to all these factors impossible. As such, the line producer (a duty rotated among three of the show's producers) gives the director notes on all these aspects throughout the shoot, though she tends to comment most often on aesthetic and creative issues over technical ones. While performance notes often originate with the producer, they are usually relayed by the director or through the floor manager at the director's request. The director is also freed from attending too closely to performance because the show has an acting coach on staff who works with the actors off-set or confers with the line producer and director in the control booth.

The distinctions in duty between the director and the line producer operate as gendered distinctions as well as efficiency-motivated time-savers. While all of the *GH* line producers are women and most of the directors are men, the gendering of their duties is not determined by the workers who fill the roles. In the *GH* production world, bodily aesthetics, questions of emotion, and delicate personnel issues are distinguished from technical matters and time constraints. The socially feminized aspects of production remain the exclusive domain of the producers and other "artistic" departments, while the more masculinized aspects are less selectively assigned. While the show certainly employs technical specialists in areas such as lighting and editing, the producers can and do dictate decisions in these areas. But technical personnel, often including the directors, remain far removed from the producers' reign over the more feminized concerns. For example, when an actress known for wanting excessive rehearsal time slowed down a scene with questions about character motivation, the technical director discounted her concerns, commenting, "That's not our business; that's not what we're here for," to his cohorts in the control booth. The production staff surrounding him agreed, emphasizing their prioritization of efficiency above all else. The line producer handled the actress.

The divisions in duty and agenda are also matters of positioning within the organizational hierarchy. Because the socially feminized areas are handled by those highest in the institutional ranks, the feminine is distinguished, but not necessarily disempowered, in this production environment. The producers have authority over so many areas, and particularly more delicate ones like talent relations, because of their prominent institutional status. Gendered distinctions meet organizational ones and result in the validation of socially feminized concerns. As the exasperation with the actress's demands suggests, resistance to such concerns is also a factor, be it in the name of efficiency, technology, or masculinized disinterest (such as when crew members watched broadcast feeds of golf matches on their camera viewfinders during particularly time-consuming scenes). Certainly, such differences in duty and agenda result from the soap opera's dual imperatives of cost- and time-efficient production and emotionally intense, time-consuming drama. But the fact that these economically motivated constraints become distinguishable elements with gendered overtones suggests that the production environment is as culturally shaped as it is economically determined.

The production environment is also shaped by those personnel less visible in the daily work process. The writing staff is one of those nearly invisible influences. During my visit, it was clear that the current head writing team was temporary, as the show worked through complicated contractual negotiations to re-hire a former, well-regarded head writer. Because the current head writers, as well as their most recent predecessors, lived in New York, and the rest of the writing team worked out of their homes, the writers held a mysterious, and somewhat revered, place within the organizational hierarchy.[2] The writers, at least according to assistant David Goldschmid (personal communication, August 11, 1997), often feel isolated from the rest of the show and are hungry for information on how their work is received in-house. The only people in-house who have contact with them are the writers' assistants, the executive producer, and the network programming executive, illustrating the physical and conceptual isolation of soap writers from the activities on the set and in the control booth.

The executive producer and the network programming executive, who hold the highest positions within the organizational hierarchy, were also physically removed from daily production. Their removal was only partial, however, as they would watch the on-set action from monitors in their offices and frequently call the line producer in the control booth with comments and suggestions. While many employees, particularly actors, claimed that executive producer Wendy Riche has an "open door" policy and that they are always welcome to speak with her about storylines and their characters, her physical door was rarely open, her physical presence rarely visible, and any physical contact with her filtered through her two protective assistants. Yet the fact that I would often be referred to her to answer my questions illustrated her controlling involvement in nearly all aspects of the work process. The isolation of Riche and the writers from the rest of the production (and from me as researcher, for that matter) was telling of the institutional hierarchy and of the physical and experiential distance between high-level decision making and daily production. Those highest in the institutional hierarchy were most removed from daily production, though they controlled it in ways unobservable to most employees.

The production environment and its complicated tensions of efficiency and creativity, hands-on labor and removed, hierarchical control, demonstrate that struggles in soap opera production occur along cultural as well as economic lines, between duties and agendas distinguished and hierarchized by gender and institutional positioning, as well as by the larger-scale constraints of ownership structure, production history, and industrial trends. All of these constraints can affect the program they're meant to produce by determining the time and attention paid to performances, the allocation of budget to salaries or equipment or production elements like sets and wardrobe, and the shifts in meaning or emphasis as the production passes through the hands of network executives, executive producer, writers, line producers, actors, and production staff and crew. The environment within which these players are positioned is crucial to an understanding of their impact on the resulting program.

Production Routines and Practices

While the weekly production meeting and the role of the director in daily tapings are some of the most significant routines and practices at *General Hospital*, a host of other routines and practices inform the production process. Such practices continue to speak to the cost- and time-efficiency demanded of soap operas. But they affect the program in other ways, as well, influencing the kinds of stories that get told and the paths by which those stories proceed. I discuss the practices of writing and production scheduling here to illustrate the way daily work routines negotiate textual meaning, at times fracturing it and at times fixing it. The continuity practices running throughout this daily work are the main method employed to stabilize such meaning before the program is offered up to audiences.

The vast quantity of stories and scripts required of a daily, hour-long dramatic production makes even the creative practice of writing a routinized one. Head writers plan stories that outline writers break down into daily segments and scriptwriters translate into dialogue and action. Despite this fractured system, continuity checks are built in to encourage consistency. Scriptwriters are given detailed, scene-by-scene summaries of each episode's happenings in the script outlines. Writers' meetings and producer notes help to hammer out questions about character motivation and plot convolutions. And continuity questions are asked and answered throughout each production day. Script continuity thus serves as the first line of defense against unstable meaning, against holes in the fictional world.

In addition to battling the writing system itself, continuity must fight against the idiosyncrasies of the daily scriptwriters, each of whom has his or her own character biases. As scriptwriter Elizabeth Korte (personal communication, August 18, 1997) admitted:

> I have a real affinity for dark, driven, really scarred, very screwed up characters. . . . However, you can't give good characters short shrift. You have to make them interesting, too . . . you have to try hard to guard against having every single scene be about the characters that you like.

Yet character consistency and balance does not happen just by writers trying very hard to be fair. Writers sometimes find alternative ways to write for "their" characters. As writer's assistant David Goldschmid (personal communication, August 11, 1997) explained:

> I've seen examples where certain writers of ours, they would love characters so much that they would trade scenes with other writers. [Say] you have writer A and writer B. Writer A will say, "Oh, I'd KILL for the Jason/Robin stuff in your day." And writer B will go, "Well, that was kind of giving me some problems. If you do those scenes for my script, can I pick up your Kevin/Lucy scenes?"

Such internal negotiation of scenes is part of the process by which *General Hospital* writing practices work to stabilize textual meaning. Jason and Robin are identifiable characters with consistent voices because of such trades and because the layering of writers builds character and story continuity checks into the writing process.

Despite such checks, however, continuity slips inevitably occur. The writing staff must sometimes make leaps of logic to keep the plots coherent. Elizabeth Korte (personal communication, August 18, 1997), who handles script continuity as well as writing scripts, explains a slip that occurred when the character of Robin said she was leaving for Paris the next day and actually left that evening:

> There's this thing called justifying where it's like, maybe we can believe that it was so traumatic that she broke up with Jason that she left earlier. Or we do this;

this is our favorite thing that we do. It's the yellow sticky. This is a willing suspension of disbelief ticket and sometimes when I'm just asking people to believe, I'm like, take a yellow sticky. It's like, that's what you get, we're doing it, it's gotta be that way.

The willing suspension of disbelief operates as a substitute for continuity when production efficiency disallows re-writes or re-takes of problematic scenes. The writing team, along with the audience, agrees to suspend their doubts about situational particularities and even the fictional status of the world itself in favor of the character and relationship motivations that drive the narratives in the first place. In both the successes and failures of continuity within the writing process, textual meaning is fractured and fixed, disputed and conceded, all before the script is even produced.

The production schedule also opens up multiple opportunities for fractured meanings and confused plots. While the ideal situation is the full production of an entire episode in one day, this is rarely the case at *General Hospital*. Because only a limited number and configuration of sets can fit on the stage on any given day, and because the cast of approximately 35 contract players has a myriad of personal and professional scheduling conflicts, each day's production schedule is organized by grouping together related scenes, not by proceeding in a linear fashion through an episode. Coordinating producer Marty Vagts and his assistants try to schedule as much of one day's episode per shooting day as possible, but inevitably plan pre- and post-tapings of other episodes because of cast or set conflicts. The implications of this production schedule are numerous. Pre- and post-taped shows mean higher fees for the director, per Director's Guild rules. The long production days (rarely less than 10 hours) mean overtime pay for the unionized crew. Actors are rarely present en masse, instead working on set for only portions of the day. The makeup and hair room oscillates between periods of intense activity and no activity. Meanwhile, actors (and the producers who guide them) must conceptually shift their focus between scenes that are not necessarily taped in chronological order, adjusting their responses and emotional ex-

pression according to the character's place in the story, a place they have not yet worked through in their performance.

Like the writing process, the production schedule requires continuity checks to secure the potentially errant meanings it might produce. Wardrobe, hair, and makeup constantly take Polaroid photos of the actors, along with extensive notes on their appearance, so that they can replicate their looks on other shooting days which are supposed to be the same story day in the on-screen world. The production office provides an item-by-item breakdown for every shooting day, noting special props, wardrobe and makeup, or special effects and unusual technological requirements. The production continuity person then carefully tracks such details throughout the day and across days, making sure, for example, that performers carry their purses in and out of rooms and that the degree of rainfall is consistent across concurrent scenes on different sets. While such details seem trivial, they occupy an immense amount of time for many different workers on the *General Hospital* set and ultimately create coherent textual meaning out of a fractured work process.

While even the most effective of continuity practices can never close down the meanings that audiences might make of a given program, they do shape those potential meanings in foundational ways. The negotiations between writing practices, production scheduling, and continuity work to make the fictional world seamless and congruous. Routinized production practices allow for the routinized reliability of the soap opera's daily textual installments, where consistent character emotions, homes, and hairstyles provide justification for the on-screen world's believability, despite its extreme plots or the extraordinary attractiveness of its inhabitants. The preoccupation with details and the persistence of assembly-line routines are in some ways necessitated by the textual form, in some ways by audience expectations, and in some ways by economic imperatives. Their effect on the text and on potential readings of it is to offer a provisional baseline of meaning on which characters and stories are built.

Production of Characters and Stories

The meanings audiences make of *General Hospital* proceed beyond a baseline of plot coherence and character consistency. They operate on more complex levels of story and character, as well, in both the world of production and that of audience consumption. The ways that characters and stories, in all their ideological intricacy, are produced involves nearly all *GH* employees to some extent. Most salient, however, are the writers, actors, and production departments that bring the characters to life and the stories to fruition. Each contributes to the characters and stories, bringing together layers of narrative significance that can be decoded in a range of ways, depending on which layers are deemed significant in any given moment of reception.

Since soap opera characters are first created through writing, the way that writers conceive of characters is an influential aspect of their generation. Scriptwriter Elizabeth Korte (personal communication, August 18, 1997) described her characters as living beings, "[Sonny] loved Brenda, but she was horrible for him. And he honored Lily but did not love her. . . . She was in every way the perfect wife for him. He wasn't unstable around her. . . . She was like human lithium. She calmed him down." But Korte also conceived of her characters as archetypes, explaining how this particular love triangle was a retelling of such classic stories as *The Godfather* and *Gone with the Wind:*

> Scarlett O'Hara, that's Brenda, is sure she's in love with Ashley Wilkes. Which, I know Sonny doesn't seem like Ashley, but if you really take a step back from it, he is, he's a person who lives according to this archaic code. . . . He's gonna be a gentleman, he's gonna be a mobster, even if the world he was raised to be in is no longer there.

Characters like Sonny and Brenda are constructed, then, not just in the minds of their creators, but through cultural constructions of tragic sagas and tortured romance. While the textual analyst or the lay audience member might make such connections by watching the program, the fact that the program's writers also view their characters in these ways suggests that similar meaning-making processes occur during stages of production, reception, and perhaps even critical analysis. The original location of the intertextual connection between Sonny and Brenda, Ashley and Scarlett, is insignificant. What does matter is that cultural archetypes consciously operate within production decisions about characters, that production processes are invested in and influenced by the surrounding culture.

Industry practice also involves itself with the surrounding culture in actors' conceptions of their characters. The fact that actors tend to discuss their characters as living beings, often as beings with experiences parallel to their own, is a telling reminder of the fluidity between lived experience and cultural production. Twenty-year cast member Jackie Zeman [personal communication, August 14, 1997) collapsed her own life, her conception of her audience's lives, and her character's life when commenting on audience reaction to her character, Bobbie:

> The first half of your life is one way and you finally hit 40 and now what becomes normal to you was never normal; it's a big deal. And so just having a husband and a child and a house and a home and a job and a family and a husband that's not fooling around or lying or drinking or taking drugs or doing any bad things, this is like, oh my God, I made it.

Zeman expressed pride in her own family life elsewhere in this discussion, assumed a similar interest in family experience for her audience, and applied both to her understanding of Bobbie's life and the audience's response to it. Such belief in the authenticity of the character's tribulations helps many of the show's actors to sustain their characters for years on end. According to *GH* acting coach John Homa, (personal communication, August 20, 1997) one of the primary difficulties of acting is that, "You as an actor must suspend your disbelief. You've got to quit bitchin' and moanin' about this being real or not real and just make it work." Much like the suspension of disbelief that the writers employ to make sometimes far-fetched events cohere, so too do soap actors suspend their disbelief, justify actions through reference to character motivation, and call on their own knowledge of human relationships to make sense of narrative events.

But neither writers nor actors solely determine the construction of characters and stories. The various production departments—Set Design & Decoration, Makeup & Hair, Wardrobe and Lighting, for instance—also produce characters and stories. For example, Sonny and Brenda's last romantic dinner before their wedding (a wedding the production staff knew would never take place) was a long and drawn out series of "items" because of the intense attention to detail during them. Not only were the actors dressed in formal-wear and elaborately coiffed, but senior supervising producer Julie Carruthers halted taping while Makeup matched Sonny's facial bruise to its previous incarnation and Props arranged the candles and table settings to look opulent, but not cluttered. Pink angels and screens were placed on the lights and the studio air conditioning was turned off because it kept putting out the candles around the set. When discussing the following day why the previous one had run so late, Carruthers (remarks made on set, August 21, 1997) explained how important it was to take the extra time to relight and perfect the romantic scene because, "It was their dance . . ." Her justification for the extra work demonstrates how production details not only support, but help to construct, narrative significance. Because this scene was lit a certain way, because special care was taken with makeup and wardrobe, because the staff used valuable production time to perfect one scene of many scheduled for that day, this scene became more important to everyone in the studio. It also became more distinctive within the flow of its episode, since it would look different than most other scenes. Because it featured the couple's final romantic moments before Sonny's last minute decision to run away by himself to save Brenda's life, it merited this extra time and attention. The meaning of the scene was constructed through writing

and performance, but also through production details. This major story and character moment was constructed as a moment about romance and poignancy (as opposed to, say, sex and excitement) because of these details.

While the production of characters and stories seems more obviously meaning-laden than other aspects of production, exploring the ways in which character and story construction *generate* meaning and significance can help to demystify the creative process. This demystification can then help to expose cultural products and their messages as constructed as opposed to real or natural. Studying the production of Sonny and Brenda's final moments in this way can allow media scholars to point out how culturally constructed ideals of love and romance are perpetuated, in this case through intertextual associations, careful attention to visual details, and extended preparation time. To understand the way characters and stories are specifically created is to understand how cultural images and narratives hold and, more significantly, execute their power.

The Audience in Production

Lurking throughout all aspects of production is the audience, the industry's conception of the audience, the processes of audience decoding that both precede and follow any given *General Hospital* production day, and the actual audience around whom so much scholarship has centered. Though the audience figures implicitly into many aspects of production, such as in continuity efforts to stabilize textual meaning, the audience can also play an explicit role at certain moments. One such moment is the handling of audience response by the production team. Another way in which audience-hood figures into production evokes Richard Johnson's (1986/87) perspective on the lack of distinction between production, text, and audience. Processes of audience meaning-making, such as speculating about future storylines and tracking character knowledge of potentially explosive information, also occur during the production process, and suggest new ways of thinking about production itself. Finally, the meaning of production, audience, and critical research, as discussed here in my relationship to *General Hospital,* can offer new insights to the role of the audience—and the media scholar—in cultural production.

The way *General Hospital* handles its audience response is telling of the limited presence of actual audience members in the production process. The show's production team fits audience responses into an established system that allows for efficient categorization and acknowledgment. When fan mail arrives at the show, those letters addressed to actors are tallied and sent unopened to the actors themselves. Those letters addressed to the writers go to one of the writer's assistants, who reads them and summarizes their responses in a monthly report that includes selected quotes from letters encapsulating what many people are saying. A large chunk of the mail is addressed to the producers or to the show itself. This mail is opened and tallied by the student interns, who register whether the response is negative (if the writer says he or she will stop watching the show), positive (even if they have specific criticisms, as long as they don't threaten to stop watching), or requires a response (to which the interns send one of a series of form letters). The writers' mail report and all the numerical tallies go to the assistant to the executive producer, who compiles them into a monthly report for the producers, head writers, and network executives. The interns are additionally responsible for summarizing the phone messages left daily on a viewer response voice-mail box. The assistant to the executive producer types and distributes these summaries to the producers and head writers. Lastly, the network sends regular summaries and choice selections from postings in the ABC Daytime Online bulletin boards about the shows. The network also conducts viewer focus groups a few times a year to get additional audience feedback.

While the system in place to handle audience response is thorough and efficient, it does not really account for most viewers' perspectives, as the letters must be neatly classified into positive or negative categories and the actual words of audience members are only rarely seen by anyone higher in the chain of command than a writer's assistant. Additionally, the writing and production schedule requires storylines to be mapped out several months in advance, so viewer responses to just-aired episodes can have little direct or immediate impact. Still, the network and the producers are interested enough in audience response that they have, on rare occasion, adjusted storylines accordingly. Predictably, the more established actors were less invested in audience response than were the newer performers and the producers were more interested in viewer feedback than were other employees. Overall, the specific opinions and perspectives of audience members were valued less than their general responsiveness. For example, the production staff appreciated the fan war being waged between those viewers wanting Brenda to be paired with Sonny versus those wanting her paired with Jax more for its vociferousness than for the specific opinions offered on the dysfunction or strength of the relationships.

But audiencehood played another, less expected, role in production, when meaning-making processes usually associated with reception were enacted by production personnel. Crew members would discuss storylines, expressing disgust with devious characters or adoration for blossoming romances as would any other viewer, despite the fact that actors were playing out those storylines in front of their very eyes. The writing staff spoke as passionately about characters and their motivations as do soap fans chatting with their peers on the Internet. As Elizabeth Korte (personal communication, August 18, 1997) in script continuity explained, her job requires her to keep track of the different characters' points of view, to know what they've done, seen, or said previously. It has been well-documented in studies such as Brown's (1994) and Allen's (1985) that audience members engage in the same kind of tracking, eagerly awaiting the revelation of some vital piece of information a character does not yet know.

The fact that show employees frequently have

as little information about future storylines as do audiences assists in this sort of audience-like speculation. In one between-takes conversation between actresses, for example, the two women debated who would turn out to be the father of Carly's baby. Like any audience members uninformed about future storyline, they weighed the ramifications of A. J. being the father instead of Tony. (Their consensus: It would most likely be A. J. because of all the future storylines with his family it would open up.) While a plethora of storylines serves production interests, it also serves audience interests, and rumination about storyline possibilities is a common feature of audience discourse on soaps (Ang, 1982; Hobson, 1982). The actresses' lack of power to control the parentage of Carly's baby, given their position within the *General Hospital* institutional hierarchy, makes their speculation and prediction more like audience activity than like producer machination. While such audience activity can be understood as "producerly" for its actions on the text, such production activity can be understood as "audience-like" for its refusal to accept textual meaning as pre-determined.

The third role of the audience in production is more accurately that of the audience in the *study* of production. If media scholars hope to research Johnson's circuit of culture (1986/87), we need to make room for ourselves within that circuit. Particularly if we choose to engage in on-site production research, media scholars should consider the role of the researcher in relation to production (much as cultural scholars have done in considering the role of the researcher in relation to audiences under study). When the media researcher is also an audience member (as most are likely to be, whether as fan or as critic), audiencehood enters into production through an otherwise non-existent channel. During my trip to *GH*, I functioned as researcher by interviewing people, sitting in on meetings, observing my surroundings, and taking notes. But I was also an audience member, coming close to tears while watching the taping of a good-bye scene between Sonny and his father and momentarily thrilling at sitting at the bar of Luke's blues club. I'm

less certain about how my presence affected the production process itself, though having a stranger sitting in the corner of the control booth or jotting on a notepad on set each day may have subtly shifted the work process.

My interpretations of the processes I observed have also undoubtedly been shaped by my long-time viewership. For example, I easily chatted with cast members in their dressing rooms due, at least in part, to my intense familiarity with their on-screen selves. Though I knew I was a stranger to them, they felt like old friends to me. Instead of challenging my researcher's professionalism or blocking my objectivity, my audiencehood provided me with a perspective on the production process potentially more valuable than that of a disinterested observer. My view of the production process was the audience view as well as the researcher's view. Since audiencehood has been historically privileged within cultural studies of media, exploring the role of the audience in production, even literally *within* the production environment as a researcher/audience member, helps to keep production scholarship from losing sight of the other spheres of cultural circulation. Analyzing the distinctiveness of production, both economically and culturally, while continuing to explore the continuities among production, texts, audiences, and social contexts, can keep cultural studies true to its theoretical models while moving the field beyond its text- and audience-centered focus.

Conclusion

These five categories for analyzing the television production process suggest one of many potential templates for organizing industry-centered scholarship. Certainly other forms of television programming, other television systems, other media, and other temporal and spatial contexts could lead to other categorizations. Neither the categories nor their implications can serve as universal truths about all cultural production or all U.S. broadcast network television production or even all soap opera production. Hopefully, however, they demonstrate the significance of production-centered scholarship to a broad understanding of the entire cultural circulation process.

Putting Johnson's model of cultural circulation into practice involves recognizing that production contains both economic and cultural elements, that it is both a distinctive process and a process intertwined with other spheres of cultural circulation. Conducting analyses of cultural production along these lines, as well as drawing on the production scholarship executed by political economists, mass communications analysts, and sociologists, can help cultural studies scholarship gain a fuller picture of the intricacies of cultural circulation. In addition, those scholars working in paradigms other than cultural studies might find new insights to the production processes they are already investigating. As a range of media communication scholars have realized and continue to realize, production-centered research can demonstrate the links between commercial media's capitalist base and their ideological messages. In addition, delineating specific production practices can alert media activists to vulnerable points at which to intervene and can assist scholars in unmasking the constructed naturalness of media images. If media researchers seek to understand the paths through which media products come to exist, if they seek to understand the constraints that shape the products available to us, then this sort of rigorous, layered attention to production processes is vital.

Notes

1. The 1995 *Critical Studies in Mass Communication* colloquy on the debate between political economy and cultural studies exemplifies this trend.

2. The scattering of soap opera writers outside the confines of the studio and even the city of production challenges traditional notions of authorship, even of television authorship, which is acknowledged to be less univocal than most. The work processes of writers, so vital to soap opera production and yet so removed from the production space, are significant elements of the production process that deserve further exploration and analysis.

References

Allen, R. (1985). *Speaking of soap operas.* Chapel Hill and London: The University of North Carolina Press.

Ang, I. (1982). *Watching* Dallas: *Soap opera and the melodramatic imagination.* (D. Couling, Trans.). London: Methuen.

Brown, M. E. (1994). *Soap opera and women's talk: The pleasures of resistance.* Thousand Oaks, California: Sage.

Cantor, M. (1971). *The Hollywood TV producer: His work and his audience.* New Brunswick: Transaction Books.

Cantor, M., & Cantor, J. (1992). *Prime time television: Content and control* (2nd ed.) Newbury Park, CA: Sage.

Colloquy. (1995). *Critical studies in Mass Communication, 12,* 60–100.

Gans, H. (1979). *Deciding what's news.* New York: Random House.

Hall, S. (1980). Encoding/decoding. In S. Hall, D. Hobson, A. Lowe, & P. Willis (Eds.), *Culture, media, language: Working papers in cultural studies 1972–1979* (pp. 128–138). London: Hutchinson.

Hobson, D. (1982). *Crossroads: The drama of a soap opera.* London: Methuen.

Johnson, K. V. (1999). Soaps in a lather. *USA Today,* 2 July, 1E.

Johnson, R. (1986/87). What is cultural studies anyway? *Social text, 16,* 33–80.

McFadden, K. (1999 24 June). Another era leaves *Another World* kaput. *The Seattle Times,* p. D1.

Parney, L., & Mason, M. S. (2000 7 July). Selling soaps. *The Christian Science Monitor,* p. 13.

Tuchman, G. (1979). *Making news.* New York: Free Press.

Ideological
Criticism
CHAPTER 11

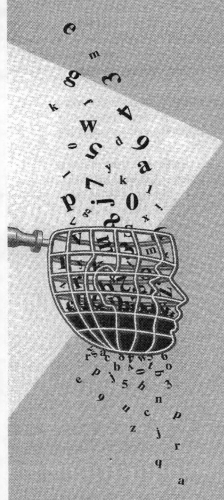

Chapter Outline

Television is the prime circulator of meanings and pleasures in our society. Meanings always have an ideological dimension; they are never neutral but always serve the interests of some social groups better than others. Television is polysemic—that is, it has multiple meanings. The critic should trace which meanings are preferred by the text; these will normally be those meanings which serve the dominant ideology. . . . Ideology works to naturalize the meanings of the social world that serve the interests of the dominant; it works to create *common* sense out of the *dominant* sense. . . . and it has to work constantly in order to establish and maintain this common sense against the social experiences of the subordinate which constantly contradict it. . . . The TV critic should be able to hypothesize the meanings that differently socially situated viewers may make and relate them to the preferred ones . . . [because] making sense of a text is an activity that is precisely parallel to making sense of social experience.
—J. Fiske (1991, pp. 445–448)

Ideological criticism, which defines *ideology* as "meaning in the service of power," investigates the ways in which "meaning mobilized by symbolic forms" serves "the vested interests of the prevalent power structure and its privileged beneficiaries" (Thompson, 1990, p. 7; Real, 1989, p. 53). Ideology is not the hidden message in a television program; rather, it is the systematic representation of ideas and beliefs that members of a society learn to regard as the normal or natural way things are—a representation that is reflected in media texts and societal institutions. Ideological criticism, then, examines the ways in which texts reflect the dominant ideas, agendas, and policies of the society in which they are produced and consumed.

As Burke (1969a, 1969b), Frye (1957, esp. p. 83), Berger (1995), and others have pointed out, ideological messages are transmitted through both content and form. In his critique of TV game shows, for example, John Fiske (1983) demonstrates how both the form and the content of game shows naturalize the "dominant ideology" of patriarchal capitalist democratic societies:

One thing quiz games provide is a face-saver; they can symbolically restore the self-image and self-esteem of the subordinate via an equivalent of the [educational and cultural] system that destroyed them in the first place. They play an important role in the educational hegemony in that their compensation for, or even denial of, the disadvantages of educational failure is achieved by reproducing and thus validating the system that produced that failure in the first place. . . . In any society knowledge (or education) equates with social power. . . . TV quizzes finally, then, reproduce the balance of social power. . . . Unequal cultural capacity, unequal cultural consumption, and unequal cultural capital all justify social inequality; the people who have earned cultural capital are, simply, more clever, more discriminating and of higher worth. Quiz shows are a symbolic enactment of this system that demonstrate it working and that give the subordinate classes a superficial taste of the rewards of the system and thus buy their loyalty to an economic and educational system that permanently disadvantages them. (1991, pp. 456–458)

Like game shows, other television texts also symbolically enact and "naturalize" various aspects of the dominant ideology. What is involved in ideological criticism is bringing both textual and social knowledge and experience to bear on the analysis of a television text (or a set of texts) in order to understand how that text is constructed and read in terms of lived social experiences and the dominant ideas, agendas, and politics of our society.

The Development of Ideological Theory and Criticism

The term *ideological* was coined by French philosopher Destutt de Tracy in 1796 to describe his new proposed science of ideas and sensations. This definition changed after a series of events in Europe[1] led to Napoleon's attacks on ideology and the people—the *idéologues*—who proposed ideas that he opposed. From its initial meaning as the science of ideas, *ideology* by the 1800s had come to refer to the ideas themselves, specifically, to "a body of ideas which are alleged to be erroneous and divorced from the practical realities of political life" (Thompson, 1990, p. 32). This is the notion of ideology that underlies Karl Marx's political economic theory.

Classical Marxist Political-Economic Theory

Karl Marx (1818–1883) was an economist whose analysis of work and society led him to develop a theory of the relationship between a society's economic structure and its social institutions and practices. Although classical Marxist criticism generally has gone the way of the Model T car, subsequent reconceptualizations and extensions of aspects of Marx's political economic theory have shaped much of contemporary ideological and cultural studies criticism.[2]

Classical Marxist theory argued that the system of economic relationships in a society (the base) was the single most powerful and fundamental shaper of all other social structures and institutions (the superstructure) in a society. Those individuals who controlled or owned the means of production (i.e., the bourgeoisie or power elite) become the ruling class.[3] Classical Marxist theory viewed ideology—the set of ideas shared by the ruling political and economic class—as "false consciousness" because such ideas seductively position ordinary members of society who are not part of the society's power elite to accept as normal and natural those ideas and institutions that maintain the subordinate status of ordinary people and the existing political and economic inequities. At the same time, the dominant ideology seduces members of the ruling classes into believing that their privileged social positions are divinely ordained and deserved.

In the case of television, a Marxist perspective would lead one to expect that television, because it is part of the vast industrial complex owned by wealthy individuals and corporations, would reflect primarily the ideas, beliefs, and values that serve the interests of these economic elites and would function to maintain the existing power structure with only minimal superficial changes. Classical Marxist

theory sees individuals who accept the beliefs and values of the most powerful social classes as their own as dupes of the dominant ideology and as participating in
their own oppression (Thompson, 1990; see also McChesney, 2000; Williams,
1979). Because not everyone accepts the existence of economic, educational, and
social resource inequities as the normal, natural way things *should* be, Marx theorized that the fundamental conflict in all societies would be the social class conflict between the haves and the have-nots. "Society as a whole," he wrote, "is more
and more splitting up into two great hostile camps, into two great classes directly
facing each other—bourgeoisie and proletariat" (1964, p. 201).

Neo-Marxist Critical Theory

Marx's concept of ideology has influenced the generations of critical theorists
writing after him. In this section of the chapter, we discuss several of the most influential refinements in the study of ideology for mass media: those of the Frankfurt School, Louis Althusser, Antonio Gramsci, and Michel Foucault.

The Frankfurt School   Neo-Marxist theory developed in the United States when
the rise of Nazism forced a group of German intellectuals to leave the Institute for
Social Research (called the Frankfurt School because of its location in Frankfurt,
Germany) in the 1930s. They fled Germany and immigrated to the United States,
where they continued their reconceptualizations of classical Marxism and tried to
explain such social and political phenomena as the rise of fascism, the dearth of
worker revolutions, and the role of the mass media—the "culture industry," as they
called it—in modern societies. The theoretical and critical work of members of
the Frankfurt School (including Theodor W. Adorno, Herbert Marcuse, Max
Horkheimer, Leo Lowenthal, Erich Fromm, and Walter Benjamin) was heavily
shaped by their own experiences with the rise of nazism and fascism in Europe
during the period between World Wars I and II. Their analytical efforts, which
came to be known as *Critical Theory,* helped focus scholarly attention on the role
of the mass media in modern societies and provided the foundation for contemporary ideological criticism of the mass media (Thompson, 1990, pp. 75–76).

Frankfurt School critics, and other scholars, have pointed out several limitations of classical Marxist theory. For example, they note that classical Marxism did
not acknowledge or account for modes of domination other than class (e.g., it ignored race and gender) and failed to explain why most European people did not
rise up in protest against fascism but instead capitulated to it. Also, they pointed
out that classical Marxism failed to explain how people might derive pleasure from
cultural productions such as television that in fact reinforce their subordinate social situations. So although classical Marxism provided an explanation for the
alienation felt by working-class members of a society, this theory has been subject
to considerable critique and revision (see Kellner, 1995; Stevenson, 1995, p. 16).

Overdetermination and Interpellation in Althusser   Louis Althusser, a French
neo-Marxist philosopher, revised classical Marxist theory by replacing Marx's
base-superstructure theory with a theory of overdetermination. In contrast to the

classical Marxist view that the economic base of society entirely controlled the superstructure—the cultural, social, and political institutions, activities, and practices of the society—Althusser's theory (1970) posited a more elastic relationship between economics and other social institutions. He argued that although the superstructure is related to the economic base, it is relatively autonomous.

Althusser proposed that we think of a collectivity or a society as a social formation[4] consisting of two sets of institutional structures and practices: *repressive state apparatuses* (RSAs) and *ideological state apparatuses* (ISAs). RSAs, which include the government with its armies, police, courts, and prisons, work on behalf of the dominant classes and use physical power and violence to oppress and maintain the economic and social power hierarchy in society. One example was the April 1914 Ludlow, Colorado massacre.[5] ISAs, which include religion, education, families, political parties, and media, reproduce the dominant ideology and its economic and social power relationships through systems of representation. Interestingly, the antipathy toward the Rockefellers that resulted from the Ludlow massacre led to the development of a campaign to replace the image of this family as rapacious murderers of women and children with one of benevolence and beneficence, and to the birth of modern public relations (see Ewen, 1996).

In Althusser's theory, ideology is a system of representation that functions through *interpellation,* that is, through social practices and structures that address or "hail" us as individuals and in so doing construct social identities for us. Consider, for example, Bud Light advertisements on TV that invite us to identify with the attractive, middle-class, physically fit young adults (men and women) in the ads whose recreational pursuits include playing friendly, often co-ed games of volleyball and basketball, and, of course, drinking beer. These symbolic representations not only naturalize the drinking of beer (see Hundley's essay in Chapter 14) but they also "hail" us to a yuppie lifestyle.

Although the influence of Althusser's theoretical notions about social formations can be seen in the work of later ideological theorists and critics such as Stuart Hall, Ernesto Laclau, and Chantal Mouffe, these critics also have called attention to some limitations of Althusser's thinking. They note, for example, that Althusser's view of how ISAs work is highly functionalist and reductionist. Althusser's work, they point out, raises additional questions—for example: "If our social identities are formed through these pervasive ideological agencies, how can we ever recognize their ideological nature? How can we ever step outside of the dominant ideology to deconstruct it?" Moreover, these later theorists regarded Althusser's answer—that scientific rigor can unmask ideology and its workings—as elitist and unworkable (see Barker, 2000; Hall, 1982, 1984, 1992).

Gramsci's Theory of Hegemony   Social thinker, working journalist, and trade union activist Antonio Gramsci developed an explanation of how ideology works that is widely used in critical media studies today. While he was in prison in Italy in the late 1920s and 1930s for supporting the failed workers' revolution against fascism, Gramsci reconceptualized Marx's notions of underlying economic and structural conditions. Historically, Gramsci's work was written before Althusser's, but it was not discovered, translated, and widely circulated until the early 1970s.

Since then, Gramsci's work has greatly shaped contemporary ideological criticism, in large part because he provided an answer to the problems Althusser's work left unanswered.

Gramsci's theory of hegemony developed out of his own political activism and his subsequent efforts to explain why the working classes in Italy had not revolted en masse but instead had capitulated to fascism. His answer was *hegemony.* As Gramsci explained, in any society, the ruling classes can use two processes to secure the consent of the rest of society: coercion and hegemony:

> The normal exercise of hegemony on the classical terrain of the parliamentary regime is characterized by the combination of force and consent, which balance each other reciprocally without force predominating excessively over consent. Indeed, the attempt is always to ensure that force would appear to be based on the consent of the majority expressed by the so-called organs of public opinion—newspapers and associations. (Gramsci, 1971, p. 80)

As we noted earlier, *ideology* refers to those "ideas, meanings and practices which, while they purport to be universal truths, are maps of meaning which support the power of particular social groups" (Barker, 2000, p. 59). Gramsci saw ideology as an intrinsic part of our everyday, material lives—as our commonsense understanding of social rules and roles and social conduct (Gramsci, 1971, p. 349). As John Fiske (1991a) cogently put it, ideology works "to create common sense out of dominant sense" (p. 447). Fiske's (1983, 1991b) study of game shows illustrates how this occurs. Game shows, Fiske explains, function ideologically as a "thirty-minute miniaturization of a social process that is crucial in a society that is class structured and socially mobile and that holds the doctrine of equal opportunity" (1991b, p. 448). They do this by removing wealth from the economic and class system and explaining economic and social inequality as a function of luck. By believing that they have a chance at that luck, game show contestants (and vicariously the audiences as well) "are led to consent to and perpetuate a system that inevitably, necessarily, disadvantages them" (pp. 452–453). In terms of Gramsci's notion of hegemony, then, game shows provide a vivid illustration of "that process whereby the subordinate are led to consent to the system that subordinates them" (Fiske, 1987, p. 40). However, ideology "has to work constantly in order to establish and maintain this common sense against the social experiences of the subordinate which consistently contradict it" (Fiske, 1991b, p. 447).

Critics study and understand hegemony by looking at the strategies through which the most powerful social groups (constituted in terms of class, sexuality, gender, race, ethnicity, or nationality) strive to maintain as the dominant "common sense" of the entire society those beliefs, values, and attitudes that privilege them and their interests. And one of the most important vehicles through which hegemony works is discourse, a structuralist concept that Michel Foucault's work extended and that television critics use in semiotic/structural, cultural studies, and ideological criticism.

Foucault, Specific Discourses, and Power/Knowledge   *Discourse* is a term used in many disciplines and in several different ways within the discipline of communication studies (and even in this book). In ideological criticism, *discourse* is "an ideological way of thinking about and representing an important topic area in social experience" (Fiske, 1991b, p. 447; see also O'Sullivan, Hartley, Saunders, Montgomery, & Fiske, 1994, pp. 92–94). French poststructuralist theorist Michel Foucault expanded the theoretical concept of discourse in his analysis of the role of specific, historically situated discourses (e.g., madness, sexuality, criminality) and discursive formations (see endnote 4) in defining fields of power/knowledge. His work has been a highly influential force in ideological as well as semiotic/ structural and cultural studies criticism.

Ideological criticism takes Foucault's concept of discourse as "an ideological way of thinking about and representing an important topic area in social experience" (Fiske, 1991a, p. 447) and uses it to study the ways in which the specific discourses (e.g., the discourse of democratic politics, the discourse of capitalist economics, the discourse of hegemonic masculinity) that structure texts present the dominant sense as the "common sense" and articulate or knit together elements of those various discourses. In doing so, though, critics must always remember that discourses are socially circulated meanings about an important topic, and as O'Sullivan et al. (1994) point out, "though discourses may be traced in texts, and though texts may be the means by which discursive knowledges are circulated, established or suppressed, discourses are not themselves textual" (p. 94). In this understanding of discourse, ways of talking become ways—limited ways—of thinking and, hence, narrowed bases for action.

Ideological Criticism and Cultural Studies Criticism

Ideological criticism and some types of cultural criticism (which we discuss in Chapter 14), especially cultural studies criticism, share a common concern with ideology and the workings of hegemony. However, these critical approaches typically differ somewhat in focus. Historically, ideological criticism has tended to focus on domination—on the disempowering and deleterious effects of ideology and hegemony. Cultural criticism and cultural studies criticism, on the other hand, often focus as much or more on strategies that individuals can use to resist ideological domination.

Cultural theory, as developed by Hall (1977, 1980, 1982, 1992), Fiske (1983, 1987, 1994a), and others, shares with ideological theory the assumption that "texts always carry the interests of the dominant classes, for those interests have developed the conditions of production, and the conditions of production are necessarily inscribed in the product" (Fiske, 1994a, p. 197). However, cultural theory often is less concerned with describing how the macro-level structural strategies of domination (ideology) structure and work through texts and is more concerned with revealing sites and strategies of resistance. In contrast, ideological criticism typically focuses on describing how the powerful forces at work in texts—

commodification, capitalist ideology, and patriarchy, for example—attempt to manufacture consent to the dominant ideology. As Fiske (1994a) explains:

> In ideology theory, subjectivity plays the role that the commodity does in political economy. Capitalism reproduces itself, in this account, in the way that the dominant ideology makes all who live under it into "subjects-in-ideology." This concept implies that the overridingly effective part of our consciousness, of our ways of understanding our identities, social relations, and social experiences, is a totally pervasive ideology. This ideology and its ways of working are institutionalized into the "ideological state apparatuses"—the law, education, the media, the political system, and so on—and in the ways they go about their daily operations; it is internalized in the consciousness, or rather subconsciousness, of the individuals who live within that society and its institutions. (p. 197)

Some Assumptions Underlying Ideological Criticism

Although ideological criticism essays can differ in terms of their focus on institutional structures or ideas, and on domination or resistance, all ideological critiques share some common assumptions:

1. *Ideological criticism has as its goal the identification and critique of media institutions, texts, and discursive practices that promote or sustain forms of oppression and domination.* Ideological criticism focuses on the ways in which media institutions and texts serve the particular interests of the dominant economic and social classes. It seeks to empower viewers to make informed judgments and choices, and it views criticism as a means to stimulate material changes in human conditions and societies (see Cloud, 1994; Hall, 1990; Kellner, 1995; Sillars & Gronbeck, 2001, pp. 266–267).

2. *Ideological criticism is rooted in the normative assumption that human freedom, democracy, individuality, and dignity are fundamental to social equality, and it regards media institutions, texts, and artifacts as playing important roles in both valorizing and undermining these values.* Whereas cultural criticism tends to be concerned as much with media as sources of individual empowerment as with media as vehicles of domination, ideological criticism focuses on domination (see Hall, 1990; Kervin, 1991; Orbe, 1998; Scott, 1998).

3. *Because ideological criticism takes as its primary objective the unmasking of the "dominant sense" as the "common sense," it often is more overtly combative in tone and less critically detached than many other types of critical analyses* (see, e.g., Cloud, 1998; Kellner, 1995). Ideological criticism does not regard media texts as innocent sources of pleasurable entertainment. Rather, it views them as products of dominant social institutions and reflections of the ideas and interests of the powerful few. Ideological criticism believes that media discourses and images have material effects on audiences, and it sees as its goal exposing and critiquing the

politics of representation. Because ideological criticism regards criticism as a form of consciousness raising, it tends, like other forms of consciousness raising, to be more explicitly evaluative and confrontational than other types of television criticism. When audiences learn to see how television and other media texts attempt to make the dominant cultural groups' values seem like cultural common sense, they will have begun to develop the critical distance needed to gain power over their culture: They will have begun to step outside the dominant ideology. Such empowerment "can help promote a more general questioning of the organization of society and can help induce individuals to join and participate in radical political movements struggling for social transformation" (Kellner, 1995, p. 61).

Writing Ideological Criticism

Television critics writing ideological criticism examine the ways in which television texts reproduce the dominant ideology of a society. They can focus their ideological criticism at one of two levels: on ideology as it is manifested in social/institutional structures or on ideology as manifested in the ideas articulated (e.g., through discourse, narrative oppositions, and narrative structure) in texts. Regardless of the focus, ideological critiques regard media institutions and texts as serving the "vested interests of the prevalent power structure and its privileged beneficiaries" (Thompson, p. 1990, p. 7).

This section of the chapter introduces you to two types of ideological criticism: structuration analysis and discursive analysis. *Structuration analyses* examine ideology at the level of social/institutional structures and power. These critiques focus on unmasking the ways that television, as set of social/institutional power structures, reproduces in its practices and produces in its texts the oppressive power hierarchy of the society. *Discursive analyses* examine ideology at the level of ideas. These ideological critiques (e.g., discourse analysis, metaphor analysis, and ideograph analysis) focus on identifying the ways in which "ideological hegemony is embedded in [such television forms as] format and formula; genre; setting and character type; slant; and solution" and other discursive formations (Gitlin, 2000, p. 577).

Structuration Analysis

Two types of ideological criticism that examine the ways in which the institutional relationships and practices of American television propagate ideologies are social/institutional power analysis and multicultural ideological critiques. Both types of structuration analysis focus on discovering and critiquing the dominant social value hierarchies and cultural ideologies that constrain television program production and the ways in which these ideological constraints are reflected in television texts. Both begin with the assumption that "dominant voices in media production include few and exclude many," and both are concerned with the ways in which the structures of media culture institutions reproduce and naturalize hegemonic politically sanctioned ideologies, including economic, sexist, hetero-sexist, and racist ideologies (Artz & Ortega Murphy, 2000, p. 63; Kellner, 1995, pp. 58–59).

Social/Institutional Power Analysis   This kind of ideological study approaches television programs as "frames and images promoted by a handful of agents authorized by hegemonic institutions" (Artz & Ortega Murphy, 2000, p. 63). This approach is closely related to the types of production context analyses we discussed in Chapter 10. There, the focus was on the production contexts through which ideological power is manifested in television productions: industry- and institutional-level structures (e.g., market and network competition), organization-level structures (decision making about news values and program adoption), and individual-level structures (the ideological power of gatekeepers in news and entertainment: producers, writers, and news directors). Such production context criticism looks behind the camera as well as in front of the camera in order to analyze the ways in which individual, organizational, media industry, and societal structures and value hierarchies that affirm (or potentially challenge) the dominant cultural ideology shape the production of television programs (see, e.g., Buxton, 1994; Collins & Clark, 1992; Ehrlich, 1995; Gitlin, 1983; Levine, 2001; Sandeen, 1997; Tucker & Shah, 1992).

Ideological critiques of institutional and social structures and power typically look not at contexts but at specific texts, sometimes augmented by interviews with production personnel, in order to explore the ways in which societal or institutional power structures shape television texts. Such analyses look at the ways in which dominant societal ideologies are written into these texts and the ways the reiteration of these power relations serves to naturalize hegemonic political positions, including economic, racial, and sexual oppression. These institutional/structural ideological critiques use the analytical constructs of narrative structures, plots, themes, character and narrator roles, narrator voice, racial stereotypes and myths, and extratextual documents to examine the ways the complicities between the dominant ideology and institutional/organizational power structures shape television texts. Examples of such ideological critiques include Tucker and Shah's study of *Roots* (1992) and Collins and Clark's study of a five-part *Nightline* series (1992).

Tucker and Shah (1992) compare the differences between Alex Haley's novel *Roots* and the 1976 television mini-series *Roots*. Their critical analysis demonstrates how the societal ideology of racism influenced the television mini-series—for example, the program creators' conscious decision to soften Haley's narrative "critique of slavery and exposition of white cruelty and indifference into one that diluted, in many ways, the horror, complexities, and seriousness of slave holding" (Tucker & Shah, 1992, p. 325). Collins and Clark (1992) examined ABC *Nightline*'s series about the Israeli-Palestinian conflict. Their combination of a structural analysis of the series' narratives with a production context analysis of the organizational role and power of the journalist-narrator of the series (Ted Koppel) enables them to explain how *Nightline*'s "structural choices privileged a particular [ideological] reading of the conflict and belied their [ABC's] overt effort to let participants tell their own story" (p. 25).

Multicultural Ideology Critique   This type of ideological criticism examines the ways in which social power hierarchies shape media representations of gender, race, sexuality, and class. Multicultural ideological criticism examines the ways in which social relationships of domination and oppression are reproduced in media texts "in the forms of images, figures, generic codes, myth, and the technical apparatus of film, television, music, and other media forms, as well as in ideas or theoretical positions" that those texts verbally articulate (Kellner, 1995, p. 93). As Kellner explains,

> Ideological texts put on display both the significant dreams and nightmares of a culture and the ways that culture is attempting to channel them to maintain its present relations of power and determination. . . . Certain media cultural texts advance specific ideological positions which can be ascertained by relating the texts to the political discourses and debates of their era, to other artifacts concerned with similar themes, and to ideological motifs in the culture that are active in a given text. (1995, p. 93).

One example of such a multicultural ideology critique is Ron Scott's (1998) analysis of television coverage of the Senate Judiciary Committee Nomination Hearings investigating Supreme Court nominee Clarence Thomas's sexual harassment of Oklahoma law professor Anita Hill when she worked for him at the Equal Employment Commission. Scott's critical essay argues that the visual argument presented by the all-white, all-male Senate Judiciary Committee foregrounded sexual stereotypes and myths, and in doing so obscured the racist ideology and three mythic stereotypes about black men—sexual superman, uninhibited expressionist, and social delinquent—that pervaded the media coverage of these hearings.

Another example of multicultural ideology criticism is Kent Ono's (1998) study of the popular children's program, *Mighty Morphin' Power Rangers*. His critical essay explores the ways in which social and ideological contexts within which this hybrid cartoon–traditional drama children's series was produced and read legitimized a neocolonialist ideology of militarism, vigilantism, (neo)racism, and (neo)sexism.

Discursive Ideological Analysis

Discursive ideological critiques focus on the ways in which social practices and power structures "are given meaning or 'brought into view' by language"; that is, on the way in which they are "discursively formed" (Barker, 2000, p. 78). Such ideological criticism focuses on ideology at the level of ideas: These types examine the ways that television texts "unite both language and practice" to "provide dominant descriptive-prescriptive formats for seeing and understanding social relationships and practices" (p. 63). The three types of discursive ideological analysis that we discuss in this section are discourse analysis, metaphor analysis, and ideographic analysis.

Discourse Analysis   One of the most widely used approaches that television critics have employed to analyze the ideological links between television texts and the sociocultural and institutional contexts in which they are produced and consumed is discourse analysis. "Critics do discourse analysis in order to make sense of the relationship between texts and the social world . . . [because] to make sense of the world is to exert power over it" (Fiske, 1994b, p. 3).

At its simplest, *discourse* is a "system of representation that has developed socially in order to make and circulate a coherent set of meanings about an important topic area. These meanings serve the interests of that section of society within which the discourse originates and which works ideologically to naturalize those meanings into common sense" (Fiske, 1987, p. 14). Discourses, as Fiske (1994b) explains, always have three dimensions: "a topic or area of social experience to which its sensemaking is applied; a social position from which this sense is made and whose interests it promotes; and a repertoire of words, images and practices by which meanings are circulated and power applied" (p. 3). We can think of discourses as ideological codes that link texts, producers, and readers: Discourses enable readers to make sense of texts, and in turn, texts reinforce social discourses through a kind of mutual validation and sense making.

As we explained in Chapter 5, a critic using discourse analysis typically begins by looking for the pattern of binary oppositions in the text. Next, the critic identifies the umbrella topic that organizes these oppositions (e.g., the discourse of democratic politics). After doing this for the central oppositions and central discourses, which structure the text, the critic looks for the ideological relationships the text articulates[6] among these discourses. Finally, the critic uses these connections to explore the relationships between the textual discourses and the social discourses that viewers could use to understand the text. Critics can make such connections, Kellner (1995) explains, because textual "representations thus *transcode*[7] political discourses and in turn mobilize sentiment, affection, perception, and assent toward specific political positions, such as the need for male warriors to protect and redeem society. . . . The binary oppositions of ideology are rooted in a system of antagonism between unequal forces and serve to legitimate the privilege and domination of the more powerful sources" (pp. 60, 61).

Ideological discourse analysis requires that the critic read television texts in terms of existing social and political debates and conflicts, and not simply in terms of some abstract "supposedly monolithic dominant ideology" (Kellner, 1995, p. 103). Furthermore, as Kellner pointedly notes, critics also need to pay attention to what is left out of texts because "it is often the exclusions and silences that reveal the ideological project of the text" (p. 113). Critics doing ideological criticism ask and attempt to answer such questions as these:

■ Whose or what point of view, feelings, and experiences are viewers invited to identify with in this television text by virtue of the camera angles, editing, narrative structure, and conclusion? In other words, in what subject position do the discursive and dramatic narrative elements place the viewer?

■ Who is the ideal viewer who is hailed or addressed by the text?

- What does the text invite that ideal viewer to regard as normal, natural, and enjoyable?
- Through what formal and technical strategies and codes is this point of view conveyed?
- Do the roles, values, actions, images, and words in this text maintain, critique/deconstruct, or reconstruct dominant cultural discourses on this topic?
- What oppositional positions, if any, does the text encourage?

Ultimately, discourse analysis is a tool that television critics can use to discover the ways in which television texts neutralize or reproduce struggles over ideological meanings, and to relate the ideological conflicts in television texts to those in our social experience. As Fiske (1983, 1984, 1986, 1987, 1991b) has demonstrated, using discourse analysis to study television texts "can reveal much not only about television, but also about our society" (1991a, p. 446).

In addition to Orbe's example essay at the end of this chapter, two other essays in this textbook use discourse analysis: Fiske's structural analysis of *Dr. Who,* in Chapter 5, and Hundley's cultural studies analysis of *Cheers* in Chapter 14.

Metaphor Analysis   A second discursive approach critics have used to examine the ideological force of television texts is metaphor criticism. This approach combines key concepts from rhetorical and narrative criticism with ideology theory in order to identify and understand the ideological positions organized by the metaphors in a text—including both the metaphoric language used in the telling (in the case of news, talk, sports, and other nonfiction programs), and the visual metaphors enacting (in the case of comedic and dramatic programs) the ideological conflicts, issues, and perspectives in television programs (see Aden, 1995; Mumby & Spitzack, 1991). Analyzing the verbal metaphors used by speakers, news reporters, or actors in television dramas and comedies, as well as the visual metaphors created by camera work, lighting, music, and other technical and production codes in a television text, enables the critic to see the ideological positions that are foregrounded and affirmed through the text and those ideological perspectives that are being hidden or marginalized.

At its simplest, a *metaphor* is the juxtaposition of two terms (or concepts) usually regarded as very different. By juxtaposing these terms, the structure of the metaphor (and the ideas evoked or entailed by the metaphor) foregrounds a particular understanding of these terms or concepts. This understanding occurs because "in allowing us to focus on one aspect of a concept, a metaphorical concept can keep us from focusing on other aspects of the concept that are inconsistent with the metaphor" (Lakoff & Johnson, 1980, p. 10). Mumby and Spitzack's (1983) analysis of television news stories, for example, shows how using different metaphors to describe politics radically alters our sense of what political activity is; what political behaviors are natural, normal, and right; and what the outcome of political conflicts should be. They point out, for instance, that the metaphor *politics is war* invites a radically different understanding (and evokes different expectations) of political activities and outcomes than do the metaphors *politics is a dance, politics is dramatic performance,* or *politics is a game.* These different understandings of what politics is occur because each metaphor includes a system of subsidiary, related concepts, called *entailments,* that together create an ideological framework.

As Mumby and Spitzack (1983) explain, the metaphor *politics is war,* for example, entails these concepts: war involves two or more enemies; war involves strategies, attacks, use of weapons, conflict, violence, a struggle for domination; war has leaders; war is dangerous; war usually ends in victory or defeat. The notion of politics here is one in which aggression, violence, danger, and negativity are presented as normal and natural, while opposing views of politics, such as cooperative democratic governing, mutual understanding, and shared social goals, are deemphasized. In contrast, the metaphor *politics is a game* entails such related concepts as play, role playing, cooperation with teammates, friendly competition, strategy, use of skill, spectators, and rules. Mumby and Spitzack explain that the ideological framework structured by this game metaphor suggests that politics is play—neither serious work nor war. It therefore is a friendly diversion rather than a serious commitment; the outcomes of political contests are a reflection of the strategic skills of the participating political teams and not necessarily their inner qualities; and political activity is something that we can watch as game spectators without becoming actively involved in it.

Richard Campbell's analysis (1987, 1991) of the TV program *60 Minutes* demonstrates how its reporters' narrative enactments of three roles—reporter as detective, reporter as analyst, and reporter as tourist—offer resolutions to ongoing cultural tensions between nature and culture, good and evil, tradition and modernity, individuals and institutions. In doing so, his analysis argues, the program functions ideologically to reaffirm the grand modernist myths of progress, human rationality, and the independence, integrity, and centrality of the heroic individual reporter to the functioning of democratic capitalism.

Mumby and Spitzack's as well as Campbell's analyses illustrate how metaphors structure our perceptions and the meanings of texts by highlighting some aspects of a topic or issue and by hiding or deemphasizing others. Metaphoric analysis, then, enables television critics to see the taken-for-granted ideological assumptions conveyed in television texts through verbal and visual metaphors. Practically speaking, as Sonja Foss (1996) explains, metaphor analysis usually involves several steps. First, critics need to examine the text carefully to identify the principal metaphors used to structure the text. In doing so, they need to pay careful attention to the context (to see if the metaphors are used ironically, comedically, or seriously, for example).

If critics identify many metaphors, they need to sort these metaphors into clusters that share entailments (those subsidiary, related metaphoric concepts). Next, they must analyze the clusters of metaphors to determine what Lakoff and Johnson (1980) call *external systematicity*—the common perceptions created when the principal metaphors share entailments. Finally, critics need to explore how these metaphors ideologically structure viewers' attitudes toward the characters, actions, and issues in the text. Critics doing metaphor analysis ask (and answer) questions such as these:

- Which ideological positions are highlighted and, equally importantly, which are hidden by the use of these metaphors?
- What view of social reality is constructed, affirmed, interrogated, or rejected by foregrounding these metaphoric understandings and obscuring others?
- In what ways does this text reinforce, question, or critique the dominant ideology?
- What alternative ideological perspectives (if any) does it present or consider?
- What insights does this analysis provide about television's hegemonic function and its empowering function?

Verbal and visual metaphors are two devices that television texts use to shape the meanings that viewers are invited to create from their viewing experiences. Metaphor analysis, then, is another tool that media critics can use to uncover and examine the hegemonic qualities of television texts and explore the connections between television texts and their societal, ideological contexts.

Ideographic Analyses   A third discursive approach critics can use to do ideological analyses of television texts is rhetorical critic Michael McGee's (1980) ideographic analysis. According to McGee, *ideographs* are common, deeply revered, ordinary language terms for "a high-order abstraction representing collective commitment to a particular but equivocal and ill-defined normative goal" (p. 15)—for example, "freedom of speech," "rule of law," and "liberty." Indeed, as McGee explains, "No one has ever seen an 'equality' strutting up the driveway." Some U.S. American ideographs that communication scholars have analyzed include <equality> (Condit & Lucaites, 1993; Lucaites & Condit, 1990), the Iwo Jima flag-raising image (Edwards & Winkler, 1990), <family values> (Cloud, 1998), public servants as "the best men" (Martin, 1983), and the cigarette (Moore, 1997). As Edwards and Winkler explain, ideographs are "culturally grounded, summarizing, and authoritative terms that enact their meaning by expressing an association of cultural ideals and experiences in an ever-evolving and reifying form within the rhetorical environment . . . [whose] meaning develops through its usages and applications" (p. 297).

According to McGee, an ideograph has four essential characteristics:

1. It must be an ordinary language term found in political discourse, which he notes includes "'popular history'. . . . [which] consists in part of novels, films, plays, even songs" (p. 11).
2. It must be a "high-order abstraction representing collective commitment to a particular but equivocal and ill-defined normative goal" (p. 15).
3. It "warrants the use of power, excuses behavior and belief which might otherwise be perceived as eccentric or antisocial, and guides behavior and belief into channels easily recognized by a community as acceptable and laudable" (p. 15).
4. It is culture bound. "Each member of the community is socialized, conditioned, to the vocabulary of ideographs as a prerequisite for 'belonging' to the society" (p. 15).

As Dana Cloud (1998) has explained, critics using ideographs to perform ideological criticism begin by identifying the ideograph in a particular set of texts. After identifying the central ideographs (e.g., liberty, freedom, free speech, individualism, family value) in a text or set of texts, critics must next do two things: locate "a society's ideographs in historical (diachronic) context" and describe "the tensions and clashes in usages in any given (synchronic moment)" (p. 390). This means that critics must research how a particular ideograph has been used historically within a society as a persuasive rhetorical trope or social construct. Critics also must look at the various ways the ideograph currently is being used in popular public discourse (e.g., critics could look for the different ways in which conflicting social groups are currently using the term *family values*). This step in ideographic critical analysis involves identifying the ways the definition of the central ideograph is shaped by clusters of other ideographs that are discursively linked with the central ideograph. In the final step in ideographic analysis, critics must analyze the rhetorical force of the tensions evoked in the ideograph's usage (i.e., in its linkage with other terms and its use in slogans) and discuss the potential implications for public policy and people's material lives.

For example, in her 1998 analysis of the ideograph <family values>, Cloud explains that she identified family values as a central ideograph in the 1992 U.S. American presidential campaign by looking at the media coverage that followed Vice President Dan Quayle's May 1992 speech in San Francisco. In it he blamed the 1992 Los Angeles riots that followed the initial verdict in the Rodney King police beating case on the rioters' lack of family values. He claimed that this lack was exacerbated by negative media images such as TV news character Murphy Brown's decision to have a baby out of wedlock. After establishing the pervasiveness of the <family values> ideograph in 1992 political campaign speeches and news coverage, Cloud next researched the development of the concept of the nuclear family. Her third step was to examine the political speeches and news coverage for clusters of ideographs and for the tensions and semantic and ideological links between these other ideographs and the <family values> ideograph. In analyzing central speeches by Dan Quayle, George Bush, Bill Clinton, and Jimmy Carter, as well as the political convention speeches and performances of Barbara Bush, Marilyn Quayle, and Hillary Rodham Clinton (and her book), Cloud identified utopian and scapegoating tensions (i.e., positive and negative understandings of the <family values> ideograph) that opposing politicians were using to try to shape public understandings and meanings of the concept of family values. Finally, Cloud analyzed politicians' articulations (linkages) of the <family values> ideograph with other ideographs and discussed the subsequent policy and concrete material implications of 1992 campaign discourse about family values, including the ways this ideograph was used to conceal and deflect attention away from the reality of the links between economic inequality and structural racism.

To date, only a few other critics have used ideographic analysis to perform ideological critiques of media texts. Celeste Condit and John Lucaites (1990, 1993) have studied the use of the ideograph <equality> in American civil rights movements; Mark Moore (1997) analyzed the use of the cigarette as representational ideograph; Martha Martin (1983) examined the political servant–public official ideograph of the <best men>; and Janis Edwards and Carol Winkler (1997) extended ideographic analysis from purely verbal discourse to visual discourse in their study of the rhetorical functions of the Iwo Jima image in editorial cartoons.

The Example Essay

In the example essay at the end of the chapter, "Constructions of Reality on MTV's *The Real World*: An Analysis of the Restrictive Coding of Black Masculinity," Mark Orbe uses discourse analysis to examine the signs through which the discourse of black masculinity is constructed in this MTV "reality" series. Orbe argues that in foregrounding images of the black male cast members during its first six seasons, the series defined black males as inherently angry, physically threatening, and sexually aggressive. This depiction of black masculinity, he explains, articulates with and reaffirms the hegemonic racist myths and ideology that historically have dominated U.S. American society.

Notes

1. These included the Jacobin terror, Robespierre, the rise of the Institut Nationale, and Napoleon's rise and opposition to de Tracy's republicanism. For more information about this period and these terms, see Thompson, 1990.

2. Dana Cloud is one contemporary rhetorical critic who has published a number of classical Marxist rhetorical critiques (see, e.g., Cloud, 1994).

3. *Class* here is defined as a category or group of individuals based on their economic resources, the social and cultural resources that their economic situation gives rise to, and their concomitant assumed positionality within the social system. Indeed, in Great Britain, for example, titled lords can be poorer than merchant class people; hence, the concept of the nouveau riche ("new rich"). It is only in the United States that class is defined in primarily economic terms.

4. Althusser's critical focus, as Stevenson (1995) cogently explains, was on the ways in which "the cultural transmission of traditions through institutions, like mass communications and the education system, helps form a dominant consensus in contemporary society [and the ways in which] hegemonic modes of dominance are also dependent upon formations within civilized society" (p. 17). *Formations* here, Stevenson explains, mean "certain conscious movements and tendencies (like literary movements) that largely work within dominant meanings and values" (p. 17).

5. In 1914 the miners working at J.D. Rockefeller's mines in Ludlow, Colorado, tried to unionize to the right to lives (with their families) in their own houses, rather in company-owned houses, and for better wages. When Rockefeller responded by ordering the miners to move out of his company houses, the miners and their families went on strike. Rockefeller then called the governor of Colorado to send the militia to move the miners off his property. He did; the militia arrived and in the ensuing melee, the militia fired on the tents housing the miners and their families, killing 53 people, including 13 women and children. The resultant

negative publicity led Rockefeller to hire former newspaper journalist Ivy Ledbetter Lee to help repair the Rockefeller family name (and to prevent losses to his Standard Oil Company), and the field of modern public relations was born.

6. In ideological and cultural studies, articulation is not the everyday notion of "speaking clearly." Instead, articulation refers to the joining of two social forces, or discourses, such that one is hierarchically dominant over the others (O'Sullivan et al., 1994, pp. 17–18).

7. As Douglas Kellner (1995) uses this term (which he coined), "the process of 'transcoding' describes how social discourses are translated into media texts, as when *Easy Rider* transcodes 1960s countercultural discourses of freedom, individualism, and community in cinematic images and scenes, when, for instance, the bikers drive through nature with the soundtrack playing 'Born to Be Wild' or 'Wasn't Born to Follow'" (p. 89; see also Kellner & Ryan, 1988).

Further Readings

Artz, L., & Ortega Murphy, B. (2000). *Cultural hegemony in the United States.* Thousand Oaks, CA: Sage. This book provides a cogent historical overview of the concept of hegemony; lucid discussions supported by ample examples of cultural hegemony and racism, hegemony and gender, and class cultural hegemony; and an exploration of how and why capitalist cultural hegemony has persisted.

Feuer, J. (1995). *Seeing through the eighties: Television and Reaganism.* Durham, NC: Duke University Press. This ideological critique explores the complex relationships between television forms of the 1980s—such as MTV ("with its transformation of U.S. network television's linear narrative structure into a postmodern concern with images as images") and *Dynasty* (with its "supply side aristocracy")—and the rise of Reaganism as a politically dominant ideology. After analyzing the populist majority, yuppies, and yuppie aesthetics, Feuer identifies the ensemble serial melodrama (and specifically *Dynasty*) as the paradigmatic expression of the political contradictions of the 1980s.

Webnotes

Opinion Pages. **http://www.opinion-pages.org/**

This web site provides access to recent opinions and editorials from 600 English-language sources. Key word searches produce a link to the editorial or opinion piece and a brief abstract of it.

Critical Social Theory. **http://www.theory.org.uk/**

This overview of critical social theory contains summaries of the theories of Foucault, Butler, Gramsci, Adorno, and Giddens.

Marxist Thought. **http://www.marxists.org**

This large collection of writing and information about Marxist theory, history, and writings is divided into main sections: a writer's archive, a history archive, a reference archive, and a non-English archive.

Learning
Activities

1. Videotape a prime-time drama series, ideally an episodic series that deals with politics, government, and justice, such as *Judging Amy,* one of the *Law and Order* series, *The Practice,* or *The Guardian.* Then, using the definition of ideographs provided in this chapter, identify the ideographs used in the episode, and examine the relationships, tensions, and clustering you see among the ideographs. Discuss the potential rhetorical functions of the presence of such ideographs in social justice series.

2. Videotape an episode of a prime-time medical drama. Then analyze the tape and identify the metaphors used to characterize medical professionals, patients, health care decisions, and health care facilities. Arrange these metaphors in related clusters and develop the entailments of these metaphors. For example, if your analysis of a videotaped episode of *ER* revealed the use of the metaphor "medicine is a business," develop some of the entailments of that metaphor. What competing metaphors do you identify? Which metaphors are used most often? Do the dominant metaphors expressed in this episode reflect one central or several competing views about medicine and health care? Which ideological positions are highlighted, and equally important, which are hidden by the use of these metaphors? What insights does this analysis provide about television's hegemonic function? About its empowering function?

References

Aden, R. C. (1994). Back to the garden: Therapeutic place metaphor in *Field of Dreams. Southern Communication Journal, 59,* 307–317.

Althusser, L. (1970). *For Marx* (B. Brewster, Trans.). New York: Vintage.

Artz, L., & Ortega Murphy, B. (2000). *Cultural hegemony in the United States.* Thousand Oaks, CA: Sage.

Barker, C. (2000). *Cultural studies: Theory and practice.* Thousand Oaks, CA: Sage.

Berger, A. A. (1995). *Cultural criticism: A primer of key concepts.* Thousand Oaks, CA: Sage.

Burke, K. (1957). *The philosophy of literary form: Studies in symbolic action* (rev. ed.). New York: Vintage.

Burke, K. (1969a). *A grammar of motives.* Berkeley: University of California Press. (Original work published 1945.)

Burke, K. (1969b). *A rhetoric of motives.* Berkeley: University of California Press. (Original work published1950.)

Buxton, R. (1994). After it happened . . : The battle to present AIDS in television drama. In H. Newcomb (Ed.), *Television: The critical view* (5th ed., pp. 117–134). New York: Oxford University Press.

Campbell, R. (1987). Securing the middle ground: Reporter formulas in *60 Minutes. Critical Studies in Mass Communication, 4,* 377–389.

Campbell, R. (1991). Methodological preface to "Securing the middle ground: Reporter formulas in *60 Minutes*." In L. Vande Berg & L. A. Wenner (Eds.), *Television criticism: Approaches and applications* (pp. 331–334). White Plains, NY: Longman.

Cloud, D. L. (1994). "Socialism of the mind": The new age of post-Marxism. In H. W. Simons & M. Billig (Eds.), *After postmodernism: Reconstructing ideology critique* (pp. 222–252). Thousand Oaks, CA: Sage.

Cloud, D. L. (1996). Hegemony or concordance? The rhetoric of tokenism in "Oprah": Winfrey's rags-to-riches biography. *Critical Studies in Mass Communication, 13*, 115–137.

Cloud, D. L. (1997). Concordance, complexity, and conservatism: Rejoinder to Condit. *Critical Studies in Mass Communication, 14*, 193–200.

Cloud, D. L. (1998). The rhetoric of <family values>: Scapegoating, utopia, and the privitization of social responsibility. *Western Journal of Communication, 62*, 387–419.

Collins, C. A., & Clark, J. E. (1992). A structural analysis of *Nightline's* "This Week in the Holy Land." *Critical Studies in Mass Communication, 9*, 25–43.

Condit, C. M., & Lucaites, J. L. (1993). *Crafting equality: America's Anglo-African word*. Chicago: University of Chicago Press.

Edwards, J., & Winkler, C. K. (1997). Representative form and the visual ideograph: The Iwo Jima image in editorial cartoons. *Quarterly Journal of Speech, 83*, 289–310.

Ehrlich, M. (1995). The competitive ethos in television newswork. *Critical Studies in Mass Communication, 12*, 196–212.

Ewen, S. 91996). *PR! A social history of spin*. New York: Basic Books.

Fiske, J. (1983). The discourses of TV quiz shows, or school + luck = success + sex. *Central States Speech Journal, 34*, 139–150.

Fiske, J. (1984). Popularity and ideology: A structuralist reading of *Dr Who*. In W. Rowland & B. Watkins (Eds.), *Interpreting television: Current research perspectives* (pp. 165–197). Thousand Oaks, CA: Sage.

Fiske, J. (1987). *Television culture*. London: Methuen.

Fiske, J. (1991a). Methodological preface [to "The discourses of TV quiz shows, or school + luck = success + sex"]. In L. Vande Berg & L. Wenner (Eds.), *Television criticism: Approaches and applications* (pp. 445–447). White Plains, NY: Longman.

Fiske, J. (1991b). The discourses of TV quiz shows, or school + luck = success + sex." In L. Vande Berg & L. Wenner (Eds.), *Television criticism: Approaches and applications* (pp. 445–462). White Plains, NY: Longman.

Fiske, J. (1994a). Audiencing: Cultural practice and cultural studies. In N. K. Denzin & Y. S. Lincoln (Eds.), *Handbook of qualitative research* (pp. 189–198). Thousand Oaks, CA: Sage.

Fiske, J. (1994b). *Media matters: Everyday culture and political change*. Minneapolis: University of Minnesota Press.

Foss, S. K. (1996). *Rhetorical criticism: Exploration and practice* (2nd ed.). Prospect Heights, IL: Waveland.

Frye, N. (1957). *Anatomy of criticism: Four essays.* Princeton: Princeton University Press.

Geras, N. (1987, May–June). Post-Marxism? *New Left Review, 163,* 40–82.

Gitlin, T. (1983). *Hill Street Blues:* Make it look messy. In T. Gitlin, *Inside prime time* (pp. 273–324). New York: Pantheon.

Gitlin, T. (2000). Prime time ideology: The hegemonic process in television entertainment. In H. Newcomb (Ed.), *Television: The critical view* (6th ed., pp. 574–594). New York: Oxford University Press.

Gramsci, A. (1971). *Selections from the prison notebooks* (Q. Hoare & G. Nowell-Smith, Eds. & Trans.). New York: International Universities Press.

Hall, S. (1977). Culture, the media and ideological effect. In J. Curran, M. Gurevitch, & J. Woollacott (Eds.), *Mass communication and society* (pp. 315–348). London: Open University/Edward Arnold.

Hall, S. (1980). Encoding/decoding. In S. Hall, D. Hobson, A. Lowe & P. Willis (Eds.), *Culture, media, language* (pp. 128–139). London: Hutchinson.

Hall, S. (1982). The rediscovery of "ideology": Return of the repressed in media studies. In M. Gurevitch, T. Bennett, J. Curran, & S. Woollacott (Eds.), *Culture, society, and the media* (pp. 56–90). London: Methuen.

Hall, S. (1984). Signification, representation, ideology: Althusser and the post-structuralist debates. *Critical Studies in Mass Communication, 2,* 91–114.

Hall, S. (1990). The whites of their eyes: Racist ideologies and the media. In M. Alvarado & J. O. Thompson (Eds.), *The media reader* (pp. 7–23). London: British Film Institute.

Hall, S. (1992). Cultural studies and its theoretical legacies. In L. Grossberg, C. Nelson, & P. Treichler (Eds.), *Cultural studies* (pp. 277–294). London: Routledge.

Kellner, D. (1995). *Media culture: Cultural studies, identity and politics between the modern and the postmodern.* New York: Routledge.

Kellner, D. & Ryan, M. (1988). *Camera politica: The politics and ideology of contemporary Hollywood film.* Bloomington, IN: Indiana University Press.

Kervin, D. (1991). Gender ideology in television commercials. In L. Vande Berg & L. Wenner (Eds.), *Television criticism: Approaches and applications* (pp. 235–253). White Plains, NY: Longman.

Lakoff, G., & Johnson, M. (1980). *Metaphors we live by.* Chicago: University of Chicago Press.

Levine, E. (2001). Toward a paradigm for media production research: Behind the scenes at *General Hospital. Critical Studies in Media Communication, 18,* 66–82.

Lucaites, J. L., & Condit, C. M. (1990). Reconstructing <equality>: Culturetypal and counter-cultural rhetorics in the black martyred vision. *Communication Monographs, 57,* 5–24.

Martin, M. A. (1983). Ideologues, ideographs and <the best men>. *Southern Communication Journal, 49,* 12–25.

Marx, K. (1964). *Selected writings in sociology and social philosophy* (T. B. Bottomore & M. Rubel, Eds.; T. B. Bottomore, Trans.). New York: McGraw-Hill.

McChesney, R. W. (1999). *Rich media, poor democracy: Communication politics in dubious times.* New York: New Press.

McGee, M. (1980). The "ideograph": A link between rhetoric and ideology. *Quarterly Journal of Speech, 66,* 113–133.

Moore, M. P. (1997). The cigarette as representational ideograph in the debate over environmental tobacco smoke. *Communication Monographs, 64,* 47–64.

Mumby, D. K., & Spitzack, C. (1983). Ideology and television news: A metaphoric analysis of political stories. In L. Vande Berg & L. Wenner (Eds.), *Television criticism: Approaches and applications* (pp. 313–330). White Plains, NY: Longman, 1991.

Ono, K. (1998). *Power Rangers:* An ideological critique of neocolonialism. In L. Vande Berg, L. A. Wenner, & B. E. Gronbeck (Eds.), *Critical approaches to television* (pp. 271–284). Boston: Houghton Mifflin.

Orbe, M. P. (1998). Constructions of reality on MTV's *The Real World:* An analysis of the restrictive coding of black masculinity. *Southern Communication Journal, 64,* 32–67.

O'Sullivan, T., Hartley, J., Saunders, D., Montgomery, M., & Fiske, J. (1994). *Key concepts in communication and cultural studies* (2nd ed.). London: Routledge.

Sandeen, C. (1997). Success defined by television: The value system promoted by *PM Magazine. Critical Studies in Mass Communication, 14,* 77–105.

Scott, R. (1998). The rearticulation of popular myths and stereotypes: The Hill-Thomas hearings. In L. Vande Berg, L. A. Wenner, & B. E. Gronbeck (Eds.), *Critical approaches to television* (pp. 302–314). Boston: Houghton Mifflin.

Sillars, M. O., & Gronbeck, B. E. (2001). *Communication criticism: Rhetoric, social codes, cultural studies.* Prospect Heights, IL: Waveland.

Stevenson, N. (1995). *Understanding media cultures: Social theory and mass communication.* Thousand Oaks, CA: Sage.

Thompson, J. B. (1990). *Ideology and modern culture: Critical social theory in the era of mass communication.* Stanford, CA: Stanford University Press.

Tucker, L., & Shah, H. (1992). Race and the transformation of culture: The making of the television miniseries *Roots. Critical Studies in Mass Communication, 9,* 325–336.

Williams, R. (1979). *Marxism and literature.* Oxford: Oxford University Press.

Constructions of Reality on MTV's *The Real World*: An Analysis of the Restrictive Coding of Black Masculinity

Mark P. Orbe

This is the true story . . . of seven strangers picked to live in a house . . . and have their lives taped . . . to find out what happens . . . when people stop being polite . . . and start being real . . . THE REAL WORLD (Opening dialogue for MTV's REAL WORLD).

In early 1992, the viewing public was introduced to MTV's newest form of innovative television programming: A series that promised to bring the real life experiences of a diverse group of young people (18–25 years old) into the homes of millions. Described by the creator/producer as a show about "real people, undirected, sharing their lives" (Huriash, 1996, p. C25), *The Real World* has now completed six seasons with the seventh season currently being underway in Seattle. The premise of the show is simple—especially attractive to television voyeurs with a specific fascination with Generation X—MTV chooses seven individuals,[1] representing diverse backgrounds, to reside rent-free in a house for three months while every aspect of their lives is taped by a multitude of cameras. The result is a Generation X fishbowl of sorts, one that is viewed by 60 million people in 52 countries every week and has become a cult hit for MTV (Sakurari, 1996). In fact, *The Real World* has launched an onslaught of capital ventures (several books, college lecture series, videos, specials, international counterparts, and commercials) and assisted in achieving celebrity status for many cast members.

For many viewers one of the most intriguing aspects of the show is the cultural diversity of each cast. In this regard, *The Real World* provides a glimpse into the social relations based on race/ethnicity, gender, sexuality, class, and religion. The objective of this article is to focus on one aspect of intergroup relations, those involving African American men.[2] Specifically, I give critical consciousness, via a semiotic analytical lens, to the totalizing rep-resentations of African American male cast members across six seasons of *The Real World*. In this respect, a primary focus on how these images work to maintain the "typification" (Lanigan, 1988; Schutz, 1967) of Black men as inherently angry, potentially violent, and sexually aggressive is maintained. Three specific points speak to the conceptual and theoretical importance of such an analysis. First, it extends the growing body of literature that critically examines stereotypical media images of African Americans in general, and African American men specifically. Second, it critiques media images (and subsequently their potential effects) created through documentary filmmaking. Like *An American Family*, the 1973 PBS series that serves as the prototype of the television docu-drama (Loud & Johnson, 1974), MTV creates a viewer expectation that *The Real World* is not about characters following a pre-determined script, but rather the real life experiences of young people negotiating a particular set of relationships in the 1990s. Third, the analysis calls into the question the self-defined liberal tendencies of MTV and explores the potential impact of "hip" media images on viewers. As an alternative network fueled by the cutting edge inspirations of young adults, MTV has provided opportunities for media images that work to unmask and deconstruct racial and gender stereotypes (see, for example, Lewis, 1994). In short, the analysis represents an important point of inquiry in that it critically examines racial/gender images that are produced in a context, both in terms of method (documentary filmmaking) and source (alternative programming of MTV), that conditions viewers to expect "realistic images." Given this objective and rationale, the remainder of the article will give attention to the unique genre that MTV's *Real World* represents and the ways in which this programming format contributes to the hegemonic power of racial images in reinforcing a general societal fear of Black men.

African American Images in the Media

In recent years, black representation in the media has received increasing attention from scholars grounded in the tradition of British cultural studies (Bailey, 1988; Hall, 1992; Julien & Mercer, 1997). Within the United States, critical/cultural studies research focusing on African American media images, both those in film (Bogle, 1994; Elise & Umoja, 1992; hooks, 1992) and television (Berry, 1992; Evoleocha & Ugbah, 1989; Gray, 1989; Harris, 1992; MacDonald, 1983; Orbe & Strother, 1996; Smith, 1993), have also appeared in the literature. Much of this work has called attention to the ways that images of Blacks in the media historically have remained largely invisible, marginalized to the point of insignificance, or been limited to specific stereotypes. The impact of such media representations has not gone unnoticed by scholars and laypersons alike (Gates, 1992; Stroman, 1991). According to Kellner (1995), these images are a central beginning in how "many people construct their sense of . . . 'us' and 'them'" (p. 1) and therefore represent an important source of exploration for those interested in the impact that mediated images have on the substance of our everyday lives (Brooks & Jacob, 1996). According to Omi (1989),

> Popular culture has been an important realm within which racial ideologies have been created, reproduced, and sustained. Such ideologies provide a framework of symbols, concepts, and images through which we understand, interpret, and represent aspects of our "racial" existence. (p. 114)

Many critics (see summary provided by Smith, 1993) have posited that the vast majority of African American media images represent portrayals of Black life as European Americans see it. In fact, Gates (1992) observes that:

> Historically blacks have always worried aloud about the image that white Americans harbor of us, first because we have never had control of those images and, second, because the greater number of those images have been negative. And given television's immediacy and its capacity to reach so many viewers so quickly, blacks . . . have been especially concerned with our images on the screen. (p. 311)

Because of the power of mediated images, characterizations of African Americans are never neutral; instead, each portrayal either "advances or retards the struggle for self-determination and empowerment" (Elise & Umoja, 1992, p. 83). Most media research has concluded that television programming continues to portray African Americans in stereotypical roles (Cooks & Orbe, 1993; Evoleocha & Ugbah, 1989; Gates, 1992). The programming format of television hinges on the success of defining characters in condensed form; this driving force has "led to the perpetuation of racial caricatures . . . [that often] serve as shorthand for scriptwriters, directors, and actors" (Omi, 1989, p. 115).

Other research, however, has focused on the potential of specific media images in advancing beyond traditional stereotypes (Berry, 1992; Brooks & Jacob, 1996; Cloud, 1992). In this regard, attention is given to the potential that television has to promote images of African Americans that represent anti-essentialist and non-stereotypical portrayals (Brooks & Jacob, 1996). The opportunity to advance the complexity of African American media images has been greatest outside of the traditional networks (ABC, CBS, and NBC). While the number of "minority-lead" characters on these network powers has shrunk in the 1990s (Atkins, 1992), other programming—most notably on BET, UPN, WB, and HBO—has provided an increasing number of diverse African American images. As MTV has extended its programming beyond music videos, they have also served as a media source, especially for young adults, for alternative images that typically are not available on network television. In this regard, *The Real World*, as well as other genres of MTV programming, holds great potential in advancing beyond the stereotypical media images most often associated with underrepresented group members. The creators/producers of the show have contrived a method for viewers to see the intricate complexities inherent in the lives of seven young people. These people are not simply actors following a script produced by others; viewers seemingly get to see real people in the context of the real world. The potential to utilize this emergent genre of alternative programming in advancing the traditional slot-casting of underrepresented group members is extremely promising. Images of Black masculinity, for instance, can be signified through non-essentializing codes and work to represent the great diversity of Black maleness that exists in the United States. It is within this conceptual backdrop that this analysis offered.

The Signification of Black Male Media Images

How are African American men represented on MTV's *Real World?* One avenue of inquiry is to critically examine the construction of black male representations within or across a specific genre. Semiotics represents a critical studies method to reveal the ways in which meaning is created and realized within mediated images (Orbe & Strother, 1996). According to Eco (1976), meaning is created and maintained through an associative process of signification where a signifier (name/image) is intentionally used to signify a specific concept. Semiotic analysis works to increase the consciousness of the process by which initial (paradigmatic) relationships between signs are made more prominent through a redundancy of associations within and outside a specific text (Stam, Burgoyne, & Flitterman-Lewis, 1992). In other words, a semiotic framework focuses on how some signifiers are foregrounded with such consistency that they come to be associated naturally with certain elements. In fact, a redundancy of these images creates a certain level of predictability that is structured into the text. The ultimate goal of a semiotic study is to increase the reader's understanding as to how seemingly straight-forward signs pick up connotative meaning (Barthes, 1972) within a preferred [dominant] reading of the text (O'Sullivan, Hartley, Saunders, Montgomery, & Fiske, 1994).

Recent work in the areas of film and television has established semiotics as a productive lens from which to explore visual mediated images (Orbe & Strother, 1996; Stam et al., 1992). A semiotic analysis of media representations promotes scholarship that works to deconstruct the indexing function of signs—how particular interpretants come to stand for (define) something else (Peirce, 1958). In addition, such inquiry reveals how the signification process of images inherently communicates the themes and values of a media text (Saussure, 1966) and ultimately affirms the ideological systems of the status quo as natural/normal (Barthes, 1972). Within such a tradition, this analysis will utilize a semiotic framework to deconstruct and interpret the signification process of Black masculinity on MTV's *Real World*. Given the broad array of diverse interactions across six different seasons, this innovative genre of programming constitutes a rich and meaningful text (Cheney & Tompkins, 1988; Ricoeur, 1976) for exploring social relations in contemporary North America.

The focus of the article will revolve around how the images of three Black men (Kevin, David, and Syrus) from different casts (New York, Los Angeles, and Boston) function to signify Black men as inherently angry, potentially violent, and sexually aggressive. Like Ang (1985) and Fiske (1994), I situate myself as a fan as well as a critical researcher of the show. As a faithful viewer, I have watched each season of *The Real World* since 1992 and have viewed each episode (depending on the content) anywhere between 4 and 10 times. Because MTV has aired each season in its entirety, as well as in special formats,[3] I have had ample opportunity to view each episode individually (within the sequential context of that particular season), collectively (within and across specific seasons) and reflectively (viewing earlier episodes with knowledge of subsequent episodes/seasons). On March 7, 1998, MTV presented a daylong special titled "MOST

DANGEROUS *Real World* EPISODES." In short, this special featured the most intense conflicts experienced by each of the six casts. My consciousness as to the potentially problematic nature of Black male representations on the show was raised during each independent season. However, within the context of this special the consistency of portraying Black men as dangerous became glaringly apparent. The focus of this analysis, therefore, will be on the signification process of Black men on these "dangerous" *Real World* episodes (within the context of events in each particular season). Through the process of cast selection, editing footage, and the creation of "documentary/soap opera," I argue that these images—presented as "real life"—work to strengthen the justification of a general societal fear of Black men.

At this conjuncture it is crucial to recognize that some scholars (e.g., Hall, 1989) posit that several readings of a text may supersede the dominant codes within the signification process, including the substitution of an oppositional code. Others, like Condit (1989) and Cloud (1992), contend that the interpretative openness of popular texts are largely bounded and "responses are contained within a binary meaning system" (Cloud, 1992, p. 314). The analysis generated here acknowledges the potential of a variety of possible readings (Siegal & Carey, 1989) of Black masculinity in *The Real World* but focuses on revealing how these powerful images, if interpreted within the preferred reading, maintain a "typification" of Black men consistent with general societal perceptions.[4]

A Restrictive Coding of Black Masculinity

Over the course of six seasons, MTV viewers have been introduced to 45 different cast members, representing a cross section of cultural diversity in the United States.[5] Among this diverse group were four African American men: (a) Kevin, a 25-year-old writer/part-time teacher from Jersey City, New Jersey who appeared on the first season in New York City; (b) David, a stand-up comic from Washington, D.C. who was part of the second season filmed

in Los Angeles; (c) Mohammed, a cast member from the third season (San Francisco) who was a 24-year-old musician/singer; and (d) Syrus, a 25-year-old self-defined "playa" from Los Angeles who appeared on the most recent season located in Boston. While this analysis of African American male representation on the show will draw from each of the episodes within each respective season, the focus will be on the images that were highlighted among the "most dangerous *Real World* episodes" aired on March 7, 1998. Of particular interest to the analysis provided here is that, while African American men constituted less than 9 percent of all cast members, they were featured in over 50% of the "most dangerous" segments presented in the seven-hour marathon. The highlights of these shows reproduced a series of intense conflicts centered around three Black men: Kevin, David, and Syrus.[6] When positioned in close proximity of one another, the redundancy of restrictive codes of the Black male images on *The Real World* become undeniably real. What was once negotiated by viewers as subtly negative portrayals of each individual African American man (representing the possibility for an elaborative code) is now replaced with a clear restrictive coding mechanism that maintains the visibility of negative images presented as consistently inherent to Black masculinity. The collective re/framing of these "most dangerous" episodes made apparent what had [been] existing in the background throughout the series: The paradigmatic signifiers of the Black male as inherently angry, physically threatening, and sexually aggressive.

Black Male as Inherently Angry

While the creators/producers of the show adamantly deny "slot casting" (Huriash, 1996), the opening episodes of the debut season reveal an ensemble of cast members representing a variety of stereotypical characters depicted in various media forms. In no uncertain terms, the cast includes a young, innocent [virgin] Southern woman (Julie); an African American [ghetto] female rapper (Heather B); a long-haired aspiring rock star (Andre); a bisexual artist (Norman); an all-[European] American jock—turned professional model (Eric); a sexually free budding musician (Becky); and the young angry Black man (Kevin). For the next 13 episodes[7] viewers get an up-close-and-personal view of these characters; for many of the characters we are able to see beyond the stereotypes that they initially represent and learn some of the complexities of their lived experiences. However, this is not the case for Kevin and the other Black men featured on *The Real World*.

From the outset, all that we learn about Kevin reifies his characterization as an angry Black man. Throughout the course of the New York season, viewers catch a glimpse of the Jersey City (NJ) neighborhood where Kevin was raised, complete with images of young African American men hanging out amidst the omnipresent presence of police. These signifiers are contextualized within Kevin's explanation that a pimp lived in his apartment complex when he was little. Kevin manages to escape the streets for the ivory towers of Rutgers University, only to later get kicked out for his "radical politics." His persona, as signified by a troubled home life, radical politics, "black revolutionary" poetry, and interactions with other cast members all give credence to his status of an angry Black man. In addition, "codes on non-verbal communication play a vital role alongside [this] restrictive code" (O'Sullivan et al., 1994, p. 102). This is made most apparent within the editing of episodes and the juxtaposition of certain images with excerpts of specific dialogue. For instance, certain interactions between Kevin and other cast members—especially when involving some sort of conflict—are intermeshed with images from Kevin's world: A poster of Malcolm X, shots of inner city life, as well as various Black and African artifacts. These signs are repeated and subsequently extended, in what viewers are shown in regards to the other African American male cast members. All wear clothing (i.e., baggy pants, gold chains, earrings, or leather jackets) associated with inner city young Black males. Syrus' shaved head and Mohammed's dreadlocks present two versions of a similar anti-establishment code; the music associated with

each person (often times this included gangsta rap), also reflect this typification of Black male power/resistance.

Throughout the New York, Los Angeles, and Boston season, viewers are given some insight into the source that fuels Black male anger. Most often, this comes from instances when the African American male cast members strive to educate the others on "what its like to be a Black man in America." In each season, we see attempts of the lone Black man in the house to enlighten his roommates (and subsequently the television viewers) as to the various problems that Black men face on a daily basis. In this regard, other members of the house learn—some, for the first time—the impact that societal stereotypes have on the life experiences of Black men (i.e., being harassed by police in areas where they do not "belong"). In different instances, we see these attempts to educate take a variety of forms. Kevin uses his poetry, confrontation of others, and less volatile means like posting provocative thoughts on a bulletin board. David uses rap lyrics and his comedic talents to drive home some issues. Finally, Syrus uses a number of "teach-able moments" to enlighten his housemates. For example when a close European American male housemate, Sean, innocently suggests using a white background for a bulletin board, Syrus jokingly questions, "What's the matter with a BLACK background?" Through this interaction and others like it (e.g., a discussion as to the symbolism of the black ball in the game of pool), Sean gets a glimpse into a new perspective and insight into the negative connotations that go with being Black in America.

The information shared by the African American cast members provided insight into the sources that contributed to feelings of anger experienced by some Black men. However, these very insights, shared as a means to educate non-African Americans also seemed to contribute to the credibility of the angry Black male stereotype. In this regard, these self-disclosures, intended as a means to enlighten others, were negotiated by the cast members as additional evidence for existing stereotypical images of African American men. From a viewer's perspective, this appeared especially to be the case with non–African Americans as seen in their interactions with their Black male housemates. For instance, in one particularly intense conflict involving Kevin and Julie, she accuses him of "having a lot of misdirected anger." In another interaction, Norman attests that "all he knows of Kevin is a pattern of aggressive behavior." David experiences similar responses from the Los Angeles cast. Irene, a Los Angeles deputy sheriff, articulates her fear of David explaining that "He has something up inside of him that's building, and building, and building." The "something," it is implied, that Irene and others sense is the Black man's response to a history of racism in the United States.

While a number of mechanisms for dealing with this inherent anger are given fleeting attention (e.g., Kevin's poetry and radical politics), what is foregrounded for the viewers are the violent ways that African American men express this "pent up rage." Most often, cast members fear that the anger of Black men will be "misdirected" at "innocent" bystanders. This point is made apparent in this conversation between New York cast members Kevin and Andre:

ANDRE: It seems like you're taking this out on us.
KEVIN: It all came out yesterday. This country is as racist as hell. That's the reality. The way that I was accused of spitting in someone's face, and picking up something that I don't even know what it is and threatening to hit somebody . . .
ANDRE: I don't think that had anything to do with you being Black, though.
KEVIN: Andre . . .
ANDRE: No, seriously, do you think that that is the cause for all of this?
KEVIN: Listen, Andre. From my perspective, whenever a Black person, including myself, has an opinion, and is assertive about it, we become threatening to White people.
ANDRE: There is racism, but you can't go about it . . . by posting signs. You're telling the wrong people, man . . . who here is racist?

Clearly, Kevin's attempt to explain how most European Americans unconsciously tap into the racist stereotypes that pervade their thinking is met with clear resistance. Racism is not constructed as a problem for most, only those most overtly associated with extreme ideologies (e.g., KKK or Aryan Nation). In one poignantly revealing exchange between Kevin and Julie, she responds to his claim that "racism is everywhere," by shouting "BECAUSE OF PEOPLE LIKE YOU, KEVIN, NOT PEOPLE LIKE ME!" Racism, therefore, is not only a problem most salient for African Americans; according to some, it is also a problem perpetuated by African Americans.

Black Male as Violent Threat

So, a primary signifier contributing to a justified societal fear of Black men is clearly maintained: Black men possess an inherent anger triggered by a past, present, and future of racism. Interposed with images that signify this intrinsic tension are self-disclosures of other cast members as to their fear of potential violence stemming from Black men with so much internal rage. In fact, several non–African American cast members confidentially[8] explain their discomfort around Black men who, in their eyes, clearly have great *potential* for violence. Interestingly, comments taken from each of the three casts that featured an African American male cast member are strikingly similar in the ways that this fear is expressed. Their articulation of a general fear of Black men is particularly compelling since—with the exception of one incident involving David and another male housemate in Los Angeles—viewers never see any violent outbursts from the Black male cast members. What appears to be happening, at least as it is deconstructed through this semiotic analysis, is that specific cast members unconsciously tap into long-established stereotypes of African American males in framing current perceptions of Kevin, David, and Syrus. Then based on these underlying stereotypes, cast members—most often European American women—work to persuade others to adopt their interpretation of certain behaviors enacted by African American men.

In Los Angeles, for example, a playful exchange

between David and Tami (an African American woman) escalated to a full-blown conflict (featured as one of the "most dangerous *Real World* episodes). Before the incident is resolved, viewers witness how this conflict triggers images of the capacity of violence by Black men. We hear from Irene, a Los Angeles deputy sheriff, who described that, "During the two days before we had our talk with David, what went through my mind was . . . how I was feeling. I had this unsafe feeling . . . I had this threatening feeling." During this time, small groups of housemates (mostly divided by sex) discussed the incident: Some agreed with Irene's perceptions while others clearly did not. When David attempts to discuss the incident with each woman individually, they refuse citing their fear of being alone with him. David cannot understand their reaction, especially since several crew members will be present recording the interaction, and jokingly asks: "You all are acting like I'm Freddy Krueger or something . . . what's going on here?" After finally convincing the entire house to sit down and discuss the incident, a consensus is achieved: The women in the house do not feel comfortable with David, so he must move out (and subsequently be replaced on the show).[9] Whereas not everyone in the house agrees with this extreme measure, they seemingly are convinced by two of the women, Irene and Beth, that no other alternative is possible. The images that follow this decision are especially revealing as to the process by which Black men are signified on the show. Viewers are exposed to a series of edited clips—presented in strikingly haunting black and white film—that show David in a series of aggressive interactions (i.e., arguing with housemates, physically going after another male housemate). With these displays of aggression, the final members of the house are convinced of David's potential for violence. In close proximity, so are *Real World* viewers.

A similar pattern is witnessed in the "most dangerous" NYC episode. Following an off-camera conflict between Julie and Kevin, Julie confesses that "I think that it's really obvious after living with Kevin, that he was capable of some physical violence." Viewers are then presented with Julie's perception

of the conflict and witness how her story convinces other housemates of Kevin's potential for violence. "Julie was really upset and hysterical . . . for her to be like that something serious really must have happened," explains one roommate (Eric). Only after confronting Kevin with these accusations do some roommates recognize that Julie's perception of what happened greatly differs from Kevin's recollection. While discussions reveal that both parties had some responsibility in the intense conflict, Julie's perceptions remain unchanged. When discussing the incident with another housemate (Eric), she states, "You can believe whatever you want or stay totally out of it." And then adds, "All I know is that I don't ever want to be left alone with him again. Ever." Later, she privately shares the following thoughts:

> I really like Kevin . . . and could never deny that. I respect him a lot, and I think that he is really intelligent and has a lot of important things to say. . . . That doesn't mean that I ever want to be alone with Kevin again . . . in my life. I will never be comfortable, and don't really understand how I can expect to be.

The third "most dangerous" episode, of the Boston season, also featured a confrontation between the African American male cast member (Syrus) and his housemates. The episode dealt more generally with a series of conflicts surrounding Montana (European American woman); however, it included a confrontation between her and Syrus. The conflict erupts over a late night call that Syrus gets while other housemates are attempting to rest. Viewers witness an exchange of words between Syrus and Montana—intense in some ways (Syrus calls Montana a bitch), but largely uneventful since both people were quite a distance from one another and leaving the room. The next day, Montana and Syrus talk about the brief incident:

MONTANA: I think that you came across a little too strong last night . . . you know what I'm saying . . . and it was like BITCH. And I got the idea that you were about to hit me, and got the impression—

SYRUS: Never. Never. I'm not a physical person like that at all . . . If I came across like that, I apologize . . .

Within the show, the visual representation of Syrus's persona is quite different than that of the other Black men on *The Real World*. Syrus does not display the social consciousness or radical politics of Kevin. Nor does he play the role of comedian, like David. Syrus is a self-proclaimed "playa" who loves to party, kick back, and "spend time with the ladies." In no episodes are viewers exposed to any hint of violence; in fact, we see that Syrus's strategy for dealing with conflict largely involves sitting down and sharing a "brew." Regardless of these personal characteristics, however, a similar sign is invoked: Black men represent a threat (especially to European American women). Although Montana and Syrus resolve the brief conflict over the late night calls, we see her confess to the camera:

> He can apologize until the cows come home, and I can say, "fine, I accept your apology," . . . but I'm not going to forget what happened. In the back of my mind, that will always be there.

Even when the possibility for violence is slim—and relatively less than for any other person—cast members articulate that the perceived potential for violence remains a salient issue for them in their interactions with Black men. In two different instances, for example, Julie and Kevin (NYC cast) are involved in a conflict when Julie makes her perceived fear of Kevin apparent by asking him if he is going to physically harm her. In one scene, Julie asks Kevin, "Why are you getting so close? Why are you getting so emotional? What are you going to do, hit me?" Kevin attempts to explain how proximity and emotional expressiveness are culture specific; Julie's response is to emphatically assert her perception that "It's not a black-white thing." Kevin then gives conscious voice to the larger question in the minds of those that recognize the subtle influence that racism has in this interaction when he confronts her perception by asking: "Do you assume that because I'm a Black man that I'm going to hit you?"

Black Male as Sexually Aggressive

A restrictive code is comprised of a system of signifiers that explicitly or implicitly governs the interpretations of the members of a using culture (O'Sullivan et al., 1994). The third interlocking signifier, one that solidifies a clear justification for societal concern/fear, involves the sexual aggression associated with Black men. Whereas this signifier works more on an inferential level with Kevin and Julie's interactions (i.e., Kevin's disclosures about his sexual fantasies in response to a light-hearted discussion on issues prompted by a "book of questions"), it is foregrounded in the ways that Syrus and David's *Real World* images are constructed.

From the onset, Syrus's persona is most clearly represented by his love for women; in fact, his life (as signified by *Real World* images) revolves around "his theory that women are like potato chips . . . [you can't have just one]." Within the first three Boston episodes, viewers witness a barrage of clips with Syrus "macking"—hugging, holding, flirting and dancing with—several different European American women. In fact, his behaviors become a house issue when he continues to bring different women home into the wee hours of the morning. Kameelah, the lone African American woman on the Boston cast, is self-admittedly annoyed because Syrus is bringing home White women (who she describes as "groupies" and "hoochie mommas"). The other women agree that he does not appear to have much respect for women; however, the larger house issue is one of courtesy. Syrus' responds to this issue by invoking his [sexual] "freedom to do whatever he wants." "I feel like I'm in a damn prison," he contends.

Questions regarding Syrus' sexual freedom to pursue a variety of women is juxtapositioned within a more problematic context during the third episode when cast members (and viewers) learn that Syrus was accused of rape while in college. Syrus adamantly denies the charge; he describes the woman as being the aggressor ("she took my clothes off") on the night in question. Whereas he appears to convince some of his housemates that, in fact, some women do "cry rape," others remain unmoved by his emotional arguments. Regardless of Syrus's guilt/innocence, the producers of the show have chosen to foreground an image that signifies him as sexually aggressive, a Black man who potentially may use rape to satisfy his sexual needs. In fact, the sign of Black male sexual aggression is made more problematic by extended images in later episodes that signify Syrus's need for sexual pleasure as largely uncontrollable. In two different scenarios, he is portrayed as succumbing to his sexual needs even when such actions put him at great risk. First, he jeopardizes his standing in the house by continuing to bring women into the house and even "doing some blonde" in his room while housemates confront his other drunk guests. Second, Syrus risks losing his job at a community center by continuing to "date" one of the child's parents'—hours after assuring his supervisor and housemates that he would no longer see the woman if it represented a conflict of interest.

Whereas Syrus's sexual appetite was foregrounded in the creation of his *Real World* persona, David's sexuality was signified in a more subtle manner. First and foremost, David is a comedian, always joking and "playing the fool" for the camera. Through his comedy, however, signs of his sexual aggression are alluded to as he jokingly discusses his love for masturbation and amusement in pulling his pants down in front of the cameras. His playful joking with housemates becomes increasingly problematic during one episode when a prank between him and Tami, an African American woman, escalates into a heated conflict. In the most replayed LA episode, David playfully attempts to pull the blanket off of Tami who is in her bed for the night wearing only her underwear and bra. For a couple of minutes, there is a lighthearted struggle; this drastically changes when David continues to try and pull the blanket off of Tami as she gets up to take a phone call. The latter part of the interaction is filled with screams of "STOP! DON'T! DAVID STOP!" from both Tami and Beth (a European American woman). The line has clearly crossed when Tami escapes to the bathroom, dons a robe, and immediately begins to re-

taliate against David. The following excerpts illustrate the conversation that ensued:

DAVID: You guys were laughing, giggling, playing—

TAMI: You can take off your pants in front of the camera, but I am not like that. It was NOT funny, okay?

DAVID: Here, hey, here you go . . . I'll take off my clothes [drops his pants to his ankles exposing himself]

IRENE: [calls from the bedroom, where she is still in bed] I'll call the police and scream rape!

BETH: We should file charges against him . . .

During this exchange, John (a young European American man from a small town in Kentucky) theorizes, "It's all about rap music, and the violence and tension that builds up . . . and this is what happens . . ."

Two salient issues are signified during this exchange. First, John associates David's aggression with the violence portrayed in rap music; in essence, his comments enact a sense-making mechanism for understanding the violent nature of Black masculinity. Second, and even more central to the fear of Black men is Irene's threatening to accuse David of rape. Interestingly, Irene's comments, contextualized within her identity as a deputy sheriff for the LA police department, invoke another powerful code from an African American male perspective. Accusations of rape, however, become more intense as Beth confronts David directly:

DAVID: You're going to press charges for me pulling a cover off of her??? For playing??? You guys were on the floor screaming [mocking their playful tone] "Stop . . . stop . . ."

BETH: Yeah, and that is what a rapist says too—

DAVID: Rape??? This hasn't anything to do with rape!

BETH: [Imitating a rapist] Yeah, you wanted it baby . . .

DAVID: I didn't try to rape—this hasn't nothing to do with rape!

BETH: No means no, okay?

DAVID: Wait a minute . . . who? . . . when? You're taking this too far; I wasn't going to rape the girl . . . I was playing . . . I was just pulling the blanket.

The power of a European American woman conjuring up metaphors of the Black male rapist is not lost on David who obviously recognizes the power of such accusations. "In the old days," he tells the group, "I would be hung. Because a woman said rape . . . not rationally hung, just hung."

Later, as the group decides to remedy the situation, David reveals his wish that the housemates could rewind the tape and review the incident. Whereas the LA cast was not privy to such an opportunity, the producers do utilize this juncture to re-play the incident for the viewers who can come to their own conclusions as to the seriousness of David's offenses. When David confronts Beth about her usage of the term, rape, she readily "takes it back." However, the signification of David as a sexually aggressive potential rapist cannot be easily erased from the minds of the female housemates. The signifier, Black male as rapist, has been successfully invoked and remains in their consciousness as they contextualize David's other behaviors (e.g., talking about masturbation, pulling his pants down, aggressively confronting other housemates). Without a doubt, David—regardless of his small physical stature and joking persona—is a person to be feared. Even the men in the house who disagree with the decision to make David move out are swayed by the intensity of these images. "I guess other incidents have occurred that I'm unaware of," explains one man. Another adds, "They [the women] explained to me that it wasn't just this one incident, but a culmination of things." Those viewers with a critical eye are left wondering if the other "things" are related to David's behaviors in the house specifically or the underlying stereotypical beliefs about African Americans generally that seem to unconciously permeate their interactions with others.

Discussion

The Hegemonic Power of Real World Images

Much has been written on the role of hegemony and the ways in which the general public utilizes mediated images in its constructions of reality. Despite its positioning as an alternative, oppositional media outlet, MTV's *Real World* contributes to a strong media tradition of signifying African American men as potentially dangerous, and in turn, intensifies the signification process of promoting a genre that strongly encourages an active "spectator-positioning" (Heath, 1979) for viewers. Based on the images presented on the show—and contextualized within the existence of a larger societal stereotype of Black men—many viewers, especially European American women, can identify with the fear articulated by some housemates. The paradigmatic signifiers (Black men as angry, violent, and sexually aggressive) work toward the reification of a syntagmatic code: Black men are to be feared. Within the context of this semiotic analysis, I argue that the mediated images of Black masculinity on *The Real World* represent a powerful source of influence because they, in fact, are presented not as mediated images, but as real-life images captured on camera. The African American men chosen for the show are passed off to the general public as—in the words of the creator/producer of the show, Mary-Ellis Bunin—"real people, undirected, sharing their lives" (Huriash, 1996, p. 35). In fact, what is displayed for the millions of viewers who watch the show each week are selectively filtered images of Black masculinity as determined by non–African Americans. The remainder of this article will explore this idea in regards to two crucial elements of the show: cast selection and editing.

For the first several seasons, the process of cast selection for the show remained largely a mystery. For the sixth season of *The Real World*, however, the creators/producers began with an hour-long "casting special" episode that documented the rigorous process by which tens of thousands of applicants were narrowed down to seven "lucky" persons. Within this hour, viewers are given insight—albeit through media images selected by the producers to represent their own efforts—into the lengthy process of reviewing videotapes, individual and group interviews, and final decisions. I argue that this special provides some important information directly relevant to the arguments presented in this article. First, viewers learn that none of the major players associated with the show (creators, producers, casting directors, assistants, and so on) are African American. Whereas this insight alone does not directly correlate to any specific conclusion, it does allow some additional contextualization of what may occur when outgroup members are responsible for decisions regarding diverse lived experiences.[10] Second, something that has long been suspected, becomes increasingly apparent: The producers of the show select cast members who have the greatest potential for cultural clash and conflict. Within the process of cast selection, for instance, viewers hear comments like, "She has a personality that polarizes others, we have to keep her." It appears that the African American men chosen for the show, in part, qualify because of the potential tension that their presence in the house will facilitate.

Within the casting special, viewers are privy to the process by which Syrus emerges as the lone African American man selected for the sixth season. Based on the footage that we see from his taped interviews, it is clear that Syrus's persona (a ladies man from the streets of LA who loves to party and play basketball) will provide ample opportunities for conflict with the others selected. These persons, in short, include a European American self-affirmed feminist from New York (Montana), a Mexican/European American 18-year-old who had led a sheltered life in Texas (Elka), and a 25-year-old lumberjack who has had no real contact with African Americans (Sean). What is especially interesting in regards to the critical analysis offered here are the other African American men who were *not* selected for the show. In fact, in addition to Syrus, two other men of African descent advanced to the final round on interviews. One man,

Q'wan was a college student in Georgia who appeared to have a healthy attitude concerning success, love, and relationships. The other applicant strongly considered for the show was Jon, a fun-loving musician with a multi-racial background. The argument posited here is that the creators/producers of the show, in attempts to create the greatest potential for tension in the house, selected the African American man who would be perceived as the largest threat to other cast members.[11] In doing so they selected Syrus, someone who they could count on for supplying the cameras all that they needed to make a compelling docu-drama. However, their decision also worked toward the perpetuation of a restrictive coding of African American men in the media, one that signifies them in a totalizing manner.

Whereas the selection of certain African American men to appear on *The Real World* fosters a certain visual representation of Black masculinity, the process that involved editing three months of footage into a series of half-hour episodes appeared to facilitate the producers' conscious or unconscious desire to signify these Black men as inherently angry, potentially violent, and sexually aggressive. The power of editing worked to force certain aspects of the African American men's lives in the foreground while others remained in the background. In order to construct a more convincing [powerful] storyline, the sequence of events or syntagmatic ordering (Stam et al., 1992) was also manipulated during editing. For example, a close reading of several conflicts involving African American male cast members reveal that the scenes did not in fact always occur in the sequence presented by the producers. Instead, as evidenced by subtle changes in an individual's appearance (clothes, hair, body positioning), it becomes clear that producers have placed comments from past or future interactions within another context in order to make that conflict seem more inflammatory.[12] Manipulation of the syntagmatic ordering of *Real World* events results in a construction of reality that reflects a storyline created by the producers of the show, and not necessarily a reflection of the reality of the three months taped for the show. The same process, it can be argued, was followed in creating the characterizations for all cast members on *The Real World*. However, it appears that the show has realized its potential for advancing non-stereotypical images of certain underrepresented groups; this especially seems to be the case with its representations of diverse Latino and gay/lesbian/bisexual cast members. Such is not the case for the African American male mediated images included in the show. In short, the signifiers that were selected to be associated with Black masculinity did little to counter the existing media stereotypes of African American men.

It is commonly understood that, despite the "hype" promoting the show as characteristic of the real world, most television viewers are discriminating enough to recognize that the interactions occurring amidst a sea of cameras and microphones are *not real*. Instead, what is seen can be deconstructed as an elaborate show put on by cast members with a clear consciousness of the millions of viewers who will have access to their lives. Following the fourth season of *The Real World*, MTV brought all of the casts together for a special reunion that, in part, asked the following question: "How real is *The Real World*?" Not surprisingly, some cast members discussed how MTV manipulated the footage by editing it in a way that portrayed them in certain ways. Others focused on the *un*realistic nature of the three months of taping: Being surrounded by cameras, living rent-free in a beautiful house/apartment, and having access to special events and places. However, other cast members maintained that the initial novelty of the cameras wore off and explained that no one could maintain a certain media persona without revealing their real selves. In responding to one comment regarding how MTV's editing worked to portray certain people in specific ways, Heather (a NYC cast member) countered by affirming the reality of the images, "They [MTV] only used what you gave them . . . they couldn't show something unless you did it." Heather's assertions are supported by the significant number of comments, behaviors, or interactions that are caught on tape by

the cameras—these are things that the viewing public is convinced that cast members (like the rest of us) have done, but would not want taped and shown repeatedly to millions of viewers. The inclusion of such clips enhances the credibility of the "realness" of the show.

The most crucial element, however, in terms of how realistic viewers perceive *The Real World* to be lies in the viewers' desire for it to be real. The primary attraction for the show is its efforts to show real people in everyday interactions, not to portray "characters" closely following a pre-determined, externally created script. Television viewers can get such contrived mediated images from countless other types of programming. The most exciting aspect of the show is the unpredictability that comes with reality; it is this very notion that draws televisual voyeurs to the show and keeps them (us) coming back for more.

> As viewers, we are privy to every detail of the cast members' lives. . . . When they scream, fight, laugh, and say unfathomably, stupid things, we are there. Because the show is pared down to half-hour episodes, most of what the producers film is edited away. And so in the end we only trust what we see on television . . . what happens off-screen might as well as never happened at all. It is the perfect existentialist production—being in nothingness, life is television. (Sakurari, 1996, p. 17)

Understanding a text, according to Gadamer (1975), consists of examining the enduring messages of the text within a larger context and apart from the creator's original intentions. The reiteration and reinforcement of similar signifiers across the various *Real World* casts, or the textual volume of such images (Bellour, 1977), connotes a fundamental truth: Black masculinity is inherently dangerous and to be feared. This stereotypical depiction of Black maleness simply adds to the hegemonic images in film and television. So, in addition to the negative characterizations of African American men in countless films and various genres of television programming, viewers now can draw from additional "real world" examples in legitimizing their discomfort around Black men. Instead of using the real life experiences of young African American men to advance viewers' understanding of the complex diversity within this large, heterogeneous group, this popular series merely cultivates the perpetuation of existing stereotypes. In making this problematic process of media signification apparent, I hope to deconstruct the arduous representations of young Black men in the media, and in doing so, challenge the cyclical process by which these images are transferred to and from the context of interpersonal interactions and accepted as accurate, natural, and true.

With a semiotic analysis, it is important to recognize "that what is absent from a text is as significant as what is present" (Fiske, 1994, p. 422). As attended to throughout this article, I argue that what is strikingly absent from the first six seasons of MTV's *The Real World* are any substantial images that signify Black masculinity in a positive, healthy, or productive manner. Certainly, there are some African American men whose life experiences do reflect those represented on the series. The redundancy of associating Black masculinity with potential violence, however, works to negate the great diversity of experiences of African American men in the United States.

> Individual subjectivity is denied because the black [male] subject is positioned as a mouthpiece, a ventriloquist for an entire social category which is seen to be "typified" by its representative. Acknowledgment of the diversity of black experiences and subject-positions is thereby foreclosed. (Julien & Mercer, 1996, p. 454)

As mentioned at the beginning of this article, the seventh season of MTV's *The Real World* is currently being filmed in Seattle. Will the producers of the show continue in their restrictive coding of African American men or will a more elaborative code—one that promotes a foregrounding of the diversity of Black men—be offered? Unofficial previews, based on a number of *Real World* sightings by Seattle internet users, describe one cast member (Steven) as "A Black guy, not much more [known] yet." Drawing from the redundancy of signifiers assigned to African American men selected

for past seasons of the show, I would suggest that the viewers have all the information that is needed to get a solid grasp on how Steven will be represented on *The Real World*.

Notes

1. For each season, seven persons are chosen from a large diverse pool of 10,000–25,000 applicants (Sakurari, 1996) who "apply" via personal videotapes, letters, or open calls held in various cities across the United States.

2. Throughout this article, I interchangeably use "African American" and "Black" to refer to those persons of African descent. However, it is important to note that when discussing the stereotypical depictions that justify the fear of "BLACK" men, I consciously use Black (and not African American) because of the connotative power associated with the term.

3. For instance, MTV will often preempt regular weekend programming and show *Real World* marathons, which in essence air all of the episodes of a given season within several continuous hours. During other times, MTV will present special programming that airs a single episode from each show around a common theme (cast introductions, vacations, or farewells).

4. Given that my interpretations of the show are undoubtedly tied to my field of experience, some identification of the cultural standpoint(s) that I bring to the analysis is appropriate. In this regard, my reading of the images of Black masculinity are inextricably linked to my identity as a non–African American thirty-something man who was raised in an ethnically diverse East Coast public housing complex. My cultural standpoint is further defined by my experiences as a: (a) researcher of intercultural/interracial communication, (b) "heavy user" of television, and (c) participant/member of various African American communities (residential, social, familial, religious, and professional) over the course of my life.

5. Throughout the various seasons, three aspects of diversity appeared to be foregrounded: sex/gender, race/ethnicity, and affectional/sexual

orientation. To a lesser degree, other cultural elements such as religion and socioeconomic status, were present but not explored with the intensity of other elements.

6. Mohammed maintains a marginal presence (at best) within these "most dangerous" episodes. This came as no surprise to *Real World* fans who watched the San Francisco season and noticed the lack of attention given to his role in the house. In fact, while Mohammed was part of the cast throughout the entire season, his prominence within the final [edited] footage is reminisce of the invisibility of Black men described by Ralph Ellison's *Invisible Man* (1947).

7. For the first season, three months of footage was edited down to 13 half-hour episodes; subsequent seasons were expanded to 19–22 episodes each.

8. One of the features of *The Real World* is the confessional room. Over the three months of their stay in the house, cast members are required to spend time alone in this room self-disclosing (only to a camera) their personal reflections of the events that are going on with others. Often times, footage from the confessional is edited into actual interactions, so that viewers gain insight into how each person perceived the interaction as it unfolds.

9. Several of the incidents portrayed within the "most dangerous episodes" marathon are marked by gender, as well as racial, dynamics. The "rape" scene analyzed here is primarily marked by gender (a man accused of raping a woman); however, it is critiqued specifically in terms of race *and* gender (a White woman accusing a Black man of rape). In this regard, my intentions are not to privilege considerations of race over those of gender, but instead to locate my focus on analyzing the media images used to signify African American men.

10. See, for example, the analysis of *All-American Girl*, a short-lived situated comedy that featured a Korean-American family but did not have any Korean-American producers or writers (Orbe, Seymour, & Kang, in press).

11. Such a clear manipulation of cast members did not only involve the African American men. Within the same season, viewers witness the selection of Elka, someone whose stereotypical views of gays and lesbians are apparent through her comments about her strong Catholic and relatively sheltered upbringing, is selected as part of a cast with a "very out" lesbian (Genesis) and anti-religion feminist (Montana).

12. This editing technique is common practice throughout the six seasons of the show. For instance, in the scenes where the conflict between David and his LA housemates unfolded, the producers take some of David's comments to housemates from earlier footage and place them within the context of the present conflict. In doing so, a more compelling drama is created, but the meanings of the comments are re-defined apart from their original context. No attention is given to identifying the specific context from which the comments were made; instead the editing team achieves their primary goal: to create a "natural" flow of events with little or no evidence of their manipulation. Through a close examination of David and Beth's dress and positioning in the house, however, some viewers may notice several inconsistencies (i.e., Beth wearing shorts when confronting David, cut to David's response, and then returning to Beth who seemingly responds directly to David but now has on long pants) that reveal how some comments made in a joking manner earlier are re-defined as hostile and threatening by inserting them into another context.

References

Ang, I. (1985). *Watching Dallas*. London: Methuen.

Atkins, D. (1992). An analysis of television series with minority-lead characters. *Critical Studies in Mass Communication, 9*, 337–349.

Bailey, C. (1988). Nigger/lover—the thin sheen of race in *Something Wild. Screen, 29*(4), 28–43.

Barthes, R. (1972). The world of wrestling. In A. Lavers (Trans.), *Mythologies* (pp. 15–25). New York: Hill & Wang.

Bellour, R. (1977). Alternation, segmentation, hypnosis: An interview. *Camera Obsura, 2,* 70–103.

Berry, V. T. (1992). From *Good Times* to *The Cosby Show:* Perceptions of changing televised images among Black fathers and sons. In S. Craig (Ed.), *Men, masculinity and the media* (pp. 111–123). Newbury Park, CA: Sage.

Bogle, D. (1994). *Toms, coons, mulattoes, mammies, and bucks: An interpretive history of Blacks in American films.* New York: The Viking Press.

Brooks, D. E., & Jacobs, W. R. (1996). Black men in the margins: Space Traders and the interpositional strategy against b(l)acklash. *Communication Studies, 47,* 289–302.

Cheney, F., & Tompkins, P. (1988). On the facts of the text as the basis of human communication research. In J. A. Anderson (Ed.), *Communication Yearbook 11* (pp. 455–501). Newbury Park, CA: Sage.

Cloud, D. L. (1992). The limits of interpretation: Ambivalence and the stereotype in "Spencer For Hire." *Critical Studies in Mass Communication, 9,* 311–324.

Condit, C. M. (1989). The rhetorical limits of polysemy. *Critical Studies in Mass Communication, 6,* 103–122.

Cooks, L. M., & Orbe, M. (1993). Beyond the satire: Selective exposure and selective perception in *In Living Color. Harvard Journal of Communications, 4,* 217–233.

Eco, U. (1976). *A theory of semiotics.* Bloomington, IN: Indiana University Press.

Elise, S., & Umoja, A. (1992). Spike Lee constructs the new Black man: Mo' better. *Western Journal of Black Studies, 6,* 82–89.

Ellison, R. (1947). *Invisible man.* New York: Vintage Books.

Evoleocha, S. U., & Ugbah, S. D. (1989). Stereotypes, counter-stereotypes, and Black television images in the 1990s. *Western Journal of Black Studies, 12,* 197–205.

Fiske, J. (1994). Ethnosemiotics: Some personal and theoretical reflections. In H. Newcomb

(Ed.), *Television: The critical view* (5th ed., pp. 411–425). New York: Oxford University Press.

Gadamer, H. (1975). *Truth and method.* New York: Seabury Press.

Gates, H. L. (1992). TV's Black world turns—but stays unreal. In M. L. Andersen & P. H. Collins (Eds.), *Race, class, and gender: An anthology* (pp. 310–316). Belmont, CA: Wadsworth.

Gray, H. (1989). Television, Black Americans, and the American dream. *Critical Studies in Mass Communication, 6,* 376–386.

Hall, S. (1989). Ideology and communication theory. In B. Dervin, L. Grossberg, B. O'Keefe, & E. Wartella (Eds.), *Rethinking communication theory* (pp. 40–52). Newbury Park, CA: Sage.

Hall, S. (1992). What is this "Black" in Black popular culture? In G. Dent (Ed.), *Black popular culture* (pp. 21–33). Seattle: Bay Press.

Harris, J. L. (1992). The portrayal of the Black family on prime-time network TV: A look at stereotypic images and disorganization of family structure. *Journal of Intergroup Relations, 19,* 45–58.

Heath, S. (1979). The truth of the subject. CINE-TRACTS, 7/8, 32.48.

hooks, b. (1992). *Black looks: Race and representation.* Boston: South End Press.

Huriash, L. J. (1996, July 10). Surreal world. *Fort Lauderdale (FL) Sun-Sentinel,* p. C25.

Julien, I., & Mercer, K. (1997). De margin and de centre. In D. Morley & K. H. Chen (Eds.), *Stuart Hall: Critical dialogues in cultural studies* (pp. 450–464). New York: Routledge.

Kellner, D. L. (1995). *Media culture: Cultural studies, identity and politics between the modern and the post-modern.* New York: Routledge.

Lanigan, R. (Ed.) (1988). A treasure house of preconstituted types: Alfred Schutz on communicology. In *Phenomenology of communication: Merleau-Ponty's thematics in communicology and semiology* (pp. 203–222). Pittsburgh: Duquesne University Press.

Lewis, L. A. (1994). Form and female authorship in

music video. In H. Newcomb (Ed.), *Television: The critical view* (5th ed., pp. 249–267). New York: Oxford University Press.

Loud, P., & Johnson, N. (1974). *Pat Loud: A woman's story.* New York: Coward, McCann, & Geoghean.

MacDonald, J. F. (1983). *Black and white TV: Afro-Americans in television since 1948.* Chicago: Nelson-Hall.

Omi, M. (1989). *In Living Color:* Race and American culture. In I. Angus & S. Jhally (Eds.), *Cultural politics in contemporary America* (pp. 111–122). New York: Routledge.

Orbe, M., Seymour, R., & Kang, M. (in press). "Ethnic humor" and ingroup/outgroup positioning: Explicating perceptions of *All-American Girl.* In Y. R. Kamalipour & T. Carilli (Eds), *Cultural diversity in the U.S. media.* Albany, NY: State University of New York Press.

Orbe, M., & Strother, K. E. (1996). Signifying the tragic mulatto: A semiotic analysis of Alex Haley's *Queen. Howard Journal of Communications, 7,* 113–126.

O'Sullivan, T., Hartley, J., Saunders, P., Montgomery, M., & Fiske, J. (1994). *Key concepts in communication and cultural studies.* New York: Routledge.

Peirce, C. (1958). In C. Hartshorne, P. Weiss, & A. Burks (Eds.), *The collected papers of Charles Saunders Peirce* (vols. 1–8). Cambridge, MA: Harvard University.

Ricoeur, P. (1976). *Interpretation theory: Discourses and the surplus of meaning.* Fort Worth, TX: Texas University Press.

Sakurari, S. H. (1996, July 17). *The Real World* is hell. *Salon,* 16–19.

Saussure, R. (1996). *A course in general linguistics.* New York: McGraw-Hill.

Schutz, A. (1967). *The phenomenology of the social world* (G. Walsh & F. Lehmert, Trans.). Evanston, IL: Northwestern University Press.

Siegal, M., & Carey, R. (1989). *Critical thinking: A semiotic perspective.* Bloomington, IN: Eric Clearinghouse on Reading and Communication Skills.

Smith, S. (1993, November). *From the junkman to the garbage man: The evolution of the African American male in the Black situation comedy.* Paper presented at the annual meeting of the Speech Communication Association, Miami, FL.

Stam, R., Burgoyne, R., & Flitterman-Lewis, S. (1992). *New vocabularies in film semiotics: Structuralism, poststructuralism and beyond.* New York: Routledge.

Stroman, C. A. (1991). Television's role in the socialization of African American children and adolescents. *Journal of Negro Education, 60,* 314–327.

PART FOUR

Reception-Centered Approaches

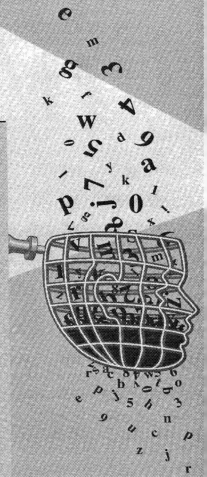

Reader-
Oriented
Criticism

CHAPTER 12

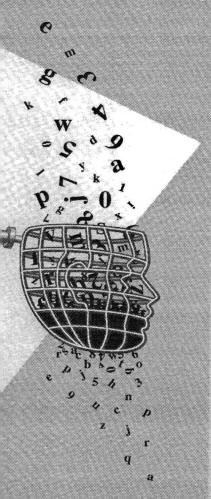

Chapter Outline

Perspectives and Assumptions

Finding the Audience in the Text
Implied Viewers
Interpretive Communities
The Addresser
Characterized Viewers
The Reading Act

Writing Reader-Oriented Criticism

Example Essay: Lawrence A. Wenner's "The Dream Team, Communicative Dirt, and the Marketing of Synergy: USA Basketball and Cross-Merchandising in Television Commercials"

J ust as television may be viewed through different lenses on the production
    process, many conceptions of the role of the audience and the dynamics of re-
    ception are seen in criticism. In the chapters that follow in Part Four, we pre-
sent four reception-centered approaches that explore the "real" and "ideal"
audience responses to television texts. *Reader-oriented criticism,* introduced in
this chapter, further explores the notion of ideological positioning, introduced in
Chapter 11 in relation to producing television. Chapter 13 presents *audience
ethnographic criticism,* a critical method involving fieldwork that the cultural
studies tradition has used to gain qualitative understandings of "the ways in which
meanings made and experienced by viewers" (Corner, 1999, p. 80). In Chapter 14
we introduce two general approaches to cultural criticism: cultural studies criticism and sociocultural criticism. Then, in Chapter 15, we present three criticism
approaches more narrowly concerned with societal reception and responses:
mythic criticism, feminist criticism, and psychoanalytic criticism.

Perspectives and Assumptions

In the 1990s, in what might be taken as the case of the "missing reader," a group of
literary critics embarked on a variety of paths to understand the roles of the reader
and the reading act. Reader-oriented criticism gained favor in literary studies during this period, in part in reaction to the autonomy of texts—texts seemingly without readers—as framed in "new criticism." However, some parts of this "new"
reader-oriented criticism were not really new. Indeed, the "return of the reader"
(Freund, 1987) was partly a return to a historically framed sociology of literature
(Holub, 1984) and partly a return to thinking about literature as a rhetorical communication act in which not just the text but also the reader and the reading act
play central roles (Richards, 1929).

Central to reader-oriented criticism are the text's characterization of the reader,
and through this, the text's attempt to control the reading act. In this approach, the
critic deduces key issues about readers and reading from the text itself. As such,
reader-oriented criticism is largely concerned with "potential" as opposed to "actualized" meanings of the text to an audience (Jensen, 1991, p. 137). Only occasionally will reader-oriented critics corroborate their interpretive conclusions
with real readers; such efforts tend to fall in the province of audience ethnographic
criticism, which is discussed in Chapter 13.

Assumptions about and characterizations of the audience can be seen in a variety of ways. Reader-oriented criticism sees the audience or readers as essential
partners to the construction of the "text" (as opposed to the "work")[1] as in the reception and interpretation of it. Standing is given to the audience through cues
embedded in the television message or text. Sometimes the audience is seemingly
on the screen. For example, when a stand-in can be seen laughing in the live audience, asking a question, or buying products that an advertiser would like you to
buy. Other times, the presence of the off-screen audience is acknowledged, as for
example, when the audience is spoken to directly by a newscaster or sports

announcer who makes assumptions about what the audience knows or how the audience feels. The audience is also constructed in other ways through the television text. For example, redundancy in the television text recognizes the viewing situation of the readers who are at home, often simultaneously engaged in other activities and who often have missed earlier episodes or scenes. Similarly, gaps in the text acknowledge the reading abilities of audience members. So, for example, a character can walk out of the house and in the next scene miraculously appear at work, without the audience's being disoriented or concerned about the character's mode of transportation or events that happened en route because the audience (the text assumes) is familiar with editing codes.[2] The reading position and characterizing of the ideal or expected audience member can also be seen through the camera's point of view. Presenting a scene from the point of view of the hero or heroine tells us something about where the audience members ideally or sympathetically should be relative to the story that is unfolding. This notion of the reader in the text (and the reader relative to the text) argues against the notion of audience as something out there and apart from the text.

Reader-oriented criticism does not represent a unified critical position (see Freund, 1987; Holub, 1984; Suleiman & Crosman, 1980; Tompkins, 1980). The approach is characterized by differences in theoretical starting points, methodological strategies, and ideological fissures. Its development can be seen in the wide-ranging work of literary critics who use the terms "reader, the reading process, and response to mark out an area for investigation" (Tompkins, 1980, p. ix). This critical approach is often called *reception theory* (or *reception aesthetics*) when framed in terms of the work of German critics (Gadamer, 1975; Ingarden, 1973; Iser, 1974, 1978; Jauss, 1982a, 1982b). In its more contemporary American castings, the approach is likely to be called *reader-response criticism*, and the influential works of Wayne Booth (1961, 1974), Jonathan Culler (1981), Norman Holland (1968), and Stanley Fish (1980) are typically cited. Although reader-oriented criticism has developed largely in reference to the reading of literature, its merits in terms of understanding the reading of television and film can be seen in the work of Roland Barthes (1973), Umberto Eco (1977), and Robert Allen (1992).

Several variants in reader-oriented literary criticism stemming from the overlapping approaches that Sulieman (1980) and others (Crosman, 1980; Freund, 1987) have identified are well-suited for analyzing television terms.

Rhetorical approaches focus on the communication situation, the meanings of the communicative transaction, its ideological significance, and its persuasive powers.

Semiotic and structuralist approaches focus on the codes and conventions that affect the process of reading, the text's readability, and ultimately how meaning is made possible.

Phenomenological approaches move questions about the reading act as a sense-making activity to the foreground and seek "to describe and account for the mental processes that occur as a reader advances through a text and derives from it—or imposes on it—a pattern" (Sulieman, 1980, p. 22).

Psychoanalytic approaches look beyond a generalizable phenomenon of reading and focus on how the personalities of ordinary readers contribute to reading strategies and interpretation.

Sociological and historical approaches focus on the social and cultural context of the reading of specific works, genres, or bodies of works by collective reading publics at a particular time.

Hermeneutic approaches bring together a variety of critical tools to explore and understand the deeper structures by which texts inscribe social meaning. Perhaps because hermeneutic criticism focuses on "the nature and possibilities of reading and interpretation as such" and deeper "unapparent" meanings, the approach is the most self-conscious, in terms of its "reflections on its own intentions, assumptions, and positions" (Sulieman, 1980, p. 38). As a result, hermeneutic analysis is likely to "deconstruct" audience experience with television (Derrida, 1976) by questioning textual authority and to be guided by diverse concerns. For example, one might blend feminism, Marxist ideology, psychoanalysis, and mythic perspectives in a hermeneutic analysis.

Finding the audience in the television text can often seem like looking for a needle in a haystack. Determining how the text attempts to manipulate the reading position can be even more problematic. As you approach your first effort in reader-oriented criticism, be aware of the many approaches, but focus on the larger issues discussed in the next section.

Finding the Audience in the Text

Reader-oriented television criticism begins with finding a television text or texts you are concerned about. Because your primary focus will be on how the text characterizes its audience and attempts to control the reading act, it is best to limit your analysis to a specific program or series. Next, articulate your vantage point on the audience. How exactly do you see the audience? Is its fate structurally determined, and if so, by what? Or is the audience ultimately rational, creative, or resilient? You will have to assess the priorities of the audience and also your priorities in doing a particular study. Are you most concerned with the characterization of the audience by the text, the process and pleasures of reading, or the text's ideological thrust and its workings to position readers relative to it? It is important to understand your underlying priorities in order to limit and focus your analysis. Beyond this, understanding your priorities can also help you identify which variant of audience-oriented criticism (e.g., rhetorical, semiotic/structural, phenomenological, sociological) you want to use as your methodological approach. After deciding on these preliminary issues, you are ready to start to examine the audience who is "written into" the text. To do that, you will need to understand several critical concepts, including implied viewers, interpretive communities, addressers, characterized viewers, and other strategies like camera position and editing codes through which texts seek to structure the process of reading/viewing and the meanings audiences construct from interactions with texts.

Implied Viewers

To begin the analysis, you will need to clarify your vision of viewers as implied by the television text and your understandings of the interpretive communities of these viewers. Narrative forms such as the novel, films, and television episodes are stories told by someone—a narrator who has a certain character. Further, stories in novels are told for the benefit and enjoyment of someone, who also has a certain character. Creators of print narratives necessarily have to think about the readers for whom their work is intended. The same is true for television. Producers don't just make television; they make a television text for certain kinds of viewers whom they expect will derive a certain type of pleasure from viewing the text. MTV, for example, was not intended for your grandparents, and football telecasts are not intended for people who know nothing about the game. Television speaks to viewers with implied characteristics. That which is spoken in the text tells the audience-oriented critic about the ideal or model viewer the producer had in mind—a viewer who is likely to garner the same meanings intended by the producer. Different reader-oriented critics have used the terms of *implied, intended, ideal,* and *model readers,* as well as others such as *superreader* and *fictive reader,* to refer to the reader who is desired by the construction of the text. Here we use the term *implied viewer* as a composite for the assumptions about the reader seen in a television text.

By looking carefully at the television text, you can discover what the implied viewer is supposed to know or is likely to believe. Knowledge may be about the program and its history or about the world pertinent to the program. Beliefs and attitudes may be about other groups of people, about entities such as government or democracy, or simply about what's popular. The audience-oriented critic needs to assess which textual, lexical, cultural, and ideological codes the text presumes are shared with viewers to understand its casting of the implied viewer. The implied viewer is somewhere relative to every shot in a television text. Thus, the implied viewer may be continuously cast throughout a program in reception: at one moment the viewer may be cast as appreciative, at others smart, offended, or scared. The text may in one instance imply that the viewer needs redundant information and in another pose that the viewer is able fill in gaps of information not directly presented.

Interpretive Communities

Having said that, however, television programs are not made solely for one implied viewer. Regular viewers of particular programs or certain kinds of programs (e.g., national news, exercise fitness shows) develop a commonality of understandings and beliefs relative to that programming. In the parlance of reader-oriented criticism, such groups are often thought of as *interpretive communities*. These communities can be conceptualized to be synonymous with tightly knit *fan communities* such as the loyal followers of *Star Trek*, a particular soap opera, or a professional football team. Alternatively, interpretive communities can be conceptualized more broadly as fans of televised science fiction, daytime soap operas, or football.

The notion of interpretive communities, as postulated by Fish (1980), attempted to overcome reliance on self-realized individual identity themes read into texts independently by reader-oriented critics. For Fish, the reader is a *social product*, constructed from a system of beliefs shared by communities of readers. From this perspective, the reading of television necessarily occurs within the situated contexts of interpretive communities. These situated contexts may be historically differentiated such as 1950s' viewers taking first runs of *Dragnet* episodes seriously in postwar America, those watching the umpteenth rerun of the show as twenty-first-century camp, or those watching reruns today in Ghana in a yet different context. Alternatively, interpretive communities may coexist at a given time, drawn by differences in gender, race, class, citizenship, or ideology. Audience-oriented television critics need to identify the character of interpretive communities for texts they are analyzing, looking for ways that the sensibilities of these communities interact with each other and with textual representations of the implied viewer.

Several other analytical concepts that will help you understand the transaction between the text and the audience and its implications concern the role of the addresser, the characterization of viewers, and the nature of the reading act.

The Addresser

According to Roland Barthes (1975) narratives work by using a series of codes that control how information is shared and received. Just as television texts are told *to* implied viewers as addressees in interpretive communities, they are told *by* an addresser. The *addresser* may be an unseen omniscient auteur fashioning a television drama, or the addresser may be seen clearly on screen as a narrator, host, or character. Just as important as the identity of the addresser is the *mode of address*. Allen (1992) distinguishes between two modes of address developed by television: the cinematic mode and the rhetorical mode.

The *cinematic mode of address*, used in television dramas and some situation comedies, mirrors the mode of address conventionally used in Hollywood feature films: It "engages its viewers covertly, making them unseen observers of a world that always appears fully formed and autonomous" (Allen, 1992, p. 117). Here, the addresser is an unidentified storyteller who is not part of the story. Still, as the story is told, the addresser continuously puts viewers somewhere relative to the action, attempting to control how they read the story by positioning these implied viewers as flies on a "fourth wall"[3] in preferred places for the desired interpretation. Thus, we may be appropriately scared, scornful, or sympathetic as the story proceeds. The story may be told from the point of view of one of the characters, but most important, the characters do not directly address the viewer.

Television's *rhetorical mode of address* simulates face-to-face communication, both recognizing and directly addressing the viewer. This form is typically seen in television news programs, talk shows, game shows, religious programs, educational programs (e.g., cooking, fitness, home repair), home shopping, standup comedy, variety programming, and many commercials. The addresser plays a variety of characterized roles, such as news anchorperson, reporter, host, guest, moderator, contestant, music video vee-jay, or live audience member. Each role uses different conventions in addressing the viewer. For example, consider the different treatment viewers receive from Dan Rather and Jay Leno. Rather and Leno not only present themselves differently but also relate to and acknowledge viewers in very different ways. In each instance, the pose of the addresser relates assumptions about the implied viewer and the way the text should ideally be read. Whereas the rhetorical mode of address provides insistent reminders that the viewer is the one being spoken to, both the rhetorical and cinematic modes of address attempt to engage and characterize the viewer. The audience-oriented critic needs to assess these strategies carefully in conjunction with characterizations of the viewer that can be seen on screen.

Characterized Viewers

While the off-screen viewer is most clearly characterized ("written into the text") when directly addressed by someone on-screen, the cinematic mode of address also characterizes the viewer by using camera positioning and point-of-view editing strategies to place him or her somewhere relative to the action, thus indicating what the viewer should know or feel. Indeed, as Allen (1992, p. 121) points out, television goes one step further by regularly providing us "with on-screen characterized viewer–textual surrogates who do what real viewers cannot: interact with other performers and respond (usually in an ideal fashion) to the appeals, demands, and urgings of the addresser." Television makes use of two types of textual surrogates: the nonfictional characterized viewer and the fictional characterized viewer.

The *nonfictional characterized viewer* can be seen in the form of the live-audience viewer on the television set, the game show contestant, or the "average person" who shows up as a guest on a talk show such as *Oprah, Sally Jessee Raphael,* or *Jerry Springer.* Here we find living, breathing, exemplary viewers who not only stand in for us but act the way we might if we were there. This nonfictional characterization of us is often capitalized on by others, such as announcers, newscasters, and talk show hosts as they employ the "fictional we" (Stam, 1983) to join our group as exemplary viewers. Thus, the talk show host roaming the audience can frame our questions (e.g., "What we really want to know is . . .") or the news reporter can join us (e.g., "We'll take a closer look at . . .").

The *fictional characterized viewer* is more clearly not a real person (that is, someone playing one's self) standing in for the audience. Rather this viewer is an actor who is playing a role that characterizes you (the audience member) as you should ideally play your role.[4] This approach is most frequently used in commercials as people like you (played by actors) act out your idealized responses for you in your role as a consumer. However, unlike your real-life response, your textual surrogate always buys the advertised product.

Over the years, television producers have crafted ways of diversifying textual surrogates so that there is something (and somebody) to identify with for everyone. This is seen in the multicultural world of commercials such as those used by Coca-Cola or AT&T, in the audiences of daytime talk shows, and in dramatic programs and soap operas that feature large ensemble casts. Somewhere in these television texts, you will find one or more characterizations of you. Reader-oriented television critics assess how these characterizations affect reading and interact with the casting of the implied viewer, who is supposedly watching television and taking all this in.

The Reading Act

Reader-oriented literary criticism, and the television criticism based on it, is particularly concerned with the process of reading. Beyond modes of address and textual surrogates, reader-oriented criticism explores the various strategies television texts use to control the reading act. In confronting television texts, viewers encounter a skeletal structure of meaning. They necessarily encounter this schemata piecemeal as they watch something on television. As a result, they progress through television texts with what Iser (1978) calls a "wandering viewpoint" from somewhere inside the schemata. An artifact of viewing television is that a program can never be experienced in its entirety while it is being viewed. However, along the way, television texts make demands on viewers, encouraging them to read the texts in a desired or ideal way. Reader-oriented critics need to assess these structural demands of the text on the readers in terms of what they say about implied readers and their interpretive communities.

The camera's position relative to the action is one of the most obvious ways the viewer is placed for a correct reading. The camera's vantage point often characterizes the interests, knowledge, allegiances, and sympathies of the implied viewer (see Butler, 1994, pp. 123–145). Redundancy in the television text can also say a number of things to and about the viewer. It can simply say that viewers are forgetful or need a reminder of something important. Alternatively, it might be a demand for a reading position, saying, "Here is something so important that we are reminding you of it again so that you will get these next things right." What appears to be needless redundancy may be restatement commanding the viewer to see how different characters in a drama react to the same information. Such retraining is necessary to read developments in a crime drama or soap opera.[5]

Redundancy aids retention. Borrowing from Iser (1978), Allen (1992, p. 106) points out that the viewing process is "an alternation between protension (expectation or anticipation) and retention (our knowledge of the text to that point)" because each shot in a television text "both answers questions and asks new ones." Answers to new questions are posed to the viewer either *sequentially* (syntagmatic organization) or *by association* (paradigmatic organization). Because of the *call of protension,* strategic juxtaposition of shots and scenes feeds on expectation and directs the reader to make desired *syntagmatic connections,* to stay with the text in the intended order. Still, strategic juxtaposition of disparate scenes regularly leaves gaps that need to be filled in by the viewer. Such gaps force the viewer to make *paradigmatic connections* between the familiar and unfamiliar in the television text. Strategic gaps occur not only between scenes but also within programs.

Perhaps the most strategic gaps in the televisual text are created for and by commercial interruptions. The commercial gap is one form of strategic interruption that aims to control the viewer. Thus, television programs often break for commercial with a cliffhanger or, put another way, heightened protension. The gap brought about by strategic interruption aims to have the viewer reflect on the situation and want to see how it is resolved and, in the process, stay put for the commercial messages. Gaps are also naturally found between episodes of programs; a strategic interruption at the close of one episode aims to call the viewer back next week after some reflective enjoyment in the gap that has been posed.

Writing Reader-Oriented Criticism

There is no cookie-cutter template for writing reader-oriented criticism essays. Writing a reader-oriented analysis does not follow one set pattern. Most critics start with a television text that is problematic in terms of what it thrusts before the audience or of what it says about the audience. Swirling texts such as music videos or commercials may pose seemingly complex challenges to the viewer. Sports programs or soap operas may imply gendered sensibilities in their audiences. Game shows may make assumptions about the value of consumerism for their fans. The problems that the television text poses will often be introduced in conjunction with what the writer knows to be true about the audience. Here, the critic may focus on a broad group of fans for particular programming, such as soap operas or sports coverage, or may focus on a subset of viewers whose relationship with the material may be complex, unusual, or disturbing.

Once material is chosen for analysis and audience focus is specified, the critic generally begins by looking at whom the text implies are viewers and the assumptions that are made of their interpretive communities. Beyond this starting point, the critic may be more interested in some things than others. Certain critics may be more concerned with understanding the addresser and the mode of address being used to approach the viewer. Others may be more concerned with how viewers are characterized, both off-screen and as textual surrogates. Still other critics may focus on the nature of the reading act and the ways in which production strategies work to manipulate the viewer and encourage certain meanings. Regardless of the areas examined, the general goal of this section of the essay is *description*—to describe and provide examples of how the text works to establish relations with the audience.

Many critics reserve the latter part of the essay to discuss the implications of the text's relationship to the audience in terms of the problems outlined early in the essay. For example, a critic might be concerned with certain programming that builds on the sexist or racist assumptions of its audience. Others may be concerned that a text is preaching to an audience cast as remarkably stupid or materialistic. Critics can use this discussion phase of the essay to identify and deconstruct a finite number of themes that characterize the audience and its relation to the televised material. Linking these themes to larger social dynamics and the problem focus of the essay in convincing fashion is often the overriding goal of reader-oriented criticism.

The major strength of reader-oriented television criticism is its ability to discern how the text characterizes and attempts to engage the viewer. By determining how the viewer is addressed, how the viewer's textual surrogates are characterized, and how the text strategically attempts to control the reading act, such criticism can illuminate in a unique way. The approach's special strengths lie in providing tools for analyzing those forms of television where the viewer is directly addressed and has readily apparent textual surrogates. As a result, reader-oriented critiques of talk shows, game shows, news programs, sports broadcasts, home shopping, and specialty educational or hobby shows (e.g., gardening, exercise, car repair) should be enlightening. Similarly, reader-oriented critiques of commercials for certain product groups (e.g., beer, luxury cars, dishwashing detergent) or commercials aimed at audiences for particular kinds of shows (e.g., news, self-help talk, sports) hold much promise.

Reader-oriented approaches to television narratives are more difficult. Because opportunities to explore the characterized reader through mode of address and textual surrogates are limited in the television narrative, the analysis must focus on the text's role in reading, and unless there is considerable knowledge about the interpretive communities, the analysis might best be subjectively derived from the critic's own reading experiences. Herein lies the most severe limitation of reader-oriented television criticism: it is dependent on deducing the reading act, and, based on the critic's own experiences, largely theorizes the reader. One can never be sure that the television text is being read as the text suggests or as your knowledge of an interpretive community might lead you to believe. Critical audience ethnography, discussed in the following chapter, seeks to resolve these issues by looking at the reading processes and interpretation of real television viewers.

The Example Essay

The essay that follows, Lawrence A. Wenner's "The Dream Team, Communicative Dirt, and the Marketing of Synergy: USA Basketball and Cross-Merchandising in Television Commercials," uses a reader-oriented approach to understanding the characterized fictional reader of commercials shown during the Olympic Games. Wenner starts his analysis with a look at how the myths and values of sport are communicated as "dirt" used in the context of selling.[6] The analysis examines how commercials attempt to control the reading act by characterizing and positioning the viewer. The critique's conclusion examines commonalities in advertisers' attempts to place viewers in a special social world.

Notes

1. This is the distinction Barthes (1975) makes between a *work* and a *text:* whereas a *work* is a message (constructed through a series of codes) that has a physical existence—like an already-printed book you can pick up, or an already-videotaped TV episode—a *text* is a set of meanings created by individual viewers.

Thus, from Barthes' perspective, a text is a "network of codes, working on a number of levels and is thus capable of producing a variety of meanings according to the socio-cultural experiences of the reader" (O'Sullivan et al., 1994, pp. 317–318).

2. The various editing conventions used in classic Hollywood film and television constitute a "code." These conventions arrange shots and scenes so that the viewer always (except in such genres as mysteries and science fiction) knows "where the characters are and when the shot is happening" (see Butler, 1994, p. 1258). Some of the editing conventions used to create temporal narrative continuity include the fade-out, fade-in, and dissolve transitions between scenes, and the use of the establishing shot (which introduces the spatial, setting, and character components of a scene, etc.) at the beginning of an episode and (sometimes) after commercial breaks.

3. Television scenes, especially indoor scenes, are staged using a convention called the invisible "fourth wall" or "fly-on-the-wall" convention . This convention, adapted from theatrical staging, presents the diegetic action as if it is not occurring in front of an audience; the audience is able to see and hear characters in private spaces because the fourth wall is, in effect, a one-way mirror through which the audience, but not the characters, can see.

4. Horace Newcomb (1974) discusses the role of regular supporting characters in texts as "stand-ins" for the audience. He describes these characters as living "somewhere between the improbable world of the central characters and the world that most of the audience experience"; thus, in response to the actions and antics of the central characters in comedies, the regular supporting characters "will react similarly to the audience," as the program creators conceptualize the program's ideal audience.

5. See, for example, Robert C. Allen's 1983 and 1985 (especially pp. 69-81) discussion of *interepisodic redundancy* in soap operas.

6. "Dirt," as Wenner explains in the following example critical essay, is a concept he and John Hartley (1984) borrowed from anthropologist Mary Douglas. It refers "to the cultural borrowing that allows one cultural entity to adopt the logic of another" (Wenner, 1991, p. 392).

Further Readings

Iser, W. (1993). *Prospecting: From reader-response to literary anthropology.* Baltimore, MD: John Hopkins University Press. The first three chapters provide an assessment of reader-response approaches to literature by one of its most important theoreticians. In particular, the chapter entitled "Interaction Between Text and Reader" will help television critics focus on key elements in the reading act.

Machor, J. L., & Goldstein, P. (Eds.). (2000). *Reception study: From literary theory to cultural studies.* New York: Routledge. A very useful contemporary collection that mixes classic essays on reader-oriented criticism with application essays, including some that analyze the media. Includes essays by Stanley Fish, Henry Louis Gates, Tony Bennett, and John Fiske.

Webnote

University of Wales Program in Media and Communication Studies. **www.aber.ac. uk/media/Sections/interp02/html**

> This site provides some of the best links to articles and other resources in reader-oriented theory. It is more comprehensive and includes more media examples than any other site.

Learning Activities

1. Join a television fan chat group at www.forums4fans.com. After participating for a few days, what surprising inferences can you make about the breadth and limits of interpretive communities of fans for a certain television show? What insights does the discussion give you about the ability of fans to fill in gaps in story lines?

2. Tape a television commercial for a product aimed directly at your demographic. Show the commercial in class, and analyze the characterized reader and the implications for what that says about you. Is the picture that is painted of you flattering, or are you shown in dire need of something that the product promises to fix?

References

Allen, R. C. (1983). On reading soaps: A semiotic primer. In E. A. Kaplan (Ed.), *Regarding television: Critical approaches—an anthology* (pp. 97–108). Frederick, MD: AFI.

Allen, R. C. (1985). *Speaking of soap operas.* Chapel Hill, NC: University of North Carolina Press.

Allen, R. C. (1992). Audience-oriented criticism and television. In R. C. Allen (Ed.), *Channels of discourse, reassembled: Television and contemporary criticism* (2nd ed., pp. 101–137). Chapel Hill: University of North Carolina Press.

Barthes, R. (1973). *Mythologies.* London: Paladin.

Barthes, R. (1975). *S/2: An essay.* (Trans. R. Miller). New York: Hill & Wang.

Booth, W. (1961). *The rhetoric of fiction.* Chicago: University of Chicago Press.

Booth, W. (1974). *The rhetoric of irony.* Chicago: University of Chicago Press.

Butler, J. G. (1994). Style and the camera: videography and cinematography. In J. G. Butler, *Television: Critical methods and applications* (pp. 121–152). Belmont, CA: Wadsworth.

Corner, J. (1999). *Critical ideas in television studies.* New York: Oxford University Press.

Crosman, I. (1980). Annotated bibliography of audience-oriented criticism. In S. Suleiman & I. Crosman (Eds.), *The reader in the text: Essays on audience and interpretation* (pp. 401–424). Princeton, NJ: Princeton University Press.

Culler, J. (1981). *The pursuit of signs: Semiotics, literature, and deconstruction.* London: Routledge & Kegan Paul.

Derrida, J. (1976). *Of grammatology.* Baltimore, MD: Johns Hopkins University Press.

Eco, U. (1977). *The role of the reader.* Bloomington: Indiana University Press.

Fish, S. (1980). *Is there a text in this class? The authority of interpretive communities.* Cambridge, MA: Harvard University Press.

Freund, E. (1987). *The return of the reader: Reader-response criticism.* New York: Methuen.

Gadamer, H-G. (1975). *Truth and method.* New York: Seabury Press.

Holland, N. N. (1968). *The dynamics of literary response.* New York: Oxford University Press.

Holub, R. C. (1984). *Reception theory: A critical introduction.* New York: Methuen.

Ingarden, R. (1973). *The literary work of art: An investigation of the borderlines of ontology, logic, and theory of literature.* Evanston, IL: Northwestern University Press.

Iser, W. (1974). *The implied reader: Patterns of reading in prose fiction from Bunyan to Beckett.* Baltimore, MD: Johns Hopkins University Press.

Iser, W. (1978). *The act of reading: A theory of aesthetic response.* Baltimore: Johns Hopkins University Press.

Jauss, H. R. (1982a). *Aesthetic experience and literary hermeneutics.* Minneapolis: University of Minnesota Press.

Jauss, H. R. (1982b). *Toward an aesthetic of reception.* Minneapolis: University of Minnesota Press.

Jensen, K. B. (1991). When is meaning? Communication theory, pragmatism, and mass media reception. In J. Anderson (Ed.), *Communication Yearbook* Vol. 14 (pp. 3–32). Thousand Oaks, CA: Sage.

Lacan, J. (1977). *Ecrits: A selection.* London: Tavistock.

Richards, I. A. (1929). *Practical criticism.* New York: Harcourt Brace Jovanovich.

Stam, R. (1983). Television news and its spectators. In E. A. Kaplan (Ed.), *Regarding television—Critical approaches: An anthology* (pp. 23–43). Frederick, MD: University Publications of America.

Sulieman, S. R. (1980). Introduction: Varieties of audience-oriented criticism. In S. Suleiman & I. Crosman (Eds.), *The reader in the text: Essays on audience and interpretation* (pp. 3–45). Princeton, NJ: Princeton University Press.

Suleiman, S. R., & Crosman, I. (Eds.). (1980). *The reader in the text: Essays on audience and interpretation.* Princeton, NJ: Princeton University Press.

Tompkins, J. P. (Ed.). (1980). *Reader-response criticism: From formalism to poststructuralism.* Baltimore, MD: Johns Hopkins University Press.

The Dream Team, Communicative Dirt, and the Marketing of Synergy: USA Basketball and Cross-Merchandising in Television Commercials

Lawrence A. Wenner

By the time all was said and done in the 1992 Olympic Games, USA basketball's bringing home the gold rang to many as tin. Novelist Stephen King called the Dream Team a horror show following a new Olympic motto: "Make Sure You're Going to Win, Then Go Ahead and Do It." What purity was left in the amateur ideals of the Olympics had been put to rest. USA basketball's team was populated by the superstars of NBA basketball. They were bigger than life. Bigger than the Olympics. They stayed in fancy hotels. They played golf as if they were on vacation. Magic was back for a victory lap, AIDS and all. Never was the outcome of the basketball competition in doubt.

It is not surprising what took center stage under such conditions. Along the way to the medal stand, we found the Dream Team quibbling with the various Olympic committees over who has what rights in the pursuit of commercialism. The issues were seemingly trivial. Charles Barkley was to be paid to write a column for *USA Today*. The International Olympic Committee (IOC) said no. Athletes may write only for their hometown paper. Michael Jordan, claiming loyalty to his Nike contract, refused to wear a Reebok outfit on the medal stand. The U.S. Olympic Committee said athletes not wearing Reebok would not be allowed on the medal stand.

In the latter dispute, international diplomacy yielded to the commercial code. Olympism recognized a new world order where new loyalties—endorsement contracts—reign. Jordan and other Dream Teamers in the Nike stable hit the medal stand, their jacket flaps consciously covering anything Reebok. In what might be taken as a perversion of Barthes's (1973) "ex-nomination" process, these athletes nominated Nike.

The struggle over commercialism, endorsement contracts, and consumer loyalties in the modern Olympic Games is a competition with stakes far greater than those between athletes. This is because Olympism is an idealized premium product. In that idealized form, the Games celebrate the virtues of amateurism, sportsmanship, international goodwill, and "healthy" nationalism, all in the context of heroic athleticism. And because of its 4-year cycle, the product's potency has built-in curbs against market fatigue.

The commercial value of the Olympics is great to sponsors and advertisers attempting to get a "cultural rub" from values associated with the Games. The growth of cross-merchandising and "synergy" as a marketing strategy among products recognizes this (Hewitt, 1991). The IOC allows only 12 worldwide Olympic sponsors. The tariff is high. It is estimated that Coca-Cola spent $33 million to become the "official" soft drink of the 1992 Games. Visa International spent $20 million to be the Olympic credit card (Beckett, 1992). NBC spent $402 million for the television rights to the 1992 Summer Games, more than double what ABC paid in 1984 (Elliott, 1992).

With such large figures at stake, the purity of Olympic ideals is necessarily compromised. *New York Times* television critic John J. O'Connor (1992) noted that it was such a big business undertaking leading to possible future payoffs for the athletes that the word *hype* was utterly inadequate. With so many jumping on the Olympic marketing bandwagon, some advertising executives feared that this amount of hype would backfire into consumer backlash as the event became archetypal of over-commercialization (Marinucci, 1992, p. E1).

Yet for most advertisers there was not enough of a good thing to go around. If they could not get in the front door, they would get in another way. A growing group of "ambush marketers" including Pepsi, Fuji, American Express, and Converse developed ads that suggested an "Olympic rub" without actually mentioning the Games. "Ambush" ads were placed in close proximity to those of official Olympic sponsors. John Krimsky, Deputy Secretary General of the U.S. Olympic Committee, angrily called the strategy "parasitic marketing" (Beckett, 1992, p. B1).

The rush to get a commercial "rub" from the Olympic Games recognizes the strong communicative power of sports "dirt" in an "interpretive community" of sports fans (Wenner, 1991). It is ironic to hear Olympic officials single out "ambush" marketers as parasitic. Official Olympic sponsors are parasitic as well; they just pay for it. Perhaps that is the difference between a sponsor and a parasite.

The sponsorship and advertising of the Olympic Games is by necessity a "dirty" one, parasitic if you will. As it is used here, the term "dirt" has no inherent negative connotation. Rather, the term refers "to the cultural borrowing that allows one cultural entity to adopt the logic of another" (Wenner, 1991, p. 392). Hartley (1984) suggests that television texts are necessarily contaminated by seepages from other parts of culture. For example, dominant ideologies expressed in sports values (nationalism, patriotism, authoritarianism) are couched in the celebration of heroism, equality, commitment, and pride in the television sports text (Wenner, 1989). Beer commercials use sports dirt—the logic and values of sport—to infuse alcohol consumption with athleticism (Wenner, 1991). Nike commercials use nostalgic dirt from the Beatles' song "Revolution" to empower their shoes (Howell, 1991).

The power of dirt ascends with its cultural primacy. At the apex of Olympic commercialism, Dream Team dirt was powerful. Through a reader-oriented analysis of the workings of dirt in commercials featuring the Dream Team, this study examines how we are characterized and positioned as readers through the use of sports dirt. Eleven commercials appearing during NBC's broadcasts of two games—USA versus Cuba's game 1 in the Tournament of the Americas and USA versus Angola's game 1 of the 1992 Olympics—are analyzed. These

11 ads were the only ones in these games that relied on Dream Team dirt as a primary strategy.

A reader-oriented approach is central to understanding the advertiser's agenda in sports. Attempts to position the reader are made easier because fans have many of the characteristics of an interpretive community (Fish, 1980; Wenner, 1990, 1991). Such group membership often contributes to a shared sense of place and cultural identity (Wenner, 1990). The resultant group cohesiveness allows sports fans exposed to commercials featuring Dream Team dirt to be more easily identified as "characterized fictional readers" (Allen, 1987, 1992). Advertisers characterize the interpretive community when fans are directly addressed. We often see on-screen characterized fans as "textual surrogates who do what real viewers cannot: interact with other performers and respond (usually in an ideal fashion) to the appeals, demands, and urgings of the addresser" (Allen, 1992, p. 121).

The structuralist version of reader-oriented criticism focuses on how the text attempts to control the reading act (Suleiman, 1980). Television ads, in particular, attempt to position the viewer "'some place' relative to the action in every shot" (Allen, 1987, p. 90). The positioning strategy attempts to blur distinctions between the characterized addressee on the screen, the implied addressee viewing at home, and the addresser. The overriding goal in this attempt is to elicit a positive answer to the addresser's question "Will you buy?" (Allen, 1987, 1992).

The reader-oriented analysis that follows focuses on the reader in the text: the Dream Team fan who is the characterized fictional reader of these commercials. It is assumed that the fan as implied reader and the advertiser as addresser both bring dirt from sport to their constructed meanings of these commercials. Because dirt from sport is highly valued by the sports fan, a position is taken that negotiated readings of these commercials will be far more dominant than oppositional (Hall, 1980). Although the study focuses on how sports dirt encourages preferred readings through characterizing the reader, it is recognized that texts are interpreted in the context of a range of "activations" (Bennett, 1982). Thus, given indications of consumer "backlash" to the "overhype" of the Olympics, likely oppositional readings from within the interpretive community are also explored.

The World of Dream Team Dirt

All 11 of the commercials that build on connections to the Dream Team fall into the category of being explicitly contaminated by sports dirt (Wenner, 1991). An earlier study (Wenner, 1991) suggests three variants of explicit sports contamination in commercials:

1. Active sports dirt focuses on portraying characterized fictional fans actively engaged in sports activities.
2. Implied sports dirt focuses on portraying fictional fans in situations that imply sports activity or demonstrate empathy for sports activities (that is, engagement in fan activities).
3. Idealized sports dirt focuses on constructing narratives that idealize activities culminating in professional sports success.

The 11 commercials featured in the two USA basketball games often blurred the genres of active, implied, and idealized sports dirt. Given the sophistication of modern merchandising, this structural "polysemy" should not be surprising. Still, a telling categorical scheme can be devised by asking, Where is the locus of the sports dirt's power in the commercial? What central logics about sports and culture empower the connection to the product? By answering these questions, the 11 commercials can be organized into three types:

1. Nationalistic sports dirt focuses on sport as a tool for promoting nationalism and the metaphor of the team as soldiers.
2. Youth sports dream dirt focuses on the idealized notion in the sports world that if one works hard enough, one's sports dreams can be realized.
3. Sports hero dirt focuses on the ideal of the sports hero as a role model and the power of

the "reflected glory" that comes from identifying with the hero.

The analysis that follows considers the workings of dirt and the characterizing of the reader in each of these categories.

Nationalistic Sports Dirt

Support the Troops (Team) and Salute the Flag (Uniform)

Champion athletic clothes chose to rely on the notion of teamwork in the context of nationalism to smear sports dirt on its product. The 30-second ad relies on a simple, unhurried, but patriotic narration:

> This summer in Barcelona, 12 of our best men will be bound by a common path, a common goal, and a common thread. Champion is proud to be chosen to make the uniform for America's team. Because we understand teams. It takes a little more to make a Champion.

The narration directly addresses the characterized reader as powerful by assuming the reader's participation in collective ownership of the team. The "bound" men are positioned in our service. Derivative of this, the reader is characterized as agreeing to the commonality of "path, goal, and thread." This positioning has entailments, used in service of characterizing the reader. The reader is a patriot, supportive of America's dream, team, uniform, and flag. Implicit is the reader's support of commonality among the variant threads of America's melting pot. Implicit is support for our team as if its members are troops. And the last logical leap makes the last and most important dirty connection. In our supporting our team, we take "pride" in the uniform our troops wear, and, as we see time and time again in the visuals, the uniform in red, white, and blue is a flag made by Champion.

Complex video imagery uses 61 shots to amplify these connections and position the reader. There are many visual juxtapositions of the USA basketball team competing and the Champion uniform being sewn. The direct address of the narrator positions us to accept the logic of this juxtaposition. As we root for our team, we root for the uniform being sewn. As we root for our powerful USA team's ball to go through the basket (5 shots), we root for the Champion's powerful needle to penetrate red, white, and blue fabric (8 shots). When the narration positions us to take "pride" in "America's team," we must take in the red, white, and blue of the uniforms. When we are positioned as having the knowledge to "understand teams," we are positioned visually to equate that understanding with a consumer sweatshirt made by Champion. In the end, the "little more" that it takes "to make a Champion" amplifies the reader's position that nationalism makes sports a little better. Supporting Champion means supporting that dirty but potent mix.

Fairy Tales of U.S. Domination

Converse athletic shoes chose to rely on a fairy tale about the power of the Dream Team as a parable for the power of its "magical shoes." In one of what is known as the "Larry Johnson's grandmother" ads, we see a grandmother sitting in a rocking chair reading a fairy tale to a multicultural group of young children. Quickly, we find sports dirt. The grandmother is a large Black mustachioed man with a gold tooth who is dressed in a prim flowered dress and high-top basketball shoes. The grandmother says,

> This is a story about two of the baddest men that ever put on little short pants. One day they were surrounded by the Russians and the dreaded Italians! Arghh! They quick put on their magical shoes from Converse and ditched them all big time! And snatched up all the gold and brought it home to Grandmama.

As the story unfolds, we find out who the "baddest men" are by seeing storybook pictures of Larry Bird and Magic Johnson. The grandmother is animated, excitedly telling the story. We see that the children are nervous and scared as the story unfolds. When the story's problem is resolved by putting on "magical shoes from Converse" we see storybook pictures of the Bird and Magic Converse shoes. We see the children pleased as the story is resolved as Bird and Magic "snatched up all the gold." In the end, a small Black boy is incredulous, asking, "Is that true, Grandmama?" The grandmother provides reassurance: "It will be, child, it will be" as we see a closing graphic of "Converse—Official Shoe of USA Basketball."

Closing the ad with the questioning of the veracity of the story formalizes dual reading positions for the characterized readers. For the adult reader, it is clear from the start that this ad is a put-on. The reader is positioned outside the scene to appreciate the pictured children being taken in. For the child, the reading position is perched delicately on the edge of plausibility. This could be a fairy tale, and this could be a grandmother. Their on-screen textual surrogates are shown to be largely suspending disbelief.

Nationalistic dirt works on both reading positions in concert with sports hero dirt. As our "bad" men are surrounded by the Russians and the "dreaded Italians," nationalism is invoked. To the child reader, "foreigners" are scary. For the adult reader, the Dream Team is an invincible national force and a foreign challenge is laughable. The child is positioned to interpret Bird and Magic as mythlike, something the adults are already positioned to bring to their interpretation. The child is positioned as well to interpret Bird's and Magic's shoes as mythlike. For the adult reader, such positioning is unlikely. More likely, the ad works to position the adult to accept and expect the child's interpretation of the shoe as inheriting mythlike qualities. Thus the reading position of the adult specifies two roles. First, the adult is positioned as parent or prospective parent, who feels good about the myth the child may value. Second, the adult is positioned as adult-child, who can play along with the fairy tale and its assumptions. In either case, dirt works in a fairly straightforward way. Bird and Magic are America's team, they will win, they will wear Converse, and you should wear Converse if you want to support America and win.

Youth Sports Dream Dirt

Lifelong Friendship as
an Olympic Value

Archetypal of the youth sports dream dirt commercials was AT&T's 30-second spot that featured a narrator telling an idealized flashback story about young Scottie Pippen and his childhood friend Ronnie Martin. The narrator speaks to us as implied readers who embrace Olympic ideals and hard work leading to athletic success. The narrator tells us that "long before Scottie Pippen was chosen for the USA Basketball team, he knew he could count on his friend Ronnie Martin." Meanwhile, we see a romanticized scene set in a warmly lit gym in Hamsburg, Arkansas, in 1976. Young Pippen and Martin take on the challenge from an older, bigger, threatening boy named Big Harold. We see young Pippen and Martin work a play together to beat Big Harold. Here, the narrator tells us "AT&T salutes all of our Olympic hopefuls and everyone that helped them get this far." We enter the present by panning up an "official" team jacket arm with signage "Pippen" and the USA basketball logo. We see Ronnie Martin asking Scottie Pippen whether "those guys in the Olympics gonna be tough?" Pippen asks, "Why? Did they sign Big Harold?" as the two laugh. Theme music comes up as we see the USA Olympic logo that transforms itself into the AT&T logo while a graphic proclaims AT&T as "Proud Sponsor of the 1992 Olympic Team."

This ad works to position the reader in three interrelated places. In direct address, the narrator positions the reader as a USA basketball fan who can be counted on in joining AT&T in "saluting" (as one would the flag) our "hopefuls." Second, we are cast as voyeurs of nostalgia, appreciative of a Horatio Alger story with a little bit of Tom Sawyer and Huckleberry Finn thrown in for good measure. Third, we are cast as privileged spectators of a private friendship, about which we share their private history. Throughout, sports dirt helps position the reader. As sports fans we are receptive to rooting for the underdog, sympathetic to the idea that hard work leads to sport success, seeing teamwork as an ideal in life, and interpreting sports histories as the culmination of these ideals. In today's sports world, we are treated to many tales of athletic prima donnas; thus the painting of Pippen as one who remains an Everyman who is true to a lifelong friend rings the bell of sports fans who likely hope that they too would remain unchanged with sports success. In short, we feel good about sport dreams, about friendship, and about AT&T. As dirt, these sport myths merely add power to a preexisting crafted connection between friendship and AT&T, amplifying both "reach out" and institutional "feel good" campaigns.

A Champion of a Young Boy's Dreams

A second Champion athletic clothes spot is more forthright in waxing poetic about a young boy's dreams of competing in the Olympics. We see a young boy alone in a gym through nostalgic soft focus and lighting. We see him fantasize playing with the Dream Team as he tells himself,

> It's Barcelona. Cautious, he came down. He brings the ball up, Drexler's open on the wing. Great pass from Malone. USA needs a basket to win. Magic goes to the hoop. Yeah!

We see the boy hit the winning basket. He jumps in celebration. The boy's hand hits a "high five" with a fantasized man's Black hand. The boy, surprised by the fantasy crossing into reality, looks at his hand and looks around. As he seemingly questions whether his dream has come true, we hear the narrator: "When USA basketball plays for the dream they'll wear the uniform Champion proudly earned the right to make." The visuals connect the Champion uniform and consumer products to the dream. As the boy leaves the gym, the shadowy outline of four of his Dream Teammates remains as the narrator tells us "It takes a little more to make a Champion."

The reader's position in this ad is as spectator to the dream, a voyeur who appreciates well-worn fantasies of young children who dream to play with their heroes. The positioning relies on the notion of the fan as one who played sports and entertained those same dreams. Specifying the Dream Team as the dirt that fuels the fantasy allows Champion to not only be equated with the best but to contribute to all of our fantasies of being the best.

If I Could Be Like Mike

One of Gatorade's generic "Be Like Mike" ads appeared during the Tournament of the Americas game. We hear singing:

> Sometimes I dream. The key is me. You've got to see that's how I dream to be. I dream I move. I dream I grew. Like Mike. If I could be like Mike. I'm gonna be, gonna be like Mike. Like Mike. If I could be like Mike. Be like Mike. If I could be like Mike.

The visuals intercut Dream Teamer Michael Jordan playing NBA basketball, multicultural girls and boys playing playground ball, and Jordan playing with the kids. The lyrics pose youthful sports dream as the driving dirty force that is energized by association with Jordan as sports hero. A variety of basketball-playing textual surrogates are seen: a teenaged Black boy (seen with Jordanesque tongue hanging), a teenaged White girl, a 5-year-old White boy, and a 10-year-old Black girl. A multicultural group of textual surrogates drinking Gatorade join Jordan as he goes to the playground. Other shots place the reader in a familiar spectator role, joining a crowd cheering Jordan as he slays the NBA. From any angle, and any age, readers are shown to like Mike and like being his friend. Only a step away is dreaming his dream and to do so is to "be like Mike." In that dream, we are those good textual surrogates shown drinking Gatorade "like Mike."

McDonald's Olympic Dream

McDonald's youth sports dream spot relies on heavy doses of nationalistic dirt and sports hero dirt to round out the dream. The narration draws a bridge between nationalism and youth sports dreams:

> The 1992 Olympic Summer Games. The year basketball trades NBA colors for red, white, and blue. For everyone who's longed to see America send nothing than their very best. For every family whose hearts still beat faster when they hear the national anthem.

For the young who dream that someday they too may soar so high. For every one of us. McDonald's is proud to sponsor the 1992 USA basketball team. To help Olympic dreams come true.

Quite simply, the commercial is dedicated to the implied reader. We are patriotic citizens. We are traditional families. We hold great hopes for our children. We share sports dreams with our children.

The visuals position us as well in the role of spectator. At the start, we see the Olympic flame and a montage of Dream Teamers on the NBA court. Our first textual surrogate is a middle-aged middle-American White couple with hands over hearts as the national anthem plays to start a game. The dreams "we" have for our young to "soar so high" are characterized by our appreciative reactions to the Dream Teamers in action. Our children with youth sports dreams are characterized by a young Black boy seen first in a stadium crowd watching action and later cheering as a championship is won.

Interestingly, the sealing of the championship for "every one of us" is accomplished by a Larry Bird shot. This ushers in McDonald's "being proud" to "sponsor the 1992 USA basketball team" as we see the McDonald's arches blend with Olympic rings encased in red, white, and blue ribbon. As spectators, McDonald's has taken the time to position us to appreciate White heroism as a Black boy looks on from the sidelines. Admittedly, this is fleeting, but from the reading position established, it is the Black boy who needs help in making "Olympic Dreams Come True." The net result is a very paternalistic, traditional reading position that embraces sport as an agency for social mobility.

Sports Hero Dirt

Almost all of the commercials discussed previously placed benefit substantially from sports hero dirt. The five commercials discussed in the sports hero dirt category de-emphasize nationalism and youth dreams. Rather, these commercials rely more directly on the importance of the sports hero as a public figure, the ideal of the sports hero, and the power of the "reflected glory" of identifying with the hero.

Visa as Player on the All-Defensive Team

The Visa credit card relies on the collective strength and power of the Dream Team to make its dirty link between the strong Dream Team defense and Visa as defense against merchants who "don't take American Express." The audio pulses as the narrator introduces individual members of the Dream Team, saying "They've been called the greatest team in Olympic history." Implied readers are positioned as spectators seeing on-court exploits of the Dream Teamers. In mid-commercial, with the lead "Olympic basketball may never be the same," the narrator queries the reader, "But if you think they're tough, wait until you see the guys at the ticket window, if you don't have your Visa card." We see tough-guy shots of Dream Teamers followed by a shot of a surly ticket seller. A textual surrogate saves the day: placing a Visa card on an elegant table emblazoned with the familiar dirty Olympic rings and telling us Visa is "worldwide sponsor, 1992 Olympic Games." When we are told that "the Olympics don't take American Express" a montage of Dream Teamers blocking shots is followed by another textual surrogate whipping out the Visa card and then a Dream Teamer getting off a tough shot. The ball goes into the basket as the narrator closes "Visa, it's everywhere you want to be."

Again, we have three main reading positions. First, we are spectators of the Dream Team. Second, we are tormented textual surrogates caught without our Visa. Third, we are elegant textual surrogates playing the Dream Team game with our forceful defense—our Visa card. We are shown to appreciate the attributes of the Dream Team, and we are characterized on-screen using the desired behavioral path to demonstrate those attributes in our consumer lives.

The Magical Ambush of Pepsi

Pepsi drew much criticism from Olympic worldwide sponsor Coca-Cola for its "ambush" ads featuring HIV-positive Dream Teamer Magic Johnson (Marinucci, 1992). Placed in the first games of the Olympics, the ad does not mention the Games. The ad is simple. It opens with inspirational classical music over the graphic "We Believe in Magic." A soft-focus shot of Magic dribbling to the basket is faded in. Dreamlike shots of Magic are intercut with a montage of shots showing a multicultural world of individuals and groups supporting him. We see Little Leaguers, a teenaged girl, a father and son, an Asian restaurant chef, a young White woman at a picnic, a Black garbage man, commercial fishermen on a boat, Pepsi employees in front of a Pepsi truck, young children in a multicultural classroom, and parochial school girls in uniform. Groups and individuals are shouting variously "Go for it, Magic! Go Magic! Go get 'em, Magic! Good luck, Magic! Magic!" And from the young woman at the picnic, "We love you, Magic!" This outburst of affection from our many textual surrogates is contextualized mid-spot by a narrator who provides a contextual "from all of us at Pepsi" to allow Pepsi to join in our fanship group and, in a sense, take ownership of it and responsibility for it. Pepsi and Magic become rallying points for our fanship group in supporting an AIDS-infected athlete in the Olympic games, although neither AIDS nor the Olympic Games need be "nominated" (Barthes, 1973).

Herein lies the inherent "ambush" problem in Olympic dirtied ads. The Olympics has reached such a point of collective excess that the need to "nominate" it only presents risks in marginalizing its marketing impact. To not mention the Olympics may be far more powerful dirt than "announcing" that the dirt was purchased for the purposes of fulfilling marketing goals. If Barthes (1973) is right, "ex-nomination" is far more powerful, and the IOC [International Olympics Committee] really has something to worry about with these ambushes. AIDS, on the other hand, remains ex-nominated for more complex reasons. To name it, Pepsi would be patting itself on the back for being politically correct. Without doing so, it may have made a stronger statement in that Pepsi signifies that they know we know the story of Magic, thereby legitimizing their role as organizers in the interpretive community.

The Magic of Skybox Cards

The shadow of AIDS remains in the interpretive background of the Skybox trading card commercials featuring Magic Johnson and his young son Andre. The opening drumbeat beckons excitement. The first visual features the official USA basketball logo and the statement "The Greatest Team Ever Assembled." Magic and Andre are excitedly dealing Dream Team player cards. Magic trades Jordan and Barkley to Andre for Ewing and Mullin. We are privileged spectators to this interaction. We see them fantasize game play. Magic claims he won. Andre disagrees, coyly posing a last-minute trade: John Stockton for Magic. Magic protests. Andre playfully explains he would sit Magic on the bench and bring in Stockton. Magic mocks being upset, gets up, and comes at Andre. The drum beats, and we see a store display of cards as the narrator announces "USA Basketball collector cards, from Skybox." The last frame shows the graphic: "Skybox, The Magic of Cards."

With regard to our spectator reading position, it is implied that we like Magic, have a preexisting relationship with him, and have sympathy for him as he struggles for a normal life as the world's most famous HIV-infected individual. For the implied child reader, the AIDS question is out of the picture. The child fan learns more insider information about what Magic really likes to do, and his role model legitimizes card trading as a worthwhile and fun activity. In both cases of implied readership, the dirt comes into play as Magic stands in for us, the characterized textual surrogate who enjoys the fantasies of card trading.

Be Like Dave

Kellogg poured Dream Team dirt on its Corn Flakes by featuring star player David Robinson in a spot aimed at promoting a "commemorative USA Olympic jacket" that was available for a couple of box tops and $4.99. The primary implied reader is a child with sports interest. A secondary implied reader might be a parent interested in fueling sports interest in a child. An announcer cues the ad: "Kellogg's Corn Flakes presents the basketball stars from the Olympic Games. Center David Robinson." We see Robinson enter, dribbling a basketball. Robinson wears basketball shorts and a tuxedo top. A comedy of errors is signaled. "Hey Dave, wrong jacket," cries the announcer. Comedic sound effects punctuate Robinson's perplexed discovery. Robinson appears back on screen wearing a red sport shirt and green plaid sport coat. The announcer cries, "No, not that jacket! This jacket, featuring you, Malone, Stockton, Bird, and Mullin." We see the stars on the jacket as the announcer makes the pitch "for you to get into the action of this basketball first." We see the jacket modeled, first by father and son cheering at a basketball game, and then by Robinson as super-surrogate. As the camera comes close to examine the jacket, the dirt of USA Olympic logo is clearly seen. The ad closes on a comedic note, with the announcer making a quip about Robinson's plaid Bermuda shorts.

The self-reflexive comedy of the sports hero works to soften the blow of an explicitly Dream Team–dirtied pitch by Kellogg. The deliberate casting of a Dream Team giant as a mere mortal who takes his frequent mistakes with good humor puts the child reader "in the know," in an "insiders" community of readers that knows something special about David Robinson. We know Dave. We like Dave. Be like Dave. Buy the Corn Flakes to get the jacket.

Be Like Mike, Part 2

The last commercial featuring sports hero dirt focused on a discussion between Michael Jordan and his father over the attributes of Hanes underwear. An opening graphic reads "Hanes. Fashion Underwear." Uptempo music accompanies Michael Jordan's entrance, shooting a basketball into an empty chair next to a man reading a newspaper. Another graphic reads "Michael Jordan & His Dad. After the Game." Jordan sits down. We see his dad pick up a pair of red underwear sitting on the floor atop blue and white underwear. Dad asks, "Michael, are these your Hanes?" Jordan smilingly nods. His dad continues, "Son, is there a reason you wear 'em?" Jordan's wife comes into the scene, hugging, then kissing Jordan, and answering the question with a fond "Definitely."

Holding the underwear up, Jordan's dad quizzes Mike, "Think Mom would like me in these?" Jordan responds, "Maybe." A graphic responds, "Definitely." Music comes up as we see a montage of shots of red, white, and blue underwear. A chorus is heard singing "Just wait'll we get our Hanes on you" while Jordan smiles and a graphic reinforces the chorus's line.

The implied reader is a privileged spectator of a drama about a superstar who can do it all. For the male spectator, the textual surrogate is likely embraced by Jordan's dad, who wonders how the Jordan-empowered underwear might work for him. For the female spectator, a textual surrogate is found in Jordan's wife. She testifies to the power of the red, white, and blue underwear. The focus of the dirtiness in this "Be Like Mike" ad is very different from the Gatorade ad. However, the workings of the dirt are similar. The power of the sports hero is transferred to the product and to the use of the product by the textual surrogate and implied reader. Both the Gatorade and the Hanes underwear make a great Jordan better, just as they could for you. Only in the Gatorade case it is fairly clean dirt. With the Hanes underwear, there is a layer of dirty dirt that commodifies and potentially reinforces cultural myths of sport and the Black male's sexual prowess (Majors, 1990). As in the case of the ex-nomination of the Olympics connection and AIDS, the nomination of the stereotype would have worked against the cultural power of the ad and made placement of the implied reader that much more difficult.

Making Sense of Dream Team Dirt

This analysis of commercials featuring the Dream Team points out that advertisers have a strong working knowledge of cultural anthropologist Ed-

mund Leach's (1976) observation "that power is located in dirt" (p. 62). The collection of Dream Team commercials is rich with the workings of sports dirt. A triad of nationalism, youth sports dreams, and sports heroism interact in most of the texts to characterize or position the reader.

Nationalism, of course, is a long-standing centerpiece of the American sports creed (Edwards, 1973). As we can see from these commercials, the characterization of the Dream Team as troops fighting the Russians and "dreaded Italians" and as emblematic of the strong personal defense we need in using credit cards in foreign countries, plays off of idealized connections between sport and national character. Implied readers and characterized textual surrogates are shown as patriots, waving flags, supporting the team as troops going to battle, embracing them as our team, and celebrating team members expectantly, as foregone (competitive) war heroes.

Youth sport dreams encapsulate the widespread social belief that there is a strong correspondence between sport participation and social mobility. This, of course, is a finding that is highly questioned in the sociology of sport literature (see Braddock, 1981; Nixon, 1984). Yet the four commercials placed in this analytic category explicitly position the reader as accepting the basic tenets of this belief. Other ads, such as Converse's fairy tale and Skybox's "Magic of Cards," also employ logics derivative of this assumption. These commercials play a role in positioning the reader to embrace a cultural belief that is at odds with what seems to be actually happening. Because marketing plays on cultural desires rather than perplexing fact, this should come as no great surprise.

The last category of commercials relies on the dirty power of the sports hero to function as a positive role model. The cultural power of sports heroes is derivative of the notion that sports builds character and that those who succeed in sports are those with the most desirable traits. Related to the myth of sport and social mobility, this notion also flies in the face of most research in sport sociology. The character that is built in sport, with its increasing focus on winning, may often be dysfunctional (see Sage, 1988). Much of the positive light that is cast on sports heroes comes from the "halo effect," extrapolating from the athletes' sport success that they are more broad-based heroes (Coakley, 1990).

In the case of these commercials, all of Klapp's (1962) five categories of heroes are enlisted. Both directly addressed implied readers and textual surrogates are cast as appreciative of sports heroes as winners, splendid performers, heroes of social acceptability, independent spirits, and group servants. Using Dream Teamers as winners, splendid performers, and independent spirits provides the core dirt in all the ads. That this is assumed by the reader also establishes our baseline reading position.

In that all of the featured heroes in the ads—Magic Johnson, Michael Jordan, Scottie Pippen, and David Robinson—are Black, they are necessarily being used as heroes of social acceptability. In a society with so few Black role models outside the sports world, characterized White readers can be more easily positioned to accept these cases as extraordinary success stories of people who have heroically fought the odds. Thus these heroes can be read as legitimate purveyors of social acceptability for Whites as well as for the minority community. Thus readers can be comfortable with these athletes breaking small but critical social acceptability rules in these commercials. The heroic David Robinson can don clownish clothes in a pitch to children, Michael Jordan can go public about the "definite" reasons for his red, white, and blue underwear, and Magic Johnson can be a role model for adults who wish to engage in the fantasies of trading cards.

Finally, it is important to recognize the positioning of the Dream Team members and the team itself as group servants. Very likely lurking beneath all of the readings of the Dream Team is the notion of the reader being aware of the team's Olympic effort being altruistic public service. It is well known to the reader that these are well-paid professionals who do not have to play in the Olympic Games for fame or fortune. Knowing this, it is likely that the reader grants some indenture for this service.

Nationalistic sports dirt, youth sports dream dirt, and sports hero dirt are all pervasive in the interpretive structures that readers bring to both the Dream Team and the commercials featuring its members. Most typically, given the sympathies of the sports fan, they may be enlisted in preferred readings. Occasionally, oppositional readings may be seized by readers attempting to make sense of intrusions into the Dream Team world. Thus knowledge about Magic Johnson's HIV infection or Michael Jordan's bouts with gambling may affect the ability of advertisers to position readers. Even with such opportunities, it can be seen that three types of Dream Team dirt interact in ways to answer questions about how the reader is cast in the wider world of sports dirt.

Where Is the Reader in the Sport Dirtied Text?

Most cultural studies theorists argue for the inherent openness or "polysemic" nature of the television text (Fiske, 1987). Savvy scholars demand that texts be seen in terms of all of their "activations" (Bennett, 1982). This reader-oriented analysis of Dream Team dirt suggests that the reader is routinely characterized in a variety of ways. If one cannot be the child in reading the Converse fairy tale ad, one can be the parent. If one is uncomfortable with being cast in the AT&T Scottie Pippen spot as patriot, we are offered alternative reading positions as voyeurs of nostalgia or privileged spectators of private friendship. The variant ways one can "be like Mike" is itself an open text.

Similarly, there are a myriad of textual surrogates offered in these Dream Team ads. Pepsi's "We Believe in Magic" spot and Gatorade's "Be Like Mike" spot offer literally hundreds of textual surrogates as opportunities to see ourselves and take comfort in the implied reading positions. Most important, the variety of textual surrogates provides opportunities for readers to see themselves in social roles in relation to these products. Of course, it is this relationship that works ultimately to contain the preferred reading position to consumer roles.

It is important to not mix up options with any inherent openness of these texts. Options, as to reading position or to one's textual surrogate, should not be confused with fuel for oppositional readings. Whereas options may facilitate multiple reading positions, the strategies employed do not cultivate oppositional reading positions. The offering of multiple reader positions does not rule out oppositional readings but, rather, reduces the likelihood of having to resort to seeking them out. If the green grass is in the near proximity, one need not go to an unfamiliar field where there is work to be done in establishing a position for interpretation. This is the inherent pleasure of sports dirt, and sports fans revel in rolling around in it (Wenner, 1990, 1991). With its archetypes of heroism in a rational world where hard work makes for success, the reader who has engaged in mediated sport as pleasure is far more likely to choose a reading position offered from the advertiser's pleasing but limited menu than to impose a special order on the sports chef.

Still, one can reach outside and off the menu. To what degree this is done cannot be answered by this study. People have variant defenses to commercials. And intertextuality with other social texts affects reading position. Advertiser try to avoid this by limiting our options. We must nominate AIDS in the interpretation of Magic Johnson, Pepsi, and Skybox. We must nominate gambling in our making sense of "Be Like Mike." How, and to what extent, this is done is beyond the purview of this study. Ethnographic study of the reading process can complement the foundational understandings about the positioning of the reader suggested in this analysis.

What Kind of Society Does the Characterized Reader Live In?

In Dream Team dirtied commercials, the implied reader and the characterized textual surrogate live in a multicultural but nationalistic society. Nationalism is explicit in the reader's characterized world not only in the two ads featuring nationalistic dirt but in three of the four youth sports dream ads that feature explicit nationalistic positioning. Only in Gatorade's generic "Be Like Mike" ad is nationalism not part of the reading position. All of the sports hero dirtied ads offer nationalism as a context for reading. It is most dominant in the Visa, Pepsi, and Kellogg's Corn Flakes ads, but it can even be seen as the interpretive frame for Michael Jordan's red, white, and blue Hanes underwear.

Multiculturalism in the reader's domain is a slightly more tricky issue. Stereotypically, multiculturalism is evoked in ads offering a wide variety of textual surrogates. Here the wide world of support for Magic by Pepsi and the "we" we see in Gatorade's "Be Like Mike" are archetypal. Converse similarly positions a multicultural audience of children for its fairy tale of U.S. domination. Ads such as these, featuring cheerfully coexisting multicultural faces in the crowd, risk calling attention to themselves with their sprinkling of self-conscious but politically correct multiculturalism. So contrived are they and so at odds are they with the prejudices and segregation of American society that they risk disruption of the suspension of disbelief necessary for the ad to work. The incredulity may evoke a resistant reading to the advertiser's advance. Still, the cultural ideal rings true, even though the construction of it may not.

Some advertisers, such as McDonald's, belly flop with multiculturalism in other ways not likely to be as evident to the reader. In McDonald's multicultural America, "we" are the patriotic middle-aged middle-class White family. Blacks are players, like Dream Teamer Malone, who mirror our characterized patriotism. Our characterized hero, however, is Larry Bird, whose shot brings the championship basket. Youth sports dreams are seen for the young Black boy, whom McDonald's positions as needing help to make his "Olympic Dreams Come True." This paternalistic stance, under the guise of multiculturalism, reinforces some very problematic stereotypes. Beyond the stereotyping of the White hero, the more serious issues lie with the subtext of throwing money at the "Black problem" and reifying the dysfunctional path of sports as an efficient agency of social mobility for Blacks.

The issue of race causes interactions with reading position in other ways. Cultural myths of the

Black male's sexual prowess (Majors, 1990) interact with the implied reading position in the Michael Jordan Hanes underwear ad and are added to the frame of AIDS infection in making sense of the spots featuring Magic Johnson. These issues are not nominated in these ads. AIDS is thoroughly avoided. Sexual prowess, while suggested in the Hanes ad, attempts to nominate the underwear more than the individual wearing them. Race-related dirt also interacts with the reading position in Kellogg's David Robinson spot. The casting of Robinson as comedic buffoon is perched on the edge of a backward-looking stereotype and a forward-looking humor that recognizes the stereotype by daring to go beyond it in an equal opportunity kind of way. The way the issue is raised gives the reader much room to maneuver.

The self-conscious nomination of multiculturalism and race helps mask the way gender interacts with reading position. In six of the ads, women are absent. Here, the texts ex-nominate men as having power in the natural order of sport. To read but not oppose these ads implicates such a worldview. In the AT&T/Pippen, Champion, and McDonald's youth sport dream ads, the dream is projected for a young boy. Women populate the multicultural mix of Pepsi's "Believe in Magic" ad and Gatorade's "Be Like Mike" ad. In the Pepsi ad, women as textual surrogates are merely supportive. In the Gatorade ad, women are actually shown competing successfully against men on the court. Even though completely in the shadow of Mike, this is as active as women get in this series of ads. In Converse's fairy tale, young girls are the most scared by the story of U.S. domination. In the McDonald's ad, the woman's role is a patriotic and traditionally supportive wife. In the Hanes underwear ad, the men talk about the powers of underwear (sex), with women positioned as goals to be scored. On a positive note, the woman's textual surrogate is actively complicit in the sexual transaction, even though the transaction is defined by men.

How Does Sport Fit into the Characterized Reader's Society?

Last, these Dream Team commercials help answer questions about how sport fits into the characterized reader's society. The categories of youth sports dream dirt and sports hero dirt address this question most directly. Here we get a very steady picture of the characterized reader. Both through directly addressing the implied reader and characterizing the textual surrogate, the reading position entails that sport promotes social mobility, that individualism and teamwork are both to be valued, that athletes provide good role models, that the power of the athletic hero or team may be transmitted through a product, and that sport is best seen as a spectacle.

As considered earlier, the sport and social mobility nexus dominates the reading position of the youth sports dream ads and is implied in most others. The emphasis in this nexus is on individualism—on transcendence through winning to become a star. This serves to give teamwork a more limited range as a value in characterized reading positions. Teamwork most dominates the reading position when we see the Dream Team members as soldiers on "our" team. Thus the two nationalism ads and the Visa ad, where the team functions as an emblem of Visa's strong defense, include us on the team. Here, teamwork is inclusive for the reader, and we are implored to take on the values of the team. In less nationalistic settings, teamwork is seen in a different light. In Champion's youth sports dream, the team helps the young boy become the hero who scores the winning basket. In the Pippen AT&T youth dream, teamwork is more personal, transformed into lifelong friendship. In the "Magic of Skybox" ad, teamwork is merely a necessary function of team sports, where teams are composed of individuals who can be freely traded in an open market.

The reader is further positioned to appreciate the power of individualism by assuming the value of athletes as positive role models. As suggested earlier, the wide range of Klapp's (1962) five types of heroes can be seen in this limited sample of

Dream Team commercials. This naturalization of such multifaceted heroism is what allows the transference of power from athlete to a wide range of products. Only in the institutional identity ads by AT&T, McDonald's, and Pepsi are there no attempts to make this transfer specifically to their products in the telecommunications, fast food, or soft drink marketplaces. Yet in all these commercials the characterized reader is positioned to accept the transfer of power. It may be close to sport, such as athletic clothing, shoes, sports drinks, or trading cards, or more far flung, bringing power to credit cards or underwear, or it may be the power to relax and feel good about a multinational corporation. In a society where heroes are decidedly hard to find, a wide range of power has been fabricated and granted to sports dirt. In these ads, reading positions are characterized as accepting that broad range of power.

The final lesson about reading position that can be extracted from these Dream Team commercials concerns the naturalization of seeing sport as spectacle. Commercials, of course, have no life apart from being spectacles. They are there to bring products to spectators. To use Stone's (1955) notion about sport, they are there to put products on "dis-play." It is not surprising in such an environment that the reader's essential interpretive frame for sport in its modern commercialized, televised forms depends on seeing it as spectacle. In the specific case, the Dream Team was the spectacle that overtook the Olympic spectacle. As DeFord (1992, p. 27) put it, the Summer Olympics were presented to us as

MICHAEL JORDAN
LARRY BIRD
MAGIC JOHNSON
in
THE DREAM TEAM GOES
TO BARCELONA
Also starring
Track and Field
Swimming
Boxing
Boris Becker and
Some Other Foreigners[1]

With this as a backdrop for the reader's interpretive frame, it is difficult not to see sport as spectacle. The Dream Teamers were megastars. They were already winners and champions before they graced the Olympics. They had transcended outcome, a key element in commercialized sport as it moves to spectacle (Coakley, 1990). The Dream Team commercials reinforce this. The individual exploits and team traits are cast to be in our service. Because the athletes don't need to be there for the fame and fortune, we feel good about them. Our textual surrogates cheer them. Our children are shown as wanting to be like them. Even corporations are shown cheering their presence by facilitating more Olympic dreams. Our reading positions entail all of this. But in reality, much of how we got there is based on dirty connections to sport, social mobility, and the wide range of power we have granted to sports heroes. But isn't that really what sport is all about?

Note

1. From *Newsweek* (July 6, 1992). © 1992, Newsweek, Inc. All rights reserved. Printed with permission.

References

Allen, R. C. (1987). Reader-oriented criticism and television. In R. C. Allen (Ed.), *Channels of discourse: Television and contemporary criticism* (pp. 74–112). Chapel Hill: University of North Carolina Press.

Allen, R. C. (1992). Audience-oriented criticism and television. In R. C. Allen (Ed.), *Channels of discourse, reassembled: Television and contemporary criticism* (2nd ed., pp. 101–137). Chapel Hill: University of North Carolina Press.

Barthes, R. (1973). *Mythologies.* London: Paladin.

Beckett, J. (1992, July 15). Struggle over Olympic ads heats up. *San Francisco Chronicle*, pp. B1, B3.

Bennett, T. (1982). Text and social process: The case of James Bond. *Screen Education, 41,* 3–15.

Braddock, J. H. (1981). Race, athletics, and educational attainment. *Youth and Society, 12,* 335–350.

Coakley, J. J. (1990). *Sport in society: Issues and controversies* (4th ed.). St. Louis: Times-Mirror/Mosby.

DeFord, F. (1992, July 6). Team of dreams. *Newsweek,* 26–28.

Edwards, H. (1973). *Sociology of sport.* Homewood, IL: Dorsey Press.

Elliott, S. (1992, Aug. 6). A top event: NBC's dash for the ads. *New York Times,* p. C1.

Fish, S. (1980). *Is there a text in this class? The authority of interpretive communities.* Cambridge, MA: Harvard University Press.

Fiske, J. (1987). *Television culture.* London: Methuen.

Hall, S. (1980). Encoding/decoding. In S. Hall, D. Hobson, A. Lowe, & P. Willis (Eds.), *Culture, media, language* (pp. 128–138). London: Hutchinson.

Hartley, J. (1984). Encouraging signs: TV and the power of dirt, speech, and scandalous categories. In W. Rowland & B. Watkins (Eds.), *Interpreting television: Current research perspectives* (pp. 119–141). Thousand Oaks, CA: Sage.

Hewitt, J. (1992). Building media empires. In A. A. Berger (Ed.), *Media USA* (2nd ed., pp. 395–403). New York: Longman.

Howell, J. (1991). "A revolution in motion": Advertising and the politics of nostalgia. *Sociology of Sport Journal, 8,* 258–271.

King, S. (1992, Aug. 9). Dream team: Just another horror show. *New York Times,* Sec. 1, p. 29.

Klapp, O. E. (1962). *Heroes, villains, and fools.* Englewood Cliffs, NJ: Prentice Hall.

Leach, E. (1976). *Culture and communication.* Cambridge: Cambridge University Press.

Majors, R. (1990). Cool pose: Black masculinity and sports. In M. A. Messner & D. F. Sabo (Eds.), *Sport, men and the gender order: Critical feminist perspectives* (pp. 109–114). Champaign, IL: Human Kinetics.

Marinucci, C. (1992, July 26). Olympics: Pinnacle of hype, hard-sell. *San Francisco Examiner,* pp. E1, E4.

Nixon, H. L. (1984). *Sport and the American dream.* Champaign, IL: Leisure Press.

O'Connor, J. J. (1992, Feb. 13). These Olympic Games are brought to you by ._._._. *New York Times,* pp. B1, B6.

Sage, G. H. (1988). Sports participation as a builder of character? *The World and I, 3,* 629–641.

Stone, G. (1955). American sports: Play and display. *Chicago Review, 9,* 83–100.

Suleiman, S. (1980). Introduction: Varieties of audience-oriented criticism. In S. Suleiman & I. Crosman (Eds.), *The reader in the text* (pp. 3–45). Princeton, NJ: Princeton University Press.

Wenner, L. A. (1989). The Super Bowl pregame show: Cultural fantasies and political subtext. In L. A. Wenner (Ed.), *Media, sports, and society* (pp. 157–179). Newbury Park, CA: Sage.

Wenner, L. A. (1990). Therapeutic engagement in mediated sports. In G. Gumpert & S. L. Fish (Eds.), *Talking to strangers: Mediated therapeutic communication* (pp. 221–242). Norwood, NJ: Ablex.

Wenner, L. A. (1991). One part alcohol, one part sport, one part dirt, stir gently: Beer commercials and television sports. In L. R. Vande Berg & L. A. Wenner (Eds.), *Television criticism: Approaches and applications* (pp. 388–407). New York: Longman.

Audience Ethnographic Criticism

CHAPTER 13

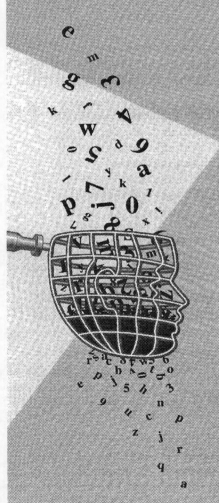

Chapter Outline

Cultural Studies and Audience Ethnographic Criticism
1970s British University Audiences in Cultural Studies
Emerging Concerns in Audience Ethnographic Criticism

Elements of Ethnographic Criticism
Basic Approach
Observations and Interviews
Other Considerations

Writing Audience Ethnographic Criticism

Example Essay: Rona Tamiko Halualani and Leah R. Vande Berg's "'Asian or American': Meanings In, Through, and Around *All-American Girl*"

When television came on the scene, the notion of the invisible mass public and its perceived vulnerability seemingly precluded thinking about television's audience in dynamic terms. With its large audience, the realism of its pictures, and dependence on a few big networks for programming, fears over the propagandizing effects of television were amplified. As a result, television, more than other popular art forms, has come under scrutiny for what it may be doing to the hearts, minds, and souls of its audience.

Early on, behavioralists used a "hypodermic needle" model (predicting direct audience effects) and empirical social science methods to study the effects of television on political and violent behavior. Encountering mixed results, behavioralists came to see the television audience as active. They found a wide range of uses made by the audience that might modify effects. Still, the behavioralists' empirical methods limited their ability to explain the dynamics behind television uses. Much simply could not be measured. Some types of behavioralist research programs, such as cultivation analysis, clearly suggested that a "powerful ideological agency" was at work (Lewis, 1991; Morgan, 1989). Evidence pointed to the political and social mainstreaming of heavy TV viewers, but little was known about the interpretive processes in television viewing.

Here was an area in where cultural studies and its approach to critical audience ethnography could make a real contribution. In cultural studies, efforts to understand and to prove the hegemonizing effects of media through demonstrations of strategic encoding of texts needed systematic study of the audience to corroborate whether "preferred" readings were indeed "dominant" with the audience (see Jensen, 1991). As Bennett (1982, p. 14) has pointed out in a classic statement, this assessment is critical because "the text is never available for analysis except in the context of its activations." As a result, *critical audience ethnography,* as inspired by cultural studies, endeavors to understand the reading processes and sense-making strategies of real people consuming television in the context of their everyday experience and relations with other people and things.

Cultural Studies and Audience Ethnographic Criticism

Critical audience study informed by British cultural studies (Turner, 1990) has debated the merits of a deductive versus an inductive approach to the audience. Ang (1991) has characterized this debate as a drawing of lines between looking at the audience as a "discursive construct" versus looking at "the social world of actual audiences." Whereas some have argued that the audience is a fictional construct and there is no real audience beyond its discursive construction (Hartley, 1987), many more culturally oriented critics are interested in understanding television viewing in the context of the lived experiences of actual viewers. Such ethnographically centered critical audience studies contrast with reader-oriented criticism, in that the former is concerned with actualized meanings of real viewers, as opposed to potential meanings of implied viewers. Critical audience ethnography moves beyond theorized conceptions of interpretive communities seen in reader-oriented criticism to the reading experiences materialized through actual practices of viewers.

Just as reader-oriented criticism was a reaction to the case of the "missing reader," where criticism routinely avoided considering reading experience, critical audience ethnography was partly a reaction to the analysis of the audience and its subject position as theorized in a tradition seen in the British journal *Screen* in the 1970s. The *Screen* theory posited that the spectator's "subject position" was naturalized through a "gaze" manufactured by the view of the camera. The implications of the enforced spectator position were interpreted through complementary concerns of Althusian Marxism and Lacanian psychoanalytical theory. Althusser (1984) saw mass media as one of the key institutions (called *ideological state apparatuses,* or ISAs) that work to sustain inequalities in industrial economies. Althusser saw ideology as a representation that hails (or *interpellates*) individuals as spectators. Lacan (1977) was similarly concerned with the "hailing" effects of discourses on the decentering of subject or spectator position. For Lacan, the gaze of movie spectators works to confuse film language with reality. As Moores (1993, p. 13) has put it, "Like speakers who misrecognize the relationship they have to language, spectators come to feel as though they are the source of 'the look.'" Unfortunately, *Screen* theory constructed a spectator with few options other than to align with the meanings as made by the film. The fact that this kind of *textual determinism* was ahistorical, avoiding both the cultural situation of texts and the relation of discourses to broader social structures, caused cultural studies to rethink their approach to understanding spectators and the audience.

1970s British University Audiences in Cultural Studies

Formative work done during the 1970s by the Media Group at Birmingham University's Centre for Contemporary Cultural Studies (CCCS) reframed critical audience study around the ethnographic method. The CCCS focus on the relationship between human agency and ideology can be seen as a response not only to mainstream (behavioral) media studies but also to *Screen* theory and reader-oriented literary theory. Focused on historically situated struggles over meaning construction, the CCCS approach looked at the wielding and imbalances of power. There was particular interest in the processes by which popular media played a hegemonizing role (Gramsci, 1971). *Hegemony* is the exercise of power by creating conditions that would have the dominant set of social relations willingly accepted by those who did not benefit by that set of arrangements. The critical audience study that emerged from the CCCS was part of a larger effort to theorize cultural power and social relations. Thus, audience activity was seen as "a network of ongoing cultural practices and relationships" that were "related to social and political structures and processes" (Ang, 1989, p. 101).

At the heart of the CCCS approach was an encoding-decoding model that blended sociological and semiotic concerns in viewing the communication process as a whole. The approach saw the media industries largely as an Althusian

ISA. Television producers, working within the confines of the norms and routines of professional practice, tended to encode preferred messages that were in line with the goals of the industrial economy. However, although encoded texts structured with semiotic meaning were put out there, the texts were necessarily interpreted by viewers engaged in their own *semiotic labor*. As a result of differences in reading, distinctions among dominant (or preferred), negotiated, and oppositional reading positions were drawn. Viewers who interpreted within the preferences of the dominant codes read the *preferred meaning*. *Negotiated readings* are made by viewers who grant legitimacy to the hegemonic set of social relations but take issue with specific assumptions or assertions in the dominant coding of the message. *Oppositional readings* are made by viewers who question fundamental assumptions in the dominant set of social relations. The oppositional position reads against the grain, bringing different contextual understandings to the fore, thus challenging the dominant text by reappropriating its meaning.

As characterization of the three reading positions suggests, different degrees of symmetry occur between the encoded text and meaning as decoded by the viewer. In its reading, the text is seen as *polysemic*, that is, open to variant readings. However, as Hall (1973, p. 13) has suggested, polysemy should not be confused with pluralism, and a "structure of dominance" remains that needs to be contended with in reading texts. Still, there can be much room to maneuver. In reading, the social semiotics of audiences can reform the dominant text and dialogically contest its meaning. As a result, the CCCS approach focused on the diversity of reading practices. It sought to locate "significant clusters" of meaning and to chart those to a "cultural map" of the audience drawn by social and discursive positions of readers (Morley, 1986, p. 12). As a result, there was a focus on understanding subcultures as actualized, interpretive communities of viewers. Key ideological differences in reading were seen to be anchored in the power disparities coming out of class and gender differences in the audience.

Emerging Concerns in Audience Ethnographic Criticism

The cultural studies approach to critical audience study begins with the selection and analysis of a television text, genre, or context of viewing that is of social concern. If the text or genre is the starting point, the text is usually deconstructed by the researcher using the tools of semiotics, although alternative methods of analyzing the text may be used to set a critical baseline. Then the researcher goes into the field, using qualitative methods and an ethnographic approach, to understand the culture, sensibilities, strategies, and sense making of the audience. It is important to understand what is going on in a context defined by viewers and to understand meaning production according to the terms and conditions they see. The researcher attempts to discover patterns, or sets of rules, that govern viewers' experiences and to relate these experiences to the workings of the text and to power in the larger set of social relations. Over the years, the cultural studies agenda with television has moved from concerns with decoding and ideology, to gendered genres and fans, to the largely domestic contexts of consumption, and most recently, to television consumption within the larger context of other communication technologies.

An archetypical example of studies focusing on the interaction between decoding and ideology is Morley's (1980) study of the audience for the British news program *Nationwide*. Morley explored the ways in which the program's preferred reading was received by viewing groups from different socioeconomic classes. He painted a cultural map that ranked the groups' decodings within a grid that characterized dominant, negotiated, and oppositional readings. Although there was evidence linking ideological workings with reading position, more evidence argued against this kind of sociological reductionism, especially the predominant reliance on class to distinguish meaning. The results from the *Nationwide* study and other studies (Dahlgren, 1988; Lewis, 1985) that looked at differential interpretation strategies pointed to two needs: (1) to focus on the viewing of people who normally watched certain programs and (2) to focus on understanding the dynamics of viewing within the context that viewing normally took place. As a result, the research moved to look, on one hand, at genres and fans and, on the other, at television viewing within broader contexts.

Brunsdon (1981) and other studies focused on female fans and their viewing of soap operas, open-ended texts with multiple layers that implied a feminine viewer. Hobson's (1982) study of *Crossroads* and Ang's (1985) study of *Dallas* focused on the pleasures of viewing for female fans. They used concepts such as *emotional realism* and *melodramatic imagination* to characterize negotiations viewers had as they engaged both the soap opera and the larger patriarchal relations of power. Female viewers brought gendered cultural competencies, a focus on their everyday lives, and experience with domestic labor to interpretations of the soap opera and the gaining of escape and compensatory pleasures. These studies and others of fan cultures (see Lewis, 1992) pointed to often contradictory dynamics of viewing; readers' meanings were not only "multiply determined" (Radway, 1987, p. 7) but also simultaneously resistant and compliant.

This gendered nature of television viewing was seen to interact with power relations within the family viewing context. Key studies by Lull (1980, 1990) and Morley (1986) examined the relational aspects of viewing as a social event situated in the family as a system. By focusing on the politics and power of the "sitting room," these studies show how differences in orientations to domestic space for wives and husbands lead to disparities in freely viewing television and to gaps between masculine and feminine styles of viewing. By examining television viewing in the larger context of family life, these studies pointed to the need to examine television viewing in still larger and comparative contexts. Consequently, audience ethnographic criticism attempted to understand television viewing within the context of audiences' use of other communications technologies in the household (Silverstone, 1991) and how viewing differs across national cultures (Liebes & Katz, 1990; Lull, 1988). Collectively, the diversity of critical audience studies has pointed to the complex dynamics of television viewing, meaning, and power and to the richness of the ethnographic method.

Elements of Ethnographic Criticism

It is fair to say that audience ethnographic criticism in the cultural studies tradition is more driven or inspired by the ethnographic tradition than it fully utilizes ethnographic methods (Allen, 1992, p. 129). As a result, critical television audience ethnographers often may not apply the elaborated protocols of ethnography as might be used by anthropologists or sociologists. Still, they share the fundamental concerns and practices of the ethnographic method. The goal is to understand cultural practices and sense making in the natural context from the point of view of people living their everyday lives.

The researcher, using commonsense knowledge and methods, becomes the primary "research instrument" (Hammersley & Atkinson, 1983, p. 18). Rather than eliminating the effects of the researcher, an attempt is made to understand them. As a result, interpretation and self-reflexivity are integral to the researcher's task. Theory, while being revealed to the researcher, does not come from the researcher. Rather, theory is inductively derived from lived experiences and their grounding in the realities and logic of people's lives (see Geertz, 1973; Glaser & Strauss, 1967; Trujillo, 1983).

Basic Approach

Doing audience ethnographic criticism means going into the field. Before one can write ethnographic criticism, a researcher must spend considerable time observing people's television viewing in the natural setting. If such "natural" observations are not possible, the researcher will need to find other ways of talking with viewers about their viewing. For example, the researcher may attempt to recreate a "natural environment" in which to observe and interact with audiences about their viewing. The aim should be to understand the characteristics of everyday viewing rather than to ferret out aberrant events.

The researcher's engagement with the viewer should be on the viewer's terms. Thus, the basic approach should be unobtrusive and nonjudgmental. Establishing good rapport and building trust with viewers is essential in getting candid, honest pictures of viewing and the viewing context. The researcher should use the pose of naiveté as a tool to approach the viewing context as anthropologically strange, as it might be seen in first stepping on the planet. Consequently, everyday happenings should not be discounted as merely normal or natural and thus without meaning.

The critical audience ethnographer needs to work to truly hear stories and listen for the context and meaning as set out by the viewer. The researcher focuses on getting "thick descriptions" of viewing experience from which a set of rules governing action can be derived (Lull, 1990). These largely implicit rules will reveal patterns in viewing and the logic behind them. Experiences of different viewers will undoubtedly reveal multiple realities that fuel differences in understanding or applying rules. *Theorizing the audience* means not only seeing these different patterns of meaning but also seeing their interrelationships and framing them in struggles over power as they relate to the lives of viewers.

It is often observed that ethnography has no standard method and is not any one method. Indeed, ethnography is usually approached using more than one method. Although extended unstructured observation and in-depth interviews are key features of most ethnographically inspired studies, so too is a triangulation of methods. *Triangulation* is the use of multiple methods. Using multiple methods protects the researcher from the biases or idiosyncrasies that arise from using a single methodology or measurement technique. Various forms of methodological triangulation exist. In critical audience study, triangulation is commonly achieved by analyzing the text, observing television viewing, and then cross-checking observation with extensive interviews.

Observations and Interviews

Just as texts may be analyzed in a wide variety of ways, observation and interview methods vary. The term *participant-observation* is itself often thought to mean the blending or combination of methods used in ethnographic inquiry (Jankowski & Wester, 1991). At the very least, participant-observation methods involve some amount of genuine social interaction in the field with television viewers, some direct observation of viewing and the viewing situation, and a goodly amount of informal interviewing. There is some controversy over how much participant-observation must be done, but it is safe to say that more is better than less (see Lull, 1988). Extensive observation of television viewing may be difficult. Gaining access to the home and, furthermore, to private parts of the home, where more and more television viewing takes place, may be perceived as intrusive. As a result, much audience ethnographic criticism relies on the interview.

The general style of the initial *qualitative interview* should be open and loosely structured. It is more useful to think of interviews as conversation rather than as directed information gathering. Allow interviewees to move in their own directions, compose their own definitions, and explain their own interpretive frameworks. Ask interviewees to tell about what happens in a certain situation, retell a story, or reconstruct a meaningful event. This approach allows you to hear experiences on the viewers' terms and allows you to be naturally curious and to ask for further explanation. Don't get impatient when interviewees go off-track because the track they are on is, for them, the right one in terms of the topic. Later in the interview or in successive interviews, a more structured or closed approach will allow you to focus on issues you would like to compare among viewers.

While one-on-one interviews will allow you to focus on individual interpretations in some detail, and these can be compared, *group interviews* are also often used. Interviewing a family group or small group of friends who share their fanship will often stimulate insights and reveal context for the common understandings. Interviewing a less intimately acquainted, and often larger, focus group of people who share some demographic or cultural attribute will provide yet a different assessment, often revealing what is publicly acceptable in reacting to television. Regardless of your research goals, triangulating interviews by interviewing in various settings or interviewing at successive points in the study will allow you to understand sense making about television at a deeper level.

Other Considerations

Triangulation of methods may be approached in a variety of other ways in critical audience ethnography. The researcher may choose to analyze documents, such as family albums, clothing, or memorabilia, and to do corresponding interviews with viewers about how these items relate to the meanings made from viewing. For example, a child's room decorations might serve as a good point of departure to contextualize his or her television viewing. Researchers such as Morley and Silverstone (1990) have also used time-use diaries and mental-mapping exercises to triangulate observational and interview data. Light may be shed on the different realities of family members by comparing their mapping of household geography, program characters, or themes.

Triangulation may also be achieved through the use of institutional data such as program ratings, broken out by demography, or other market research data. Finally, it is important not to overlook that triangulation may be achieved by validating viewers' responses at different times or by comparing accounts of different participants in a setting. In short, the ethnographic enterprise in critical audience study may be enhanced by triangulation of the "time, space, and analytical level in which information is obtained" (Jankowski & Wester, 1991, p. 62).

Writing Audience Ethnographic Criticism

Because the sheer amount of qualitative data collected in critical audience ethnography can be overwhelming, getting one's bearings in writing the essay is essential. Strategies on how to analyze data and write a useful report vary considerably. Lofland (1971, p. 5) proposes that four overarching tenets guide the report:

1. It is close to the data and based on substantial inquiry and observation.
2. It is written in good faith and aims to be truthful.
3. It uses much description and relies on illustrative quotations from those studied.
4. It states explicit procedures for analyzing data.

In terms of writing style, Agar (1980) has suggested that the report be accessible to the group studied so that it may be useful in their lives. Often, audience ethnographic criticism is written as much as a story as a report. The story motif can be crafted as either a realist or "confessional" tale (van Mannen, 1988). The more common *realist tale* is told from the vantage point of those studied. The story is framed in terms of the everyday lives of the viewers being studied. To illustrate reasoning and provide context, liberal quotations are used for comparison and contrast.

The less common *confessional tale* stresses the critic-fieldworker's vantage point. Here, the critic's activities, intentions, and perceptions are featured in clear relation to the data. This, for example, is what John Fiske (1994) does in his ethnosemiotic analysis of *the Newlywed* Game, and Ellen Seiter (1989) does, to a lesser extent, in her study of white middle-class, middle-aged male soap opera viewers. Although there has been much discussion about the merits of either "writing in" or "writing out" of the identity of the writer-researcher (Ang, 1989, 1991; Lull, 1990; Moores, 1993), there is no question that the writer is part of the story and that some revealing of identity can help the reader. However, regardless of the type of tale being fashioned, writing the critical audience study relies on art as much as science. Consequently, literary techniques such as the use of metaphor and analogy are key features of ethnographic writing.

Beyond style, the critic's analysis will need to (1) reduce a tremendous amount of qualitative data, (2) display those data in an organized and illustrative way, and (3) use articulated procedures to draw conclusions (Miles & Huberman, 1984). Systematically taken field notes will need to be organized by person, topic, and theme and then reduced to a set of topics that emerge as most significant in the context of viewers' lives. Instead of reducing data by topic, descriptive case studies of individuals or groups may be chosen to characterize overarching patterns of experience.

Conclusions may be drawn through the use of analytic induction or grounded theory. *Analytic induction* works from the researcher's initial assumptions to examine cases or situations systematically to determine whether a goodness of fit occurs and causal generalizations hold. In the absence of goodness of fit, the description is modified so that the case or situation is excluded from analysis or the researcher's hypotheses are revised. Experiences with analytic induction inspire the use of grounded theory to guide conclusions.

Grounded theory arises from the data, and thus should be relevant and fit the context under study (Glaser & Strauss, 1967). Wester (1987) sees four phases in developing grounded theory:

1. The exploratory phase aims to identify "sensitizing concepts" from the material that has been collected.

2. The defining phase aims at constructing variables based on the concepts.

3. The reduction phase aims to provide the contours of workable theory.

4. The integration phase relates the concepts to one another, and these relationships are tested on the data.

Conclusions drawn at each stage are iteratively reviewed through each phase until the data have exhausted theoretical formulation.

The main strengths of audience ethnographic criticism come from the depth of its description and the fact that it depends on understanding meanings about television through the eyes of viewers. The richness of audience perceptions stimulates the critic to see television in new ways. The face validity gained from being "on the ground" with viewers takes the critic away from the ivory tower and the structural biases of academic presupposition. The related advantages of basing conclusions on analytic induction or grounded theory ensure that audience ethnographic criticism grows naturally as an organic process.

The primary weaknesses in critical audience ethnography stem from its dependence on a small sample of viewers. When such select samples are used, it often takes a leap of faith to generalize to the experiences of broader group of viewers in culture at large. Further, while meaning is approached on terms that are generated by viewers, the larger cultural significance of these meanings is necessarily seen through the interpretive eyes of the researcher. Facing this issue head-on is the key to successful audience ethnographic criticism. The researcher must acknowledge her or his own powers in the critical act. Researchers should be self-reflexive about their own biases, incompleteness in data gathering, and even gaps that can be seen when data were gathered.

There are special dangers that come from making the critic part of the story in audience ethnography. The pull toward self-indulgence on the part of a critic who is using the style of the confessional tale can be considerable. Although there should be no fear in unmasking the researcher in postmodern autoethnographic approaches, overly subjective and self-reflexive exercises in psychoanalysis can pose new problems and shift focus away from more common audience interpretations. When the experiences of the researcher overshadow those lived experiences of real viewers, the grounding of meaning, and consequently the critical method, changes in ways that may not have been intended and can obfuscate stability of generalizations.

The Example Essay

In the example essay at the end of the chapter, "'Asian or American': Meanings In, Through, and Around *All-American Girl*," Rona Tamiko Halualani and Leah R. Vande Berg examine some of the serious sides to polyvalence in the situation comedy text of *All-American Girl*. Their audience ethnographic criticism is set in the political-economic context of multiculturalism and inferential racism. While their findings show the remarkable range of critical sensibilities brought by viewers with different backgrounds as they attempt to negotiate and deconstruct a text that has the experiences of a typical young Asian American woman as its centerpiece, they present telling arguments about why these audience experiences still very much cast a colonialist shadow.

Further Readings

Morley, D. (1992). *Television, audiences, and cultural studies.* New York: Routledge. This book provides the best overview of the cultural studies approach to doing audience ethnographic criticism of television. Background is provided on the cultural studies approach to class, ideology, and interpretation, gender and viewing practices, family television viewing, and the role of television in domestic life.

Thomas, J. (2001). *Doing critical ethnography.* Thousand Oaks, CA: Sage. This short book provides a terrific set of skills and strategies for the critical ethnographer. Although the book does not frame its examples in the television audience setting, it will help researchers in understanding conceptual differences between critical and conventional ethnography. It sets out good advice on selecting topics, interpretation and analysis, the discourse of critical writing, and traps and tricks to be avoided.

Webnotes

The Qualitative Report. **www.nova.edu/ssss/QR/qualres.html**

> Up for more than a decade, this site has provided a compendium of "Qualitative Research Resources on the Internet." Overseen by Ron Chenail at Nova Southeastern University, links are provided to journals, discussion groups, publications, and other resource sites of use to critical ethnographers.

University of Wales Program in Media and Communication Studies. **www.aber.ac. uk.media.Sections/interp01/html**

> This site provides links to a great set of articles and other sites on active interpretation on the part of the media audience, with particular reference to studying the television audience.

Yahoo Television Chat Groups. **http://dir.yahoo.com/News_and_Media/Television/ Programming/Chats_and_Forums/Chats/**

> This web address will get you directly to Yahoo! chat groups on television programs. Joining one of these groups and participating in the chat will give you some good ideas in framing a more extensive critical audience ethnography.

Learning Activities

1. Interview three friends about their interpretations of their favorite television program. Have them tell you why the show is their favorite, how they get ready for viewing it, the setting in which they usually do their viewing, and their reactions to the show. Make sure to inquire about deeper meanings that they may read into the show, their projections about what they would like to see develop in future episodes, and about the difficulties they have had with some of the recent plot lines and characterizations. Compare and contrast your findings with a focus on differences in viewing style and the degree to which you see oppositional strategies at play in your friends' viewing strategies.

References

Agar, M. (1980). *The professional stranger: An informal introduction to ethnography.* New York: Academic Press.

Allen, R. C. (1992). Audience-oriented criticism and television. In R.C. Allen (Ed.), *Channels of discourse, reassembled: Television and contemporary criticism* (2nd ed., pp. 101–137).

Althusser, L. (1984). *Essays on ideology.* London: Verso.

Ang, I. (1985). *Watching "Dallas": Soap opera and the melodramatic imagination.* London: Methuen.

Ang, I. (1989). Wanted: Audiences, on the politics of empirical audience studies. In E. Seiter, H. Borchers, G. Kreutzener, & E.-M. Warth (Eds.), *Remote control: Television, audiences, and cultural power* (pp. 96–115). London: Routledge.

Ang, I. (1991). *Desperately seeking the audience.* London: Routledge.

Bennett, T. (1982). Text and social process: The case of James Bond. *Screen Education, 41,* 3–15.

Brunsdon, C. (1981). 'Crossroads': Notes on soap opera. *Screen, 22*(4), 32–37.

Dahlgren, P. (1988). What's the meaning of this? Viewers' plural sense-making of TV news. *Media, Culture, and Society, 10*(3), 285–301.

Fiske, J. (1994). Ethnosemiotics: Some personal and theoretical reflections. In H. Newcomb (Ed.), *Television: The critical view* (5th ed., pp. 411–425). New York: Oxford University Press.

Geertz, C. (1973). *The interpretation of cultures.* New York: Basic Books.

Glaser, B. G., & Strauss, A. L. (1967). *The discovery of grounded theory: Strategies for qualitative research.* Chicago: Aldine.

Gramsci, A. (1971). *Selections from the prison notebooks.* New York: International Publishers.

Hall, S. (1993). Encoding and decoding in the television discourse. In A. Gray & J. McGuigan (Eds.), *Studying culture* (pp. 28–34). London: Edward Arnold. [Originally published in 1973 as CCCS Stenciled Paper 7, University of Birmingham.]

Hammersley, M., & Atkinson, P. (1983). *Ethnography: Principles and practice.* London: Tavistock.

Hartley, J. (1987). Invisible fictions: Television audiences, paedocracy, pleasure. *Textual Practice, 1*(2), 121–138.

Hobson, R. (1982). *Crossroads: The drama of a soap opera.* London: Methuen.

Jankowski, N. W., & Wester, F. (1991). The qualitative tradition in social science inquiry: Contributions to mass communication research. In K. B. Jensen & N. W. Jankowski (Eds.), *A handbook of qualitative methodologies for mass communication research* (pp. 44–74). London: Routledge.

Jensen, K. B. (1991). When is meaning? Communication theory, pragmatism, and mass media reception. In J. Anderson (Ed.), *Communication yearbook* (Vol. 14). Thousand Oaks, CA: Sage.

Lacan, J. (1977). *Ecrits: A selection.* London: Tavistock.

Lewis, J. (1985). Decoding television news. In P. Drummond & R. Paterson (Eds.), *Television in transition: Papers from the First International Television Studies Conference* (pp. 205–234). London: British Film Institute.

Lewis, J. (1991). *The ideological octopus: An exploration of television and its audience.* New York: Routledge.

Lewis, L. A. (Ed.). (1992). *The adoring audience: Fan culture and popular media.* New York: Routledge.

Liebes, T., & Katz, E. (1990). *The export of meaning: Cross-cultural readings of "Dallas."* New York: Oxford University Press.

Lofland, L. (1971). *Analyzing social settings: A guide to qualitative observation and analysis* (2nd rev. ed.). Belmont, CA: Wadsworth.

Lull, J. (1980). The social uses of television. *Human Communication Research, 6,* 197–209.

Lull, J. (Ed.). (1988). *World families watch television.* Thousand Oaks, CA: Sage.

Lull, J. (1990). *Inside family viewing: Ethnographic research on television's audiences.* London: Routledge.

Mannen, J. Van (1988). *Tales of the field: On writing ethnography.* Chicago: University of Chicago Press.

Miles, M. B., & Huberman, A. M. (1984). *Qualitative data analysis: A sourcebook of new methods.* Thousand Oaks, CA: Sage.

Moores, S. (1993). *Interpreting audiences: The ethnography of media consumption.* Thousand Oaks, CA: Sage.

Morgan, M. (1989). Television and democracy. In I. Angus & S. Jhally (Eds.), *Cultural politics and contemporary America* (pp. 162–184). New York: Routledge.

Morley, D. (1980). *The nationwide audience.* London: British Film Institute.

Morley, D. (1986). *Family television.* London: Comedia.

Morley, D., & Silverstone, R. (1990). Domestic communication: Technologies and meanings. *Media, Culture, and Society, 12*(1), 31–55.

Radway, J. (1987). *Reading the romance: Women, patriarchy, and popular literature.* London: Verso.

Radway, J. (1988). Reception study: Ethnography and the problems of dispersed audiences and nomadic subjects. *Cultural Studies, 2*(3), 359–376.

Seiter, E., Borchers, H., Kreutzner, G., & Wurth, E-M. (1989). "Don't treat us like we're so stupid and naïve": Toward an ethnography of soap-opera viewers. In E. Seiter, H. Borchers, G. Kreutzner & E.-M. Wurth (Eds.), *Remote control: Television, audiences, and cultural power* (pp. 204–222). New York: Routledge.

Silverstone, R. (1991). From audiences to consumers: The household and the consumption of information and communication technologies. *European Journal of Communication, 6*(2), 135–154.

Trujillo, N. (1993). Interpreting November 22: A critical ethnography of an assassination site. *Quarterly Journal of Speech, 79,* 447–466.

Turner, G. (1990). *British cultural studies: An introduction.* Boston: Unwin Hyman.

Wester, F. P. (1987). *Strategies for qualitative research.* Muiderberg: Coutinho.

"Asian or American": Meanings In, Through, and Around *All-American Girl*

Rona Tamiko Halualani and Leah R. Vande Berg

The opening credits of the television series *All-American Girl* provide a fitting visual metaphor for the diverse meanings of this "ethnicom." The opening credits featured a white backdrop against which alternating thin and thick royal blue stripes lay atop a red stripe—all waving and rippling as if a gust of wind has just passed. Accompanied by a jumpy musical beat, the words "All-American Girl" slowly glide across the stripes. The moving landscape of the series credits metonymically signifies both the American flag and the imposed "fixed" cultural terrain of meaning that is played out *in, through,* and *around* the ABC/Disney 1994 *All-American Girl* sitcom text: the opposition between "American" and "non-American" or "Asian."

The dualism set up between "American" and "Asian" is not new. For at least six decades, Asians and Asian Americans have been constructed as "foreign" and "Oriental"; both dangerous invaders and inferior subjects from the East (Choy, 1978; Farquhar & Doi, 1978; Fung, 1994; Hamamoto, 1994; Kim, 1986; Paik, 1971).[1] Asians and Asian Americans have been constructed as the antitheses of everything "American." In this way, the racist "American" ideological system of a purely "Anglo Saxon monoculture" can be strategically preserved (Hamamoto, 1994).

Asian Americans, who are both born in this country and of Asian descent, are often forced to choose between "American" and "Asian." Either way, both extremes—an "American" identity stripped of any racial and ethnic significance, or that of an unassimilable "Asian" alien—ultimately point to the superiority of a "white," Anglo American–dominated social system. Inevitably, any attempt to shape a fluid, multicultural identity of being both Asian and American is constrained. Thus, the dichotomous terrain of "American" ver-

sus "Asian" that is continually reproduced in public discourse serves as a hegemonic vehicle to perpetuate an entrenched color-caste system of inequalities (see Hamamoto, 1994; Kim, 1986).

This essay argues that meanings *in, through,* and *around All-American Girl* move between the dualistic poles of "American" and "Asian," thereby reflecting a discourse "tightly organized around [white American] social power" (Fiske, 1990, p. 126). *In, through,* and *around* refers to the many different "voices" that take part in a dialogic struggle for meaning about *All-American Girl*. For instance, the meanings *in* refers to the divergent readings of the televisual text by the two differently situated critic authors. The meanings *through* represent diverse Asian and Asian American viewers' responses to the sitcom. Meanings *around* pertain to texts from the production context (e.g., press interviews with *All-American Girl* actors and creators, journalistic comments about the show) and from Asian/Asian American activists, journalists, and scholars. The participating voices either affirm an "American" position or demand more of an "Asian" perspective. Although a few reject such a dualism, the majority are confined within a socially created framework of racial identity that secures status quo (Anglo American) power arrangements.

We decided to study *All-American Girl* because, for television critics, "firsts" are interesting and important to study and this series was a first—the first time that an American prime time television series starring an Asian female and featuring an almost entirely Asian American cast had aired on network television. However, as we began to watch episodes together, we increasingly became convinced that it was important for us to study together the multiple meanings various audience members created in viewing the series.

To do this we use an approach we term a critical multicultural studies ethnography. In this essay, we explain briefly some of the assumptions and processes involved in using this method of critical analysis. Next, we summarize some of the textual interpretations or meanings created *in, through,* and *around All-American Girl* by various Asian American viewers of the series, television series' producers and actors, Asian American journalists, and Asian American scholar activists. We support our critical analysis with descriptions of scenes and story lines, transcripts of interviews with viewers, and commentary from producers, actors, journalists, and activists. We conclude with an assessment of the efficacy of this approach for studying the case of *All-American Girl.*

Although *All-American Girl* (1994) was the first American prime-time television series starring an Asian female and featuring an almost entirely Asian American cast, the half-hour comedy's title reflected the series' entrenched dualism and its ultimate denial of the possibility of a truly fluid, multicultural identity. At the center is the series' central character, Korean-American Margaret Kim (comedian Margaret Cho), and behind her (left to right) are her young brother, her television-watching grandmother, her older, high-achieving brother Stuart, and her parents.

A Critical Multicultural Ethnographic Approach

This approach to audience-centered research has developed from the assumption made by cultural studies that textual meaning is the result *both* of the preferred meanings encoded into a text *and* of interpretations created by audience members as a result of their viewing positions. As Stevenson (1995) and other scholars have explained, "This does not mean, however, that the audience is able to read any meaning into the text." Rather, it means that "the text acts as a structured polysemy" which is open to the creation of a number of possible meanings, depending upon the audience members' cultural identity or position (Stevenson, 1995, p. 79). Gender, ethnicity or race, social class, religion, and nationality all affect the reading strategies and meanings that are created.

Critics often have been guilty of what Pierre Bourdieu (1990) has labeled the "scholastic fallacy": the assumption of critics that everyday readers create the same meanings from texts that the critics do. One way of avoiding the scholastic fallacy is to use audience-centered approaches in which critics present their personal interpretations of the text in conjunction with those created by audience members. In doing so, critics must talk with audience members about the television text, learn about their reading positions, and understand their sense-making processes.

In this essay we explore the meanings and interpretations created by viewers who come to the text from multiple, diverse cultural positions. These "spectator positions" include those of an Anglo-American upper middle-class feminist critic (the second author), a Japanese American/Hawaiian/ English graduate student/feminist critic (the first author), and a diverse group of 20 Asian and Asian American viewers, females and males ranging in age from their mid-teens to their late 50s, with different cultural backgrounds (e.g., Korean, Korean American, Chinese, Chinese American, Japanese American, Pilipina American, Hawaiian, Indonesian).[2]

Microlevel cultural studies ethnographies frequently avoid addressing the political economic context (see Beezer & Barker, 1992; Kellner, 1995; Philo, 1995). We attempt to address this weakness by providing some description of the social and political economic context within which *All-American Girl* was produced and by reflecting on commentary about the ideological import of the meanings constructed *in, through,* and *around* the series.

The Political/Economic Context of *All-American Girl*

Kellner (1995) has observed that "the system of production often determines what sort of artifacts will be produced, what structural limits there will be as to what can and cannot be said and shown and what sort of audience effects the text may generate" (p. 9). *All-American Girl* is located within a multidimensional context that is constituted by political and economic factors. Debuting in fall 1994 on ABC, the sitcom arose from a sociopolitical scene of neoconservative leanings and overtly racist sentiments (Marin & Lee, 1994; Zoglin, 1994). Rising racial tensions could clearly be seen in the anti-Mexican/anti-"foreigner" legislation and strong attacks on affirmative action programs. Beneath such measures, the ideological message was clear: minorities would not be tolerated in a "reinvigorated," xenophobic America. Many—led by Anglo-American males—felt this threat to the existing power structure needed to be contained (Marin & Lee, 1994; Zoglin, 1994).

Economically, the mainstream comedy *All-American Girl* represented a product of the profit-oriented Disney Touchstone Television, a major player in a Hollywood culture industry increasingly driving the American economic engine. Disney is a multinational entertainment conglomerate with a legacy of materially entwining entertainment and political ideology ever since its inception.[3]

In the Hollywood entertainment industry environment that produced *All-American Girl*, the norm for film, literary, and televisual representations of Asians has been what Edward Said (1978) has called the "Orientalized" other. These "Orientalist" depictions have included such stereotypes as the dangerous Asian invader (historically the samurai warrior and more recently the ruthless, wealthy Japanese banker/real estate invader), the mysterious and cryptic Charlie Chan, the simultaneously subservient and hypersexualized "Oriental Butterfly" woman, and the Kung Fu master of powers seen and unseen. As various media critics have noted, these images have consistently represented Asians, and by extension Asian Americans, as subordinate "Oriental" subjects justifiably dominated by the superior Anglo West (Choy, 1978; Farquhar & Doi, 1978; Fung, 1994; Hamamoto, 1994; Kim, 1986; Paik, 1971; Said, 1978; Salvador-Burris, 1978; Tajima, 1989).

However, the 1990s have been labeled the "Asian American decade" because of the influx of progressive "Asian chic" Hollywood films which revolved around Asia-Pacific themes (Corliss, 1992, p. 14; Hagedorn, 1994, p. 76; Simon, 1993). This view has been countered by others who see these newer Hollywood images of Asians in films such as *Rising Sun* and *Heaven and Earth* merely as updated versions of Oriental stereotypes (Cacas, 1995).[4] Some, like playwright Kan Gotanda, have taken the argument further and have suggested that the effects of decades of mediated stereotypes of Asians are evident "in acts of anti-Asian hate violence, as well as sophisticated forms of racism evinced in how Asian Pacific American actors are cast" (p. 14). It was against this background, then, that *All-American Girl* premiered in fall 1994.

Based on comedienne Margaret Cho's stand-up comedy material, *All-American Girl* was a thirty-minute prime time situation comedy whose story lines centered around Margaret Cho's character, Margaret Kim, her two-generational Korean American family, and her friends. The Kim family, who owned, ran, and lived above a bookstore in San Francisco, included brash, valley girl–talking twentysomethingish college student Margaret, her high-achieving brother Stuart—a medical resident—her fifth grade brother Eric, her grandmother, and her parents, Ben and Katherine. According to the series' central actor, Margaret Cho, the anticipated goal of the series was to bring "Asians and Asian Americans in focus and to bring their traditions and attitudes into national view" (Shields, 1995, p. 23). Further, ABC promotion touted *All-American Girl* as the "first situation comedy in television history based on the trials and tribulations of an Asian American family" (Mendez, 1994, p. 28).

That the series was produced by Hollywood giant Disney and aired on ABC is somewhat surprising in a media culture industry whose history has been dominated by the oppressive Asian/Asian American images. In light of this, the series would seem to be quite progressive. However, close analysis of the text indicates that the progressiveness hoped for in this television "first" was undercut by the series' actual content. Our interpretive analysis of the text led us to conclude that the series' cultural insensitivity toward the diversity of Asian American cultural identities and its privileging of "American" over "Asian" identities in an ongoing theme of cultural dualism merely perpetuated the hegemony of the Anglo-American monoculture.

Meanings In, Through, and Around *All-American Girl*

> The text does not determine meaning so much as delimit the arena of the struggle for that meaning by marking the terrain within which its variety of readings can be negotiated. (Fiske, 1992, p. 303)

The dichotomy of "American" versus "Asian" is a floating public text that historically has helped to secure the Anglo American political, economic, and cultural power structure (see, e.g., Radhakrishnan, 1994). Popular representations of Asians/ Asian Americans in the media have repeatedly oversimplified Asian American identities as binary terms: as "conflicts between those who identify closely with the immigrant or nationalist positions versus those who are more Americanized and assimilated" (Lowe, 1991, p. 32; Osajima, 1995, p. 81). This categorization hegemonically mirrors white nationalist power in that "nation" is privileged over "ethnicity" (see, e.g., Radhakrishnan, 1994). To be "American" is to both disavow one's Asian ancestry,

history, and cultural background(s) and uphold a colonialist social system. To choose on the side of "Asian" is to comply with the dominant construction of the invading, foreign, and "homogenized" Asian. For Asian Pacific Americans, being "forced" to "choose" between these poles restrains the defining of their own richly dynamic subjectivities. Asian Americans are therefore deprived of discursive space which represents their varied identities and experiences while "American" versus "Asian" dualism is continually reproduced in public discourse (including this television series). That is why, despite the apparent progressiveness signaled by a prime time series featuring an almost all Asian American cast, many viewers argue that *All-American Girl* merely perpetuates an entrenched color-caste ideology of inequalities (see, e.g., Hamamoto, 1994; Kim, 1986).

The master narrative pitting American (nation) over Asian (ethnicity) moves *in, through,* and *around All-American Girl.*[5] Such a cultural text is not determinate or completely polysemous (Condit, 1989; Fiske, 1992). Instead, the television sitcom, like most mainstream televisual texts, delineates an area of containment for meaning. Scholarly critics, television viewers, journalists, and production participants are drawn into dichotomies which help shape their meanings of the text. Indeed, the very terms of the struggle between "American-ness" and "Asian-ness" legitimize an (Anglo) American capitalistic system undergirded by static oppositions and racialized/genderized inequalities.

In this struggle, the critics' readings of *All-American Girl,* the production texts (e.g., actors' comments, publicity, journalistic accounts, press interviews of cast), the readings of Asian/Asian American activists and scholars, and the Asian/ Asian American viewers' responses do not lie in a textual hierarchy, but rather move intertextually.[6] Fiske (1990) explains intertextuality as the way in which texts are read in the context of other texts in order to create meanings. The meanings of *All-American Girl* are shaped by a variety of texts: the sitcom text itself, past mediated Asian images, previous roles of the actors, social discourses, and personal experiences. Because intertextuality connotes a sense of movement among meanings, the circulated meanings for *All-American Girl* are best presented as a collage of participating voices.

De-Orientalized and "American": One Critical Reading of *All-American Girl*

Many audience members—viewers, journalists, reviewers, and one of the critics authoring this essay—interpreted *All-American Girl* as a progressive text that showcased positive, "deorientalized" portrayals of Asians as "Americans." Specifically, these viewers of *All-American Girl* "read" the show as depicting the Kims as real people and Asian women as strong, independent females. Some of these readers lauded the sitcom primarily for bringing Asian Americans to network television as a symbol of movement away from the invisibility of Asians in mainstream culture.

Asian/Asian Americans as "Real"

Some viewers celebrated *All-American Girl*'s portrayal of the Kim family as a "universal" family as opposed to Asian American. They saw the sitcom as breaking away from Asian stereotypes to portray Asian Americans as "normal" people with the same pleasure, pains, fears, and hopes as other Americans. In effect, they saw *All-American Girl* as doing for Asian Americans what *The Cosby Show* did for African Americans. For instance, the series' executive producer and co-creator Gary Jacobs explained that the show's "stories will demonstrate how many of their [Kims'] experiences are universal and immediately comprehensible to all" (Mendez, 1994, p. 28). Production members such as lead actor Margaret Cho emphasized the Kims' universal appeal in her statement that, "aside from their cultural uniqueness, the Kims are also an identifiable, individual family as well, with the same problems, communication barriers, and the same love" (Mendez, 1994, p. 28). Cho hailed her show as successfully "taking away some of the mystery about Asian Americans and demonstrat[ing] that we're like everybody else" (Mendez, 1994, p. 28).

Two Japanese American male college students shared this view:

VIEWER A: For once, we see Asians—the Kims—as just like everybody else. No different from other people in this society. We are not odd, not freaks, just normal people who go about life.

VIEWER B: Yeah, you see that family as a typical American family. You know, just like other families around us. They fight, laugh, and come together when they have to. But, those kids and the star. They want to break away from their parents. You know, just like how normal teenagers do. And sometimes they do not always want to be together. Like the time, the father wants a family night and grandma runs away. You see, Asian families aren't always tight-locked, you know. They are just normal people.

Another viewer, a Pilipina American mother, located the source of her positive response in the series' "human" portrayals of Korean Americans:

I really like the treatment of the Korean characters as real people, as humans. They are not speaking in Confucian lingo or appearing in tight silk sams. The Asian is not made into such a big spectacle—they are just real. They are Americans here. You don't see that much, do you?

These positive responses to the show's portrayal of Asian Americans as "universal," "normal people," "just like everybody else," "real," and "typical" reflect the series' broad appeal for audience members desiring a "normalizing" first. That the show de-ethnicizes and obscures the unique aspects of Korean American culture is, for these viewers, progressive and laudatory.

The appeal of an "Asian-stripped" *All-American Girl* for Asian American audience members is understandable within the context of past stereotyped images of Asian and Asian Americans as ruthless, threatening infidels, as mysterious and inscrutable other, and as "Oriental Butterflies." For these audience members, replacement of the symbolic annihilation[7] of Asian Americans with normalizing albeit "whitened" representations is seen as positive.

A critical, multicultural studies perspective requires that we ask what is ignored, eclipsed, or marginalized in and through audience perceptions of these homogenized images. When these audience members describe the Kims as Americans and "typical American family," what they are missing are descriptions of these characters as "real" Asian American people. Here the show is being embraced for its "white" American portrayals of Asian/Asian Americans, and as Toni Morrison (1992) explains, "American means white" (p. 47).

A whitened/colorless *All-American Girl* is a marketable media product providing some measure of acceptance and relief from a history of racist stereotypes. That for once Asian characters are not dehumanized or demonized, for these readers, represents a victory of great magnitude. Alternatively, however, producer Jacobs' (1995) hopes that "people will stop seeing" the Kims as "Asian Americans" (p. F3) can be viewed as merely another socially sanctioned strategy for denying race and ethnicity and the accompanying racial biases that are the foundation of the dominant American social/political, ideological order.

"American Asian" Women as Independent

Other audience members read the series as positive because they interpreted it as a decolonialist presentation of independent "American" Asian women. One of the authors of this article saw in several of the narratives a counter to the subservient "Oriental Butterfly" stereotype of the exotic and hypersexualized yet "quiet, unassuming, and non-threatening doll" whose submissiveness reaffirms traditional Asian and American patriarchal authority (see Halualani, 1995; Lai, 1988). For this critic/audience member textual analysis revealed episodes which modeled feminist awakening and provided empowering anti–"Oriental Butterfly" images. To illustrate, this critic points to the episode in which Stuart and his Asian American girlfriend Amy announce their engagement

and Margaret is pressed into taking her new sister-in-law-to-be out with her friends for a female celebration. This critic argues that the change depicted in Amy (and Stuart) over the course of the half-hour—from Amy's initial identity as a submissive, self-effacing traditional "Oriental" female to her evolution into a modern, independent female—is a positive, feminist, and counterstereotypical depiction of Asian American womanhood.

In this episode, when we first meet Amy she is self-effacing, enthusiastically subservient, old-fashioned, wholesome, and demure, despite being well-educated and economically well-to-do. She wears modest, dowdy, ankle-length, old-fashioned floral dresses. She sits demurely on the couch next to Stuart, her hands folded on her lap. She allows Stuart to answer questions directed to her, and nods in delight when Stuart announces their engagement. These narrative details constitute Amy as an "Oriental Butterfly."

However, this stereotype is shattered after Margaret takes Amy out with Margaret's friends for a final "girls' night out," and Amy accepts Margaret's advice to take control of her life and be "free" to be her own person. At the bar, Margaret, dressed in her usual black miniskirt and leather jacket, advises Amy, "Don't start every sentence with 'Stuart and I.' " Margaret chastises Amy about her clothes and doormat-like behavior. Amy comes to realize that she has subsumed her identity to Stuart's, and that she has never explored who Amy is. Exchanging her traditional dowdy dresses for new miniskirted leather attire, Amy rebels against Stuart's kindly but patriarchal treatment of her and demands "to be treated as an equal." By the end of the episode, Amy "sees" how disempowered she was, and learns that she does not have to "settle for less" than she wants. She learns that she does not have to pretend to be "decorative, invisible, or one-dimensional" (Hagedorn, 1994, p. 79). This feminist narrative of Amy's empowerment debunks American and Asian patriarchal stereotypes and enacts a feminist image of an empowered American Asian female not content to be merely an appendage.

A mixed Chinese/Japanese American female audience member, who shared this critic's view, said she liked the show because of its "strong Asian women":

> TV does not place minority women, especially Asians, in seats of power. They are just tools for a greater end. *All-American Girl* captures a sense of autonomy among the women. Margaret Cho is both independent and entertaining. She does not have to hide her wild side and she doesn't take crap as a strong American woman. That is good to see.

While these audience members lauded the images of "strong" Asian women as progressive, an alternative (critical multicultural) interpretation of the show notes that the strength, power, and independence of this portrayal is derived largely through the character's choice of an "American" over an "Asian" female identity. In fact, both the critic's and viewer's readings of the text highlighted the series' feminist counter-"Oriental Butterfly" images and identified these as essentially "American." The dualism of identity is again brought forth by "the positive equals American" readings, reaffirming the dominance and superiority of an American liberal democratic ideology. However, such a reading foregrounds the national/ethnicity opposition over the contemporary/traditional opposition.

Presence as Positive: Countering Symbolic Annihilation

As we discussed earlier, many positive readings were based on the show's mere existence in mainstream television. One Korean male viewer, for instance, saw the show as a landmark because it "shows our faces":

> My children grow up watching white faces. Here I saw one time it had our faces and I immediately loved it. It is a first. You know how important that is?

Throughout his interview, this reader did not describe any of the episodes or characters that struck him as particularly important. In fact, it came out later that he saw the show only once at the beginning of the season. His interpretation revolved around placing the show in juxtaposition to past oppressive Asian stereotypes. For him, *All-*

American Girl symbolized an "upturn." That he "immediately" loved the sitcom's presentation of Asians suggests that the show provides a mark of Asian empowerment and presence in society.

Two Chinese American professionals, one male and the other female, also viewed the series as a "breakthrough" for Asian Americans:

VIEWER C: It was refreshing to see Asian images in mainstream TV. American television. Now that's a switch. I am surprised it even happened.

VIEWER D: It finally happened. That is the point. For decades, we have been excluded from the screen. And such politics of exclusion is damaging because people do not see Asians/Asian Americans as complex individuals. The show is actually pretty stupid. The characters, story lines, everything is based on silly stuff. But it is good in the sense that it made its way to TV. That is what we should recognize.

VIEWER C (nodding head): The Asian Pacific community should look at the show in that way—as gaining major ground in an industry that we are purposefully kept out of. Although *All-American Girl* is no winner of quality material, the fact that it is here is extremely important.

Here even audience members who disliked the sitcom's content looked beyond the substance of the show to its ground-breaking role. These viewers created positive interpretations of the text because they saw the series as strategically important as a reversal of the ethnically exclusionary history of American media. Production members, Asian/Asian American activists, and scholars also interpreted the mere fact that the show existed on prime time as positive and significant for Asian American viewers. For example, cast member B. D. Wong (Stuart Kim) explained that he felt that the show's presentation of Asians was progressive because: "When I was little, whenever there was an Asian person on television, everyone in the family had to stop what they were doing and come see. That's how unusual it was" (Mendez, 1994, p. 28).

Guy Aoki, the president of the Media Action Network for Asian Americans, shared the sentiment that the sitcom "is positive because it is the first television series to feature an Asian American family" and countered Asian American criticism of the show by focusing on how "Seeing ourselves on television gives validity to our existence" (Price, 1994, p. 129).

For these culturally situated Asian American readers, the fact that *All-American Girl* brought Asian faces to the television screen outweighed all other aspects of the show, including the quality of the representations. Yet from a critical multicultural interpretation, these portrayals are isolated exceptions. From this vantage point, until we see substantial numbers of Asian American actors cast in all sorts of roles, not just ethnic roles, such depictions remain tokens that reaffirm the dominance and the moral legitimacy of the Anglo-American-dominated political economic order.

"Bleaching Asian-ness": The Americanization of All-American Girl

In contrast to these audience members' interpretations, other viewers "read" the series more negatively. A number of interpretations characterized the series as erasing Asian-ness. These viewers interpreted the series' portrayals as assimilating ("Americanizing") or "bleaching" the Korean American family to make them resemble white (Anglo) Americans. For these audience members, *All-American Girl* signified not a turning point but rather a confirmation of "Oriental" stereotypes and the subtle ways the Anglo-American status quo is preserved and authentic representations of Asian American-ness are denied.

All-American Girl as an "Orientalized" Text: A Different Critical Reading—

Long Live the American Dream. For example, one of the authors of this chapter read the program as an attempt to encourage seeing Asian/Asian Americans as a homogenized mass of assimilated "American" citizens. For this viewer, the Kims were

symbolic devices celebrating the dominant American capitalist order and distracting from the racialized, genderized, and sexualized inequalities of American institutions. This critic points to several episodes which confirmed the "Oriental" stereotypes of the "model minority," the "Oriental Butterfly," and the American liberal democratic myth of "Individual Freedom" (i.e., the myth that all citizens are free to be whoever/whatever they want to be).

All-American Girl's confirmation of Asian Americans as a "model minority" can be seen in an episode in which a commercial bookstore franchise offered to buy out the Kims' bookstore. The narrative here overtly reinforced the American Dream myth (and work ethic) that holds that in America those who work hard, obey the law, and are committed to education will succeed economically.

> FATHER: Your mother and I came to this country with nothing. That bookstore represents everything we've become.
>
> MARGARET: Dad, this is the American Dream. I mean, this is why you worked so hard for thirty years. You've built something of value and now you can cash in.

This scene affirms the efficacy of the American Dream myth that impoverished immigrants who come to America and work hard can achieve economic success. Absent from this episode are references to the difficulties caused by prejudices ethnic minorities have experienced in establishing their own businesses in America, an omission that implies that all immigrants can succeed through determination, commitment, and a solid family environment. From this critical multicultural perspective, this omission obfuscates the inequalities due to prejudice that ethnic immigrants face and uses them to confirm the working of the current ideological system. They become, as Hamamoto (1992) points out, an example to other ethnic minorities of how a formally disadvantaged group can overcome limited life chances, social discrimination, and economic hardship through self-reliance, personal discipline, and mutual assistance, all within the opportunity structure afforded by a liberal democracy (p. 36).

The sitcom text suggests that if ethnic groups like Korean Americans can succeed, the American system of individualistic capitalism truly works for everyone. As Nakayama (1988) argues, "Asian American success affirms the workability of American social institutions" and that the problems of "minority groups are a result of their own neglect." Hence, race and the intersecting of race/gender are constructed as *not* impeding the pursuit for mobility and status (p. 70). According to this interpretation, *All-American Girl* participates in legitimizing a hegemonic social order under attack by ethnic, women's, and gay and lesbian civil rights groups since the 1960s.

Interactions between the parents, Katherine and Ben Kim, and their son, Stuart, further reinscribe the Model Minority stereotype. Stuart, the mid-twentyish obedient son and hard-working medical resident, represents the quintessential Model Minority figure as do his hard-working parents who hold high educational aspirations for their son. In one episode, Katherine boasts to Stuart, "I am so proud of you. Today ranking resident, tomorrow chief resident. And someday, the cover of the *New England Journal of Medicine*." In this episode, because of pressure to achieve from his parents, Stuart nearly collapses trying to keep up his grueling resident physician work schedule. As he explains, "You can't make chief resident by slacking off." Pained by the emotional pressure that she sees Stuart is feeling to be the perfect "model minority" son, Margaret has the following conversation with her mother:

MARGARET: Mom, you're starting to do to Eric exactly what you did with Stuart.
MOM: What? Motivate him toward excellence? I hope so.
MARGARET: It's just too much pressure. Look at Stuart. When he screws up, his whole world crumbles.
MOM: Well, you are the ones who took him to Skid Row when he was six, pointed to a bunch of winos and said, "That's what happens when you get an A minus in phonics."

Later in this episode, an exhausted Stuart, who has been working literally night and day to please

his parents by becoming chief resident, mixes up two files. When he is temporarily suspended because of a mishap, Stuart explains to Margaret his fear of the "look" he gets from their parents, "a look reserved for the eldest son who has gravely disappointed his parents." With Margaret's encouragement, Stuart sheds the debilitating burden of being the "model minority" his parents want him to be by singing "Yankee Doodle Dandy," thereby exorcising the haunting memory of a childhood recital in which he sang "Yankee Doodle Dandy" flatly and disappointed his parents. However, Stuart's defiant singing of the refrain, "I am that Yankee Doodle Boy" ironically corroborates rather than debunks the Asian Model Minority myth. Here again, "Yankee Doodle Dandy" symbolically links Stuart's newfound feeling of autonomy to the American tenets of independence/freedom and justice in opposition to his parents' "old country" expectations of the eldest son. Again, then, American (nation) and contemporary are opposed to ethnicity (Asian) and traditional, and the former are preferred while the latter are rejected.

This interpretation views *All-American Girl* as ironically affirming the Oriental Butterfly myth as well. This occurs in an episode in which Margaret's mother finally succeeds in persuading Margaret to date an eligible young Asian professional listed in Mrs. Kim's "Marriage" computer file. Margaret's date, Raymond Han, is a successful Korean American doctor from a traditional family. Margaret forgoes her usual black leather punk attire and dresses in conservative, demure clothing when she is with Raymond. However, when Margaret begins to giggle with her hand over her mouth and softly respond, "Whatever you say, Raymond," in her conversations with him, her Anglo friends Ruthie and Gloria confront her:

MARGARET: He treats me great. So, if in return, he wants me to be a little bit . . .
GLORIA: Subservient.
RUTHIE: Doormatish.
MARGARET: Demure, then it's my business.

After several dates, Raymond invites Margaret to dine with his family. To prepare her for this, Margaret's mother and brother Stuart spend several days coaching her on traditional Korean etiquette. At the dinner, she is "looked over" by Raymond's parents who eventually indicate that they agree she would be a suitable wife when they deliver a traditional, patriarchal toast:

MRS. HAN: May you have the joy that comes from selfless devotion to your husband!
MR. HAN: May you swell with the bounty of many masculine children!

Once they return to Margaret's house a horrified Margaret tells Raymond that this relationship will never work. As she explains to him, because "I like you, I wanted it to work out so I tried to become the person you wanted me to be." When Raymond asks what Margaret is really like, she answers, "I'm really opinionated and I say exactly what I think. And frankly, I have no immediate plans to swell with the bounty of any children, masculine or otherwise." Having heard this, Raymond then admits that he could never live with the "real" Margaret (or any American girl who would just say what she thought), and they part ways.

This episode reflects the continued vitality of the subservient Oriental Butterfly myth. This episode, as well as the earlier episode which depicted Amy's evolution from subservient Butterfly to empowered modern woman (and the concomitant efforts of Stuart to develop a more feminist, egalitarian relationship with her), reaffirmed traditional Asian culture as oppressively patriarchal in contrast to the democratic, egalitarian, even feminist American culture. For example, in the Margaret/Raymond episode Raymond negatively contrasted traditional, demure Asian girls (which he thinks Margaret is) who keep their opinions to themselves with "American girls who are going to say what's on their minds," and Margaret tartly reminded him that she was "American." Here again, the "Oriental Butterfly" stereotype reinscribes Asian/Asian American culture as sexist and thus, legitimates the superiority of the contrasting "American" way of life.

Another way in which All-American Girl reflected the essentializing dichotomy of American

(nation) over Asian (ethnicity) was in its casting of the series. Although the series claimed to focus on the lives of the members of a Korean American family in the 1990s, Margaret Cho was the only member of the cast who was actually Korean. Cho's older brother on the show was played by B. D. Wong who is actually Chinese, and her grandmother was played by Amy Hill, who is Japanese-Finnish (Marin, 1994). Apparently Disney-Touchstone and ABC felt that most Americans wouldn't notice this. Such collapsing and essentializing of multiple Asian and American ethnic identities into a singular "Asian American" identity is a version of the racist stereotype that all (fill in the ethnic minority group—here Asians) look alike. The series' casting, thus, reflects the dominant American culture's homogenization of diverse Asian cultures and contributes to the difficulty Asian Americans face in establishing their own truly multicultural identities.

Many Asian/Asian American viewers objected to the "model minority" and Oriental Butterfly stereotypes depicted in *All-American Girl*. One Pilipino male said:

All-American Girl is totally a sell-out. The question is—Where are the Asians? Where are the Asian Americans? You see none of it. It's all bleached white. I saw the film episode, when Margaret Cho is in the film class and the teacher gives her a "D" cuz he had different expectations for someone like her. Let me spell it out for you—M O D E L M I N O R I T Y. Model minority, plain and simple. Of course, the Asian American student is held up to a different standard than all the others. Even a "D" student is placed with those kinds of stereotypical expectations. I mean, come on.

To illustrate the source of his interpretation he referred to an episode in which Margaret's (Anglo male) writing teacher told her that because she had great potential he would be judging her work by a "different standard." The outraged viewer interpreted this as unequal treatment based on the "Model Minority." His critical reading of the episode was that the performance of Asian American students was being measured by a racist standard couched in the socially laudable form of the overachieving "Model Minority."

Another Korean American male viewer also saw the series' depictions as "extremely insulting":

> Asian American men and women are jokes in the show. All that stuff about the Korean guy she is set up with and Stuart. And they are supposed to be these incredibly domineering men. What is communicated is that all Asian men, Asian American men, especially Korean American men, are oppressive. This is so incredibly misleading. All my life, people have either expected that from me or told me that was how I should be. I grew up in a household where my father split the child-rearing/home duties. Where the sons and daughters were both expected to treat each other with respect and love. I respect all of those around me. My significant other is my best friend. She is not this object who I speak for. My mother is a college professor and my father is a civil engineer who endured stereotypes like this.
>
> Even the Asian women are portrayed as ridiculous. The mother is completely devoted to her family. While this is true in many Asian families, this is not always the case. But Margaret is supposed to be this really radical woman who rebels against oppressive Asian men and does not want to be like her mother. If that isn't adding credence to stereotypes, I don't know what is.

This reader used personal experiences to interpret representations in the series as stereotypical constructions of oppressive Asian/Asian American men and acquiescent Asian women. This viewer felt such stereotypes had affected his life and he critiqued Margaret Cho's seemingly "radical stance" as an "insulting" attempt to reinforce "Orientalized" images. Equally critical of the series was a female Vietnamese viewer who rejected the series' privileging of national/American over ethnic cultural/Asian identities:

> I knew I would never watch the show when I saw it that one night. When the mother tells Margaret how much she hated her making fun of them in public, Margaret said something like "this isn't Korea, it is America and I have freedom of speech." Just slap Asians in the face, why don't you? The creation of comments like that are negative for Asians. It makes America seem like this great, redeeming place that allows minorities to speak their mind. And we know

that isn't so. We are muted in the media, in politics, in colleges. The show made a lot of those digs into Asian culture. So much so that at the end all you see is an assimilated, Americanized, white family with "black hair."

This viewer denounced the text's oppositional contrasts between an old world, repressive Korea and an American nation of boundless freedom. She interpreted the show as an assimilationist effort that effaced Asian race and ethnicity, except for the Kims' black hair as a signifier of racial difference. She "read" the series' promotion of American ideals in the narrative content as reinforcing Anglo superiority and a nonthreatening Asian inferiority (see Fiske, 1992, pp. 287–288).

A mixed Japanese/African American male viewer concurred and pointed to the title of the sitcom and the grandma character as signs of the series' affirmation of "Americanization" and rejection of Asian identity:

> The title explains much: *All-American Girl*. Not *All-Asian-American-Girl*. Or *Asian Girl*. Or *Asian-American Girl*. But, *All-American Girl*. Meaning all and completely, totally American and not at all Asian. I think that says much about the show. When the show first came out, all my friends raved that this would be a new focus. *All-American Girl* would look at Asian American stories. Now, we come to find out that there is an extremity being taken. Total Americanization is the ploy, the catch. And the grandma falls into this ploy. No one notices this. You may have? She watches TV all the time. American TV. Day and night. She lives within that tube. Everybody laughs but it's such a ploy. That grandma is the most despicable evidence of complete assimilation to American culture.

This audience member deconstructed the show's title, which he saw as a reflection of the text's assimilationist ideology. He explained that his oppositional reading was based on the implication that the word "All-American" meant "all and completely and totally American and not at all Asian." He interpreted the show's "Americanization" as a manipulative effort to embrace assimilation to American culture as a most desirable choice for Asian Americans because it wouldn't threaten Anglo Americans.

All of these viewers critically interrogated the sitcom's presentation of admirable Asians/Asian Americans as those who embrace only the "American" portion of their identity. Without explicitly using the critical vocabulary that critics use, both the Vietnamese female and the Japanese/African American male viewer argued that the series naturalized the characters' assimilationist actions and, thus, were examples of hegemony in action (e.g., Gray, 1995).

Commentary about the series in the popular media reflected tensions between production members who positively interpreted *All-American Girl* as affirming "American-ness" and Asian American journalists and activists who attacked the sitcom for its totalizing emphasis on American ideals and its rejection of Asian cultural values. For example, one preview of *All-American Girl* featured a picture of Margaret Cho wearing an American flag as an apron and holding up an apple pie. The caption read "Miss Korean-American Pie." Although this caption specified "Korean-American," it was contradicted by the picture of an Asian American woman adorned in the quintessential emblem of American-ness—the flag. The potential for representing Asian American-ness was further defused by the hyphenated term "Korean-American," which reproduced "a metaphor that highlights the boundary between minority Americans and white Americans" (Chen, 1994, p. 9). Margaret Cho's comment that if her show was renewed, "then I think that we have arrived at hot dog-baseball-American cheese status" reiterated this focus (Chin, 1994, p. A12). For Asian American journalists and activists, the emphasis on American rather than Asian symbols in these production texts implied *All-American Girl* was designed to represent and encourage the assimilation of Asians into the homogenized Anglo-American culture, not to endorse the inclusion of Asian culture as part of the national (American) culture.

The meanings constructed by Asian American journalists and activists contradicted the preferred readings proffered by the sitcom text and its surrounding production texts. For example, *Asian Week* columnist Bill Wong (1994) condemned the show as "ethnically inauthentic" and proof that "Asian Americans can be part of banal, uninspired entertainment. Equal Opportunity mediocrity" (p. 9). According to Wong, the show's featuring of a generic "American" shell inferiorized Asian/Asian American voices under the rubric of "Equal Opportunity." Wong also attacked the series' "ethnic inauthenticity" and raised the question, "What is a true Asian/Asian American experience(s)?" Wong's interpretation suggested that essentializing ethnic identity is problematic because it encourages using a standardized criterion for affirming or negating cultural identity and experience. In so doing, individual identity construction is denied. Furthermore, tensions among various Asian/Asian American groups are fostered by attempts to determine authentic Asian American experience and identity.

Asian American activist/journalist Cacas (1994) attacked the sitcom because in a multicultural San Francisco setting the character Margaret Kim interacted predominantly with only Anglo Americans:

> Will the non–Asian Pacific American persons she has contact with eventually include Latino Americans, African Americans, Native Americans, Gays and Lesbians? Or will they continue to be European Americans exclusively? Only time will tell just how All-American "All-American Girl" will be. (p. 23)

Cacas ironically retitled the show, "All European American in Margaret Kim's World" (p. 23), to illustrate his criticism of the series' limiting Margaret's interactions primarily to Anglo Americans (e.g., Ruthie, Gloria, Casey, Margaret's mostly Anglo American male dates and roommates, and Eric's little Anglo American female friend). His comparison of the show's ethnic landscape with the flourishing multicultural Bay Area population underscores the disparity between the series' representation and Asian American social reality. Cacas' reading reveals an interpretive strategy used by a number of viewers who feel that if images do not fit actual experience(s), they should be discarded and branded as (whitened) "Americanized."

Many audience members left their encounter with the series deeply resentful of what they interpreted as "bleaching" (i.e., Anglo "Americanization") of its Asian American representations. Like Hamamoto (1989), they saw *All-American Girl* as typical of commercial television in its "packag[ing]," "market[ing]," and reproducing the "affirmative aspects" of American liberal democratic ideology: freedom, equality, and social and economic opportunity (pp. 2, 4). From these Asian American viewers' perspectives, "true" Asian/Asian American experience was subverted by the sitcom's binary framework of "American" versus "Asian," the concomitant essentialization of Asian/Asian American identities, and the privileging of American over Asian.

Ironically, despite the diversity among the meanings viewers created *in, through,* and *around All-American Girl,* all shared the view that the series was a politically charged program. These Asian American cultural readers felt there was little choice in identity or reading position—either one had to affirm the dominance of the Anglo American socioeconomic order and subordinate one's Asian ethnicity or accept perpetual alien status in the country of one's birth. Either they must hail *All-American Girl's* portrayals as "real" and "American" or denounce the text's erasure of Asian ethnicity and hardship as an American televisual assimilationist effort to elevate "color-blind" or rather "bleached white" American-ness over "yellow" Asian-ness.

Chow (1990) has explained that ethnic identity in America is not "voluntary," but rather "a matter of history" (p. 45). The history of political, economic, and social subordination of Asian Americans and their "Orientalist" media representations have propagated a social marginality and dualism that is actively reflected in the meanings many viewers constructed from *All-American Girl.* However, affirmation of Asian American experiences as cultural hybrids also was articulated by some viewers (e.g., Lowe, 1991; Osajima, 1995). Indeed, some viewers, including this Korean American female viewer and avid Margaret Cho fan, rejected this dualism and called instead for articulating and representing the diverse, hybrid experiences of Asian Americans:

> I was disappointed with the show. It did not capture the real complexities in being a Korean American, or

an Asian Pacific American. The terms—Asian, American—become useless at some point. Sometimes I do not always feel just Asian or American or just half of each. It is always both at the same time. Does that make sense? You can't even describe it. I have watched all of Margaret Cho's comedy specials; saw her perform in the city once and ABC should have just filmed her routines; that is where she gets at the complexities of being diversely Asian American.

This reader stressed that the multiple identities that she experiences as an Asian American led her to resist *All-American Girl's* dichotomized and preferred "American" versus "Asian" identity. That is, her lived cultural position led her to reject the situation comedy's preferred reading and to affirm instead Cho's stand-up comedy routines because in the latter Cho mocks this dichotomy and affirms a multicultural Asian American identity. This viewer recalled this portion of Cho's stand-up comedy routine in which Cho explained to the audience her frustration with being constantly cast as a "forever foreign" Asian:

> I was supposed to go on the show and tell jokes. What was I supposed to do. (She speaks with an exaggerated accent): "My husband is so fat that when he sits around the hopaku, he really sit around hopaku! Gong!"

This excerpt reflected the viewer's frustration with the series, a frustration generated not only from the content of the series or published commentary about the series but from the viewing self she brought to the series. Like all viewers of *All-American Girl*—including the authors of this essay—this viewer brought to her viewing of the series her previous experiences with literary texts and her knowledge of other texts, her social self, her life experiences, and her self-identity. And in consequence, she constructed a reading of the text which disrupted the "American" versus "Asian" identity framework.

Final Observations

Condit's (1989) concept of polyvalence describes one of the major findings in this critical ethnographic study of the meanings of *All-American Girl.* Condit's (1989) essay critiqued Fiske's (1986) concept of polysemy and posited the concept of polyvalence as a corrective. Fiske's concept of polysemy posited that popular texts are constructed in ways that enable audience members—especially members of gender, ethnic, cultural, political, and economic minorities—to use the "openings" or ambiguity in texts to resist the text's expressions of dominant ideology and to negotiate alternative, pleasurable, and empowering interpretations of the text. Condit (1989) offered another explanation for negotiated readings; she argued that perhaps the empowering process of audience interpretation has less to do with attributing entirely new meanings to textual signifiers than it does with audience members choosing to evaluate the meanings differently. Thus, she advanced the notion that audiences indeed may recognize the preferred meanings encoded in texts and may simply differ in the positive or negative valence they give these meanings.

Condit's notion of polyvalence seems to describe our finding that although all the audience members whose interpretations are discussed in this study—the Asian American critic, the Anglo American critic, and the Asian and Asian American audience members—all acknowledged at some level that the series privileged (Anglo) American (national) over Asian (ethnic) representations, values, and norms, these viewers differed greatly in their interpretation of this as positive/empowering or racist/constraining. Some viewers—including a number of Asian American audience members and the Dutch American author of this essay—saw *All-American Girl* largely as positive, a progressive first through which past overtly racist Asian and Asian American stereotypes were rejected. These audience members gave the series a positive valence for its legitimization of images of Asians as normal, regular albeit Americanized humans, and for its strong, feminist Asian female protagonist. Other viewers—including the Japanese Hawaiian American author of this essay and a number of Asian American audience members—interpreted the same text as yet another neocolonialist text whose inferential racism subtly affirmed the dominant

Anglo cultural ideology in which Asian Americans are forever viewed as foreign "others" despite rejection of their Asian identity and attempts to assimilate into Anglo American society.

Cloud's (1992) essay, like Stuart Hall's (1981/ 1990) essay "The Whites of Their Eyes," points out that polyvalent readings of ambivalent stereotypes are not necessarily subversive of the dominant ideology. In contrast to Fiske's (1986) focus on the subversive pleasures that viewers can find in popular texts, Cloud cautions critics and cultural studies ethnographers "that we cannot simply assume that ambivalent or contradictory articulations of racial difference are in and of themselves subversive" of the dominant social structure and ideology. Indeed, Cloud argues that "the playful discovery in popular texts of moments of contradiction and opposition" (such as some viewers found in *All-American Girl*) "is perhaps not as vital a critical task as coming to an understanding of how a carefully structured cultural variance can work in support of an oppressive society" (p. 322).

This is Stuart Hall's (1981/1991) point as well. Hall argues that as critics, we need to think about "the way[s] in which the media—sometimes deliberately, sometimes unconsciously—define and construct the question of race in such a way as to reproduce the ideologies of racism" (p. 8). In doing so, he reminds us, we must remember that "ideologies 'work' by constructing for their subjects (individual and collective) positions of identification and knowledge which allow them to 'utter' ideological truths as if they were their authentic authors" (p. 9).

Cloud's (1992) essay reminds us that our obligation in audience-centered criticism, as critical ethnographers, is to step back and recontextualize texts and viewers' interpretations of texts—to read them against the backdrop of the sociopolitical and economic context in which they were produced. From such a perspective, then, we can conclude that the Orientalist colonialist stereotype is still alive and well in *All-American Girl.* As Bhabha (1983) has explained, "The colonial stereotype is a complex, ambivalent, contradictory mode of representation [whose] predominant strategic function is the creation of a space for a 'subject peoples' through the production of knowledges in terms of which surveillance is exercised and a complex form of pleasure/unpleasure is incited" (pp. 22–23).

One important way this is accomplished, as Hall (1981) explains, is through media "representations of the social world, images, descriptions, explanations and frames for understanding how the world is and why it works as it is said and shown to work" (p. 11). And some of these are "apparently naturalized representations of events and situations relating to race, whether 'factual' or 'fictional,' which have racist premises and propositions inscribed in them as a set of unquestioned assumptions . . . [and which therefore] enable racist statements to be formulated without ever bringing into awareness the racist predicates on which the statements are grounded" (p. 13). Hall terms this *inferential racism,* and he cautions that it is both widespread and insidious (p. 13) and also that "neither a unifiedly conspiratorial media nor indeed a unified racist 'ruling class' exist in anything like that simple way" (p. 12). For example, our textual analysis of *All-American Girl* revealed a number of examples of such inferential racism, including the series' title "All-American Girl," the casting of only one Korean American actor in this situation comedy about a Korean American family, Stuart Kim's singing of "I'm a Yankee Doodle Dandy" as his song of liberation from conformity to his parents' expectations, and Margaret's assertion to Raymond Han that "I am an American girl."

Clearly, the evaluations audience members attached to these representations were polyvalent. Despite the series' apparent opposition to Orientalist or colonialist stereotypes, close textual analysis revealed the insidious and largely invisible presence of the series' racist premises. Some audience members resoundingly rejected the series when their own readings of it revealed this unapparent inferential racism. However, other viewers who also recognized the underlying racist premises and assumptions, attached a positive valence to the series' recoding of Orientalist stereotypes. For these viewers the series, however imperfect,

was nonetheless a positive and empowering step—a revolutionary first—in combating racist ideological assumptions about Asian Americans. And indeed, as Hall (1981/1990) has observed, "the argument that *only* 'deconstructivist' texts are truly revolutionary is as one-sided a view as that which suggests that forms have no effect" (p. 21).

We agree with Hall (1981/1990) that one of the most difficult problems cultural theorists and critics face is that of finding effective strategies and tactics to use in challenging "media construction of race, so as to undermine, deconstruct and question the unquestioned racist assumptions on which so much of media practice is located" (p. 8). The two critics authoring this chapter disagree about the overall efficacy of this series as an antiracist strategy. Our ethnographic analysis, however, suggests this is not solely the result of occupying different subject positions. One author is a third generation Dutch American middle class heterosexual woman for whom her university education was an intellectually, emotionally, and ideologically liberating experience, and as a scholar and professor she strives to create a climate which can enable all of her students and her readers to have similarly empowering experiences. The other author is an ethnically mixed fourth generation (yonsei) Japanese American/Hawaiian/English female graduate student who strives to work for the social emancipation of the silenced and the suppressed. Like many of the audience members we interviewed, we "read" the series differently. Using Cloud's (1992) term, we attached different valences to its representations. We both agree, however, that critical readership studies such as this encourage all viewers—Asian Pacific/Asian Pacific American, African American, Latina/Latino American, Chicana/Chicano, and Anglo American—to recognize and challenge inferiorizing representations that appropriate and marginalize dynamic, multicultural social identities.

Notes

1. We struggled with the identifying terms and labels we use throughout this essay. We recognize

the problems and limitations in our linguistic choices; however, despite our sincere attempts we were not able to find a satisfactory linguistic means of communicating our awareness that identity is a multifaceted construct that certainly is not simply or solely a function of national origin, ethnicity, and culture. We acknowledge that throughout this essay the distinction between "Asian" and "Asian American" is oftentimes blurred. Broadly speaking, in this chapter, "Asian" refers to those of Asian descent from different parts of the world while "Asian American" refers to those of Asian descent who are born in the United States. Used mostly as a mobilizing device, "Asian American" is a problematic "essentializing" term in that it both fails to represent the ever-present diversity in and among Asian cultures and excludes a large population of Asians who live in other parts of the world (e.g., Canada). Thus, in this essay, the "Asian American" term is used as a strategic discursive device to disrupt the dichotomy of "American" versus "Asian" and represent multiple, heterogeneous Asian subjectivities.

2. Open-ended single person and group ethnographic interviews were conducted with 20 diverse Asian and Asian American viewers. Participants represented various ages (e.g., from the mid-teens to late fifties) and different Asian cultural groups (e.g., Korean, Korean American, Chinese, Chinese American, Japanese American, Pilipina American, Hawaiian, Indonesian), and included both females and males. Each interview averaged forty minutes in length and was audiotaped with the permission of the interviewees. Participants had the option of watching the 14 analyzed episodes before the interviews. Interviewees authorized the inclusion of interview excerpts in this paper.

3. Disney's founder, Walt Disney, served as FBI informant (Eliot, 1993) and accepted federal government underwriting of military training films, propaganda cartoons, and shorts designed to sway public and government opinion in favor of strategic bombing during World War II (Holliss & Sibley, 1988; Jewett & Lawrence, 1977). Subsequently, while overseeing his growing entertainment empire, Walt Disney served as a U.S. State Department goodwill ambassador to South America and produced a series of films related to this which were intended to "show the truth about the American way [and] carry a message of democracy and friendship below the Rio Grande" (Burton, 1992, p. 55). In addition to Disneyland, Disney World, and Euro Disney, the corporate Disney also owns Childcraft, an educational toy company (Bell, Hass, & Sells, 1995) and the ABC television network. Recently, Disney opened a new enterprise also explicitly designed to combine education (ideology) and entertainment—The Disney Institute in Lake Buena Vista, Florida. At the Disney Institute's vacation campus guests can choose to take courses from 80 different programs (including story arts, television broadcasting, lifestyles, environment, etc.) as well as enjoy the recreational offerings of Walt Disney World (Clarke, 1996). Clearly, Disney is intimately involved in the commercial combining of entertainment and educational experiences.

4. In the 1990s, several mainstream films that portrayed Asians were released. Some of these were *Dragon* (1994), *Golden Gate* (1993), *Farewell, My Concubine* (1994), *Rising Sun* (1992), *The Joy Luck Club* (1993), *Heaven and Earth* (1993) and *M. Butterfly* (1994). However, most of these reinscribed "Orientalist" stereotypes of the past, creating one-dimensional, "foreign" Asian characters. Cacas (1995) documents the panel meeting of Asian Pacific American scholars, playwrights, and artists who concluded that "Charlie Chan," "taken as a collective conscious of all the negative images of Asians in this country," is still alive and well (p. 14). This designation of an Asian male stereotype to represent all Asian images unjustly glosses over the degradation of Asian female images. Tragically, in film and television, Asian women have been appropriated as "mirrors" of Anglo American male supremacy (Halualani, 1995). The tendency to protest some stereotypes over others is just as oppressive as the negative images themselves. A glaring example lies in Hamamoto's (1994) misguided attack on Asian woman as enjoying "favorable exposure" in the media in their frequent pairings with Anglo males.

5. Seventeen episodes of *All-American Girl* were aired during 1994–1995. Of these, we managed to acquire 14 for textual analysis, thanks to the gracious assistance of Guy Aoki, co-founder and president of the Media Action Network for Asian Americans (MANAA).

6. Fiske (1990) describes cultural studies analysis of a text as involving three levels: primary (i.e., reading of the text on screen), secondary (i.e., reading fan gossip, publicity, journalistic comments, feature articles), and tertiary (i.e., reading audience talk about the show). Fiske's terminology hierarchically privileges the meanings drawn from the primary text and oversimplifies the complex task of analyzing the ways cultural readers (and critics) move among these different but interrelated levels to activate meanings. In addition, texts from grassroot-based ethnic communities (outside the production context) are not considered in Fiske's discussion; however, such texts are also integral to the creation of meaning for some viewers.

7. The concept of *symbolic annihilation* was used by sociologist Gaye Tuchman (1978) to describe the way in which women are marginalized and kept in their proper place—by their absence—neither seen nor heard. This strategy also describes the way in which television has symbolically annihilated minorities and reaffirmed the normal, natural dominance of Anglo American society—by simply excluding images of minorities from the television screen.

References

Allen, R. C. (1992). Audience-oriented criticism and television. In R. C. Allen (Ed.), *Channels of discourse, reassembled* (pp. 101–137). Chapel Hill: University of North Carolina Press.

Bell, E., Hass, L., & Sells, L. (Eds.). (1995). *From mouse to mermaid: The politics of film, gender and culture.* Bloomington: Indiana University Press.

Bhabha, H. (1983). The other question: The stereotype and colonial discourse. *Screen, 24*(6), 18–36.

Bordieu, P. (1990). *In other words: Essays toward a reflexive sociology.* Cambridge, MA: Polity Press.

Burton, J. (1992). Don (Juanito) Duck and the imperial-patriarchal unconscious: Disney studios, the good neighbor policy, and the packaging of Latin America. In A. Parker, M. Russo, D. Sommer, & P. Yaeger, (Eds.), *Nationalism and sexualities* (pp. 21–41). New York: Routledge.

Cacas, S. (1994, September 23). How all-American is *All-American Girl? Asianweek, 12*, 23.

Cacas, S. (1995, November 10). Charlie Chan is alive and well. *Asianweek, 17*(12), 14–15

Chen, V. (1994). (De)hyphenated identity: The double voice in *The Woman Warrior.* In A. Gonzalez, M. Houston, & V. Chen (Eds.), *Our voices: Essays in culture, ethnicity, and communication* (pp. 3–11). Los Angeles: Roxbury.

Chin, C. (1994, Sept. 11). Asian American goes prime time. *San Francisco Examiner,* B2.

Chow, R. (1990). Politics and pedagogy of Asian literatures in American universities. *differences, 2*(3), 29–51.

Choy, C. (1978). Images of Asian-Americans in films and television. In R. M. Miller (Ed.), *Ethnic images in American film and television* (pp. 145–155). Philadelphia: The Balch Institute.

Clark, J. (1996, February 25). Disney Institute breaks new ground: Learning and fun combine at Florida "vacation campus." *Sacramento Bee,* travel sec., pp. 1, 5.

Condit, C. M. (1989). The rhetorical limits of polysemy. *Critical Studies in Mass Communication, 6*, 103–122.

Corliss, R. (1992, October 4). Betrayal in Beijing. *Time,* 14.

During, S. (1993). Introduction. In S. During (Ed.), *The cultural studies reader* (pp. 1–25). London: Routledge.

Eliot, M. (1993). *Walt Disney, Hollywood's dark prince: A biography.* Secaucus, NJ: Carol/Birch Lane Press.

Farquhar, J., & Doi, M. L. (1978, Fall). Bruce Lee vs. Fu Manchu: Kung fu films and Asian American stereotypes in America. *Bridge: An Asian American Perspective, 23–32.*

Fiske, J. (1990). *Television culture.* London: Routledge.

Fiske, J. (1992). British cultural studies and television. In R. C. Allen (Ed.), *Channels of discourse, reassembled* (pp. 101–137). Chapel Hill: University of North Carolina Press.

Fung, R. (1994). Seeing yellow: Asian identities in film and video. In K. Aguilar-San Juan (Ed.), *The state of Asian American: Activism and resistance in the 1990's* (pp. 161–172). Boston, MA: South End Press.

Gray, H. (1995). Television, black Americans, and the American dream. In G. Dines & J. M. Hunez (Eds.), *Gender, race and class in media: A textreader* (pp. 430–437). Thousand Oaks, CA: Sage.

Hagedorn, J. (1994, January/February). Asian women in film: No joy, no luck. *Ms.,* 10–12.

Hall, S. (1980/1993). Encoding/decoding. In S. During (Ed.), *The cultural studies reader* (pp. 90–103). London: Routledge, 1993. [Originally published in S. Hall et al. (Eds.), *Culture, media, language* (pp. 128–138). London: Hutchinson.]

Hall, S. (1981/1990). The whites of their eyes: Racist ideologies and the media. In M. Alvarado & J. O. Thompson (Eds.), *The media reader* (pp. 7–23). London: British Film Institute. [Originally published in G. Bridges & R. Brunt (Eds.), *Silver linings* (pp. 28–52). London: Lawrence and Wishart.]

Halualani, R. T. (1995a). *Hollywood film's construction of "Asian femininity."* Unpublished master's thesis, California State University, Sacramento, Sacramento, CA.

Halualani, R. T. (1995b). The intersecting hegemonic discourses of an Asian mail-order bride catalog: Pilipina "Oriental Butterfly" dolls for sale. *Women's Studies in Communication, 18,* 45–64.

Hamamoto, D. Y. (1989). *Nervous laughter: Television situation comedy and liberal democratic ideology.* New York: Praeger.

Hamamoto, D. Y. (1992). Kindred spirits: The contemporary Asian American family on television. *Amerasia Journal, 18*(2), 35–53.

Hamamoto, D. Y. (1994). *Monitored peril: Asian Americans and the politics of TV representation.* Minneapolis: University of Minnesota Press.

Holliss, R., & Sibley, B. (1988). *The Disney studio story.* New York: Crown.

Jacobs, G. (1995, March 20). In defense of the *All-American Girl. Los Angeles Times,* F3.

Jewett, R., & Lawrence, J. S. (1977). *The American monomyth.* Garden City, NY: Anchor Press/Doubleday.

Kellner, D. (1995). Cultural studies, multiculturalism and media culture. In G. Dines & J. M. Humez (Eds.), *Gender, race and class in media* (pp. 5–17). Thousand Oaks, CA: Sage.

Kim, E. H. (1986). Asian Americans and American popular culture. In H. C. Kim (Ed.), *Dictionary of Asian American history* (pp. 99–113). Westport, CT: Greenwood Press.]

Lai, T. (1988). Asian American women: Not for sale. In J. Cochran, D. Langston, & C. Woodward (Eds.), *Changing our power: An introduction to women's studies* (pp. 163–171). Dubuque, IA: Kendall-Hunt.

Lowe, L. (1991). Heterogeneity, hybridity, multiplicity: Marking Asian American differences. *Diaspora, 1*(1), 24–44.

Mendez, C. (1994, August 26). Margaret Cho ushers in a new era for "All-American" television sitcoms. *Asianweek, 16*(1), 28.

Morrison, T. (1992). *Play in the dark: Whiteness and literary imagination.* Cambridge, MA: Harvard University Press.

Nakayama, T. K. (1988). "Model Minority" and the media: Discourse on Asian America. *Journal of Communication Inquiry, 12*(1), 65–73.

Osajima, K. (1995). Postmodern possibilities: Theoretical and political directions for Asian American studies. *Amerasia Journal, 21*(1 & 2), 79–87.

Paik, I. (1971). That oriental feeling: A look at the caricatures of the Asians as sketched by

American movies. In A. Tachiki, E. Won, F. Odo, & B. Wong (Eds.), *Roots: An Asian American reader* (pp. 30–36). Los Angeles: University of California Press.

Price, D. L. (1994). *All-American Girl* and the American dream. *Critical Mass, 2*(1), 129–146.

Radhakrishnan, R. (1994). Is the ethnic "authentic" in the diaspora? In K. Aguilar-San Juan (Ed.), *The state of Asian America: Activism and resistance in the 1990s* (pp. 219–233). Boston: South End Press.

Said, E. W. (1978). *Orientalism.* New York: Vintage Books.

Salvador-Burris, J. (1978, Spring). Changing Asian American stereotypes. *Bridge: An Asian American Perspective,* 29–40.

Shields, M. (1995, May 14). Margaret Cho returns to her roots in stand-up. *Sacramento Bee,* Encore sec., pp. 23–24.

Simon, J. (1993, November 15). Chinoiserie. *National Review,* 61–62.

Stevenson, N. (1995). *Understanding media cultures: Social theory and mass communication.* London: Sage.

Tajima, R. E. (1989). Lotus blossoms don't bleed: Images of Asian women. In Asian Women United of California (Eds.), *Making waves: An anthology of writings by and about Asian American women* (pp. 308–317). Boston: Beacon Press.

Tuchman, G. (1978). The symbolic annihilation of women. In G. Tuchman, A. K. Daniels, & J. Benet (Eds.), *Hearth and home: Images of women in the mass media* (pp. 3–38). New York: Oxford University Press.

Wong, B. (1994, September 23). Column. *Asianweek, 12,* 9.

Cultural Criticism:
General Approaches

CHAPTER 14

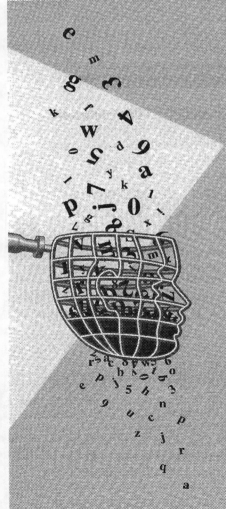

Chapter Outline

A Brief History of Cultural Criticism

A Cultural Studies Approach to Television Criticism

Television, Popular Culture, and Viewers' Resistance to Power

Some General Concepts in Cultural Studies Criticism
    Textualization
    Performance and Embodiment
    Ideology
    Hegemony
    Race, Class, and Gender
    Discourse

Sociocultural Criticism
    Social Role Analysis
    Image/Depiction Analysis
    Social Values Analysis

Some Central Concepts in Sociocultural Criticism
    Roles
    Stereotypes
    Values
    Sex and Gender
    Race and Ethnicity
    Social Class

Writing Cultural Criticism

Cultural Studies Example Essay: Heather C. Hundley's "The Naturalization of Beer in *Cheers*"

Sociocultural Example Essay: Cathy Sandeen's "Success Defined by Television: The Value System Promoted by *PM Magazine*"

Acultural anthropologist such as Clifford Geertz (1973) defines *culture* as "the systematic way of construing reality that a people acquires as a consequence of living in a group." From this perspective, culture is "the social production of sense, meaning, and consciousness" (O'Sullivan, et al., 1994, p. 68). References to a people's construction or construal of reality or to the social—that is, public and shared—production of meaning, however, are not very specific. Such definitions suggest we ought to be studying the ways human beings organize themselves and make sense out of their environments, but they do not really tell us how to study collectivities. Different approaches to Western culture, cultural theory, and cultural analysis in the twentieth century provided vocabularies for that work. Some were macro-approaches, that is, attempts to define culture in general, while others were micro-approaches, that is, approaches to more particular cultural products (e.g., myths), cultural divisions (e.g., the male-female divide), or cultural layers (e.g., relationships between the public and private or psychoanalytical layers of life).

We are devoting two chapters to cultural criticism because we first want to set up (in this chapter) two of the macro-approaches to cultural theory and criticism—what are called British Cultural Studies and sociocultural theory—and then devote a second chapter to more self-consciously micro-approaches: mythic, feminist, and psychoanalytical theory and criticism. We begin with a short overview of the historical development of cultural criticism in the United States, England, and the European continent. Then we talk about the two general approaches most critics doing cultural analysis of television use: sociocultural criticism and cultural studies analyses.

A Brief History of Cultural Criticism

> Culture [is] a pursuit of our total perfection by means of getting to know, on all the matters which most concern us, the best which has been thought and said in the world; and through this knowledge, turning a stream of fresh and free thought upon our stock notions and habits, which we now follow staunchly but mechanically. [T]he culture we recommend is, above all, an inward operation.
> —ARNOLD (1869/1916, p. x)

This statement by British poet and essayist Matthew Arnold expresses what is probably the English-speaking world's first fully developed theory of culture. As this quotation demonstrates, that theory was strongly normative: it asserted that there was *one* correct set of habits, behaviors, and attitudes that "properly cultured" British should evince, and that what made people cultured was an inward operation—a kind of subjectivity. Furthermore, Arnold used the United States as an example of the deplorable kind of society that results when citizens of a country lack proper instruction in what it means to be a cultured person, noting that the absence of cultural training results in superficiality, vulgar manners, and intellectual mediocrity (1869/1916, p. xxii).

At about the same time as Arnold made his pronouncements, an alternative view of culture based not on the aesthetic and religious views of educated males from the upper classes but on democratic views of society and politics emerged in the rhetorical discourse of the famous British political radical John Bright, and in the theoretical writing of Yale University sociologist William Graham Sumner. In 1906, Sumner published *Folkways: A Study of the Sociological Importance of Usages, Manners, Customs, Mores, and Morals*, in which he argued that the proper study of the cultural character of a country emerges from an examination of the everyday or ordinary beliefs and actions of people:

> Folkways are habits of the individual and customs of the society which arise from efforts to satisfy needs; they are intertwined with goblinism and demonism and primitive notions of luck. . . , and so they win traditional authority. Then they become regulative for succeeding generations and take on the character of a social force. They can be modified, but only to a limited extent, by the purposeful efforts of men. In time they lose power, decline, and die, or are transformed. While they are in vigor they very largely control individual and social undertakings, and they produce and nourish ideas of world philosophy and life policy. (Sumner, 1906/1911, p. iv)

Sumner's more descriptive and observationally based understanding of culture is closer to our current ordinary understanding of culture, understandings that have been developed by cultural anthropologists such as Geertz. From such perspectives, culture is what holds a society together: those beliefs, habits, values, and customary ways of acting collectively that distinguish Americans from the British and both from the people of East Timor. Culture is how people make and use everyday and sacred symbols to understand themselves and the world around them.

Thus, coming into the intellectual world of the twentieth century there were two conceptions of culture, the one normative and reformative and the other descriptive and preservational. Cultural criticism as an academic practice today unites aspects of both of these traditions. It generally focuses on the everyday, on meaning-making processes that are practiced by portions or all of society, and yet it has a normative or reformative edge as well, though today this normative edge has less to do with aesthetics than with politics. Cultural criticism also is audience centered because it concerns how human understandings of identity, relationships, and the universe come to be and to make demands on members of a society.

In Chapter 2, we discussed the mass society popular culture debate, a recurring historical debate between "high-brow" and "low-brow" art. This debate, we noted, dominated criticism of the new medium of television in the 1950s and 1960s (see, e.g., Rosenberg & White, 1957). However, over the past 50 years, these aesthetic concerns have largely been replaced with concerns about cultural and political oppression, and a people's role in its own subjugation to authority and societal institutions (issues discussed in detail in Chapter 11).[1] Within the British intellectual, aesthetic cultural tradition, Matthew Arnold's vision was last seen in the 1970s' television series *Civilisation*, when Kenneth Clark took audiences through the magnificent, progressive evolution of British politics, society, architecture, and art.

Since then British studies of culture—sometimes referred to in capital letters as

British Cultural Studies to identify its populist politics—have followed the discursive turn of most of the humanities and focused on the production and circulation of meanings in society (Hall, 1997). Today, most British scholars studying culture use tools from psychoanalysis, neo-Marxist views about society and politics, together with feminism and semiotic/structuralism, to analyze cultural rules, roles, and ideas manifested in texts. (Recall that we reviewed institutional studies done in the British tradition in Part III of this book.) Television is one of these cultural institutions, and its texts are among those cultural forms studied by Raymond Williams (see, especially, 1974) and his followers, as well as those of his two principal students: Stuart Hall, primarily from his days at the University of Birmingham's Centre for Contemporary Studies, and John Fiske, primarily from his teaching at Australian and American universities.[2] Following the work of Williams and his students (Hall, 1980, 1982; Hall, Critcher, Jefferson, Clark, & Roberts, 1978; Fiske, 1987, 1994c; Fiske & Hartley, 1978), cultural studies criticism in the United States, Britain, Australia, and many other countries today engages society's cultural institutions but primarily through studies of their discourses. (For a somewhat different history of British and Australian approaches to television criticism, see Fiske, 1986b.)

The French developed their own strand of cultural analysis, which has been dominated by anthropologist Claude Lévi-Strauss (1958) and social thinker Roland Barthes (1968, 1973, 1977). Lévi-Strauss was the structural anthropologist who understood the cultural world as one we use to structure—organize, interpret—everyday life, whereas Barthes was the critic who taught that all kinds of symbol systems (road signs, clothing, eating practices, sporting events) embody significant aspects of popular culture. Their work has been supplemented by three later sorts of French cultural studies: the anticultural (postmodern) critiques of the masses, sign systems, and politics (Debord, 1970; see also Baudrillard, 1983, 1988); the intensive, introspective scrutiny and detailed subjective interpretation of highly particularized pieces of social behavior (deCerteau, 1984); and, in an opposite move, the sweeping visions of societal shifts in practices of discoursing, knowledge making, and power over time (Foucault, 1972, 1977, 1980). French cultural studies generally focus less on institutional presence and power than do those of British scholars; French scholars are generally more interested in perceptual-interpretive-persuasive patterns of meaning making and meaning circulation in public discourse (see During, 1999, esp. p. 9).

American cultural studies, particularly the cultural study of mass communication practices, often is dated from Park's (1938) "Reflections on Communication and Culture," although the master text of the Americanist view is Edward Hall's (1959) *The Silent Language*. Here, we are shown that culture—social behavior—can be analyzed, like a text, by breaking the behavior down into units that are much like words and organized into sets that are much like sentences. In Hall's view, "Communication is culture and culture is communication," because one can communicate with others only when one knows their culture, and yet cultures are revealed or exhibited only in communicative behaviors. Human communication, in this view, is both the ground for relationships and the process by which those relationships are maintained (see Gronbeck, 1999).

Edward Hall's views became the bases of social-scientific studies of cultures and subcultures (e.g., Smith, 1966) and of critical studies of popular novels and movies and of everyday social practice. For example, his ideas undergird many of the writings in the late 1960s volumes of the *Journal of Popular Culture* and the anthologies of media studies edited by Lewis (1972), Voelker and Voelker (1972), and others. The American tradition of cultural studies, therefore, was more descriptive and celebratory of democratic politics than its continental relatives, perhaps because of its sociological and anthropological, scientist outlook in all aspects of academic practice and probably because American scholars were less concerned with critiquing and reforming social process and institutions than their transatlantic counterparts. The Americanist cultural studies tradition largely informs what in this chapter we define as sociocultural studies.

By the late 1970s and early 1980s, both the British and the French approaches to cultural studies invaded the continental United States. American cultural studies became interested in semiotics, institutional critique, and power relationships between people based on race, class, and gender, even getting caught up in the concern for political correctness and multiculturalism as agendas for social reform (see Aronowitz, 1993, for a telling of the story of the invasion). America once again became a kind of melting pot, blending bits and pieces of European thought but adapting them to the particular personal-social-political climate of the new world. And so, in this chapter what we'll identify as "cultural studies" or "cultural television criticism" has its roots in European thought (for another view of American studies, see Hartley, Pearson, & Vieth, 2000).

A Cultural Studies Approach to Television Criticism

For our purposes, we can think of cultural television criticism as grounded in four assumptions:

1. *A culture is a social group's system of meanings.* Following Sumner, earlier anthropologists and social commentators thought of culture as particular behaviors and thought patterns possessed by a people, often broken down into the categories of habits, beliefs, and artifacts (e.g., Chase, 1956, p. 64). Such a view is too confining, for it separates some behavior as cultural from some that is not. Today, culture is seen as the ways in which anything and everything shared by people in some temporal or spatial grouping is thought to be meaningful. *Meanings* and *meaningfulness* are socially derived understandings and accounts of things people take shared perspectives on: persons, places, things, ideas, routines, rituals, and strategic behavior (social action). Individuals generally are taught from infancy on to conform their understandings and their behaviors to social standards for meaning when communicating with others. Although ideological criticism, as we discussed it in Chapter 11, tends to focus on ways that external institutions or practices shape discourse, cultural criticism generally focuses more directly on the discourses themselves and how it is that they give meaning to lived experience.

2. *To study culture is to study meaning systems both descriptively and normatively.* Descriptively, students of culture outline the meaning systems of societies or social groups, seeking to comprehend better the "webs of signification" that Geertz (1973, p. 6) says comprise our social relationships. Inventorying the meanings attached to objects and actions or, for our purposes, arrayed in a television show is the beginning of cultural studies. Additionally, the culturalist often goes a step further, exploring the ways in which meaning systems, whether understood institutionally or textually, control the perceptions, thoughts, or actions of people. So, descriptively, you might inventory the celebrities Larry King interviews on his show for a year, but then, normatively, you could talk with viewers to see how their understandings of the world seem to have been affected by the kind and range of guests he has featured. You might ask, Whose voices are heard often, and whose voices are never heard? In this view, the meanings of television lie not in what is shown but in how that showing is understood by viewers. That second activity would allow you to argue that King's impact on the country is positive or negative, depending on what sorts of voices you believe ought to be guiding American social and political thought.

3. *Members of a society usually are complicitous in their own subjugation to meaning systems.* If you ask people why they pay taxes, they're likely to say, "Well, because I have to" or "Because that's the way the system works" or "That's just the way things go in this country." In recognizing social obligation ("I have to") or a general acceptance of social demands ("the way the system works"), people signal that they've internalized the demands of society. "That's the way things are done around here" is a signal that someone has adopted what is called "the natural attitude": social convention has been made to seem natural (see the final essay in Barthes, 1973, for a discussion of *naturalization*). Individuals' tolerance of institutional control over their lives—schools, banks, churches, places where one buys and sells goods—is amazing. That tolerance allows society to function—to keep us from killing each other or eating our young, and working together for mutual protection and growth. Thus, although it is easy to document personal, social, economic, and political injustices all over the country, most of us shrug our shoulders and get on with our lives; only a few individuals (we call them revolutionaries, anarchists, or radicals) get disturbed enough to want to overhaul the system. Cultural stability cannot be maintained by force; most people have to go along with social practices for these practices to continue. And in our time, one of the mechanisms for encouraging people to go along, to get along, is television.

4. *The goal of most culture-centered criticism is critique.* Going along, getting along can lead to individual demoralization, social stagnation, economic inequality, and political injustice. The goal of most culture-centered critics, therefore, is change—change associated with such socially charged concepts as liberation, empowerment, and freedom. Almost all aspects of such change are tinged with politics. In an era when "the personal is political" (individual control of self-identity) and "the social is political" (the fights for the self-determination of people of varying racial, class, and gender backgrounds), it is little wonder that the final paragraphs of cultural studies almost inevitably deal with power.[3]

Television, Popular Culture, and Viewers' Resistance to Power

Cultural studies is an interdisciplinary, transdisciplinary, and sometimes counter-disciplinary field that operates in the tension between its tendencies to embrace a broad anthropological and a more narrowly humanistic conception of culture. Unlike traditional anthropology, cultural studies has grown out of analyses of modern industrial societies. It is typically interpretive and evaluative in its methodologies, but unlike traditional humanism, it rejects the exclusive equation of culture with high culture. Instead, cultural studies argues that all forms of cultural production need to be studied in relation to other cultural practices and to social and historical structures. Cultural studies therefore is committed to the study of the entire range of a society's arts, beliefs, institutions, and communicative practices (Grossberg, Nelson, & Treichler, 1992, p. 4).

Contemporary television cultural studies combines neo-Marxist concerns about economic power, political power, and social class with concerns about race, gender roles, and equity. Grounded in Marxism and semiotics, cultural studies scholars believe that intellectual labor—critical practice—matters and can make a difference in people's material lives (see Cloud, 1994; Grossberg et al., 1992, p. 6). Thus, the goal of television cultural studies criticism is to examine the relationships between social relationships and meanings in order to "understand how culture (the social production of sense and consciousness)" makes social divisions meaningful; represents and naturalizes class, gender, race, and other inequalities; and how various subordinate groups ("the subaltern") live with and resist such cultural "common senses" (O'Sullivan et. al, 1994, p. 71). As O'Sullivan et al. (1994) explain, "The production of knowledge is always done either in the interests of those who hold power or those who contest that hold" (p. 73).

Cultural studies, then, is centrally concerned with hegemony; this makes it an audience-centered kind of study. However, in contrast to ideological criticism, cultural studies criticism often focuses on the ways in which groups and individuals read culture and cultural texts "against the grain," creating what Stuart Hall (1980) calls negotiated or oppositional readings. Cultural studies has been little concerned with the grand theorizing of Marxist and neo-Marxist political economic studies and, especially in its American and Australian versions, has been influenced by the anthropological and rhetorical interest in agency. As a result, contemporary cultural studies arguably has been focused on studying the empowering meanings and pleasures individuals and social groups create from popular culture (including television) texts. Put another way, unlike ideological criticism, cultural studies criticism has been as interested in resistance as in domination.

This has led a number of scholars to critique what they see as cultural studies' "fetishism of audience pleasure" and its "fetishism of struggle" (see Kellner, 1995, pp. 38–43; Stevenson, 1995). These critics argue that the "tendency in cultural studies to celebrate resistance per se without distinguishing between types and forms of resistance" results in a displacement of political struggle into a "struggle for meanings and pleasure"; as a result, "modes of domination are occluded, and resistance and struggle are depoliticized and rendered harmless, thus providing an ideology of 'popular culture' perfectly congruent with the interests of the powers that be" (Kellner, 1995, pp. 38–39). Defenders of cultural studies counter that cultural studies is not blind to the possibility that focus on pleasure by viewers or scholars can serve to deflect attention away from or even reinforce conservative, racist, sexist cultural perspectives. Neither does it regard ordinary audience members as cultural dupes who are incapable of anything other than uncritical acceptance of the meanings and pleasures served up by television and other cultural forms (see Fiske, 1986a, 1987, 1994a, 1994b). As Fiske (1994a) explains:

> In both ideology and psychoanalytic theories, texts became agents of domination. Cultural studies attempts to be multilevel in its methodology and in particular to explore the interface between the structuring conditions that determine our social experience and the ways of living that people devise within them. . . . Although cultural studies differs from other critical theories, it shares with them the most important characteristic of all—the critical. The basic assumption of all critical theories is that the inequalities of capitalism need to be changed and that the world would be a better place if we could change them. (pp. 197–198)

Two recent approaches to television cultural studies criticism that John Fiske has used, audiencing (1994a) and ethnosemiotics (1994b), acknowledge these concerns. *Audiencing* combines ethnographic analysis of audiences' meaning-making interactions with a critic's own political-economic analysis. Audiencing is not, Fiske (1994b) explains, a full-blown social scientific, anthropological ethnography because it does not attempt to acquire a full understanding of audience members' general interactions with television. Rather, audiencing provides "glimpses of culture in practice" by analyzing audience members' specific viewing experiences (e.g., of a particular television series). Audiencing criticism approaches television texts as "neither commodities nor agents of the dominant classes, but as sites of struggle where the subordinate can engage in contested relations with the social interests that attempt to subordinate them" (p. 197). *Ethnosemiotics* is Fiske's term (1994b) for a cultural studies critique that combines semiotic/structural analysis of a television or film text with a political/ideological analysis of the social context within which that text is produced and viewed. Ethnosemiotic critiques use structural/semiotic analysis to examine the discourses through which texts and audiences make sense of social topics "called up" by programs and the relationship between these discourses and the larger symbolic environment to which both texts and audience members belong. Fiske explains that the critic using this approach does a semiotic reading of texts and auto- and audience- ethnographic data "because the popular text is where the potential meanings, pleasures and politics of the industrial text are actualized, and it is only in their actualizations that we can identify them" (pp. 419, 423). In other words, the "macro-politics of the social structure are made concrete in the practices of everyday life," including our everyday interactions with popular media texts (p. 423).

Some General Concepts in Cultural Studies Criticism

So far, we have talked about cultural studies without getting too far into the actual vocabulary used by culturalists. As you read and practice culture-centered criticism, you'll need to understand the concepts discussed next.[4]

Textualization

Cultural studies arose in part out of a particular branch of literary studies (Raymond Williams taught literature at Cambridge). Not surprisingly, then, the concept of a text is central to cultural studies criticism. Thanks to literary theorists with strong social concerns, we have come to understand that television texts are sequences of verbal, visual, acoustic, or behavioral signs that can be understood or interpreted in multiple ways (see Chapter 5). Cultural studies takes the notion of text further and assumes that many kinds of human activities or even natural events can be turned into texts.

Performance and Embodiment

Textualization is related to two other concepts that are important to cultural analysis: performance and embodiment. *Performance* is the enactment of social roles, roles, and identities. Cultural lessons about rules and roles can often be framed in words: in aphorisms ("Birds of a feather flock together"), orders ("Buckle up!"), and warnings ("All backpacks subject to search as you leave this store"). However, in a culture where "seeing is believing," seeing cultural performances of roles, rules, and social identities is a vital form of social learning. On television we see such cultural performances every night.

Embodiment is a process whereby ideas, attitudes, values, and social character are given corporeal existence in texts (and the characters in texts). In television news, in international ceremonies, and on *The West Wing*, we see the presidency and learn about the powers and responsibilities of this social role. On *Friends* and *Girlfriends*, we see embodiments of friendship and how positive and empowering a social support network of friends can be.

Ideology

Televisual texts, along with so many other texts in your experience, naturalize (Barthes, 1973) the power of social, economic, educational, religious, and political institutions. You accept those institutions as legitimate influences, as institutions with the right, even obligation, to control significant aspects of your life. That power is expressed in ideologies; systems of thought that embody social values and perceptual orientations to life, role relationships, and the authority to enforce them; and the very rules of thinking themselves. Cultural studies criticism is centrally concerned with ideology. (For an extended discussion of ideology, see Chapter 11.)

Hegemony

As we noted in Chapter 11, cultural studies and ideological criticism uses Italian Marxist Antonio Gramsci's (1971) term *hegemony* to explain the everyday mechanisms whereby an elite or dominant class or group exercises control over a lower or subordinate class or group. As Gramsci noted, the force of hegemony is not so much coercive as social; thus, an essential aspect of a hegemonic relationship between peoples or classes is *complicity:* the acceptance of power relationships as normal, as the way things are done in a society. Hegemony is less concerned with how social change is produced than in how the existing social order is maintained through voluntary compliance, through acceptance of one's place as normal or natural. Television critics with avowedly cultural interests often explore the ways in which social, economic, and political—which is to say, power—relationships are reinforced again and again in television programs.

Race, Class, and Gender

Recognizing that the social is political, the United States has lived through a series of revolutionizing movements that have critiqued the systematic domination of racial groups (civil rights), one gender group (women's rights), and America's underclasses (the right to social services regardless of ability to pay). Over the past forty years especially, the United States has tried to make sense of the idea that racial, gendered, and class-based marks of one's social identities in fact are political matters. Because hierarchical power is always best witnessed materially, in the historical or temporal-spatial specificity of concrete actions in particular moments, television is a great weapon in the struggle to redefine racial, gender, and class relationships. One can study Madonna's MTV videos to see an assault on traditional gender roles or *Seventh Heaven* and *Everybody Loves Raymond* to see them reaffirmed. The very lack of racial commentary on *Friends* is as significant as its presence is on *NYPD Blue*. Police dramas almost always show police officers chasing lower-class rather than middle- or upper-class perpetrators, while the white, male, seemingly upper-class narrator still is the preferred presenter of television's advertising fare. Questions of monoculturalism and multiculturalism, homogenization and diversity, political correctness and hate speech—all of these matters are raised in cultural studies of race, class, and gender by television critics.

Discourse

Discursive acts, as we noted in Chapters 5 and 11, are tools of power relations; they are "ideological ways of thinking about and representing an important topic area in social experiences" (Fiske, 1991, p. 447). Recognizing that much social sense making is accomplished through ideological conflicts between discourses—for example, between the legitimated, naturalized discourse of patriarchy and the marginalized, subordinated discourse of feminism—cultural studies critics have used the construct of discourse to analyze how "particular texts take up elements of different discourses and articulate them (that is, 'knit them together')" (O'Sullivan et al., 1994, pp. 93–94). Television critics use discourse analysis to examine the ways in which television texts circulate, affirm, counter, and suppress various social discourses and the structured social relationships (discursive subjectivities) these discourses reproduce.

Sociocultural Criticism

Let us now offer a somewhat more abbreviated overview of a variant of cultural criticism that is native to the United States. *Sociocultural criticism* is a special subclass of cultural criticism that focuses on the ways in which television programs and television viewing reflect the structured patterns and organizations of social life. It is concerned with the social roles, social rules, social relationships, and social processes displayed in television texts; it offers interpretations of the lessons viewers may learn from their encounters with television texts and the ways in which television viewing may function for individuals, groups, or societies as a whole.

One of the fundamental assumptions underlying all variants of sociocultural analysis is that television is an important social and cultural force because its stories offer lessons about rules and roles that portray idealistic and realistic visions of society, social organizations, social norms, and social experiences. This assumption is based on Albert Bandura's (1986, 1994) social cognitive theory, which argues that human beings learn social roles, rules, norms, and values both directly (through personal experience) and indirectly (through observing others) in real life and in the media. Applied to television, then, social cognitive (social learning) theory leads critics to assume that viewers can learn social roles and rules—can be socialized—through watching the actions (and the results of the actions) of people in newscasts and characters in entertainment programs. Thus, sociocultural critics look at the same kinds of social phenomena that (especially American) sociologists and cultural anthropologists do: the roles that social actors play in various settings, the norms and values represented by sequences of characters' actions, and the social rules and advice being communicated through the negative and positive outcomes in these portrayals.

All sociocultural criticism assumes that television is a social institution and set of practices that both reflects and shapes the ideological context within which viewers make sense of their world. That is, sociocultural analyses of television texts regard television as the context within which viewers see affirmed and disconfirmed particular views of social, occupational, and sexual roles; social class; deviance and conformity; and race and ethnicity. It thus uses existing sociological, anthropological, and cultural concepts to examine television texts in order to understand television program portrayals of the social, mythic, and ideological worlds and then to make inferences about the potential implications of these representations for individuals and groups in societies.

There are many types of sociocultural analysis. Three types of analyses useful to television critics are social role analysis, image/depiction analysis, and social values analysis.

Social Role Analysis

This type of sociocultural television criticism uses the sociological construct of roles (e.g., occupational roles, social roles, sex and gender roles, family roles) to analyze television texts. A *social role* is a stable pattern of expected conduct, a cluster of learned behaviors, connected to a particular position in a social structure or organization. The notion of social roles is based on a dramatistic view of social life: we enact various social roles. Social role analysis uses the metaphor of theatrical roles to examine the depictions of the various roles individuals can play (in real life and on television): student, worker, boss/supervisor, friend, daughter, son, father, mother, sibling, companion, neighbor, colleague, teammate, police officer, physician, and others.[5] Sociocultural critics use social roles analysis to examine (1) the types of roles presented in television texts; (2) the particular attributes, attitudes, behaviors, and values characters in these roles display; (3) the nature of the role portrayals—that is, which roles are presented as psychologically, emotionally, socially, or economically rewarding and which roles are not; and (4) what social rules and lessons are directly or indirectly enacted, and hence potentially learned, through these dramatic portrayals.

Image/Depiction Analysis

Another type of sociocultural television criticism involves the analysis of the recurring types of images and social types of characters in television texts. This type views characters in television texts not just as representations of particular individual people, but as social types of characters (Burke, 1969, pp. 215–217). Image or depiction analysis views television texts as realistic because they reproduce a socially convincing sense of the real through a dramatic style (verisimilitude) that faithfully reproduces the physical, sensorially perceived details of the external world. And in so doing, television texts encourage viewers to accept the values affirmed through realistic images and depictions. Critics using this type of sociocultural analysis critical perspective analyze television's portrayals of aspects of our social world (e.g., occupations, lifestyles, family roles, races and ethnicities, social class) in order to see what these images affirm as valued, desirable, and esteemed (as well as devalued, undesirable, and despised). As John Fiske and John Hartley explain (1978, p. 24):

> The world of television is clearly different from our real social world, but just as clearly related to it. . . . We might clarify this relationship by saying that television does not represent the manifest actuality of our society, but rather reflects, symbolically, the structure of values and relationships beneath the surface. So the high proportion of middle-class occupations is not a distortion of social fact, but an accurate symbolic representation of the esteem with which a society like ours regards such positions and the people who hold them.

For example, a sociocultural image/depiction analysis might look at how adulthood on television is presented; the critic might analyze several series about "adults" to see what views of "grownups" or "adults" are being positively affirmed and which are being (humorously or seriously) critiqued and, thus, rejected. Rosenblatt (1979) did just such a critical analysis of adulthood on prime-time TV twenty-five years ago. Given the recent spate of "adult" programs (see the cover story of the October 23–30, 1999 *TV Guide*) on television, it may be time to see whether, how, and in what ways (if at all) television images of adults in "family" shows have changed 25 years later.

Critics undertaking this type of sociocultural analysis might look at how the elderly and aging, African Americans, gays and lesbians, Latinos, women, the poor, and religion are depicted in particular prime-time television texts in order to gain some insights into television's potential socializing function—its messages about these social groups. Bonnie Dow's *Prime Time Feminism* (1996) is just such a book about women.

Social Values Analysis

A third type of sociocultural analysis is concerned with the values displayed in television programs. *Values* are attitudes people have about what is desirable and undesirable, good and bad. As we discussed in Chapter 2, many individuals and groups are concerned about television's role as a social and moral value educator. Critics do social values analysis to study the values affirmed (and rejected) in television texts; a good example is Cathy Sundeen's (1997) inventory of the values reinforced regularly on the TV program *PM Magazine*. Other social values studies work within alternative frameworks.

In her critical analysis comparing values in children's television cartoons of 1985 with theatrical film cartoons of 1945, Suzanne Williams (1991) develops a narrative approach for analyzing the depiction and enactment of values in any television narrative. She explains that critics who are trying to understand the values enacted and endorsed by a narrative need to analyze three aspects of the text: (1) what the characters say their values are, (2) what the characters' actions imply that their values are, and (3) what the narrative conclusion affirms as the dominant cultural values through its portrayal of the outcome (success or failure) of the actions of the characters whose words and behavior reflect their instrumental and terminal values.

Kevin Ryan (1976) also developed an approach for analyzing whether a television narrative may function as positive moral educator values in television texts. His approach, which, like Suzanne Williams's, is grounded in Bandura's (1986/1994) social learning/social cognitive theory, combines narrative analysis with psychologist Lawrence Kohlberg's (1968) theory of moral development to explore the possibility that television might function as a positive moral educator by showing individuals grappling with moral dilemmas and moving from lower (at the beginning of an episode) to higher (at the end of the episode) levels of moral thinking. Ryan (1976) explains this method of values analysis and illustrates its application with an analysis of the original *Kung Fu* television series.

Some Central Concepts in Sociocultural Criticism

Among the sociocultural constructs television critics use to analyze the ways in which television texts articulate ideology through the social structures they display and enact are roles, stereotypes, values, sex and gender, race and ethnicity, and social class.

Roles

Roles are "socially defined positions and patterns of behavior which are characterized by specific sets of rules, norms, and expectations which serve to orient and regulate the interaction, conduct, and practices of individuals in social situations" (O'Sullivan et al., 1994, p. 270). We all have many different roles, each connected to different contexts. For example, there are social roles (e.g., citizen, neighbor, friend), occupational roles (teacher, doctor, lawyer), and family roles (parent, spouse, sibling, child). We learn sets of expectations related to these roles and their proper performance. We are socialized (i.e., we learn about these roles) through various institutions: the family, the school, religious institutions, and the media. Sociocultural analysis explores television's depiction of roles and analyzes the meanings conveyed through them about power, status, and identity.

This is not to say that we learn how to behave solely by watching *The Real World, Boston Public, Friends,* or *Late Show with David Letterman.* But we do learn much about "types"—about what are called "social, cultural, and discursive *formations*" (Hayes, 1992, p. 361). Others around us (our social connections), the rules for living (cultural tenets), and discourses (e.g., social topics appearing in television texts) have considerable power in forming us into various kinds of subjects, that is, into a person or spectator with particular relationships to others. Those formations are usefully thought of as roles, and more particularly, as roles we play in relation (reciprocally) to others: a child to another's parental role, a male to someone's femaleness, a friend to another's role as friend.

Stereotypes

Stereotypes are implicitly or explicitly judgmental ways of categorizing particular individuals and groups based on oversimplified and overgeneralized features or signs. Stereotypes can be positive (e.g., Officer Friendly, the policewoman, or the kind, dedicated family physician) or negative (the crooked politician or the dumb jock), and they can be based on racial, occupational, sex, or gender characteristics. Their intensity and perniciousness may vary, but they "generally represent underlying power relations, tensions or conflicts . . . encourage an intuitive belief in their own underlying assumptions, and play a central role in organizing common sense discourse [ideology]" (O'Sullivan et al., 1994, pp. 299–301).

Values

In sociocultural studies, values are attitudes we have about what behaviors and goals are desirable and undesirable, good and bad, and about the means of obtaining them. According to Milton Rokeach (1980), values are "shared prescriptive or proscriptive beliefs about ideal modes of behavior and end states of existence that are activated by, yet transcend object and situation" (p. 262). Values, then, are social or cultural, not strictly personal. Rokeach (1973) distinguishes between terminal (or "ends") values, such as freedom, security, and salvation, and instrumental (or "means") values, such as honesty, courage, and ambition. Robin Williams (1970) has described a set of 15 major clusters of value orientations that, he argues, have long been salient in American society: achievement and success, activity and work, morality, humanitarianism, efficiency and practicality, progress, material comfort, equality, freedom, external conformity, science and secular rationality, nationalism, democracy, individual personality, and group superiority.

Sex and Gender

Sex is a bio/physiological term, based on primary and secondary biological and reproductive differences, that differentiate females from males. *Gender* is a cultural term that includes social concepts of the traits, roles, and behaviors deemed typical and desirable for females and males. Sociocultural analysis examines how discourses and other textual devices such as language, character, settings, narrative structure, camera work, laugh tracks, and musical soundtracks construct gender ideologies that reflect, maintain, or challenge dominant cultural notions of gender and sex roles (see Kervin, 1991; Trites, 1991).

Race and Ethnicity

Race is "a social category of people who are supposedly distinguished by inherited and invariable characteristics," while *ethnicity* "assumes the further addition of cultural characteristics for a group of people" (O'Sullivan et al., 1994, pp. 255–257). The concept of race also "carries a hidden ideological agenda" about the nature of racial stereotyping. (See discussions of racist ideologies and the media in Hall, 1990, and Fiske, 1994b.) Sociocultural analysis examines how discourses, narratives, and other textual devices overtly and/or covertly (inferentially) reflect racism, unthinking Eurocentrism (Shohat & Stam, 1994), and racial and ethnic equality.

Social Class

Social classes "are those distinct social formations made up of groups of people who have a similar relationship to the means of production in a society and, as a result, a common social and cultural position within an unequal system of property ownership, power and material rewards the term refers to the fundamental determinant of social stratification within modern industrial societies"

(O'Sullivan et al., 1994, pp. 39–42). As we noted in the discussion of classical and neo-Marxist ideology theory in Chapter 11, the major social division is between the class of owners and the class of workers or producers. According to Marxist theory, social classes can be distinguished by the ideologies or forms of consciousness they characteristically possess as a function of their position in the socioeconomic system. However, even Marx recognized other class divisions and that classes often are divided and at odds (e.g., conflicts between skilled and unskilled workers). The key is that different class positions "confer what Weber called different 'life chances' upon individuals" because they "govern access to a wide variety of scarce and valued products and services in society" (p. 41). Sociocultural analysis examines the strategies through which class conflicts and inequities inherent in the dominant ideology and social institutions are naturalized and legitimized.

Among scholars of television criticism, culture-centered studies are tremendously popular. The critique of domination and the critique of freedom are heady enterprises. For some critics, there is sheer pleasure to be had in blasting a politically and economically motivated network for its right-wing ideology. And for almost all culture-conscious analysts, the feeling that one is working on the side of angels in attempting to improve society through criticism is undeniable. Rooting out racism, sexism, classism, selfishness, ruthlessness, and megalomania seems today like a near-perfect justification for a career in television criticism; the joy one can feel in trying to ennoble the powerless in society justifies the long hours of analysis and composition. There is a happiness to be found, too, in the very act of writing cultural criticism: the prose of such critics can be fearsomely rhetorical. As Michael Parenti (1994, p. 173) was completing his cultural study of connections between American politics and economic institutions, he wrote the following passage:

> In 1907, the sociologist E. A. Ross noted that as society develops so does sin. With commerce comes piracy and smuggling; with banking comes embezzlement and forgery. Many latter-day sins are impersonal. The victimizer is far removed by an elaborate organizational system from the victim. Rather than using the gun or bludgeon, as might the brigand, the impeccable gentlemen who preside over great business empires resort to bribery, false claims, safety violations, child labor, toxic dumping, war profiteering, and the like, causing material loss, physical injury, misery, and death to persons whom they never see. While their actions and decisions may harbor no malicious intent toward specific individuals, they are guilty of neglect, deception, illegality—and liability. Still, these estimable individuals never think of themselves as criminals, nor does the press or any other established opinion-maker. On the contrary, the "systemic sinners" sit on the boards of foundations, museums, churches, and universities, are given honorary degrees, and are welcomed into the best clubs.

You can hear this passage in your mental ears. You can almost imagine a great pipe organ and chorus blasting out the concluding coda of a magnificent oratorio in these words. Parenti's sensitivity to pain and the obliviousness of established opinion makers, his rhythmic prose, his ironic references to foundations, museums, churches, and universities, and above all his devotion to the victims of politically and economically empowered victimizers make this passage a good read. And he undoubtedly had a wonderful time writing it. His joyful state of mind shows in the words.

Parenti's *Land of Idols* illustrates many of the strengths and potential weaknesses of cultural criticism. For example, he wants to build the argument that, politically, black-white differences are less a matter of race than of class: America has a system of class power that privileges whites. To build that argument, he textualizes class differences by analyzing mortality rates between blacks and whites of all classes, examining television depictions of stereotyped black fathers who refuse to pay child support, looking at court decisions that talk exclusively about race and not class inequalities, and quoting African American leaders W. E. B. Du Bois and Malcolm X on relationships between class and racism (1994, pp. 135–138).

What is visible in this section of Parenti's book, however, is an example of case building, not analysis. Parenti obviously looked for examples that would help him build a case for the idea that class, not race, is the key cultural factor dividing black and white. This argument is important to the overall argument of this book: that economics determines in many ways what our political and social relationships are all about. Looking at different dimensions of black-white relationships (where people sit or stand in public buildings, scores on standardized intelligence tests, gerrymandering or the construction of congressional districts), one could come to the opposite conclusion: that racism in social and political matters, regardless of class, is alive and well in America.

The point here is not to disparage Parenti's fascinating book, for it is very enlightening and, yes, a good read. Rather, the point is that the best critics always start with the texts or textualizations and see where they take them, rather than starting with some judgments and then searching out evidence to support them. If a critic seems always to be case building, he or she certainly is writing a critical essay but is not really doing criticism as we have defined it in this book. Because cultural criticism ends in judgment, it's very tempting to start with the judgment and then work more or less backward. *Resist that temptation.* As we have noted more than once, the promise of cultural analyses and assessments of television programs comes in the careful execution of both description, as William Graham Sumner did, and normative judgment, as Matthew Arnold did.

Writing Cultural Criticism

The central challenge in writing culture-centered criticism, whether in its British or American form, as you might guess, is to negotiate description and assessment, or, if you prefer, fact-based and value-based argument. Sumner and Arnold must be made to work together. Working only descriptively or only judgmentally makes for less-than-satisfying criticism. Merely describing cultural rules and roles, ideological orientations and hegemonic mechanisms, or the moves an institution makes in performing or acting out some perspective on life is not enough. In the face of mere description, readers cry out, "So what?" "So what if *Cheers* is set in a bar and no one on the series ever suffers any negative effects—physical, legal, or relational—from consuming immense quantities of beer?" As we noted in Chapter 4, for the good critic, descriptions of typical and usual action from programs become evidence for both generalizations about programs and judgments about their beauties and ugliness, their force for justice or injustice, and their political force. Descriptions without judgments are sterile; judgments without descriptive evidence are mere expressions of taste or preference. Sumner's description of cultural practices, together with Arnold's normative assessments of those practices, comprise a complete piece of cultural criticism.

Writing cultural criticism thus calls for great discipline, bringing together both the critic's analytical skills and sense of injustice yet hope for the future. This judgment will become more concrete as we examine more focused sorts of cultural studies in the next chapter.

What we have done in this chapter is provide general orientations to cultural/sociocultural studies/criticism. You now have in hand the general vocabulary of ideology and hegemony, social role and class, textualization and performance, naturalization and power.

The Example Essays

The first example essay, Heather L. Hundley's "The Naturalization of Beer in *Cheers*," examines the ways in which the discourse of beer in the television series *Cheers* was naturalized through its characters, dialogue, action, consequences, settings, and narrative strategies of humor, camaraderie, and detoxification. Taking as her focus the final year of the series' eleven-year run, she explains how the discourse of excessive consumption of beer was made to seem a normal, natural social practice. She presents evidence from outside the show's framing to support her argument that its endorsement of excessive beer drinking served the economic interests of the beer producers at the expense of consumers, who were taught no negative consequences and several positive consequences—social and relaxation—associated with serious drinking. Texts working in service of the economic establishment, then, become the exposé that Hundley pursues.

Next, in Cathy Sandeen's "Success Defined by Television: The Value System Promoted by *PM Magazine*," Sandeen analyzes the value system underlying the nationally syndicated *PM Magazine* to show how the dominant cluster of values—personal and financial success, professional achievement, material acquisition, excitement and power (for men) and physical attributes (for women)—reinforced existing power structures in American society. She used as evidence her examination of the values and value patterns expressed through the content and production techniques in thirteen weeks (225 feature stories) of the news magazine that aired in summer 1995, supplemented by interviews with *PM Magazine* production personnel and public relations and promotional brochures. Sandeen argues that the conservative, capitalist, material values celebrated in *PM Magazine* stories clearly serve the interests of the white, middle-class professional classes. By promoting this worldview and suggesting people who valued individuality, community and compassion rather than acquisition and conformity were trivial and ineffective, she concludes, the news magazine functions culturally to "discipline" diversity and reinforce existing traditional, conservative values needed to maintain corporate culture power structure. In the next chapter, we'll examine narrower, more focused approaches to three popular sorts of cultural studies of television programming.

Notes

1. Just as Horace Newcomb (see Chapter 3) asserted that television, in fact, does have an aesthetic, so have some critics continued to do aesthetic studies of television programming. Examples of aesthetic critiques include Thompson's (1983) study of *Love Boat*, Gitlin's (1983) analysis of *Hill Street Blues*, and Gronbeck's (1985) examination of *Family*. Most normative studies of television programming, however, are much more concerned about social and political than aesthetic issues.

2. One branch of British Cultural Studies has a strong focus on audience modes of meaning making; it was given direction by John Morley's work on the British news magazine program *Nationwide*. Excellent summaries of this orientation can be found in Ang (1991) and Morley (1992). See also Ang's (1996) rethinking of her work five years later.

3. Power/knowledge, as Foucault (1980) conceived of that term, is found in two modes of critique: (1) the *critique of domination*, analyses that strip away the imprisoning institutional, social, and linguistic forms that control individual word and deed (these kinds of analyses prevail in ideological criticism, as we discussed in Chapter 11), and (2) the *critique of freedom*, analyses that urge the individual on to a sense of empowerment, the courage to act constructively with and through others, once one is liberated, in a call for new social awareness (see McKerrow, 1989).

4. As Berger (1995) explains, beginning critics should not be intimidated or put off by unfamiliar concepts they encounter in criticism. In general, when critics and theorists use the term *concept or construct*, they mean "an idea, theory, or hypothesis, or notion that someone who is interested in cultural criticism uses to interpret, understand, make sense of, find meaning in, and see relationships in (1) what characters say and do in texts (and what people in real life say and do in their everyday lives); (2) data about the world and the role of institutions in the world; (3) the behavior of individuals and groups of individuals; (4) the way the human mind, psyche, and body function, and the relationship between the psyche and the body; and (5) the role of texts (works of elite and public art) in the development of individuals and the impact of these texts on society and culture" (Berger, 1995, p. 5).

5. See Gronbeck's (1980) discussion for the debate over dramaturgical versus dramatistic theory and criticism.

Further Readings

During, S. (Ed.). (1999). *The cultural studies reader* (2nd ed.). New York: Routledge. This is the best of the British Cultural Studies readers. Part I offers classic essays on cultural theory and method, and then the remaining parts offer essays on space and time; nationalism, postcolonialism and globalization; ethnicity and multiculturalism; science and cyberculture; sexuality and gender; carnival and utopia; consumption and the market; leisure; culture–political economy and policy; and "media and public spheres."

Hartley, J., & Pearson, R. E (Eds.). (2000). *American cultural studies: A reader.* New York: Oxford University Press. The introduction provides an excellent orientation to Americanist intellectual outlooks, and the chapters in Part II offer readings illustrating some prototypical approaches to American cultural analysis.

Webnotes

Cultural Studies. **http://www.culturalstudies.net**

This excellent collection of information and dialogue boxes built by the Department of Communication at the University of South Florida since 1996 is a good place to start bibliographical research. It also allows you to access the online journal *popcultures.com.*

Cultural Studies Conversations. **http://www.cas.usf.edu/communication/rodman/ cultstud**

This site takes you to CULTSTUD-L, a listserv devoted to discussion and exchange of information with other culturalists. A great place to play.

Resources in cultural Studies **http://www.uiowa.edu/~commstud/resources/ index.html**

This is the home for one of the most complete listings of cultural studies sites available on the Web.

Learning Activities

1. Examine a so-called reality show—from *Survivor* to *Meet the Parents* to *Fear Factor* to whatever else is still on the air when you're taking this class. On the bases of thoughts and behaviors that are positively and negatively valued on that program, construct its cultural rules. How must one think, and what must do to survive and prosper? What kinds of thinking and actions doom a person? What, then, is attractive about those cultural rules for a viewer? That is, why watch?

2. Now do the same exercise for a popular situation comedy. Check the ratings page in a newspaper that publishes the weekly Nielsen ratings of top 50 programs, and pick a sitcom in the top 10 for your analysis. In addition to answering the same questions as noted in the first learning activity, add two more: Why is this program a top 10 this year? What does its rating tell you about the state of American society?

References

Ang, I. (1991). *Desperately seeking the audience.* New York: Routledge.

Ang, I. (1996). *Living room wars: Rethinking media audiences for a postmodern world.* New York: Routledge.

Arnold, M. (1869/1916). *Culture and anarchy: An essay in political and social criticism.* New York: Macmillan.

Aronowitz, S. (1993). *Roll over Beethoven: The return of cultural strife.* Hanover, NH: University Press of New England.

Bandura, A. (1986). *Social foundations of thought and action: A social cognitive theory.* Englewood Cliffs, NJ: Prentice-Hall.

Bandura, A. (1994). Social cognitive theory of mass communication. In J. Bryant & D. Zillman (Eds.), *Media effects: Advances in theory and research* (pp. 61–90). Hillsdale, NJ: Lawrence Erlbaum.

Barthes, R. (1968). *Elements of semiology.* London: Cape.

Barthes, R. (1973). *Mythologies.* London: Paladin.

Barthes, R. (1977). *Image-music-text* (S. Heath, Ed. & Trans.). New York: Hill & Wang.

Baudrillard, J. (1983). *In the shadow of the silent majorities, Or, the end of the social, and other essays.* New York: Semiotext(e).

Berger, A. A. (1995). *Cultural criticism: A primer of key concepts.* Thousand Oaks, CA: Sage.

Baudrillard, J. (1988). *The ecstasy of communication.* New York: Semiotext(e).

Black, E. (1973). Electing time. *Quarterly Journal of Speech, 59,* 125–129.

Bormann, E. G. (1985). *The force of fantasy: Restoring the American dream.* Carbondale: Southern Illinois University Press.

Burke, K. (1969). *A rhetoric of motives.* Los Angeles: University of California Press.

Chase, S. (1956). *The proper study of mankind* (rev. ed.). New York: Harper & Row.

Debord, G. (1970). *The society of the spectacle.* Detroit: Black and Red.

deCerteau, M. (1984). *The practice of everyday life.* Berkeley: University of California Press.

Dow, B. (1996). *Prime time feminism: Television, media culture, and the women's movement since 1970.* Philadelphia: University of Pennsylvania.

During, S. (Ed.). (1999). *The cultural studies reader* (2nd ed.). New York: Routledge.

Fiske, J. (1986a). Television: Polysemy and popularity. *Critical Studies in Mass Communication, 3,* 391–408.

Fiske, J. (1986b). Television and popular culture: Reflections on British and Australian critical practice. *Critical Studies in Media Communication, 3,* 200–216.

Fiske, J. (1987). *Television culture.* London: Methuen.

Fiske, J. (1991). Methodological preface to "The Discourses of TV Quiz Shows," or school + luck = success + sex. In L. Vande Berg & L.A. Wenner (Eds.), *Television criticism: Approaches and applications* (pp. 445–447). White Plains, NY: Longman.

Fiske, J. (1994a). Audiencing: Cultural practice and cultural studies. In N. K. Denzin & Y. S. Lincoln (Eds.), *Handbook of qualitative research* (pp. 189–198). Thousand Oaks, CA: Sage.

Fiske, J. (1994b). Ethnosemiotics: Some personal and theoretical reflections. In H. Newcomb (Ed.), *Television: The critical view* (5th ed., pp. 411–425). New York: Oxford University Press.

Fiske, J., & Hartley, J. (1978). *Reading television*. London: Methuen.

Foucault, M. (1972). *The archeology of knowledge and the discourse on language* (A. M. Sheridan Smith, Trans.). New York: Harper & Row.

Foucault, M. (1977). *The order of things*. London: Tavistock.

Foucault, M. (1980). *Power/knowledge: Selected interviews and other writings, 1972–1977* (C. Gordon, Ed.). New York: Pantheon.

Geertz, C. (1973). *The interpretation of cultures*. New York: Basic Books.

Gitlin, T. (1983). *Hill Street Blues:* Make it look messy. In T. Gitlin, *Inside prime time* (pp. 273–335). New York: Pantheon.

Gramsci, A. (1971). *Prison notebooks*. New York: International Publishers.

Gronbeck, B.E. (1980). Dramaturgical theory and critism: The state of the art (or science)? *Western Journal of Speech Communication, 44,* 315–330.

Gronbeck, B. E. (1985). Audience engagement in *Family*. In M. J. Medhurst & T. W. Benson (Eds.), *Rhetorical dimensions in media: A critical casebook* (pp. 4–32). Dubuque, IA: Kendall/Hunt.

Gronbeck, B. E. (1999). The triumph of social science: *The silent language* as master text in American cultural studies. In T. Rosteck (Ed.), *At the intersection: Cultural studies and rhetorical studies* (pp. 266–291). New York: Guilford Press.

Hall, E. (1959). *The silent language*. New York: Doubleday.

Hall, S. (1980). Encoding/decoding. In S. Hall, D. Hobson, A. Lowe, & P. Willis (Eds.), *Culture, media, language* (pp. 128–139). London: Hutchinson.

Hall, S. (1982). The rediscovery of ideology: The return of the repressed in media studies. In M. Gurevitch, T. Bennett, J. Curran, & J. Woollacott (Eds.), *Culture, society, and media* (pp. 56–90). London: Methuen.

Hall, S. (1990). The whites of their eyes: Racist ideologies and the media. In M. Alvarado & J.O. Thompson (Eds.), *The media reader* (pp. 7–23). London: British Film Institute.

Hall, S. (Ed.). (1997). *Representation: Cultural representations and signifying practices*. Thousand Oaks, CA: Sage.

Hall, S., Critcher, C., Jefferson, T., Clark, J., & Roberts, B. (1978). *Policing the crisis: Mugging, the state, and law and order*. London: Macmillan.

Hartley, J., Pearson, R. E., & Vieth, E. (Eds.). (2000). *American cultural studies*. New York: Oxford University Press.

Hayes, J. (1992). Afterword. In R.C. Allen (Ed.), *Channels of discourse, reassembled: Television and contemporary criticism* (pp. 354–385). Chapel Hill: University of North Carolina Press.

Kellner, D. (1995). *Media culture: Cultural studies, identity, and politics between the modern and the postmodern.* New York: Routledge.

Kervin, D. (1991). Gender ideology in television commercials. In L. Vande Berg & L. Wenner (Eds.), *Television criticism: Approaches and applications* (pp. 235-253). White Plains, NY: Longman

Kohlberg, L. (1968). Moral development. *International Encyclopedia of the social sciences* (pp. 489–494). New York: Crowell, Coller & MacMillan.

Lévi-Strauss, C. (1958). The structural study of myth. In T. A. Sebeok (Ed.), *Myth: A symposium* (pp. 81–106). Bloomington: Indiana University Press.

Lewis, G. E. (Ed.). (1972). *Side-saddle on the golden calf: Social structure and cultural character.* Pacific Palisades, CA: Goodyear.

Lippmann, W. (1920). *Liberty and the news.* New York: Harcourt Brace Jovanovich.

McKerrow, R. E. (1989). Critical rhetoric: Theory and praxis. *Communication Monographs, 56,* 91–111.

Morley, J. (1980). *The "nationwide" audience.* London: BFI.

Morley, J. (1992). *Television, audiences, and cultural studies.* London: Routledge.

O'Sullivan, T., Hartley, J., Saunders, D., Montgomery, M., & Fiske, J. (1994). *Key concepts in communication and cultural studies* (2nd ed.). New York: Routledge.

Parenti, M. (1994). *Land of idols: Political mythology in America.* New York: St. Martin's Press.

Park, R. (1938). Reflections on communication and culture. *American Journal of Socialism, 45,* 187–208.

Rokeach, M. (1973). *The nature of human values.* New York: Free Press.

Rokeach, M. (1980). Some unresolved issues in theories of beliefs, attitudes, and values. In H.E. Howe, Jr., & M.M. Page (Eds.), *Nebraska symposium on motivation (1979)* (pp. 261–304). Lincoln: University of Nebraska Press.

Rosenberg, B., & White, D. M. (Eds.). (1957). *Mass culture: The popular arts in America.* New York: Free Press.

Rosenblatt, R. (1979). Growing up on television. In H. Newcomb (Ed.), *Television: The critical view* (2nd ed., pp. 350–362). New York: Oxford University Press.

Ryan, K. (1976). Television as a moral educator. In R. Adler & D. Cater (Eds.), *Television as a cultural force* (pp. 111–127). New York: Praeger.

Shohat, E., & Stam, R. (1994). *Unthinking Eurocentrism: Multiculturalism and the media,* London: Routledge.

Smith, A. E. (Ed.). (1966). *Communication and culture.* Englewood Cliffs, NJ: Prentice Hall.

Stevenson, N. (1995). *Understanding media cultures: Social theory and mass communication.* London: Sage.

Sumner, W. G. (1906/1911). *Folkways: A study of the sociological importance of usages, manner, customs, mores, and morals.* Boston: Ginn.

Thompson, R. (1983). *Love Boat:* High art on the high seas. *Journal of American Culture, 6,* 59–65.

Trites, R. (1991). Disney's sub/version of Andersen's *The Little Mermaid. Journal of Popular Journal of Film and Television, 18,* 145–152.

Voelker, F. H., & Voelker, L. A. (Eds.). (1972). *Mass media: Forces in our society* (4th ed.). New York: Harcourt Brace Jovanovich.

Williams, R. (1974). *Television: Technology and cultural form.* London: Fontana.

Williams, R.M., Jr. (1970). *American Society: A sociological interpretation* (3rd ed.). New York: Knopf.

Williams, S. (1991). Bugs Bunny meets He-Man: A historical comparison of values in animated cartoons. In L. Vande Berg & L. A. Wenner (Eds.), *Television criticism: Approaches and applications* (pp. 201–219). White Plains, NY: Longman.

The Naturalization of Beer in *Cheers*

Heather L. Hundley

Alcohol consumption in the United States is related to a variety of safety and health risks.[1] Because of the problems associated with alcohol, it is important to examine how it is portrayed in the media. Of particular concern to many health and safety officials is the portrayal of beer consumption since 1) drinkers underestimate the negative consequences of beer consumption, and 2) beer consumption is an integral part of the socialization routines of young drinkers (Strate, 1992).

Cultivation theory posits that repeated exposure to consistent media portrayals and themes may influence viewers' perceptions so that they become congruent with media portrayals (Gerbner, Gross, Morgan, & Signorielli, 1980). Gross and Morgan (1985) explain that the more time one spends living in the world of television, the more likely one is to report conceptions of social reality that can be traced to television portrayals. Krugman and Hartley (1970) concur, arguing that "the mass media have taught our society what it needs to know in order to have attitudes on a thousand serious matters" (p. 189). Similarly, Bandura's (1977) social learning theory holds that viewers can learn a variety of attitudes and behaviors by observing behaviors and then modeling the observed behavior. Both of these theories suggest that over its eleven television seasons, *Cheers* may have "cultivated" some of its millions of viewers to accept the perception that excessive beer drinking is an unproblematic activity.

Critical Approach

The structural method used in this analysis is the application of the construct of discourse. Fiske defines discourse as "both a topic and a coded set of signs through which that topic is organized, understood, and made expressible" (1984, p. 169). Later, Fiske (1991) elaborates on the utility of examining discourse within texts because it is "an ideological way of thinking about and representing an important topic area in social experience" (p. 447). This study examines the discourse of beer in the television series, *Cheers*. The approach is well suited to the purpose of the study because, as Fiske (1987) argues, "to understand both the production of the programs and the production of meaning from them, we need to understand the workings of discourse" (p. 14). Discourse works ideologically to naturalize particular meanings in social topics within a text. The discourse of beer, then, is used by viewers not only in making sense of *Cheers*, but also in making sense of their social experiences (Fiske, 1987).

This method and this analysis stem from Fiske's theoretical development. To analyze various television programs and genres, Fiske (1984; 1986; 1987) uses such semiotic constructs as discourse and codes. Fiske has studied a variety of discourses such as sex, politics, and education, among others. For him, codes are conventionally shared meanings in a culture for a system of signs. In his television analyses he examines (1) social codes of appearance, dress, speech, (2) representation codes of camera, lighting, narrative character, and (3) ideological codes such as individualism, sex, and alcohol (Fiske, 1987).

Fiske's (1986) study notes that in order for television programs to be popular (like *Cheers*), they have to be open to multiple readings; the dominant ideology of the culture will be structured in both popular texts and the social system. The structure of meanings in a text is much like the structure of subcultures in society, that is, as Fiske argues, "both exist in a network of power relations, and the textual struggle for meaning is the precise equivalent of the social struggle for power" (p. 392).

Although a text must be open to different readings, Fiske explains that "the text can appeal to this variety of audiences only if there is a common ideological frame that all recognize and use, even if many are opposed to it" (p. 399). The identification of this common ideological frame is the focus of this study of the portrayal of beer drinking in *Cheers*.

While Fiske notes that there is a seemingly endless array of discourses that a reader can bring to a text, he explains that there are limits to a text's polysemy. Fiske's (1986) metacritical essay elaborates on the relationship between popularity and the semiotic construct of polysemy, which he first notes in

his (1984) analysis of *Dr. Who*. Fiske's (1984) essay greatly contributes to this work in that connections are drawn between the symbolic television world and the social world, as I attempt to explain how the naturalization of beer on television stereotypes reality's concept of masculinity. Additionally within the *Dr. Who* essay is a definition of discourse, a discussion on polysemy, and an understanding of popularity. Specifically regarding popularity, Fiske believes that in order to be popular, a television program's textual signs must evoke social or ideological meanings which resonate with a wide diversity of audience members, all of whom must find the program appealing. While I acknowledge the polysemic possibilities presented by the *Cheers* text, I concentrate the analysis on the dominant reading encoded in the text's narrative structures (Fiske, 1984; 1986).

The Television Text

Cheers was an eleven-year-long prime time situation comedy set in a Boston bar named Cheers. It was television's longest-running situation comedy, having first appeared on September 30, 1982, and ended on May 20, 1993, totaling 275 episodes. During the 1989–1990 season, *Cheers* was among the top ten most watched prime-time shows in the United States, and in the 1990–1991 season it was "the top-rated show of the year" (*Facts on File*, 1991). *Cheers* received more Emmy nominations than any series, 111, and received 28 total Emmys.

During its last season (1992–1993), *Cheers* featured seven regular characters (four employees and three patrons); the bar in this season was co-owned by Sam Malone (a recovering alcoholic) and Rebecca Howe. *Cheers'* only cocktail waitress was Carla LeBec. Working as *Cheers'* bartender, Woody Boyd served regular bar patrons Norm Peterson, Cliff Clavin, and Frasier Crane. Norm was known for his outstanding bar tab, his non-existent relationship with his wife, and his frequent unemployment. Cliff was a letter carrier known for sticking his foot in his mouth and for his penchant for trivia—both factual and fictional. Frasier, a well-known, respected psychiatrist, was the "brains" of the *Cheers* group.

As of December 1994, 170 individual stations ran *Cheers* in syndication. The November 1993 sweeps showed that *Cheers*, in syndication, earned a 5.6 rating in 168 markets, and in its continuing popularity, "the show's license price [had risen] from $1.3 million to roughly $2.3 million in its second cycle" (Tobenkin, 1994, p. 18). *Cheers'* immense popularity has earned the greatest revenue in Paramount's history, more than any other television product (Chagollan, 1993). *Cheers* is one of the few television series that has kept the interest of a diverse audience for over a decade with few character and setting changes (Galloway, 1990). Because of the show's popularity, the Bull and Finch (the real bar in Boston after which *Cheers* was designed) made at least $7 million a year selling *Cheers* T-shirts, ashtrays, Bloody Mary mix, etc. (Gliatto, 1990).

Numerous content analytic studies have pointed to the excessive consumption of beer on television (Cafiso, Goodstadt, Garlington, & Sheppard, 1982; DeFoe, Breed, & Breed, 1983; Fernandez-Collado, Greenberg, Korzenny, & Atkin, 1978; Signorielli, 1987; Wallack, Breed, & Cruz, 1987; Wallack, Grube, Madden, & Breed, 1990). Interestingly, without *Cheers* the situation comedy genre would move from second highest to lowest in the portrayal of alcohol consumption. These studies afford documented evidence of *Cheers'* alcohol-related content and hence underscore the suitability of *Cheers* for purposes of this critical investigation.

This essay argues that over its eleven seasons *Cheers* naturalized beer drinking, presenting it as a normal, natural everyday activity. To explore the naturalization of beer in the last season of *Cheers*, 23 half-hour episodes and one hour-long episode, plus the one and one-half-hour-long finale are analyzed. The last season was chosen because the final season of any series is the last opportunity for the producers to change or alter the presentation of characters and/or topics before the show's end, and leaves the audience with a sense of closure regarding the characters' behaviors, traits, and motives (Piccirillo, 1986).

Naturalization is, as Fiske (1987) explains, the self-disguising process of "exnomination." A "naturalized" subject "present[s] itself as common sense,

as an objective, innocent reflection of the real" (p. 42). Thus, "the only views that need no explanation or defense are those that have been naturalized or exnominated into common sense" (p. 134).

Even casual viewers should have been able to recognize at a glance that alcohol is an important and essential element of *Cheers*, since the setting for their sitcom is a neighborhood bar. However, a more critical examination suggests that beer, unlike other alcohol in the bar, is naturalized. Characters sit for hours and swill beer, seemingly without feeling any effects, in contrast to characters who drink wine, champagne, scotch, and other types of alcohol. In short, beer drinking is presented as a normal, acceptable behavior, naturalized through the use of three narrative devices: humor, camaraderie, and detoxification.

Strate (1992) points out that "often, beer is shown to be a product that is natural and pure, implying that its consumption is not harmful, and perhaps even healthy" (p. 83). I agree and argue in the remainder of this essay that *Cheers* naturalizes beer in that viewers are encouraged to think of beer not as a potentially harmful alcoholic beverage, but rather as a beverage no more dangerous than soda pop or water.

Humor as a Naturalization Strategy

Berger's (1987) psychoanalytic approach to humor suggests that jokes pertaining to alcohol, for example, "make possible the satisfaction of an instinct in the face of an obstacle that stands in its way" (p. 101). The logic of humor includes laughing at obstacles that stand in the way of masked desires which are ridiculously presented in excess. While excessive beer drinking is not an instinctive need of most people, it is presented as a virtually instinctive, pervasive, and apparently satisfying activity of most of the *Cheers* characters. However, the human body cannot tolerate the quantity of beer Norm consumed. "Such excesses," Palmer (1989) argues, "are implausible because excesses pursued more modestly are normal" (p. 151).

Norm provides the most exemplary portrayal of

the use of this strategy to naturalize beer. In the 10/8/92 episode, for instance, Norm participated in a beer taste test and critique. After sampling beers, A, B, and C, and critiquing them, Norm then asked to be really challenged. The marketing representative responded by offering him samples D through V. Beer, apparently, had little effect on this seasoned drinker and after tasting 22 beers, Norm went to *Cheers* to "hoist a few" as his lunch.

This portrayal of Norm's drinking implies that beer could be consumed in excessive amounts. Furthermore, the equivalence with which other characters respond to Norm's drinking in general and his drinking while describing his beer testing strongly affirms beer drinking as a normal, natural, and acceptable activity.

Overindulgence which allows the audience to laugh at the (non)consequential effects of excessive beer drinking as well as the characters' apparent inability to learn lessons from overindulgence were, for example, in the 4/29/93 episode. After a night of drinking too much hard liquor, Norm returned to the bar and Rebecca asked, "How are you doing?" Norm responded, "Terrible, I've got a splitting headache and I think I might be sick. Can I have a beer, Sammy?" At this point the laugh track sounded, positioning the viewers to regard drinking beer as the "natural" thing to do, despite having a hangover and being nauseous. Berger (1987) explains that while characters "may often be 'low' and motivated by relatively trivial concerns, the function of humor is not trivial by any means" (p. 14). Applying Berger's ideas to the above example then, we see that one seriously important function of this vignette is the naturalization of beer drinking, regardless of one's health.

Another humorous device used to naturalize beer in this comedy is the use of quick one-liners strewn throughout each episode regarding beer drinking. For example, in the 10/1/92 episode Norm and Cliff were sent to retrieve Carla who was temporarily employed at Mr. Pubb's while *Cheers* was being rebuilt after a fire. The two were amazed at the vast selection of beers from every country, so before returning to *Cheers*, Norm suggested a "trip around the world." The laugh track and Cliff's ap-

Pictured here in the "Cheers" bar, where "everybody knows your name," is bartender/owner, former Red Sox pitcher, eternal womanizer, and recovering alcoholic Sam Malone, enjoying humor and comraderie with Cheers' regulars.

proval suggest that consuming a great amount of beer, which is physically impossible, is humorous. In the 3/18/93 episode, Rebecca remarked that Norm had been making green beer for three hours to prepare for the St. Patrick's Day celebration, to which Norm responded, "And I'm prepared to work on it all night long if I have to because, damn it, I care!" The laugh track again indicates that Norm's affixation to beer is humorous. Both of these examples reflect the acceptability of beer drinking by using humor as a strategic device.

Camaraderie as a Naturalization Strategy

Cheers centers on the relationships of characters in a bar. Strate's (1992) study of beer commercials describes the typical bar setting which closely resembles the *Cheers* bar: It is generally portrayed as a relaxed and comfortable context for male socializing, as well as a place where a man can find entertainment and excitement. The bars are immaculate and smokeless, and the waitresses and bartenders are always friendly; thus, bars are the ideal male leisure environment. (p. 84)

This male camaraderie both enables male viewers to parasocially relate to *Cheers'* characters and functions as another narrative strategy by which beer drinking is naturalized. People are brought together within this "boys club" to fraternize, to share the joys and sorrows, and to drink. In the Cheers bar, where "everybody knows your name," beer is the common link among patrons and employees who are quite diverse in age, education, and socioeconomic status. For example, Frasier, who is an educated, white collar patron, befriended Norm, an unemployed accountant/painter. While it might seem that the two have little in common, they drink beer together at Cheers and in the rare occasions they meet outside the bar, beer is still present. Strate (1992) explains the role of beer as a medium of male bonding and as a facilitator of group solidarity. Both of these aspects are quite clear and present in *Cheers*.

That this (primarily male bonding) process evolves while tippling beer together is illustrated over several episodes, it cumulatively naturalizes beer drinking as a positive social activity. For example, Frasier at first drank Manhattans and was not welcomed as part of the Cheers gang. However, over time as he began quaffing drafts, he became increasingly accepted as part of the Cheers "family." Indeed, by the final season, when he and his wife, Lilith, separated, the Cheers gang gave him a surprise divorce party at the bar. Later they went to his house (Norm brought beer) to keep him from feeling lonely and depressed.

Montgomery (1989), DeFoe and Breed (1986), and Strate (1992) note that heavy drinking on television is a macho activity and, in fact, often a requirement for proving oneself as a man, and gaining membership into one's social environment. Woody illustrated this rite of passage to join the membership and camaraderie of the "boys club" in the 2/11/93 episode. Specifically, Al (a minor character) saw Woody serving himself a beer and queried Woody about his drinking. Woody's response, "Why not? I'm a grown man. I'm an adult. I can handle my alcohol," suggests that drinking beer is a normal, natural indicator of male adulthood. Furthermore, the rest of Woody's explanation, "Plus, we're out of chocolate milk," suggests that his decision to drink beer is a conscious attempt to prove that he is an adult, a "manly man."

Subsequently, though, we saw that Woody's attempts to gain the respect of others by drinking like the men only resulted in his passing out, as affirmed later by Cliff's comment, "He's still out cold. Should we wake him?" Norm, Sam, and Frasier join Cliff in looking at Woody who had passed out on a bar table, and responded by shaking their heads no, and smiled indulgently at the "kid's" inability to hold his liquor. However, while Woody's attempt to drink beer like the other men in the bar failed, nonetheless, his beer drinking is positively acknowledged by the other patrons as an effort to join the beer brotherhood and share the camaraderie since "beer functions as a symbol of initiation and group membership" (Strate, 1992, p. 85).

This "boys club" is the crux of naturalizing beer in *Cheers*. Drinking beer is the socializing agent which bring together a diverse group of people, primarily men. Beer drinking is the "secret code" that indicates to the audience which members of the club are "cool" and serve as role models.

Detoxification as a Naturalization Strategy

A third strategy through which beer is naturalized in *Cheers* is by the paradigmatic opposition of its harmlessness with the strong effects of other alcoholic beverages, a strategy which in essence detoxifies beer. By repeatedly portraying characters who drink beer all day without showing any signs of drunkenness, *Cheers* exnominates and naturalizes beer's alcoholic content.

Norm arrives when the bar opens and shortly thereafter Cliff stops in. Both patrons usually do not leave the bar until closing time. Sam often has to tell them to go home because he must close the bar for the evening. During this daily ritual Cliff and Norm always have a beer with them indicating that they spent the entire day at Cheers drinking beer.

Frasier increasingly spent more time at the bar in the final *Cheers* seasons and he too would be seen drinking beer throughout the day and night. These characters do not show any signs of drunkenness after the day-long beer drinking ritual and thus allow the audience to understand beer to be a relatively harmless beverage.

Cheers further naturalizes beer by contrasting its harmlessness with the debilitating effects of other types of alcoholic beverages such as wine, champagne, scotch, and mixed drinks. An example of this strategy occurred in the 4/29/93 episode. In it Carla was left in charge of the bar and proceeded to make everyone a drink called "I Know My Redeemer Liveth." This Long-Island-Iced-Tea-like drink came from a recipe that Carla had learned from her grandfather. Everyone enthusiastically tried it, and Norm asked Carla to "make mine a double." Subsequently, however, everyone who drank Carla's grandfather's concoction became drunk and suffered a hangover the next morning.

In addition to this depiction of the negative effects of alcohol other than beer, several episodes feature characters becoming drunk after consuming other alcoholic drinks while their beer drinking companions apparently are unaffected. For example, although Frasier became intoxicated from drinking scotch, his beer drinking bar companions, Norm and Cliff, appeared to suffer no ill effects (11/5/92).

Indirect contrasts between bar and other alcoholic drinks are provided in episodes in which Frasier drank too much champagne at his divorce party (2/11/93), and when Rebecca drank too much wine at Mr. Gaines' home (5/6/93), while the guys drinking beer back at Cheers had no such problems (5/6/93). Indeed, the only character whoever was shown suffering any unpleasant consequences from drinking too much beer was Woody, who was passed out at the bar (2/11/93). As evident in these examples *Cheers* detoxifies beer and highly toxifies other alcoholic beverages; by doing so it naturalizes beer and presents it as if it were water. In sum, beer is naturalized in *Cheers* by contrasting its non-effects with the powerful effects of other alcohol.

Conclusions

"Television is a subtle, continuous source for learning about the rules of life and society" (Huston,

1992 pp. 57–58) and popular shows like *Cheers* can educate the masses. *Cheers'* final season presented a humorous, tolerantly accepting attitude toward beer that was amplified by *Cheers'* failure to depict any serious economic, social, or emotional consequences due to regular or excessive beer consumption. The absence of beer-related deaths, accidents, D.U.I.s, alcoholism, or other body dysfunctions and diseases invites viewers to disassociate the possible consequences of beer consumption from drinking and encourages them to instead associate only sociability and relaxation with beer drinking.

Such portrayals of beer are certainly those endorsed by the beer industry. Approximately $839.6 million is spent each year on beer advertising (*Advertising Age*, 1992) which celebrates friendship and good times (e.g., "Proud to be your bud, Budweiser," "Here's to good friends, tonight is kind of special Michelob"). Strate (1992) notes that like *Cheers*, "the emphasis on the group in beer commercials plays on the common misconception that drinking, when it is done socially and publicly, cannot be harmful" (p. 88). The conclusions in his analysis of beer commercials are quite similar to the findings in this study, thus acknowledging that naturalizing strategies can be found in other forms of media. Strate (1992) argues that beer commercials stereotype masculinity, and in order to prove oneself as a man, one must drink beer. Consequently, beer commercials and *Cheers*, which support the American male myth, promote masculinity which, in turn, promotes alcoholism.

Television plays an important role in American lives. It is pervasive; it accounts for an average of 28.5 hours of human (in)activity per week (Kubey & Csikzentmihaly, 1990). And for many Americans, viewing *Cheers'* naturalization of beer is part of this weekly activity. In the case of *Cheers,* the dominant ideological position affirmed throughout the series and in the final season is that beer drinking is normal, natural, and harmless. No matter what quantity of beer consumed, there are few risks and intoxication is rare.

As noted, Cheers is very much a man's haven. Even though Rebecca is very much part of the bar, she is not included in the antics of the male patrons and employees. Carla asserts herself as part of the male camaraderie, but nonetheless, her sole purpose in Cheers is to serve the men. As found in beer commercials, the same is true for *Cheers* in that "women tend to be passive, not participating but merely watching as men perform" (Strate, 1992, p. 91).

Drinking beer is not only presented as a man's activity, but as stereotypically masculine and upholding the male working class. For example, unlike Rebecca, Lilith, and Diane, Carla is more accepted as part of the group because she is more like the working class males. Strate's (1992) study explains the types of occupational roles that are shown in beer commercials, including cowboys, construction workers, and lumberjacks. At the end of a hard day's work, these laborers are rewarded with beer. Although Cheers patrons are not all from the working class, and represent a variety of occupational roles, the common thread of the portrayal of beer drinking is their maleness. Drinking beer supports masculinity which, according to Strate (1992), favors the working class; however, it cannot be determined whether beer drinking stereotypes the working class like it certainly stereotypes masculinity. This is especially apparent since women are also part of the working class force.

Even though *Cheers* is polysemic, the dominant reading is from a white, male, working class perspective. In fact, the majority of audience members consist of males 18 to 34 years old. The humor is primarily directed toward women, homosexuality, white collar workers, and non-beer drinkers. Gender, race, and class are definitely underscored in the *Cheers* narratives.

This analysis discussed three strategies—humor, camaraderie, and detoxification—through which "layers of encoded meaning were constructed into [the] television program" *Cheers* (Fiske, 1987, p. 6). Fiske (1987) explains that television uses a variety of social and technical codes, including camera work, lighting, editing, music, casting, setting, costume, make-up, action, dialogue, and ideology, to create realistic representations. He also notes that television "shows have to serve the economic interests of their producers and distributors, and, as these are capitalistic institutions, their economic interests must be aligned with capitalistic (and patriarchal) ideology" (1991, p. 445). *Cheers'* "drink and make merry" message certainly parallels and serves the economic and ideological interests of the beer producers and the television networks who profit from beer advertising time purchased.

It is important and valuable for critics to understand how audiences read texts, and a variety of methods must be employed to do so. Because survey research such as uses and gratifications, as well as audience effects research, have been scrutinized for their constrained and simplistic responses, more innovative research methods need to be employed to further develop this study. Focus groups that consist of die-hard *Cheers* fans could provide great insights on their experience of watching *Cheers*. The naturalization strategies identified in this work can be "tested" in such focus group discussions to determine whether or not audiences identify the same or other strategies. Contrasting the responses from groups of males to those of groups of females may reveal further evidence to support the naturalization strategy of camaraderie via the male bonding process found in this research. Shaefer and Avery's (1993) essay is one such example of how focus groups can be implemented in research. While the focus groups added depth and revealed insight into their understanding of the talk show *Late Night with David Letterman*, the same can be accomplished with *Cheers* and other television programs. Along with focus groups, audience ethnographies (see, e.g., Ang, 1985; Morley, 1980, Radway, 1985) would also be an appropriate methodology with which to explore audience understandings of the portrayals of beer drinking in the media.

Note

1. Alcohol consumption in the United States is related to 2,000,000 deaths per year, which accounts for 10% of the annual mortality rate ("Message From," 1992). Driving under the influence arrests have increased over time (U.S. Department

of Commerce, 1992). Long and short term abuse of alcohol affect virtually all body systems ("Message From," 1992).

References

Advertising Age. (1992, September 23). [CD ROM]. *World almanac and book of facts.* Crain Communications, Inc.

Ang, I. (1985). *Watching* Dallas: *Soap opera and melodramatic imagination.* New York: Methuen.

Bandura, A. (1977). *Social learning theory.* Englewood Cliffs, NJ: Prentice Hall.

Berger, A. A. (1987). Humor: An introduction. *American Behavioral Scientist, 30*(1), 6–15.

Cafiso, J., Goodstadt, M. S., Garlington, W. K., & Sheppard, M. A. (1982). Television portrayal of alcohol and other beverages. *Journal of Studies on Alcohol, 43,* 1232–1242.

Chagollan, S. (1993, May 17). Audiences say goodbye to old friends at "Cheers." *Broadcasting and Electronic Media,* p. 1.

DeFoe, J. R. & Breed, W. (1986). The family, research, and prime-time television in alcohol education. *International Quarterly of Community Health and Education, 7*(1), 33–40.

DeFoe, J. R., Breed, W., & Breed, L. A. (1983). Drinking on television: A five year study. *Journal of Drug Education, 13*(1), 25–38.

Facts on file. (1991). New York: Facts on file.

Fernandez-Collado, C. F., Greenberg, B. S., Korzenny, F., & Atkin, C. K. (1978). Sexual intimacy and drug use in TV series. *Journal of Communication, 28*(3), 30–37.

Fiske, J. (1984). Popularity and ideology: A structuralist reading of *Dr. Who.* In W. D. Rowland Jr. & B. Watkins (Eds.), *Interpreting television: Current research perspectives* (pp. 165–198). Beverly Hills: Sage.

Fiske, J. (1986). Television: Polysemy and popularity. *Critical Studies in Mass Communication 3,* 391–408.

Fiske, J. (1987). *Television culture.* London: Methuen.

Fiske, J. (1991). The discourses of TV quiz shows, or school + luck = success + sex. In L. R. Vande Berg & L. A. Wenner (Eds.), *Television criticism: Approaches and applications* (pp. 445–462). White Plains, NY: Longman.

Galloway, S. (1990, November 3–9). The gang at *Cheers* toast their most memorable moments. *TV Guide,* pp. 20–25.

Gerbner, G., Gross, L., Morgan, M., & Signorielli, N. (1980). The "mainstreaming" of America: Violence profile no. 11. *Journal of Communication, 30*(3), 10–27.

Gliatto, T. (1990, November 12). The taproom that inspired *Cheers* tries to change its name, until barflies cry, "Bull— & Finch!" *People Weekly,* 81–82.

Gross, L., & Morgan, M. (1985). Television and enculturation. In J. Dominick & J. Fletcher (Eds.), *Broadcasting research methods* (pp. 221–234). Boston: Allyn & Bacon.

Huston, A. C., et al. (1992). *Big world, small screen: The role of television in American society.* Lincoln, NE: University of Nebraska Press.

Krugman, H. E., & Hartley, E. L. (1970). Passive learning from television. *Public Opinion Quarterly, 34,* 184–190.

Kubey, R. W., & Csikzentmihaly, M. (1990). *Television and the quality of life.* Hillsdale, NJ: L. Erlbaum Associates.

Message from the president. (1992, July). Summary of health consequences of alcohol and other drug use, pp. 1–2. [Available from CSUS Division of Student Affairs and Alumni Insurance Agency—Seymour Canter, C.L.U. 6000 J Street, Sacramento, CA.]

Montgomery, K. C. (1989). The Hollywood lobbyists. In K. C. Montgomery (Ed.), *Target: Primetime* (pp. 174–256). New York: Oxford University Press.

Morley, D. (1980). *The nationwide audience: Structure and decoding.* London: British Film Institute.

Palmer, J. (1989). Enunciation and comedy: "Kind Hearts and Coronets." *Screen, 30,* 144–158.

Piccirillo, M. S. (1986). On the authenticity of televisual experience: A critical exploration of parasocial closure. *Critical Studies in Mass Communication, 3,* 337–355.

Radway, J. (1985). Interpretive communities and variable literacies: The functions of romance reading. In M. Gurevitch & M. Levy (Eds.), *Mass communication yearbook, Vol. 5* (pp. 337–361). Beverly Hills: Sage.

Schaefer, R. J., & Avery, R. K. (1993). Audience conceptualizations of *Late Night with David Letterman. Journal of Broadcasting & Electronic Media, 37,* 253–273.

Signorielli, N. (1987). Drinking, sex, and violence on television: The cultural indicators perspective. *Journal of Drug Education, 17,* 245–260.

Strate, L. (1992). Beer commercials: A manual on masculinity. In S. Craig (Ed.), *Men, masculinity, and the media* (pp. 78–92). Newbury Park, CA: Sage.

Tobenkin, D. (1994, April 4). Sitcoms: On a laugh track to profitability. *Broadcasting and Cable,* pp. 15, 18.

U.S. Department of Commerce, Bureau of the Census. (1992). *Statistical Abstract of the United States.* Washington, DC: U.S. Government Printing Office.

Wallack, L., Breed, W., & Cruz, J. (1987). Alochol on prime-time television. *Journal of Studies on Alcohol, 48,* 33–38.

Wallack, L., Grube, J. W., Madden, P. D., & Breed, W. (1990). Portrayals of alcoholism on prime-time television. *Journal of Studies on Alcohol, 51,* 428–437.

Success Defined by Television: The Value System Promoted by *PM Magazine*

Cathy Sandeen

Promoted for its unique production style, syndication arrangement, appeal to regionalism and local community needs, PM Magazine *was a fixture in early evening television throughout the 1980s. But was the program really unique in terms of its overall message? What values did the program promote as being most important? By examining the value system present within a large group of* PM Magazine *stories broadcast during the summer of 1985, a clear picture emerged. The program was hardly just a random mix of upbeat local stories from around the US. Instead,* PM Magazine *emphasized and promoted a dominant personal success value system that revolved around recognition, achievement, financial success, excitement, and physical attributes. Arguably, this value system existed because it appealed to a particular demographic, making the program highly marketable to national advertisers; on a broader level, the value system functioned to reinforce existing traditional and conservative power structures within American society.*

PM Magazine, a 30-minute early evening weekday television program that premiered in 1976, was, ten years after its creation, a fixture in early evening television schedules. Known largely for its upbeat "soft news" style, *PM Magazine* actually contributed many "firsts" to the field of television, from the structure of its production and marketing organization, to its production techniques.

The typical *PM Magazine* feature was a fast paced, brief glimpse at a soft news topic, usually an interview with a celebrity or a feature on a person involved in a humorous, quirky or dangerous situation. The typical feature was composed of a variety of shots, usually set to music. The overall effect was light and entertaining. The soft news orientation was an explicitly stated goal for the program, as expressed in a portion of a *PM Newsletter* from April 1981:

> Send good public affairs topics over to your public affairs department. . . . People watch our show as they are winding down from a hard day at work, after the hard news of the day is over. We want to remind them of what's positive and bright about life. Stories that offer viewers "a look at living with asthma" or "new educational advances for the learning disabled" are turnoffs to our audience. (Turow, 1983, p. 116)

The program formula proved to be so popular in one Westinghouse-owned station that other stations in the ownership group developed their own versions of the show. Eventually, the program became syndicated nationally to a total of 97 stations in the early 1980s and developed a unique national production organization that at any given time included more than 1,000 production personnel. A *PM Magazine* national office press release described the program's evolution:

> In 1976, KPIX, the Group W station in San Francisco, launched what was then considered a risky venture— a nightly, prime time access strip called "Evening Magazine." The locally-produced program was to be the station's alternative to game shows and sit-com re-runs. A year later, the other Group W stations in Baltimore, Boston, Philadelphia, and Pittsburgh premiered their own versions of "Evening Magazine." The rest, as they say, was history.

In September of 1978, one station's bold programming effort evolved into a nationwide cooperative under the title *"PM Magazine,"* and currently boasts a lineup of nearly 80 stations and was frequently rated #1 among all syndicated television programs. (*PM Magazine* National Office, "About *PM Magazine*")

The Production Cooperative

The cooperative production organization of *PM Magazine* was a novel idea and represents one of the major development of U.S. television syndication in the 1980s. *PM Magazine* was not produced by one national production staff as were most magazine feature programs of the time. Instead, personnel at smaller local markets affiliated with the program produced a significant portion of the show. A *PM Magazine* press release described the way the programming cooperative worked:

> When a station joins the *PM* cooperative, it doesn't merely purchase the rights to a series. More importantly, the station gets the right to significantly participate in the production of the series. In addition to providing staff and equipment, the station must supply its own on-air hosts. Each station then chooses from among the national pool of selected stories for inclusion in its own locally produced and assembled program. (*PM Magazine* National Office, "How the Cooperative Works," undated)

The local *PM*-affiliated station also submitted some or all of its locally produced features to the *PM Magazine* national office for possible inclusion on the weekly national reel. The national reel was a week's worth of feature stories, organized into five separate *PM* episodes, along with promotional material for the week, provided to the local *PM*-affiliated stations from which they constructed their own version of the show. Although the *PM Magazine* national office produced some of its own feature stories for inclusion in the national reel, the majority of stories on the national reel were produced by different local stations throughout the country.

Besides providing the staff and equipment and contributing to the national reel, each *PM Magazine* affiliated station also had to pay a licensing fee to the national office. This fee varied according to the size of the station. According to Turow, one station within the top 25 broadcast markets reportedly paid $840 per episode in 1981 (1983, p. 115). In addition, each local station made available at no charge to the *PM Magazine* national office, one 30-second advertising spot from their local market that *PM* in turn sold to national advertisers. For its part of the equation, the *PM Magazine* national office provided its affiliated stations with a national reel of *PM* feature stories each week, advice on how to produce the program as well as promotional materials, music and graphic elements that were incorporated into each local *PM* show.

Promotional material from the *PM Magazine* national office, used to market the program to other stations, emphasized the show's potential contribution to the station's local programming and community service efforts. General managers of sizable television stations around the US who were quoted within the brochure stressed *PM*'s link to a specific locale, as one general manager explained:

> We're proud of our reputation for local and national news coverage. We know our present success, and our future survival, depend upon how well we inform the community we serve. Not only with hard news coverage, good investigative reporting and provocative documentaries. But also with the informative and upbeat content of *PM Magazine*. It's like a nice dessert after a healthy meal of news. (*PM Magazine* National Office, brochure, undated)

Another general manager echoed the sentiment:

> We're delighted to be producing a show using beautiful southern Florida as our stage and the interesting people who live and work here as our cast. *PM Magazine* affords us a handclasp with the community that just can't be found in other programming. The good will generated is proof enough *PM*'s benefits to a station are not measured in dollars. *PM* keeps paying back long after the half-hour is over. (*PM Magazines* National Office, brochure, undated)

Yet another general manager wrote:

> Ours is a television station built on excellence in local informational programming. We recognized *PM Magazine* would contribute to a strong local image when we became the first station to join the *PM Magazine* cooperative five years ago. In today's busy electronic marketplace, that proved to be a wise decision. (*PM Magazine* National Office, brochure, undated)

As a nationally syndicated show, *PM Magazine* received numerous accolades. By 1980, the show had received three "Irises" given by the National Association of Television Program Executives (Droesch, 1980). Nicholas Johnson, a former Federal Communications commissioner, reportedly praised *PM Magazine* as "a point for our side, especially when you look at what else was on" (Droesch, 1980). *Washington Post* television critic Tom Shales, agreed: "they're exemplary as access shows, practically a godsend when compared to what the stations had been running" (Droesch, 1980).

Developmental Factors

Two factors directly or indirectly may have contributed to the development of *PM Magazine*. First, in 1970 the Federal Communications Commission (FCC) issued a regulation called the "Prime Time Access Rule," which sought to increase the number of hours of local programming during the prime time. To do this, the FCC required that television stations in the top 50 markets by size broadcast no more than three hours of network-originated programming each weeknight. Network programming was limited to 7–10 p.m. or 8–11 p.m., depending on the area of the country, leaving the early evening time between the news and the beginning of the network programs free for the local stations to program themselves. Most of the local stations filled this time by purchasing syndicated programs, usually game shows or network reruns. In some cases, however, stations attempted to produce their own local shows to fill in some of the time. *PM Magazine* provided a rather convenient and relatively inexpensive way for a local station to produce a high quality, national-level program to air with its own early evening time slots.

Besides filling a need for non-network programming, another factor, the development of portable video cameras and recording equipment and improvements in videotape editing technology, also contributed to making *PM Magazine* the successful venture it was. The use of outside locations for the entire program, a taken-for-granted technique today, was fresh and novel back in 1976 when the program was first developed. The general manager of KPIX-TV in San Francisco, where the *PM* prototype *Evening Magazine* was produced, admitted,

> There's nothing new about the concept of a magazine show, but our execution was. We did it on all videotape, we did everything outside with no studio work, we used bright young people as hosts and we used flashy editing techniques. It set a pattern that's been copied by many other reality programs across the country. (Buck, 1984, p. 36)

An early *PM Magazine* national executive director elaborated on this point: "We certainly put Sony in business. It was the first show to use 3/4-inch technology in the field, come back, edit it and put it on the air. . . . We made it mandatory that this show be done totally on video, so people had to experience the equipment" (*Broadcast Week*, 1983). The unique mix of upbeat stories that one former national executive producer described as a "show that takes you places" (Droesch, 1980), would not have been possible without the invention of relatively portable video production technology.

To many, *PM*'s main claim to fame appears to have been that it helped stations fulfill certain FCC requirements in effect at the time and it was considered to offer more than the game shows and reruns broadcast during its time slot. Yet, for its time period, *PM*'s ratings were fairly substantial. According to the November 1982 Arbitron syndicated program analysis, which listed 481 syndicated programs, *PM Magazine* was listed as the number one rated of all syndicated programs in the United States.

Naturally, *PM Magazine* was not without its detractors. Most criticism focused on *PM*'s upbeat, what many called "lightweight," approach. Critic Tom Shales articulated this particular criticism: "It's franchised like McDonalds. . . . Just like all airports look alike, all *PM*s look alike" (Droesch, 1980). *San Jose Mercury News* television critic Ron Miller also admitted he watched the program "and my complaint has always been its once-over-lightly approach to things." Despite these complaints, *PM Magazine* was generally considered a highly successful effort that continued to be broadcast until well into 1990.

Value Analysis Approach

The goal of this analysis is to delve beneath the overt "lightweight" content of *PM Magazine* to describe and interpret the underlying value system of the program. The program emerged in a regulatory environment ostensibly designed to increase programming diversity and local or regional involvement in television programming during the early evening time period. Because the program originated from San Francisco, a highly diverse community that tends to embrace alternative lifestyles, and because large portions of the program originated from all across the United States, one would expect to see a broad range of values promoted. On the surface, *PM Magazine* appeared to be vastly different from the network reruns it competed against. But on a deeper, more fundamental level, was *PM* truly diverse in the values it portrayed? What elements defined the value system within *PM Magazine*? What does this value system tell us about what was considered important to certain segments of American culture who watched or produced the program during the spring of 1985, a high point in the program's evolution?

Value analysis is an especially useful tool to recognize and describe patterns within a text like *PM Magazine*. Because it allows the critic to focus on messages inherent beneath the surface of many other program elements, value analysis helps to make sense of a message that at first seems to lack cohesiveness. Value analysis provides several additional specific advantages for the critic.

First, values are everywhere. Value analysis begins with the assumption that people inherently attach a value or varying degree of importance to what they encounter. Robin Williams (1982) elaborated on this point:

> Values merge affect and concept. Persons are not detached or indifferent to the world; they do not stop with a sheerly factual view of their experience. Explicitly or implicitly, they are continually regarding things as good or bad, pleasant or unpleasant, beautiful or ugly, appropriate or inappropriate, true or false, virtues or vices. (Rokeach, 1979, p. 16)

Both from the perspective of those people involved in creating the *PM Magazine* message and from the perspective of the viewers "consuming" the message, such value assignments constantly occur. Within the *PM Magazine* text, certain topics, elements, and ideas were included more than were other topics, elements, and ideas. Selection, ordering, and emphasis can be determined directly from the text itself.

The approach is also useful because values represent a relatively finite group of core ideas. Milton Rokeach defined a value as "an enduring belief that a specific mode of conduct or end-state of existence is personally or socially preferable to alternate modes of conduct or end-states of existence" (1968, p. 160). These modes of conduct or end states of existence are most commonly recognized in explicitly stated value terms like *freedom, equality, courage,* and *progress.*

More commonly, however, value statements are implied through other statements and elements and the critic must dig to uncover them. For example, a group of stories that contains a preponderance of positive values over negative values may be said to imply *optimism.* Television programming that contains an abundance of statistical or numerical evidence could be said to imply the values of *reasonableness* or *rationality.* Whether directly expressed or implied through other elements, values can be recognized in texts and described.

A major advantage of value analysis is that it allows a critic to distill from a broad textual base that spans a variety of subject areas (like *PM Magazine*) a manageable number of core ideas or values for analysis. Rokeach observed that "an adult probably has tens or hundreds of thousands of beliefs, but only dozens of values" (1968, p. 124). Value analysis focuses on the "dozens of values" available within a text.

Even though value analysis allows the critic to reduce the core ideas of a text into manageable proportions, it still provides the means for building a rich analysis. The goal is to identify not only the individual values present, but also the values not present and the priorities and relationships among values—what is generally referred to as "defining a

value system." Individual value terms tend to cluster together as a beginning point for describing how combinations of values exist within a text in a deep and complex way.

By conducting a value analysis of a particular text within a culture, the critic is also identifying values of importance to the culture—or more frequently the subculture—that produces or uses the message. In this way, a close value analysis of a text makes a statement beyond the text itself. Nevertheless, value analysis does not require the critic to stray far from the text. As Patricia Ganer has observed, value analysis does not "require that one get into the minds" of the source of the text to analyze the text or the culture (1988, p. 15). A number of critics have used forms of value analysis to understand a variety of texts, including children's literature (Field & Weiss, 1987), baseball stories (Dagavarian, 1987), investigative journalism (Glasser & Ettema, 1989, 1994); broadcast and print news operations (Gans, 1979); Tuchman 1978); newspaper sportswriting (Trujillo & Ekdom, 1985), presidential debates (Ganer, 1988), and other television programming (Gitlin, 1983; Stein, 1979).

Textual Base and Critical Orientation

This analysis is based on 225 individual *PM Magazine* feature stories, representing thirteen weeks (April through June 1985) of the *PM Magazine* national reel. Each "reel" is actually two hours of videotape and contains approximately twenty feature stories per reel (each ranging from three to five minutes in length) along with promotional advertisements for the week.[1]

This study did not rely upon an existing inventory of American values to use as a standard against which to "measure" *PM Magazine.* The basic critical orientation was to allow values to emerge directly from the text itself. Yet, it is essential to familiarize oneself with values uncovered in texts by other critics prior to embarking on a value analysis. Applicable to this analysis of *PM,* for instance, Malcolm Sillars (1991, p. 14) described a common value system reflected in American culture that he labeled the "personal success value system." Sillars argued that this value system was implied in terms like career, health, family, recreation, economic security, among other terms (141). Though they studied cultural values people acknowledged via self-report data rather than values reflected in cultural texts, Robert Bellah, *et al.* (1986, p. 21), also discussed a potent mix of contemporary American values, similar to Sillars' "personal success value system," that revolved around the pursuit of individual happiness and financial success, or what the authors called "radical individualism" (21). Ultimately, these and similar values appeared in *PM Magazine* to varying degrees.

Few Americans would fail to recognize terms like "equality," "freedom" and "courage" as core values, yet within *PM Magazine*, and many other artifacts of contemporary popular culture, values terms are rarely stated directly. Instead, values are implied by informational statements, by visuals emphasized in the story, by clothing worn and by a myriad of other elements that, taken individually, do not assign a value to a final goal or mode of conduct. Taken together, these seemingly minute elements combine in such a way that the critic can argue persuasively that the elements do place a value on an end state or mode of conduct. How does the critic identify those elements that might contribute to the value system?

Formal Elements

A number of different formal elements besides direct value statements were noted, including general subject and the length of each feature. Certain values may be implied by patterns or emphasis in topics covered. Longer stories naturally represent a certain degree of emphasis over shorter stories. However, certain values may take on prominence through means other than length of the story that contained the value. For example, a strong negative value like *death* or *failure* may be used as an opposing value to emphasize positive values like *life* or *success*. The strong, emotion-provoking negative value both calls attention to and emphasizes the corresponding positive value. People represented in the features for their approximate age,

gender, and ethnicity also were examined and noted. Certain values can be inferred through patterns in such representations. Or, a group of stories that ignores certain ethnic groups may be said to imply a negative value of *inequality*.

Production variables such as the number of locations in each feature, the number of people interviewed, the form of narration used, whether special effects were included, and where and how music or sound effects were incorporated into the feature were noted as well as were forms of argument or evidence used within each story. For the most part, *PM* stories were structured in a fairly straightforward way, presenting evidence or information relating to particular situations. Some stories included a noticeable preponderance of numerical or statistical evidence. This form of information was out of the ordinary. Certain forms of argument or evidence tended to correspond to certain values. For example, a statement supported by numerical evidence might imply a positive value of *reason*.

Individual Values

In viewing the *PM Magazine* stories, I focused most of my attention on value statements. The vast majority of the *PM Magazine* stories did reflect at least one easily recognizable value and most of them reflected two or three values.

Occasionally, a story contained a directly stated value. For example, a story that featured the founder of the organization, Mothers Against Drunk Driving, contained a number of stated values. In the story, the woman declared: "Finally, someone here realizes the value of human life and for once we're putting that right, that value, ahead of the right of the individual."

More often than not, values were implied through other types of statements. An example of implied values was a story that featured a pair of six-year-old twin models. The introductory narration to the story contained the statement: "They're identical twins, six-year-old bundles of energy. . . . [They're] handled by the prestigious Ford agency, and over the last two years, they've landed assignments in enough prominent magazines to make many a grown model envious. Their potential to earn lots of money is tremendous." Phrases like "the prestigious Ford agency," "prominent magazines," and "potential to earn lots of money," along with other story elements, strongly imply the positive values of professional *achievement* and *financial success*.[2]

Whether a value was expressed in positive or negative terms was also noted. Most values within *PM Magazine* were predominantly positive. For instance, within a celebrity interview story, one actress stated: "*Knotts Landing* has brought me a lot of nice things, a lot of financial rewards and therefore a wonderful kind of peace of mind." This statement promoted the value of *financial success* or *happiness* as a positive goal toward which to aspire.

Somewhat less often, values would be stated in negative terms. A negative value was contained in the narration of a story about a young man who commutes on a kayak to his job in downtown Chicago: "For six miles to the mouth of the Chicago River, [the man featured] cuts through the Great Lake's power and escapes the grit and grime of big city life." The phrase "grit and grime of big city life," along with other elements in the story, implied the negative values of pollution and overpopulation and further implied the negative elements of *progress*.

Whether a value defined an end state or a mode of conduct, two terms developed by Rokeach, was also noted. Rokeach used "terminal" for values that referred to final goals and "instrumental" for values that referred to modes of conduct. In her study of values in arguments used in the 1980 presidential campaign, Ganer (1988) examined the relationship of terminal and instrumental values and how different emphases and relationships among instrumental and terminal values contributed to the effectiveness of a candidate's message. For example, Ganer concluded that

Reagan placed a great deal of emphasis on terminal values while both Anderson and Carter gave most of their consideration to instrumental values. Since the instrumental values are only a means to an end, it is not surprising to expect a public to be more concerned about the ends themselves (1988, p. 214)

Within *PM Magazine*, the relationship between instrumental and terminal values also played a role in helping to define the value system.

Defining the Value System

Identifying values, whether they are stated or implied, positive or negative, terminal or instrumental, is just an initial step in a value analysis. Within this interpretive stage, the critic must develop a persuasive argument that defines a complex system or arrangement of values within the text under examination. Recognizing patterns among values, developing an argument about values that are emphasized and given more priority, describing the relationship between instrumental and terminal values and role of formal elements—supported by numerous examples of the text itself—are important steps in the process.

In the case of *PM Magazine*, after repeated careful viewing of each story, a system of values emerged quite clearly. By far, the most prevalent values present in the program centered on the individual: *personal and financial success, professional achievement*, and *material acquisition*. Subordinate clusters of values included *family, happiness, relationships, individuality, community*, and *compassion*.

Personal Success Values

The dominant cluster of values found within the *PM Magazine* stories examined revolved around the idea of *personal success*, articulated through constant use of terms, images, and production techniques that promoted *recognition, financial success, professional success, physical attributes* (for women), *excitement* and *power* (for men), and, to a lesser degree, *happiness, family*, and *relationships*.

Recognition was given a strong voice in a large portion of the *PM* stories. Within the stories that focused on entertainment topics, *recognition* was expressed through the quest for or achievement of fame and celebrity status. Common phrases like "becoming a star," "signing autographs," or "having a hit movie" directly articulated the *recognition* value and were emphasized repeatedly.

A model or a designer achieved *recognition* by appearing on the cover of popular fashion or women's magazines like *Vogue* or *Cosmopolitan*. Certain clothing or hair styles were consistently described as "the latest," "the hottest," "best selling," and similar superlatives. In a group of sports and action stories, terms like "the bravest," "the finest," "world-class climbers," "number two in the world," and the like were used to boost the status of the people and activities featured. Even the rather dubious sport of racing cars and trucks through mud, called "mud racing," was described within the context of a *PM Magazine* story as "the fastest-growing off-road motor sport in America," thereby assigning a high degree of status to a relatively marginal activity.

Not surprisingly, *financial success* was also an integral part of the *personal success* group of values. Entertainment stories emphasized highly-paid television actors and established their wealth through inventories of expensive personal possessions such as large homes, artwork, grand pianos, and Jacuzzi bathtubs. A substantial group of stories also described and promoted expensive items, activities, or travel destinations, such as Rolls Royce automobiles, thoroughbred race horses, caviar, expensive clothing and perfume, and vacations in French chateaux or at exclusive spa resorts.

For example, "Paris Party" centered on the 30-year anniversary party for the Paris nightclub Regine's. An aura of exclusivity and wealth was established in the opening narration: "People flew in from around the world" to attend the party, and "anyone who is anyone is here at [Regine's] Paris club." *Financial success* was further implied in statements that defined Regine, the owner of the club, as a "success story" who "makes life fantasy" by sharing "opulence" and the "good life" with her jet-set customers. Videotaped footage taken inside the club featured numerous celebrities with recognizable symbols of the "good life": an abundance of sequined dresses, jewelry, tuxedos, and champagne.

In another story, "Summer Estates," a tour of multimillion-dollar mansions on New York's Long Island, also implied a value of *financial success*. Phrases within the story such as "certain level of lifestyle" and "exclusive beach community favored by the internationally famous and the wildly wealthy" reinforced the *financial success* theme.

The narrator toured several beach-front mansions that were selling for several million dollars and that rented for $65,000 to $75,000 for the summer months only. Other terms like "exclusive," "wealth," and "success" were used frequently throughout the story, and the visuals—shots of fabulous homes and private tree-lined drives—recorded from the back seat of a large Mercedes Benz added weight to this value.

Similarly, "Ultimate Auto," a look inside the factory where Rolls Royce automobiles are manufactured, further underscored the *financial success* value in a very direct and explicit way. The narrator described the car as a "symbol of success," "the best in the world," "as far as you can go," and "the top of the line." *Wealth, success* and *"social position"* dominated the story both through language used as well as visual techniques, such as numerous closeup shots of some of the expensive materials used in making Rolls Royce automobiles—gleaming chrome and velvety leather. Even though other traditional values—*quality, pride of workmanship, heritage* and *reputation*—were promoted to a certain degree within "Ultimate Auto," the dominant value stressed *wealth* and especially *financial success*.

A story called "Fallon Returns" featured an interview with Emma Samms, a young actress from the primetime serial, *Dynasty*. Set in Samms' Los Angeles condominium, the story opened with a description of Emma's big break, "moving up with the big boys to ABC's number-one primetime soap." The narration mentioned that Samms, like many young hopefuls in Hollywood, "put in time as a waitress" before getting her "big break" as an actress.

The viewer was taken on a tour of Samms'

home, including shots of her white grand piano, her works of art and the sunken Jacuzzi tub in her bathroom. A brief segment focused on the relationship between Samms and her boyfriend (himself a popular daytime serial actor). The story closed with a segment of Samms taking an ice skating lesson with friends. The narrator reminded the viewer that Samms was encouraged to take up ice skating by her "buddy, Olympic gold medalist, Scott Hamilton." As the viewer watched Samms skating, the narrator reported that "Emma's life is progressing nicely."

Success was defined in a number of ways within this story: explicit descriptions of *financial success;* a contrast between higher and lower socioeconomic status; and, of course, *optimism* linked to *financial success*. The narration included numerous references to Samms' "financial independence" expressed as a positive quality. The portion of the story that inventoried Samms' possessions, both visually and through the accompanying narration or interview segments, further reinforced the *financial success* value. Samms did not live in just any old condominium, but rather a "post LA condo." The possessions featured within the story (the piano, art, and Jacuzzi) functioned as symbols of *luxury* and *success,* a visual shorthand that appeared repeatedly within *PM Magazine*.

Like the "Fallon Returns" story, the celebrity interview story called "Dynasty Princess," featured an interview with a young star of another prime-time serial and also reflected *financial success, optimism* as well as other related values. The story centered on an interview with Catherine Oxenberg, the *Dynasty* actress who played Joan Collins's daughter, technically a "real" princess because her mother is an exiled Yugoslavian princess. Other information revealed within the story included a description of Oxenberg's youth in England and her close contact with celebrities like Richard Burton and Elizabeth Taylor. Viewers learned that Oxenberg was accepted into Harvard University but chose instead to pursue a modeling career. The viewer was shown cutaway shots of Oxenberg posing for a magazine photo shoot in glamorous makeup and gown.

In this story, as in the Emma Samms's interview, *financial success* and high socioeconomic status were positive values. But unlike the feature on Emma Samms, in this interview of Catherine Oxenberg, the *financial success* value was more implicit than explicit.

Having a British accent, having a title (especially that of "princess"), having been raised with famous celebrity friends around, and having been accepted to an ivy-league school implied high socioeconomic status. The royal theme was reinforced in a more subtle way by the use of royal fanfare music throughout the story. Although the shots showing Oxenberg wearing expensive clothing and jewelry, modeling for a famous fashion magazine, did positively promote the *financial success* value to a certain degree, for the most part within this story Oxenberg's own personal *financial* or other *success* brought from her role on *Dynasty* was not emphasized. Instead, the idea of long standing "old money," a form of *financial success* brought about by her privileged upbringing took prominence. *Financial success* was implied rather than explicitly described, as was the actual source (a family trust fund or her own salary?) of Oxenberg's *financial success*.

Interestingly, in one interview segment, Oxenberg seemed to contradict the importance of *wealth, class status,* and *luck* in favor of personal *initiative* and *equal opportunity*. Oxenberg stated that "anyone can be a princess" but that she was proud that she "achieved something through talent." This naive comment contained a strong assertive statement reflecting on *achievement* and *ability* over *luck* and *privilege*. However, the statement also appeared greatly out of context within the remainder of the story that promoted a different set of values. For one, the story stated Oxenberg chose to pursue a modeling career, a path that naturally glorifies certain physical attributes, over attending Harvard University, a path that represents a relatively high level of *intellectual achievement* and ability. Oxenberg's own reported choice in this case represented rejecting an arena in which participants have more equal opportunities for *academic achievement* and *success* and embracing an arena in which a more random arrangement of physical characteristics that define the current notion of "beauty" prevailed.

The "Dynasty Princess" and "Fallon Returns" stories were representative examples of *PM* stories that positively promoted *financial success*. At seemingly every opportunity within these stories, the viewer was reminded that Oxenberg and Samms and many others were not like us. These two young women were richer, more beautiful, more successful, had more famous friends and luxurious belongings. Like the primetime serials on which they were cast members, the Oxenberg and Samms interviews provided viewers of *PM Magazine* an escape from their more dreary lifestyles to a place where "fairy tales come true."

Besides *financial success, professional achievement* was another important element within the *personal success* value system. Within those stories that focused on career and work, *recognition* was expressed more in response to concrete professional activities, rather than as an element of achieving the vaguer appellation of "celebrity status." "Pavarotti the Great," an interview with the opera singer Luciano Pavarotti, was such a story. Pavarotti was a well-known opera singer, rather than the more typical film or television star more often singled out for attention in *PM Magazine*. The story was constructed around an on-camera interview with the singer, intercut with film or videotape footage of past performances and a brief segment about Pavrotti's past.

Success, achievement, and *professional satisfaction* were established by contrasting Pavarotti's present professional achievements with his humble beginnings. Pavarotti was the son of a baker in Italy. He became a teacher, then an insurance salesman before achieving his tremendous success as an opera singer. Professional *achievement* through *work* and *discipline* was emphasized over other possible values.

Recognition, financial success, and *achievement* are, by and large, terminal values or end states. Patterns in instrumental values, or values that provide guidance about how to attain desired end states, also emerged from the *PM* stories. *Work* often

emerged as a significant instrumental value. An interview with the actor, Michael Douglas, for example, emphasized the *work ethic* and *discipline* necessary to succeed. *Work, discipline,* and *training* were principal values in stories that emphasized athletic endeavors and military action. *Recognition, financial success,* and *achievement* were often strongly linked to *work, discipline,* and *training*.

In direct contrast with *work, discipline,* and *training,* the instrumental value of *optimism* was also given strong voice within *PM Magazine* stories. The stories analyzed contained numerous examples of a celebrity's career framed in terms of "a dream come true," a "big break," a "fairy tale come true," or "a rags-to-riches story." Stories about successful business entrepreneurs or lottery winners implicitly contained *optimism* as a key value. The stress on positive values over negative values overall within the value system also implied *optimism*.

The *personal success* range of values with *PM Magazine* stories emphasized the values of *recognition, financial success, achievement, progress, work, discipline, training* and *optimism*. However, other subordinate important values also functioned within the *personal success* group of values—*happiness, family, relationships, physical attributes* (for women), and *excitement* and *power* (for men)—and deserve more detailed discussion as well.

Success Defined by Happiness, Family, and Relationships

Surprisingly, the values *happiness, family,* and *relationships* were most strongly articulated in a group of celebrity interview stories, the same group of stories that also promoted *recognition, financial success,* and *achievement*. These values also called attention to themselves, because they seem somewhat out of place within the cohesive materialistic version of *personal success* in *PM Magazine*.

The values of *recognition, financial success,* and, to a lesser degree, *achievement* were more often implied through topic or other program elements or directly expressed through narration rather than directly expressed by the celebrity him or herself. When it came to *happiness, family,* and *relationships,* however, *PM* stories appeared to have been edited to allow the celebrity to articulate the values in a clear and direct way. An interview with Michelle Lee, an actress in another primetime serial, *Knotts Landing,* was a good example of such a link. The narrator introduced Lee with the observation that with her role in *Knotts Landing,* "big success has finally come to the actress." The interview was set in the actress' home where viewers got a "tour," via the camera, including the *PM*-style inventory of traditional icons of financial success.

Moreover, within interview segments, Lee was open and direct about her *financial success:* "[my career] has brought me a lot of nice things, a lot of financial rewards and therefore a wonderful kind of peace of mind that a lot of people don't get to have," and "I don't have to *work* again in my life— ever!" In the story Lee was also quick to add, "of course it [financial success] doesn't bring happiness."

Like many *PM Magazine* celebrity interview stories, *financial success* was an explicitly and positively stated value. Both the narration and interview segments with Lee herself reflected values and beliefs that promoted the idea of *financial success* as a valuable end state. However, this story also explicitly promoted the positive value of personal *happiness* and *satisfaction* as something toward which to aspire in addition to *financial success.*

Happiness and *satisfaction* were certainly positive terminal values, values that, ideally, everyone, regardless of financial status, can achieve. The overall message portrayed in most *PM Magazine* celebrity interview stories, however, emphasized the *financial success* values over the personal *happiness* and *satisfaction* values. *Financial success* values were often more prominent in the stories, due both to number and prominence of references to *financial success.* In addition, *financial success* and *happiness* were linked in this story; Lee herself connected the two values in her statement that financial rewards bring "a wonderful kind of peace of mind."

Family also emerged as a component of personal success. An interview with Christopher Reeve, called "Closeup on Superman," addressed the *family* value in an explicit way. Set in a sumptuous living room or hotel suite, long before his debilitating accident, Reeve pondered the dilemmas of becoming a celebrity, focusing on the changes he felt in his own life once he became a father: "I'll trade security for adventure any day of the week. . . . Once you have children, other values take over."

In this way, *family* and *security* were overt values within "Closeup on Superman." But the audience was also reminded of Reeve's many expensive hobbies like sailing and glider flying. The setting of the interview communicated an aura of wealth. Viewers were reminded of the actor's success; he's one of the "hottest box office attractions." Like many other *PM* stories, although interview segments emphasized the importance of *family* and *happiness,* the viewer took away the implicit message that such happiness can best and most easily be achieved when one has the financial wherewithal a role in a box-office hit will bring.

These and similar stories that stressed *happiness* were often strongly linked to other values such as *financial success* and *achievement.* Certainly, one may argue, it is easy to focus on concerns such as *happiness* and *family* once the more traditional trappings of professional middle-class life are assured. However, direct statements about *happiness, family,* and *relationships* appeared with so much regularity within the *PM Magazine* stories; they could not be that easily dismissed.

Success for Men in *PM Magazine*

The *personal success* group of values within *PM Magazine* also contained elements of some additional values: *physical attributes, excitement,* and *power.* These values were strongly segregated along gender lines.

Excitement and *power* were promoted as an element of *success* and were overwhelmingly associated with men and men's activities. Story selection emphasized inherently exciting and action-oriented topics. Dangerous sports like cliff diving and rock climbing were featured. Stories featuring less dangerous sports, such as bicycle riding or surfing, increased the *excitement* and *power* level by framing the sport in highly competitive terms—cross-country bicycle races and world-class surfing competitions. Military and police stories contained footage of training sessions or special reenactments involving flooding, shooting, and rampaging fires that, again, tended to increase the action and excitement inherent within the stories. Of course, the nature of the television medium itself encourages a certain degree of excitement through the visuals incorporated in much of its content. Whatever the reason, within *PM* highly suspenseful treatments of the topics of Big Foot or Mount St. Helens' served to increase the excitement level associated with these stories to an even greater degree.

In addition, certain production decisions, like a preponderance of exterior footage, extreme camera angles, rapid editing, and the use of rock music, also served to increase the perception of *excitement* and *power* within a significant number of stories. Forms of argument and evidence stressed the value of *reasonableness. Reasonableness,* linked with *excitement* and *power,* tended to lend credibility to the activities featured.

Although many of the stories within the action category included value statements that revolved around a certain definition of *personal success,* many stories within this category seemed to ignore *personal success.* Instead, they contained the terminal value of attaining *an exciting life* as a principal value statement.

"Tall Trucks" was one such story. At under two minutes in length, this was a relatively brief story that centered around pickup trucks that have been modified by the addition of extra large tires. The story opened with a montage of closeup shots of truck components, set to rock and roll music, while the narrator began: "Car crunchers, mud racers, monster mashers . . . they jack 'em up so high, they're anything but practical; . . . everybody's talking about the latest thing in wheels—at least in Texas!" Dynamic names like "car crunchers" as well

as drawing a distinction between the tall trucks featured in the story and the value *practicality,* were good examples of how many *PM Magazine* stories glorified a quest for excitement in even a short and relatively simple story.

"Radio Racers" was another brief (less than three-minute) *PM Magazine* story in which the positive value of *excitement* predominated. This story began with closeup, slow motion shots of race cars circling a dirt track. The shots were set to loud rock music. The camera cut to a shot of a person holding one of the cars, revealing that the cars were really miniature radio-controlled race cars.

Excitement and *competition* were emphasized within the story. Brief interview segments with some of the spectators of the race expressed the excitement and competition angle. One fan said, "I think it's fun because you get to see them crash." Another stated, "I like the jumps the best." These statements were followed with cuts to closeup shots of the cars' crashing and jumping. The narrator reinforced this theme: "winners, jumps, crashes—this is what they come to see." The story concluded with the progress of the championship race series. The narrator summed it up: "Competition is so heavy, the atmosphere so intense, the fans are getting just what they came for." As in many of the *PM Magazine* stories, *excitement* was the core value implied through narration, interview segments, camera and editing techniques, and sound.

A story called "Off the Edge" also emphasized *excitement.* "Off the Edge" featured two brothers, Xavier and Christophe, whom the narrator identified as "two of the [French] Alps' most able hang gliders." The story contained spectacular videotape footage of hang gliders soaring through the French Alps. Xavier and Christophe had "devised a way to make it possible for ordinary groundlings to experience what up till now only their eyes has seen." Essentially, the brothers had created a way to "piggy-back" another person down to the valley floor in their hang gliders.

The story showed one of the camera operators join in on a tandem hang glider ride. The narrator reinforced the positive feeling *excitement* communicated in part by acknowledging the negative, dangerous aspects of the activity: "Imagine it's your turn to take the giant step with Christophe. You've never done anything like this in your life and as you secure your skis, your heart pounds so hard your chest hurts." Visuals showed the camera operator taking off in the hang glider and included videotape footage taken from the hang glider itself on the trip down. After the uneventful trip down to the valley floor, the camera operator was interviewed on camera, again emphasizing *excitement:* "Hanging in space with nothing around me—I've been in a lot of small planes, but nothing like this." Through selection of the topic itself, to the visuals, sound, and narration that accompanied the story, like other stories that focused on athletic competition, the quest for *excitement* was a dominant value.

Excitement and *power* took the place of *financial success,* creating a hybrid of *personal success* within these male-oriented action stories. Principal values included *recognition, achievement, excitement,* and *power.* These values were associated almost completely with men. Men were active, outdoors, doing important work protecting others from military invasion, crime, and fire.

Further, this group of stories focused entirely on external activities or on reasonable, logical arguments and clearly avoided the self reflection and degree of emotionalism present in many other stories. The men featured in action stories did not talk about their personal satisfaction or *happiness,* nor did they reflect on the importance of *family* or *relationships* at all.

In fact, the men featured within the action stories were remarkably unemotional. Language employed within many male-oriented stories served effectively to "de-emotionalize" potentially highly charged situations. Within a story about the Los Angeles Police Department anti-terrorist squad, or SWAT team, this strategy was obvious. The SWAT team leader used the terms "neutralize them" or "surgical shooting" in place of terms "maiming" or "killing." Even stories that focused on dangerous sports adopted a similar *reasonable* approach to emotional situations.

Within the *PM* value system, men were shown involved with exciting, active work. *Danger* and *lack of security* were present but were implied to be controllable, largely through the use of unemotional, sanitized terms and language. Women were completely uninvolved with this important work.

Success for Women in *PM Magazine*

Whereas *personal success* for men was defined by the values of *recognition, achievement, excitement,* and *power,* influenced by conservative notions of the proper male role, *personal success* for women took on a different dimension. *Recognition, financial success,* and *achievement* were dominant values related to [male] *personal success,* but for women, these values tended to be linked to *physical attributes.*

Physical attributes were emphasized by story selection; a large number of the stories focused on professions such as modeling, acting, and dancing, that very often require specific *physical attributes* for women to be successful. Other story elements reinforced careful scrutiny of a woman's physical characteristics. The stories that focused on men, even male models, came nowhere near to the level of physical inspection rampant in stories about women.

A story called "Playmate Revealed" is a good example. From the selection of this particular topic for the national reel and the values automatically associated with *Playboy* magazine, to the numerous shots of the women featured as she posed in a bathing suit, *physical attributes* were the predominant value statement.

"Bikini Queen," a story about a bathing suit designer, illustrated the strong presence of the *physical attributes* value as well. Even though this story ostensibly was about the design and business accomplishments of a slightly overweight woman in her fifties, the main message of this story, as implied through the visuals, was that the most valuable attribute one should strive for is a beautiful, tall, thin, tanned body. The selection of this specific story topic, coupled with numerous shots of models in bikinis, glorified *physical attributes.* The designer's business and design acumen were dramatically overshadowed by the stress on *physical attributes* that featured designer herself clearly did not possess. Within the *PM Magazine* value system, it is not what one does that is important; it is how one looks.

Further, the *PM* stories glorified only a limited range of desirable *physical attributes*. With the exception of the rare male model, the child models in "Twin Terrors," and another story on baby models, most of the models featured in *PM Magazine* were women. Specifically, the stories focused on women who were young, tall, blonde, white, with long hair, long legs, and trim but curvaceous bodies. Women who deviated from these characteristics were specifically singled out for additional scrutiny. In "Playmate Revealed," an interview segment with a *Playboy* magazine photographer called attention to the fact that the model featured in the story, was unique from most other "Playmates" because she was brunette rather than blonde. Another story called "Petite Elite" specifically focused on a modeling agency that marketed models 5'7" tall or less.

Women within these stories were also subjected to intense, almost microscopic inspection of their physical characteristics. A modeling agent in "Petite Elite" mentioned that the proportion of body parts, specifically the relative size of legs, torso and arms rather than height determined success in modeling for print advertisements. In "Playmate Revealed," the photographer who was interviewed in the story analyzed the model's "exotic" facial features in great detail. One story featured two models, one who specialized in hand display modeling and another who specialized in lingerie modeling. The story included a detailed inventory of characteristics that contribute to beautiful hands: smooth skin, long fingers and long fingernails and fingernail polish. The lingerie model went so far as to reveal her bra size on camera. Weight, specifically maintaining a low weight, was strongly implied in the large amount of footage of thin (and in the case of the "Riviera Bikini" story, clearly anorexic) models and placed a positive value on *thinness*. The value of *thinness* was more explicitly addressed in "Bikini Queen." Within the story, the featured

bikini designer punctuated the importance of a good body: "I think ladies from the age of 16 to about 45 or 50 could wear our suits [pause], ah, women that really keep themselves intact."

Certain production techniques used routinely within *PM Magazine* reinforced the intense scrutiny of and subsequent glorification of *physical attributes*. Many of the stories, especially the modeling and fashion designer stories, opened with a montage of shots, edited together to rock music, composed of closeup shots of various body parts—face, eyes, lips, hair, legs, breasts, and so forth. This technique focused on individual physical attributes in an extremely graphic manner and implicitly communicated that the whole was of less value than was a collection of individual body parts. Another visual technique, a slow pan or tilt across the model's body with the camera lens zoomed into a closeup shot, also emphasized physical attributes by focusing the viewer's attention on relatively minute details of a model's body.

In a somewhat different, but equally demeaning way, the story, "Dream Teen," equated a young female model with a commodity. An interview segment with the model's New York–based modeling agent revealed this element: "For us to try to create a career is very costly in terms of the investment on our part. So we're very careful of who we take into this agency and we would not have her in this agency if she wasn't going to be a star."

As discussed previously, many *PM Magazine* stories focused on *professional achievement* and *success*. Although this was also true for stories about women within *PM Magazine*, the range of professions available to women was severely restricted. Women were shown primarily as actresses, models, dancers, or fashion designers. Success within these professions was strongly linked to how a woman looked.

A separate story about yet another female bathing suit designer, went a step deeper into the psyche of American women by articulating a strong link between certain physical characteristics and a woman's self-esteem. Like others, this story was punctuated by numerous camera shots of very tall, thin, and blonde models while the designer commented that when a woman wears one of her designs, "the woman feels she is the most beautiful on the beach" and "the woman is happy as she wears it." Because of the attention given to the models in the story, the subtext of the designer's comments might be, "the woman is happy as she wears it" as long as she looks like the models in this story; and conversely, if the woman does not look like the models (more than likely the case), the woman cannot be happy.

The focus on women's *physical characteristics* echo many of the observations about an American "beauty myth" popularized by Wolf (1991) and others. Since the late 1960s, American women have received a constant and strong cultural inoculation that makes them feel ugly by promoting a specific beauty ideal through images in popular culture, through advertising claims to sell products, through public relations efforts promoting cosmetic surgery, and through court cases codifying employment discrimination on the basis of a woman's appearance. This inoculation has reinforced the notion that *ideal beauty* is necessary for employment, marriage, and happiness—and that anything less than this ideal represented a severe character flaw.

Not surprisingly, elements of this cultural trend were clearly present within *PM Magazine*. The heavy emphasis on women involved in beauty professions, particularly fashion modeling, sent a strong message to women about the relationship between appearance and earning potential. Even though the professional, middle-class view predominated *PM*, the program may actually function to lower the professional aspirations of women who use the show by promoting members of the highly paid display professions above all other possible professions.

Individuality Values

Personal success in all its permutations—*financial success* and *professional achievement* and the special definitions of *personal success* for men and women—was the overwhelmingly dominant voice within *PM Magazine*. Nevertheless, three subordi-

nate groupings of values, *individuality, community,* and *compassion* did emerge to a certain degree as well.

The *personal success* range of values revolved around *individualism*—the strong focus on the self, de-emphasizing any attachments to a broader social context. Although related to *individualism, individuality,* as the term is employed here, is synonymous with *eccentricity* and the *freedom* to be oneself and to do what one pleases.

In contrast, the *individualism* reflected in the dominant *personal success* values in many ways imposed the opposite of *individuality*. The elements of *personal success*—professional level employment and the material manifestations of *success*—actually required a high level of *conformity* to achieve *success*. In some portions of the *PM Magazine* national reel, however, a different form of *success*—not linked to a certain job or certain material possessions—began to emerge.

A small group of stories focused on people who were clearly not members of the professional middle class or who were not famous celebrities from the entertainment industry. But these "average" people were not average in all respects. Like other types of *PM* stories, many of the people featured in the show were shown at their jobs. Rather than professional-level employment, the jobs featured in some of the stories tended to be from a lower socioeconomic class or were interesting because they were inherently unusual jobs rather than highly paid jobs.

For example, jobs featured included the owner of a small locksmith shop; an announcer in a New York train station; a small town librarian; a small town mail carrier; and a woman who earned her living by pitching to men in exhibition baseball games, to name a few. These people did not represent members of the professional middle class. They were not featured to promote *work, self-discipline, financial success,* masculine *power* or feminine *beauty* to any great degree. These people were featured because they were unique. They did not fit the standard *PM* definition of *success.*

A story called "Eagle Express" exemplified the interplay between *freedom* and *individuality.* The story featured an artist who traveled around the country in a special bus that had been adapted to include a home-made glass enclosure around the front portion of the vehicle, making it look like, as the narrator put it, "an antique spaceship." The narration revealed the artist began to build his "dream bus" after a fire destroyed his home, studio, and all his possessions. The artist featured in the story was not employed in a traditional job, but traded drawings for food and other necessities. Reinforced by choices in music (Willie Nelson's "On the Road Again") and visuals of wide open spaces, "Eagle Express" stressed *individuality*—in the sense of having the *freedom* to "do one's own thing."

"Capping the Stars" featured an individual with a quirky hobby, a woman who knitted personalized ski caps that she sent to show business personalities in exchange for an autographed photograph. This story included panning shots of walls filled with black and white glossy photographs of various celebrities and public figures, including the Pope. The woman reported she had knitted three hats per week and estimated that 50 per cent of the people she'd sent hats to responded to her request for a photo and autograph.

Another classic *PM* story within this genre was "Rainbow House," a story about a "former barnstormer and construction worker and now house painter extraordinaire." The man featured had painted his house, alternating horizontal stripes on red, green, yellow, blue, and white, using over 1,000 cans of spray paint in the process. The story began with a panning shot of a fairly typical urban or suburban, lower middle class neighborhood. As the camera panned across the uniform gray and white houses, it finally stopped at the uniquely painted residence.

The story provided additional details about the featured house: the multicolored gas meter; the interior of the house, replete with loud flocked wallpaper, beads, mirrored walls, dolls dressed in flamenco-type outfits hanging from every possible corner; and the backyard that sported a miniature "Dodge City," based on the classic television western, *Gunsmoke*. The focus on the house, the symbol of American prosperity and the domain of the individual, underscored the *individuality* value within this story. The rainbow house was promoted as a symbol of *freedom*—the freedom to embellish one's prize possession as one wished. The story's concluding narration underscored this point: "It may be strange, it may be bizarre, it may be outlandish; but be it ever so humble, there's no place like home."

Work, whether it be at a professional level or not, was clearly not the point within stories that focused on unique individuals. A large majority of the people in stories that emphasized the *individuality* value did not appear to be employed at all. A man who collected video equipment was retired, as was the man who spray painted his house. The woman who knitted personalized ski caps for celebrities did not appear to be employed, and so on. Instead, success was defined principally by *freedom*, the *freedom* to break the dominant cultural view, to be oneself, and to do what makes one happy.

The unique individuals who emerged with some regularity within the national reel may not have been completely on the outside of society—though they were certainly near the fringes—but they may have represented the emergence of mythic heroes within an example of contemporary American popular culture. The fact that stories about these "mythic individuals" were outnumbered by the *personal success* stories may help reconcile their incongruity with the prevailing view of *success* within *PM*. These "mythic individuals" may not have been completely respected or used as role models by the dominant culture, but like the cowboy figure, the "mythic individuals" within *PM* were at least tolerated and accepted for their quaint entertainment value.

Community Values

Also in contrast with the dominant view of *personal success*, another small group of values emerged within the *PM* stories: *community* values. Individual values associated with this group included *tradition, history, neighborliness,* and *connection.*

The organization of the *PM Magazine* production

cooperative itself purposely gave rise to a certain feeling of *community*. The title of each individual *PM* program almost always included a regional reference—*PM Baltimore, PM Atlanta* or *PM Utah*. The "wraps," or short narratives that introduced each story, were delivered by recognizable local personalities at recognizable local landmarks. The structure of the show automatically encouraged a feeling of community and connectedness. As the viewer initially tuned into the program, a sense of being part of a special region or community was encouraged.

Story selection also promoted *community* values. A number of stories were situated in relatively small communities. An extreme example was a story set in the town of Crabb, Texas, described as "a small community, just south of Houston on Farm-to-Market Road 762." The narrator further described Crabb as an "itty-bitty city [that] has a population of sixty people and covers six square miles."

Small towns and small-town life were described in overwhelmingly positive terms. A statement by the twelve-year-old mayor of Crabb, Texas, encapsulated the *PM* vision of small town life: "People in Crabb are nice enough to talk to you; even if they can't stand you, they're nice enough to talk to you." *Acceptance, niceness, politeness* were hallmarks of the community range of values. Stories about a county fair, a kite festival, a crawfish cookout, and other features of rural life also positively articulated these *community* values.

Small-town life and a sense of *community* were prominent values in "Postcards Please." This story began with a shot of an American flag, flapping in the breeze, from where the camera tilted down to reveal the post office in the small town of Boswell, Pennsylvania. The narrator introduced, "Skittles," the nickname for Boswell's "most recognized citizen; everyone knows the 74-year-old who gets mail from note writers from all over the world."

The story was constructed around an interview with the mail carrier for the town and did not overtly promote positive values associated with small communities. Nevertheless, *community* values, like *neighborliness* and *connection*, were im-

plied through statements the mail carrier made: "I couldn't believe there'd be that many people out there concerned enough about Skittles back here in Pennsylvania to send him postcards."

Small town concern and the idea that everyone knows what everyone else is doing in a small community were reinforced at the story's conclusion. Viewers were invited to send their own postcards to Skittles. The mail carrier provided instructions: "Just put 'Skittles' on like everybody else and put 15531—that's the zip code for Boswell, Pennsylvania; they know where it goes." The thought that even in the fast-paced and modern mid-1980s one could address a piece of mail with only someone's nickname punctuated the personal, protective nature of *community* within this story.

The positive promotion of *community* values within the *PM Magazine* value system was similar to what Conal Furay (1977) identified as the "small town ethos." Furay explored what he called stable mentalities or modes of belief that have emerged historically through elements of American popular culture. Specifically, he claimed the shift of the population from urban to suburban communities represented a quest for rural roots or what sociologists call a "Gemeinschaft" (literally "community") system, meaning "a society characterized by closer personal connections between members, along with a valuing of sentiment above individual efficiency" (1977, p. 64). Stories that promoted a set of *community*-related values in a positive way may have represented a pull toward this "Gemeinschaft" or community orientation.

Compassion Values

Perhaps even rarer in number than stories that promoted *individuality* and *community* values were stories that promoted a range of values labeled *compassion*. *Compassion* values included the individual values of *humanitarianism, equality, sharing, conservation,* and *nature*.

Stories containing *compassion* values included a story about a blind sailor that articulated *equal opportunity;* a story about a woman naturalist and "eagle watcher" that articulated *conservation* and *nature;* a story about a young mother who donated her dead son's kidney to another young woman articulated *humanitarianism, equality* and *sharing;* and a story about the founder of the organization, "Mothers Against Drunk Drivers" (MADD), that articulated *humanitarianism, equality* and a dedication to *broader social good.*

A specific group of production values was associated with *compassion* values. Visually, stories tended to use stable camera shots of longer duration and incorporated fewer edits. The soundtracks of these stories tended to rely upon slower, melodic music rather than faster paced rock or jazz music so common in most *PM* stories. Such production choices tended to communicate a level of seriousness associated with the *compassion* stories and tended to lend credibility to the topics and values contained therein.

The positively expressed *compassion* values of *humanitarianism, equality, sharing, conservation,* and *nature,* more than any other group of positive values within the *PM* value system, were almost always contrasted with a negative value. The many stories that positively promoted *conservation* and *nature* also tended to include negative values associated with *progress,* such as *pollution, overpopulation, industrialization, irresponsibility,* and *environmental damage.* The story on the founder of MADD contained the negative values of *death, loss,* and *irresponsibility.* Similarly, the story about the mother who donated her son's kidney contained the negative values of *death, loss,* and *unfairness.*

Negative values can be strong devices in defining a value system. Within *PM Magazine,* negative values stood out even more strongly because of the overwhelming emphasis on positive values within value system overall. The use of negative values associated with positive *compassion* values tended to give those values a certain prominence so, at the very least, the *compassion* values were not completely overwhelmed by the dominant value system.

The negative values promoted in these stories, *pollution, overpopulation, death, irresponsibility, environmental damage,* and *loss* also issued a strong warning. It was no coincidence that many of the negative values revolved around environmental damage caused in large part by contemporary western culture's strong *progress*-oriented and *personal success* orientation. The *compassion* stories that focused on *conservation* and *nature* both articulated the danger of the damage and reflect efforts to reverse the damage. In this way, the dominant *personal success* oriented value system in *PM* was mildly challenged.

Discussion

Despite these brief nods to *individuality, community,* and *compassion,* the value system in *PM Magazine* painted a picture of a world where *personal success* in all its permutations—*recognition, achievement, financial success, excitement, physical attributes,* and to a lesser degree, *happiness, family* and *relationships*—was given priority. In a program that arguably had the potential to show a broad range of diverse voices and values, *PM* clearly did not. Instead, it focused, like much of popular television programming, on a narrow, traditional, and conservative world view.

Strict, traditional gender roles were honored and few underrepresented groups graced the *PM* program. For the most part, *PM* stories glorified white people who achieved their status in life by pursuing a highly-paid and/or glamour profession: actors, directors, producers, film and television technicians, and dancers. Other stories focused on models, fashion designers, perfume creators, caviar importers, or management-level people involved in the production and marketing of luxury items.

Work, discipline, and *training,* although obviously necessary for *success* in any of the professions listed above, were deemphasized within *PM.* Instead, *optimism,* expressed through comments on the role of luck and good fortune, was granted prominence. Of course, the role of *optimism* has always been an element within American cultural thought, but not to the exclusion of other values like *discipline* and *work. PM Magazine*'s value system created the unsettling impression that culturally defined positive goals, such as *recognition, financial success*, and *achievement*, were afforded only to a special group of lucky people, like the princesses and lottery winners featured in the show.

The emphasis placed on the acting and modeling professions, of all the possible professions the program could promote, reinforced a certain "spark" or degree of talent that cannot be acquired strictly through education and training. Modeling requires certain physical attributes that, again, largely cannot be acquired through individual initiative. Even in *PM* stories featuring people in other professions, such as engineering or business management, where *education* and *training* play a stronger role in *success*, the element of *luck* tended to be emphasized over *discipline* and *hard work*.

Stories that emphasized action and sports, however, served to tip the scale within the *PM Magazine personal success* value system away from the role of good fortune and back toward promoting a more traditional utilitarian view. Stories about athletic, military, and para-military activities gave strong voice to the values of *discipline* and *training*. With the exception of those stories featuring "fad" sports and activities, the people featured within these types of stories tended to be members of the white, professional middle class.

Only a group of stories that centered on unusual, but "regular" folk varied greatly from the predominant emphasis on the white, professional middle class, spanning a much broader cross section of America in terms of age, ethnicity, and apparent socioeconomic status. Although the value of *recognition* was emphasized within such stories by promoting only those people who had achieved a high degree of status in their fields of expertise, clearly the rank of "bubble gum-blowing champion" or "house painter extraordinaire" does not fit neatly into the same category as "one of the hottest models in the world," "world class diver," or "the greatest tenor of our time." However wonderful, unique, and charming these people appeared to be, in comparison with the majority of the topics and people featured on *PM Magazine*, the bubble gum–blowing champion and the house painter extraordinaire could not offer a viable alternative to the dominant white, middle-class view.

The special type of consumerism inherent in the professional lifestyle was also strongly reflected in those *PM Magazine* style stories that described luxury commodities, such as expensive cars, jewelry, perfume, hobbies, vacation destinations, or food and restaurants. Such stories served to illustrate the "good life" by providing fairly clear instructions about what material possessions were associated with membership in the promoted class.

The vast majority of *PM* stories illustrated a world inhabited by young, white, financially secure, thin, attractive, educated, articulate and lucky "stars," or as Bellah, *et al.*, put it, "the uniquely successful and admirable one[s]" (1986, p. 285). The smaller group of stories that focused on the day-to-day life of more average people, illustrated a world filled with older, ethnic, working class (or poorer) uneducated, often overweight, unique-looking, inarticulate "ordinary folk who don't know how" (1986, p. 285). Within the substantial *personal success* component of the *PM* value system, this group of "regular people" stories served as a poignant counterpoint, reinforcing the dominant positive message about white, professional middle-class ideals and values by showing what the promoted class has risen above.

Commercial Market Influences

PM's corporate parent and the local stations that aired *PM Magazine* may have wanted to promote the impression that the program amounted to a half-hour public service announcement. But the value system that emerged from individual stories revealed that *PM* was designed, like all other commercial television programs, to attract the largest and most demographically-desirable audience possible. It was only a happy coincidence for the program's producers that *PM* arguably appeared to meet a public service need or helped fulfill a regulatory policy in effect at the time. *PM* was programmed against syndicated off-network reruns, largely situation comedies and game shows. The so-called "unique format" was not an end in itself, but rather was a means to providing an alternative to competing programs in the time period—and, ultimately a sizable audience.

In its heyday, the program was very successful in meeting its commercial objective. By the mid-1980s, *PM* was frequently rated the number one syndicated program in the nation. Beyond audience numbers alone, looking more closely at the value system within the program, one can infer that the *quality* of that audience—from a demographic standpoint—was highly appealing as well. Recall that the *PM* syndication arrangement required *PM*-affiliated local stations to surrender one of their thirty-second spots each weeknight to the national *PM* organization, who in turn, sold the time to national advertisers for more than the local stations could have commanded for the same spot. *PM* offered national advertisers a more tightly targeted national demographic and an alternative to traditional television network advertising.

Naturally, maintaining adequate audience size was an overarching goal. The role of the national production office in screening and combining individual stories served a normative function, ensuring a degree of consistency in topics, the overall "look," and, ultimately, the values promoted within the program. Local feature stories sent to the national office by *PM*-affiliated stations were screened by "coordinating producers" who were responsible for eliminating stories deemed unsuitable for the national reel.

In addition to controlling the selection of individual stories, the national office staff was also responsible for *combining* stories into the daily shows. Individual stations were allowed to substitute their own local stories for certain national stories, but they were not allowed to further alter the sequencing of stories for a given day, week, or month. Both the selection and ordering functions gave the *PM Magazine* enormous power in shaping the look, the message, and the values promoted within the program in such a way that would maximize, through deliberate effort or through trial and error, the audience size and demographics sold to national advertisers.

Very general guidelines determined whether or not a story would be selected for the national reel.

Csaplar described the criteria articulated by one *PM Magazine* assistant creative services director:

> She [the assistant creative services director] specified four criteria for national reel materials. First, does the story have a hook—a reason the mass audience would want to watch? Second, does it have a story line—a beginning, middle and end, and enough suspense to sustain six minutes? Third, is there visual interest—action, motion, pictures? Fourth, is the story memorable—will people talk about it the next day? (1983, p. 129)

PM Magazine production personnel readily articulated market-driven criteria as justification for programming choices. This process occurs almost naturally in commercial media organizations. As Ettema and Whitney observed, "individual communicators work within the context of organizational structures and processes. These structures and processes in turn operate within the contexts of the economic, political, legal, ideological and other institutional arrangements of society" (1994, p. 7). Raymond Williams elaborated how market influences, in particular, establish their impact:

> The contrast between market-originated and producer-originated work cannot be made absolute, once market conditions have been generalized. For producers often *internalize* known or possible market relationships, and this is a very complex process indeed, ranging from obvious production for the market which is still the work the producer "always wanted to do," through all the possible compromises between the market demand and the producer's intention. . . . (1982, pp. 105–106)

Because the actual producers of *PM Magazine* represented a collaboration of many individuals, most of whom were either employed by or were financially linked to a large for-profit media conglomerate (Westinghouse), on the spectrum between individual intention and market demand, no doubt choices about *PM* were firmly situated on the side of market demand.

These same market forces affected choices made in early stages of program development. As Williams elaborated, "in addition to the general process in which the market registers people's choices and these feed back into selected or discontinued types of production, there is an evident pressure, *at or before* the point of production, to reduce costs: either by improving the technical means of reproduction, or by altering the nature of the work or pressing it into other forms." (1982, 104) This interplay between market influences, producers' conception of the actual or perceived audience, and product has been explored by Ettema, Whitney and others (1994).

We see this interplay at work as *PM* coordinating producers encouraged segment producers in *PM*-affiliated stations to mimic successfully rated national reel stories. Having internalized market forces, local producers themselves would tend to select topics, treatments, and values likely to make it onto the national reel. Even the much touted "unique production values" of *PM Magazine*, which relied on videotape technology and shooting the entire program outside the traditional television studio setting were as much the result of market-driven factors as they were a product of aesthetic choices. For creating a "new" look for *PM* cannot be isolated from the fact that shooting the program segments outside the television studio also allowed the production organization to bypass labor unions, relying on a large pool of non-union—and no doubt lower paid—workers to produce their product.

Supporting Existing Power Relationships

Just as production choices about story selection and basic production values cannot be separated from market forces at work within the television industry, neither can the value system within the program be separated from dominant cultural forces at work within the surrounding culture. For one, by promoting the *personal success* value system as the predominant value system, *PM Magazine* helped reinforce basic forces at work within capitalist society and reflected not-so-subtle control mechanisms.

At first glance, *personal success*, as defined by

PM, seems to impart a high degree of freedom to those who share the value system. Indeed, Barbara Ehrenreich pointed out that members of middle class professions exhibit certain traits: "most are salaried employees . . . [an individual who is] granted far more autonomy in his or her work and is expected to be fairly self-directing much of the time" (1990, p. 13). However, this so-called freedom is not without a price.

> The professional and managerial occupations have a guildlike quality. They are open, for the most part, only to people who have completed a lengthy education and attained certain credentials. The period of study and apprenticeship—which may extend nearly to mid-life—is essential to the social cohesion of the middle class . . . this long training period requires the discipline and the self-direction that are essential to the adult occupational life of the class. (1990, p. 13–14)

John Fiske (1993) explained what he called the "paradox" between American's basic belief in freedom and the high degree of control necessary for entry to the dominant class:

> The paradox between the tightly disciplined nature of respectable US society and its deeply held belief in freedom is defused by the willing entry of people into its disciplinary systems. The result is that the system is experienced not as repressive, but as enabling and productive. If discipline, the belief appears to run, is "freely" entered into, it cannot limit freedom. (p. 76)

Discipline, like that required for entry into the class promoted by *PM*, is not a means to obtain individual freedom via financial stability and material acquisition; it has more to do with the control the dominant culture has a vested interest in maintaining. Fiske elaborated:

> Disciplined individuals (or docile bodies) are essential to the smooth running of an elaborate society and so those components of individuality which can best be disciplined are the ones which the power-bloc promotes as those which matter. Those over which its control is less effective are, conversely, defined as trivial and denied, as far as possible, social effectivity. (1993, p. 66)

By promoting values that resonate with the highly disciplined professional middle class, *PM Magazine* also functioned to reinforce existing control mechanisms and dominant power structures. Within the program, *personal success* values were promoted as "those which matter."

Indeed, the group of *PM* stories that gave voice to *individuality* showed what the professional middle class is not, in terms of *freedom*. For to a certain degree, *freedom* was something the lower classes actually had more of and of which the upper middle classes may have had less. Members of the professional middle class may easily reconcile this insight by dismissing the people associated with *individuality* as eccentric weirdoes to avoid at all costs—or by rationalizing that financial security guarantees an adequate level of *freedom*. Ultimately, stories that promoted *individuality, community,* or *compassion* within *PM* were in the minority and failed to counter the show's prevailing *personal success* orientation. To use Fiske's terminology, people contained within stories promoting *individuality, community,* or *compassion* were presented as "trivial" and "ineffective" compared with the dominant or promoted class.

This analysis began with the notion that *PM Magazine* national reel stories over a three-month period would reflect a large degree of diversity, not only in topics, but in people represented and values promoted. The localism or regionalism, promoted by the program at both the corporate and the station level supports this view. The show's magazine format incorporated a variety of topics, offering "soft news," or something relatively benign to fill the gap between television news programs and the primetime network schedule.

Instead, the *personal success* value system adopted by 1980s white, professional middle-class Americans was soundly reaffirmed in the symbolic world created by *PM Magazine* for those who believe in these values as well as for those who do not. Although it was not always right on the surface, the personal success view threaded its way throughout a majority of the program. So prevalent was this view that one might come to the conclusion that *PM Magazine* should be preceded by a message:

Warning. This program promoted a specific conservative world view that may inflate your expectations, limit your level of satisfaction, and erode your self-esteem. If you are interested in anything other than a high-profile, highly-paid professional occupation, you may feel like there is something wrong with you. If you do not own an expensive home, car, or clothing, you may feel abnormal. If you are a woman who fails to meet the beauty ideal promoted within the show, you may feel deflated. If you are a man occupied in anything other than a male-dominated military or police endeavor, or dangerous athletic competition, you may feel effeminate. If you are older, poorer, eccentric, or "average" in any way, you may feel tolerated, but outside the mainstream. If you are African-American, Asian, Hispanic, or Native American, you may feel invisible.

Such hypothetical warnings aside, the strong *personal success* value system present within the program supports the notion that *PM Magazine* was really not much different than the programs it followed and preceded—it was a national program "packaged" as a local program in order to sell it to other stations. Those stations, in turn, produced a large and demographically-sound audience whose time could be sold to advertisers. On the surface the program may appear to offer something different, but as a product of the American commercial television industry, it is no surprise that *PM* could not break out from its links to the industry and culture that created it.

Notes

1. Tapes of national reel stories were obtained directly from the *PM Magazine* national office in San Francisco. Interviews with production personnel at the *PM* national office, as well as sales and public relations materials used to market the program to potential syndicators, provided additional background for this value analysis.

2. A minority of stories did not contain any easily recognizable values. In these cases, one implied value initially was assigned to each story. For example, the tapes analyzed included five very brief stories called, "Mind Game." These stories featured a magician who presented an

audience-participation guessing game on the screen, accompanied by scary-sounding music. The overall feeling of the stories was one of mystery or lack of security—the opposite of the positive value of *security*. Ultimately, the "Mind Game" stories, and a few other stories that did not contain a value or did not follow the typical *PM* formula, were rare, inconsequential, and were vastly overshadowed by other stories and other values.

References

Assis, K. (1983, April). Behind the scenes at *PM Magazine*. New Orleans, n.p.

Ball-Rokeach, S., Rokeach, M., & Grube, J. (1984). *The great American values test: Influencing behavior and belief through television.* New York: Free Press.

Ball-Rokeach, S. & Tallman, I. (1979). Social movements as moral confrontations: With special reference to civil rights. In M. Rokeach (Ed.), *Understanding human values: Individual and societal* (pp. 82–94). New York: Free Press.

Bellah, R., Madsen, R., Sullivan, W., Swidler, A. & Tipton, S. (1986). *Habits of the heart: Individualism and commitment in American life.* New York: Harper.

Buck, J. (1984, July 23). The success of *PM Magazine. San Francisco Chronicle*, p. 36.

Csaplar, N. R. (1983). Local television: The limits of prime-time access. *Journal of Communication,* 33(2), 124–31.

Dagavarian, D. (1987). *Saying it ain't so: American values as revealed in children's baseball stories 1880–1950.* New York: Peter Lang.

Droesch, P. (1980, March 1). Stalking Bigfoot, meeting mystics and marinating beef. *TV Guide,* n.p.

Ehrenreich, B. (1990). *Fear of falling: The inner life of the middle class.* New York: Harper.

Ettema, J., & Whitney, D. C. (1982). Mass communicators in context. In Ettema and Whitney (Eds.), *Individuals in mass media organizations: Cre-*

ativity and constraint (pp. 7–10). Beverly Hills: Sage.

Ettema, J., & Whitney, D. C. (Eds.). (1994). *Audiencemaking: How the media create the audience.* Beverly Hills: Sage.

Field, C., & Weiss, J. (1987). *Values in selected children's books of fiction and fantasy.* Hamden, CT: Library Professional.

Fiske, J. (1993). *Power plays. Power works.* New York: Verso.

Furay, C. (1977). *The grass-roots mind in America.* New York: New Viewpoints.

Ganer, P. (1988). An analysis of the role of values in the argumentation of the 1980 presidential campaign. *Dissertation Abstracts International* (#8908172).

Gans, H. (1980). *Deciding what's news.* New York: Vintage.

Gansberg, A. (1983, February 24). *PM Magazine* number one in Arbitron's syndie ratings. *The Hollywood Reporter,* n.p.

Gitlin, T. (1983). *Inside prime time.* New York: Pantheon.

Glasser, T. (1995). Communicative ethics and the aim of accountability in journalism. *Social Responsibility: Business, Journalism, Law. 21,* 31–51.

Glasser, T. & Ettema, J. (1994). The language of news and the end of mortality. *Argumentation 8,* 337–334.

Glasser, T. & Ettema, J. (1989). Investigative journalism and the moral order. *Critical Studies in Mass Communication 6,* 1–20.

Miller, R. (n.d.). Inside the prize judging for *PM Magazine* show. *San Jose Mercury News, n.p.* [Article reprint from *PM Magazine* press package.]

PM Magazine National Office (n.d.). *About PM Magazine.* San Francisco, CA: *PM.*

PM Magazine National Office. (n.d.). *And now for a few words about PM Magazine.* San Francisco, CA: *PM.*

PM Magazine National Office (n.d.). *How the cooperative works.* San Francisco, CA: *PM.*

PM Magazine sets trends for the future. (1983, March 14). *Broadcast Week, n.p.*

Rokeach, M. (1968). *Beliefs, attitudes, and values: A theory of organization and change.* San Francisco: Jossey-Bass.

Rokeach, M. (1973). *The nature of human values.* New York: Free Press.

Rokeach, M. (1979). Change and stability in American value systems, 1968–1971. In M. Rokeach (Ed.), *Understanding human values: Individual and societal* (pp. 129–147). New York: Free Press.

Sillars, M. (1991). Messages, meanings, and culture: Approaches to communication criticism. New York: Harper.

Stein, B. (1979). *The view from Sunset Boulevard.* New York: Basic Books.

Trujillo, N., & Ekdom, L. (1985). Sportswriting and American cultural values: The 1984 Chicago Cubs. *Critical Studies in Mass Communication, 2,* 262–281.

Tuchman, G. (1978). *Making news: A study in the construction of reality.* New York: Free Press.

Turow, J. (1983). Local television: Producing soft news. *Journal of Communication, 33*(2), 111–123.

Williams, R. (1982). *The sociology of culture.* New York: Schocken Books.

Williams, R. (1974). *Television: Technology and cultural form.* New York: Schocken Books.

Williams, R. M., Jr. (1979). Change and stability in values and value systems: A sociological perspective. In M. Rokeach (Ed.), *Understanding human values: Individual and societal* (pp. 15–46). New York: Free Press.

Wolf, N. (1991). *The beauty myth.* New York: Morrow.

Cultural Criticism: Mythic, Feminist, and Psychoanalytical Approaches

CHAPTER 15

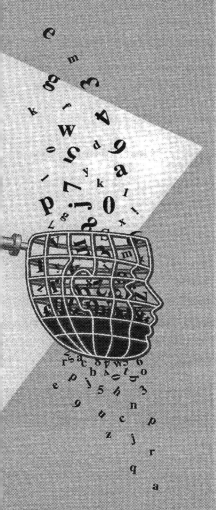

Chapter Outline

Within the general orientations of British Cultural Studies and sociocultural theories of mass media, especially television, narrower critical approaches to analyzing particular aspects of cultural life have developed. By "narrower," we mean that critical theories and approaches that deal not with all of culture but with partial but highly significant realms or regions of social processes. Actually, we could develop a relatively long list of arenas of social relations that have been examined by television critics: for example, race (Gray, 1995; Means Coleman, 2000, 2002), the workplace (Dow, 1992; Japp, 1991), politics (Curtin, 1995, Hartley, 1992; Hart, 1999), advertising (Fowles, 1996; Frith, 1997; Goldman, 1992; Twitchell, 1996), TV music (McGrath, 1996; Schwichtenberg, 1992; Turner & Sprague, 1991), and non-Western cultures (Appadurai, 1990/1999; Kottak, 1990; Naficy, 1999).

Given that range of micro- or narrow approaches to cultural studies, we have had to make some choices in which orientations to feature in this chapter. We have selected three: *mythic criticism,* to give you examples of one of the most expansive kinds of cultural study; *feminist criticism,* to illustrate one of the demographically generated approaches, one of the Big Three (race, class, and gender); and *psychoanalytic criticism,* to probe relationships between television and subterranean, subjective aspects of cultural life. Given our general overview of the assumptions governing cultural and sociocultural criticism in the previous chapter, we won't stop here to do that again. Rather, we'll move right into each of the three kinds of audience-centered approaches.

Mythic Criticism

Popular among TV critics especially of the 1970s and 1980s, and still practiced today, is mythic criticism. Our word *myth* comes from the Greek *mythos,* which was Aristotle's word for plot or story. While we sometimes use the word to distinguish truth from falsehood, as when Edwin Black (1973) accused Richard Nixon in 1972 of *mythifying* his hometown, Whittier, California, by trying to construct it as an environment characterized by rich, positive values, we usually think of myths as particular kinds of stories. More useful is the idea that myths become the stories that societies tell themselves in order to construct a past, ethical guides for the present, and a vision of a future or destiny. In the 1980s, Hal Himmelstein (1984) demonstrated the pervasiveness of myths on American television, and mythic criticism has been an especially important part of culturally oriented television studies ever since.

Myths are stories often set in the past, with virtuous and villainous, larger-than-life characters whose actions have *morals;* that is, they can teach us how to behave in our own world (this understanding of myth is grounded in Lévi-Strauss, 1958). Myths are set in the past, yet are endlessly translatable into present-day circumstances. Thus, the myth of Faust, the man who sold his soul to the devil for power only to regret it later, was first recorded in a play by Thomas Kidd in the sixteenth century. It later appeared as a German drama in the eighteenth century by Goethe, a twentieth-century novel by German-American writer Thomas Mann, and even a 1978 episode of the cartoon *Thundarr the Barbarian*. Whether the Faust persona was a philosopher (Kidd), a scientist (Goethe), a musician (Mann), or a wizard (*Thundarr*) made no difference; each was a hero whose excessive desires to know and have power over others brought about his own downfall. The lesson in each case was the same: Don't try to reach too far outside your own circumstances or too far beyond the abilities of others. The Faust story is an excellent example of the socializing powers of myth.

Myths become the sources of lessons about-life. As audience members, we use the mythic frames to make sense of what we're shown. Myths work at multiple levels: as localized accounts (say, of your own family), regional or national stories about valued or despised actions and characters, or even universal stories about struggles that all human beings face in making their way through life (see Gronbeck, 1989). At all levels, myths have been made to seem like the "way things are"; they are naturalized in our perceptual equipment (Barthes, 1972). As they become so large as to account for a people's (a culture's) understanding of life as a whole, their place in the universe, their origins, and their destinies, myths become what Ernest Bormann (1972, 1985) calls *rhetorical visions*—a people's way of seeing social life and using that way of seeing as an orientation to the world.

Mythic analysis represents an important kind of cultural criticism because myths can become constraints that work to prevent social change or rationales that drive people to act, even violently, against "the other." Most of prime-time television in the 1950s and 1960s featured domestic dramas and sitcoms that reaffirmed as the mythic "ideal American family" ones in which two white heterosexual parents raised their biological children lovingly and wisely (see Coontz, 1992, for a debunking of this mythical conceit). Such programs constrained Americans' views of family life: We were not allowed to explore alternative family arrangements, the family life of nonwhites, or the conditions experienced by children being raised in less-than-loving environments. Furthermore, the myths that justify whites' sense of superiority over blacks, males' belief in their superiority over "the weaker sex," and America's destiny and mission to democratize in capitalistic ways the rest of the world often appear in television programs as the way things are, that is, as naturalized. Few programs feature African Americans in leadership roles (*NYPD Blue* and *Boston Public* stand out as exceptions). In few programs are women stronger, wiser, and more adroit than men (*Ink* in 1996 was launched with that myth as its central premise, and *Alias* is a rare, recent exception). And rarely are the poor shown as superior to the rich (though the *Beverly Hillbillies* was constructed on that premise, and shows such as *Hazel* and *Benson* represent a genre featuring the superiority of hired help).

One of the cultural critic's primary tasks is to problematize and strip away such myths. This is done on the assumption that myths regularly reinforced on multiple television programs in fact reflect their viewing audience's limited, even prejudicial, outlooks. Hence, in such circumstances, the mythic critic comes to unmask those views to show them off for what they are: rationales for domination, even subjugation.

Specifics of Mythic Criticism

Television is rife with mythic allusions in such overt political communication as presidential messages about America's mission or campaign ads about the virtues of small-town origins, or more subtly in the mythic narratives that frame the action of prime-time shows. Saturday cartoons teach the myths of gender differences to the young (Schrag, 1991). Game shows, as the Fiske (1983) essay discussed in Chapter 11 noted, embody the myths for success: knowledge (*Jeopardy*), an understanding of everyday truisms (*Wheel of Fortune*), common sense (*Family Feud*). Mythic analysis helps critics dig into the unarticulated assumptions about good and bad thinking and the behavior undergirding so much of television programming. A number of media scholars have used mythic criticism to analyze films critically (e.g., Frentz & Rushing, 2002; Rushing 1985, 1989; Rushing & Frentz, 1989; Trites, 1991). Far fewer, however, have done mythic analyses of television texts. Cultural critics doing mythic criticism often use literary analogue criticism, structural analysis, or a monomythic frame to examine television's enlarged narratives.

Analog Mythic Criticism

Beginning with a definition of myth such as Rollo May's—"Myth is a story in which the symbols are brought together and portrayed in the experiences of a living person. A myth embodies the symbol in historical experience and forms it into a drama which carries the values of our society" (1976, p. 22)—critics doing analogue mythic criticism deconstruct a television text comparatively. That is, they compare and contrast the characters, events (actions and happenings), and settings of the television narrative with those of at least one additional mythic narrative, in order to analyze the extent to which the televisual retelling is a faithful reenactment of the mythic narrative and to explore different kinds of myth that come together in some body of works.

One example of analog mythic criticism is Gronbeck's (1991) analysis of the mythic portraits that 1988 presidential candidates tried to paint in the biographically oriented political advertisements they ran prior to the Iowa caucus. For example, Gronbeck's analysis explains how Bob Dole's two Iowa biographical advertisements (bioads) recast Dole as a contemporary Job, surviving and gaining strength through various adversities, while Bruce Babbit's bioads cast him as the frontier sheriff who was raised in the West and ran for public office so that "the rules will be the same for everyone." Another analog mythic narrative is Trites's (1991) analysis of the potential cultural significance of the differences between Hans Christian Andersen's telling of the "Little Mermaid" myth and Disney's telling of this narrative in *The Little Mermaid*.

Analog mythic studies are done, then, both to identify a range of possibilities (e.g., what are the stories of origin told by politicians?) and to offer judgments about which stories seem to work more effectively and more powerfully than others. A large-scale analog study is Joanne Morreale's (1993) examination of presidential biographical and résumé films and videos, which have been made since 1924 and constructed specifically for television broadcast since 1984. In her book-length critique, she compares and contrasts biographical and résumé films, those that are more person-centered with those that are more career-centered, and those that are more pessimistic with those that radiate optimism. According to Morreale, the coming of film, particularly for televised political conventions, created new kinds of biographical, mythic, political products.

Structural Mythic Analysis

Fiske and Hartley (1978), Barthes (1968, 1973), and others have explained that signs and clusters of signs can convey different levels of meaning—in semiotic terms, different orders of signification. Myths are second-level, or second-order, cultural meanings. They are cumulative clusters of signs that develop mythic significance in a particular society "when the first order meanings of the sign meet the values and established discourses of the culture" (O'Sullivan, Hartley, Saunders, Montgomery, & Fiske, 1994, p. 286).

Critics undertaking structural mythic analyses focus primarily on the paradigmatic structure of binary oppositions and discourses in a text—the chain of opposing concepts that cumulatively explain a particular topic or social experience. As O'Sullivan et al. explain, "Our myth of the countryside, for example, consists of a chain of concepts such as it is good, it is natural, it is spiritually refreshing, it is peaceful, it is beautiful, it is a place for leisure and recuperation" (p. 287). We learn to understand this countryside or rural myth primarily by its paradigmatic opposition to "our myth of the city," which "contains concepts such as unnaturalness, constriction, work, tension, and stress." Critics using structural approaches to analyze myth, then, typically examine the sets of paradigmatic oppositions in a text in order to explore the relationship of the myth to the culture's ideology, between a first-order or manifest set of meanings with a second-order or deeper/mythic set (as in Lester, 1997). Indeed, as Fiske and Hartley (1978), explain, "myths . . . are themselves organized into a coherence that we might call a *mythology* or an ideology" (p. 46).

One example of a structural mythic analysis is Michael Real's analysis of the annual televised Super Bowl. The Super Bowl is the most widely viewed (and the most lucrative) annual spectacle in American mass culture.[1] This is not an accident, but rather, as Real (1977) explains, because the Super Bowl is the perfect marriage between the ideology and dominant institutional structures of television and American culture. To understand the meanings and the popularity of the Super Bowl, Real analyzes the relationship between the televised Super Bowl and American culture and notes their shared similarities: Both focus on the physical, the body, and dramatic action. Both valorize acquisition, territoriality, and immediate and violent responses to challenges. Both have clearly delineated occupational and social roles that reflect the sexual, racial, and organizational hierarchy of American power structure and the institutional organization of American business. Both are shared cultural experiences. As a result of these homologies, Real explains, the Super Bowl functions as a mythic spectacle that "structurally reveals specific cultural values proper to American [myth,] institutions and ideology" (p. 92):

> The Super Bowl combines electronic media and spectator sports. . . . The structural values of the Super Bowl can be summarized succinctly: American football is an aggressive, strictly regulated team game fought between males who use violence and technology to win monopoly control of property for the economic gain of individuals within a nationalistic, entertainment context. . . . In other words, the Super Bowl serves as a mythic prototype of American ideology collectively celebrated. (1977, pp. 92, 115)

Monomythic Analysis

The theory of monomyths is based on the idea that a single, broad, somewhat variable yet consistent mythic frame dominates a social unit, a society, or even hemispheric units of collectivities. Monomyths are used to explain both cultural foundations of peoples as well as powerful stories within the culture. For example, the romantic quest myth is taken by Joseph Campbell (1968) as the most basic story undergirding the West's conception of itself as always pursuing some object (the holy grail) or objective ("progress") so as to purge itself of weakness/pessimism and move itself forward to positions of strength/optimism. The Israelites who wandered the desert for 40 years in search of the Promised Land, the Crusades bent on recapturing Constantinople for Christian civilization and the Holy Grail as a sacred representation of that civilization, and even whole television series in our time all draw on the monomyth of the romantic quest: Richard Kimble's search not only for a killer but for more humane institutions in the 1960s *The Fugitive*; the Asian American Caine's search for identity and peace in *Kung Fu* in the 1970s; the drive to civilize the frontier in the 1970s and 1980s *Little House on the Prairie*; even the push for fairness and justice in the 1990s *Power Rangers*. The quest myth is romantic in the sense that it celebrates honor codes and demonstrates how high motives and perseverance will pay off—the sort of happy ending characteristic not only of children's literature but also serious dramatic, novelic, and televisual literature. A variation of the quest—the "chosen people" theme—accounts for many depictions of Western countries, especially the United States (Lewis, 1987).

More narrowly constructed social units also can be subjected to monomythic analysis. Richard Slotkin (1973) has argued that American society at base is grounded in the regeneration-through-violence monomyth that is seen everywhere, from the John Smith/Pocahontas story through all of the western tales of subjugating savagery and the wilderness (Rushing, 1983), to thousands of revenge stories. Violence begats justifiable retaliation, which then purges society of pollution and evil. This monomyth is regularly depicted in such televised legal-political actions as the capture and trial of Patty Hearst (Mechling, 1979) and in police and detective dramas, where we are allowed voyeuristically to look safely at a violent yet controllable underworld (Newcomb, 1974). *NYPD Blue* is an excellent example of such a TV drama, and the various *Law and Order* series also critique the myth regularly.

The latest variations on monomythic study are less concerned with discovering foundational myths of social units than in exploring how myths guide the representation of segments of a society. For example, Gray's (1995) *Watching Race: Television and the Struggle for "Blackness,"* Cuklanz's (2000) *Rape on Prime Time: Television, Masculinity, and Sexual Violence,* and Projansky's (2001) *Watching Rape: Film and Television in Postfeminist Culture* all work to expose iron-clad myths that govern public representations of peoples and that must be broken before social relations between races and genders can become tranquil.

Other approaches to mythic analysis could be used by television critics (see Doty's 1986 inventory), but these three are sufficient to introduce the range of possibilities for cultural studies based on the enlarged stories that audiences use to comprehend their places in the world historically, socially, politically, and personally.

Feminist and Gender Ideology Criticism

Feminist and gender ideology criticism moves us into a particular mythic realm: the myths that affirm persistent patterns of patriarchal power: "Men own and control the media and it is their ideas, viewpoints and values which dominate the systems of production and representation in broadcasting, the press, and advertising. . . . Television does not present innocent, neutral pictures of the world; rather, its views are selective, schematic, and constructed" (Dyer, 1981, pp. 6–7). It should come as no surprise, then, that what is presented on TV carries viewpoints to which males have been acculturated. The Radio Television News Directors Association reports that women television news directors earn 34 percent less, on average, than men do. Furthermore, the Directors Guild of America (DGA) reports that of the 65,000 hours of prime-time television aired between 1959 and 1980, women directed 115. In 1986, women directed 348 of the 3,180 television programs produced in the United States. However, from this 11 percent, women received 24 percent of the DGA director's award nominations (Real, 1996, p. 178).

In culturally oriented television studies, feminist and gender ideology criticism is concerned with analyzing gender ideology: the structure of beliefs, principles, and practices that define, organize, and interpret what we regard as the normal attributes, roles, and spheres of activity, and characteristic behaviors appropriate for men and women that so permeate our culture that the interests of the most powerful social group, men, are equated with the natural and commonsense, even by those individuals and groups who are disadvantaged and repressed by these beliefs and practices.

As Bryson (1992) explains, cultural constructions of gender are accomplished rhetorically, through the use of verbal and visual symbols. Through the use of symbols, signs, codes, and discourses, cultures (including American culture) have divided the world into male and female traits (independence, competitiveness, logic, versus dependence, cooperation, emotionality, nurturance), roles (financial provider versus nurturance provider/relationship maintainer), and appropriate and socially sanctioned spheres of activity (public/world of work and politics versus private/home, domestic world). Historically, male traits, roles, and spheres of activity have been valued, and female traits, attitudes, roles, and spheres have been devalued. For example, prime time is when most men are primarily available to watch television; daytime is the non–prime time when the TV audience consists of far more women than men.

While feminism, as Foss (1996) explains, includes a diverse range of theories and perspectives, feminist theories and critical approaches generally share the following fundamental tenets:

- Feminist theories are theories of, by, and for women and are firmly based in women's own experiences.
- The oppression of women is the most fundamental and universal form of domination, and the central aim of feminism is to end this domination.
- Women as a group have interests opposed to those of male power and male-dominated institutions. These interests unite women in a common sisterhood that transcends divisions of class or race and motivates women to struggle together to achieve equality and liberation for all women.

Feminist and gender ideology criticism uses terms and concepts from semiotics and psychoanalytic film criticism because both of these methods are concerned with showing how meaning is structured in a text and how texts attempt to position viewers to adopt a particular viewing position toward the text's subject (Dyer, 1981, pp. 11–12). Following are some of the concepts central to a feminist criticism vocabulary.

Gender versus Sex

Feminist and gender ideology criticism make a distinction between sex and gender. *Sex* is understood to be a biological term that defines people by primary and secondary biological characteristics, while *gender* is a cultural term understood to include society's conceptions and expectations of traits, roles, and behaviors deemed typical, appropriate, or desirable for females and males (see Reeder, 1996).

Gender Roles

Roles, as we explained in Chapter 14, are socially defined sets of expectations associated with positions in particular contexts. Gender roles, then, are the different sets of rules, norms, and expectations deemed desirable for women and for men to perform (see Janeway, 1971; Kimmel, 2000).

Voyeurism

In Freudian psychoanalytic terms, *voyeurism* is any kind of sexual gratification obtained from vision. It usually applies to vision from a hidden vantage point. In feminist film and television criticism, it is one of the pleasures that television texts provide the ideal "male spectator" through their depiction of women as erotic objects of desire (see Mulvey, 1975, 1989).

Scopophilia

Taking other people as objects and subjecting them to a controlling, curious gaze is not simply sexual but generally pleasurable as well. There is, in this analysis, a sheer pleasure in looking, which fuels the contention that television is a "window on the world," a site for gazing pleasurably (see Parry-Giles & Parry-Giles, 2002, esp. pp. 27–30). That pleasure may also produce the numbing of one's critical facilities that Hart (1999) worries about.

Femininity

Femininity is that set of traditional, patriarchal notions of ideal qualities of "True Womanhood." Historically, as Welter (1966) explains, femininity referred to four ideal characteristics: purity, piety, domesticity (wanting more than anything to have a beautiful wife and mother serving one's family in the home), and submissiveness.

Feminism

This is an umbrella term for various perspectives (and attendant theories and social and political activities) that seek social, economic, political, and legal equality for women (see Wood, 2003, esp. pp. 50–87).

Hegemonic Masculinity

This is the particular patriarchal model of what it means to be a man that is so pervasive that it operates at the level of "common sense." It is the "culturally idealized form of the masculine character that emphasizes toughness, competitiveness, dominance, subordination of women and the marginalization of gay men" (Hanke, 1990, p. 232; see also Connell, 1990, pp. 83, 94).

The Gaze

Laura Mulvey's (1975) classic film essay used the concept of the (male) *gaze* to describe what she and many other film scholars saw as the dominant cinematic apparatus through which the unconscious of the patriarchal society structures film form by presenting and displaying women as erotic objects of desire for the characters in the screen story and through the camera work, for the television and film spectators.[2] The male gaze works through three structures: (1) that of the character types (men are actively doers and lookers, while women are the passive acted-on and looked-at objects) in the narrative, (2) that of the camera (which may not coincide with the point of view of any one character, but may be that of a fly-on-the wall in the classic fourth-wall convention), and (3) that of the audience (whose attention is directed to what the camera permits it to see). This understanding of the gaze not only limits vision to what is shown within the screen, but it also positions the audience to view what is framed in a particular way. This three-part filmic and televisual apparatus attempts to position viewers to look at scenes from a particular perspective. The gaze, perhaps paradoxically, controls not only what you see but how you're allowed to see. Hence, your interpretive processes—the mechanisms of any audience-centered approach to criticism—are strongly influenced by televisual apparatuses and their habitual use in various genres of programs.

Patriarchy

Literally, *patriarchy* means "rule of the fathers." Theorists and historians differ in terms of whether patriarchy developed as a consequence of evolutionary events stemming from women's weakness during pregnancy, childbirth, and lactation that concomitantly resulted in men's greater strength, or as a consequence of the discovery of the male role in reproduction and the subsequent attempts of men to control women in order to ascertain who are their children, or some other explanation (see Delphy, 1984; Firestone, 1972; French, 1992; Hartmann, 1976). Regardless of origin, male authority in most societies still is enforced through political, economic, social, and religious institutions (Gamble, 1999).

However, patriarchy, as Bryson (1992, pp. 186–193) notes, "does not necessarily imply that all individual men oppress all women, that every male person is to be considered an enemy incapable of reform, or that the total elimination of the male sex would be the desired consequence of an improvement in sperm bank technology." Rather, it enables us to distinguish between the male power structures and institutions that maintain patriarchy as well as its physical and psychological dominance, and individual men, who may be feminists or themselves dominated or disenfranchised by hegemonic masculine patriarchy (e.g., African American men, Latino men, Asian American men, gay men).

Among the questions that feminist and gender ideology criticism asks (and tries to answer through a close analysis of television texts) are these:

- With whose point of view, feelings, and experiences are viewers invited to identify in this television text by virtue of the camera angles, editing, narrative structure, and conclusion?

- Are women presented as objects of voyeuristic pleasure? (For a study of a gaze-sensitive campaign that backfired, see Goldman's analysis of the 1988 Reebok campaign, 1992, pp. 205–214.)

- Are men presented as objects of voyeuristic pleasure?

- What attributes and attitudes are presented or portrayed as appropriate for and/or desirable in women? Men? Both?

- Do the roles, values, and actions in this text maintain, deconstruct, or reconstruct dominant cultural notions of gender?

- Does the text present women, feminists, lesbians, and gays as "other"? Does it "naturalize" these depictions or critique or interrogate them (see, e.g., Dow, 2001)?

- What oppositional readings, if any, does the text encourage?

- What lessons about gender roles might the text teach viewers? Are these lessons affirming and empowering or disconfirming and disempowering?

- What might some of the potential consequences of such social lessons be?

- In what ways do the text's representations and "lessons" affirm the dominant political and economic power structures and institutions of American society? In what ways do they question these patriarchal power structures? (See Projansky's 2001 study, esp. Chap. 2.)

Such questions probe the audience's understanding of televisual texts as informed or guided by feminist perspectives.

Psychoanalytic Criticism

Psychoanalytic criticism is an outgrowth of the soaring interest especially in the lectures and thought of Sigmund Freud in the late nineteenth and early twentieth centuries. Certainly Freud was concerned with various sorts of mental deviations—neuroses and psychoses—and their treatment; his work focused on the study of and therapeutic approaches to individuals' psychological illnesses. Yet even in the 1920s and 1930s, his vocabulary and ways of thinking came to be applied in public print to matters of public concern: the perversions of Hollywood lifestyles, social activities in the 1920s, and the sexual dimensions of violence, for example. It seemed that anything could be and was psychoanalyzed. Then, as the work of Carl Jung, Alfred Adler, and Jacques Lacan circulated in more recent years, an enlarged vocabulary, suited even better to analyses of public, shared texts, and experiences, gave new life to psychoanalytic study, especially of fictive and nonfictive works. Psychoanalytic criticism has gained in popularity especially over the past quarter-century. And it found in television a communication medium particularly well suited to its assumptions. This point was made strongly by Peter Wood as early as 1976 in his essay, "Television as Dream." Television the dream machine, he argued, could do the same sort of work for a society that nocturnal dreams do for individuals.

Assumptions Guiding Psychoanalytic Criticism

Three assumptions inferred by psychoanalytic critics from psychoanalysis are especially important:

1. *Human thought and behavior are derived from both the conscious and the unconscious psychological worlds.* Freud (1904/1966) built his central theory of the human psyche around the influence of the *id, libido, ego,* and *superego* on human beings. The *id* is an unconscious repository of human desires and needs; the *libido* is the drive to gratify those desires and needs. Governing the id and libido are the *ego* (the conscious, reasoning portion of mind) and the *superego* (the subconscious storehouse of what a person has learned from experience); its subcon-

sciousness means that we don't so much reason from the superego as react with it. Finally, then, it is the relationships existing between and among these four forces of mind that produce interactions between the conscious and unconscious worlds. In the battles between and among the id, libido, ego, and superego, we find humans' reactions to environmental stimuli, including television. Sexually charged relationships, whether in dramas such as *Providence* or sitcoms such *Will and Grace,* have drawn such large audiences, we can assume, because they showcase those battles.

2. *Both the individual and the shared or social aspects of psychological life are important to people.* Given the roots of psychoanalysis in individual illness and therapy, this mode of criticism certainly has been used to explain individuals' stories. A 2001–2002 episode of *Judging Amy* used psychoanalytic discourses to explain the behaviors of Amy's cousin, runaway teenagers, and a young man who was caught impersonating a police officer in a high school incident. But especially because of the theories of Carl Jung (1968), critics can argue that the superego is a repository of social rules that Jung called the *collective unconscious,* which "generated mythic heroes for the primitive and still generates similar individual fantasies for the civilized man, and which focus its chief expression in a relatively familiar and timeless symbolism endlessly recurring" (Hyman, 1955, p. 133). That familiar and timeless symbolism endlessly recurring he termed *archetypes,* or residue left in the mind after numerous experiences of the same type. The collective unconscious becomes the source of individual fantasies that are shared by large numbers of people: say, the fantasy of athletic achievement as a route to fame and riches that stereotypically govern many corners of ghetto life. The popularity for so many years of NBC's hit *Friends* can be explained, from this viewpoint, by the collective fantasies that it helped twentysomethings live through.

3. *Dreamwork is central to human life.* Dreams, to psychoanalytic critics, are not simply routes for escaping reality but important mechanisms for working through the problems people confront in their real lives. Dreams are imaginative places for exploring alternative lifestyles, even universes; wishes can be fulfilled, for good or ill, in dreams, and hence explored in a safe way, as can one's most primal fears. For Christian Metz (1976), films are waking dreams, fulfilling the same personal and collective functions that sleeping dreams do. The same argument applies to television programs. Some programs are especially dreamlike. *Xena, Warrior Princess* and *Buffy the Vampire Slayer* explicitly plot confrontations between the fearful worlds of the nonhuman and the individual-social lives of ordinary mortals. For Buffy Summers, her adopted town of Sunnydale, California, unfortunately was built on a Hellmouth, which could unleash torrents of not only vampires but also demons and every other kind of antisocial being that has inhabited the underworld, all seeking the Glory of the Dawn that only a vampire slayer could stop. Monsters, vampires, demons: all of these psychologically become the villains that our good and constructive selves (our egos and superegos) must slay in our dreams to keep us on course in our waking lives. It is little wonder that the early 1970s saw a television program entitled *The Great American Dream Machine,* for that it is.

Writing Psychoanalytic Criticism Within a Cultural Framework

An important difference between literary and most kinds of psychoanalytically oriented criticism is that the TV critic seldom focuses on individual characters. While one of course could psychoanalyze the disciplining dominatrix of *The Weakest Link* or the voyeuristic host of *America's Funniest Videos* in order to explain the central thrust or function of such shows, it usually is within a dreamlike frame of examining characters acting in particular ways within particular settings that most psychoanalytic study of television takes place. This means that you write psychoanalytic analyses as you would general narrative studies, but with psychoanalytic concepts used in interpretive ways.

For example, Sasha Torres (1989) studied the program *thirtysomething* as therapy. Examining an episode out of its first season, Torres noted that it was constructed as a quite normal melodrama focused on issues of family, suburban home life, and the healthy maintenance of sexual and emotional lives. Yet she found the program working the world of dreams and fantasies, particularly the world of gendered identities and relationships. Her analysis of an episode led her to explore relationships between sexuality and parenting, relationships between a fun-loving female sexuality (symbolized in a tattoo) and the conservative sexuality of a married woman (who had it done), and the gender contrasts that were played out in a husband-and-wife therapy session. She concluded that, overall, the fear of feminizing masculinity leads the show to explore—give voice to, yet critique—the traditional vision of suburban family life. Here, then, the dreamworld of *thirtysomething* not only depicted marriage therapy but, more important, worked therapeutically within the social environment of the 1980s by calling into question gendered roles within family and work settings through discussions of sexuality, parenting and income responsibilities, gender relationships, and personal autonomy.

Torres's essay illustrates that the sort of psychobabble that abounds in many Woody Allen movies need not invade critical essays. Her psychoanalytic touch is light. She introduces the vocabularies of therapy, repression and expression, inversion, and so on easily and only when needed. The psychoanalytic example essay that we include in this chapter, Sonia Livingstone and Tamar Liebes's "Where Have All the Mothers Gone? Soap Opera's Replaying of the Oedipal Story," plunges more deeply into psychoanalytic thought. It compares and contrasts soap operas as fairy tales for grown-up girls and as therapeutic discourses for girls who are separated from mothers. As you read the essay, notice their care in grounding the most important arguments in analyses of episodes from *The Young and the Restless*, and yet the efforts to apply their conclusions to soap operas in general. (You'll have to decide whether you think their attempts to generalize their interpretations are justifiable.) This is a complicated, thoughtful, and yet understandable example of psychoanalytic criticism.

Particular Kinds of Critical Cultural Studies

Mythic, feminist, and psychoanalytic criticism are but three of the possible ways to narrow cultural studies and focus on the lives of particular groups of people. These three approaches fit together because psychoanalytic thought has invaded them all: myth as a way of working out individual and collective repressions, the psychoanalysis of the gaze, and of course the subjective aspects of waking dreams. Much more could and probably should be said about each, but perhaps you've read enough into all three to better understand such essays when you encounter them. And with a little fortitude, you'll be able to tackle these kinds of critical analysis yourself.

In all three kinds of micro- or narrow cultural studies, critics must be able to unmask and probe beneath the surface—to explore not just what is manifest in televisual works but what is latent as well. That which is latent certainly has markers—the reference to a mythic hero, gendered pronouns, the close-up camera shot of a troubled personality—though building interpretive arguments, where those markers become evidence of a cultural truism, power relationship, or underlying fear, represents the central tasks of the cultural critic. "The cultural" usually is hidden beneath the surface, so taken for granted that it's not said or explained. Mythic accounts of life are learned by the young and then submerged in the lives of the old. Gendered power relationships function in deed, not word; the life of the libido and the ego is carried out in dreams and fantasies.

That's what unmasking is all about: articulating such accounts, relationships, and subjectivities to account for some of the ways in which television programming functions to culturally powerful ends.

The Example Essays

We include three example essays in this chapter. The first is A. Susan Owen's feminist postmodern critique of *Buffy the Vampire Slayer.* Owen argues that Buffy is a feminist heroine who transgresses the action-adventure genre conventions in two ways: as a female who controls the narrative and as a female whose power, strength, and assertiveness enable her to literally punch out the (usually male) vampire villains who prey on females and feminized "others." Owen's analysis demonstrates how the series ironically displays the failure of the grand social narratives of heterosexual traditional family, justice and the rule of law, and science through the surrogate family formed by Buffy and her adolescent friends in the face of fractured nuclear families and largely clueless, helpless adults.

Robert Westerfelhaus and Teresa Comb's mythic analysis of *X-Files,* like Owen's analysis of *Buffy,* argues that this series questions the grand narrative of modernism by raising questions about the privileged position of science in the face of its inability to explain human experience and in the face of its costs: alienation from ourselves, others, nature, and the divine. Their essay looks at how the series deconstructs the myths of scientific progress and knowledge as well as the mystery of spirituality. They argue that *X-Files'* narratives and visual symbolism (e.g.,

Scully's and Mulder's flashlights as the stolen, sacred flame) extend the ancient Promethean myth about the dangers of rational, scientific knowledge, but they conclude that the series ultimately recuperates both scientific and spiritual explanations of human experience.

Finally, Sonia Livingstone and Tamar Liebes's essay, "Where Have All the Mothers Gone? Soap Opera's Replaying of the Oedipal Story," provides an example of a psychoanalytic critique. Using Freud's theories of the mother-daughter relationship, they examine the differential treatment of sons and daughters/males and females in soap operas. They conclude that soap operas, through camera techniques, characterization, and narrative structure, provide adults with the same sort of psychological socialization that fairy tales offer children. Specifically, they argue that both soaps and fairy tales infantilize women, that all the events and acts in story types have hidden sexual meanings, and that the narrative force in both fairy tales and soaps stems from the protagonists' attempts to return to the time of innocence before the inevitable psychic separations between mother and daughter, mother and son, and a woman and her own body occur. These culturalism truisms, they argue, explain soaps' and fairy tales' focus on kinship networks, the lineage of children, and the competition between women for the ultimate goal, which is always a man.

Notes

1. According to Robin Roberts' *CBS evening news* report on January 25, 2003, the 2003 Super Bowl would be seen live in 222 countries by 800 million viewers.

2. For a discussion of alternative scopic schemata that disrupt the male gaze, see Foss and Foss's (1994) analysis of Garrison Keillor's monologues.

Further Readings

Brunsdon, C., D'Acci, J., & Spigel, L. (Eds.). (1997). *Feminist television criticism: A reader.* New York: Oxford University Press. This collection of 23 essays provides a wide range of examples of the types of feminist analysis of television. The essays are divided into three sections: (1) housewives, heroines, and feminists; (2) audiences and reception contexts; and (3) private bodies and public figures. Each section is preceded by an introduction of the issues the essays in that section engage, and the book's Introduction provides a splendid overview of the history, critical approaches, and major issues addressed by feminist television criticism since the 1970s.

Helford, E. R. (Ed.). (2000). *Fantasy girls: Gender in the new universe of science fiction and fantasy television.* Lanham, MD: Rowman & Littlefield. The 11 essays examine television's contradictory representations of gender politics as displacements of and commentary on the cultural debates about feminism and women's roles. They critically examine television science fantasy series in order to explore television's sometimes empowering, often reactionary negotiation of cultural politics.

Kellner, D. (1995). *Media culture: Cultural studies, identity and politics between the modern and the postmodern.* London: Routledge. This book uses examples ranging from *Miami Vice* to presidential press conferences to Madonna and Laurie Anderson music videos to examine the intersections of media culture and society. The critical analysis illustrates how the myths, discourses, and images of media culture provide both hegemonic and empowering resources for helping individuals create cultural identities and negotiate political and social relationships and roles.

Webnotes

Women's Studies. **http://www.inform.umd.edu/Ed.Res/Topic/WomensStudies/**

This University of Maryland women's studies database provides an excellent starting point for gathering information about gender issues. In addition to directing users to other web sites dealing with feminist issues, it provides a reading and reference room with additional sources.

Feminism. **http://www.cddc.vt.edu/feminism**

This feminist theory web site is divided into three sections. The first section, Fields within Feminism, includes bibliographies, links, and names of people working in women's theory and thought in over 30 fields. The second section, National/Ethnic Feminism, provides similar information for countries grouped into seven regions. And the third section, Individual Feminists, provides short bibliographies, discussions of major feminist themes, and an alphabetical listing of more than 80 links to web sites focused on individual feminists.

Culture Studies Center. **http://www.mcs.net/-zupko/popcult.htm**

Sarah Zupko's "Cultural Studies Center" web site offers online articles, book reviews, and many links to resources on cultural studies. Sections include information on cultural studies theorists and critics, academic programs, bibliographies, and journals. Links to other sites are divided into five areas: television, film, international, mass media/communication, and cyberspace/sci-fi.

The Mind Book. **http://www.clas.ufl.edu/users/nnh/mindbook.htm**

This site provides an overview of literary psychoanalytic criticism.

Mythic Crossroads. **http://www.mythiccrossroads.com/default.htm**

This site provides links to myths from around the world, though most fully developed are the sections on myths in Great Britain. It also links into a variety of sites with products, secondary sources, and the like.

Mythic Realm. **http://www.folkstory.com/contentsmain.html#articles**

This useful site is devoted to scholarly and informational sources. It takes you into the pages of the journal *SAGA* and other writings that include mythic history and criticism.

1. An important skill for any critic seeking to uncover, unmask, or objectify that which is taken for granted culturally—a mythic assumption of origin, a gendered power relationship, a subconscious desire—is that of identifying *markers*. Markers are manifested pieces of visualization, dialogue, plot structure, and technological convention (e.g., a freeze frame or shot/reverse-shot) that probe identification of or focus on a first-order sign that also has a second-order significance—that is, cultural meaningfulness. To practice identifying markers that will be useful in building arguments about gendered power relations, examine an episode of *Friends* or a similar sitcom with clearly developed male and female roles. Look for markers of gender identity: stereotyped male or female references, facial expressions or bodily movements, clothing styles, references to activities (e.g., touch football versus shopping), suggestions of counter-stereotypical thought or behavior (men who don't like sports, women who say they're going to kick some butt), and anything similar you can identify in shot selection, dialogue, visualized behavior, plot structure, and the like. Given the markers you have found, what critical propositions could you defend, using the markers as evidence?

2. Execute the first exercise by pursuing mythic markers in *The West Wing*, *Law and Order*, or some similar profession-focused program.

3. Execute the first exercise pursuing psychoanalytic markers in a daytime serial, *Will and Grace*, *Ally McBeal*, or any other show that features discourses about desire and dread.

References

Appadurai, A. (1990/1999). Disjuncture and difference in the global cultural economy. In S. During (Ed.), *The cultural studies reader* (2nd ed., pp. 220–230). London: Routledge.

Barthes, R. (1968). *Elements of semiology.* London: Cape.

Barthes, R. (1972). *Mythologies* (A. Lavers, Trans.). London: Cape.

Bathes, R. (1973). *Mythologies.* London: Paladin.

Black, E. (1973). Electing time. *Quarterly Journal of Speech, 59,* 125–129.

Borman, E. (1972). Fantasy and rhetorical vision: The rhetorical criticism of social reality. *Quarterly Journal of Speech, 58,* 396–407.

Borman, E. (1985). *The force of fantasy: Restoring the American dream.* Carbondale, IL: Southern Illinois University Press.

Bryson, V. (1992). *Feminist political theory: An introduction.* New York: Paragon.

Campbell, J. (1968). *The hero with a thousand faces* (2nd ed.). Princeton, NJ: Princeton University Press.

Connell, R.W. (1990). An iron man: The body and some contradictions of hegemonic masculinity. In M. A. Messner & D. F. Sabo (Eds.), *Sport, men, and the gender order: Critical feminist perspectives* (pp. 83–95). Champaign, IL: Human Kinetics.

Coontz, S. (1992). *The way we never were: American families and the nostalgia trap.* New York: Basic Books.

Cuklanz, L. M. (2000). *Rape on prime time: Television, masculinity, and sexual violence.* Philadelphia: University of Pennsylvania Press.

Curtin, M. (1995). *Redeeming the wasteland: Television documentary and cold war politics.* New Brunswick, NJ: Rutgers University Press.

Delphy, C. (1984). *Close to home: A materialist analysis of women's oppression* (D. Leonard, Ed. & Trans.). London: Hutchinson.

Doty, W. G. (1986). *Mythography: The study of myths and rituals.* Tuscaloosa: University of Alabama Press.

Dow, B. J. (1992). Femininity and feminism in *Murphy Brown. Southern Communication Journal, 57,* 143–155.

Dyer, G. (1987). Women and television: An overview. In H. Baehr & G. Dyer (Eds.), *Boxed in: Women and television.* New York: Pandora Press.

Dow, B. J. (2001). *Ellen,* television, and the politics of gay and lesbian visibility. *Critical Studies in Media Communication, 18,* 123–140.

Firestone, S. (1979). *The dialectic of sex.* London: Woman's Press.

Fiske, J. (1983). The discourses of TV quiz shows, or school + luck = success + sex. *Central States Speech Journal, 34,* 139–150.

Fiske, J., & Hartley, J. (1978). *Reading television.* New York: Methuen.

Foss, S.K. (1996). *Rhetorical criticism: Exploration and practice* (2nd ed.). Prospect Heights, IL: Waveland.

Foss, S.K., & Foss, K.A. (1994). The construction of feminine spectatorship in Garrison Keillor's radio monologues. *Quarterly Journal of Speech, 80,* 410–426.

Fowles, J. (1996). *Advertising and popular culture.* Thousand Oaks, CA: Sage.

French, M. (1992). *The war against women.* New York: Summit Books.

Frentz, T., & Rushing, J. H. J. (2002). Mother isn't quite herself today: Myth and spectacle in *The Matrix. Critical Studies in Media Communication, 19,* 64–86.

Freud, S. (1966). *Standard edition of the complete psychological works.* London: Hogarth.

Frith, K. T. (Ed.). (1997). *Undressing the ad: Reading culture in advertising.* New York: Peter Lang.

Gamble, S. (Ed.). (1999). *The Routledge critical dictionary of feminism and postfeminism.* New York: Routledge.

Goldman, R. (1992). *Reading ads socially.* New York: Routledge.

Gray, H. (1995). *Watching race: Television and the struggle for "blackness."* Minneapolis: University of Minnesota.

Gronbeck, B. E. (1989). Mythic portraiture in the 1988 Iowa Presidential Caucus bio-ads. *American Behavioral Scientist, 32* (4), 351–364.

Hanke, R. (1990). Hegemonic masculinity in *thirtysomething. Critical Studies in Mass Communication, 7,* 231–248.

Hart, R. P. (1999). *Seducing America: How television charms the modern voter* (rev. ed.). New York: Oxford University Press.

Hartley, J. (1992). *The politics of pictures: The creation of the public in the age of popular media.* New York: Routledge.

Hartmann, H. (1976). Capitalism, patriarchy and job segregation by sex. *Signs, 1,* 137–168.

Himmelstein, H. (1984). *Television myth and the American mind.* Westport, CT: Praeger.

Hyman, S. E. (1955). *The armed vision.* New York: Vintage.

Janeway, E. (1971). *Man's world, woman's place: A study in social mythology.* New York: Dell.

Japp, P. M. (1991). Gender and work in the 1980s: Television's working women as displaced persons. *Women's Studies in Mass Communication, 15,* 49–74.

Jung, C. (1968). *Man and his symbols.* Garden City, NY: Doubleday.

Kimmel, M. (2000). *The gendered society.* Cambridge, MA: Oxford Press.

Kottak, C. P. (1990). *Prime time society: An anthropological analysis of television and culture.* Belmont, CA: Wadsworth.

Lester, E. P. (1997). Finding the path to signification: Undressing a Nissan Pathfinder direct mail package. In K.T. Frith (Ed.), *Undressing the ad: Reading culture in advertising* (pp. 19–34). New York: Peter Lang.

Levi-Strauss, C. (1958). The structural study of myth. In T. A. Sebeok (Ed.), *Myth: A symposium* (pp. 81-106). Bloomington, IN: Indiana University Press.

Lewis, W. F. (1987). Telling America's story: Narrative form and the Reagan presidency. *Quarterly Journal of Speech, 73,* 280–302.

Livingstone, S., & Liebes, T. (1995). "Where have all the mothers gone?" Soap opera's replaying of the Oedipal story. *Critical Studies in Media Communication, 12,* 155–175.

May, R. (1976). *Existential psychotherapy.* Toronto: CBC Learning.

McGrath, T. (1996). *MTV: The making of a revolution.* Philadelphia: Running Press.

Means Coleman, R. R. (2000). *African American viewers and the black situation comedy: Situating Racial humor.* New York: Garland.

Means Coleman, R. R. (Ed.). (2002). *Say it loud! African American audiences, media, and identity.* New York: Routledge.

Mechling, E. W. (1979). Patricia Hearst: MYTH AMERICA 1974, 1975, 1976. *Western Journal of Communication, 43,* 168–179.

Metz, C. (1976). The fiction film and its spectator: A metapsychological study. *New Literary History, 8,* 75–105.

Morreale, J. (1993). *The presidential campaign film: A critical history.* Westport, CT: Praeger.

Mulvey, L. (1975). Visual pleasure and narrative cinema. *Screen, 16* (3), 6–18.

Mulvey, L. (1989). *Visual and other pleasures.* Bloomington: Indiana University Press.

Naficy, H. (1999). The making of exile cultures: Iranian television in Los Angeles. In S. During (Ed.), *The cultural studies reader* (2nd ed., pp. 537–563). London: Routledge.

Newcomb, H. (1974). *TV, the most popular art*. Garden City, NY: Anchor Press/ Doubleday.

O'Sullivan, T., Hartley, J., Saunders, D., Montgomery, M., & Fiske, J. (1994). *Key concepts in communication and cultural studies*. New York: Routledge.

Parry-Giles, S. J., & Parry-Giles, T. (2002). *Constructing Clinton: Hyperreality and presidential image-making in postmodern politics*. New York: Peter Lang.

Projansky, S. (2001). *Watching rape: Film and television in postfeminist culture*. New York: New York University Press.

Real, M.R. (1977). *Mass-mediated culture*. Englewood Cliffs, NJ: Prentice-Hall.

Reeder, H. (1996). A critical look at gender differences in communication research. *Communication Studies, 47,* 318–330.

Rushing, J. H. (1983). The rhetoric of the western myth. *Communication Monographs, 50,* 14–32.

Rushing, J. H. (1985). *E.T.* as rhetorical transcendence. *The Quarterly Journal of Speech, 71,* 188–203.

Rushing, J. H. (1989). Evolution of "the new frontier" in *Alien* and *Aliens*: Patriarcal co-optation of the feminine archetype. *The Quarterly Journal of Speech, 75,* 1–24.

Rushing, J. H., & Frentz, T. (1989). The Frankenstein myth in contemporary cinema. *Critical Studies in Mass Communication, 6,* 61–80.

Schrag, R. (1991). Sugar and spice and everything nice versus snakes and snails and puppy dog's tails: Selling social stereotypes on Saturday morning television. In L. Vande Berg & L. A. Wenner (Eds.), *Television criticism: Approaches and applications* (pp. 220–235). White Plains, NY: Longman.

Schwichtenberg, C. (Ed.). (1992). *The Madonna connection: Representational politics, subcultural identities, and cultural theory*. Boulder, CO: Westview.

Slotkin, R.C. (1973). *Regeneration through violence: The mythology of the American frontier, 1600–1860*. Middleton, CT: Wesleyan University Press.

Torres, S. (1989). Melodrama, masculinity and the family: *thirtysomething* as therapy. *Camera Obscura, 19,* 87–106.

Trites, R. (1991). Disney's subversion of Andersen's *The Little Mermaid. Journal of Popular Film and Television, 18,* 145–152.

Turner, K. J., & Sprague, R. (1991). Musical and visual intervention in *Miami Vice*: Old genre, new form. In L. Vande Berg & L. A. Wenner (Eds.), *Television criticism: Approaches and applications* (pp. 273–288). White Plains, NY: Longman.

Twitchell, J. B. (1996). *Adcult USA: The triumph of advertising in American culture*. New York: Columbia University Press.

Vande Berg, L., & Trujillo, N. (1989). *Organizational life on television*. New York: Ablex.

Welter, B. (1966). The cult of true womanhood: 1820–1860. *American Quarterly, 18,* 151–174.

Wood, J. (2003). *Gendered lives: Communication, gender, and culture*. Belmont, CA: Wadsworth.

Wood, P. H. (1976). Television as dream. In R. Adler (Ed.), *Television as a cultural force* (pp. 17–35). Westport, CT: Praeger.

Vampires, Postmodernity, and Postfeminism: *Buffy the Vampire Slayer*

A. Susan Owen

In this article, I explore the popular series *Buffy the Vampire Slayer* through the intersections of postfeminism, postmodernity, and the vampire metanarrative. In particular, I discuss the manner in which this television narrative appropriates body rhetorics and narrative agency from traditionally masculinist metanarratives in the horror and mystery genres. Moreover, I examine how the fictional characters negotiate the politics of feminism and postmodernity in contemporary American suburban life. Social and mystical powers (on the side of good) are matrilineal in the series: only females can be vampire slayers, only females can have supernatural powers, and only females can discern who the predators are. (The sole exception is the "Watcher," Giles, a decidedly feminized male.) Through the narrative frame of the series, each episode is grounded in the tension between the embodied female heroine and the varied embodiments of evil she and her friends encounter. Each encounter requires the heroine to count the costs of leadership (primarily for girls and women), to mark "evil" as the consequence of modernity's faith in science and rationalism, and to depend upon the cooperation of a community of friends. Most of the series' humor derives from the (sometimes contrived) irony of postmodern teens dealing with premodern monsters, without the assistance of the clueless or complicitous adults.

This series has much in common with other popular dramatic teen series such as *Dawson's Creek*, *Felicity*, and *Party of Five*. The humor is edgy

As Owen explains, this prime-time teen serial drama about California valley girl Buffy (with Sarah Michelle Gellar as the heroic Vampire Slayer) ironically explores the social and psychic horrors of American adolescence (the high school with vampires) while ideologically and aesthetically transgressing action-adventure genre conventions by having a female control the narrative and deliver the kicks and punches.

and the story lines are serialized (to varying extents). The narratives illustrate that friends are family, because the traditional family unit has fragmented. Ironically, the story lines are steeped in television nostalgia, the public forum in which the idealized American family was imagined and perfected.[1] *Buffy* differentiates itself from market competitors by showing American adolescence and a variety of genres: action-adventure, mystery, horror and the occult, and comedy. The series offers transgressive possibilities for reimagining gendered relations and modernist American ideologies. At the same time, however, the series reifies mainstream commitments to heteronormative relationships, American commodity culture, and a predominantly Anglo perspective.

Character Composition and Ideological Tensions

This television series is premised on the novelty of a California valley girl who kicks ass, literally. The character of Buffy ruptures the action-adventure genre, in that a female is controlling the narrative and delivering the punches. Moreover, Buffy's embodied strength, power, and assertiveness destabilize the traditional masculinist power of the vampire character in the horror genre, in effect policing those who prey on the feminized. The series gleefully transposes conventional relations of power between the body-that-bleeds and the bloodsuckers. (The narrative implies that slayers are initiated at menarche, though Whedon and his writers are silent on the subject of menstruation in the television series.) The playful irony of the dramatic setting—a high school with vampires—explores the social and psychic horrors of American adolescent rites of passage. Sometimes comedic, sometimes farcical, sometimes tragic, the series meanders from the deadpan to the deadly. An episode in the third season, for example, parodies *Night of the Living Dead* as a vehicle for humorous, yet pointed, commentary on self-destructive rites of passage in male urban youth gangs. By contrast, earlier in the series, viewers were invited to reflect upon violence committed toward teen females by teen males.

Buffy begins the series as a loner, the quintessential outsider in the high school scene. In the first season, she is marked as both familiar and different; her name emphasizes the ambivalence of the character. Although she does not do well in school and does not get along well with her peer group, she is physically strong and regularly faces death with steely determination. She longs for safety and stability—to be like "other girls"—but she is frequently distracted from school and family life by her social and moral obligations to fight "evil." She generally experiences intense pleasure in physically challenging encounters with various monsters. And heretofore in television, we have not seen the adolescent female body in this way—signifying toughness, resilience, strength, and confidence. Nor have we seen adolescent female pleasure embodied as "a supremely confident kicker of evil butt" (Katz, 1998, p. 35). It is worth noting, however, that Buffy's body is a site of considerable struggle in the narrative. She is recognizably coded as slim, youthful, fit, and stylish; her body is a billboard for American commodity culture.[2] Sometimes her face and body are dominated by the camera; sometimes she fills and dominates the frame. But there can be little doubt that Buffy's agency drives the narrative and saves the world. Moreover, she talks back, she looks back, and she can take a blow as well as she can land one.

Pivotal relationships with two adults and three teens further refine the complexity and ambivalence of Buffy's character. She is most carefully supervised by her Watcher and mentor, Giles, who is marked as comically "foreign" in the postmodern world of Sunnydale High School. Giles is fortysomething, speaks with a British accent, and is an expert on antiquities and arcane medieval mysticism; he is absent-minded, ambiguously gendered, fussy, and resistant to most late-twentieth-century technology. In the first two seasons of the series, Giles is the only (responsible) adult who knows about the monsters. By contrast, Buffy's mother is marked as "ordinary"—she is emblematic of second-wave liberal bourgeoisie feminism.[3] Curator of a local museum, she provides a lavish upper-middle-class lifestyle for Buffy. She is divorced from

Buffy's father, she is white, she articulates liberally progressive perspectives, and she is utterly clueless about Buffy's closeted identity as a vampire slayer. Like the maternal character in the film, *The Lost Boys*, Buffy's mother unwittingly (and repeatedly) exposes her child to danger (Auerbach, 1995, p. 159).

The contrasts between the two adults are noteworthy. The feminized adult male both instructs and nurtures Buffy; his generational and cultural eccentricities function primarily to connect the youthful slayer to a historical past contained in rare books about mystical monsters that walked the earth prior to the age of reason. The feminized adult female is well intentioned but largely ineffectual; her efforts to nurture and instruct frequently are framed as misguided or naive. For example, in the final episode of the first season, she mistakes Buffy's apprehension about death at the hands of a powerful vampire as teen angst over going to the prom. Giles hones Buffy's physical and mental prowess in preparation for the showdown; Buffy's mother buys an expensive (white) prom dress to boost Buffy's confidence. Throughout the episode, the dress draws ironic commentary from all the characters, including the murderous vampire king. "Nice dress," he sneers. Buffy's mother (known occasionally as "Joyce") functions as a measure of Buffy's struggle to conceal her identity as a slayer, and as an exemplar of how clueless suburban parents (especially mothers) are about the dangers their children face.

Buffy's emotional and social life is most clearly seen in her interaction with three teen friends: Willow, Xander, and Cordelia. The contrasts provided through structured oppositions between and among these characters offer subtle shading for Buddy's character. In the first season of the series, Willow and Xander are "outsiders" at Sunnydale High School; hence, they initiate interaction with the odd new student (Buffy). Willow is conventionally gendered in most dimensions of her character. She is an excellent student, nonassertive, and concerned with the feelings and perspectives of others. She is the moral voice of the group, although she stutters and stammers through much of her dialogue. Her mode of dress and grooming is more

childlike than any of the other teen characters. Significantly, however, Willow is re-gendered as a creative and fearless computer hacker; later in the series, she discovers additional creative powers through witchcraft. Xander possesses no capacity for mystical power. He is a feminized heterosexual male who is anxious about heteronormative masculinity (he does not succeed in bonding with alpha males, and he is disparaged by the female teens he desires). Xander's character makes ironic and self-mocking commentary on the perils and challenges of masculine social scripts, giving voice to the anxieties invoked by the presence of the capable, confident super-heroine, Buffy. Xander and Willow play *les femmes* to Buffy's butch performance, each yearning for the super-heroine from a related, yet different, position in the gender matrix of the narrative.

Cordelia comes to the group reluctantly and gradually, over the course of the first and second seasons of the series. Her character is a sly parody of the bitch-cheerleader stereotype, the consummate high school "insider."[4] Cordelia is utterly confident in the power of conventional femininity, performed well, and in the celebration of commodity culture. She is flashy, vain, shallow, mean-spirited, narcissistic, fetishistic and generally fearless. Her relentless self-centeredness provides comic relief in the face of whatever monstrosity is served up by the narrative. Cordelia's embodied social power is an important contrast to Willow's girlishness and Buffy's re-gendered power; the scenes between and among these three characters set up the possibilities for exploring the transfer of social power from the bounded performance of a given social script, to the transgressive re-visioning of the script. Cordelia's hostility to Buffy's unconventional power is structurally aligned with Xander's anxieties about heteronormative masculinity; Cordelia mocks Xander because he is not able or willing to perform as alpha male. (The caustic, comic edginess to Cordelia's character is historically indebted to the literary tradition of *Lysistrata*.) Still, Xander's characteristic ironic dialogue suggests that he is aware of the paradigmatic shifts in gendered relations; thus, although Cordelia's taunts wound, they are framed as out of bounds. Cordelia castigates Buffy and Willow for their shortcomings as feminine commodity consumers, and her critique frequently hits the mark. In the context of the narrative, her words have the power to mark deviance; failure to accessorize femininity is on par with failures to *act* (convincingly) like a man. These character intersections invite viewing audiences to consider cultural changes, and resistance to change, in feminine social power and gender politics.

Buffy's relationship with these three teens establishes narrative momentum toward collectivity and away from the individualist quest narrative typical of the action adventure, mystery, and horror genres. Most problems and challenges are evaluated and solved through cooperation and shared responsibility. The constructed social conflicts and competing desires between and among characters underscore the necessity of social cooperation and tolerance. Buffy is the keystone signifier of a youth community that fights Evil and deals with reconstructed problems of middle-class, Anglo, heteronormative, North American teenage socialization: shifting gender scripts, sexual maturation, sexual violence, drug use, peer pressure, clueless adults, the numbing banality of educational systems, the fragmented heterosexual, middle-class family unit, and the failures of the national world paradigm. The two adult (parental) characters articulate the social boundaries of civil society; the teens test the boundaries to determine whether they will hold in the face of irrationality and chaos. Each episode negotiates the claims of a rational world view in the context of social fragmentation and institutional failure; each crisis illustrates the incommensurability of rational claims (God is dead) with the lived experience of everyday life in urban America (the devil is undead). In each episode, postmodern playfulness is juxtaposed with the narrative demand for social order.

Buffy's sexual and emotional entanglement with a male vampire provides an interesting twist to the series, further complicating the possibilities for narrative play and underscoring the deep-rooted ambivalence of her character. "Angel" appears in the first season of the series as a self-appointed guardian and secret admirer of the young slayer, Buffy. As the series unfolds, we learn that he has been a vampire for over two hundred years, and that he has been cursed by gypsies to feel moral loathing for his predatory desires (he is a vampire with a conscience). Should he ever experience true happiness, he will revert to his former amoral state. (This particular contradiction is never addressed by any of the characters, and Angel is far too shallow a character to notice the loophole in his curse.) Angel is arguably the most sexualized and eroticized of all the characters in the series; this beast is a real beauty. His body invites the constructed consumer gaze of romance novel covers, soft-core pornography, and mass circulation advertising. Angel is appropriately (and humorously) named, in that he functions in the narrative as the object of teen fantasies and anxieties. Played woodenly by David Boreanaz, Angel is the only character in Buffy's inner circle (other than her mother) who lacks wit, savvy, or special talent.

Angel is primarily a plot-enabler. In relation to Buffy, Angel's presence enables various clichés of heterosexual romance, such as the redemptive power of dyadic love, the agony and angst of star-crossed lovers, the allure of secret trysts, and the deflowering of the female virgin. Because of her relationship with Angel, Buffy will betray her friends' trust, experience the anguish of putting community before self-interest, and enact social alienation by running away from home. For Xander and Cordelia, Angel is the site of perfected masculine appeal; they each fret over his devotion to Buffy. Willow and Buffy talk endlessly about Angel; their conversations rehearse the assumptions of heteronormative scripts. Giles and Angel, of course, are paradigmatically vested in Buffy, and frequently are at odds in the narrative. In them, Buffy finds fractured paternal patronage: Giles is the sexually repressed brains, Angel is the eroticized brawn. Periodically, Buffy plays out the fantasy of being a damsel in distress, needing to be rescued by her hunky boyfriend. Ultimately, however, Buffy chooses Angel's fate and her own path.

The other vampires in the series merit commentary here, as they are a composite characterization of danger and desire. Like the humans, the vampires are homogeneous in some respects and diverse in others. The predators are oddly corporeal; embodied as beneficiaries of a healthclub aesthetic, they are uniformly muscled, trim, and agile. They generally do not appear as mist, shadows, rotting corpses, or animal forms.[5] Rather, they are smartly attired in trendy fashions or campy gothic costumes, and they are athletically vigorous and aerobically fit. They leap from bushes, vault off various perches, or burst forth from sewer openings and fresh graves. Encounters with Buffy include several minutes of kickboxing, acrobatic bodyslams, and artistically choreographed punching. When the vampires are staked by Buffy and her assistants, they desiccate into powder, leaving no messy residue or unpleasant trace of death and decay. Occasionally, the overpowered vampires simply run away from their encounters with Buffy. Among the more interesting variabilities in vampire "social" relations is the generational tension between the ancient ones, and the younger, hip monsters. For example, sassy British punk vampires, Spike and Drucilla, are far more dangerous to Buffy and friends than the ancient ones, precisely because Spike and Drucilla are no strangers to the postmodern condition. In what is surely one of the high moments of visual and narrative satire in the first season of the series, Buffy sarcastically advises the king of the vampires (an ancient one) to save his hypnotic gaze "for the tourists."

Vampires generally lurk in the "bad places"— cemeteries, dark alleys, basements and tunnels, abandoned buildings, and suburban parks.[6] In Sunnydale, however, they also lurk in the ordinary spaces where contemporary teens are exposed to urban threats: dance clubs, high school locker rooms, classrooms, lounges, and parking lots, shopping malls, and private homes. In this narrative, vampires conceal their identity until they are aroused; then, their seemingly human faces morph into a contorted mask of rage and desire (with obligatory fangs, of course). Like their literary and filmic forebears, these vampires infiltrate human social gatherings to stalk prey. To some extent,

their presence in the narrative rehearses lingering cultural anxieties about hidden danger, contamination, and infection.[7] But most of Sunnydale's vampires are always already enraged—their identities fixed and known. They are the foot soldiers of the vampire leaders, or the highly stylized loners and adventure seekers, all desiring battle with the "girl" slayer. Gone is the hypnotic gaze, the stately posturing, the otherworldliness of Hollywood filmic vampires. Diminished, too, is the cast of shrinking, screaming, swooning female victims. Contamination and infection metaphors are faint traces in the narrative; crucifixion icons, holy water, biblical injunctions, and mirrors are generic fragments, relegated to mere scene. Giles is all that remains of the foreign other embodied by Lugosi and Langella, who were at once contamination threat and sexual fantasy. Giles is "foreign" to the postmodern culture of Buffy and her friends because he is an embodied relic, a repository of historical knowledge.

Overall, Sunnydale's vampires are hip, campy, and cartoonish—more goofy than ghoulish manifestations of what truly is to be feared. This is consistent with how Whedon describes himself, saying, "I was a comic book boy. I tend to create universes with the kind of sophomoric emotional bigness that really exists only in comic books and TV" (Lippert, 1997, p. 25). In Sunnydale, the threat is inherent within the culture; reason, science and social order fail in the face of predation, because predation is part of the modern project.[8] In this narrative, vampirism is the inverted human face of power and domination. Significantly, when vampires are on the scene, the name of the game is creepy fun. Vampires are signifiers at play: they invite the audience to play with matters that seem frightening. But when those matters emerge in the interactions of human characters, that sense of play largely disappears.

Stepford Fathers, Cyborgs, and Domestic Terror

In the second season of the series, Buffy faces one of many of the "real" monsters in the series; this time, it is her mother's "boyfriend." In an episode broadcast on 8 December 1997, John Ritter plays a computer salesman who seduces Joyce and threatens Buffy's life. As the episode unfolds, "Ted" works his way into Joyce and Buffy's private lives. To Joyce, Ted seems like the perfect, sensitive new age guy (SNAG). In addition to his wildly successful career as a computer salesman, Ted is skilled in the domestic arts, especially cooking. (Viewers familiar with seventies television programming probably appreciate this playful association with Ritter's role as aspiring chef Jack Tripper on *Three's Company*.) Ted charms Joyce, and even Buffy's friends, with his flattering talk and culinary prowess. Only Buffy is wary. As the episode unfolds, Ted begins to isolate Buffy from family and friends to utter ugly threats to her. He is disgusted and enraged by her independence and unruliness; moreover, he views Buffy as a threat to his relationship with Joyce. None of the other characters ever witnesses the very human face of Ted's rage in these narrative interludes; the viewing audience always does.

The tension builds between Ted and Buffy for almost one-half of the hour-long episode. Then, in a pivotal scene, witnessed only by the viewing audience, Buffy returns from patrolling for vampires late at night to find Ted sitting in her darkened bedroom. Moreover, Ted has read Buffy's diary and knows about her slayer identity. He threatens to expose Buffy to her mother and to school authorities. Shocked and angered, Buffy demands that Ted return her diary and leave her room. Ted's dialogue becomes increasingly abusive and threatening, escalating inexorably toward the moment when he strikes Buffy in the face with his fist, knocking her down. More angry than frightened, Buffy gets up and says to Ted: "I was so hoping you would do that." And then she kicks and punches Ted until he falls down the stairs, to his death. Only after Buffy has defended herself from Ted's assault does Buffy's mother appear, shocked by her daughter's actions.

Most seasoned television viewers can guess that something is amiss with Ted's apparent death: he is killed off too early in the episode; his death, although potentially satisfying to some viewers, nonetheless violates the genre boundaries for application of deadly force; and, the death poses a moral dilemma

for Buffy, who cannot kill a "human." Buffy's friends rally around her and begin to investigate Ted's life. Buffy once again is a pariah at school, but this time she's in "real" trouble because she has killed her potential stepfather. None of the adults believes Buffy's account of Ted's abuse and assault. The police believe Buffy killed Ted in a fit of jealous rage; school officials state, with some satisfaction, that she has finally gone "too far"; and Buffy's mom (as always) is bewildered and upset by her daughter's conduct. The viewing audience, however, has been positioned to root for Buffy, because they know Ted is a monster—of the human variety.

Predictably, Ted pops back into the narrative as one of the "undead." Significantly, however, he is not a vampire but a self-made cyborg. Once again, he and Buffy struggle in verbal and physical confrontation. The scene owes much to Ridley Scott's 1979 *Alien*, in which the most famous action-adventure heroine of American cinema, Sigourney Weaver's "Ripley," does battle with the murderous android Ash.[9] Like Ash, Ted has been damaged by his first confrontation with the female heroine. Like Ash, Ted malfunctions in speech and head movement, revealing the terrifying truth of his technological re-birth. Unlike Ash—and this is noteworthy—Ted ultimately is subdued by the youthful heroine. (Recall that Ripley was rescued from Ash's phallic rape by a male character.) When Ted threatens Joyce's life, Buffy "kills" him again, this time with a blow to the head with his favorite skillet. The killing blow exposes the metallic machinery under Ted's skin, verifying what viewers were encouraged to suspect. Meanwhile, Buffy's friends have located Ted's apartment; and in the closet they find the grisly remains of his first three wives. Thanks to the wariness and toughness of her daughter, Joyce narrowly escapes lethal entanglement with a serial murderer of women.

In the denouement of the episode, social order is restored in the context of postmodern play. Tongue in cheek, the teens muse about whether Willow (the computer expert) has kept any of Ted's technological "parts," making reference to the narrative premise of *Terminator 2* (*T2*). In the context of narrative closure of the episode, with all regular characters and relationships restored to stability, such playfulness invites the audience's wandering gaze to reread the episode ironically as a humorous pastiche of stage, film, and television fragments. Recirculated as a Willie Lomanesque, free-floating signifier, Ted the super-salesman refuses to die; rather, as in *Terminator 2,* we realize the possibility of the perpetual presence of Ted's walking—and stalking—in American commodity culture. In a humorous and rare slap at American commodity culture, this episode suggests that those able to merge themselves with technology will be successful, and potentially deadly. *Death of a Salesman* intersects with *Fatal Attraction;* only here, the gendered roles are reversed so that male to female violence is framed as the "real" predation. As an exposed predator, Ted is dispatched from this life by a teenage female kickboxer, imitating Linda Hamilton in *T2* and Sigourney Weaver in *Alien.* The monster in this *Fatal Attraction* narrative reveals Jack Tripper as Jack the Ripper.

Ideological tensions typical of the series are played out in this episode. The collectivized, matrilineal social order (Buffy and company) is disrupted by patriarchal culture. Ted's character is coded as politically conservative. He favors Christian prayer at the dinner table and rigid gender roles and conventional relations of power for men and women. What drives him to batter and kill women is their assertion of independence and autonomy. Where women and girls are concerned, Ted embodies manipulative, abusive, violent force. Hence, Buffy provokes his rage from the moment they meet; Joyce resists him only near the end of the episode, when she finally recognizes danger. Like many of the vampires Buffy encounters, Ted, too, is able to conceal his identity—from authority figures such as parents, teachers, and law enforcement agencies. Unlike the vampires, however, Buffy has no authority over human monsters, and so life with Ted is not a game. He cannot be dispatched with ease or moral certainty. There are no special books, no sacred objects, no incantations with which to destroy his power; even a well placed kick, a tumble down the stairs, and a broken neck fail to stop Ted. The logic of this narrative poses a dilemma for the rational world paradigm: Either social institutions are incapable of detecting and constraining predators such as Ted, or social institutions create and foster the predation.

Final Reflections

A hard-edged, humorous assault on the shortcomings of liberal reform and the inherent flaws of American civil society, the series is most challenging to mainstream culture when it manipulates irony and fragmentation as modes of critique. The series reconfigures some of the relations of power in the body rhetorics of horror and action by relocating narrative agency from masculine to feminine. Vampires are cartoonish figures standing in for the failed grand narratives of middle America: stable family life, equanimity, justice, rule of law, and the conquest of nature. Buffy and her friends wage a hyperreal war against the vampires, with all the playfulness and imagination of a video game aesthetic. Vampires also stand in for the demonic faces of adult rage. The ultimate fantasy in *Buffy* is that teens can develop the metaphysical power and social cohesion necessary to shield themselves from these demons. As illustrated in the episode with Ted, the teens are less sanguine about their chances with the adult humans. The series is most poignant when dramatizing the adolescent passage from innocence to worldliness. In Sunnydale, young people must take on adult responsibilities before they have finished being children.

The series is most conventional in its uncritical embrace of American capital culture. Assumptions about social relationships are predicated on the very commodity culture that television helps to construct and mediate. Buffy's power is domesticated by her oft articulated longing to be "normal"—to have a steady boyfriend (with all that entails) and to consume life uninterrupted by the demands of civic obligation. The narrative opposes the costs of leadership and political potency, with intimacy, stable relationships, and material comfort. The quality of a woman's private life is diminished by the burden she bears to participate in civil society. Moreover, in spite of Buffy's narrative agency and physical potency, her body project remains consistent with the rescripted body signs of American commodity advertising.[10] In other words, political potency is imagined and then reduced to matters of consumer style. Racially, the series is very conservative; whiteness is not marked but rather constitutes the presumptive grounds of the series. A postfeminist perspective is constructed through Buffy's relationship with her mother, Joyce.[11] Although Joyce and Buffy clearly enjoy benefits from the first and second waves of the American feminist movement, little is ever said about the history of women's struggle in American culture.[12] More to the point, Joyce is emblematic of parental and feminine limitation in the series. Buffy's strength and confidence are not learned from the vast experiences of past generations of women; rather, they are her mystical birthright as a slayer. The series plays at transgression; as such, it is quintessential television.[13] But it remains to be seen whether transgressive play can challenge institutional relations of power.[14]

Notes

1. See Owen. *Gen X TV: The Brady Bunch to Melrose Place.*

2. See Katz: "Death Becomes Her," 42; Michael Stroud, "WB Tops UPN Season to Date," and Jennifer Graham, "Slay Anything."

3. See Fargonis, "Postmodernism and Feminism."

4. See Butler, *Gender Trouble.*

5. See Auerbach.

6. See Clover, *Men, Women, and Chainsaws: Gender in the Modern Horror Film.*

7. See Waller, *The Living and the Undead: From Stoker's Dracula to Romero's Dawn of the Dead.*

8. Owen and Ehrenhaus, "Animating a Critical Rhetoric: On the Feeding Habits of American Empire."

9. It is worth noting here that Whedon has screenwriter credit for *Alien: Resurrection.* See Lippert, p. 25.

10. For a historical analysis of the institutional relations between adolescent females and commodity culture, see Joan Jacobs Brumberg, *The Body Project: An Intimate History of American Girls.* Also see Griselda Pollock, "Missing Women: Rethinking Early Thoughts on Images of Women."

11. For an excellent discussion of post-feminism and television, see Dow, *Prime-Time Feminism: Television Media Culture, and the Women's Movement since 1970.*

12. On the importance of memory, history, and women, see Bordo, *Unbearable Weight: Feminism, Western Culture, and the Body,* p. 283.

13. See Meehan, "Conceptualizing Culture as Commodity: The Problem of Television." Meehan discusses the tension between art and commodity in American television broadcasting.

14. See Bordo, "Postmodern Subjects, Postmodern Bodies." In a review of Judith Butler's *Gender Trouble,* Bordo argues that Butler may have overstated the case for the subversive power of textual play. Bordo writes, "I want to make clear that my criticism of the abstract nature of Butler's argument does not entail a denial of the fact that subversive elements are continually at work (or play) in our culture. My point is that subversion is contextual, historical, and above all social. No matter how exciting the 'destabilizing' potential of texts, bodily or otherwise, whether those texts are subversive or recuperative or both or neither cannot be determined in abstraction from actual social practice" (1992, p. 172).

References

Auerbach, N. (1995). *Our vampires, ourselves.* Chicago: University of Chicago Press.

Bordo, S. (1992). Postmodern subjects, postmodern bodies. *Feminist Studies, 18,* 150–175.

Bordo, S. (1992). *Unbearable weight: Feminism, western culture, and the body.* Berkeley: University of California Press.

Brumberg, J. (1997). *The body project: An intimate history of American girls.* New York: Vintage Books.

Butler, J. (1990). *Gender trouble.* New York: Routledge.

Clover, C. J. (1992). *Men, women, and chainsaws: Gender in the modern horror film.* Princeton: Princeton University Press.

Dow, B. J. (1996). *Prime-time feminism: Television, media culture, and the women's movement since 1970.* Philadelphia: University of Pennsylvania Press.

Fargonis, S. (1994). Postmodernism and feminism. In D. R. Dickens & A. Fontana (Eds.), *Postmodernism and social inquiry* (pp. 101–126). New York: Guilford Press.

Graham, J. (1998, January). Slay anything. *Young and Modern,* pp. 56–60.

Katz, A. (1998, April 6). *Buffy the Vampire Slayer. Nation,* pp. 35–36.

Katz, A. (1998, June 8). Death becomes her. *Brandweek,* p. 42.

Lippert, B. (1997, December 15). Hey, there, warrior girl. *New York,* pp. 24–25.

Meehan, E. (1986). Conceptualizing culture as commodity: The problem of television. *Critical Studies in Mass Communication, 3,* 448–457.

Owen, R. (1997). Gen X TV: *The Brady Bunch* to *Melrose Place.* Syracuse: Syracuse University Press.

Owen, A. S., & Ehrenhaus, P. (1993). Animating a critical rhetoric: On the feeding habits of American empire. *Western Journal of Communication, 57,* 169–177.

Pollock, G. (1990). Missing women: Rethinking early thoughts on images of women. In C. Vance (Ed.), *The critical image: Essays on contemporary photography* (pp. 202–219). Seattle: Bay Press.

Stroud, M. (1998, 23 February). WB tops UPN season to date. *Broadcasting & Cable,* pp. 41–43.

Waller, G. A. (1986). *The living and the undead: From Stoker's* Dracula *to Romero's* Dawn of the Dead. Urbana: University of Illinois Press.

Criminal Investigations and Spiritual Quests: The *X-Files* as an Example of Hegemonic Concordance in a Mass-Mediated Society

Robert Westerfelhaus and Teresa A. Combs

As the twenty-first century approaches, many Westerners have begun to question what social psychologist Kenneth Gergen (1991) calls the *"grand narrative of modernism"* (p. 30).[1] As Gergen explains it, this narrative "is a story told by Western culture to itself about its journey through time. . . . The grand narrative is one of continuous upward movement—improvement, conquest, achievement—toward some goal" (p. 30).

The narrative's defining feature, then, is its promise of perpetual progress. This promise provides the West with a means of understanding its past as well as a road map for its future. Neither we humans nor the world in which we live are perfect, so the narrative goes, but both have the potential to be improved.

Beginning with the Englightenment, many of the West's most influential thinkers came to view reason as the way of improving ourselves and the social and physical worlds in which we dwell. Throughout most of this century, a particular application of reason—that of modern science—has been touted as the means through which the grand narrative's prom-

Authors' Note: The authors wish to thank Roger Aden for useful comments he made regarding an earlier draft of this article.

ised improvements, conquests, and achievements would be realized. As Gergen (1991) puts it, "Because of the individual's capacities for reason and observation, as expressed in the scientific attitude, utopias were now within our grasp" (p. 31). And indeed, for a time it seemed as though science was fulfilling the promises made on its behalf. Inventions made life easier, diseases were conquered, and humans landed on the moon. Gradually, however, the West's optimism regarding scientific progress became tempered by a growing recognition that the benefits of science come with a cost. The products and processes that science makes possible take a toll on the environment (Carson, 1962; Gaarder, 1994) and on the humans whose interests science ostensibly serves (Gergen, 1991; Ritzer, 1996).

Disillusioned by science's betrayal of its promise of unlimited progress and dissatisfied with the world science helped create, many Westerners have spurned science and turned to nonscientific belief systems for explanation and consolation. Indeed, according to Nicholas Humphrey (1996), more than half of the American population admit to believing in such things as astrology, clairvoyance, faith healing, past lives, and psychokinesis. This trend is not unique to Americans, however; as Norwegian philosopher Jostein Gaarder (1994) observes, many Europeans also subscribe to these nonscientific beliefs. This belief in astrology, clairvoyance, and so forth does not necessarily imply an outright rejection of science. What such belief does suggest, however, is that there are human needs that science cannot fulfill; and, in addition, there are limits to what we can know and understand through science. This suggestion poses a challenge to science's privileged position within Western culture. And when that which is privileged is challenged, tension results.

In this article, we identify the *X-Files* (Carter 1996), a television series broadcast on the Fox network, as a site where the tension between Western science and nonscientific ways of knowing is depicted through drama, dialogue, and metaphor. Through this depiction, we argue, the *X-Files* is a reflection of contemporary concerns while it gives new expression to an age-old dialectic between scientific

skepticism and a spiritual faith that accepts, and at times even embraces, the mysterious (i.e., that which defies explanation). In the West, the dialectic between these two alternative ways of knowing and coping with the world can be traced back more than two and a half millennia to ancient Greece, where Western science first took root. In contributing to this dialectic, the *X-Files* reflects contemporary ecological, political, and social concerns.

Our examination of this dialectic is informed by Condit's (1994) model of hegemony in a mass-mediated society. Condit offers this model of consent formation as an extension of Gramsci's (1987) conception of hegemony and as an alternate to contemporary critical approaches to hegemony that emphasize ideology and domination (e.g., Bodroghkozy, 1991; Dow, 1990; Hanke, 1990; Trujillo, 1991). Condit argues that this theoretical extension is needed for a late twentieth-century American historical context that differs significantly from the context in which and for which Gramsci developed his theory of consent.[2] Condit also expresses the hope that her alternative model will, in her words, "make hegemony more than simply a synonym for dominant ideology" (p. 226).

Condit's (1994) model of consent formation is evolutionary rather than revolutionary. As she explains, the "hegemonic position presumes that contradictions are inevitable in all human political entities" (p. 221). These contradictions reflect polyvocal concerns and are never fully resolved; instead, they serve as the basis of a series of accommodations that result in an ever-evolving and never-concluded concord. According to Condit, this "concord is neither harmonious nor inevitably fair or equitable, it is simply the best that can be done under the circumstances. Concordances are therefore always open to dispute and in play" (p. 210). As a site that gives fictitious expression to such dispute and play, the *X-Files* is worthy of serious critical attention.

The *X-Files* as a Site of Tension

The *X-Files* focuses on the exploits of two FBI agents, Dana Scully and Fox Mulder, who specialize in investigating unconventional crime cases, especially those with paranormal features. The cases Scully and Mulder investigate range from cannibalism to necrophilia, from UFO abductions to murders committed through the use of shamanic spells or voodoo practices. The perpetrators of these crimes are just as diverse; they include solitary loners and genetic freaks, multinational conspirators, as well as their extraterrestrial collaborators. The series premiered on the Fox network in fall 1994, "with little hope and less hype" (Wild, 1996, p. 40). According to Nollinger (1996), the series garnered critical acclaim and acquired a dedicated cult following during its debut season, while the second season saw the popularity of the show rise. Reflecting this popularity, the *X-Files* has been featured on the cover of numerous magazines, has won several awards (e.g., the 1994 Golden Globe Award for best dramatic series), and has been nominated for many more. Yet another sign of the *X-Files'* popularity is the devoted band of cyberspace followers the series has attracted who communicate via the Internet and refer to themselves "the X-Philes."

The *X-Files* is more than a critically acclaimed and popularly favored series, however; it is also a site of tension between alternative ways of knowing—between a Western science based on skepticism (i.e., the need to prove) and a faith that acknowledges those things science denies or ignores (i.e., a willingness to accept). This dialectic has been a major focus of the show since its beginning. In the pilot episode, FBI agent Scully is assigned by her superiors to accompany another FBI agent, Mulder, during the course of his investigations. Scully is a medical doctor with a strong background in science (her senior thesis was titled "Einstein's Twin Paradox: A New Interpretation"). Scully's training as a doctor and education as a scientist have brought her to the attention of her superiors, who charge Scully with the mission of reporting on and assessing Mulder's work, which has as its focus the paranormal. (Cases that involve the paranormal are referred to as X-Files; hence, the series' name.) As she is presented with this assignment, Scully asks, "Am I to understand that you

want me to debunk the X-Files project, sir?" To which inquiry the man replies, "Agent Scully, we trust that you will make the proper *scientific* analysis" (emphasis added). In assessing the validity of Mulder's work, then, Scully is to use the criteria employed by science.

Mulder, an Oxford-educated psychologist, is obsessed with the paranormal because, as a child, he witnessed (or thinks he witnessed) his sister's abduction by aliens (i.e., extraterrestrials). Spurred on by this obsession, Mulder has taken on himself the responsibility of investigating cases brought to the FBI's attention that have paranormal features. The bureau has grudgingly permitted Mulder the time and resources required to pursue these nonconventional cases, because he has proven himself a good agent and because, as he cryptically puts it, "connections in Congress allowed me a certain freedom to pursue my interests."

From the series' beginning, the differences between the two agents' world views are clearly defined. The following exchange, which takes place during their first meeting, is typical and clearly delineates their differences:

MULDER: Do you believe in the existence of extraterrestrials?

SCULLY: Logically, I would have to say no. Given the distance needed to travel from the far reaches of space, the energy requirements would exceed the spacecraft's capabilities.

MULDER: Conventional wisdom. You know when convention and science offer us no answers, might we not finally turn to the fantastic as a plausibility?

SCULLY: What I find fantastic is the notion that there are answers beyond the realm of science. The answers are out there, you just have to look.

This belief is echoed in the series' motto: "The truth is out there." The search for this truth is what drives both Scully and Mulder as well as the series itself.

However, although Scully and Mulder do not dispute that there is truth to be found, as the dialogue cited above indicates they disagree regarding what this truth is and how it can best be sought.

Scully is the *X-Files'* resident skeptic; Mulder, the series' believer.[3] In the dialectic between science and faith, Scully represents impersonal science and the skepticism that informs it, while Mulder represents a faith that is shaped by and understood through personal experience. In their encounters with paranormal phenomena and their conversations with one another, Scully and Mulder participate in what amounts to a late twentieth-century morality play in which science and faith, rather than good and evil, are pitted against one another.

This morality play unfolds in episode after episode as Scully and Mulder use forensic science and modern technology in an ongoing attempt to understand and negotiate a world filled with things that do not readily lend themselves to scientific explanation or control (e.g., ghosts, prophetic premonitions). Scully relies on science to dismiss those things that science itself cannot explain or control. Mulder, on the other hand, hopes that science will confirm the existence of those things he already knows but cannot prove and, in the process, convince others—and perhaps himself—that such things do indeed exist. As a narrator puts it in one episode, Mulder is searching for "the one piece of undeniable evidence that will make us all believers" (i.e., evidence that meets the standards of science). To date, Mulder's search has failed to yield the kind of conclusive evidence for which he has been looking.

Ironically, in searching for such evidence, Mulder and Scully have uncovered more mysteries than they have solved. Indeed, as the same unnamed narrator notes, "Scully and Mulder have explored mysteries from the outer reaches of space to the inner reaches of the mind." They have looked beyond and within. In investigating such wide-ranging mysteries, Scully and Mulder encounter and seek an understanding of the mysterious, that which defies rational scientific explanation and yet demands to be acknowledged. In this respect, then, their cases are as much spiritual quests as they are criminal investigations. In their encounters with the mysterious, Scully and Mulder are constantly searching for a truth that transcends the immediate concerns of the particular case with which they are currently involved.

In this respect, Scully and Mulder function in the role of mythic heroes. As Berger (1992) explains, "One of the basic functions of mythic heroes is to solve contradictions, to mediate between opposing forces" (p. 25). The opposing forces between which Mulder and Scully mediate are those of the natural and the supernatural. The former lends itself to the scientific scrutiny valued by Scully; the latter can only be approached experientially and requires, at times, a degree of faith. Tension arises between the two approaches when both vie to explain phenomena that straddle the contested boundary that lies between the natural and the supernatural worlds. This tension between skepticism and faith, between science and nonscientific ways of knowing, is not new; indeed, this struggle has been a central feature of Western civilization since Western science first emerged in ancient Greece. At times, faith has had the upper hand (e.g., during the Middle Ages); at other times, science has been predominant (e.g., during the Enlightenment). At no time has either managed to exclude the other from societal discourse. This is in keeping with Condit's (1994) observation that societal discourse is polyvocal; although one voice might achieve a degree of dominance over others, no voice is completely silenced.

The *X-Files*, then, is a contemporary contribution to a dialogue that has a long history in the Western world. The following is an early account (circa early second century C.E.) of the dispute and play between science and faith as told by the ancient historian Plutarch (1960); this account succinctly sums up some of the main issues that define the conflict between the two:

> There is a story that Pericles was once sent from his country estate the head of a one-horned ram. Thereupon Lampon the soothsayer, when he saw how the horn grew strong and solid out of the middle of the creature's forehead, declared that the mastery of the two dominant parties in the city . . . would be concentrated in the hands of one man. . . . Anaxagoras, on the other hand, had the skull dissected and proceeded to demonstrate that the brain had not filled its natural space, but had contracted into a point like an egg in the cavity from which the horn grew. (p. 170)

In commenting on this incident, Plutarch has this to say:

> In my opinion . . . there was nothing to prevent both the scientist and the prophet from being right, since the one correctly diagnosed the cause and the other the meaning of the prodigy. It was the business of the first to observe why something happens and how it becomes what it is, and the second to foretell the purpose of an event and its significance. (p. 170)

Plutarch's comment is an early attempt to achieve a balance between scientific skepticism and religious faith. Almost two millennia later, Westerners are still striving to strike a balance between the two. We have yet to reach an accommodation, however, that satisfies the conflicting demands of science and of faith. At best, we struggle along with a tenuous and never-concluded concordance that makes room for both without attempting to reconcile the two.

As Plutarch (1960) points out, the focus of science is on the *how;* the focus of faith is on the *why.* In the *X-Files,* this dialectic is a critical one. In explaining the how of the unusual phenomena she encounters, Scully as a scientist strives to bring the paranormal into the realm of the normal and the supernatural into the realm of the natural. This is an attempt to control through definition. To render the extraordinary ordinary robs phenomena of its supernatural significance. To use an example from the series, an object cannot be the product of extraterrestrials if its chemical composition suggests a terrestrial origin. In the clash between science and faith, the adherents of both seek to claim control over meaning. As Condit (1994) notes, such a contest over "symbolism is at stake throughout the formation of concordance" (p. 224).

The *X-Files* as Mythic Extension

In continuing the centuries-old dialectic between science and faith, the *X-Files* assumes the form of what Rushing (1986) refers to as "transitional 'hybrids'—that is, stories which fuse old mythic values onto a new scene" (p. 282). The *X-Files* blends the contemporary police story (which is a modern adaptation of those myths in which the hero/heroine searches for truth and seeks to right wrongs)

with tales of the supernatural (another mythic form in which humans encounter beings and forces that defy rational explanation). In blending these disparate genres, the series casts two contemporary American law enforcement agents in the role of inquirers into the supernatural. Or, to put it another way, the *X-Files* fuses two traditional mythic themes—the search for some truth and encounters with the supernatural—onto the contemporary American cultural and physical landscape. Rushing suggests that such transitional hybrids sometimes contain "the seeds of a more advanced mythic phase" (p. 282). Since the seeds of this particular hybrid have yet to sprout, we can only guess at what the new mythic phrase, of which the *X-Files* is a harbinger, might look like. At this point, we venture such a guess.

The *X-Files* represents partial rejection of the grand narrative of modernism (i.e., progress through reason—in particular, the application of reason that is science) in favor of a return to the ancient Greeks' more complicated understanding of reason as both dangerous and beneficial. In this respect, the series reflects the current suspicion on the part of many Westerners concerning the ability of science to improve life as well as their appreciation of and search for nonscientific sources of comfort and understanding. In the *X-Files,* this suspicion of science and search for alternatives is often portrayed through metaphor.

Light and the absence of light play a central role in the *X-Files.* Indeed, beams of light piercing darkness is one of the show's most frequently recurring motifs. This motif is realized as Scully and Mulder wander about dark open spaces or enter confined and maze-like dark spaces armed with high-powered flashlights. Their flashlights probe the mysterious darkness, but only a portion of the darkness is illuminated at any given time; for this reason, the darkness surrenders only a few of its secrets if it surrenders any at all. The light proves useful but it is inadequate to the task.

We suggest that the show's use of light is a metaphor for human reason in general and science in particular, while the darkness represents the realm of the mysterious. To extend this metaphor, the open spaces represent that which extends beyond the human, while the confined spaces represent that which is within. In the West, reason is frequently represented as light (e.g., "the light of reason"). The flashlights used by Scully and Mulder to probe dark spaces and be metaphorically understood, then, as an attempt to use reason to probe life's mysteries. Such mysteries reside within and without us; they are the stuff of which myths are fashioned.

Myths play a central role in the life of any culture (Campbell & Moyers 1988). They provide continuity between past and present while offering a road map for the future. Myths enable us to make sense of our world and to act within it. When a culture's circumstances radically change and its traditional myths no longer serve the purpose for which they were originally created, the traditional myths become little more than curious old stories that no longer speak to the concerns of a living generation. During times of significant cultural transition, traditional myths are sometimes discarded in favor of new myths, or they are salvaged by expressing the myth's content in new form. The *X-Files* is an example of such a salvaging.

In ancient Greece, the dangers of rational, scientific knowledge were mythically represented by the Promethean myth. We contend that the *X-Files* is an extension of this ancient myth. As such, the series is not merely a contemporary adaptation of that myth that depicts, in contemporary terms, the consequences of Prometheus's actions.[4] The sacred flame stolen by and then given to the human race by Prometheus can be understood to represent the light of reason (in the same way that Scully's and Mulder's flashlights do; indeed, these flashlights are contemporary substitutes for fire's illumination). The punishment meted out to Prometheus and to the humans he aided is a mythological acknowledgment that, although beneficial, the human capacity for reason comes with a cost.[5] Fire is a dangerous possession, according to the myth, and so too is reason. Like fire, reason can be used to create or destroy. In much the same way, our modern application of reason through science has also been used to create or destroy. The miseries unleashed with the opening of Pandora's box

in the Promethean myth have their counterpart in those miseries we have inflicted on ourselves and our environment through our exercise of reason in the form of science.

Perhaps the most tragic of these miseries is that of alienation. Science separates us from ourselves, from others, from nature, and from the divine.[6] As animals that possess reason, then, we are creatures of Prometheus; and as such, we now live with the consequences of his theft. Week after week, the *X-Files* gives dramatic expression to this fact and depicts some of its implications. In doing so, the series illustrates the limits of scientific reason as well as science's alienating effects. These limitations and effects are among the reasons that many Westerners currently question, if not outright spurn, science as a way of knowing and coping with the world.

As we noted earlier, light and the absence of light play a central role in the *X-Files*. Through this metaphor, the limits of science are depicted. In an especially amusing episode, for example, Mulder and Scully are stranded at night on a small rock. For light, they have only a lantern that feebly illuminates a small portion of the vast darkness surrounding them. Throughout the night, Mulder and Scully tenaciously cling to the rock. Just before dawn, a voice calls out to them. They learn that the rock to which they had clung was in shallow water only a few yards from shore. Had they known this earlier, Mulder and Scully could have waded easily to the safety of shore. Their knowledge of the world was confined, however, to that small circle of light cast by the lantern; in much the same way, our Western knowledge of the world is currently confined to that meager portion of the world illuminated by science.

In addition to depicting the limits of science, the *X-Files* depicts as well the alienating effects of science. As depicted in the series, science separates us from ourselves. As a result, we discount our personal experience and intuition in favor of that which can be measured by and subjected to the standards of science. We will illustrate and expand on this theme in the next section.

Science also separates us from others. It provides us with technologies that simultaneously keep us connected with and distant from others. We watch strangers on television and ignore our friends and family. We type out messages on the computer for people whom we have never met. In the *X-Files*, this simultaneous connectedness and separation is a recurring theme. Mulder and Scully frequently communicate with one another via cellular phones, although they are separated by large distances.

Science separates us from nature. We live in climate-controlled environments, insulated from the elements. We move from one such environment to another insulated in cars and other modes of transportation that are themselves climate controlled. We not only live in isolation from, but in opposition to, nature. One of the underlying assumptions of the West's grand narrative was that improvement of our species and its living conditions would result from the conquest of nature to satisfy our needs and wants. This isolation from and antagonism to nature is another of the *X-Files'* recurring themes. In one episode, for example, the Navajo's knowledge of and easy relations with nature are depicted in sharp contrast to the lack of knowledge and uneasy relations with nature that are characteristic of the American civilization that surrounds the Navajo. By observing and interpreting signs offered by nature (e.g., circling birds), the Navajo were able to locate Mulder, while agents of the American government, with all their high-tech paraphernalia, were not. In other episodes, the West's antagonistic relation with nature is also represented. We wound nature, and nature wounds us. We pollute nature; in turn, nature gets even by producing parasitic, genetic mutants—such as the Flukeman—that exploit and eventually kill their human hosts. Other examples of the wrath of nature are included in episodes featuring deadly viruses that have been brought into contact with civilization from pristine areas, such as the tropics and the arctic, where the technology science made possible enabled us to intrude.

Finally, science separates us from the divine. It dismisses the unheard, the unseen, the untouched in favor of a gross materialism that gives credence to only those things that can be sensed (directly or by instruments) and measured. In taking the power of voodoo, the presence of poltergeists, and the existence of legendary creatures (e.g., the Jersey Devil, modern inland sea serpents) seriously, the *X-Files* touches on a dimension of human experience that science ignores. These phenomena are manifestations of something greater than themselves, something beyond explanation, something mysterious. To the series' credit, that mysterious something is never defined; it is only suggested. As humans, we tend to approach the mysterious in a posture of reverence and awe, an attitude that some describe as spiritual. This attitude, however, stands in sharp contrast to the skeptical inquiry of science. Where science offers only biological explanation regarding the how of life, faith provides answers regarding the why. These latter answers are the ones that keep most people going; they offer a hope that science cannot provide.

Concordance as Process: The *X-Files* as a Site of Dispute and Play

Although the *X-Files* appears to challenge science's privileged position within Western culture as the sanctioned means of developing an understanding of and control over natural phenomena, we argue that the show serves instead to reaffirm the dominance of science while making room for other ways of knowing. In this respect, we see the show as an example of the kind of accommodation that Condit (1994) says makes concordance possible.

As we pointed out earlier, Scully is the *X-Files'* skeptic: "What I find fantastic," she admits, "is that there are any answers beyond the realm of science." In episode after episode, however, Scully confronts phenomena that challenge her belief in science's ability to provide answers and define the parameters of what is possible. Scully encounters such phenomena during the first mission she works with Mulder, in which they investigate a series of teenage deaths in which the victims bear two strange marks on their backs. When the body of one of the victims is exhumed, the two agents uncover a shriveled semihuman form occupying the casket in which they expected to find a human body. On further investigation, the agents discover and remove a metallic device that has been implanted in the nose of the body. Mulder contends that the marks and the metallic device are consistent with what he knows of alien abduction and experimentation. Scully, however, rejects Mulder's contention, arguing that "there has got to be an explanation" (that is, an explanation in keeping with what Scully believes to be within the realm of scientific possibility). Mulder's explanation is later given credence, however, when he and Scully are blinded by the bright light of what appears to be an alien spaceship, after which experience another victim bearing the same two strange marks turns up dead.

When reporting back to her superiors regarding the case, Scully says that she has reason to believe Mulder's explanation in this instance but cannot support her belief because most of the evidence she and Mulder gathered was destroyed in a motel fire. In commenting on Scully's report, one of her superiors tells her, "What we have read in your reports—the scientific basis and credibility seem wholly unsupportable—you're aware of that?" "Yes sir," she replies, "my reports are personal and subjective." The superior goes on to state, "I see no evidence that justifies the legitimacy of these investigations. You have no physical evidence." From a scientific perspective, one's personal and subjective knowledge are not deemed admissible as evidence.

This devaluing of personal experience in deference to what science counts as evidence is a frequent theme throughout the series. In one episode, for example, a woman is mysteriously marked with the identical bruises, cuts, and other injuries as those that are inflicted on an abduction victim who is suffering many miles away. On one occasion, Mulder witnesses this strange occurrence happening. When he shares his observations with Scully, however, she dismisses them with the observation that he is "too close to the case." Later, however, the woman inexplicably dies as a result of drowning (at the same time the abduction victim is submerged in water), although she is near no source of water.

Despite an eye-witness account of the event, no one except for Mulder entertains the possibility of her having drowned until an autopsy confirms it; five gallons of water were found in her lungs.

In valuing scientific confirmation over personal experience, this episode is not unique. In yet another episode, for example, Mulder witnesses a young man draw electricity to himself and wield it as a murderous weapon. When tests come back from the lab, however, they report normal results. The prosecutor confides to Mulder that, based on the evidence at hand (which consists exclusively of Mulder's personal observation of the event and the lack of corroborating scientific data), he could not build a convincing case.

The paranormal phenomena that Scully and Mulder encounter in the first and subsequent episodes of the *X-Files* expand Scully's notions as to what is possible. In working with Mulder, Scully investigates cases involving voodoo curses, shape-shifting shamans, protective spirits, evolutionary throwbacks, extraterrestrials, and insects that trap and devour humans. These phenomena are drawn from a variety of sources: non-Western religious traditions, prescientific belief systems, contemporary folklore, and the imaginations of the series' writers. With the exception of the latter, the phenomena that inhabit the world of the *X-Files* are the products of and are values by different ways of knowing than that of Western science. Their inclusion in the show seems to challenge the Western notion that science is the only way to know, a challenge that is in keeping with the West's contemporary preference for plurality. However, as we suggest below, the series actually serves to reconfirm the dominance of science within Western culture.

As a result of her encounters with a variety of paranormal phenomena, Scully reluctantly comes to accept that there exist in this world things that her scientific training has not prepared her to expect. However, although she acknowledges as a result of her experiences that there are new things to know, Scully continues to reject the notion that there are new (i.e., nonscientific) ways of knowing. Scully's faith in science is shaken but not shattered.

Indeed, in commenting on a case involving an alien hit man, Scully affirms her need for faith in science:

> Several aspects of this case remain unexplained, suggesting the possibility of paranormal phenomena. But I am convinced that to accept such conclusions is to abandon all hope of understanding the scientific events behind them. Many of the things I have seen have challenged my faith and my belief in an ordered universe. But this uncertainty has only strengthened my need to understand, to apply reason to those things which seem to defy it.

Scully admits that some of the things she has seen have challenged her faith in science and presented her with disturbing possibilities. For Scully, however, to witness personally paranormal phenomena, or to receive reports of such phenomena from other witnesses, is not enough to warrant her belief in them. She needs other evidence as well, the impersonal objective kind valued by science. Scully concludes the monologue cited above by singing the praises of science: "It was science that isolated the retro-virus that Agent Mulder was exposed to. And science allowed us to understand its behavior. And ultimately, it was science that saved Agent Mulder's life." Perhaps this litany of praise is Scully's way of reaffirming her faith in the face of challenges to it.

As employed by Scully, science is used to confirm or deny the plausibility of paranormal phenomena, the very existence of which science is currently unable to explain. In the end, then, science remains the final arbiter of what is and is not real. In the concord of which the *X-Files* is a reflection, science may not be able to explain certain phenomena, but it is still the only acceptable means by which the existence of such phenomena can be authenticated to the satisfaction of those authorities whose opinions count (e.g., scientists, government officials). Even Mulder, in searching for "the one piece of undeniable evidence that will make us all believers," hopes to find the kind of proof that will satisfy the demands of science and will validate his beliefs.

Conclusion

We find it ironic that science now exercises such hegemonic power in the West. After all, modern science as originally conceived was an emancipatory project, not an enslaving one. Modern science emerged as a means of challenging repressive authority; science was counterhegemonic, not hegemonic. In addition, science was promoted as an egalitarian enterprise in that one's proof, and not one's position, was the criterion against which claims were judged. In this way, science freed the human race, or so the argument went, from the repressive authority of religious tradition and ancient philosophy (Burke, 1985). Freed from such restraints, science promised improved material circumstances and a better social world in which to live. However, as we noted in our introduction, many Westerners have begun to question these promises.

The *X-Files* offers a fictive space within which room is made for the inclusion of those paranormal phenomena that have become part of our cultural and spiritual landscapes and yet are at odds with Western science. The series accommodates these while subjugating them to the stringent scrutiny of Western science. Paranormal phenomena are deemed real only to the extent that science says they are. Science, then, is still the final arbiter. Lived experience and alternative means of evaluation are dismissed as irrelevant. Faith is called into question. The spiritual dimension of the human experience is suspect. In this way, the *X-Files* reaffirms the privileged position of science within Western culture while seeming to accommodate other ways of knowing. By making room for certain paranormal phenomena (i.e., those subject to scientific validation), science manages to maintain its preeminence within the West, at least for the present. In doing so, science as portrayed in the *X-Files* effects the kind of accommodation that Condit (1994) argues makes hegemony possible in a mass-mediated society.

Notes

1. We suggest that this questioning of the grand narrative of modernism reflects dissatisfaction

with both the narrative's broken promises (i.e., the narrative's *content*) and a postmodern suspicion of metanarratives in general (i.e., the narrative's *form*). In discussing this latter suspicion, Lyotard (1994) writes, "I define postmodern as incredulity toward metanarratives. This incredulity is undoubtedly a product of progress in the sciences: But that progress in turn presupposes it. . . . The narrative function is losing its functors, its great hero, its great dangers, its great voyages, its great goal" (p. 27). Interestingly, in expressing incredulity toward metanarratives, Lyotard uses the very language of the grand narrative of modernism: "progress in the sciences." A major theme of the grand narrative is that applications of this progress in the sciences are expected to lead to progress in the material and social worlds that are the foci of scientific study. During the 1950s and 1960s, this expectation was given expression in such phrases as "better living through science" and the "war on poverty." In this article, we focus on the *X-Files* as a response to the broken promises made on behalf of science. Although we acknowledge that the series is also a site of tension between the modernist metanarrative and postmodern suspicion of such narratives, an examination of this tension is beyond the scope of this article.

2. Citing Buci-Gluckman (1982), Condit (1994) observes that "hegemony functions differently in different times and places" (p. 211). As described by Condit, "Gramsci's theory of consent was elaborated for Italian politics in a proto-fascist context. It focused primarily on the change of regimes in a nation that was not fully industrialized, not evidently driven by technology as a first order engine of social change, and in which televised and other 'objective journalism' was not a primary means by which 'the public' was informed" (Clark, 1977, p. 208). To make the model of consent formation Gramsci developed in pre–World War II Italy relevant to the historical realities of the contemporary American sociopolitical landscape, Condit suggests several modifications: First, she points out that "the norm of political discourse is mass mediation, rather than direct one-on-one or even one-

on-arena contact" (p. 209). Second, drawing on the work of Laclau and Mouffe (1985), Condit argues that "in light of contemporary multicultural conditions, economic universalism must give way to less totalized assumptions about the ability of one class to represent or speak for others" (p. 210). And finally, Condit contends that "current conditions suggest that the model of revolutionary change that suffused Gramscian perspectives . . . is not a necessary one" (p. 210). In other words, change can be, and often is, evolutionary rather than revolutionary.

3. To the series' credit, Scully and Mulder are depicted as complex, and at times contradictory, characters. Scully is not only a scientist but a nominal Roman Catholic who occasionally struggles with questions regarding her religious faith. Still, during moments of intense doubt, Scully most often turns to science, and not religion, for the comfort that comes from a sanctioned source of certainty. Unlike Scully, Mulder is unsympathetic to organized religion, and indeed, he is sometimes downright hostile. However, although Mulder is not religious (that is, he is not a professed adherent of a particular system of religious beliefs and practices), we argue that he is deeply spiritual as we define spirituality, in that he is willing to encounter the mysterious. Mulder's spirituality manifests itself in his ongoing quest for "the truth" and his desire for a faith that eludes him—a desire that is poignantly expressed in the words of a poster Mulder keeps in his office: "I want to believe."

4. For ancient accounts of this myth, see Hesiod (1983) and Plato (1991). Hamilton (1940) provides a modern rendering.

5. As a punishment for his theft, Prometheus was chained to a rock and his entrails were devoured by birds. Humans were punished when Pandora's box was opened, through which act every form of suffering known to the human race was introduced into the world, as was the concept of hope.

6. The notion of science as an alienating influence is yet another echo of the Promethean myth.

References

Berger, A. A. (1992). *Popular culture genres.* Newbury Park, CA: Sage.

Bodroghkozy, A. (1991). A Gramscian analysis of entertainment television and the youth rebellion of the 1950s. *Critical Studies in Mass Communication, 8,* 217–230.

Buci-Gluckman, C. (1982). Hegemony and consent. In A. S. Sassoon (Ed.), *Approaches to Gramsci* (pp. 116–126). London: Writers & Readers Publishing Cooperative Society.

Burke, J. (1985). *The day the universe changed.* Boston: Little Brown.

Campbell, J., & Moyers, B. (1988). *The power of myth.* New York: Doubleday.

Carson, R. (1962). *Silent spring.* Boston: Houghton Mifflin

Carter, C. (Producer). (1966). *The X-Files* [Television broadcast]. Vancouver, B.C., Canada: Thirteen Productions.

Clark, M. (1977). *Antonio Gramsci and the revolution that failed.* New Haven, CT: Yale University Press.

Condit, C. M. (1994). Hegemony in a mass-mediated society: Concordance about reproductive technologies. *Critical Studies in Mass Communication, 11,* 205–230.

Dow, B. J. (1990). Hegemony, feminist criticism, and *The Mary Tyler Moore Show. Critical Studies in Mass Communication, 7,* 261–274.

Gaarder, J. (1994). *Sophie's world: A novel about the history of philosophy.* New York: Farrar, Straus & Giroux.

Gergen, K. J. (1991). *The saturated self: Dilemmas of identity in contemporary life.* New York: Basic Books.

Gramsci, A. (1987). *Selections from the prison notebooks.* New York: International.

Hamilton, E. (1940). *Mythology.* New York: New American Library.

Hanke, R. (1990). Hegemonic masculinity in *thirtysomething. Critical Studies in Mass Communication, 7,* 231–248.

Hesiod. (1983). *Theogony, works and days, shield.* Baltimore: John Hopkins University Press.

Humphrey, N. (1996). *Leaps of faith: Science, miracles, and the search for supernatural consolation.* New York: Basic Books.

Laclau, E., & Mouffe, C. (1985). *Hegemony and socialist strategy: Toward a radical democratic politics.* London: Verso.

Lyotard, J-F. (1994). The postmodern condition. In S. Seidman (Ed.), *The postmodern turn: New perspectives on social theory* (pp. 27–38). New York: Cambridge University Press.

Nollinger, M. (1996, April 18–24). 20 things you need to know about the *X-Files. TV Guide,* p. 4.

Plato. (1991). *Protagoras.* New York: Oxford University Press [Rev. ed. Originally published in 1976].

Plutarch. (1960). *The rise and fall of Athens.* New York: Penguin.

Ritzer, G. (1996). *The McDonaldization of society* (Rev. ed.). Thousand Oaks, CA: Pine Forge Press.

Rushing, J. H. (1986). Mythic evolution of "the new frontier" in mass mediated rhetoric. *Critical Studies in Mass Communication, 3,* 265–296.

Trujillo, N. (1991). Hegemonic masculinity on the mound: Media representations of Nolan Ryan and American sports culture. *Critical Studies in Mass Communication, 8,* 290–308.

Wild, D. (1996, May 16). The *X-Files* undercover. *Rolling Stone,* pp. 38–42, 74.

Where Have All the Mothers Gone?
Soap Opera's Replaying of the Oedipal Story

Sonia Livingstone and Tamar Liebes

Despite recent arguments for the empowering, resistant or feminist content of the soap opera for women viewers, we argue that the dominant tendency is for the American daytime soap opera to represent a traditional conception of women's psychological development. We explore parallels between the soap opera and both fairy tales and therapy. Fairy tales and soaps use analogous permutations of characters and themes to socialize women to the oedipal paradigm. Therapy and soaps both articulate relations of (male) dominance and (female) dependence through the situation of contact and their thematic framing. We develop the connections between soap narratives and the commonly accepted, psychoanalytically informed view of women's psyche through the detailed analysis of a recurrent narrative element in soaps—that of the "bad" and/or missing mother of young women heroines (in contrast with the mothering of sons) in The Young and the Restless. *Our conclusions emphasize the repressive over the liberating aspects of soap opera.*

Soap opera—one of television's most researched genres—has been found to supply their women viewers with advice for coping with the daily problems of mothering husbands and children (Arnheim, 1943; Herzog, 1944; Katzman, 1972; Turow, 1974). Such analyses focus on this genre's realistic rather than its melodramatic aspects. While occasionally social problems such as abortion or AIDS are included, it is in a highly personalized fashion. For American soap operas, with which we are primarily concerned here (Liebes & Livingstone, 1992), the genre is primarily melodramatic (Feuer, 1984). It enacts a fantasy world of changing mates, prohibited loves, and the constant vanishing and reappearing of long-lost or newly discovered family members. As Ang (1985) argued, soaps follow a logic of emotional rather than literal realism. A restricted repertoire of narratives is repeatedly enacted by different permutations of the characters. The atmosphere is a hermetic world—as if out of time and out of society. Yet the soap opera is more popular than ever—the genre with the highest ratings in Britain, heavily viewed throughout Europe, the staple fare of American daytime schedules, and increasingly available around the world with the growth of terrestrial and satellite broadcasting. Rather than being viewed casually, soap opera viewers are highly involved. Loyal fans discuss episodes with friends, record missed episodes, take lunchtime breaks according to the time of broadcast, and make use of telephone agencies with daily updates (for example, Ang, 1985; Brown, 1990; Geraghty, 1990; Hobson, 1982). Little empirical evidence has yet been gathered to examine the socializing role of the soap opera for its viewers, although suggestive findings can be seen in Liebes and Katz (1990), Pingree (1979), and Press (1991).

We will address the widespread and considerable constancy in the soap opera's appeal through a series of interconnected arguments. In their conventional content, soaps continue where fairy tales for children leave off, using similar habit-forming contexts to drive home the message—socializing women to the oedipal paradigm through the different permutations of characters and variations on basic narrative themes. The messages children gain from fairy tales are also those addressed more explicitly through therapy. We suggest that soaps act not unlike psychotherapy sessions as diffusers of psychologically accepted wisdom. We identify the structural similarities between soap and therapy in the way that each articulates relations of (male) dominance and (female) dependence through both the situations of contact and their thematic framing.

In order to explore the connection between the narratives of soaps and the psychoanalytically informed, broadly accepted view of women's psyche, the major focus of the paper is an analysis of a recurrent narrative element—that of the "bad" and/or missing mother. This motif is often told as the disappearance, at an early stage, of the mothers of the young women heroines, sometimes followed by a no less unfortunate reappearance once the daughter has grown. To understand the ideology underlying the asymmetrical mothering of sons and daughters in soaps, we relate psychoanalytic theories of the mother-daughter relationship to the ways in which the soap opera represents a traditional conception of women's psychological development, as revealed through missing mother narratives analysed in *The Young and The Restless*.

In our conclusions, we consider the possibilities within the genre for liberating as well as repressive responses to soap opera by women viewers. We argue that part of its appeal can be explained by tracing how the genre tends to reproduce, popularize, and value psychoanalytic accounts of women's relations with others. But that does not imply approval of such images or theories; nor do we mean to imply that all the meanings of soaps are captured by such theories. The appeal of the genre also lies in its ambivalences and openness and hence in the potential for alternative audience responses.

Our analysis is based on soap opera texts, informed by our previous research on the soap opera viewer (Liebes & Katz, 1990; Livingstone, 1990), although we do not present research on audience interpretations here. Audience research argues for meaning as a process of negotiation between text and reader. Texts attempt to position viewers in a certain, typically hegemonic, manner (see Hall's preferred reading, 1980); the hegemonic readings of women's popular culture have been examined by Modleski (1982) and Radway (1984). Through the act of interpretation, viewers attempt to use the

text's openness or polysemy to negotiate readings which satisfy their own purposes and accord with their own experience; while these are sometimes oppositional or subversive in nature (Brown, 1990), they more often accept the normative meanings offered to them (Morley, 1980), making referential readings which—while shifting between modes of fantasizing, moralizing, and so forth—nonetheless are not critical of the text's ideological positioning (Liebes & Katz, 1990). Active viewers, making multiple readings, are not necessarily oppositional or critical of the text (Livingstone, 1990).

At present, audience research is in danger of replacing textual analysis by studies of audience response without asking what viewers are responding to. A related danger is that of simplifying our understanding of the text while complexifying our understanding of audiences. Of course, this was a vital move several years ago, when audiences were neglected in favor of texts. Now the time has come for both texts and audiences to be analyzed in parallel and in the light of each other, without assuming either complete heterogeneity or homogeneity in audience readings. Only through such an approach can a more sophisticated study of the socializing and cultural impacts of soap opera be undertaken (Liebes and Livingstone, 1994).

Soaps as Fairy Tales for Grown Up Girls

> [It] clearly does not refer to the outer world, although it may begin realistically enough and have everyday features woven into it. The unrealistic nature of these tales . . . is an important device, because it makes it obvious that the fairy tale's concern is not useful information about the external world, but the inner processes taking place in an individual (Bettelheim, 1976, p. 25).

While the genre of soap opera has its own distinctive features (Allen, 1985; Livingstone, 1990), we suggest here that in addressing women's problems of relationship, parenting, identity and sexuality, the soap opera continues the themes that were developed in children's genres, particularly the fairy tale. In terms of narrative structure it is easy to classify fairy tales as concerned with action and adventure (Propp, 1968) and soaps as concerned with emotions and relationships, fairy tales as "closed" narratives and soaps as "open" ones. While undoubtedly many differences between the genres exist, significant similarities have gone hitherto unrecognized. Dilemmas of identity, emotional anxieties, and other personal conflicts do not all reach resolution at the end of childhood. Thus, once grown up women have left behind the period when they may legitimately listen to fairy tales; other forms of popular culture are needed to provide a space where they may deal with these existential problems. Bettelheim (1976, p. 25) argues that "the fairy tale is therapeutic because the patient finds *his own* solutions, through contemplating what the story seems to imply about him and his inner conflicts at this moment in his life." The literature on the active listener and viewer of soap opera similarly started with the idea of how the viewer puts the texts to psychological use, contemplating what the soap says about her inner conflicts (Herzog, 1943). We suggest below that structurally and psychologically the two genres share a number of important attributes.

Narrative Structure

As regards the context of reception, both fairy tales and soaps tend to form a daily habit; both are repetitive and their audiences expect them to remain so in order to meet the continuing agenda of psychological anxieties in the viewer. Just as fairy tales "state the existential dilemma briefly and pointedly" (Bettelheim, 1976, p. 8) so as to not confuse matters for the child, soaps consist of a sequence of extremely short scenes, each making a single narrative statement (a boyfriend has left, the mother has reappeared, and so forth). Children prefer their favorite tales (selected from a well known, relatively limited repertoire) endlessly retold verbatim. Soaps also repeat the same formulae—centered around the key crises of birth, identity, love, separation, loss—albeit with different characters or with the same characters over time. Similarly, reception studies show that readers

of romance and soap opera insist on strict adherence to the conventions of the genre and are intolerant of deviations (Hobson, 1982; Radway, 1984).

Characterization

As in the fairy tale, soap characters are typical rather than unique. The main subjects of the soap—whose perspective is adopted by the viewer—are young pretty women and boyishly handsome men, similar in age to the heroes and heroines of fairy tales. While other staple types populate the soaps (the reliable father-figure, the grandparental matriarch or patriarch), the object position—that of the "other"—is taken by evil schemers who try to penetrate and destroy the family. These are often the bad, long-time missing mother (for example, Alexis Carrington of *Dynasty*, Jill Abbott in *The Young and The Restless*). In the fairy tale, too, the mother is frequently missing. Snow-white and Cinderella's problems start with their wicked stepmother; in other tales the heroine's adventure begins when the mother dies. The characters in soaps are not as black and white as in fairy tales, for adults prefer more complexity in characterization and because the narrative extends over years. Yet they too personify the oppositional poles of key dualities—good/bad, kind/selfish, powerful/weak (Liebes & Livingstone, 1992; Livingstone, 1987). As in fairy tales, evil is as omnipresent as virtue, and the struggle between evil and virtue personified in the characters is vital and endless.

**The Fifty Minute Hour:
Soaps and Therapies**

If soap opera addresses, though not necessarily resolves, women's emotional agenda of fears and anxieties, we can also make a broader parallel between soap opera and therapy. At the risk of sounding disrespectful, we argue that soaps and therapies may be regarded as two genres of popular culture (White, 1992), addressed mainly to women, with a somewhat similar situation of contact and rules for playing the game. Both are constant features of a working day—an installment in a private story, a liminal moment contained within well-defined limits that interrupts the drudgery of mundane chores; both are voluntarily chosen to serve a symbolic rather than an instrumental function. In both situations, there is a similar focus on childhood experiences, parents, sexual identity, relationships, communication problems, dreams and fears, and so forth. While soap opera is seen by many as harmful to women, seducing them into an escapist habit of reality avoidance, for critics of psychoanalysis, the working out of the real or imagined traumas, and the sometimes lifelong dependence on the therapist, also offers no end-point, no cure, no escape. Indeed, it may be seen as enslaving (Masson, 1990). While the differences between soap and therapy are many, we explore below some little recognized parallels.

The Constitutive Rules

The frameworks of both soap and therapy involve a fixed, daily, time slot, extending over a typical 50 minute period. In both cases, it may be argued, the show goes on regardless of the client's attendance, and there is a price to pay for breaking the rules. In the case of therapy, a fee is still due, and the missed session itself becomes something to be accounted for in the ongoing narrative. Similarly in soap operas, catching up on missed episodes is built into the repetitive structures of the narrative (Modleski, 1982), and there are penalties in terms of lost involvement and not being able to participate in conversations about the soap opera.[1] The patient/ viewer herself is, of course, free to quit or to choose another therapist or another soap, only to discover that these too abide by the same rules. While patients and viewers do leave, both therapy and soap are structured to try and prevent this.

Therapy and Soap as Gendered Forms

The situations both of therapy and soap viewing, with their unequal division of power, are gendered. The patient or viewer typically is a woman, and the therapist/producer, though often a woman, speaks with the voice of dominant patriarchy. In the case of psychoanalysis (Lakoff & Coyne, 1993; Masson, 1990), the theory is anchored in patriarchy: women are assumed to be inferior biologically, and therefore psychologically and morally. Passivity and receptivity are appropriate rather than problematic responses (Scheman, 1988). Opposition to the analyst's interpretation is doomed, being incorporated into the theoretical framework as instances of psychological resistance. In spite of the massive feminist criticism of the psychoanalytic understanding of women's sexuality, the basic premises are still mostly accepted even by more feminist psychologies of gender (for example, Benjamin, 1990; Chodorow, 1978).

In most genres of popular culture, including soaps, we are dealing with patriarchal texts which assume passive women viewers (Arnheim, 1943; Katzman, 1972; Turow, 1974). The feminist effort to endow a subversive potential to the soap (Ang, 1985; Brown, 1990; Brunsdon, 1993; Geraghty, 1990) has shown some opportunities for oppositional readings against the grain. Studies of viewers reveal that their interpretations, while these can be diverse and oppositional, are nonetheless heavily constrained by a broadly hegemonic framework (Livingstone, 1990; Liebes & Katz, 1990). Most statements are referential, accepting the dilemmas faced by the characters and elaborating on their motivations rather than challenging them, enjoying the emphasis on appearance, romance, relationships, and so forth.

Terms of Mediation

At a first glance therapy seems the more tightly controlled text. The therapist is discreet in order to make the act of mediation less salient and so to naturalize the interpretation. The mediation of the physically absent producer of a soap opera is even less obtrusive and is scarcely ever acknowledged by the viewer. After all, the viewer, unlike the patient, has not identified herself as having a problem relevant to her activity of viewing soap opera. Yet the problems portrayed (for example, unrequited love, sibling rivalry, clinging mother) and the patterns of dealing with them (through the hopes, dreams, and forever-reversible actions of the heroines) are designed to address the viewers' own concerns.

Psychoanalytic film theory would conceive of therapists as taking up the position of the camera, which is regarded as the focus of identification for film viewers (Flitterman-Lewis, 1987; Houston, 1985), while patients are constructed as the object of the masculine gaze (Mulvey, 1975).[2] In soap opera, women also learn to see themselves through the eyes of men as the soaps fetishize women's glamorous appearance and focus on woman as spectacle (especially in weddings); consequently women are portrayed as competitive and self-hating. Incidentally, the theory of the male gaze is problematic when the hero is female. In the soap opera, the daughter/viewer are constructed as subject of the male (producer's) gaze, but the daughter's gaze further constructs the mother as other. Similarly, Bottigheimer (1987) argues, against Bettelheim, that fairy tales with male and female hero(in)es must be interpreted differently.

The subject position of women in soaps, as in therapy, is a child rather than adult. We have noted elsewhere that one rarely sees any babies in American soaps (Liebes & Livingstone, 1992), maybe because this would construe mother as self rather than mother as other. As the mothers generally are older, and have adult children, viewers are encouraged to identify with the daughter[3] not the parent. The experience of viewing soap therefore prioritizes the therapeutic focus on the child's (viewer's) fears and fantasies in an alien world where grown-ups have the power and control. This relates to the soap's (and therapy's) fascination with secrets, particularly secrets concerning prohibited sexual relations (the third party listening outside the door or the interruption of the telephone imitates the shock and thrill of the child listening outside the parents' bedroom door). The interpretive frame used in soaps, as in psychoanalysis, assumes that the only kind of love is sexual love. Nothing is innocent; all events and acts have sexual readings (both soaps and psychoanalysis are criticized for seeing sex in everything). Soaps express the desire to re-turn to the time before the loss of innocence by re-living the shock of discovery and of abandonment.

Where Have All the Mothers Gone?

We have argued above that soaps and therapies can be seen as expressions of hegemonic popular culture, both of which socialize women to their dependency on men. Both constitute a daily fix, administered to women by therapists and producers, with soap's audience representing more lower class women, although certainly both men and middle class women also view.[4] Both promote similar patriarchal messages, comforting to viewers who, in the intimacy of the situation of contact, preserve the illusion that they are being individually listened to and addressed. The soap presents fairy-tale-like narratives, complete with the networks of primary attachments and the psychological attributes needed for experimenting with the limited number of options for feminine emotional development available to women. Of the various recurring narratives in soaps, we examine the central motif of the disappearance of the mothers of the young women heroines.

In foregrounding this theme, the soap opera draws on the earlier genre of the Hollywood melodrama (Feuer, 1984), in which the mother/daughter relationship has been downplayed in favor of that of the mother and son (see Cavell, 1981; Scheman, 1988; Walters, 1992). Scheman (1988) argues that the absent mother story promotes the argument that mother/daughter separation is a necessary step for growing up, that is, for falling in love. In the 1940s, the popularization of psychoanalytic theory together with women's entry into the work force provided the context for the appearance in film of the bad and often missing mother who is held responsible for her daughter's neuroses (for example, *Stella Dallas*, the symbol of self-sacrifice in favor of the daughter, and *Mildred Peirce*, who struggles against her daughter; Walters, 1992). From the Hollywood melodrama to the 1990s soap opera, the psychoanalytic theme is re-enacted. A daughter is painfully separated from her mother but emerges from suffering into a feminine sexual identity, proved by her desire for a man and celebrated through the wedding.

When charting the kinship structures in soap operas, one relationship that stands out by its frequent absence is that of the mother/daughter relationship (Liebes & Livingstone, 1992). Although mothering is still considered the most important role for women and it plays a major part in the daily lives of many viewers, whether as mothers and/or daughters, soap opera heroines are often motherless. How can this be explained? Instead of bringing up their own daughters, mothers abandon them to uncaring, sometimes cruel, stepmothers, other female relatives, or awkward fathers, in order to wield power in the world outside or to engage in new romance. The disappearing mothers—deserted, escaped, or dead—are often wholeheartedly hated and "bad" but are sometimes longed for and idealized. Their eventual possible reappearance facilitates a narrative pattern of either rejection and competition or of symbiosis and victimization.

Mother/Daughter Relationships in Psychoanalysis: Mother as Other

As Moscovici (1984) has shown, through the popularizing function of the mass media, psychoanalytic theory has filtered into ordinary understanding (see also White, 1992). As a consequence, commonly held assumptions about identity, sexuality, the family, and relationships, as reinforced and legitimated through popular culture, are heavily influenced by ideas from psychoanalysis—the Oedipal story, the unconscious, the crucial role of motherhood, and the significance of dreams. We suggest that the soap opera, along with other genres of popular culture (White, 1992), is implicitly informed by such ordinary understandings. Its narratives provide a convenient site for the playing out of traumas, for expressing the ways in which they are repressed or denied, and for representing the dreams and aspirations to which they give birth. Soap operas portray a cycle of longing for ideal relationships, crashing into a reality of de-

structive ones, only in order to start a new quest for a perfect, unachievable love.

Before offering our analysis of a soap opera narrative, let us consider in more detail the psychoanalytic theory which has filtered into the soap opera and popular culture more generally, resulting in the repeated absence or problematic presence of mother/daughter relationships in the texts. To what traumatic psychological processes do these texts refer and what emotional resonances or commonsense assumptions do they encourage or legitimate in their viewers?

In the psychoanalytic scheme, the mother/daughter relationship is part of the oedipal struggle, conceived within a biologically determined psychology in which the penis reigns as the symbol of power (Freud, 1988; Mitchell, 1986). Girls, on discovering their lack, blame their mother for condemning them to remain powerless, like her, and turn to the father, first with the hope of becoming like him (by having a penis), and then with the hope of having a baby. While feminists do not accept that girls feel physically castrated, they do accept that girls attach cardinal symbolic importance to the penis which, in Benjamin's (1990) words, they regard as an "emblem of the father who will help them to individuate." But fathers withdraw from their daughters, seeing them as "a sweet adorable thing, a nascent sex object," and so girls are pushed back to the mother, angry about the father's nonrecognition, and, "unprotected by the phallic sign of gender difference, unsupported by an alternative relationship, they relinquish their entitlement for desire" (Benjamin, 1990).

A crucial issue for psychoanalytic theories is that of separation from the mother as the basis for individuation (Bowlby, 1965). While boys emerge out of the oedipal stage completely separate from their mothers, for girls there is no such automatic process: "women must . . . confront the paradoxical requirement to simultaneously separate from and identify with the mother" (Benjamin, 1990, p. 121). Moreover, as Chodorow (1978) has shown, mothers are ambivalent about passing on their own unsatisfactory gender identity to their daughters and are therefore less clear about drawing the boundaries between themselves and their daughters; they keep their daughters both more attached and less nurtured than their sons.

Consequently, a conflict between daughter and mother, leading to total separation (literal and symbolic), comes to be seen as necessary and crucial to the daughter's growing up.—It is "a wrenching experience" involving a "renunciation of her belief in her mother's power, and her hope for her own" (Benjamin, 1990), but has to be suffered in order to get to "the other side" of men and marriage. A continuing mother/daughter bond is the sign of immaturity in the daughter, and of clinging, possessiveness or overprotectiveness in the mother (Benjamin, 1990). Thus, the mother is culturally posited as "the other," as regressive, archaic, and irrational, in opposition to the progressive, oedipal, rational father (and husband). Rich (1977) accuses patriarchy for making the mother/daughter relationship into a form of repression which alienates women from their own bodies. The mother's victimization passes on to her daughter and many daughters are angry at their mothers' passive submission to their lot. Women cannot respect themselves or their mothers in a society which humiliates them. Many of the pleasures which women find in soap opera may implicitly socialize them to the subject positioning for women central to this psychoanalytic account. The patriarchal relations between men and women which Chodorow and others describe are thus reinforced, without providing space for oppositional voices or alternative accounts of these relations and identities.

The generational conflict depicted in this scene from *The Young and the Restless* affirms Livingstone & Liebes' essay findings about psychoanalytic and narrative parallels between soap operas and fairy tales, including their patrilineal framework (concern with lineage and family membership) and the repressive portrayal of mothering: "bad" or absent mothers (for daughters) contrasting with present, often "good" and caring, mothers (for sons).

Missing Mothers in Soap Opera Narratives

Proceeding inductively from an analysis of a randomly selected series of episodes from *The Young and the Restless*, we examined the soap's treatment of the mothering of young women in comparison to the mothering of young men. *The Young and The Restless* fits the category of true soap opera (Cantor & Pingree, 1983). Produced since 1973 for CBS, it is

targeted at housewives, with an emphasis on dialogue rather than visual content. Our analysis, presented below, was checked against episodes and storylines from a range of other, mainly American, daytime soap operas such as *Guiding Light, As the World Turns, General Hospital, One Life to Live,* and primetime soaps such as *Dallas* and *Dynasty,* and the Australian soap opera *Neighbours.* The frequent absence of the mother provides a significant clue in our analysis, demonstrating that the soap opera is not a "realistic" genre. It is exactly the unnaturalness of this pattern that signals a culturally significant representation. Through missing mother narratives soaps express popular resonances of the convoluted emotional path of the mother/daughter relationship.[5]

Two storylines alternate throughout the selected episodes of *The Young and the Restless* (our examples are drawn mainly from the former). (1) Nina Webster is on the point of marriage to Phillip Chancellor, who is the father of her new baby (Phillip Jr.). Phillip's adoptive parents who raised him, the infertile Catherine and Rex, are making arrangements for the wedding. His returned biological mother, Jill Abbott, attempts to prevent it by paying Chase, a former lover of Nina, to seduce Nina. Danny (Rex's son) and Cricket (Phillip's ex-girlfriend) support Nina and Phillip over their planned wedding, and eventually Nina and Phillip are married. (2) Paul Williams is having an affair with Cassandra Rollins, who, initially unknown to Paul, is married to his business associate, George Rollins. Paul's mother persuades him to end the affair, but before Paul can tell Cassandra, George dies, apparently murdered. Paul's father is the detective who investigates George's death, following the alert by George's niece and Paul's friend, Brittany. Suspicion that Paul has killed George grows; we later discover it was suicide, designed to incriminate Paul.

Witches and Bitches

The parallel between fairy tale witch and soap opera "bitch" (often a stepmother in both fairy tale and soap) may be seen through Bettelheim's analysis of Hansel and Gretel. The child's (viewer's) fears that her parents will desert her because of her own badness are expressed through projection, resulting in a belief that the (step)mother has become unloving and selfish. Bettelheim offers a similar analysis of Cinderella, showing how sibling rivalry results from the child's fear of parental rejection, while the vileness of the stepmother and stepsisters reassures the child that she or he has value despite feelings of worthlessness. As most adult women have been socialized into feelings of guilt and inadequacy, the evil characters in the soaps may similarly express these anxieties, and maybe serve to reassure.

Like the fairy tale, the soap opera teaches that one must move forward rather than turning back, and that one must rely on peers rather than parents (although sibling relations are often treacherous), as seen in the predominance of horizontal rather than cross-generational links between characters in the soap kinship structures (Liebes & Livingstone, 1992). Having constructed the (step)mother as other, often as bitch, the soaps

(and fairy tales) offer some images of women's active resistance (Gretel pushes the witch into the oven). Yet the soap teases rather than reassures, as the lack of resolution in soaps means that the viewer is never sure whether the witch will return (Houston, 1985).

Mothers and Patrilineage

The missing mother in soap opera supports the broadly patriarchal framework which is concerned with lineage, inheritance, and definitions of the family boundaries (Liebes & Katz, 1990).[6] Women in soap operas, as elsewhere, join the husband's family on marriage (and bear rather more baby sons than daughters). For Cavell (1981), the focus on patrilineage perpetuates the myth that women are created by, and belong to, men. Male characters (especially the rich ones) more often have one or both parents present while young women often come from unknown backgrounds and must rely on peers or in-laws. In *The Young and the Restless*, Nina lacks a mother and is about to gain two mother-in-laws, one of whom is very unsupportive. Consequently, adult daughters and male babies have different concerns about their parentage. The adult daughter is concerned for her identity (understood through relations with the mother) and so asks, "who (or where) is my real mother?" The patriarchal community is concerned to ask of the male baby, "who is his real father?"

Gilligan (1993) argues that "since masculinity is defined through separation while femininity is defined through attachment, male gender identity is threatened by intimacy while female gender identity is threatened by separation" (p. 8). Soaps explore the negotiation of identity for both genders by having mothers, typically, present for sons and absent for daughters. Thus women struggle with femininity in soaps—as explored through the missing mother and the problem of merged ego boundaries between mother and daughter (Chodorow, 1978). Meanwhile men struggle with masculinity—as explored through their relations and conflicts with their sometimes multiple present/real/good mothers or mother-figures.

Mothers of Sons

In our episodes from *The Young and the Restless*, the three mothers all look after their sons. Paul has a good and real mother to lean on, as well as two grown up women concerned for him (Cassandra and Brittany). Phillip has two mothers organizing his life—a bad (that is, sexual) but "real" (that is, biological) mother and a good (that is, caring), but less "real" (that is, adoptive) one. The narratives illustrate the dangers for sons of intimacy with women. Both men are deeply attached to and respectful of their mothers. As Paul says to his mother: "I listen to you. Even though I don't necessarily agree with what you're saying. Because you're my mother and because I have an awful lot of respect for you." Phillip expresses no anger at his mother's disappearance and is grateful to her, ironically, for returning and organising his wedding. Yet, this respect for the mother leads us to question the maturity and manliness of both men: one sacrifices his lover for his mother,[7] one fails to suspect his mother's treachery over his wedding. Phillip has believed Jill when she says:

> See, you have to understand something about mothers, about this mother. I only want what's best for you. And for that reason it may sometimes seem that I intrude on your life a little bit, become too involved, maybe a touch manipulative. But it's only that I care so much for you.

Mothers of Daughters

In general, we know little of the mothers of central female compared to those of male characters.[8] The three main "daughter" characters in this soap opera, Nina, Cricket, and Brittany, have no apparent mothers. We already know that Cricket was abandoned by her mother,[9] we learn in the present episode that Nina too was rejected by her mother when young (consider also Pam and Sue Ellen in *Dallas*, Phoebe in *Neighbours*). They have had to

find men to care for them: Brittany lives with her uncle George; Cricket has Danny, and Nina is choosing a husband from Phillip and Chase (similarly, Jim Robinson, whose wife Anne died, brings up Lucy in *Neighbours*).

Mothers of daughters in soaps are rarely good, real and present. Rather different combinations of these characteristics are combined in any one mother-figure: they are good or bad (frequently color-coded blonde and brunette, as in fairy tales); they are real (that is, biological mothers) or unreal (that is, foster or adoptive mothers, or other relatives, especially aunts, and sometimes mistakenly supposed to be "real" by the daughters); and they are present or absent (disappearing and reappearing for long periods at a time). The absence of real, good and present mother poses problems for their daughters. Who is the real mother, whom can she trust, will she disappear, can she be forgiven, will one reproduce her problems? The soap opera thus represents the daughter's perennial complaint against the mother: "You were never there for me when I was growing up." Her "absence" in the soap opera is literal, emotional or moral.[10]

When Danny and Cricket suggest bringing her mother to the wedding, Nina gives a passionate rejection of the bad mother:

> Danny, I don't want to seem ungrateful, but my mother is the last person I'd want to see at my wedding. . . . Even if I knew how to get hold of her, I wouldn't bother. She couldn't care less. . . . Look, I know I sound terrible, but I can't help the way I feel. I can't just forgive and forget. . . . You know, I was just a kid when she shoved me out the door and said "Good luck, you're on your own." From then on, I blocked that part of my life out of my mind. I just decided I didn't have a family, you know?

In the soap opera, opposed aspects of the mother remain separate and in conflict, appearing and disappearing and thereby continuing the unchanging narrative. One aim of therapy is to help the daughter perceive the complexity of her mother with both good and bad aspects, and to resolve her own ambivalence towards her mother. The soap opera provides a therapeutic space for women to face their anxieties about being valued or deserted, but the viewer is never impelled to overcome the splitting of the mother or to recognize (and possibly challenge) their desire for the father and for romance. While the absent mother allows the viewer (in the subject position of daughter) to enjoy a sense of freedom and a separate identity independent of her mother (which Chodorow, 1978, argues is elusive in reality), the return of the soap mother tests this autonomy. At this point the daughter is often shown to fail as the mother returns to manipulate or undermine the daughter's life.[11]

Motherhood Versus Romance

We have argued elsewhere (Liebes & Livingstone, 1992) that soap opera presents the relations between women's roles—as mother, lover and careerist—as conflictual. The pre-wedding scenes in *The Young and the Restless* present two opposed images of the woman as mother which differently prioritize motherhood and romance by personifying a contradiction between the real mother and the good mother. The struggle between Jill and Catherine dramatizes the difficulties for women in being both caring and sexual, selfless and self-independent. Jill, the biological mother is a younger, sexual, glamorous, dynamic brunette, while Catherine, the adoptive mother is older, quiet, rather faded. Jill, having had her illegitimate son, Phillip, then abandoned him to engage in a series of romantic affairs. She returns to prevent his marriage and so re-establish her powerful bond with her now-adult, attractive son. The good mother is shown as weak, barely understanding what is going on—a position with which the viewer can identify. For example, Jill ridicules Catherine to Rex: "Oh Rex, you must admit she does watch over you like a mother-hen; the poor woman must be terribly insecure," at which point she adjusts his tie flirtatiously. The women are seen competing for the same man: Jill says to Rex, "how does it feel to be standing next to a real woman?" and describes Catherine as "too old for him."

As Nina and Phillip also have a baby son, the conerns over motherhood continue into the next generation. Will Nina mother baby Phillip Jr. as Catherine did his father or will she choose to abandon his welfare and follow the path of Jill and of her own mother? Paradoxically, Jill tries to push Nina towards her own position—the romance with the rogue (Chase)—but for the wrong reasons, out of her own motherly concern for Phillip (for she considers Nina not worthy of him). The conversation between Nina and Chase on the eve of the wedding directly contrasts motherhood and romance as a woman's goal:

NINA: I've got a baby to think about.

CHASE: Well, babies grow up, Nina, and then what?

NINA: So what am I supposed to do? A child needs his father. I can't just keep thinking about myself and good times.

CHASE: Would you listen to what you are saying? You are marrying Phillip to give your child a father.

NINA: What's wrong with that?

CHASE: I will tell you what's wrong with that. What happens when the kid grows up and goes off to school? What are you left with? Just you and Phillip. And then you are going to realize that that guy you're married to, to be a father to your baby is not your best friend, is not your lover. Can you really spend the rest of your life with the guy? . . . You want excitement and passion, not just a father for your baby. Come on, just admit it.

In reaching her decision, Nina fantasies about life with Phillip and with Chase through two dream sequences which contrast security/motherhood and romance. Viewers know that both dreams are flawed. Nina doesn't love Phillip, Chase doesn't love Nina. The twin fantasies reflect the split woman. With Phillip, Nina fantasizes being the loving, secure, domestic mother; with Chase, the baby has disappeared and Nina can indulge her selfish, romantic, sexual self. Viewers hear the above scene from a position of knowledge regarding Chase's dishonest motives and so they are drawn to favor the security offered by Phillip, flirting with the idea of romance while acknowledging its impossibility. After an inner struggle, Nina opts for security and for becoming a good/real/present mother. The subject position of the viewer is Nina's. We are invited to worry for her that Jill will triumph over Catherine and disrupt her marriage, and we know that in the never-ending soap, marriages don't last. (It is not accidental that the story of Nina and Phillip's marriage is alternated with that of Paul and Cassandra's adultery.) While the mothers are concerned with the male line—husband, son and grandson[12]—viewers are concerned for the daughter in the middle, Nina, and care little for Phillip or the baby.

Missing Mothers and Grown-up Daughters

Motherless women are portrayed as still suffering from their loss, offering a voice to the continuing pain and anger felt by daughters in the audience toward their own mothers. The soap daughters are shown to need further nurturing, and the conventions of the soap (and of the culture more broadly) prescribe that they seek it through relations with men. However, as men rarely offer sufficient, sustained nurturing (Chodorow, 1978), women continually desire new romance; their vulnerability makes them appear immoral. In addition to seeking dependency relations with men, women in soap sustain competitive rather than nurturing relationships with women. The suggestion is that women have weak identities, lack power, cannot trust each other, and do not respect each other (Benjamin, 1990; Chodorow, 1978). In the narratives, empathetic relations between women are continually undermined through women's primary concerns with men. For example, when Cricket and Danny help plan her wedding, far from assuming their caring concern for her, Nina suspects a conspiracy and reacts with hostility: "what are you whispering about?" (Indeed, Nina is surrounded by female conspiracies, as Jill has paid Chase to prevent the wedding and as Cricket is a previous lover of Phillip.)

Through these narratives, the soap opera offers viewers several psychological theories. The first concerns the power of childhood experiences. The absence of the mother affects the daughter in her subsequent relationships, forever recycling the original trauma. The second is that feminine maturity is achieved only through marriage (for the viewer knows that the exciting, sexy image of adventure and romance with Chase cannot be sustained).

By her meeting with Phillip Nina has been transformed from an insufferable, material girl to a mature, self-aware woman. If she accepts selfless femininity with a safe and reliable man, she need never be alone again, a need betrayed in childhood when her mother deserted her. As the first theory has a built-in recycling of narratives, it can be sustained, but the genre both promotes and undermines the second theory. While the ideal of marriage is continually held out for women, it cannot be sustained (the soap must go on, and, as Chodorow argues, men cannot succeed in the nurturing role). A third theory is also relevant here, namely that repressed desires will resurface at a later time in a disruptive fashion.

For example, Cricket and Danny discuss Nina's unhappy childhood but are optimistic because "now she's got her man, her life is going to be roses from now on." Yet the viewer is uncertain: can Nina provide the stability for her child that she herself lacked, or will she be swayed into romance with Chase or future lovers? As she already has a child, she "should" sacrifice her own romantic desires. But repressed desires will, the viewer knows, erupt at some point to destroy the hoped-for future stability.

Marriage as (Temporary) Resolution

The wedding in soap opera provides a focal event which triggers a range of traumas and conflicts. Old alignments must be renegotiated and everyone redefines his or her position. The wedding makes apparent the kinship network that connects them all. It is also, therefore, a moment in which the primacy of patriarchal themes are re-established over matriarchal or subversive messages in the soap opera (Liebes & Livingstone, 1992).

The wedding is also an emotional focus, drawing out everyone's feelings—competition, seduction, hatred, love, jealousy. The effect is heightened by a classic tension over whether or not the bride will appear. In our example from *The Young and the Restless*, during this prolonged moment of uncertainty, Chase seduces Nina, Jill seduces Rex, Catherine denies that the baby is Nina's, and some of the wedding guests relive their own weddings. Weddings, then, provide a vehicle for replaying past and future traumas, for making visible identities and relationships, for expressing emotions. While conventionally a wedding is a positive outcome, evidencing emotional maturity and the achievement of appropriate sexual and gender identity, in soaps this outcome is only temporary. As the viewers know, while marriages form the goal of soap relationships, they nearly always break down, repeatedly demonstrating immaturity, problematic identity, and emotional conflict.

Conclusions

We have drawn on the psychoanalytic paradigm not in order to assert its usefulness in accounting for mother/daughter relationships but to analyze the soaps as telling a cultural story which ensnares women. Through dissemination and legitimation in popular culture, we suggest that psychoanalysis informs and supprots the patriarchal framework through which women understand themselves. This cultural narrative is made visible through its relentless repetitiveness, despite many variations and permutations, throughout the genre of soap opera.[13]

Never-ending Repetition

While the soap opera appears open in its never-ending narratives—all digressions, no final conclusions—nonetheless each new narrative recycles the same underlying conservative message concerning women's psychic problems. Repetitiveness is the dominant impression—of missing mothers, dependence on men, self-destructiveness in women, failure of romantic and nurturing

relationships, impermanence of marriage, self-sacrificial good mother versus the egoistic bad mother, and so forth, with no hope of escape or alternative resolutions. The soap cannot emerge from its world of fantasy and so the viewer cannot get to work on the nitty gritty of achievable relationships. To sustain the drama the soap must stay within the fantasy. There is no therapeutic endpoint, only another crisis for another day, and the promise of happiness is always deferred or betrayed (Cavell, 1981). In this respect, the lack of resolutions celebrated in the feminist literature as openness, as potentially subversive and empowering (for example, Nochimson, 1992; Seiter, 1981), becomes negative (as indeed, the early critics of soaps argued).

Fathers and Daughters, Mothers and Daughters

The mother-daughter relationship in soap opera is continually downplayed in comparison with the father-daughter relationship. While mothers represent regression to narcissim and infantilism, fathers represent acceptance of femininity and the achievement of a mature gender identity. Here the soap opera continues the socialization of little girls in the fairy tale. Hansel and Gretel vanquish both stepmother and witch and return to their father; Cinderella and the Sleeping Beauty triumph over their female adversaries and marry the handsome prince. The daughter often must undergo her own journey, but the goal is always a man; he completes the woman and the story. According to psychoanalysis, this resolution offers the opportunity for the child/viewer to face her fears of loss or inadequacy and to accept the (patriarchal) solution open to her.

Therapeutic Explorations of the Self

Within this overall restrictive framework, it can also be argued that while therapy is available only to the rich, soap opera may provide therapy for the poor. It provides a sense of exclusivity and space to express one's fantasies, and although the genre encourages women to make use of those fantasies prescribed to women by culture, it allows for some recognition of and engagement with their desires and anxieties. For example, in soaps, the continual coupling, uncoupling, aligning and disappearing allows an exploration of the social definition of self, as problematically both separate and yet connected. As Hoggart (1957) noted, the period before marriage represents a temporary freedom for women, before they settle down to the routine ignored by American soaps. The soap opera maximizes this period of freedom in women's lives through the cycle of marriage and remarriage (Liebes & Livingstone, 1992), and it recognizes that "happy ever after" is a fantasy. However, it explores the processes of separating and connecting, with their momentary freedoms and attendant emotions, but fails to offer any specific sense of self. The genre treats relationships as a game of musical chairs. Relations among women are treacherous rather than supportive, relations between women and men remain selfless for women and selfish for men, and all relationships lack content. It is the fact of relationship which is significant, rather than the exploration of ways of relating which permit the construction of satisfactory or problematic identities. Thus the soaps maintain a paradox, recognising and yet never fulfilling women's need for a sense of self.

The Viewers' Experience

We suggest that women view the soap opera on two levels. On one level, the soap opera viewer is active (Hobson, 1982; Liebes & Katz, 1990; Livingstone, 1990). She talks of becoming involved in the characters' lives, of following and predicting the narratives, of speculating about the details of relationships, of drawing analogies with their own lives, and so forth. The fascination is that of the minutiae of relationship development (she did such and such, and then he said this, and then she . . .) through which Gilligan (1993) suggests that women negotiate their connectedness to each other and hence generate a contextualized, relational sense of self. This aspect of viewing is concerned with the "realism" of soaps, and with a playful pleasure in their narratives and characters.

But this is not to contradict viewing on a more unconscious level in which viewers may respond also to the repetitive socializing messages of women's dependence on men, of their location in the personal sphere, their unreliability (they may disappear at any time) and their uncertain relations with others (treacherous relations with women, temporary relations with men).[14] While the active level of viewing allows the viewer to adopt a variety of subject positions—engaging in parasocial interaction with diverse characters in a complex kinship network, on the more unconscious level, the viewer is expected to take for granted being constructed as the daughter, dealing with the mother as other, and yet accept the legitimate prioritization of motherhood over romance and career.

For example, the soap opera uses dramatic irony (for example, when Danny calls Nina, torn between Phillip and Chase, "the happiest girl in the world") to draw in the viewer tightly, heightening the tension, flattering them that they know more than the characters. This enticement of the "active viewer" generates the intimacy which is central to the therapeutic, maybe emancipatory, function of the viewing experience. But this intimacy also encourages acceptance of the soap's normative framing of the characters' (and viewers') dilemmas; indeed, this acceptance is required if viewers are to share the pleasurable emotions—tension and relief—of the narrative.

Women's Voices in the Soap Opera

Gilligan (1993) argues that women, experiencing their self-identity crisis later than men (in adolescence rather than early childhood), articulate the crisis of identity development and authentic voice for both genders. One might then expect women's popular culture to express these crises. And, indeed, if as Gilligan argues, men learn to leave out women, while women learn to leave out themselves, the soap opera is liberating for putting women's experience and struggles center stage. Soaps both promote traditional ideals of femininity and counter these by expressing and legitimating women's desires. We have argued that mothers of daughters in soaps are rarely present, real and good, yet this makes visible the contradiction inherent in this triple expectation of mothers: to be good, woman must be absent (selfless), to be real, she must be good and bad (not split). Narratives of the missing mother explore the consequences of women's disappearances and reappearances. When absent, women see how their men and family become fickle, when present, they are rejected as selfish.

However, the lesson to be learned by women viewers is not hopeful. Men—via romance—dominate the whole scheme of things, even if their roles in the narrative are secondary. The narratives tell of woman's place in the male narrative and of the consequences for her of accepting or resisting that position. The texts are not closed; spaces exist for women's authentic voice and for women to explore central emotional issues (Livingstone, 1990; Liebes & Katz, 1990). However, in the soap opera, *all* that women can ultimately do is to repeat the same mistakes over and over again. Everything is subordinated to the never-ending desire for identity through relationships with men, and conflicts can never be finally resolved as they must remain to perpetuate the narrative for another day.

Notes

1. For example, a Russian immigrant in Israel notes that without watching *Dallas* regularly, one cannot take part in conversation the next day and thus one has no chance of becoming an Israeli (Liebes & Katz, 1990). The same is said to be true of *The Young and the Restless* in Trinidad (Miller, 1992).

2. There is a problem in the theory of the male gaze when the hero is female: In the soap opera, the daughter and viewer are constructed as subject of the male (producer's) gaze, but her gaze further constructs the mother as other. Similarly, Bottingheimer (1987) argues against Bettelheim's analysis of fairy tales, that fairy tales with male heroes must be interpreted differently from those with female heroines. The two are not equivalent.

3. This is not true in British soap operas, where babies are highly visible, and so the subject position is that of adult woman as mother, facing the difficulties of balancing the needs of herself, her family, and her career (Liebes & Livingstone, 1992).

4. Audience ratings show consistently that soap operas are watched significantly more often by women than men and by lower class than by middle class viewers (Livingstone, 1990).

5. Baudrillard argues that disappearance is the major trait of our times, signifying the end of history, of progress, of grand narrative (Bauman, 1992, p. 49).

6. For example, in *The Guiding Light*, one episode alternates between three stories centering on (patriarchal) fathers (Hampton Speakes' attempt to control the sexual activities of his daughter Catherine, Alan Michael Spalding's concern for his unborn child—assumed to be a son and heir, and Michelle's caring for her sick father, Ed Bauer, explicitly taking the place of her absent mother at the cost of school attendance).

7. One might say that he fails to resolve the Oedipal situation he faces by transferring his love for his mother to a sexual partner.

8. To give examples from one other soap opera, in *General Hospital*, we know the mothers of Dr. Tom Harding, Dr. Alan Quartermain and his sons A. J. and Jason. While Leila Quartermain's daughter Tracy is present, Lucy Coe has no mother, having been brought up by her aunt Charlene. Dr. Monica Quartermain, Felicia Jones, Honor Domain, Simone Harding and others have no visible mothers. Further, as Lucy's aunt supports her sons more than her neice, as Monica's mother-in-law is not particularly supportive of her, as Tracy's mother is continually critical of her, in none of these cases is any positive mother-daughter relationship portrayed, in contrast to the relationships between mothers and sons.

9. Cricket's mother later reappears, a prostitute who contracts AIDS. In this example and many others, the theme of punishment for "bad" mothers is strong.

10. Split conceptions of mothers circulate in the culture more generally. A study of real life mother/daughter relationships reveals similarly dichotomous discourses of adult daughters regarding their mothers (Henwood, 1993)—as bad, overprotective, neglectful.

11. For example, in *General Hospital*, Dr. Monica Quartermain abandoned her daughter to an orphanage some 25 years ago and repressed any memory of her existence. Eventually the daughter reappears to form a good relationship with her mother, but this serves to break up the mother's marriage. A few years later the daughter drowns. In *One Life to Live*, Vicky Buchanan abandons her daughter Megan under pressure from her father. When Megan returns as an adult, she expresses her anger to her mother, but later dies in an accident.

12. This is a common theme in soap opera. For example, Miss Ellie in *Dallas* and Alexis Carrington in *Dynasty* have similar worries (Liebes & Katz, 1990).

13. Storylines which parallel that analyzed here from *The Young and the Restless* abound in soap opera. For example, in recent episodes of *Neighbours* (5/11/93, BBC1), Phoebe and Steve decide to get married so as to provide a family for their future baby (she is 7 months pregnant). Phoebe declares that she will not invite her mother, who abandoned her as a baby, to the wedding.

14. While much audience research on the soap opera has been conducted to date, researchers have of late been so concerned to explore divergent or oppositional readings that viewers' responses to the underlying hegemonic aspects of the genre have been neglected. Our present analysis would suggest that future audience research should examine more closely the relation between normative and oppositional aspects of viewers' interpretations (although see Livingstone, 1990; Radway, 1984).

References

Allen, R. C. (1985). *Speaking of soap operas*. Chapel Hill: University of North Carolina Press.

Ang, I. (1985). *Watching Dallas: Soap opera and the melodramatic imagination*. New York: Methuen.

Arnheim, R. (1943). The world of daytime serial. In P. Lazarsfeld & F. Stanton (Eds.), *Radio research* (pp. 34–85). New York: Duell, Sloan & Pearce.

Bauman, Z. (1992). *Intimations of postmodernity*. London: Routledge.

Benjamin, J. (1990). *The bonds of love: Psychoanalysis, feminism and the problem of domination*. London: Virago.

Bettelheim, B. (1976). *The uses of enchantment: The meaning and importance of fairy tales*. Harmondsworth, England: Penguin.

Bottingheimer, R. (1987). *Grimms' bad girls and bold boys: The moral and social visions of the tales*. New Haven and London: Yale University Press.

Bowlby, J. (1965). *Child care and the growth of love* (2nd ed.). Harmondsworth, England: Penguin.

Brown, M. E. (Ed.). (1990). *Television and women's culture: The politics of the popular*. London: Sage Publications.

Brunsdon, C. (1993). Identity in feminist television criticism. *Media, Culture and Society, 15*(2), 309–320.

Cantor, M., & Pingree, S. (1983). *The soap opera*. Beverly Hills, CA: Sage Publications.

Cavell, S. (1981). *Pursuits of happiness: The Hollywood comedy of remarriage*. New York: Cambridge University Press.

Chodorow, N. (1978). *The reproduction of mothering: Psychoanalysis and the sociology of gender*. Berkeley: University of California Press.

Feuer, J. (1984). Melodrama, serial form and television today. *Screen, 25*(1), 4–17.

Flitterman-Lewis, S. (1987). Psychoanalytic approach to television. In R. C. Allen (Ed.), *Channels of discourse* (pp. 172–210). Chapel Hill: University of North Carolina Press.

Freud, S. (1988). *The interpretation of dreams*. The Pelican Freud Library (vol. 4). Harmondsworth, England: Penguin.

Geraghty, C. (1990). *Women in soap operas*. London: Polity Press.

Gilligan, C. (1993). *In a different voice: Psychological theory and women's development* (2nd ed.). Cambridge, MA: Harvard University Press.

Hall, S. (1980). Encoding/decoding. In S. Hall, D. Hobson, A. Lowe, & P. Willis (Eds.), *Culture, media, language* (pp. 128–138). London: Hutchinson.

Henwood, K. (1993). Women in later life: The discursive construction of identities within family relationships. *Journal of Aging Studies, 7,* 303–319.

Herzog, H. (1944). What do we really know about daytime serial listeners? In P. F. Lazarsfeld & F. Stanton (Eds.), *Radio research, 1942–1943* (pp. 3–33). New York: Duell, Sloan & Pearce.

Hobson, D. (1982). *Crossroads: The drama of a soap opera*. London: Methuen.

Hoggart, R. (1957). *The uses of literacy*. London: Chatto and Windus.

Houston, B. (1985). Viewing television: The metapsychology of endless consumption. *Quarterly Review of Film Studies, 9,* 183–195.

Katzman, N. (1972). Television soap operas: What's been going on anyway? *Public Opinion Quarterly, 36,* 200–212.

Lakoff, R., T., & Coyne, J. C. (1993). *Father knows best: The use and abuse of power in Freud's case of "Dora."* New York: Teachers College Press.

Liebes, T., & Katz, E. (1990). *The export of meaning*. Oxford, England: Oxford University Press.

Llebes, T., & Livingston, S. M. (1992). Mothers and lovers: Managing women's role conflicts in American and British soap operas. J. B. Lumler, J. M. McLeod, & K. E. Rosengren (Eds.), *Communication and culture across space and time: Prospects of comparative analysis* (pp. 94–120). Newbury Park, CA: Sage Publications.

Liebes, T., & Livingstone, S. M. (1994). The structure of family and romantic ties in the soap opera: An ethnographic approach. *Communication Research, 21,* 717–741.

Liebes, T., & Grissek, R. (in press). Television news and the politicization of women. In D. Paletz (Ed.), *Political Communication*. Np:Np.

Livingstone, S. M. (1987). The implicit representation of characters in *Dallas:* A multidimensional scaling approach. *Human Communication Research, 13,* 399–420.

Livingstone, S. M. (1990). *Making sense of television: The psychology of audience interpretation*. Oxford, England: Pergamon.

Masson, J. (1990). *Against therapy*. London: Fontana.

Miller, D. (1992). *The Young and the Restless* in Trinidad: A case of local and the global in mass consumption. In R. Silverstone & E. Hirsch (Eds.), *Consuming technologies* (pp. 163–182). London: Routledge.

Mitchell, J. (1986). *The selected Melanie Klein*. Harmondsworth, England: Penguin.

Modleski, T. (1982). *Loving with a vengeance: Mass-produced fantasies for women*. New York: Methuen.

Morley, D. (1980). *The nationwide audience: Structure and decoding*. British Film Institute Television Monograph No. 11. London: British Film Institute.

Moscovici, S. (1984). The phenomenon of social representations. In R. M. Farr & S. Moscovici (Eds.), *Social representations* (pp. 3–69). Cambridge, England: Cambridge University Press.

Mulvey, L. (1975, Autumn). Visual pleasure and narrative cinema. *Screen, 16,* 6–18.

Nochimson, M. (1992). *No end to her: Soap opera and the female subject*. Berkeley: University of California Press.

Pingree, S., Starrett, S., & Hawkins, R. (1979). *Soap opera viewers and social reality*. Unpublished paper.

Press, A. (1991). *Women watching television: Gender, class and generation in the American television experience*. Philadelphia: University of Pennsylvania Press.

Propp, V. (1968). *The morphology of the folktale.* Austin: University of Texas Press.

Radway, J. (1984). *Reading the romance: Women, patriarchy and popular literature.* Chapel Hill: University of North Carolina Press.

Rich, A. (1977). *Of woman born: Motherhood as experience and institution.* London: Virago.

Scheman, N. (1988, Autumn). Missing mothers desiring daughters: Framing the sight of women. *Critical Inquiry, 15,* 62–89.

Seiter, E. (1982). Eco's TV guide—the soaps. *Tabloid, 5,* 35–43.

Turow, J. (1974, Spring). Advising and ordering: Daytime, primetime. *Journal of Communication, 24*(2), 138–141.

Walters, S. D. (1992). *Lives together/worlds apart.* Berkeley: University of California Press.

White, M. (1992). *Tele-advising: Therapeutic discourse in American television.* Chapel Hill: University of North Carolina Press.

PART FIVE

Ethics and the Critical Approach

CHAPTER 16   Television, Ethics, and Criticism

Television, Ethics, and Criticism

CHAPTER 16

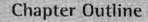

W e began the first chapter of this book by framing the context of television criticism in the relationship between television and society. It is not happenstance that we confronted the powers of television—to entertain, to socialize and educate, to inform, and to create community and consensus—prior to delving into the foundations of television criticism and the approaches that may be taken to analyze television texts. Our focus on the powers of television mirrors broadly felt social concern over the influence of the media. Television, in part because it has had remarkably broad and unfettered access to our homes for so long, deserves special consideration. Even critics approaching television with the most "micro" preoccupations over aesthetic form and function must do so cognizant of the long social shadow cast by the medium's social, cultural, and economic force.

This issue of special social concern over television presses critics to look through and beyond aesthetics to basic questions of value. Questions about the value or social worth of television and our engagement with it are raised throughout this book, explicitly in some approaches and less so in others. Such concerns are easy to find. For example, when we look at television through the lens of rhetorical criticism, we are examining not only issues of suasive force but also the efficacy of the rhetorical strategies used, the appropriateness of motives behind the strategies, and whether the net result of being moved in the intended direction is more a good thing than bad. Similar issues are raised in semiotic/structural criticism, reader-oriented criticism, and many other places when we interrogate how the text interacts with the reader, what positioning results, and we try to assess the ultimate fairness and harm in what likely has transpired.

Other issues crystallize as we assess resistant strategies seen in audiences examined through critical ethnography. Such viewers often negotiate value conflict and engage in struggles over the artistic merit and moral tenor of programming. In other areas, such as production context criticism, we necessarily look at issues of equity throughout the production process. Here, when we are confronted by imbalances of power between creative personnel and their corporate overseers, we are forced to evaluate the merits of the resulting constraints on both artistic freedom and the circulation of ideas in a democracy. When we think about television and its criticism in ways that consider such variant matters of valuation, we are looking at the intersection of aesthetics and ethics.

While the "long conversation" over ethics in the annals of moral philosophy has yielded many disagreements, the core concerns of ethics may be drawn in succinct terms. Put most directly by Merrill (1999, p. 1): "Ethics is the study of what we ought to do." Casting a wider net, Josephson (2002) explains, "Ethics refers to standards of conduct, standards that indicate how one should behave based on moral duties and virtues, which themselves are derived from principles of right and wrong." Thus, in ethical inquiry, we necessarily sift through moral understandings in the course of rendering evaluation or judgment about what ought to be done or, put in the past tense, what has been done. These concerns may be reframed in terms of television and its criticism. On a basic level, an ethical focus would implore consideration of what television ought to be doing. Such ethical engagement with television concerns itself with a familiar set of issues that frame social and professional ethics. Here, we find questions about consequence and creating the greater good; questions over duties, loyalties, and the right thing to do; questions of finding a "righteous" middle ground through exercising character and temperance; questions over acting out of compassion and care to avoid inducing harm; and questions about being fair to all and providing justice.

Although there is little disagreement that such weighty questions are of universal importance, raising ethics in the context of criticism can be slippery. Passing moral judgment in the course of making aesthetic evaluations makes many critics nervous. As we discuss later, the role of ethics in criticism has been much debated in art and literary criticism (see Carroll, 1998a, 2000; Gregory, 1998; Levinson, 1998). In comparison, the role of ethics in the criticism of the mass arts, such as film, television, and popular music, has been less explicitly examined (see Carroll, 2000). However, outside the academic realm, it is clear that the vast bulk of journalistic and media advocacy group criticism of commercialized mass art forms, such as television, have ethical evaluations at their core. Answers to commonly asked questions of how television should treat something, of whether its stories distort the truth, of whether its use of sex, violence, and stereotype may be harming us, of whether its news coverage is fair, and the like all are based in ethical judgment and evaluations of moral appropriateness.

In the next sections, we offer some ideas about how the ethical dimensions of television criticism. We look first at the broader traditions of media ethics and consider how themes seen here are relevant to television criticism. Following this, we provide a brief overview of approaches to moral reasoning commonly used in considerations of media ethics that can inform television criticism. Finally, we close by looking at the climate for the ethical criticism of television and the prospects for its' melding with other approaches we have considered in this book.

The Tradition of Media Ethics

The media ethics tradition in journalism dates back to the turn of the twentieth century and the rise and fall of yellow journalism (Englehardt & Barney, 2002). Codes of ethics for journalists began to appear in the 1920s (led by the American Society of Newspaper Editors' "Canons of Journalism"), and concerns over the social responsibilities of the press were heightened most by the work of the Hutchins Commission (Commission on Freedom of the Press, 1947).[1] It is fair to say that tensions between freedom and responsibility propelled consideration of media ethics. Worries over curbs to freedom of expression in the media gave rise to strategies that would minimize the likelihood they would be invoked. In this vein, by the latter part of the twentieth century, the nascent academic area of media ethics had taken hold. While gaining a toehold first in journalism, ethical analysis of media has fanned out to examine issues in the communication advocacy professions (such as advertising and public relations) and the media entertainment marketplace (including radio, television, film, and popular recordings).

Much in the media ethics tradition stems from concern over the producer or worker as moral actor. This is because mediated texts or audiences, for television or other forms, do not appear out of thin air. Both texts and audiences are, in a sense, manufactured. Thus, as Merrill (1999, p. 1) suggests:

> Media ethics concerns right and wrong, good and bad, better and worse actions taken by people working for the media. Media themselves, of course, cannot be ethical or unethical—only their staff members can. When we deal with *media ethics*, we are really concerned with ethical standards of media *workers* and what kinds of actions they take.

In television criticism, such a claim might suggest that producer-centered approaches are best suited for ethical criticism. Indeed, it may be fruitful to start by examining the ethical contours of action throughout the production context (by actors at varying power roles and levels of hierarchical control) or by considering the special influence of the auteur. However, when we think about the ethical ramifications of what kinds of actions they take, it is clear that we are also talking about the resulting ethical propositions in television narratives and texts and the nature and consequences of audience engagement.

By the turn of the twenty-first century, a set of universalized concerns could be seen emerging from the growing treatments of media ethics. While the fleshing out of these issues has centered on journalism and the reporter as media worker, virtually all of the issues apply across media settings, including television. For example, basic issues of truth telling, honesty, fairness, and deception pertain not only to news and basic business practices, but just as readily to television's reality and docudrama programming. Privacy questions are raised when television uses hidden cameras, gets "up close and personal" at a time of tragedy, "outs" or "ambushes" someone, or merely includes an "innocent bystander" in framing a docudrama. Questions of keeping promises, remaining loyal, bestilling confidentiality, and avoiding conflicts of interest come up daily in the television business as well as in the course of its news and dramatic programming. Here, the economic pressures of "winning" the television game often force players into untenable ethical positions in order to control risk and gain competitive advantage. When economic interests come first, ethical considerations may take a back seat.

Other recurring issues pertain to television's treatment of antisocial behavior and the airing of material that may be morally offensive. Here, familiar questions are raised over the ethos of violence in the context of storytelling, discomforts caused by portrayals of sexual displays or relations, the complexities of drug, alcohol, and tobacco use, and more plainly, uncivil behavior. Our core concerns over harm are raised in other areas as well. When we evaluate television differently for children and juveniles in the audience, ethical criteria are at play. Similarly, when we evaluate how television is doing in terms of its treatments of race, ethnicity, and gender or other forms of discrimination or stereotyping, both on screen and off, we are raising social justice questions that evoke issues of fairness and harm. While issues such as these reflect an emerging consensus of concerns in media ethics (see Day, in press), just as significant has been an emerging reliance on five approaches to guide resolution of ethical dilemmas through moral reasoning (Christians, Fackler, Rotzoll, & McKee, 2001; Day, in press).

Approaches to Moral Reasoning

Television offers many opportunities for ethical interrogation in the course of criticism. Ethical considerations can be folded into almost any approach to television criticism. Depending on the critic's focus, the ethical contours can be a major or minor concern. Once identified, ethical problems raised in the production process, by treatments in the televisual text, or through audience positioning or interpretation can be clarified through the use of ethical theories in the course of moral reasoning (see Carroll 1998b, 1998c). These five perspectives, while not exhaustive of the approaches that may be used, have wide applicability to illuminating ethical dimensions in critical evaluation. Coming at ethical assessment from different directions, they may be used individually or conjointly in informing the critic's assessments. These approaches to ethical and moral reasoning are most often used in deciding what to do when confronted with a dilemma that requires prospective resolution. They may as readily be applied in post-hoc critical reflection on the possibilities of what might have been done in the course of shaping television texts or consuming them.

Utilitarian Perspectives

With origins in the thinking of eighteenth- and nineteenth-century British philosophers Jeremy Bentham (1948) and John Stuart Mill (1861), utilitarianism has been adopted as the most common ethical yardstick of modern times; it is used routinely in the course of setting public policy. With its emphasis on the outcome, it is often referred to as "ends-based thinking." It is a form of "consequentialism" that may be thought of as "teleological," from the Greek *teleos*, meaning "end" or "issue." The approach is best known for the "utility principle," which says one should strive, in the face of an ethical dilemma, to act to create "the greatest good" for the "greatest number." A utilitarian facing the issue of what to do in an ethical dilemma would first ask: What would be the consequences of making a judgment or decision in this situation? In finding an ethical answer, all possible outcomes of all possible actions on all parties would need to be explored.

From this perspective, the first goal of any decision should be to produce the greatest good or most favorable consequences that create the greatest happiness or pleasure. Here, ethical action promotes outcomes with the greatest possible balance of good over evil. Equally important is the second goal of any decision: to distribute this good as widely as possible so that the good consequences affect the greatest number, not a lesser number or the few who may be around you or include you. An inherent risk in a utilitarian approach is that the ends focus can justify morally questionable means. To curb this, utility theory invokes a "minimization of harm" corollary, where harm (as a means) is justifiable only if it is necessary or essential in promoting the "greater good." Thus, in a television comedy, the greatest happiness for more viewers is problematic if it comes on the backs of stereotypical portrayals of a minority group that are deemed harmful.

Still, from the utility perspective, ethical action is largely judged by the quality and breadth of the good that results.

Nonconsequentialism: Duty Perspectives

In direct contrast with utilitarianism's focus on consequences, theories based on duty are often called *nonconsequentialism*. An advantage of such theories is that they avoid the uncertain guesswork needed to predict consequences when faced with an ethical dilemma. Advocates argue that because anticipating consequences is such an imperfect art, it is far better to rely on that over which the individual has more control: acting righteously. Influenced heavily by the ideas of the eighteenth-century German philosopher Immanuel Kant (1959), such an approach has its basis in "rules for action" and may be thought of as "deontological," from the Greek *deon*, meaning "duty" or "obligation." The nature of the obligation is expressed in Kant's notion of the *categorical imperative*, which commands people to "act so your choices could be universal law." For Kant, *categorical* means "unconditional," with moral laws being "unconditionally binding" on all rational beings. In Kant's view, these higher truths or "noumena" are born in each person and must be obeyed. With such assumptions, Kant places a heavy burden on the individual to act ethically. More practically, he is really asking people to check the principle that is underlying decisions to see whether they would want that principle applied universally. If we act according to whatever law we would like everyone else to follow in similar circumstances, we act based on what kind of world would be best to live in. For Kant, individual righteous action matters, and he has little concern over what other individuals may do or the consequences of the action. He argues that although we can't predict consequences, we can act out of duty to do the right thing. As a result, his focus is, on one hand, actions that are wrong, such as cheating, lying, stealing, dishonesty, deception, or doing harm, and on the other, actions that are universally right, such as truth telling, benevolence, freedom, and respect for others and for life.

Although Kant's brand of moral absolutism stands in contrast to today's "anything goes" culture that encourages moral relativism, it can help the critic draw lines in seemingly ever moving sand. Some approaches, such as political-economic critiques of the production context or neo-Marxist ideological criticism that routinely focus on abuses of power, deception, or dishonest business practices, are necessarily derived from duty-based assessments. Other topics, such as deception in political advertising, the routine use of violence to harm in action shows, or the lack of respect for others implied by the use of stereotyped characters in situation comedy can be informed by considering the universal duties, obligations, and loyalties of the creative and business people that shape television, quite apart from what the consequences may be or what the competition is already doing.

Virtue Perspectives: Finding the Golden Mean

The building of character is central to virtue ethics. Focused on *phronesis,* or the development of practical wisdom in citizens, the virtue ethics stems from the work of Aristotle (1953) in the fourth century B.C. in Greece (see Reid, 1999) and that of Confucius and his students more than 100 years earlier in the fifth century B.C. in China (see Reid, 1999). Both embrace the notion of virtue seen in a "golden mean" or, more accurately, a "temperate" point in between extremes that would be found by a person of practical wisdom in determining the right or ethical thing to do. Finding the mean is not a mathematical exercise, but rather one of finding the "right place" between excess and deficiency, between overdoing and underdoing. Such temperance stresses rational and pragmatic solutions to issues that embrace a "fair" or "right" compromise that is sensitive to competing interests. In focusing on the actor rather than the outcome, as in utility theory, or the action, as in duty-based theory, virtue comes through character-building practice.

Ethical evaluation from the virtue approach starts by identifying the opposing options or extremes that would be possible in handling a situation or resolving a dilemma. In reporting a television news story, this may mean doing nothing at one extreme, while reporting everything at the other. In a television drama, it may mean showing no blood in a violent scene in contrast to being very graphic about the violence and its aftermath. In each of these situations, the virtue ethicist strives to find a tempered mean action that would be both right and fair. While the compromises that come from a virtue approach are often intrinsically sensible, they can as easily blunt the critic's sword. Taking the middle ground infrequently produces great art, and critical assessments may benefit from taking a stand for that which is right on one extreme or the other. Certain compromises, such as stealing a million dollars as a mean between stealing nothing and stealing many millions, defy moral standing. When confronted by an egregious mean, utility, duty, care, or justice approaches may be more useful to the critic.

Ethic of Care Perspectives

Often thought of as the central tenet to Judeo-Christian ethics, the ethics of care is embraced in the Golden Rule of loving your neighbor as you would yourself. Here, the notion of reversibility fuels treating others as you would want to be treated in similar circumstances. More than a Judeo-Christian ideal, this goal of "other respecting care" is seen across the world's great religions (Kidder, 1996). The normative idea of "loving thy neighbor" has special formulation in Christian tradition in the concept of *agape,* or unselfish "other directed love" that embraces a loyalty to others shown in loving them as they are. Often this means caring for "neighbors," which in the Old Testament was a term reserved for those less fortunate or powerful (Christians et al., 2001).

In more contemporary times, the ethics of care underlies much feminist scholarship that stresses cooperation, compassion, and the primacy of human dignity in resolving conflicts (Gilligan, 1982; Noddings, 1984). For the care-centered critic, the ethics of love and caring brings a supreme obligation from which all other duties are seen as derivative. For the television critic, thinking in care-based terms means putting yourself in the shoes of others and asking how you would want to be treated. From such a stance, it is easy to enlighten evaluations concerning the injustices of stereotype, privacy invasions, humiliating or less than human portrayals from the perspective of care ethics.

Social Justice Perspectives

With its origins in social contract theory, justice-based moral reasoning is often centered in egalitarianism. The social contract, guaranteeing equal protection, provides a foundation to law in democratic societies. Here, the ideal of fairness and the elimination of arbitrary distinctions guide judgment. We know, however, that in practice, some people have more resources and power than others and that this can skew the social contract. Toward remedying this, Rawls (1971) added the twist of a "veil of ignorance" in pursuit of a strategy that not only achieves "justice for all" but ensures equity for those most vulnerable. With the goal of eliminating social and role differentiation when confronting an ethical dilemma or decision, Rawls asks that all those involved or affected by the decision step back from who they are in that situation to an "original position" behind the veil. The "veil" is one of ignorance because, once behind it, you don't know who you are: you may be young or old, rich or poor, male or female, black or white, gay or straight, famous or obscure. This stripping of identity goes beyond the decision-making process behind the veil and continues as the veil is lifted, when you may emerge as anyone who entered. Thus, in making a decision, resolutions should be comfortable and just to anyone you may emerge as being.

Behind the veil, two goals are sought in deciding action. First, basic liberty, freedom, and dignity should be equally and maximally distributed. With this first goal achieved, other social goods (such as wealth and power) should be distributed inequitably to benefit the least advantaged party. Through such a process, this notion of justice seeks to level the playing field. Similar to care-based theory, this conception of justice invokes reversibility as in the Golden Rule. However, instead of it always being "you" treating someone "as you would want to be treated," your vantage point (including power and paternalism) is destabilized with this justice approach, as you may walk away "in the shoes of others."

A key strength of this approach is that it works to strip away bias, but the exercise is challenging in practice because in real life, people have stable stakes and positions. In the hands of the critic, "going behind the veil" is a powerful strategy that can engage the critic in multiple perspectives simultaneously. For example, assessing the rhetoric of humor in *The Man Show* from the perspective of the "female butt" of jokes, rather than the point of view of the male rhetor may foster new sensibilities. Similarly, considering the omniscient vision of an auteur, such as Dick Wolf in his view of *Law and Order* in New York City, through the eyes of all those who may be involved or affected by the criminal justice system may add perspective. Questions of justice or fairness can become central to almost any critique of television, from structural inequities, to semiotic choices that benefit some more than others, and narrative voices that empower. In production context and reception-centered analysis, inequities are frequently voiced by participants. Critics who have their ears attuned to fairness and justice are far more likely to give these voices standing in their analyses.

Making the Link to Television Criticism

Collectively, the lenses of utility, duty, virtue, care, and justice offer a good way to assess whether an ethical hook (or at least some reflection) might be appropriate to your critical interrogation of television. They raise big questions that might otherwise be overlooked:

- Does the television work, its production, and/or its reception promote the greatest good for the greatest number, while minimizing harm?
- Are the duties, obligations, and loyalties exercised in the television work, its production, and/or its reception those that are "righteous," such that, if universally followed, the world would be a better place?
- Is a virtuous temperance exercised or encouraged in the television work, its production, and/or its reception when confronted by possibilities that would be extreme in excess or deficiency?
- Is other regarding care exercised or promoted in the television work, its production, and/or its reception?
- Are fairness, equity, and justice valued and encouraged in the television work, its production process, and/or in its reception?

These questions, affirmatively framed, provide a good starting point in assessing whether ethical or moral dimensions might add to your analysis. They may alternatively be framed conversely, or negatively, in order to pinpoint more clearly ethical shortcomings that need stocktaking in television analysis. Is the good that is created selfish or fatally limited? Is more harm than good being propagated? Are the duties, obligations, or loyalties being followed (or avoided) morally off-base or compromised? Is excess (extreme options) or deficiency (no action) so naturalized as to exclude temperate and more virtuous options? Does preoccupation with self, success, or competition compromise or devalue other regarding care? Does an "ends mentality" with a focus on winning perpetuate a norm of self-serving justice at the expense of equity and fairness, especially to vulnerable parties?

These questions merely open the door to adding an ethical dimension to the critic's considerations of television texts, their creation, and their consumption. The possibilities for incorporating ethical and moral reflection in criticism extend well beyond the issues they raise and the limits of the five approaches we have briefly outlined. The critic should recognize that there are many more approaches to communication and discourse ethics that might be brought to bear on television (see Christians, 2000; Merrill, 1999).

The Climate for Ethical Criticism of Television

In today's critical climate, there is renewed interest in ethical criticism, although in certain quarters, there remains opposition to any ethical turn in aesthetic criticism. As advocates have pointed out, ethical criticism has been with us for many millennia (Booth, 1988, Carroll, 2000). Plato's indictment and banishment of the poets as ethically suspect stands as a major landmark in this tradition. Much art has explicitly embraced ethical and moral concerns. As a result, certain common forms, such as religious or political art and narratives, make little sense if approached on purely aesthetic grounds, without being informed by ethical and moral understandings. It is only in more recent times, in the light of such movements as art for art's sake and new criticism, that bringing ethics to bear on critical evaluation was seen as problematic (Carroll, 1998b, Gregory, 1998).

Advocates have argued for the "inescapability of ethical criticism" for a broad range of art and literature (Gregory, 1998, p. 196). While it is often admitted that there are art works (such as abstract paintings or orchestral music) for which ethical criticism is inappropriate or irrelevant, there are many forms, such as narratives, that inherently make claims about how to live or how not to live. As Burke (1967, pp. 294–304) has put it, literary forms (and he would include television programs) are "equipment for living." In naming situations, narratives press us to "define and create our own moral agency " (Gregory, 1998, p. 213). In this light, Booth (1988, p. 11) has argued for the central tendencies of ethical criticism:

> If "virtue" covers every kind of genuine strength or power, and if a person's ethos is the total range of his or her virtues [to behave badly or well], then ethical criticism will be any effort to show how the virtues of narratives relate to the virtues of selves and societies, or how the ethos of any story affects or is affected by the ethos—the collection of virtues—of any given reader.

More recently, Booth (1998, p. 353) has reflected on what he sees as a near universal applicability of ethical criticism: "I can think of no published story that does not exhibit its author's implied judgments about how to live and what to believe about what to live." One would be hard pressed to think of a television form that does not include those same implied judgments about living. Given this, it might be argued that the ethical criticism of television is one of those things that is "inescapable."

Even so, there are varied objections to the prospects for and proprieties of ethical criticism. A chief fear is that inducing moral judgment in aesthetic evaluation is the tip of the censorship iceberg. While a serious concern, as Carroll (2000, p. 301) cogently points out, this is a bit of a red herring: "Something can be morally wrong and not warrant coercive enforcement by the state." Put more forthrightly, critics engaged in ethical assessments can quite reasonably be staunchly anticensorship.

Other objections to ethical criticism are philosophical ones. Carroll (2000) has characterized and refuted three classes of argument against ethical criticism: autonomism, anticonsequentialism, and cognitive triviality. The autonomist argues that art and ethics are distinct spheres, and so ethics should not be imposed in evaluating aesthetics. Autonomists rely on a "common denominator argument" that art should be evaluated by standards that can be applied to all works, and because "not all art concerns ethical matters, the standard cannot be ethical" (Carroll, 2000, p. 352). This may be responded to by agreeing that ethical assessments of some art may be inappropriate, but that does not rule out its appropriateness in evaluating forms, such as television, that inherently have a moral dimension.

The anticonsequentialism argument poses that ethics should not be brought into criticism because we cannot reliably know the moral and behavioral consequences of a work. To use a television example, we can't reliably know that a child watching *Beavis and Butthead* would actually be inspired to set another child on fire (which unfortunately happened). Here, too, advocates of ethical criticism may agree, even admitting to ambiguities in research over social learning from television. Still, it may be argued that behavioral consequences do not need to be firmly established for ethical criticism to proceed. Ethical criticism can move forward based merely "on the pathways we are invited to follow" in the text, and the "ethical critic can focus on the probity of the moral experience that an artwork shapes or prescribes as a condition for correctly assimilating it" (Carroll, 2000, p. 370). Thus, ethical criticism can assess the terms of engagement: the moral contours of the prescriptions and identifications that are encouraged by interacting with a text.

The cognitive triviality objection to ethical criticism stems from the observation that artworks tend to deal in moral truisms that are already known by the reader or viewer rather than revealing any new moral discoveries. As such, art works offer no new knowledge, and thus ethical criticism can similarly add nothing new. From this position, ethical criticism would be commenting more on what the reader brought to bear than that which originated in the work. In responding to the cognitive triviality argument, the ethical critic may agree that art is unlikely to offer much new "knowledge" that a moral position exists. Nonetheless, ethical criticism may proceed based on examining how the work engages the reader in a different kind of moral knowledge. Here, through "acquaintanceship" with the work, a moral "knowledge for" and "knowledge of what it would be like" is fostered. Ethical critics argue that through engagement with the work, moral insights are refined and "cultivated" and may, in some instances, be "subverted" as we "call into question" our moral assumptions through the reading or viewing experience (Carroll, 2000, pp. 360–369).

These responses to the autonomist, anticonsequentialist, and cognitive triviality arguments provide a foundation for a position on ethical criticism that is one of "moderate moralism" and "clarificationism." As Carroll (2000) argues, *moderate moralism* is a response to a more tempered version of autonomism. Moderate moralism poses that aesthetic and ethical criticism may be done conjointly and "that sometimes a moral defect in an artwork can be an aesthetic flaw and that sometimes a moral virtue can be an aesthetic virtue" (p. 377). Under such circumstances, a moral defect in a work can be severe enough to render a judgment of aesthetic defect, although the mere existence of a moral defect does not necessarily lead to such a judgment. For example, one might find Fox's *Temptation Island* aesthetically engaging, but the premise of the program in tempting couples into infidelity may be so morally objectionable that it must be judged as aesthetically defective. While moderate moralism is concerned with how moral evaluations interact with aesthetic ones, it readily recognizes that works with moral virtues can have considerable aesthetic flaws.

A *clarificationist* position on ethical criticism grows from responses to the cognitive triviality and anticonsequentialist arguments. On one hand, clarificationism encourages the critic to explore the terms of moral engagement that are encouraged, and on the other, the character of the "knowledge for" that might result. As Carroll (1998b) outlines, from the clarificationist's view,

> Moral assessments of narrative artworks can be grounded in the quality of our moral engagement with and experience of the narrative object. This engagement can be positive, where our moral understanding and/or emotions are deepened and clarified, or it can be negative, where the moral understanding is misled, confused, perverted, and so on (p. 151). . . . Clarificationism does not claim that in the standard case, we acquire interesting, new prepositional knowledge from artworks, but that [they] can deepen our moral understandings by, among other things, encouraging us to apply our moral knowledge and emotions to specific cases. (p. 142)

For the television critic, taking the clarificationist view means exploring how television frames and encourages moral engagement and, beyond this, what kind of moral refinements are likely to be mobilized or reoriented as a result. As most of what we encounter on the television screen provides cues to what it means to be a good or bad human being, the clarificationist vantage point is a readily accessible one.

It is not necessary for the ethical critic of television to adopt the position of moderate moralism or become a clarificationist. However, the stance and goals of these positions are consonant with critical approaches that have been introduced in this book. As Gregory (1998, p. 194) has argued, there is a "general need [for] an ethical criticism that is intellectually defensible, not to replace or displace other critical approaches but to complement them." We agree with this assessment and are supportive of the position that ethical judgment can and should influence the aesthetic evaluation of much television work. You may find that much television criticism, done under other guises, qualifies as ethical criticism. Clausen (1986, p. 22) argues that "much conservative criticism is overtly or covertly moral. So is most radical and feminist criticism, even if it is disguised as ideological critique." Gregory (1998, pp. 199–200) goes one step further, suggesting that criticism engaged with the "language of power, colonization, or marginalization," such as much postmodern and poststructural criticism has been, has merely masked ethical criticism in the course of taking a political position about right or wrong. As Gregory (1998, p. 200) points out:

> Such views constitute ethical arguments because their main burden is ethical arguments about better and worse ways of living and acting. What these arguments deliver are not just analyses of power but *moral judgments* about power: judgments that power *ought* to be reconfigured and that rest on the authority of the frequently

unspoken but always present moral assumption that the desired reconfigurations of power would make the world a *better* place for someone or some group.

Because television is perhaps the most social and commercial of art forms, to routinely evade considering the ethical and moral contours of its texts, their production, and their reception would be an unfortunately uncritical act. In pondering the possibilities for an engaged television criticism that confronts the human condition, ethical criticism can supply some of the answers to what will be the post-postmodern turn in criticism. Booth (1998, p. 355) has argued: "Ethical judgments are by their very nature controversial; the very point of uttering them is to awaken or challenge those who have missed the point." Because awakening others and making sure they do not miss your point is a main goal of doing television criticism, ethical reflection may be one way to ensure that when a tree falls in your critical forest, it is heard.

Note

1. Led by Robert W. Hutchins, Chancellor of the University of Chicago, the Hutchins Commission on Freedom of the Press featured a blue-ribbon panel of educators. The commission's report outlined a contemporary ethos for media responsibility in a democracy that was anchored in truthtelling, criticism, and diversity.

Further Readings

Carroll, N. (1998). Is the medium a (moral) message? In M. Kiernan (Ed.), *Media ethics* (pp. 135–151). London: Routledge. Carroll's work in the area of ethical criticism and the treatment of moral agency in art is seminal. In this publication, Carroll refutes, on logical and philosophical grounds, a series of commonly alleged structural moral defects attributed to television.

Johannesen, R. L. (2002). *Ethics in human communication* (5th ed.). Prospect Heights, IL: Waveland. This is perhaps the fullest treatment of ethics in varied communicative situations. It provides particularly useful treatment of the ethical contours for political communication and for discourse ethics, including treatment of Habermas.

Kidder, R. M. (1996). *How good people make tough choices: Resolving the dilemma of ethical living.* New York: Fireside. This is a guide to using ethics in the course of making everyday decisions. The reflections are commonsensical, and the criteria used in resolving life's dilemmas are readily applicable to situations confronting the television critic.

Valenti, F. M. (2000). *More than a movie: Ethics in entertainment.* Boulder, CO: Westview. This book deals with ethics in more than movies. This practical treatment of the ethical challenges confronting creative personnel in the shaping of entertainment for film and television offers reflection on ethical treatment of violence, stereotypes, sex, substance use, children's programming, docudrama, and reality programs.

Webnotes

Ethics Update. **http://ethics.acusd.edu/**

> This web site is perhaps the "major domo" web site for practical and applied ethics.Run by Professor Lawrence Hinman of the University of San Diego, this site archives and links major works and applications for the ethicist and ethical critic concerned with the real world.

RTNDA Codes. **http://web.missouri.edu/~jourvs/rtcodes.html**

> This site, facilitated by Vernon Stone at the University of Missouri, provides a chronology and discussion of the evolution of the Code of Ethics endorsed by the Radio and Television News Directors' Association. Useful in any analysis of television news.

Centre for Applied Ethics. **http://www.ethics.ubc.ca/resources/media/topics.html**

> This site, run by the Centre for Applied Ethics at the University of British Columbia, provides media ethics resources. Links to major centers, organizations, and other sites are included.

Learning Activities

1. Pick three prime-time shows that you find particularly morally objectionable. Assess what you find to be morally problematic or ethically questionable. What does this suggest about your core values or the duties, obligations, or loyalties that you believe should be universally followed? Are there other interpretations that could be made of the ethics in the shows you have picked? How might the clarificationist look at the quality of the moral engagement?

2. What's right and what's wrong about Saturday morning cartoons? Assess the vice and virtues of major characters in a sampling of animated programs. Make a similar assessment of the characters in *South Park* or *The Simpsons*. Assess the moral choices made by characters in these latter shows in comparison to the choices made in the Saturday morning sampling. Do you see a significant difference? Is there anything to suggest that there are ethical defects in the evening programming that would influence your being able to recommend them for viewing by children?

References

Aristotle. (1953). *Nichomachean ethics. An Introduction to Aristotle.* (pp. 333–423). New York: Modern Library.

Bentham, J. (1948). *An introduction to the principles of morals and legislation.* New York: Hafner.

Booth, W. C. (1988). *The company we keep: An ethics of fiction.* Berkeley: University of California Press.

Booth, W. C. (1998). Why ethical criticism can never be simple. *Style, 32,* 351–364.

Burke, K. (1967). *The philosophy of literary form: Studies in symbolic action* (2nd ed.). Baton Rouge: University of Louisiana Press.

Carroll, N. (1998a). *A philosophy of mass art.* Oxford: Clarendon Press.

Carroll, N. (1998b). Art, narrative, and moral understanding. In J. Levinson (Ed.), *Aesthetics and ethics* (pp. 126–160). Cambridge: Cambridge University Press.

Carroll, N. (1998c). Is the medium a (moral) message? In M. Kiernan (Ed.), *Media ethics* (pp. 135–151). London: Routledge.

Carroll, N. (2000). Art and ethical criticism: An overview of recent directions of research. *Ethics, 110,* 350–387.

Christians, C. G. (2000) An intellectual history of media ethics. In B. Pattyn (Ed.), *Media ethics: Opening social dialogue* (pp. 15–46). Leuven, Belgium: Peeters.

Christians, C. G., Fackler, M., Rotzoll, K. B., & McKee, K. B. (2001). *Media ethics: Cases and moral reasoning* (6th ed.). New York: Longman.

Clausen, C. (1986). *The moral imagination: Essays on literature and ethics.* Iowa City: University of Iowa Press.

Commission on Freedom of the Press. (1947). *A free and responsible press.* Chicago: University of Chicago Press.

Davis, T. F., & Womack, K. (1998). Introduction: Reading literature and the ethics of criticism. *Style, 32,* 184–193.

Day, L. A. (in press). *Ethics in media communications: Cases and controversies* (4th ed.). Belmont, CA: Wadsworth.

Englehardt, E. E., & Barney, R. D. (2002). *Media and ethics: Principles for moral decisions.* Belmont, CA: Wadsworth.

Gilligan, C. (1982). *In a different voice: Psychological theory and women's development.* Cambridge, MA: Harvard University Press.

Gregory, M. (1998). Ethical criticism: What it is and why it matters. *Style, 32,* 194–220.

Josephson, M. S. (2002) *Making ethical decisions.* Marina del Rey, CA: Josephson Institute of Ethics. Available online at: http://www.josephsoninstitute.org/MED/MED-1/makingsense.htm.

Kant, I. (1959). *Foundations of metaphysics of morals* (L. W. Beck, Trans.). Indianapolis: Bobbs-Merrill. (Original work published 1785.)

Kidder, R.M. (1996). *How good people make tough choices: Resolving the dilemma of ethical living.* New York: Fireside.

Levinson, J. (Ed.). (1998). *Aesthetics and ethics.* Cambridge: Cambridge University Press.

McKeon, R. (Ed.). (1947). *Nichomachean ethics. An introduction to Aristotle.* (pp. 333–423). New York: Modern Library.

Merrill, J. (1999). Overview: Foundations for media ethics. In A. D. Gordon & J. M. Kitross, *Controversies in media ethics* (2nd ed., pp. 1–25). New York: Longman.

Mill, J. S. (1861). *Utilitarianism.* London: Dent.

Noddings, N. (1984). *Caring: A feminine approach to ethics and moral education.* Berkeley: University of California Press.

Rawls, J. (1971). *A theory of justice.* Cambridge, MA: Harvard University Press.

Reid, T.R. (1999). *Confucius lives next door: What living in the East teaches us about living in the West.* New York: Random House.

Index